THE ANATOMY OF TORTURE

A Documentary History of Filartiga v. Pena Irala

William J. Aceves

Martinus Nijhoff Publishers
Leiden / Boston

Library of Congress Cataloging-in-Publication Data

Aceves, William J.
    The anatomy of torture : a documentary history of Filartiga v. Pena-Irala
/ by William J. Aceves.
      p. cm.
    Includes bibliographical references and index.
    ISBN-13: 978-1-57105-352-7
      1. Trials—United States. 2. Aliens—United States. 3. Torts—
United States. 4. Torts (International law). 5. Crimes against humanity.
6. Filartiga, Joelito, 1959–1976, I. Title.

KF226.A25 2007
341.4'8—dc22

To Dolly, for your courage.
To Joel, for your compassion.
To Joelito, for your legacy.

TABLE OF CONTENTS

ACKNOWLEDGMENTS

I would like to thank the following individuals for their assistance and encouragement throughout this long project: Michael Bazyler, Débora Benchoam, Christina Cerna, Sandy Coliver, Vienna Colucci, James Cooper, Rhonda Copelon, Lori Damrosch, Drew S. Days, III, Matt Eisenbrandt, Dolly Filártiga, Dr. Joel Filártiga, Jerry Gray, Jennie Green, Rick Herz, Paul Hoffman, John Huerta, Harold Hongju Koh, Brian Landsberg, Jose Gonzalez Macchi, Michael Maggio, Pamela Merchant, John Noyes, Steven Schneebaum, Kathryn Sikkink, Jim Silk, Beth Stephens, Peter Weiss, David Weissbrodt, and Katie Zoglin. I owe Paul Hoffman and Jennie Green a special debt of gratitude for inspiring me to work in this field. The following law students provided excellent research assistance throughout this project: Julie A. Bally, Lauren Bortolotti, Amanda Bradley, Lindsey Burcham, Brian Crane, Marin Dell, Shaun Dunning, Tobey Goldfarb, Alexandra L. Grosse, Kevin Gupta, Lisa Hendricks, Victor Herrera, Klayton Khishaveh, Jennifer Lane, Anton Lakshin, Melissa Robbins, Zachariah Rowland, Marni Rubin, Hansdeep Singh, and Heather Zuber. I would like to thank Dean Steven Smith and Associate Dean Janet Bowermaster of California Western School of Law for their support. I also appreciate the work of Faculty Support Services and the library staff at California Western School of Law: Bill Bookheim, Debra Compton, Ana Contreras, Laurie Farid, Joyce Stallworth, Diane Sopko, Liliana Torres, Linda Weathers, and Bobbi Weaver. I am indebted to the following organizations for their assistance in locating relevant documents: Amnesty International, Association of the Bar of the City of New York, California Western School of Law Library, Center for Constitutional Rights, Center for Justice & Accountability, *Centro de Documentacion y Archivo* in Asunción, Paraguay, Inter-American Commission on Human Rights, the Special Collections Department of the University of Virginia Law Library, the Special Collections Division of the University of Washington Libraries, and the U.S. National Archives and Records Administration.

Above all, I am thankful to the Aceves and Sharma families for their devotion throughout these many years and to Seema and Sonia for giving me hope at what still lies ahead.

PREFACE

It has been over 30 years since Joelito Filártiga was tortured and killed in Asunción, Paraguay. But the pain still follows his family. They remain marked by the tragic events of March 29, 1976, a day that scarred their lives forever.

When I first met Dr. Joel Filártiga and his daughter, Dolly, I was struck by their warmth and kindness. They welcomed me with an enthusiasm generally reserved for an old friend. I met Joel in Asunción and Dolly in New York. Throughout our many meetings, they opened their hearts and their memories to me. These were difficult conversations. I asked them to recall events that no one should have to live through even once or be forced to relive a second time. They smiled and laughed as they recalled Joelito's vibrant life. There was sadness and deep grief as they recounted his brutal death and described its effect on their family. And while Joel and Dolly remain passionate about life and the search for justice, there is a silent melancholy that always hovers nearby.

Filartiga v. Pena-Irala is arguably the most significant and iconic human rights case in American history. But how many students who read the case know that Dr. Filártiga was also tortured or that Dolly was jailed by the Paraguayan government? How many students are told that Dolly cleaned houses during her first few years in the United States, not only to earn money but also in a symbolic and self-acknowledged effort to wipe clean the brutality that had stained her life? How many students learn about the Center for Constitutional Rights, whose attorneys first thought of using the Alien Tort Statute on behalf of the Filártiga family and who worked throughout the night to draft the complaint so it could be filed and served before Americo Peña-Irala was deported?

It is one thing to read a case; it is quite another to meet the people whose lives make up that case. In law school, we teach our students about the law. But the case method, which forms the pedagogical core of our teachings, is flawed, because it distances students from the very lives of the people they seek to serve. Textbooks never tell the whole story of the cases they present, and classes seldom delve into the details.

I wrote this book to address these issues—to remind us that every case tells a story. And every story marks a life. And every life has meaning.

FOREWORD: *FILARTIGA'S* WAY

Harold Hongju Koh*

Some cases spawn new ways of looking at the law. One such historic decision was the landmark 1980 ruling of the United States Court of Appeals for the Second Circuit in *Filartiga v. Pena-Irala*,[1] which inaugurated the era of human rights litigation in which we now live. Supported by an important Carter administration amicus brief pressing the administration's human rights policy, *Filartiga* held that an obscure federal law, the Alien Tort Claims Act,[2] conferred district court jurisdiction over a suit by two Paraguayan nationals—Joel and Dolly Filartiga—against a Paraguayan official who had tortured young Joelito Filártiga to death in Paraguay, while acting under color of governmental authority. On remand, U.S. District Judge Eugene Nickerson awarded the Filártigas a judgment of nearly $10.4 million, comprising compensatory damages based on Paraguayan law and punitive damages based on U.S. cases and international law.[3]

In *Filartiga*, human rights litigants finally found their *Brown v. Board of Education*.[4] "[F]or purposes of civil liability," Judge Irving Kaufman declared, "the torturer has become—like the pirate and slave trader before him—*hostis humani generis*, an enemy of all mankind."[5] By so saying, the Second Circuit reaffirmed the Nuremberg ideal—that like genocide, torture can never serve as a legitimate instrument of state power. Under the court's reasoning, official torturers may not invoke comity nor cloak themselves in state sovereignty to avoid individual responsibility to their victims before a court of law. Nor, the *Filartiga* court held, must such cases invariably be dismissed under the doctrine of separation of powers. Even if the Executive Branch had not supported adjudication, the court found, the core issue in the case was quintessentially legal—whether the victims had a

---

* Dean and Gerard C. & Bernice Latrobe Smith Professor of International Law, Yale Law School; U.S. Assistant Secretary of State for Democracy, Human Rights and Labor, 1998–2001.

[1] Filartiga v. Pena-Irala, 630 F.2d 876 (2d Cir. 1980).

[2] 28 U.S.C. § 1350 (federal courts "shall have original jurisdiction of any civil action by an alien for a tort only, committed in violation of the law of nations or a treaty of the United States.").

[3] Filartiga v. Pena-Irala, 577 F. Supp. 860, 864–67 (E.D.N.Y. 1984).

[4] Brown v. Bd. of Educ., 347 U.S. 483 (1954).

[5] Filartiga v. Pena-Irala, 630 F.2d 876, 890 (2d Cir. 1980).

right to be free from torture that was actionable in federal court. Resolution of that question required standard judicial determinations—construction of the Alien Tort Claims Act and human rights treaties—and a
conclusion that because the customary international law norm against torture was definable, obligatory, and universal, it constituted an actionable
"tort in violation of the law of nations" for purposes of the statute. In addition, *Filartiga*'s ruling on remand created a federal common law remedy
against torture, which fell squarely within the Supreme Court's prior recognition that issues "in ordering our relationships with other members of the
international community must be treated exclusively as an aspect of federal
law," made by the federal courts, binding on the states, but subject to legislative revision.[6]

Filartiga has become seminal, not just for what it held, but also for what
it triggered—what I have elsewhere called an era of "transnational public
law litigation," a novel and expanding effort by state and individual plaintiffs to fuse international legal rights with domestic judicial remedies.[7]
Transnational public law litigation couples a substantive notion—individual and state responsibility—with the process of adjudication in pursuit of
a normative goal—promotion of universal norms of international conduct.
International tort plaintiffs such as the Filártigas pursue not only norm-
enunciation, but also compensation, deterrence, and denial of safe haven
to the human rights violator defendant. In *Filartiga*, the court acknowledged that "transnational litigation," which had originated in the context
of private commercial suits in U.S. courts against foreign governments, had
properly migrated into the realm of public human rights suits against foreign governments and officials.

The *Filartiga* decision has spawned more than a quarter century of
human rights litigation in U.S. courts. In subsequent cases, the lower federal courts held that torture, genocide, summary execution, disappearance,

---

6 Banco Nacional de Cuba v. Sabbatino, 376 U.S. 398, 425 (1964). For elaboration,
see Harold Hongju Koh, *Is International Law Really State Law?*, 111 HARV. L. REV. 1824
(1998).

7 *See* Harold Hongju Koh, *Transnational Public Law Litigation*, 100 YALE L.J. 2347
(1991), from which the ideas in this Foreword derive. Transnational public law litigation
is characterized by: (1) a *transnational party structure*, in which states and nonstate entities equally participate; (2) a *transnational claim structure*, in which violations of domestic
and international, private and public law are all alleged in a single action; (3) a *prospective focus*, directed as much upon obtaining judicial declaration of transnational norms
as upon resolving past disputes; (4) the litigants' strategic awareness of the *transporta-
bility of those norms* to other domestic and international fora for use in judicial interpretation or political bargaining; and (5) a subsequent process of *institutional dialogue*
among various domestic and international, judicial and political fora to achieve ultimate
settlement.

and other kinds of gross violations also fit within *Filartiga*'s actionable category of specific, definable, universal, and obligatory offenses. Courts in four of the U.S. circuits—the 1st, 2d, 9th, and 11th—all adopted *Filartiga*'s theory of the Alien Tort Claims Act.[8] These cases culminated on the last day of the U.S. Supreme Court's 2003 Term in the decision in *Sosa v. Alvarez-Machain*.[9] While the Supreme Court's decision did not embrace *Filartiga* unquestioningly, six Justices—Justices Souter, Stevens, O'Connor, Kennedy, Ginsberg, and Breyer—did reaffirm *Filartiga*'s core insight: when there is a norm of international character accepted by the civilized world, and defined by specificity comparable to recognized paradigms, an alien can sue for violations of that norm in a federal court under the Alien Tort Claims Act.[10]

In this important volume, Professor William J. Aceves, a deeply committed human rights scholar and advocate, collects the key documents and opinions that underlay the *Filartiga* litigation. This documentary history provides the definitive detailed account of the case and its background, relying on many previously unseen primary sources: litigation documents from the Center for Constitutional Rights, U.S. government documents from the National Archives, and documents from Paraguayan government archives. Professor Aceves' remarkable documentary appendix takes the reader from the first days of the case—the Police Summary of the Crime Scene in March 1976—through the notification of government authorities on both sides of the equator, filing, briefing, and opinions, and the ultimate damages award in the case in 1984. This stirring collection mixes litigation and diplomatic documents in a rare way that will educate legal scholars and students, inspire human rights activists, and inform courts around the world.

Textbooks sometimes obscure more than they illuminate. But Professor Aceves' book shows how the law, wisely invoked, can illumine life and redress pain. In the war on terror, we too often hear the claim that terror must be met with torture, violence with more violence. Professor Aceves' volume shows us instead *Filartiga*'s way: an anatomy of how the law—and the human beings it touches—can rise above torture to heal, and ultimately to teach.

---

[8] *See, e.g.*, Kadic v. Karadzic, 70 F.3d 232 (2d Cir. 1995); Abebe-Jira v. Negewo, 72 F.3d 844 (11th Cir. 1996); Trajano v. Marcos, 978 F.2d 493 (9th Cir. 1992); Xuncax v. Gramajo, 886 F.Supp. 162 (D. Mass. 1995).

[9] Sosa v. Alvarez-Machain, 542 U.S. 692 (2004).

[10] *Id.* at 729.

ABOUT THE AUTHOR

William J. Aceves is a Professor of Law and Director of the International Legal Studies Program at California Western School of Law, where he teaches Civil Procedure, Comparative Law, Foreign Affairs Law, and Human Rights Law. Professor Aceves has written numerous articles on human rights and international law. His publications have appeared in the *American Journal of International Law, Columbia Journal of Transnational Law, Harvard International Law Journal, Michigan Journal of International Law, University of Chicago Legal Forum, University of Pennsylvania Journal of International Economic Law,* and the *Virginia Journal of International Law.* Professor Aceves frequently works with Amnesty International, the Center for Justice & Accountability, the Center for Constitutional Rights, and the American Civil Liberties Union on projects involving the domestic application of international law. He has also represented several human rights and civil liberties organizations as *amicus curiae* counsel in cases before the federal courts, including the U.S. Supreme Court. These cases include *Acree v. Republic of Iraq, Beharry v. Reno, DeMore v. Kim, Doe v. Unocal, Ma v. Reno, Medellin v. Dretke, Rasul v. Bush, Republic of Paraguay v. Gilmore, Sanchez-Llamas v. State of Oregon, Sosa v. Alvarez-Machain,* and *United States v. Lindh.* He is the principal author of the 2002 Amnesty International USA report on torture and impunity in the United States. He has served on the Board of Directors of Amnesty International USA and is presently the Ombudsperson for AIUSA. He is a member of the National Board of the American Civil Liberties Union and serves on the Board of the Center for Justice & Accountability. He is also a member of the Executive Committee of the American Branch of the International Law Association and a member of the Human Rights Committee of the International Law Association. Professor Aceves has appeared before the Inter-American Commission on Human Rights, the U.N. Special Rapporteur on Migrants, and the U.S. Commission on Civil Rights.

LIST OF ABBREVIATIONS

ATA	Anti-Terrorism Act
ATS	Alien Tort Statute
CCR	Center for Constitutional Rights
D.E.A.	Drug Enforcement Administration
FSIA	Foreign Sovereign Immunities Act
ICJ	International Court of Justice
MOGE	Myanmar Oil and Gas Enterprise
RICO	Racketeer Influenced and Corrupt Organizations Act
SLORC	State Law and Order Restoration Council
TRC	Truth and Reconciliation Commission (South Africa)
TVPA	Torture Victim Protection Act

CHAPTER 1
INTRODUCTION

When the First Congress of the United States met in 1789, it drafted a statute that would have a profound impact on international law and human rights almost 200 years later. The Alien Tort Claims Act, or Alien Tort Statute (ATS), codified as part of the First Judiciary Act, originally provided that the federal courts shall "also have cognizance, concurrent with the courts of the several States, or the circuit courts, as the case may be, of all causes where an alien sues for a tort only in violation of the law of nations or a treaty of the United States."[1] After minor revisions, the statute now reads: "[t]he district courts shall have original jurisdiction of any civil action by an alien for a tort only, committed in violation of the law of nations or a treaty of the United States."[2] The ATS and the litigation it has spawned have generated an extraordinary amount of interest, culminating in the U.S. Supreme Court's 2004 opinion affirming the statute and its attendant litigation.[3]

Despite its contemporary prominence, the legislative history of the ATS remains unclear.[4] Indeed, it has been referred to as "a kind of legal

---

[1] Act of Sept. 24, 1789, ch. 20, § 9(b), 1 Stat. 79. *See generally* WILFRED J. RITZ, REWRITING THE HISTORY OF THE JUDICIARY ACT OF 1789 (1990); ORIGINS OF THE FEDERAL JUDICIARY: ESSAYS ON THE JUDICIARY ACT OF 1789 (Maeva Marcus ed., 1992).

[2] 28 U.S.C. § 1350.

[3] *See* Sosa v. Alvarez-Machain, 542 U.S. 692 (2004). *See generally* Julian G. Ku, *The Third Wave: The Alien Tort Statute and the War on Terrorism*, 19 EMORY INT'L L. REV. 105 (2005); Ehren J. Brav, *Recent Development: Opening the Courtroom Doors to Non-Citizens: Cautiously Affirming Filartiga for the Alien Tort Statute*, 46 HARV. INT'L L.J. 265 (2005); Harold Koh, *The Supreme Court Meets International Law*, 12 TULSA J. COMP. & INT'L L. 1 (2004); Gary Clyde Hufbauer, *What's the Sequel to Sosa v. Alvarez-Machain?* 12 TULSA J. COMP. & INT'L L. 77 (2004); Note, *The Offenses Clause After Sosa v. Alvarez-Machain*, 118 HARV. L. REV. 2378 (2005); Ralph G. Steinhardt, *Laying One Bankrupt Critique to Rest: Sosa v. Alvarez-Machain and the Future of International Human Rights Litigation in U.S. Courts*, 57 VAND. L. REV. 2241 (2004); Beth Stephens, *Sosa v. Alvarez-Machain: "The Door Is Still Ajar" For Human Rights Litigation in U.S. Courts*, 70 BROOK. L. REV. 533 (2004); Eugene Kontorovich, *Implementing Sosa v. Alvarez-Machain: What Piracy Reveals About the Alien Tort Statute*, 80 NOTRE DAME L. REV. 111 (2004).

[4] *See generally* Jordan Paust, *The History, Nature, and Reach of the Alien Tort Claims Act*, 16 FLA. J. INT'L L. 249 (2004); Curtis A. Bradley, *The Alien Tort Statute and Article III*, 42 VA. J. INT'L L. 587 (2002); William S. Dodge, *The Historical Origins of the Alien Tort Statute: A Response to the Originalists*, 19 HASTINGS INT'L & COMP. L. REV. 221 (1996); Joseph Sweeney, *A Tort Only in Violation of the Law of Nations*, 18 HASTINGS INT'L & COMP. L. REV. 445 (1995); William Casto, *The Federal Courts' Protective Jurisdiction over Torts Committed in*

Lohengrin . . . no one seems to know whence it came."[5] Some scholars argue it was adopted to ensure the United States could prosecute violations of international law that posed a threat to international peace and national security. Anthony D'Amato suggests the ATS was considered an important part of U.S. national security in 1789.[6] "Acutely recognizing that denials of justice could provide a major excuse for a European power to launch a full-scale attack on our nation, the Founding Fathers made sure that any such provocation could be nipped in the bud by the impartial processes of federal courts."[7] William Casto highlights the role of the notorious Marbois incident in the adoption of the ATS. The 1784 assault on the French consul in Philadelphia provoked a significant outcry and threatened U.S. relations with France.[8] "When the Constitutional Convention was convened in Philadelphia three years after the Marbois incident, the issue of compliance with the law of nations was fresh on the minds of the delegates . . . The Continental Congress's impotence when confronted with violations of the law of nations had been clearly established."[9] Other scholars have asserted that the ATS was adopted as a "badge of honor," representing a U.S. commitment to comply with and uphold international norms.[10] Anne-Marie Slaughter views the ATS as having been adopted in "an era in which national policymakers, charged with the leadership of a younger and much

---

Violation of the Law of Nations, 18 CONN. L. REV. 467 (1986); Anthony D'Amato, *What Does Tel-Oren Tell Lawyers? Judge Bork's Concept of the Law of Nations Is Seriously Mistaken*, 79 AM. J. INT'L L. 92 (1985); Alfred P. Rubin, *What Does Tel-Oren Tell Lawyers? Professor D'Amato's Concept of American Jurisdiction Is Seriously Mistaken*, 79 AM. J. INT'L L. 105 (1985).

5   IIT v. Vencap, Ltd., 519 F.2d 1001, 1015 (2d Cir. 1975). Lohengrin is the mythical German knight whose mysterious story forms the basis for Richard Wagner's opera *Lohengrin. See* RICHARD WAGNER, THE AUTHENTIC LIBRETTOS OF THE WAGNER OPERAS (1938).

6   Anthony D'Amato, *The Alien Tort Statute and the Founding of the Constitution*, 82 AM. J. INT'L L. 62 (1988).

7   *Id.* at 65.

8   *See* Respublica v. De Longchamps, 1 U.S. (1 Dall.) 111 (1784). *See also* 28 JOURNALS OF THE CONTINENTAL CONGRESS 1774–1789, at 314 (J.C. Fitzpatrick ed., 1933). A similar incident involving a Dutch diplomat occurred four years later in New York City. *See* 34 JOURNALS OF THE CONTINENTAL CONGRESS 1774–1789, at 111 (R.R. Hill ed., 1937).

9   Casto, *supra* note 4, at 492–93. *See also* Thomas H. Lee, *The Safe-Conduct Theory of the Alien Tort Statute*, 106 COLUM. L. REV. 830 (2006).

10   Anne-Marie Burley, *The Alien Tort Statute and the Judiciary Act of 1789: A Badge of Honor*, 83 AM. J. INT'L L. 461 (1989). *Cf.* Ariel N. Lavinbuk, *Note, Rethinking Early Judicial Involvement in Foreign Affairs: An Empirical Study of the Supreme Court's Docket*, 114 YALE L.J. 855 (2005); Harold Hongju Koh, *Agora: The United States Constitution and International Law: International Law as Part of Our Law*, 98 AM. J. INT'L L. 43 (2004); Kenneth C. Randall, *Federal Jurisdiction over International Law Claims: Inquiries into the Alien Tort Statute*, 18 N.Y.U. J. INT'L L. & POL. 1 (1995).

more vulnerable nation, nevertheless factored 'honor' and 'virtue' into their calculus of the national interest."[11]

For almost 200 years, the Alien Tort Statute lay dormant and was seldom used by litigants. Occasional references in the case law failed to generate much interest in the statute. The first reported case involving the ATS, *Moxon v. The Fanny*, was decided in 1793 and involved a libel action seeking restitution for a ship and its cargo taken in violation of the law of nations.[12] The reference to the ATS, however, was by implication, as the district court recognized that it was "vested with authority where an alien sues for a tort only in violation of the laws of nations,—and this is a case falling under that description."[13] Another case, *Bolchos v. Darrel*, was decided in 1795 and involved a lawsuit seeking restitution for the value of slaves taken from a captured Spanish ship.[14] The district court again made only a brief reference to the ATS, although it recognized the plaintiff's right to seek compensation for a violation of substantive rights under the law of nations.[15] In these early years of the American republic, the ATS was also recognized in the opinions of the U.S. Attorney General. In 1795, for example, U.S. Attorney General William Bradford was asked to consider the potential liability of U.S. citizens who had aided the French in attacking a British colony in Sierra Leone. The opinion, issued six years after the adoption of the First Judiciary Act and the ATS, recognizes that torts in violation of the law of nations would be cognizable at common law, just as any other tort would be.

[T]here can be no doubt that the company or individuals who have been injured by these acts of hostility have a remedy by *civil* suit in the courts of the United States; jurisdiction being expressly given to these courts in all cases where an alien sues for a tort only, in violation of the law of nations, or a treaty of the United States.[16]

---

[11]   Burley, *supra* note 10, at 493.

[12]   Moxon v. The Fanny, 17 F. Cas. 942 (D. Pa. 1793) (No. 9895).

[13]   *Id.* at 943.

[14]   Bolchos v. Darrel, 3 F. Cas. 810 (D.C.S.C. 1795) (No. 1607).

[15]   *See* JORDAN PAUST, INTERNATIONAL LAW AS LAW OF THE UNITED STATES 229, 300–01 (2d ed. 2003).

[16]   Breach of Neutrality, 1 Op. Att'y Gen. 57, 59 (1795) (emphasis in original). *See also* Mexico Boundary—Diversion of the Rio Grande, 26 Op. Att'y Gen. 250, 253 (1907) ("I repeat that the statutes thus provide a forum and a right of action."); Abduction and Restitution of Slaves, 1 Op. Att'y Gen. 29, 30 (1792) (apparent reference to a possible civil action under the ATS where the defendant had committed piracy by stealing slaves from a French colony).

Beyond these occasional and rather limited references, the ATS did not receive significant attention for almost 200 years.[17]

In 1979, a lawsuit was filed in the federal district court for the Eastern District of New York that breathed new life into the ATS and signaled the birth of transnational litigation in the United States. Transnational litigation involves the use of domestic litigation to affirm international norms.[18] While it seeks to vindicate the rights of individual litigants, Harold Koh posits that transnational litigation also pursues a broader agenda.

> [T]ransnational public lawsuits focus retrospectively upon achieving compensation and redress for individual victims. But as in traditional international law litigation, the transnational public law plaintiff pursues a prospective aim as well: to provoke judicial articulation of a *norm* of transnational law, with an eye toward using that declaration to promote a political settlement in which both governmental and nongovernmental entities will participate. Thus, although transnational public law plaintiffs routinely request retrospective damages or even prospective injunctive relief, their broader strategic goals are often served by a declaratory or default judgment announcing that a transnational norm has been violated. Even a judgment that the plaintiff cannot enforce against the defendant in the rendering forum empowers the plaintiff by creating a bargaining chip for use in other political fora.[19]

---

17 Prior to 1979, most case references to the ATS were cursory in nature. *See* Huynh Thi Anh v. Levi, 586 F.2d 625 (6th Cir. 1979); Benjamins v. British European Airways, 572 F.2d 913 (2d Cir. 1978); Dreyfus v. Von Finck, 534 F.2d 24 (2d Cir. 1976); Nguyen Da Yen v. Kissinger, 528 F.2d 1194 (9th Cir. 1975); IIT v. Vencap, Ltd., 519 F.2d 1001 (2d Cir. 1975); Abiodun v. Martin Oil Serv., Inc., 475 F.2d 142 (7th Cir. 1973); Valanga v. Metro. Life Ins. Co., 259 F. Supp. 324 (E.D. Pa. 1966); Damaskinos v. Societa Navigacion Interamericana, S. A., Panama, 255 F. Supp. 919 (S.D.N.Y. 1966); Lopes v. Schroder, 225 F. Supp. 292 (E.D. Pa. 1963); Upper Lakes Shipping, Ltd. v. Int'l Longshoremen's Ass'n, 33 F.R.D. 348 (S.D.N.Y. 1963); Adra v. Clift, 195 F. Supp. 857 (D. Md. 1961); Khedivial Line, S.A.E. v. Seafarers' Int'l Union, 278 F.2d 49 (2d Cir. 1960); O'Reilly DeCamara v. Brooke, 209 U.S. 45 (1908). Prior to 1980, there were only a handful of scholarly references to the ATS. *See* Jay M. Lewis Humphrey, *Note: A Legal Lohengrin: Federal Jurisdiction Under the Alien Tort Claims Act of 1789*, 14 U.S.F. L. REV. 105 (1979); Thomas P. Crotly, *The Law of Nations in the District Court: Federal Jurisdiction Over Tort Claims By Aliens Under 28 U.S.C. § 1350*, 1 B.C. INT'L & COMP. L.J. 71 (1977).

18 *See generally* William J. Aceves, *Liberalism and International Legal Scholarship: The Pinochet Case and the Move Toward a Universal System of Transnational Law Litigation*, 41 HARV. INT'L L.J. 129 (2000); Harold Hongju Koh, *Transnational Legal Process*, 75 NEB. L. REV. 181 (1996); Lea Brilmayer, *International Law in U.S. Courts: A Modest Proposal*, 100 YALE L.J. 2277 (1991). *Cf.* PHILIP JESSUP, TRANSNATIONAL LAW 2 (1956).

19 Harold Hongju Koh, *Transnational Public Law Litigation*, 100 YALE L.J. 2347, 2349 (1991) (emphasis in original).

Several developments offered a receptive climate for transnational litigation in the United States, including the burgeoning public law movement, a growing awareness of international law, and the strong human rights agenda of the Carter administration.[20]

Filartiga v. Pena-Irala involved the torture and murder of Joelito Filártiga, the son of a prominent Paraguayan political dissident, in Asunción, Paraguay.[21] When the alleged perpetrator, Americo Peña-Irala, was discovered living in the United States, the Filártiga family, through the Center for Constitutional Rights, filed a civil lawsuit using the ATS in the federal district court for the Eastern District of New York.[22] The district court dismissed the action on jurisdictional grounds, holding that the term "law of nations," as employed in the ATS, excludes the law that governs a state's treatment of its own citizens.[23] On appeal, the Second Circuit Court of Appeals reversed that decision in a landmark ruling, holding that "whenever an alleged torturer is found and served with process by an alien within our borders, [the ATS] provides federal jurisdiction."[24] According to the Court, establishing civil liability for such acts "is a small but important step in the fulfillment of the ageless dream to free all people from brutal violence."[25]

Initially, the *Filartiga* decision did not "open the floodgates" for ATS litigation.[26] Only a handful of ATS lawsuits were filed between 1980 and 1990.

---

[20] *Id.* at 2364–68.

[21] Diacritic marks are used on the Spanish names "Filártiga" and "Peña-Irala" except when these names are used to describe the case *Filartiga v. Pena-Irala.*

[22] The Center for Constitutional Rights (CCR) was established in 1966 as a nonprofit legal organization dedicated to protecting human rights and civil rights. Its docket includes several landmark civil rights cases, including *Monell v. Department of Social Services, NOW v. Terry,* and *Rasul v. Bush.* In addition to *Filartiga v. Pena-Irala,* CCR has litigated many other ATS cases, including *Doe v. Karadzic, Doe v. Unocal, Prosper v. Avril,* and *Wiwa v. Royal Dutch Petroleum.*

[23] Filartiga v. Pena-Irala, No. 79 C 917, slip op. (E.D.N.Y. May 15, 1979).

[24] Filartiga v. Pena-Irala, 630 F.2d 876, 878 (2d Cir. 1980).

[25] *Id.* at 890.

[26] In contrast, the *Filartiga* decision led to a significant scholarly response. *See, e.g.,* Jeffrey M. Blum & Ralph G. Steinhardt, *Federal Jurisdiction over International Human Rights Claims: The Alien Tort Claims Act After Filartiga v. Pena-Irala,* 22 HARV. INT'L L.J. 53 (1981); Michael Daneher, *Case Comment: Torture as a Tort in Violation of International Law: Filartiga v. Pena-Irala,* 33 STAN. L. REV. 353 (1981); Edward J. Rosen, *Decision: Filartiga v. Pena-Irala,* 75 AM. J. INT'L L. 149 (1981); William T. D'Zurilla, *International Responsibility for Torture Under International Law,* 56 TUL. L. REV. 186 (1981); Gordon A. Christenson, *The Uses of Human Rights Norms to Inform Constitutional Interpretation,* 4 HOUS. J. INT'L L. 39 (1981); Jeffrey Hadley Louden, *Note: The Domestic Application of International Human Rights Law,* 5 HAST. INT'L & COMP. L. REV. 161 (1981); Lisa A. Rickard, *Filartiga v. Pena-Irala: A New Forum for Violations of International Human Rights,* 30 AM. U. L. REV. 807 (1981); Steven

Several developments eventually raised the profile of ATS litigation and promoted the development of transnational litigation in the United States. First, the success of *Filartiga* and several other ATS cases in the 1980s emboldened a growing network of human rights lawyers, activists, and organizations to pursue transnational litigation, seeking redress for victims of human rights abuses and the affirmation of international law. While some of these lawsuits addressed contemporary abuses, others sought redress for historical wrongs, including atrocities perpetrated during the Holocaust.[27] Second, Congress adopted legislation extending the reach of transnational litigation beyond the narrow parameters of the ATS. For example, Congress adopted the Torture Victim Protection Act (TVPA) in 1992 to provide U.S. citizens the right to sue for torture and extrajudicial killing.[28] Significantly, the legislative record of the TVPA affirmed the *Filartiga* precedent, indicating congressional approval of ATS litigation. Other legal developments extended transnational litigation, including the adoption of the Anti-Terrorism Act (ATA) and amendments to the Foreign Sovereign Immunities Act (FSIA). Third, ATS litigation soon extended beyond individual defendants and direct perpetrators. Courts began to recognize indirect liability for human rights abuses through principles of command responsibility and accomplice liability. In addition, multinational corporations were sued for human rights abuses and environmental harms that occurred in their overseas operations.[29] These lawsuits alleged that the cor-

---

M. Schneebaum, *International Law as a Guarantor of Judicially-Enforceable Rights: A Reply to Professor Oliver*, 4 HOUS. J. INT'L L. 65 (1981); Daniel S. Dokos, *Enforcement of International Human Rights in the Federal Courts After Filartiga v. Pena-Irala*, 67 VA. L. REV. 1379 (1981); *Symposium—Federal Jurisdiction, Human Rights, and the Law of Nations: Essays on Filartiga v. Pena-Irala*, 11 GA. J. INT'L & COMP. L. 305 (1981); Susan Relyea-Bowman, *Second Circuit Expands Reach of Alien Tort Claims Act and Rejects Statist Definition of "Law of Nations,"* 12 INT'L PRAC. HANDBOOK 10 (Nov. 1980). Not all commentary on the *Filartiga* decision was positive. *See, e.g.,* Alfred P. Rubin, *U.S. Tort Suits By Aliens*, 21 INT'L PRAC. HANDBOOK 19 (1983); Farooq Hassan, *A Conflict of Philosophies: The Filartiga Jurisprudence*, 32 INT'L & COMP. L.Q. 250 (1983); Covey T. Oliver, *Problems of Cognition and Interpretation in Applying Norms of a Customary International Law of Human Rights in United States Courts*, 4 HOUS. J. INT'L L. 59 (1981); Frank A. Russo, *Recent Development: The Alien Tort Statute of 1789—International Law as the Rule of Decision*, 49 FORDHAM L. REV. 874 (1981).

[27] *See generally* Michael J. Bazyler, *Nuremberg in America: Litigating the Holocaust in United States Courts*, 34 U. RICH. L. REV. 1 (2000); Harold Koh, *Civil Remedies for Uncivil Wrongs: Combatting Terrorism Through Transnational Public Law Litigation*, 22 TEXAS INT'L L.J. 169 (1987).

[28] 28 U.S.C. § 1350 (note).

[29] *See generally* SARAH JOSEPH, CORPORATIONS AND TRANSNATIONAL HUMAN RIGHTS LITIGATION (2004); David Kinley & Junko Tadaki, *From Talk to Walk: The Emergence of Human Rights Responsibilities for Corporations at International Law*, 44 VA. J. INT'L L. 931 (2004); Terry Collingsworth, *Separating Fact from Fiction in the Debate over Application of the*

porations were complicit in international law violations committed by foreign governments through their joint ventures or other cooperative arrangements. Fourth, several ATS cases were filed as class action lawsuits, further raising the profile of these cases.[30] These lawsuits revealed that human rights cases often involved widespread and systematic abuses against civilian populations. They also raised the financial stakes for corporate defendants. In response to these developments, the U.S. government and, in particular, the George W. Bush administration, became increasingly involved in ATS litigation, often filing Statements of Interest on behalf of defendants.[31] In these filings, the Bush administration argued that ATS litigation harmed U.S. foreign policy and was often in conflict with the economic and political interests of the United States. By 2004, 24 years after the *Filartiga* decision, human rights lawyers were regularly invoking the Alien Tort Statute and other statutes to litigate "international human rights principles in United States courts."[32]

In 2004, the U.S. Supreme Court upheld the *Filartiga* precedent and the legitimacy of ATS litigation in *Sosa v. Alvarez-Machain.*[33] The *Sosa* decision was significant because the Supreme Court acknowledged that federal courts have jurisdiction over certain claims that allege violations of international law. Indeed, the Supreme Court recognized that the ATS had been adopted with this goal in mind, and Congress had taken no action to rescind the ATS or limit the nature and scope of the *Filartiga* precedent.

Alien Tort Claims Act to Violations of Fundamental Human Rights by Corporations, 37 U.S.F. L. REV. 563, 586 (2003); Steven R. Ratner, *Corporations and Human Rights: A Theory of Legal Responsibility,* 111 YALE L.J. 443 (2001); Richard L. Herz, *Litigating Environmental Abuses Under the Alien Tort Claims Act: A Practical Assessment,* 40 VA. J. INT'L L. 545 (2000); Gregory G.A. Tzeutschler, *Corporate Violator: The Alien Tort Liability of Transnational Corporations for Human Rights Abuses Abroad,* 30 COLUM. HUM. RTS. L. REV. 359 (1999).

[30] *See generally* Beth Van Schaack, *Unfulfilled Promise: The Human Rights Class Action,* 2003 U. CHI. LEGAL F. 279; Morris A. Ratner, *Factors Impacting the Selection and Positioning of Human Rights Class Actions in United States Courts: A Practical Overview,* 58 N.Y.U. ANN. SURV. AM. L. 623 (2003); Catherine A. MacKinnon, *Collective Harms Under the Alien Tort Statute: A Cautionary Note on Class Actions,* 6 ILSA J. INT'L & COMP. L. 567 (2000).

[31] Most U.S. filings in ATS cases have been submitted on behalf of defendants. One notable exception is the Memorandum for the United States submitted on behalf of the plaintiffs in *Filartiga. See generally* Beth Stephens, *Upsetting Checks and Balances: The Bush Administration's Efforts to Limit Human Rights Litigation,* 17 HARV. HUM. RTS. J. 169 (2004); Brian C. Free, *Comment: Awaiting Doe v. Exxon Mobil Corp.: Advocating the Cautious Use of Executive Opinions in Alien Tort Claims Act Litigation,* 12 PAC. RIM L. & POL'Y J. 467 (2003).

[32] U.S. Dep't of State, Initial Report of the United States of America to the U.N. Committee against Torture, U.N. Doc. CAT/C/28/Add.5 (2000), at para. 278.

[33] Sosa v. Alvarez-Machain, 542 U.S. 692 (2004).

[N]o development in the two centuries from the enactment of §
1350 to the birth of the modern line of cases beginning with
Filartiga v. Pena-Irala, has categorically precluded federal courts
from recognizing a claim under the law of nations as an element
of common law; Congress has not in any relevant way amended §
1350 or limited civil common law power by another statute.[34]

As the U.S. Department of State subsequently indicated, the *Sosa* decision
adopted "a restrictive interpretation of the range of civil actions that could
be brought under this statute consistent with the intent of the legislators
who originally enacted it."[35] However, the decision also "left open the possibility that federal courts may recognize as a matter of federal common law
claims for damages based on alleged violations of the law of nations."[36]

Between *Filartiga* and *Sosa*, approximately 100 ATS cases were filed in
U.S. courts.[37] The plaintiffs hailed from countries such as Argentina,
Burma, Chile, China, El Salvador, Ethiopia, Guatemala, Haiti, Indonesia,
Nigeria, Sudan, the Philippines, and Yugoslavia.[38] These plaintiffs alleged
numerous violations of international law, including arbitrary detention,
slavery, forced disappearance, torture, extrajudicial killing, genocide, war
crimes, and crimes against humanity. The defendants in these cases
included government officials, private individuals, foreign governments,
and multinational corporations. Several of these lawsuits resulted in significant damage awards, although few awards have ever been collected,
because defendants typically lack significant assets or the assets are otherwise unavailable.[39] The effectiveness of transnational litigation cannot be

---

34 *Id.* at 724–25 (citations omitted).

35 U.S. Dep't of State, Second Periodic Report of the United States of America to the
U.N. Committee against Torture, U.N. Doc. CAT/C/48/Add.3 (2005), at para. 81.

36 *Id.*

37 *See generally* Jeffrey Davis, *Justice Without Borders: Human Rights Cases in U.S. Courts*,
28 LAW & POL'Y 60 (2006); Kathryn Lee Boyd, *Universal Jurisdiction and Structural
Reasonableness*, 40 TEX. INT'L L.J. 1 (2004); EARTHRIGHTS INTERNATIONAL, IN OUR
COURT: ATCA, SOSA AND THE TRIUMPH OF HUMAN RIGHTS (2004); Beth Stephens,
*Translating Filartiga: A Comparative and International Law Analysis of Domestic Remedies for
International Human Rights Violations*, 27 YALE J. INT'L L. 1 (2002); THE ALIEN TORT
CLAIMS ACT: AN ANALYTICAL ANTHOLOGY (Ralph G. Steinhardt & Anthony D'Amato
eds., 1999); BETH STEPHENS & MICHAEL RATNER, INTERNATIONAL HUMAN RIGHTS LITI-
GATION IN U.S. COURTS (1996); KENNETH RANDALL, FEDERAL COURTS AND THE INTER-
NATIONAL HUMAN RIGHTS PARADIGM (1990).

38 Several organizations have played a prominent role in ATS litigation, including
the Center for Constitutional Rights, Center for Justice & Accountability, Earthrights
International, and International Labor Rights Fund.

39 *See* Edward A. Amley, *Sue and Be Recognized: Collecting § 1350 Judgments Abroad*, 107

measured in simple economic terms, however. It also requires reference to practical results: "the norms declared, the political pressure generated, the government practices abated, and the lives saved."[40]

For most victims of human rights abuses, the purpose of these lawsuits is not to seek financial compensation—it is to find justice.[41] In this respect, it is important to recognize that money is not the only goal of civil litigation.[42] Reparations for human rights abuses can encompass several goals, including compensation as well as rehabilitation, restitution, and guarantees of nonrepetition.[43] For Dolly Filártiga, who filed the ATS action against Peña-Irala, the purpose of the lawsuit was to seek justice on behalf of her brother and to honor his memory. "The essential *leit-motif* for me was to disperse the cinders of memory in the name of my brother and his unjust martyrdom, articulating my innate faith for justice and my firm conviction of the one thing that does not exist—oblivion."[44] Reflecting on the *Filartiga* legacy, Dolly is "grateful that justice was done and proud that her name has gone down as marking a giant step forward in the annals of international

---

YALE L.J. 2177 (1998); Richard B. Lillich, *Damages for Gross Violations of International Human Rights Awarded by U.S. Courts*, 15 HUM. RTS. Q. 207 (1993). There are, however, some notable exceptions where ATS plaintiffs were able to collect compensation from defendants. *See e.g.*, Press Release, Center for Justice & Accountability, Judgment Final Against Generals Responsible for Torture in El Salvador (July 10, 2006); Press Release, Earthrights International, Historic Advance for Universal Human Rights: Unocal to Compensate Burmese Villagers (Apr. 2, 2005). Difficulties in the enforcement of awards are not unique to ATS litigations. *See, e.g.*, THE REDRESS TRUST, ENFORCEMENT OF AWARDS FOR VICTIMS OF TORTURE AND OTHER INTERNATIONAL CRIMES (2006).

[40] Harold Hongju Koh, *Reflections on Refoulement and Haitian Centers Council*, 35 HARV. INT'L L.J. 1, 16 (1994).

[41] ATS plaintiffs seldom expect to collect any money in a successful judgment. If collection is possible, they often offer to donate the proceeds to charities in their home countries. *Compare* ROBERT H. BORK, COERCING VIRTUE: THE WORLDWIDE RULE OF JUDGES 25 (2003) ("These suits do not really seek recompense; rather, they aspire to make a propaganda point appear more morally compelling by the decision of a U.S. court.").

[42] Elizabeth J. Cabraser, *Human Rights Violations as Mass Torts: Compensation as a Proxy for Justice in the United States Civil Litigation System*, 57 VAND. L. REV. 2211 (2004). *Cf.* Eric A. Posner & Cass R. Sunstein, *Dollars and Death*, 72 U. CHI. L. REV. 537 (2005); Samuel Issacharoff, *The Content of our Casebooks: Why Do Cases Get Litigated?*, 29 FLA. ST. U. L. REV. 1265 (2002).

[43] *See generally* DINAH SHELTON, REMEDIES IN INTERNATIONAL HUMAN RIGHTS LAW (2d ed. 2006); THE REDRESS TRUST, REPARATION: A SOURCEBOOK FOR VICTIMS OF TORTURE AND OTHER VIOLATIONS OF HUMAN RIGHTS AND INTERNATIONAL HUMANITARIAN LAW (2003).

[44] Letter from Dolly Filartiga to William Aceves (July 31, 2000).

human rights law."[45] Another family member, Analy Filártiga, offers a similar explanation.

> The importance of the Filartiga case does not reside so much in the uniqueness of the murder, for many men and women before and after Joelito suffered torture, were assassinated, or disappeared. The fundamental point here is that family members did not cover their pain under a cloak of resignation. They could have—and many people think they should have—mourned in silence, isolated by the suffering and pain they felt. But they decided to cry out a denunciation, knowing nonetheless that they would never recover their beloved son and brother. They did it because the tragedy touched them deeply, because they needed to get out in some way from the rancor and ire that enveloped them, but above all because they believed that somewhere they would find justice. They would seek it until the end as an act of faith.[46]

Not all victims of human rights abuses may share the same goals in their search for justice. Indeed, victims of abuse are not a homogeneous group.[47] But all victims share a common interest in justice, although their search may take different paths.

For many lawyers involved in ATS litigation, their work is also motivated by the search for justice.[48]

> In addition to demanding recognition and justice for those who have suffered, our human rights activism also strives for a future in which the atrocities we describe will be no more. . . . Our work thus serves as an indictment of those responsible for human rights abuses: those who wield the instruments of torture and who give the orders, but also those who condone and cover up such abuses, in our own government as well as around the world. Only if those

---

[45] Brief for the Center for Justice and Accountability et al. at 7–8, Sosa v. Alvarez-Machain, 542 U.S. 692 (2004) (No. 03–339). *See also Taking Tyrants to Court*, AM. LAW., Oct. 1991, at 56.

[46] ANIBAL MIRANDA & ANALY FILARTIGA, EL CASO FILARTIGA 95 (1992).

[47] THE REDRESS TRUST, TORTURE SURVIVORS' PERCEPTIONS OF REPARATION 62 (2001). *See also* WHEN SORRY ISN'T ENOUGH: THE CONTROVERSY OVER APOLOGIES AND REPARATIONS FOR HUMAN INJUSTICE (Roy L. Brooks ed., 1999).

[48] Unlike some civil rights statutes, the ATS does not offer attorneys' fees to successful litigants. Thus, attorneys often take these cases on a *pro bono* basis or through a contingency fee arrangement. But like many of their clients, these attorneys seldom expect to collect any fee for their work. There are, of course, some exceptions.

individuals are brought to justice, if we put an end to impunity, can we foresee the beginning of the end of human rights atrocities. . . . Not only must we pursue these lawsuits in the United States, but every country must make a priority of bringing torturers to justice. May our work hasten the day in which human rights abuses rarely occur and are promptly punished when they do, so that future generations will look upon these evils as relics of an uncivilized past.[49]

To ATS lawyers, accountability is a critical factor in the search for justice. Litigation is thus viewed as a valuable mechanism for enforcing human rights norms. Relying on alternative mechanisms—whether international or regional organizations, diplomatic pressure, or public protests—is unsatisfactory.

I have sat through a few too many academic discussions about ideal normative standards, and I have interviewed too many victims of human rights abuses, only to feel the frustration, if not the embarrassment, of explaining that their stories will be told to the world in reports. . . . I believe that developing a clear mechanism, short of war, to enforce internationally accepted norms is the breakthrough issue for the future of human rights.[50]

While ATS lawyers recognize the limits of litigation, they also believe in its potential.

---

[49] STEPHENS & RATNER, *supra* note 37, at xi. Beth Stephens and Michael Ratner have participated in numerous ATS cases through the Center for Constitutional Rights. *See* Center for Constitutional Rights, *available at* www.ccr-ny.org. *See also* Michael Ratner & Beth Stephens, *The Center for Constitutional Rights: Using Law and the Filartiga Principle in the Fight for Human Rights, in* ACLU INTERNATIONAL CIVIL LIBERTIES REPORT 29 (Dec. 1993).

[50] Terry Collingsworth, *The Key Human Rights Challenge: Developing Enforcement Mechanisms,* 15 HARV. HUM. RTS. J. 183, 185 (2002). Terry Collingsworth has litigated several ATS lawsuits through the International Labor Rights Fund. *See* International Labor Rights Fund, *available at* www.laborrights.org. *See also* Paul Hoffman, *Symposium Panel: War Crimes and Other Human Rights Abuses in the Former Yugoslavia,* 16 WHITTIER L. REV. 433, 439 (1995) ("All in all, United States courts should be able to effectively insure that people receive fair compensation. It may not have a huge effect on the elimination of genocide or war crimes, but this kind of legislation is more about the kind of country the United States claims to be. America should not be a safe haven for human rights violators. Rather, it should work to create a system of compensation and reparation to replace the ineffective system that victims of torture and war crimes currently struggle against."). Paul Hoffman has litigated numerous ATS lawsuits in conjunction with the Center for Constitutional Rights, the Center for Justice & Accountability, and the American Civil Liberties Union.

I am well aware of the limitations of civil lawsuits in the United States. They are nowhere near "perfect" justice, and it is certainly debatable whether they provide any widespread deterrence. However, to individual victims, they can be life-changing experiences. They allow people who were powerless, who were tortured, who were in prison, who had family members killed, and who had no power to do anything, to now turn the tables on those who used to be powerful. Moreover, these cases are just a first step in a much larger movement. U.S. cases are a part of the global march toward accountability that includes the International Criminal Court; the ad hoc tribunals concerning Yugoslavia, Rwanda, Sierra Leone and Cambodia; the national courts in Europe and elsewhere exercising universal jurisdiction to criminally prosecute perpetrators; and the domestic courts of the countries where the abuses actually happened. The ATS and TVPA are merely the tools we use in the United States to carry out our part of this mission.[51]

This book examines the development of transnational litigation in the United States through a case study of *Filartiga v. Pena-Irala*.[52] Chapter 2 describes the birth of transnational litigation, beginning with the seminal *Filartiga* decision. It describes the torture and murder of Joelito Filártiga in Asunción, Paraguay, and chronicles the Filártiga family's efforts to seek justice in Paraguay. It then examines their search for justice in the United States, which culminated in the landmark 1980 ruling by the Second Circuit. Chapter 3 then reviews the development of the *Filartiga* precedent. It examines the expansion of transnational litigation by Congress through the adoption of other statutory mechanisms that provide redress for victims of human rights abuses. It then reviews several cases that followed *Filartiga*, which further extended transnational litigation. It also examines the U.S. Supreme Court's 2004 decision in *Sosa v. Alvarez-Machain*. The key documents of the *Filartiga* litigation appear in the Appendix. From the initial complaint to the final judgment, the actual pleadings and related legal documents are presented with minimal editing. Other documents from the

---

[51] Letter from Matt Eisenbrandt (Litigation Director, Center for Justice & Accountability), to William Aceves (June 1, 2006). Matt Eisenbrandt has litigated several ATS lawsuits on behalf of the Center for Justice & Accountability. *See* Center for Justice & Accountability, *available at* www.cja.org. *See also* Steven M. Schneebaum, *Human Rights in the United States Courts: The Role of Lawyers*, 55 WASH. & LEE L. REV. 737 (1998).

[52] Despite its prominence, there are relatively few detailed works on the *Filartiga* decision. *See, e.g.*, RICHARD ALAN WHITE, BREAKING SILENCE: THE CASE THAT CHANGED THE FACE OF HUMAN RIGHTS (2004); Richard Pierre Claude, *The Case of Joelito Filártiga and the Clinic of Hope*, 5 HUM. RTS. Q. 275 (1983). The *Filartiga* story was subject to a 1991 film. *See* ONE MAN'S WAR (HBO Studios 1991). *See also* Larry Rohter, *Dramatizing a Family That Took on Dictatorship*, L.A. TIMES, Apr. 18, 1991, at C15.

United States and Paraguay, such as declassified government telegrams and correspondence, are also included to add context to the legal documents.

Unlike traditional casebooks and academic studies, this book emphasizes the contextual nature of law. It is part of a growing movement in legal literature that provides detailed studies of prominent cases in U.S. and international litigation.[53] In the field of human rights, a handful of detailed case studies have been written on prominent litigation.[54] This approach to legal scholarship complements the traditional case law method that has been used in legal education for over 100 years.[55] It does so, however, by recognizing the importance of studying law in context.[56] While it acknowledges the relevance of process and procedure, this book also recognizes

---

[53] For similar examples, see LEWIS A. GROSSMAN & ROBERT G. VAUGHN, A DOCUMENTARY COMPANION TO A CIVIL ACTION (3d ed. 2006); IMMIGRATION STORIES (David A. Martin & Peter H. Schuck eds., 2005); CIVIL PROCEDURE STORIES (Kevin M. Clermont ed., 2004); CONSTITUTIONAL LAW STORIES (Michael Dorf ed., 2004); JONATHAN L. ZITTRAIN & JENNIFER HARRISON, THE TORTS GAME: DEFENDING MEAN JOE GREENE (2004); NAN D. HUNTER, THE POWER OF PROCEDURE: THE LITIGATION OF JONES V. CLINTON (2002); DAVID CRUMP & JEFFREY B. BERMAN, THE STORY OF A CIVIL CASE: DOMINGUEZ V. SCOTT'S FOOD STORES (3d ed. 2001). This approach to legal scholarship has received significant commentary. *See, e.g., Symposium: Teaching Law Stories,* 55 J. LEGAL EDUC. 108 (2005); Kevin M. Clermont, *Teaching Civil Procedure Through its Top Ten Cases, Plus or Minus Two,* 47 ST. LOUIS L.J. 111 (2003); *Symposium, Legal Archaeology,* 2000 UTAH L. REV. 183.

[54] *See, e.g.,* THE PINOCHET PAPERS: THE CASE OF AUGUSTO PINOCHET IN SPAIN AND BRITAIN (Reed Brody & Michael Ratner eds., 2000) (assembling documents from the Pinochet litigation); PETER KORNBLUH, THE PINOCHET FILE: A DECLASSIFIED DOSSIER ON ATROCITY AND ACCOUNTABILITY (2003) (assembling documents from the Pinochet era); GENOCIDE IN CAMBODIA: DOCUMENTS FROM THE TRIAL OF POL POT AND IENG SARY (Howard J. De Nike et al., eds. 2000) (assembling documents from the trial of prominent Khmer Rouge officials). *See also* BRIAN DOOLAN, LAWLESS V. IRELAND: THE FIRST CASE BEFORE THE EUROPEAN COURT OF HUMAN RIGHTS (2001) (describing the history of *Lawless v. Ireland*); KEN ENGLADE, BEYOND REASON (1990) (describing the history of *Soering v. United Kingdom*).

[55] *See* W. David Slawson, *Changing How We Teach: A Critique of the Case Method,* 74 S. CAL. L. REV. 343 (2000); Russell L. Weaver, *Langdell's Legacy: Living with the Case Method,* 36 VILL. L. REV. 517 (1991).

[56] *See, e.g.,* BRANDT GOLDSTEIN, STORMING THE COURT: HOW A BAND OF YALE LAW STUDENTS SUED THE PRESIDENT—AND WON (2005) (describing the litigation in *Sale v. Haitian Centers Council,* 509 U.S. 155 (1993)); RICHARD DANZIG & GEOFFREY R. WATSON, THE CAPABILITY PROBLEM IN CONTRACT LAW: FURTHER READINGS ON WELL-KNOWN CASES (2d ed. 2004) (describing several prominent contract cases); ALLAN GERSON & JERRY ADLER, THE PRICE OF TERROR: LESSONS OF LOCKERBIE FOR A WORLD ON THE BRINK (2001) (describing the litigation over the bombing of Pan Am Flight 103); DEBORAH BLUM, BAD KARMA: A TRUE STORY OF OBSESSION AND MURDER (1986) (describing the background of *Tarasoff v. Regents of University of California,* 17 Cal. 3d 425 (1976)); GERALD M. STERN, THE BUFFALO CREEK DISASTER (1976); RICHARD KLUGER, SIMPLE JUSTICE (1975) (describing the history of *Brown v. Board of Education,* 349 U.S. 294 (1955)).

that "we need, like archaeologists, gently to free these fragments from the overburden of legal dogmatics, and try, by relating them to the evidence, which has to be sought outside the law library, to make sense of them as events in history and incidents in the evolution of the law."[57] Litigation is complex, and published opinions seldom reveal the whole story.

> The facts as set forth by the court, for example, are often unrecognizable to either side. Sometimes they represent elements of the presentations of each or a compromise of the two. They have likely been pared down, edited as it were, by the court to reflect its view of relevance. . . . Similarly, any lawyer knows that the course and often the outcome of a case is affected, sometimes indeed determined, by strategic considerations.[58]

While litigation involves tactical decisions and strategic considerations, the documentary approach also reveals how chance—from the discovery of critical evidence to the assignment of a particular judge to hear the case—can affect the development and outcome of litigation.

The documentary approach highlights the diffuse network—victims and their families, activists, lawyers, judges, and government officials—that makes litigation possible. In *Filartiga*, the documentary approach reveals the development of a transnational advocacy network that emerged to pursue the case and promote human rights norms through domestic litigation.[59] The documents reveal a network of public interest lawyers, nongovernmental organizations, and law professors that worked together to pursue the case. The advocacy model developed in the *Filartiga* case became the standard for other ATS cases.[60]

The documentary approach is advantageous for other reasons as well. "Because the archaeological approach to storytelling is based on the avail-

---

[57] A.W. Brian Simpson, Leading Cases in the Common Law 12 (1995).

[58] Patricia D. White, *Afterword and Response: What Digging Does and Does Not Do*, 2000 Utah L. Rev. 301, 301.

[59] *See generally* Harold Hongju Koh, *The 1998 Frankel Lecture: Bringing International Law Home*, 35 Hous. L. Rev. 623 (1998); Margaret Keck & Kathryn Sikkink, Activists Beyond Borders: Advocacy Networks in International Politics (1998).

[60] *See generally* Naomi Roht-Arriaza, The Pinochet Effect: Transnational Justice in the Age of Human Rights 211 (2005); Ellen Lutz & Kathryn Sikkink, *The Justice Cascade: The Evolution and Impact of Foreign Human Rights Trials in Latin America*, 2 Chi. J. Int'l L. 1 (2001). While lawyers and legal professionals play a significant role in transnational litigation, their contributions to the movement are also subject to some criticism. *See* Richard J. Wilson, *Book Review: The Pinochet Effect*, 28 Hum. Rts. Q. 528, 536 (2006).

able objective historical record of litigated cases, it avoids a recurrent criticism of narrative scholarship—that it is based on subjective stories by individual authors and, thus, cannot be tested and replicated by others."[61] While this book accepts the legitimacy of the *Filartiga* precedent and supports transnational litigation as a tool for promoting human rights, it allows readers to review the documents and the history of the litigation and make their own determination about its legitimacy and effectiveness.[62]

---

[61] Paul L. Caron, *Back to the Future*, 71 U. CIN. L. REV. 405, 409 (2003).

[62] Scholars have both praised and criticized *Filartiga* and its progeny since the case was decided by the Second Circuit in 1980. The debate has addressed various issues, including the constitutionality of the ATS, the types of international norms that can be pursued, and the legitimacy of transnational litigation. *See, e.g.*, Ralph G. Steinhardt, *International Humanitarian Law in the Courts of the United States: Yamashita, Filartiga and 9–11*, 36 GEO. WASH. INT'L L. REV. 1 (2004); Note: *An Objection to Sosa—And to the New Federal Common Law*, 119 HARV. L. REV. 2077 (2006); Julian Ku & John Yoo, *Beyond Formalism in Foreign Affairs: A Functional Approach to the Alien Tort Statute*, 2004 SUP. CT. REV. 153; Harold Hongju Koh, *Is International Law Really State Law?*, 111 HARV. L. REV. 1824 (1998); Ryan Goodman & Derek P. Jinks, *Filartiga's Firm Footing: International Human Rights and Federal Common Law*, 66 FORDHAM L. REV. 463 (1997); Curtis A. Bradley & Jack L. Goldsmith, *Customary International Law as Federal Common Law: A Critique of the Modern Position*, 110 HARV. L. REV. 815 (1997); Alfred P. Rubin, *U.S. Tort Suits By Aliens Based on International Law*, FLETCHER F. 66 (Summer/Fall 1994); Steven Schneebaum, *Freedom from Torture Is a Legal Right*, ABA J. 34 (Feb. 1990); Richard A. Hibey, *U.S. Courts Shouldn't Meddle in Foreign Policy*, ABA J. 35 (Feb. 1990).

CHAPTER 2

FILARTIGA V. PENA-IRALA:
THE BIRTH OF TRANSNATIONAL LITIGATION

Federal Rule of Civil Procedure 3 provides that "[a] civil action is commenced by filing a complaint with the court."[1] While this is legally accurate, the search for justice begins well before the parties reach the courthouse door.

A. DEATH IN PARAGUAY

For many years, Dr. Joel Filártiga ran a modest medical clinic in Ybycuí, Paraguay, which was located approximately 50 miles from the capital of Asunción.[2] The clinic, *Sanatorio La Esperanza*, served a largely rural and indigent population in central Paraguay. The Filártiga family also owned a home in the Sajonia neighborhood of Asunción. A local police official, Americo Peña-Irala, lived two houses from the Filártiga home in Asunción along with his common law wife, Juana Villalba, her daughter, Charito Villalba, and Hugo Duarte, who was Charito's husband. Prior to March 1976, the Filártiga family and Peña-Irala did not interact, although the Filártiga children were friends with Charito.

Throughout his medical career, Dr. Filártiga had criticized the regime of General Alfredo Stroessner for its brutal treatment of indigenous groups in Paraguay.[3] He even used his foreign trips to denounce the Stroessner

---

[1] FED. R. CIV. P. 3.

[2] Dr. Filártiga was born in Ybytymi, Paraguay on August 15, 1932. *See generally* Richard Pierre Claude, *The Case of Joelito Filartiga and the Clinic of Hope*, 5 HUM. RTS. Q. 275 (1983); Michele Burgess, *Physician-Artist Is the Schweitzer of Paraguay*, MARYKNOLL 8 (Sept. 1978). For a description of Paraguayan history, see JOHN GIMLETTE, AT THE TOMB OF THE INFLATABLE PIG: TRAVELS THROUGH PARAGUAY (2003).

[3] *See generally* INTERNATIONAL HUMAN RIGHTS LAW GROUP & COMITE DE IGLESIAS PARA AYUDAS DE EMERGENCIA, PARAGUAY: HUMAN RIGHTS AND THE TRANSITION TOWARDS THE RULE OF LAW (1996); FATIMA MYRIAM YORE, LA DOMINACION STRONISTA: ORIGENES Y CONSOLIDACION (1992); CARLOS R. MIRANDA, THE STROESSNER ERA: AUTHORITARIAN RULE IN PARAGUAY (1990); Andrew Nickson, *The Overthrow of the Stroessner Regime: Re-establishing the Status Quo*, 8 BULL. LATIN AM. RES. 185 (1989); VIRGINIA M. BOUVIER, DECLINE OF THE DICTATOR: PARAGUAY AT A CROSSROADS (1988); PAUL H. LEWIS, PARAGUAY UNDER STROESSNER (1980).

regime while also seeking funds for his medical clinic in Paraguay.[4] Because of his political activism, Dr. Filártiga was often the target of harassment and intimidation by Paraguayan officials.[5] On several occasions, Dr. Filártiga was detained by Paraguayan officials. On three occasions, he was tortured.[6] Dr. Filártiga often feared that Paraguayan officials would target his family to punish him for his political activism or to deter him from further criticizing the Stroessner regime.

On March 29, 1976, Dr. Filártiga, his wife Nidia, and daughter Katia were at the medical clinic in Ybycuí. Joelito Filártiga, Dr. Filártiga's 17-year-old son, was living at the Filártiga home in Asunción along with his 20-year-old sister Dolly and younger sister Analy.[7] In subsequent court filings, the Filártigas presented a graphic description of what happened that night.[8]

[I]n the middle of the night, seventeen year old Joelito Filartiga was kidnapped from his bed while his three [sic] sisters and a sailor lay sleeping in the house. He was taken two doors down to the house of Americo Norberto Pena-Irala (Pena), then Inspector General of Police of Asuncion, Paraguay and the defendant herein. He was whipped, beaten, slashed across his body and appeared to have been subjected to extremely high levels of electric shock. An aluminum wire was placed in his penis for the pur-

---

[4] In January 1976, Dr. Filártiga visited the United States and offered several public lectures about his work in Paraguay and the difficulties of living under the Stroessner regime.

[5] The Stroessner regime kept detailed records of its internal security investigations, which documented the surveillance and persecution of political opponents, including Dr. Filártiga. These records became public following the overthrow of the Stroessner regime in 1989. *See generally* Katie Zoglin, *Paraguay's Archive of Terror: International Cooperation and Operation Condor*, 32 U. MIAMI INTER-AM. L. REV. 57 (2001); Keith M. Slack, *Operation Condor and Human Rights: A Report from Paraguay's Archive of Terror*, 18 HUM. RTS. Q. 492 (1996); ALFREDO BOCCIA PAZ ET AL., ES MI INFORME: LOS ARCHIVOS SECRETOS DE LA POLICIA DE STROESSNER (1994); Stella Calloni, *The Horror Archives of Operation Condor*, 50 COVERT ACTION 7 (Fall 1994).

[6] In 1958, Dr. Filártiga was detained for several days without food and was subjected to forced labor. In 1963, he was detained for several days. During this detention, he was forced to stand for long periods of time. He was beaten, submerged underwater, and subjected to electric shocks. Transcript of Hearing Before the Honorable John L. Caden at 31–32, Filartiga v. Pena-Irala, 577 F. Supp. 860 (E.D.N.Y. 1984) (No. 79 C 917).

[7] In addition, a family friend of the Filártiga family, who served in the Paraguayan Navy, stayed at the Filártiga home in Asunción.

[8] There are slightly different accounts of Joelito's initial location on the night of March 29. According to Analy Filártiga, Joelito arrived at home at 10:30 p.m. After dinner, he received a telephone call and left the house. ANIBAL MIRANDA & ANALY FILARTIGA, EL CASO FILARTIGA 52 (1992).

pose of applying electric shock. He was tortured in this manner for approximately forty-five minutes until his young body reached its endurance limit and he died. The torture of Joelito was in retaliation for the political activities and opinions of his father.

At approximately 4:00 a.m. in the morning, Dolly Filartiga, the sister of Joelito and one of the plaintiffs herein was awakened by a loud knock on the front door. The person knocking was Galeano, the Chief of Police for the precinct in that area. He informed her that "there was a small problem with [her] brother at Pena's house." She followed Galeano to Pena's house which was surrounded by land filled with policemen. She asked for her brother and was told he was in the back room.

Knowing the house, she walked to that room and there she was confronted with the brutally tortured body of her beloved brother. The body lay on a mattress in a pool of blood.

In disbelief, she ran to her brother and tried to awaken him. She wanted to cry, but they did not let her. She wanted to ask for help, but she was stopped. She was told to take her brother's body and bury it quickly. But she could not think of what to do. In desperation, she ran to the street.

On her way out, Dolly Filartiga met defendant Pena in the hall of the house. She asked him what he had done to her brother and he replied with a confession and a threat: "here you have what you have been looking for for so long and what you deserved. Now shut up." He further threatened Dolly with a similar fate. With this, Dolly ran into the streets in circles, finally finding her way home where she and a younger sister consoled each other and attempted to call relatives. Still Pena insisted that Dolly remove the body of her brother, or it would be thrown into the streets. With the help of the sailor and a policeman, Dolly took Joelito's body home on the bloody mattress on which she found it.[9]

On the morning of March 30, 1976, Dr. Filártiga and his wife were notified at the clinic in Ybycuí that Joelito had "suffered a tragedy."[10] They

---

[9] Plaintiffs' Post-Trial Memorandum of Law and Facts at 3–4, Filartiga v. Pena-Irala, 577 F. Supp. 860 (E.D.N.Y. 1984) (No. 79 C 917) (citations omitted). *See also* Alberto Cabral, *Political Murder in Paraguay*, AMERICA, Apr. 23, 1977, at 376. Alberto Cabral was a pseudonym for Richard Alan White, a friend of the Filártiga family.

[10] Transcript of Hearing, *supra* note 6, at 37.

immediately drove back to Asunción. As they neared their home, they found it surrounded by military personnel and police officers. On entering the house, they found Joelito's body placed on a table in one of the main rooms. When he examined Joelito's naked body, Dr. Filártiga noticed marks associated with torture, including cuts, burns, bruises, and stab wounds. To document the evidence of torture, he asked three friends who were doctors to conduct a preliminary autopsy.[11] Their autopsy report identified numerous wounds and injuries. It concluded that Joelito died of acute anemia due to internal hemorrhaging. Dr. Filártiga then took photographs of the body to provide further evidence of the torture. At the request of Dr. Filártiga, a second autopsy was performed two weeks after Joelito's death, which documented other injuries, including burn marks, mutilation of the genitals, and revealed that the fingernails and toenails had been pulled from their settings.[12] This autopsy report was subsequently reviewed by two doctors in the United States, who provided the following forensic observations.

> The photograph of the body of Joelito Filartiga shows direct evidence of torture in the form of whipping and beating. The patterned marks over the right side of the body are classical for whip marks by a looped flexible cord. The injuries to Joelito were deliberately forceful, multiple and inflicted over a period of time. For example, the mark on the right thigh appears to be older than others. The other marks on the skin were certainly inflicted during life and were intended to produce severe pain. The cause of death probably was not a single stab wound but rather the result of shock and hemorrhage due to multiple traumatic injuries. If the burns were caused by electricity, the amount of current used may have caused his death by cardiac arrest. An intracerebral bleed may have also been responsible. This possibility must be raised because of the fracture of the temporal bone of the skull. To my knowledge no examination of the internal organs or the brain was made. While the pain associated with the beating and stabbing can be

---

11 Affidavit of Dr. Joel Filartiga at 1–2, Filartiga v. Pena-Irala, 577 F. Supp. 860 (E.D.N.Y. 1984) (No. 79 C 917). *Cf. El estudiante no murio a las 2,30,* HOY (Asunción), Apr. 9, 1979, at 11.

12 This autopsy was performed on April 13, 1976, by Lorenzo Hernan Gody Garcia at the request of Dr. Filártiga. In a July 24, 1979, communication to the Inter-American Commission on Human Rights, the Paraguayan government denied that Joelito had suffered these injuries. In fact, the Paraguayan government indicated that the autopsy report specifically stated that "the genital organs were not mutilated" and that "the nails of the hands and feet were not torn." Letter from Francisco Barreiro Maffiodo, Paraguayan Ambassador, to Edmundo Vargas Carreño, Executive Secretary, Inter-American Commission on Human Rights (July 24, 1979).

imagined to some degree by anyone, the amount of pain from the considerable number of wounds inflicted upon Joelito must be outside the experience of any of us.[13]

The Filártiga family was convinced that Joelito was tortured by Paraguayan officials seeking information on Dr. Filártiga's political activities. His death, perhaps inadvertent, occurred during the torture. Joelito's murder had a profound impact on the Filártiga family. Dolly suffered severe emotional trauma because of her brother's death.

> For a full year following my brother's death, I could not believe he was dead. I kept thinking he would come back and that I heard the sound of his footsteps or of his voice. This happened often and each time I would rush to see if he was there; each time he did not appear filled me with terrible fear and despair.

> I also constantly had the same dream—almost every night and I still have this dream from time to time. I dream that Joelito is rising from the blood-soaked mattress upon which I found him with all his wounds and that he is telling me that nothing happened. It is like I am continually confronted with the vision of my brother as he was when I was led to him. I wake up screaming. When I was home I would put pillows in my mouth so my mother wouldn't hear my screams and turn on the water faucets in the bathroom so that she couldn't hear me sobbing. During that first year I could hardly sleep. I guess I slept actually about one hour a day. When I couldn't sleep I would start cleaning in a frenzy. Cleaning the house, sweeping the pavement in front of the house. I would clean the same thing over and over and I still am a compulsive cleaner. I cannot stand anything messy.[14]

One year after Joelito's death, Dolly tried to commit suicide by overdosing on medication. She suffered constant sadness and guilt because of her brother's death, and this continued for many years. Dr. Filártiga also suffered emotional and physical effects from his son's murder.[15] He recalled

---

[13] Affidavits of Dr. Glenn Randall & Dr. Jose Quiroga at 6–7, Filartiga v. Pena-Irala, 577 F. Supp. 860 (E.D.N.Y. 1984) (No. 79 C 917). Drs. Randall and Quiroga reviewed the autopsy reports and accompanying photographs in 1982. Their report indicated that the fingernails appeared intact in the photographs, suggesting that the loosened fingernails described in one of the autopsy reports may have been caused by postmortem changes. *Id.* at 5.

[14] Affidavit of Dolly Filartiga at 1–2, Filartiga v. Pena-Irala, 577 F. Supp. 860 (E.D.N.Y. 1984) (No. 79 C 917).

[15] Transcript of Hearing, *supra* note 6, at 32–33.

his own experiences with torture. He also expressed feelings of guilt that he was responsible for Joelito's death because of his own political views and his support of Paraguayan peasants. The entire Filártiga family shared similar symtoms and grief.[16]

The official Paraguayan version of Joelito's death is quite different. According to Paraguayan police, Joelito was killed in a jealous rage by Hugo Duarte when he discovered Joelito in bed with his wife. Duarte and his young wife, Charito Villalba, lived in Peña-Irala's house. On the night of March 29, 1976, Duarte was working at the Hotel Guaraní and returned home at 2:00 a.m. Upon entering his bedroom, Duarte alleged he discovered Joelito in bed with his wife. Duarte's purported confession to police describes how he attacked Joelito and eventually killed him.

> [T]hey got into a hand-to-hand fight for several minutes, and during the fighting Derlis [Hugo Duarte] had taken possession of a knife located on a small table in the bedroom, with which he stabbed [Filartiga] in the back running through his chest, the consequences of which Filartiga fell in a faint. Taking advantage of this and while being blinded by his nerves, Duarte stabbed him in the back and sides on many occasions. With only the desire to kill and realizing that nothing could be done, he hit him several times with a thick cable from a bedside lamp, leaving him dead.[17]

Paraguayan officials quickly accepted Duarte's confession, and they strongly denied the torture charges or allegations of police complicity. The official coroner's report prepared on March 30, 1976, did not identify any bruises or injuries to Joelito's body. It simply stated: "Joel Filartiga—March 30, 1976. Acute anemia, (wound) penetrated thorax; Fifth space in left intercostals made by a knife." A formal inquest subsequently confirmed the official explanation: Joelito had been murdered by Hugo Duarte in a jealous rage. Duarte also confessed to the murder and denied any government involvement.[18] However, Charito Villalba, Duarte's wife and a key witness

---

16 Affidavit of Dr. Joel Filartiga, *supra* note 11, at 9–13.

17 Paraguayan Crime Scene Report (undated).

18 On April 21, 1979, Duarte gave an interview in prison to a Paraguayan newspaper where he reaffirmed his guilt. "Do you think that I would be here in jail if I wasn't the perpetrator of the murder? Do you think I would take responsibility for the murder if I wasn't the perpetrator? Like I have said, neither money nor threats would keep me quiet. Someone who thinks otherwise is mistaken. . . . During the fight, Joel Filartiga died just like I could have died. It was a crime of passion. It was the result of an intense anger, a profound pain that I felt when I found my wife in the company of Filartiga." *Duarte Arredondo habla en prision*, ULTIMA HORA (Asunción), Apr. 21, 1979, at 10.

who could corroborate the government position, disappeared soon after Joelito was murdered.

The Filártiga family refused to accept the official government version of Joelito's death. They remained convinced that Joelito was tortured and killed by Paraguayan police. On April 7, 1976, they instituted legal proceedings in Asunción to identify the perpetrators who were involved in Joelito's murder.[19] They were assisted by several attorneys, including Horacio Galeano Perrone.[20] Perrone received numerous threats because of his work on the Filártiga case. He was subsequently disbarred, allegedly for engaging in fraudulent activities, although the Filártiga family remained supportive of his work on their case.[21] Two other lawyers hired by the Filártiga family withdrew from the case after they were threatened. The Filártiga family was also targeted with threats and abuse. Military personnel monitored the Filártiga home. The family received numerous telephone calls threatening them with further acts of violence if they continued to pursue their inquiry into Joelito's death. One month after Joelito's death, Dolly and her mother were arrested and jailed, accused of breaking into Peña-Irala's house. They were released the following day, although Dolly remained under house arrest for several months. At one point, Katia Filártiga was kidnapped, allegedly by a police officer, and was returned after the family contacted the U.S. Embassy in Asunción.

Despite their efforts, the Filártiga family was unable to get Paraguayan authorities to prosecute Peña-Irala. He disappeared for several months and

---

[19] Under Paraguayan law, crime victims may participate as parties in a criminal investigation. For background on the Paraguayan proceedings, see RICHARD ALAN WHITE, BREAKING SILENCE: THE CASE THAT CHANGED THE FACE OF HUMAN RIGHTS (2004).

[20] On several occasions, Perrone contacted the U.S. Embassy to discuss developments in the case. *See* Telegram from the American Embassy in Asunción, Paraguay to the U.S. Department of State (Feb. 18, 1977). In an October 12, 1976 letter to U.S. Ambassador George Landau, Perrone challenged the Paraguayan government's version of Joelito's death. Letter from Horacio Galeano Perrone, to George Landau, U.S. Ambassador to Paraguay (Oct. 12, 1976). He asserted that Joelito was tortured by the police in order to gain information about a suspected insurgency group. Perrone then requested that the U.S. government investigate the Filártiga case and publicize its findings. In March 1977, Perrone sent another letter to the U.S. Ambassador, retracting his previous statements about the case and absolving the police of complicity in Joelito's death. The letter also expressed support for the Stroessner regime. In a subsequent meeting at the U.S. Embassy, however, Perrone renounced his second letter, indicating he sent it in response to repeated threats arising out of his work on the Filártiga case. *See* Letter from Philip C. Gill, American Embassy, Asunción, Paraguay, to Richard Graham, U.S. Department of State (Mar. 29, 1977).

[21] DAVID M. HELFELD & WILLIAM L. WIPFLER, MBARETÉ: THE HIGHER LAW OF PARAGUAY 134–35 (1980).

was eventually discovered living in the United States. Duarte served five years in prison before he was released under a Paraguayan law that absolves husbands who commit a murder *in flagrante delicto.* Duarte then sued Dr. Filártiga for slander and defamation of character and was awarded approximately $30,000 in damages. In 1985, the Paraguayan Supreme Court of Justice upheld Duarte's civil action against Dr. Filártiga.[22]

Because of the human rights implications, the U.S. Embassy in Asunción expressed its concerns about the Filártiga case to the Paraguayan government.[23] On several occasions, Embassy officials met with Dr. Filártiga to discuss the case. In September 1976, the Embassy even sponsored an exhibition of Dr. Filártiga's drawings at the Paraguayan American Cultural Center in Asunción. The event received significant media coverage, and pictures of U.S. Ambassador George Landau's meeting with Dr. Filártiga appeared in several Paraguayan newspapers. Robert White, who became U.S. Ambassador to Paraguay in 1977, met the Filártiga family soon after his appointment and was regularly apprised of developments in the case. According to White,

> [w]e became very interested in the Filartiga case, not only because it was our mandate under the Carter administration to be vigilant about human rights and to report on them and to do whatever we could to protect them, but also because we were deluged with letters from the United States after every trip that Dr. Filartiga made here and we would get letters from university professors, human rights organizations and just ordinary citizens, Senators, Congressmen, etc., in effect saying, please do everything you can to protect Dr. Filartiga.[24]

Gradually, the U.S. Embassy developed its own understanding of the Filártiga case. On February 18, 1977, the U.S. Embassy sent the following description of the case to the U.S. State Department.

> [O]n March 30, 1976, the body of Joel Filartiga, the 16 [sic] year old son of Dr. Joel Filartiga, medical doctor and one of Paraguay's leading painters, was found at the home of a young married

---

[22] *See generally* INTERNATIONAL LEAGUE FOR HUMAN RIGHTS, MBARETE: TWO YEARS LATER 113 (1982).

[23] *See, e.g.*, Telegram from the U.S. Department of State to the American Embassy in Asunción, Paraguay (Dec. 15, 1977); Telegram from the U.S. Department of State to the American Embassy in Asunción, Paraguay (Dec. 10, 1977); Memorandum from Philip C. Gill, American Embassy, Asunción, Paraguay to Files (Oct. 21, 1976).

[24] Transcript of Hearing, *supra* note 6, at 78–79.

woman. That the body was badly mutilated is attested to by the many photos of it published in the local press. The woman's husband was subsequently charged with the murder and brought to trial. The trial has not yet been completed. (Such a delay is not unusual in the Paraguayan legal system.)

Beyond this, there is no generally agreed upon version of what transpired. Because of some obvious discrepancies, such as the condition of the body and the fact that the young woman reportedly was still in bed with the corpse when the police allegedly arrived, and shortly thereafter disappeared never to give testimony in the case, created serious doubts regarding the murder charges.[25]

Subsequently, the U.S. Embassy developed various other accounts of the case. A January 23, 1978, memorandum from the U.S. Embassy in Asunción presented a detailed overview of the case and offered an "educated guess" on what took place.

There was an adulterous relationship between Duarte's wife and Filartiga. Police officials were involved in a scheme of personal revenge through torture but not premeditated murder. Either the torture or Duarte killed Filartiga. Unless the missing Rosario [Charito] Villalba de Duarte is found and will talk, it will be impossible to find out what actually happened.[26]

On April 7, 1979, the U.S. Embassy offered further elaboration on the case.

It is probable that Duarte is guilty. It is almost certainly not possible that he committed the barbaric acts alone and in a fit of passion. It is probable that he has confessed and shielded others out of fear of consequences similar to those visited on young Filartiga if he did not cooperate. There are legitimate, solid reasons to suspect police involvement. The possibility also exists of political persecution but it appears to be based more on inherent suspicion of this government rather than any real evidence.[27]

---

[25] Telegram from the American Embassy in Asunción, Paraguay, to the U.S. Department of State (Feb. 18, 1977).

[26] Telegram from the American Embassy in Asunción, Paraguay, to the U.S. Department of State (Jan. 23, 1978).

[27] Telegram from the American Embassy in Asunción, Paraguay, to the U.S. Department of State (Apr. 7, 1979).

The Filártiga case was profiled extensively in the Paraguayan media. But its notoriety extended beyond Paraguay. Several organizations publicized the case, including Amnesty International, the Washington Office on Latin America, the Committee on Hemispheric Affairs, and the International League for Human Rights. In 1977, Amnesty International issued a report on political repression in Paraguay that highlighted the Filártiga case.[28] As part of its Campaign against Torture, Amnesty International issued an appeal for its members to contact the Paraguayan government and request action in the Filártiga case. In November 1977, Amnesty International co-sponsored Dr. Filártiga's visit to the United States, providing him with a forum to speak about his son's death and the brutality of the Stroessner dictatorship.

In 1977, a petition concerning the Filártiga case was filed with the Inter-American Commission on Human Rights.[29] The petition charged the Paraguayan government with violating the American Declaration on the Rights and Duties of Man by failing to investigate Joelito's torture and murder. The Inter-American Commission referenced the case in its 1978 *Report on the Situation of Human Rights in Paraguay*, although it declined to offer substantive comments on the case since an investigation was pending.[30] The Commission did indicate, however, that it had received several photographs of Joelito's body "in which the signs of physical mistreatment can be seen."[31] In response to the petition, the Paraguayan government denied the allegations and asserted that Hugo Duarte killed Joelito in a jealous rage.

> Joel Filártiga was killed during a dramatic episode by the husband of an unfaithful wife discovered in a flagrant act of adultery with the deceased. The murderer, [Hugo] Duarte Arredondo, confessed his guilt during the judicial proceeding being conducted in the Regular Courts. All the background information on this case is public knowledge and the events are followed by the citizenry in

---

[28] *See* AMNESTY INTERNATIONAL, DEATHS UNDER TORTURE AND DISAPPEARANCES OF POLITICAL PRISONERS IN PARAGUAY (1977).

[29] The Inter-American Commission on Human Rights received two communications regarding the Filártiga case. On March 24, 1977, Martin Ennals, the Secretary-General of Amnesty International sent a letter to the Commission describing human rights abuses in Paraguay, including the Filártiga case. Based on this communication, the Commission opened an individual case and forwarded the pertinent parts of the communication to the Paraguayan government. On July 28, 1977, Harold R. Berk, an Amnesty International USA member, submitted a second communication to the Commission regarding the Filártiga case.

[30] Inter-Am. C.H.R., OEA/Ser.L/V/II.43, Report on the Situation of Human Rights in Paraguay, doc. 13 corr. 1 (1978). The case was designated Case 2158.

[31] *Id.*

the newspaper, due to the obvious attraction that this type of incident has for most of the public. It is totally false that the police participated in this crime; the clarification of which, moreover, is now the responsibility of the judges of the Judicial Branch.[32]

The Paraguayan government reiterated its denials in a July 1979 submission to the Inter-American Commission on Human Rights.[33] In September 1983, however, the Commission closed its investigation of the case without taking action against Paraguay. The public files maintained by the Commission do not reveal why the case was closed.

In the United States, several members of Congress used the Filártiga case to criticize the Stroessner regime and highlight the Carter administration's commitment to human rights. On February 1, 1977, Senator Edward Kennedy described the Filártiga case in the U.S. Senate and submitted an article about the case into the *Congressional Record*.[34]

I have spoken out in the past of my concern for the problems of human rights in Paraguay. Recently, I received material documenting another sad and shocking case involving the kidnapping, torture, and murder of a 17-year old youth, Joelito Filartiga, in Asuncion, Paraguay.

This young man could have been any one of the victims each year who disappear from their homes in the dead of night, or who fail to come home from work one day and are never seen again, as testimony before the House International Relations Subcommittee disclosed last year. What was different about this boy is that his father, an internationally renowned Paraguayan artist, decided that his son would not just be quietly buried and forgotten. Instead he has risked his own life, and the safety of his family to do all that he could to bring this ugly incident to public attention. The photographs that he has taken of the pitifully scarred body of his son, Joelito, speak more deeply and powerfully of the savagery of such practices than volumes of testimony. Once seen, it cannot be forgotten or ignored.[35]

---

[32] *Id.*

[33] Letter from Francisco Barreiro Maffiodo, Paraguayan Ambassador, to Edmundo Vargas Carreño, Executive Secretary, Inter-American Commission on Human Rights (July 24, 1979).

[34] Senator Kennedy submitted the 1977 article, *Political Murder in Paraguay*, written by Richard Alan White under the pseudonym Alberto Cabral.

[35] 123 CONG. REC. 3048 (Feb. 1, 1977) (statement of Sen. Kennedy). A similar article was inserted into the *Congressional Record* by Congressman Ed Koch on February 9,

B. JUSTICE IN AMERICA

On July 21, 1978, Americo Peña-Irala entered the United States on a tourist visa along with Juana Villalba, his common law wife.[36] They were accompanied by their three-year-old son and Villalba's niece, Blanca Fernandez. From their point of entry in Miami, they soon traveled to New York, where they rented an apartment in the Borough Park section of Brooklyn. They remained there for nine months, long after their visas had expired.

In September 1978, the Filártiga family discovered that Peña-Irala was living in New York when they received a misdirected letter sent from Blanca Fernandez to her father, who lived in the same neighborhood as the Filártigas in Asunción.[37] The letter was delivered by mistake to the Filártiga home. When the Filártiga family opened the letter, it revealed that Blanca Fernandez was living in New York with her aunt, Juana Villalba, and Peña-Irala. The letter included a return address for Peña-Irala in New York. According to Dolly Filártiga,

> When the letter from Pena was delivered to our house, I decided that the only thing I could do was to come to the United States to find him. I had no life in Paraguay. I could not study, I could not live, I could not work, I had no friends, and I felt constantly per-

---

1977. *See* 123 CONG. REC. 4014 (Feb. 9, 1977) (statement of Rep. Koch). In response to the *Congressional Record* story, the State Department requested information about the case from the U.S. Embassy in Asunción. On February 18, 1977, the American Embassy sent the following telegram in response.

> Joel Filartiga, 16 [sic] year old son of prominent physician and artist, was murdered last March. It is unclear who committed the crime; trial of the accused is still in progress. Although there are rumors of sex, drugs and/or political motives and that Filartiga was actually killed by police, GOP [Government of Paraguay] officials and opposition leaders (including Chairman of Paraguayan Human Rights Commission) as well as high church officials to date do not RPT [repeat] do not believe case involves a human rights violation, but rather was a common crime. In view of allegations of HR [human rights] violations in U.S., however, Embassy has urged GOP to investigate fully and take appropriate measures if warranted.

Telegram from the American Embassy in Asunción, Paraguay to the U.S. Department of State (Feb. 18, 1977).

[36] Affidavit of Dolly Filartiga at 2, Filartiga v. Pena-Irala, 630 F.2d 876 (2d Cir. 1980) (No. 79 C 917). Peña-Irala entered the United States along with a Paraguayan tour group, ostensibly to visit Disney World.

[37] Transcript of Hearing, *supra* note 6, at 11.

secuted. I knew if I came here I might never be able to go back, but I had no choice.[38]

In October 1978, Dr. Joel Filártiga and Dolly Filártiga came to the United States as part of an Amnesty International sponsored tour.[39] Their goal was also to locate Peña-Irala. While Dr. Filártiga returned to Paraguay in December 1978, Dolly remained in the country to search for Peña-Irala. Unfortunately, she misplaced Peña-Irala's address and was forced to start her search anew. This was a difficult time for Dolly since she was without her family and had no means of financial support. She moved to Washington, D.C. and took several part-time jobs to support herself. During this time, Dolly cleaned houses to make money but also in a cathartic effort to wipe clean the brutal memories that continued to haunt her. Soon after she arrived in Washington, D.C., Dolly contacted Michael Maggio, an acquaintance of the Filártiga family, who had recently graduated from law school and had established his immigration law practice in Washington, D.C. She discussed with him the possibility of filing a political asylum application. When her tourist visa expired, Dolly decided to remain in the United States to search for Peña-Irala.

In January 1979, Richard Alan White, a scholar of Paraguay and close friend of the Filártiga family, who had spent several weeks living with the family after Joelito's death, became increasingly active in the search for Peña-Irala.[40] White was a senior fellow at the Washington-based Council on Hemispheric Affairs (COHA), an organization that promotes human rights in Latin America. Through their contacts with the Paraguayan community in New York, Dolly and White located an exiled Paraguayan national, Gilberto Olmedo Sanchez, who had information about Peña-Irala's whereabouts. On March 1, 1979, they contacted Sanchez, who provided them with Peña-Irala's address in Brooklyn.[41]

On March 8, 1979, Maggio contacted the Immigration and Naturalization Service (INS) to notify it of Peña-Irala's presence in the United

---

[38] Affidavit of Dolly Filartiga, *supra* note 14, at 4.

[39] *See* Janet Koch, *Dr. Filártiga—A Picture of Hope*, NEW HAVEN JOURNAL-COURIER, Nov. 11, 1978, at 41.

[40] WHITE, *supra* note 19, at 189–92.

[41] Affidavit of Dolly Filartiga, *supra* note 36, at 2; Affirmation of Gilberto Olmedo Sanchez, Filartiga v. Pena-Irala, 630 F.2d 876 (2d Cir. 1980) (No. 79 C 917). Olmedo Sanchez published a newsletter, *El Paraguay Libre*, which denounced the Stroessner regime and called for political reform in Paraguay.

States.[42] The INS then began an investigation to confirm Peña-Irala's location and identity. It requested that the U.S. Embassy in Asunción ascertain how Peña-Irala entered the country.[43] It also asked the Embassy to investigate Peña-Irala's alleged participation in Joelito's torture and murder. As part of the investigation, INS agents secretly photographed Peña-Irala and Villalba to verify their identities.[44] On April 1, 1979, the INS presented the photographs to Dolly Filártiga in Washington, D.C., who confirmed their identities.[45]

On April 4, 1979, Peña-Irala and Villalba were arrested by the Immigration and Naturalization Service as they walked out of their apartment in Brooklyn.[46] The following day, they appeared at a deportation hearing before an immigration judge. At the hearing, Peña-Irala indicated to the judge that they wanted to "return as soon as possible to Paraguay."[47] After acknowledging they had overstayed their tourist visas, Peña-Irala and Villalba were ordered deported. They were held at the Brooklyn Naval Yard detention facility pending their deportation.[48]

The decision to file a civil lawsuit under the Alien Tort Statute against Peña-Irala was made soon after his identity was confirmed. Michael Maggio contacted several organizations about the possibility of initiating civil proceedings against Peña-Irala.[49] Through Gerhard Elston, the Executive

---

[42] Interview with Michael Maggio, in New York, New York (July 16, 2002).

[43] According to the State Department, Peña-Irala was eligible for a tourist visa because he had never been indicted in Paraguay. *See* Letter from Barbara M. Watson, Assistant Secretary of State, Bureau of Consular Affairs, to the Deputy Secretary of State (Apr. 12, 1979); Letter from Hume Horan, Acting Assistant Secretary of State, Bureau of Consular Affairs, to the Honorable Robert F. Drinan (Apr. 29, 1979); Letter from the Honorable Robert F. Drinan, to Barbara M. Watson, Assistant Secretary of State, Bureau of Consular Affairs (Apr. 6, 1979). In addition to the Peña-Irala case, the State Department became involved in a broader investigation concerning the issuance of visas by the U.S. Embassy in Asunción. *See generally* Jeff Nesmith, *U.S. Probe of Visas Resisted*, ATLANTA CONSTITUTION, Apr. 9, 1979, at 1–A.

[44] Affidavit of Dolly Filartiga, *supra* note 36, at 2.

[45] Interview with Dolly Filártiga, in New York, New York (July 16, 2002).

[46] *See generally* Selwyn Raab, *Paraguay Alien Tied to Murders in Native Land*, N.Y. TIMES, Apr. 5, 1979, at B1; Lee Lescaze, *Paraguayan Police Figure is Arrested in New York*, WASH. POST, Apr. 5, 1979, at A17.

[47] Selwyn Raab, *Judge Rules Pena Can Be Sued Here on Death in Paraguay*, N.Y. TIMES, Apr. 10, 1979, at B1.

[48] Peña-Irala was held on a $75,000 bond, and Villalba was held on a $25,000 bond. Their child was turned over to social service agencies during the pendency of their detention.

[49] Interview with Michael Maggio, in New York, New York (July 16, 2002). Several

Director of Amnesty International USA, Maggio was placed in contact with
Peter Weiss, a Vice-President and cooperating attorney at the Center for
Constitutional Rights (CCR).[50] On April 5, 1979, Weiss called Maggio,
expressing his interest in the case and his thoughts of using the Alien Tort
Statute against Peña-Irala. Weiss had previously considered using the ATS
in cases involving war crimes in Vietnam.[51] He had discovered the statute
while investigating the possibility of filing a civil lawsuit regarding the My
Lai massacre of 1968. In fact, the Center for Constitutional Rights had
raised the ATS, albeit unsuccessfully, in a 1975 case involving children who
had been evacuated from Vietnam.[52] Weiss then asked Maggio to bring
Dolly from Washington, D.C. to New York in order to file the civil lawsuit
against Peña-Irala. Because they feared that Peña-Irala would soon be
deported, they decided to file the complaint the next day. The complaint
was put together within 24 hours at the Center for Constitutional Rights by
Weiss and three other CCR attorneys, Rhonda Copelon, John Corwin, and
Jose Antonio Lugo.[53]

---

organizations, including Amnesty International USA, the Washington Office on Latin
America, and the Committee on Hemispheric Affairs, subsequently publicized the case
and called on government officials to assist the Filártiga family. *See, e.g.,* Press Release,
Council on Hemispheric Affairs, The Strange Case of Americo Pena (Apr. 17, 1978).

[50] Interview with Peter Weiss, Vice-President, Center for Constitutional Rights, in
New York, New York (July 15, 2002). *See also Proceedings: Conference on International Human
Rights Law in State and Federal Courts,* 17 U.S.F. L. REV. 1, 57 (1982). According to Peter
Weiss, "one day the phone rings and it's Gerhard Elston from Amnesty International who
says, 'They just arrested a Paraguayan torturer. He's being held at the INS detention center in Brooklyn and he is going to be deported in 48 hours. What can we do to keep him
here?' . . . That's how *Filártiga* started. Nobody had time to think about what the implications were, where it was going to lead or even what the theory was going to be. All we
knew was that something had to be done within 48 hours." *Id.*

[51] Peter Weiss, Vice-President, Center for Constitutional Rights, Remarks at the
Association of the Bar of the City of New York (Nov. 2, 2005); Interview with Peter Weiss,
Vice-President, Center for Constitutional Rights, in New York, New York (July 15, 2002).

[52] *See* Nguyen Da Yen v. Kissinger, 528 F.2d 1194 (9th Cir. 1975). In *Nguyen Da Yen,*
the Ninth Circuit considered the possibility that the ATS might be available in a lawsuit
filed with respect to the mass transfer of children from Vietnam at the end of the
Vietnam War. "The illegal seizure, removal and detention of an alien against his will in
a foreign country would appear to be a tort, and it may well be a tort in violation of the
'law of nations.' . . . We are reluctant to decide the applicability of § 1350 to this case
without adequate briefing. Moreover, we are reluctant to rest on it in any event. The
complaint presently does not join the adoption agencies as defendants. While the present defendants' involvement in the airlift would certainly constitute them as joint tortfeasors, Fed. R. Civ. P. 19 might dictate joinder of the agencies in order to litigate the
suit under § 1350 or § 1331. We are unaware whether such joinder is feasible." *Id.* at
1201–02 (citations omitted).

[53] Maggio and Dolly Filártiga worked on her affidavit through the evening of April
5. They also filed Dolly's political asylum application on that day. On the morning of

On April 6, 1979, the lawsuit was filed in the federal district court for the Eastern District of New York.[54] The case was assigned to Judge Eugene H. Nickerson. The complaint, which was only six pages long, was personally served by Maggio on Peña-Irala in his detention cell at the Brooklyn Naval Yard.[55] Dolly Filártiga and Dr. Joel Filártiga were listed as the plaintiffs, and Peña-Irala was named as a defendant. Because Peña-Irala was under a deportation order, the complaint also named Leonel Castillo, the INS Commissioner, and George Vician, the District Director of the INS, as defendants. Federal jurisdiction was premised on several statutes, including the Alien Tort Statute.[56]

The complaint alleged that Peña-Irala had kidnapped, tortured, and murdered Joelito. It described how Dolly was summoned by Paraguayan police officials to Peña-Irala's house and led to Joelito's mutilated body. It noted how Peña-Irala had announced to Dolly, "[h]ere you have what you have been looking for for so long and what you deserve. Now shut up."[57] The complaint indicated that the Filártigas had been unable to pursue their investigation into Joelito's death in Paraguay. It noted their attorney had been arrested and threatened. It also indicated that Peña-Irala had threatened them with further retaliation if they continued to pursue the investigation. The complaint then raised two causes of action. The first cause of action asserted that Peña-Irala's acts constituted violations of U.S. treaties and the law of nations. The second cause of action alleged that Peña-Irala's acts constituted violations of wrongful death statutes. Both causes of action were based on the same facts. They alleged that Joelito Filártiga had sustained pain and suffering and bodily injuries, which were

---

April 6, they took an early morning flight from Washington, D.C. to New York. When they arrived at the Center for Constitutional Rights, they continued working on the complaint until 4:00 p.m. Correspondence from Michael Maggio, to William Aceves (Sept. 13, 2000).

[54] Verified Complaint, Filartiga v. Pena-Irala, 630 F.2d 876 (2d Cir. 1980) (No. 79 C 917).

[55] Several exhibits were attached to the complaint: (1) two photographs of Joelito's body; (2) a January 16, 1978, communication from Harold Berk, an Amnesty International USA activist, to the Inter-American Commission on Human Rights describing the Filártiga case; and (3) two *New York Times* articles on Peña-Irala's arrest in New York. In addition, Professor Richard Arens of Temple University submitted a short affidavit stating that torture is considered a tort in violation of the law of nations. Professor Arens had previously edited a book on Paraguay. *See* GENOCIDE IN PARAGUAY (Richard Arens ed., 1976).

[56] Jurisdiction was premised on 28 U.S.C. §§ 1331, 1350, 1651, 2201, and 2202 as well as the doctrine of pendent jurisdiction.

[57] Verified Complaint, *supra* note 54, at 3.

the result of the acts of Peña-Irala. They further alleged that Dolly Filártiga had suffered emotional pain and suffering as a result of the deliberate confrontation with the tortured body of her brother. Dolly had also suffered deprivation of liberty and emotional pain as a result of her unlawful detention in Paraguay. In the jurisdictional statement, the Filártigas alleged that these causes of action arose under the U.S. Constitution, several federal statutes, wrongful death statutes, the U.N. Charter, the Universal Declaration of Human Rights, U.N. Declaration on the Protection of All Persons from Being Subjected to Torture and Other Cruel, Inhuman or Degrading Treatment or Punishment, the American Declaration of the Rights and Duties of Man, and customary international law. The Filártigas requested several forms of relief. They asked for compensatory and punitive damages of $10 million along with interest, costs, and disbursements. They also asked the court to enter an order prohibiting INS Commissioner Leonel Castillo, and all persons acting in concert with him, from deporting Peña-Irala.

On April 9, 1979, the Filártigas sought an order from the district court seeking a stay of deportation as well as an order permitting depositions of Peña-Irala and Villalba.[58] In an accompanying affidavit, Dolly Filártiga explained the significance of the lawsuit. She noted that justice was unavailable in Paraguay because the judiciary was not considered an independent branch of government. In addition, she described how her family had been threatened and harassed in its efforts to pursue the case in Paraguay. "Because the defendant Pena will never be brought to justice in Paraguay, this lawsuit presents a crucial and the only means by which I can seek justice for my brother's death and my injuries."[59] Dolly also expressed con-

---

[58] An amicus brief supporting the Filártigas' request for a temporary restraining order staying the defendants' deportation and ordering their depositions was submitted by several groups, including the Council on Hemispheric Affairs, the Letelier-Moffitt Human Rights Fund of the Institute for Policy Studies, the Clergy and Laity Concerned, and the International Human Rights Law Group. *See* Brief Amici Curiae in Support of Plaintiffs' Motion to Restrain Defendant Immigration and Naturalization Service from Enforcing Defendant Pena-Irala's Departure from the United States, Filartiga v. Pena-Irala, 630 F.2d 876 (2d Cir. 1980) (No. 79 C 917). In addition, Amnesty International USA sent a telegram to the Department of State urging it to exercise its legal authority to delay Peña-Irala's deportation and to hold him in custody pending trial. *See* Telegram from David Hinkley, Chairman AIUSA, to Warren Christopher, Deputy Secretary of State (Apr. 11, 1979). In response, Assistant Secretary of State Barbara Watson indicated that the Department "is not in a position to comment on a case which is before our courts." Letter from Barbara M. Watson, Assistant Secretary of State, Bureau of Consular Affairs, to David Hinkley, Chairman AIUSA (Apr. 18, 1979).

[59] Affidavit of Dolly Filartiga, *supra* note 36, at 3. Paraguayan government officials responded to Dolly Filártiga's assertions by stating that legal proceedings in the case had been transparent and appropriate. *See Nuestra justicia no trabo a nadie*, HOY (Asunción),

cerns about the implications if Peña-Irala was released. "If this Court allows Pena to return without investigation of and accountability for his violation of the most fundamental principles of human rights, it will be touted in Paraguay as an endorsement of Pena's innocence."[60] While the Filártiga attorneys recognized it was unusual to seek Peña-Irala's continued detention because of a pending civil action, they feared he would leave the country and not participate in the lawsuit if he was released.[61]

In response, Judge Nickerson immediately issued an order that the INS "shall refrain from deporting" Peña-Irala and Villalba.[62] The district court also issued an order authorizing the plaintiffs to take depositions of the two detainees while they were in INS custody. The depositions were taken on April 12, 1979, although both Peña-Irala and Villalba declined to answer any questions without a lawyer.

Soon after these preliminary proceedings, the law firm of Fragano, Rebollo & Barone began representing Peña-Irala. It was never established who contacted the law firm or who paid the legal bills. Subsequently, the law firm of Lowenstein, Sandler, Brochin, Kohl, Fisher & Boylan joined as co-counsel. According to Murry Brochin, who represented Peña-Irala, "I was intrigued by the case for several reasons. I thought it was wrong that Mr. Peña-Irala could be detained because of a pending civil matter. I was also troubled by the case because it appeared to me that the plaintiffs only wanted to pursue a 'show trial.' In addition, I found the Alien Tort Statute to be excessive in its jurisdictional grant."[63] A prominent Paraguayan attorney, Jose Emilio Gorostiaga, flew to New York to assist in the proceedings.[64] Gorostiaga had previously represented Peña-Irala in Paraguay. He denounced Peña-Irala's detention as a violation of Paraguayan sovereignty.

May 9, 1979, at 1; *La justicia nunca tuvo trabas*, HOY (Asunción), May 9, 1979, at 9.

[60] Affidavit of Dolly Filartiga, *supra* note 36, at 5.

[61] Interview with Professor Rhonda Copelon, in New York, New York (July 16, 2002).

[62] Order to Show Cause and Stay of Deportation, Filartiga v. Pena-Irala, No. 79 C 917 (E.D.N.Y. Apr. 9, 1979).

[63] Telephone conversation between Murry D. Brochin and William Aceves (Aug. 2, 2000).

[64] Peña-Irala's detention and the subsequent ATS lawsuit garnered significant media coverage in Paraguay. *See* Telegram from American Embassy, Asunción, Paraguay, to U.S. Department of State (Apr. 12, 1979). *See also Sonado caso Filartiga reactivan ante Corte Superior neoyorquina*, ULTIMA HORA (Asunción), Aug. 6, 1979, at 26; *El juez Nickerson postergo la audiencia por dos semanas*, ABC (Asunción), May 1, 1979; *Informaran hoy sobre el caso Pena a periodistas de EE.UU.*, ABC (Asunción), Apr. 18, 1979; *El estudiante no murio a las 2,30*, HOY (Asunción), Apr. 9, 1979, at 11.

He also argued that the U.S. proceedings were inappropriate because the Filártigas were already pursuing a similar action in Paraguay.[65] Throughout the U.S. proceedings, Gorostiaga communicated with the Paraguayan government about the status of the litigation.

On May 7, 1979, Peña-Irala filed a motion to dismiss the lawsuit.[66] First, he argued that the district court lacked subject matter jurisdiction because the murder of a Paraguayan national in Paraguay did not give rise to a violation of the law of nations, a prerequisite for jurisdiction under the Alien Tort Statute. Second, he argued that the INS could not detain him in order to compel his testimony in the civil proceedings. Peña-Irala's briefing on this point was emphatic.

> To anyone concerned with civil rights in the United States, the proposition that a man, a woman, and their child can be kept in federal confinement against their will as the result of a civil case so that they may participate in a show-trial would be shocking indeed! Our laws will not sustain so egregious a violation of due process![67]

Finally, Peña-Irala argued that the district court should decline jurisdiction pursuant to the doctrine of *forum non conveniens* since none of the key witnesses and evidence were located in the United States. In addition to these substantive arguments, Peña-Irala also raised a broader policy consideration, expressing concern about the implications of allowing ATS litigation in U.S. courts.

> Even if this court possessed jurisdiction—and it does not—it should seek to avoid a precedent which would encourage every Kurdish rebel, every West Bank Palestinian, every Soviet dissident—the list is endless in a turbulent world—to appeal to our courts for redress of politically motivated injuries which he claims to have sustained in his own country. Consider what a justifiable outcry would be aroused in the United States if one of our citizens were detained and tried in Moscow—or in Paraguay—upon the allegation that he was responsible for a racially motivated killing perpetrated against another American in the United States! Fortunately, our laws do not compel this court to act the role of

---

[65] *See Es un ataque a nuestra soberanía*, HOY (Asunción), Apr. 19, 1979, at 11.

[66] Defendant Pena-Irala's Memorandum of Law in Support of Motion to Dismiss Complaint and Vacate Stay, Filartiga v. Pena-Irala, 630 F.2d 876 (2d Cir. 1980) (No. 79 C 917).

[67] *Id.* at 1.

Don Quixote seeking to cure the ills of the world. In fact, our laws prohibit this court from undertaking such an adventure and we are confident that the court will reject the proffered role.[68]

In support of the motion to dismiss, Peña-Irala submitted three affidavits. The first affidavit was prepared by a Paraguayan government official who indicated that the Filártigas had not instituted civil proceedings against Peña-Irala or any other individuals for the death of Joelito.[69] The second affidavit was prepared by a Paraguayan law professor who indicated that Paraguayan law allows "persons directly or indirectly damaged for an offense committed in the national territory" to claim a corresponding indemnity before the Paraguayan courts.[70] The third affidavit was prepared by Jose Emilio Gorostiaga, who was Peña-Irala's attorney in Paraguay.[71] Gorostiaga described the Paraguayan criminal proceedings against Peña-Irala and Hugo Duarte pending in Paraguay. He also indicated that the Filártigas could have filed a civil action against Peña-Irala in Paraguay but had not done so.

Because the Filártiga complaint also named INS officials as defendants, the U.S. Attorney for the Eastern District of New York, Edward Korman, submitted a separate response to the district court. He joined in Peña-Irala's motion to dismiss "to the extent that it seeks to vacate the preliminary injunction order that prohibits the deportation of Peña-Irala."[72] Korman argued that an alien cannot enjoin his own deportation in order to pursue a civil action in the United States. By implication, therefore, a third party cannot enjoin an alien's deportation in order to pursue a civil action against that alien. Korman also argued that the district court lacked the authority to enjoin the INS from deporting Peña-Irala. Finally, he noted that it was unreasonable to maintain the injunction against Juana Villalba and her infant child since they were not a party to the lawsuit and they did not oppose deportation to Paraguay.

In response to these filings, the Filártigas argued that the Alien Tort Statute was constitutional.[73] They noted that the ATS requirements were

---

68   *Id.* at 2.

69   *Id.* at C-4 (statement of Remigia Villalba).

70   *Id.* at D-7 (statement of Ramiro Rodriguez Alcala).

71   *Id.* at D-2 (Affidavit of Jose Emilio Gorostiaga).

72   Letter from Edward R. Korman, United States Attorney, to the Honorable Eugene H. Nickerson (May 9, 1979).

73   Plaintiffs' Memorandum of Law in Opposition to Defendant Pena-Irala's Motion

met since the case involved a tort committed in violation of the law of nations. In support of their argument that torture constituted a violation of the law of nations, the Filártigas submitted affidavits from four international law scholars: Richard Falk, Thomas Franck, Richard Lillich, and Myres MacDougal. The affidavits asserted that torture was firmly prohibited under international law. In addition, the Lillich and Falk affidavits asserted that U.S. courts could invoke and apply this international norm in domestic litigation. Finally, the Filártigas argued that dismissal under the doctrine of *forum non conveniens* would be inappropriate, because it would leave them with no available remedy. In a subsequent submission, the Filártigas argued that the district court's stay of deportation was appropriate.[74] Pursuant to the All Writs Act, a federal court has the authority to issue all necessary writs to preserve its jurisdiction in the case.

> Plaintiffs are asking this Court to issue orders restraining defendants from leaving this Court's jurisdiction only until plaintiffs can depose Pena and Villalba concerning the brutal murder of Joelito Filartiga and Pena's ability to satisfy any judgment which might be rendered against them. Plaintiffs do not seek to have defendants incarcerated pending the outcome of this litigation, but merely to have this Court issue those writs "necessary or appropriate in aid of . . . [its] jurisdiction in order to prevent defendant's flight from justice and the complete frustration of the power of this Court."[75]

Throughout these proceedings, the *Filartiga* case was profiled extensively by the Paraguayan media, and numerous articles appeared in Paraguayan newspapers and magazines. These articles addressed the *Filartiga* case from various angles. On May 13, 1979, for example, the Paraguayan magazine, *ABC*, interviewed U.S. Ambassador Robert White and asked him about the pending litigation.[76] Ambassador White noted that the U.S. proceedings against Peña-Irala were consistent with international human rights law. He also challenged the assertion that these proceedings were an affront to Paraguayan sovereignty, noting that certain violations of international law can be punished by any state regardless of

---

to Dismiss Complaint and Vacate Stay, Filartiga v. Pena-Irala, 630 F.2d 876 (2d Cir. 1980) (No. 79 C 917).

[74] Plaintiffs' Memorandum in Opposition to Point II of Defendants' Memorandum Urging Vacatur of the Stay of Deportation, Filartiga v. Pena-Irala, 630 F.2d 876 (2d Cir. 1980) (No. 79 C 917).

[75] *Id.* at 7.

[76] Pepa Kostianovsky, *La democracia es la unica vacuna contra el comunismo*, ABC REVISTA (Asunción), May 13, 1979, at 4.

the defendant's nationality.[77] Extensive interviews were also conducted by the Paraguayan media with Duarte in Paraguay as well as Jose Emilio Gorostiaga and Michael Maggio in the United States.

On May 14, 1979, a hearing was held before Judge Nickerson on the motion to dismiss. Dr. Filártiga, his wife Nidia, and Dolly attended the hearing. Oral argument focused on whether the Filártigas could pursue similar litigation in Paraguay and the implications of allowing ATS litigation in U.S. courts. On the following day, Judge Nickerson issued a memorandum and order dismissing the lawsuit. In his brief four-page ruling, Judge Nickerson indicated that he was bound by two Second Circuit rulings concerning international law: *IIT v. Vencap, Ltd.* and *Dreyfus v. von Finck.*[78] "Those decisions held that conduct, though tortuous, is not in violation of the 'Law of Nations,' as those words are used in 28 U.S.C. § 1350, unless the conduct is in violation of those standards, rules or customs affecting the relationship between states and between an individual and a foreign state, and used by those states for their common good and/or in dealings *inter se.*"[79] While Judge Nickerson acknowledged the Filártigas' arguments regarding the development of customary international law with respect to torture, "this court feels bound by the Second Circuit decisions cited above."[80] Judge Nickerson allowed the stay of deportation to be continued for 48 hours after entry of the order to enable the Filártigas to appeal the decision.

The Filártigas immediately filed a motion for interim relief pending appeal with the Second Circuit, seeking to stay Peña-Irala's deportation until his deposition could be taken.[81] According to the Filártigas, they "will be irreparably harmed, and the future capacity of this Court to meaningfully exercise its jurisdiction and adjudicate this complaint will be irreparably undermined if the defendant and a material witness to the torture and death charged are deported to Paraguay without first being required to submit to depositions."[82] The request for interim relief was denied by the Second Circuit, and an application for a stay of deportation was also denied

---

[77] *Id.* at 7. *See also* Telegram from the American Embassy in Asunción, Paraguay, to the U.S. Department of State (May 17, 1979).

[78] *See* IIT v. Vencap, Ltd., 519 F.2d 1001 (2d Cir. 1975); Dreyfus v. von Finck, 534 F.2d 24 (2d Cir. 1976).

[79] Filartiga v. Pena-Irala, No. 79 C 917, slip op. (E.D.N.Y. May 15, 1979).

[80] *Id.* at 3. The decision was immediately publicized in Paraguay. *See Peña: Rechazaron la demanda y dejarian libre al ex policía,* ULTIMA HORA (Asunción), May 16, 1979, at 14.

[81] Notice of Motion and Motion for Interim Relief Pending Appeal, Filartiga v. Pena-Irala, 630 F.2d 876 (2d Cir. 1980) (No. 79 C 917).

[82] *Id.* at 5.

by the U.S. Supreme Court. Peña-Irala was deported to Paraguay soon thereafter on May 25, 1979.

While the request for interim relief had been dismissed, the primary appeal remained before the Second Circuit. Both parties filed appellate briefs with the Court of Appeals, addressing the constitutionality of the Alien Tort Statute as well as the policy implications of the litigation. The Filártigas emphasized that the ATS was adopted to ensure federal jurisdiction over torts alleging violations of international law and that such jurisdiction was necessary in light of the international implications of these cases. Otherwise, jurisdiction would be vested exclusively in the state courts, which were subject to parochial interests and may not consider the national or international implications at stake. They added that vesting U.S. courts with jurisdiction in these cases was entirely consistent with the principle of transitory torts, which had a long history and was recognized in both Anglo-American jurisprudence and private international law. In addition to its appellate submissions, the Center for Constitutional Rights contacted several organizations and worked with them to submit two amicus briefs on behalf of the Filártigas with the Second Circuit.[83] The Center also contacted the U.S. State Department and the Justice Department seeking government intervention in the case.[84] While lawyers in both departments expressed interest in the legal issues raised by the litigation, they were unable to finalize their position before the case was argued.

On October 16, 1979, the case was argued before a three-judge panel of the Second Circuit. The panel consisted of Judges Wilfred Feinberg, Irving Kaufman, and John Smith.[85] Peter Weiss argued on behalf of the Filártigas; Murry Brochin argued for Peña-Irala.

Peter Weiss began his argument by addressing the historical foundations of the Alien Tort Statute.[86] Weiss noted the ATS was adopted at a time

---

[83] Two groups filed amicus briefs on behalf of the Filártigas. One brief was filed by the International Human Rights Law Group, The Council on Hemispheric Affairs, and the Washington Office on Latin America. The other brief was filed by Amnesty International USA. Both amicus briefs argued that the federal courts could assert subject matter jurisdiction for acts of torture pursuant to the Alien Tort Statute.

[84] Interview with Professor Rhonda Copelon, in New York, New York (July 16, 2002); Interview with Peter Weiss, Vice-President, Center for Constitutional Rights, in New York, New York (July 15, 2002).

[85] Judge Smith died on February 16, 1980. He was replaced on the panel by Judge Amalya Kearse.

[86] Transcript of Oral Argument, Filartiga v. Pena-Irala, 630 F.2d 876 (2d Cir. 1980) (No. 79 C 917).

when the law of nations was considered a part of the common law, and the ATS drafters were well-versed in the law of nations. He added Congress adopted the ATS to ensure that the United States complied with its obligations under the law of nations. Judge Kaufman then asked Weiss whether the State Department had been invited to intervene or file an amicus brief in the case. Weiss indicated that they had communicated with the State Department on several occasions. While State Department officials had expressed great interest in the case, they did not take a position on submitting any materials to the Court. Weiss added, however, that the opinions of the State Department should not be controlling since only the Court could determine its jurisdiction.

Arguing on behalf of Peña-Irala, Murry Brochin addressed the policy implications of allowing human rights violations to be litigated in U.S. courts. He expressed concern that ATS cases could be used as propaganda by individual litigants involved in private disputes. He also questioned whether Congress had sought to incorporate international human rights norms into federal common law by adopting the Alien Tort Statute. While several cases had recognized that some areas of law can be incorporated into federal common law, these cases were inapposite because federal legislation was already extensive in these areas. In contrast, Congress and the Executive Branch had indicated that human rights treaties are not self-executing and, therefore, they are not incorporated into U.S. law. Brochin argued that recognizing jurisdiction in this case would federalize international law and bind the United States to norms that had not been adopted by Congress.

On rebuttal, Peter Weiss argued that recognizing jurisdiction in the case would not federalize international law. In fact, international law is already an integral part of the law of the United States. In addition, he argued that this case addressed a narrow issue of law—the prohibition against torture—and allowing the case to proceed would not open the floodgates of litigation. "Far from [the] opening of floodgates, . . . we think this case would . . . serve notice on the torturers of this world that they have no haven in the United States and that they [should] not come here and the courts will not have [to] deal with this kind of case."[87]

Following oral argument, the Second Circuit sent a letter to the Office of the Legal Adviser at the U.S. State Department seeking its position on the *Filartiga* litigation.[88] Because the case involved "questions of foreign pol-

---

[87] *Id.* at 24.

[88] Letter from Daniel Fusaro, Clerk, Second Circuit of Appeals, to Robert Owen, Legal Adviser, U.S. Department of State (Oct. 29, 1979).

icy," the Second Circuit asked the State Department to "submit a memo-randum setting forth its position concerning the proper interpretation of 28 U.S.C. §1350 in light of the facts of this case."[89] In fact, the State Department had been considering filing an amicus brief well before it received the Second Circuit's request.[90] Soon after the district court had issued its decision dismissing the *Filartiga* case in May 1979, the Center for Constitutional Rights had contacted officials in the State Department urging them to submit a brief in the case.[91] In August 1979, two months before oral argument at the Second Circuit, Stephen M. Schwebel, the Deputy Legal Adviser at the State Department, contacted the Civil Rights Division in the Justice Department and expressed the desire of the State Department to file an amicus brief in the *Filartiga* case.[92] Schwebel expressed concerns about the district court's obsolete views that failed "to take account of 20th century (and earlier) developments of international law which firmly establish that all natural persons are entitled to funda-mental human rights."[93]

> The position of the Department of State on the question of inter-national law immediately relevant to the District Court judgment in *Filartiga* is that acts of torture violate an individual's rights under international law not to be tortured. That an individual has this right is a conclusion founded on provisions of the United Nations

---

[89] *Id.*

[90] The State Department legal team in the Office of the Legal Adviser included Roberts B. Owen (Legal Adviser), William T. Lake (Principal Deputy Legal Adviser), Stephen Schwebel (Deputy Legal Adviser), Charles Runyon (Assistant Legal Adviser for Human Rights), Stefan Riesenfeld (Counselor in International Law), Linda Bauman (Attorney-Adviser), and Lori Damrosch (Special Assistant to the Legal Adviser). The Justice Department legal team included Drew S. Days, III (Assistant Attorney General), John Huerta (Deputy Assistant Attorney General), Brian K. Landsberg (Chief, Appellate Section, Civil Rights Division), Irving Gornstein (Attorney, Appellate Section), and Joan Hartman (Attorney, Appellate Section).

[91] As early as July 1979, the Center for Constitutional Rights was in contact with the State Department, seeking its intervention in the case. *See* Letter from Charles Runyon, Assistant Legal Adviser for Human Rights, U.S. Department of State, to Rhonda Copelon, Center for Constitutional Rights (July 24, 1979).

[92] In the Justice Department, the Civil Rights Division was charged with responsi-bility for matters pertaining to international human rights. This included reviewing com-plaints involving alleged human rights abuses in the United States. The Civil Rights Division also served as the Justice Department liaison with the State Department on these matters.

[93] Letter from Stephen Schwebel, Deputy Legal Adviser, U.S. Department of State, to John Huerta, Deputy Assistant Attorney General, Civil Rights Division, U.S. Department of Justice (Aug. 9, 1979).

Charter and authoritative interpretations of those provisions, on other treaties, on international custom and practice and on the general principles of law—all as recognized by the United States and other nations. It derives also from international and national judicial decisions.

In order that the Second Circuit may have before it the reasoned legal views of the United States Government, we request that the Department of Justice seek to file a brief amicus curiae setting forth the position of the United States on these important questions of international law.[94]

In response to the State Department request, the Justice Department prepared a draft amicus brief and sent it to the State Department and U.S. Solicitor General for comments. The draft brief argued that torture violates international law and that the ATS should be interpreted to authorize a private suit for breach of that international norm.

Briefly, the court's holding that the law of nations can never touch the relations between a nation and its citizens fails to take into account the growth in international law since World War II, and particularly since the signing of the United Nations Charter. Section 1350, which must be given a dynamic interpretation, incorporates this development. The Second Circuit decisions relied upon by the district court, did not arise in a human rights context, and did not thoroughly analyze the proper reach of Section 1350. Application of proper legal standards leads us to conclude that official torture is prohibited by the law of nations. Finally, the defendant's argument that such an interpretation of section 1350 would render it unconstitutional is without merit.[95]

For these reasons, the Justice Department recommended that the United States seek leave to file an amicus brief with the Second Circuit.

In response to the Justice Department brief, the State Department prepared a memorandum identifying seven points that should be addressed in any U.S. submission.

---

94 *Id.*

95 Memorandum from Drew S. Days, III, Assistant Attorney General, Civil Rights Division, Justice Department, to the Solicitor General 1–2 (Aug. 29, 1979). *See also* Memorandum from Irving Gornstein, Attorney, Appellate Section, Justice Department to Brian K. Landsberg, Chief, Appellate Section, Justice Department 1 (Nov. 7, 1979).

1. Contemporary international law is not limited to the relationships between States and between States and aliens. On the contrary, it does embrace relations between a State and its own nationals insofar as those relations comprehend universal respect for and observance of fundamental human rights and freedoms.

2. Torture of an individual by an agent of a State or a person acting under the color of the authority of a State is a violation of one of the most fundamental human rights and freedoms—that of being free of the physical and emotional trauma of torture. Such torture accordingly is a violation of international law.

3. The reference in 28 U.S.C. §1350 to "the Law of Nations" should be read as referring to international law as it evolves (and not as it existed in the Eighteenth Century), and therefore must encompass certain relations of a State to its nationals. The rationale of the District Court therefore contains a serious error, and one that may prejudice the United States' efforts to promote and develop the international law of human rights. However, the reference in §1350 not only embraces the substantive but the procedural rules and practices of international law.

4. Under customary international law, States do not ordinarily enjoy and observe universal jurisdiction in respect of violations of international law; on the contrary, they and their courts will normally exercise jurisdiction only where, in the least, their interests or those of their nationals are directly affected by the acts complained of. One exception to this rule is universal jurisdiction over the crime of piracy. States have not customarily exercised jurisdiction over criminal or civil actions flowing from allegations of acts of torture carried out beyond their territorial jurisdiction and not involving their officials or citizens.

5. While torture is proscribed expressly by some international treaties in force (notably, the International Covenant on Civil and Political Rights and the Geneva Conventions for the Protection of War Victims) and, by reasonable construction, by other treaties (notably, the Charter of the United Nations), among treaties currently in force only the Geneva Conventions entrust the remedy for violations of this proscription to national courts. The United Nations Charter is not self-executing; and the International Covenant on Civil and Political Rights has created a Human Rights Committee which is charged with pursuing remedies which conduce to observance of the Covenant's provisions. Enforcement of

that Covenant's provisions by national courts is not provided for (though it is not excluded).

6. There is currently under negotiation in the Commission on Human Rights of the United Nations a draft Convention on the Protection of All Persons from Being Subjected to Torture and Other Cruel, Inhuman or Degrading Treatment or Punishment. That Convention, should it be concluded and brought into force, seems likely to establish the obligation of States Parties to provide for their national courts exercising jurisdiction over acts in violation of its prescriptions wherever and by whomever committed, where there is *in personam* jurisdiction over the defendant.

7. Pending the conclusion of such a convention and ratification of it by the United States, or the evolution of customary international law as evidenced by a widespread practice of States conferring on their own courts jurisdiction over aliens' tort claims for alleged acts of torture abroad, 28 U.S.C. §1350 should be construed as not according federal courts the jurisdiction to entertain suits by an alien in tort for acts of torture allegedly committed by another alien abroad. This conclusion, it should be emphasized, does not derogate from the conclusion stated above that international law embraces the treatment by a State of its nationals in some respects and that one such critical respect is the torture by a State agent of an individual.[96]

The State Department thus sought to recognize the rights of individuals and the status of torture under international law. But, it also sought to preclude individual enforcement of this international norm through the ATS. The State Department then forwarded the memorandum to the Justice Department and the Solicitor General for review.

It took over eight months before the Solicitor General, State Department, and Justice Department could agree on a final position.[97] According

---

[96] Letter from Stephen Schwebel, Deputy Legal Adviser, U.S. Department of State, to Richard Allen, Office of the Solicitor General, Department of Justice (Sept. 14, 1979).

[97] In September 1979, the U.S. Solicitor General received a letter from eight members of Congress urging him to file an amicus brief in the Second Circuit supporting the Filártiga position. Letter from Congressman Toby Moffett et al., to Wade H. McCree, Solicitor General of the United States, Department of Justice (Sept. 28, 1979). In addition, several organizations contacted the State Department Legal Adviser seeking similar support. *See, e.g.*, Letter from Amy Young-Anawaty, Executive Director, International Human Rights Law Group, to Roberts Owens, Legal Adviser, U.S. Department of State (Nov. 21, 1979).

to Wade H. McCree, the Solicitor General, "written and oral discussions between lawyers in this Office, in the Civil Rights Division, and on the staff of the Legal Adviser to the Department of State have revealed serious difficulties in formulating a satisfactory legal position, in light of the implication a filing by the United States on this subject would have for the treatment of our own nationals in foreign courts."[98] Concerns were raised "about the uncontrollability of litigation under the Act and possible repercussions such as suits against U.S. officials in foreign courts."[99] It was also recognized that the ATS "could play a significant role in the enforcement of international human rights standards and it seemed appropriate for U.S. courts to hear cases involving acts that occurred elsewhere when the international norm involved had achieved true universality."[100]

During the final stages of the drafting process, Roberts B. Owen, the State Department Legal Adviser, proposed a compromise to Deputy Secretary of State Warren Christopher that would address the competing concerns of the State Department, Justice Department, and Solicitor General. In a March 5, 1980, letter, Owens proposed that U.S. courts could recognize jurisdiction and yet dismiss the *Filartiga* case on judicial abstention grounds.[101]

The courts probably should abstain in this case, for a number of reasons. Decisions under other statutes hold that U.S. courts should not entertain suits where both parties are aliens and the injury occurred abroad, as long as a foreign forum is available. That rule seems to apply here, unless plaintiffs can prove (as they assert they can) that the [pending criminal] proceedings in Paraguay [against Pena] are a sham. And the defendant could argue with some force that it would be unfair for the courts to pro-

---

[98] Letter from Wade H. McCree, Solicitor General of the United States, Department of Justice, to Congressman Toby Moffett et al. (Oct. 3, 1979). The Solicitor General also noted that both parties had already submitted their appellate briefs to the Second Circuit. Accordingly, "only the most compelling considerations would make it appropriate for the government to seek leave to file an amicus brief" at this late stage. *Id.*

[99] *Id.*

[100] John Huerta, General Counsel, The Smithsonian Institution and Former Deputy Assistant Attorney General, Department of Justice, Remarks at the Association of the Bar of the City of New York (Nov. 2, 2005); Correspondence from William T. Lake, former Principal Deputy Legal Adviser, Department of State, to William Aceves (May 13, 2001).

[101] Letter from Roberts B. Owen, State Department Legal Adviser, to Warren Christopher, Deputy Secretary of State (Mar. 5, 1980), *reprinted in* CUMULATIVE DIGEST OF UNITED STATES PRACTICE IN INTERNATIONAL LAW 1979, at 524–25 (Marian Nash (Leich) ed., 1983).

ceed with the case after the United States Government itself has deported the defendant [on May 25, 1979], thus preventing a proper defense. We propose to suggest that these considerations support abstention and that the trial court should consider that issue on remand. . . . If the courts are going to dismiss the case, the correct way to do it is to uphold jurisdiction (on the ground that international law does condemn torture) but to abstain from exercising it on the facts of this case. The advantages of the United States Government's advocating this position are: (1) it would be faithful to the language of section 1350; (2) it would help to establish that international law prohibits denials of basic human rights; and (3) our suggestion of abstention would show that we are sensitive to the fact that the exercise of jurisdiction will often be inappropriate in cases that lack U.S. connections.[102]

The final version of the amicus brief addressed judicial abstention although it did so only in a footnote placed at the end of the brief.

In subsequent remarks about the drafting process, Roberts Owen acknowledged the political struggles and pragmatic considerations that influenced the amicus brief.

The briefing process was not easy. I quickly discovered that there were strong views both in the State Department and in the Justice Department as to whether or not a Federal Court should take jurisdiction of a case based upon Paraguayan torture of a Paraguayan citizen in Paraguay. As among the personnel of the two Departments, the international lawyers were generally of the view that the District Court's ruling was simply wrong as to the present state of international law. This group was persuaded that . . . international law today prescribes a number of basic standards to which a state must adhere in its treatment of its own citizens. More specifically, there seems to be a consensus that customary international law now imposes upon every government an obligation to refrain from torture. In fact, if you were searching around to find a practice which would be universally condemned, torture would obviously be at or near the top of everybody's list.

Nevertheless, there was considerable resistance in both State and Justice to the idea that the jurisdiction of our courts should be invoked in a situation of this kind—where a foreign government had abused one of its own citizens within its own borders—there was deep concern about the possibility that our courts and our gov-

---

[102] *Id.*

ernment would gradually become self-appointed policemen for the world—and that such a role would place severe strains on our international relations generally. If our courts were to pass judgment on the conduct of foreign officials, arguably the courts of other countries would assert jurisdiction over traveling American officials and accuse them of an open-ended range of perceived abuses.

In any event, after much internal soul-searching and debate, we filed an amicus brief in support of the plaintiff's position—that is, supporting the notion that the 1789 statute conferred jurisdiction in the Filartiga case.[103]

Throughout the drafting process, the Center for Constitutional Rights was in regular contact with the State Department and Justice Department. As early as July 1979, the Center had contacted the Office of the Legal Adviser in the State Department to seek its intervention in the case. Subsequent communications also occurred with the Civil Rights Division of the Justice Department. On several occasions, lawyers at the Center even reviewed drafts of the U.S. amicus brief and offered comments on its development and argumentation. They also emphasized to U.S. government lawyers the benefits that a U.S. submission would provide their case.

On May 29, 1980, the Memorandum for the United States as Amicus Curiae was submitted to the Second Circuit.[104] The brief was submitted jointly by the State Department and the Justice Department. It addressed two issues: the status of torture under international law and the right of individuals to pursue judicially enforceable remedies under the ATS.

In Part I of the amicus brief, the United States argued that official torture violates the law of nations. As a preliminary matter, the United States indicated that the law of nations was not a static concept but was constantly evolving, and the ATS should be interpreted accordingly.[105] Otherwise, only

---

[103] Address by the Honorable Roberts B. Owen, The Legal Adviser, U.S. Department of State, at the Annual Dinner of the American Branch of the International Law Association, The Princeton Club, New York City (Nov. 14, 1980), *reprinted in* PROCEEDINGS AND COMMITTEE REPORTS OF THE AMERICAN BRANCH OF THE INTERNATIONAL LAW ASSOCIATION 11, 16 (Theodore R. Giuttari ed., 1982).

[104] Memorandum for the United States as Amicus Curiae, Filartiga v. Pena-Irala, 630 F.2d 876 (2d Cir. 1980) (No. 79 C 917). *See also* Lee Lescaze, *Justice and State Back Right to Sue in Torture Cases*, WASH. POST, June 3, 1980, at A10.

[105] The United States cited the Supreme Court's ruling in *The Paquete Habana* to illustrate its view of the evolutionary development of international law. *See* The Paquete Habana, 175 U.S. 677 (1900). "Since the law of nations had developed in large measure

state courts would have jurisdiction to enforce recent developments in the law of nations, and this would undermine federal uniformity over such significant matters. "Accordingly, the district court's jurisdiction in this case turns not on whether the conduct alleged in the complaint would have been a violation of the law of nations in 1789, but on whether it is customarily treated as a violation of the law of nations today."[106]

The United States then challenged the district court's assertion that violations of international law do not occur when the aggrieved parties are nationals of the acting state. Historically, the United States noted that international law did not regulate a state's treatment of its own citizens. Beginning in the 20th century, however, states began to recognize an obligation to respect human rights. In support, the United States cited numerous developments, including the adoption of the League of Nations Covenant in 1919 and the U.N. Charter in 1945. It referred to various postwar treaties and declarations, including the Universal Declaration of Human Rights, International Covenant on Civil and Political Rights, European Convention for the Protection of Human Rights and Fundamental Freedoms, American Convention on Human Rights, and several U.N. General Assembly resolutions. The United States also cited the expert affidavits submitted by the Filártigas as well as the State Department's own *Country Reports on Human Rights Practices* for the proposition that human rights obligations are firmly established under international law. Even "[g]eneral principles of law recognized by civilized nations also establish that there are certain fundamental human rights to which all individuals are entitled, regardless of nationality."[107] With the advent of human rights law, therefore, a wide recognition developed "that certain fundamental human rights are now guaranteed to individuals as a matter of customary international law."[108]

Having established the status of international law and its protection of human rights, the United States then addressed the prohibition against torture. It noted that every multilateral treaty addressing civil and political

---

by reference to evolving customary practice, the framers of the first Judiciary Act surely anticipated that international law would not be static after 1789." Memorandum for the United States as Amicus Curiae, *supra* note 104, at 5.

[106] Memorandum for the United States as Amicus Curiae, *supra* note 104, at 5.

[107] *Id.* at 10. In support of its assertion that fundamental human rights were universally recognized, the United States noted that over 75 countries had incorporated principles set forth in the Universal Declaration of Human Rights into their national constitutions or domestic law between 1948 and 1973. The United States also noted that the Universal Declaration was referenced by national courts in 16 different countries during this same time period.

[108] *Id.* at 6.

rights proscribes torture, including the International Covenant on Civil and Political Rights, the American Convention on Human Rights, the European Convention for the Protection of Human Rights and Fundamental Freedoms, and the 1949 Geneva Conventions.[109] "This uniform treaty condemnation of torture provides a strong indication that the proscription of torture has entered into customary international law."[110] The status of the prohibition against torture was confirmed by additional sources, including the Universal Declaration of Human Rights and the U.N. Declaration on the Protection of All Persons from Being Subjected to Torture, which provided a precise definition of torture. National constitutions and legislation, including U.S. constitutional and statutory law, affirmed the proscription.[111] Finally, judicial opinions and the commentary of experts "confirm that official torture violates international law" and that this conclusion "is inescapable."[112]

In Part II of the amicus brief, the United States argued that acts of official torture give rise to a judicially enforceable remedy in the United States. The United States acknowledged that individuals, in certain situations, may sue to enforce their rights under international law.[113] "The more recently evolved international law of human rights . . . endows individuals with the right to invoke international law, in a competent forum and under appropriate circumstances."[114] This right is evident in those countries, such as the United States, that have incorporated international law as part of the law of the land.[115]

---

[109] The United States acknowledged that not every treaty provision constitutes a norm of customary international law. "Where reservations have been attached by a significant number of nations to specific provisions or where disagreement with provisions is cited as the ground for a nation's refusal to become a party, the near-unanimity required for the adoption of a rule into customary international law may be lacking." *Id.* at 14. The United States also distinguished between aspirational treaty provisions and those treaty provisions that codify existing rights and obligations.

[110] *Id.* at 13.

[111] While the United States acknowledged that torture occurs, it knew of "no assertion by any nation that torture is justified." *Id.* at 16. Countries confronted with allegations of torture either denied such claims or argued that the alleged acts did not constitute torture.

[112] *Id.* at 19, 20.

[113] However, the United States acknowledged that not all violations of international law constitute torts within the meaning of the ATS.

[114] Memorandum for the United States, as Amicus Curiae, *supra* note 104, at 21.

[115] In support, the United States referenced a decision from the Constitutional Court of Germany (*In Matter of the Republic of the Philippines*), which recognized the right of individuals to invoke international law in domestic litigation. Additional references

The United States then addressed several possible challenges to the litigation. While it did not specifically reference the political question doctrine or the act of state doctrine, its analysis identified and analyzed the case law underlying these two doctrines of judicial abstention.[116] The United States noted, for example, that lawsuits against foreign officials "unquestionably implicate foreign policy considerations."[117] It acknowledged, however, that foreign policy implications should not always preclude judicial review. While some matters of political significance are delegated to the political branches of government, "the protection of fundamental human rights is not committed exclusively to the political branches of government."[118] In addition, the United States noted that courts must find "a consensus in the international community that the right is protected and that there is a widely shared understanding of the scope of this right."[119] Establishing the existence of these two conditions would minimize the foreign policy implications of the case.[120] "When these two conditions have been satisfied, there is little danger that judicial enforcement will impair our foreign policy efforts."[121] Indeed, the United States indicated that the

---

were made to case law from the Philippines (*Borovsky v. Commissioner of Immigration; Chirskoff v. Commissioner of Immigration*) and Belgium (*Judgment of Court of First Instance of Courtrai*). *Id.*

[116] The United States referenced *Baker v. Carr* and *Banco Nacional de Cuba v. Sabbatino* in its analysis of the political implications of the litigation. *See Baker v. Carr*, 369 U.S. 186 (1962); *Banco Nacional de Cuba v. Sabbatino*, 376 U.S. 398 (1964). The political question doctrine allows courts to dismiss lawsuits that require them to consider matters that extend beyond the purported realm of judicial competence. The act of state doctrine provides that courts should refrain from judging the acts of a foreign state when such acts are committed within that state's territory. *See generally* CURTIS A. BRADLEY & JACK L. GOLDSMITH, FOREIGN RELATIONS LAW 47–60, 90–111 (2d ed. 2006); THE CONSTITUTION AND THE CONDUCT OF AMERICAN FOREIGN POLICY (David G. Adler & Larry N. George eds., 1996).

[117] Memorandum for the United States as Amicus Curiae, *supra* note 104, at 22.

[118] *Id.*

[119] *Id.*

[120] The United States noted that Paraguayan law prohibited torture and even authorized a tort action as an appropriate remedy. In addition, the prohibition against torture was firmly established under international law. In the *Filartiga* case, therefore, "[t]he compatibility of international law and Paraguayan law significantly reduces the likelihood that court enforcement would cause undesirable international consequences and is therefore an additional reason to permit private enforcement." *Id.* at 24. For these reasons, the United States also indicated that principles of comity would not require a different result.

[121] *Id.* The United States noted this would also reduce the likelihood that U.S. courts would become "Commissions to evaluate the human rights performance of foreign nations." *Id.* at 22.

failure to recognize a private cause of action in these cases "might seriously damage the credibility of our nation's commitment to the protection of human rights."[122] For these reasons, private enforcement of the international prohibition against torture was appropriate under the ATS.[123]

The United States also addressed the possibility of judicial abstention in a footnote at the end of the brief.[124] While the district court had not addressed the doctrine of *forum non conveniens*, the United States noted "that when the parties and the conduct alleged in the complaint have as little contact with the United States as they have here, abstention is generally appropriate."[125] The United States also challenged the assertion that judicial abstention would be inappropriate in the case since any legal proceedings conducted in Paraguay would be a sham. "For reasons of comity among nations, however, such an assertion should not be accepted absent a very clear and persuasive showing."[126] Finally, the United States noted that it was relevant to consider the fact that the defendant had been deported.[127] Another footnote at the end of the amicus brief addressed the constitutionality of the ATS. The United States asserted that "[c]ustomary international law is federal law, to be enunciated authoritatively by the federal courts."[128] Accordingly, "[a]n action for tort under international law is therefore a case 'arising under . . . the laws of the United States' within Article III of the Constitution."[129]

On June 30, 1980, the Second Circuit issued its groundbreaking ruling in an opinion drafted by Judge Irving R. Kaufman.[130] The opinion addressed

---

[122] *Id.* at 22–23.

[123] The United States cited two cases invoking customary international law and the prohibition against torture: *Ireland v. United Kingdom* (European Court of Human Rights) and *Auditeur Militaire v. Krumkamp* (Belgian court). However, it acknowledged the paucity of case law enforcing the customary international norm against torture.

[124] The decision to place the issue of judicial abstention in a footnote at the end of the brief reveals a cursory effort to implement the recommendations offered by Roberts Owen in his March 5, 1980, letter to Deputy Secretary of State Warren Christopher.

[125] Memorandum for the United States as Amicus Curiae, *supra* note 104, at 25.

[126] *Id.*

[127] *Id.*

[128] *Id.*

[129] *Id.*

[130] Filartiga v. Pena-Irala, 630 F.2d 876 (2d Cir. 1980). Judge Kaufman was appointed to the Second Circuit in 1961. Prior to the *Filartiga* case, he was most well known for his role as the trial judge in the criminal proceedings involving Julius and Ethel Rosenberg.

two issues: the status of torture under international law and the constitutionality of the ATS.[131] The analysis and accompanying sources presented in the opinion were clearly influenced by the Filártiga submissions and the accompanying amicus briefs.

The court reviewed the history of the *Filartiga* case in Part I of the opinion, accepting as true the allegations in the complaint for purposes of its jurisdictional analysis. In Part II of the opinion, the court examined whether subject matter jurisdiction existed under the Alien Tort Statute.[132] This required an assessment of whether the alleged conduct violated the law of nations. To answer this threshold question, the court began by reviewing the primary sources of international law, including treaties, state practice, judicial decisions, and the works of jurists.[133] Each was considered an acceptable source for determining the status of international law. To become binding, however, the court indicated that a rule must command the general assent of civilized nations. "Were this not so, the courts of one nation might feel free to impose idiosyncratic legal rules upon others, in the name of applying international law."[134] The court also noted that international law is not static. "Thus it is clear that courts must interpret international law not as it was in 1789, but as it has evolved and exists among the nations of the world today."[135]

The court then examined the status of torture under international law. It noted that the U.N. Charter makes clear that "a state's treatment of its own citizens is a matter of international concern."[136] While the provisions of the U.N. Charter regarding human rights and fundamental freedoms

---

See RONALD RADOSH & JOYCE MILTON, THE ROSENBERG FILES (2d ed. 1984). *See also* United States v. Rosenberg, 195 F.2d 583 (2d Cir. 1952).

131 The *Filartiga* decision received significant commentary in the United States. *See, e.g.,* Marcia Chambers, *Court Says Alien Can Sue for Torture in Paraguay*, N.Y. TIMES, July 1, 1980, at B3; Alan Kohn, *1789 Alien Tort Act Invoked To Allow $10 Million Suit*, NEW YORK L.J., July 1, 1980, at 1. It was also highly publicized in Paraguay. *See, e.g., Un precedente en la justicia de EE.UU.*, ABC (Asunción), July 4, 1980, at 9.

132 The court noted that the Filártigas alleged jurisdiction under the "law of nations" component of the Alien Tort Statute. Nonetheless, it was permissible for them "to reference treaties and international instruments as evidence of an emerging norm of customary international law." Filartiga v. Pena-Irala, 630 F.2d 876, 880 (2d Cir. 1980).

133 *Id.* at 880–81 (citing United States v. Smith, 18 U.S. (5 Wheat.) 153 (1820) and The Paquete Habana, 175 U.S. 677 (1900)).

134 *Id.* at 881.

135 *Id.* (citing Ware v. Hylton, 3 U.S. (3 Dall.) 198 (1796)).

136 *Id.* at 881.

are not considered self-executing, the court noted that there is no dissent from the prohibition against torture. Indeed, this prohibition is now part of customary international law. In support, the court referenced numerous multilateral, regional, and national sources of law. It noted, for example, that the Universal Declaration of Human Rights provides that "no one shall be subjected to torture."[137] This prohibition is also found in the International Covenant on Civil and Political Rights, the American Convention on Human Rights, and the European Convention for the Protection of Human Rights and Fundamental Freedoms. The U.N. Declaration on the Protection of All Persons from Being Subjected to Torture was particularly relevant and, significantly, it had been adopted by the U.N. General Assembly without dissent. Apart from international practice, the court also considered the domestic practice of individual countries. It noted how the international prohibition against torture is codified in domestic statutes and constitutions. By one estimate, over 55 countries, including the United States and Paraguay, had prohibited torture expressly or by implication in their national constitutions. The United States, in its annual country reports on human rights as well as its amicus brief submitted to the court, acknowledged the universal status of the prohibition against torture. The court recognized that the prohibition against torture was not always respected by individual countries. But, "[t]he fact that the prohibition of torture is often honored in the breach does not diminish its binding effects as a norm of international law."[138]

For these reasons, the court determined that torture was firmly prohibited by international law. "Having examined the sources from which customary international law is derived—the usage of nations, judicial opinions and the works of jurists—we conclude that official torture is now prohibited by the law of nations."[139] This violation can occur regardless of the nationality of the victim and, therefore, there is no distinction between citizens and aliens for purposes of determining whether torture violates international law. "The prohibition is clear and unambiguous, and admits of no distinction between treatment of aliens and citizens."[140]

---

[137] *Id.* at 882 (citing Universal Declaration of Human Rights, G.A. Res. 217 (III), U.N. GAOR, 3d Sess., at 76, U.N. Doc. A/810 (Dec. 12, 1948)).

[138] *Id.* at 884.

[139] *Id.*

[140] *Id.* The court noted that the dictum in *Dreyfus v. von Finck* distinguishing between aliens and citizens, which was relied on by the district court, was "clearly out of tune with the current usage and practice of international law." *Id.* (citing Dreyfus v. von Finck, 534 F.2d 24, 31 (2d Cir. 1976)).

In Part III of the opinion, the court considered whether federal courts could exercise jurisdiction pursuant to the Alien Tort Statute consistent with Article III of the U.S. Constitution. The court recognized that U.S. courts "regularly adjudicate transitory tort claims between individuals over whom they exercise personal jurisdiction."[141] This principle had long been recognized by common law courts and its policy justifications were evident: "A state or nation has a legitimate interest in the orderly resolution of disputes among those within its borders."[142] In addition, the court acknowledged the unique role of the ATS, "as part of an articulated scheme of federal control over external affairs . . . for federal jurisdiction over suits by aliens where principles of international law are in issue."[143]

The court also recognized the constitutionality of the jurisdictional grant contained in the Alien Tort Statute. Article III of the U.S. Constitution provides that the judicial power extends to all cases that arise under the "laws of the United States."[144] The court found that the common law is part of the "laws of the United States" for purposes of Article III. Furthermore, it found that "[t]he law of nations forms an integral part of the common law, and a review of the history surrounding the adoption of the Constitution demonstrates that it became a part of the common law of the United States upon the adoption of the Constitution."[145] Because the law of nations is part of the common law of the United States, the grant of federal jurisdiction under the ATS was authorized by Article III of the Constitution.[146] Thus, the ATS did not grant new rights to aliens; it simply

---

[141] *Id.* at 885.

[142] *Id.*

[143] *Id.* (citations omitted). The court acknowledged, however, that such actions could conceivably be brought in state courts. "Here, where *in personam* jurisdiction has been obtained over the defendant, the parties agree that the acts alleged would violate Paraguayan law, and the policies of the forum are consistent with the foreign law, state court jurisdiction would be proper. Indeed, appellees conceded as much at oral argument." *Id.*

[144] U.S. CONST. art. III, § 2.

[145] Filartiga v. Pena-Irala, 630 F.2d 876, 886 (2d Cir. 1980). The Court reviewed several cases and legal authorities to support its assertion that the law of nations was part of the common law. *See, e.g.,* The Paquete Habana, 175 U.S. 677, 700 (1900); The Nereide, 13 U.S. (9 Cranch) 338, 422 (1815); Respublica v. DeLongchamps, 1 U.S. (1 Dall.) 113, 119 (1784). *See also* Edwin D. Dickinson, *The Law of Nations as Part of the National Law of the United States,* 101 U. PA. L. REV. 26, 27 (1952).

[146] The Court recognized that it could also sustain jurisdiction under the federal question statute. "We prefer, however, to rest our decision upon the Alien Tort Statute, in light of that provision's close coincidence with the jurisdictional facts presented in this case." Filartiga v. Pena-Irala, 630 F.2d 876, 887 (2d Cir. 1980).

opened "the federal courts for adjudication of the rights already recognized by international law."[147] This interpretation of the ATS would affirm the intent of the Framers of the Constitution and the drafters of the First Judiciary Act to assert national control over international affairs.[148]

The court acknowledged that the Alien Tort Statute had not been used extensively in the past. It explained that the paucity of ATS case law was "readily attributable to the statute's requirement of alleging a '*violation* of the law of nations' at the jurisdictional threshold."[149] Because the ATS required the plaintiff to allege a violation of international law as a jurisdictional requirement, courts must engage in a "more searching preliminary review of the merits than is required, for example, under the more flexible 'arising under' formulation."[150] Unlike prior ATS cases, the international norms raised in the *Filartiga* case were well-established and universally recognized.[151] "Here, the nations have made it their business, both through international accords and unilateral action, to be concerned with domestic human rights violations of this magnitude."[152]

Having resolved the jurisdictional challenges, the court then dismissed Peña-Irala's remaining arguments in Part IV of the opinion. Peña-Irala had argued that customary international law, as reflected in non-self-executing treaties, should not be applied as rules of decision by U.S. courts. The court noted, however, that Peña-Irala had confused the issue of federal jurisdiction with the issue of choice of law, which would be addressed by the district court on remand: "Our holding on subject matter jurisdiction decides only whether Congress intended to confer judicial power, and whether it is authorized to do so by Article III. The choice of law inquiry is a much

---

[147] *Id.*

[148] *Id. See also id.* at 878 (citations omitted) ("Implementing the constitutional mandate for national control over foreign relations, the First Congress established original district court jurisdiction over 'all causes where an alien sues for a tort only (committed) in violation of the law of nations.'").

[149] *Id.* (emphasis in original).

[150] *Id.* at 887–88.

[151] *Id.* at 888. The Court distinguished between violations of municipal law and violations of international law. For example, theft was not considered a violation of the law of nations even though it was prohibited by the municipal law of every state and so "the Eighth Commandment" was not incorporated into the law of nations. *Id.* (quoting IIT v. Vencap., 519 F.2d 1001, 1015 (2d Cir. 1975)). But, "where the nations of the world have demonstrated that the wrong is of mutual, and not merely several, concern, by means of express international accords, that a wrong generally recognized becomes an international law violation within the meaning of the state." *Id.*

[152] *Id.* at 889.

broader one, primarily concerned with fairness."[153] Peña-Irala also argued that the act of state doctrine should preclude the lawsuit if the underlying acts of torture were perpetrated by the Paraguayan government. While this issue had not been raised before the lower court, the court indicated that the act of state doctrine would probably not apply: "[W]e doubt whether action by a state official in violation of the Constitution and laws of the Republic of Paraguay, and wholly unratified by that nation's government, could properly be characterized as an act of state."[154] The court also indicated that it would not consider the doctrine of *forum non conveniens* because it had not been addressed by the lower court.[155]

The final portion of the court's opinion considered the development of international law since the Second World War and the status of human rights.

> In the twentieth century the international community has come to recognize the common danger posed by the flagrant disregard of basic human rights and particularly the right to be free of torture. Spurred first by the Great War, and then the Second, civilized nations have banded together to prescribe acceptable norms of international behavior. From the ashes of the Second World War arose the United Nations Organization, amid hopes that an era of peace and cooperation had at last begun. Though many of these aspirations have remained elusive goals, that circumstance cannot diminish the true progress that has been made. In the modern age, humanitarian and practical considerations have combined to lead the nations of the world to recognize that respect for fundamental human rights is in their individual and collective interest. Among the rights universally proclaimed by all nations, as we have noted, is the right to be free of physical torture. Indeed, for purposes of civil liability, the torturer has become like the pirate and slave trader before him *hostis humani generis*, an enemy of all

---

[153] *Id.*

[154] *Id.*

[155] *Id.* at 880, 890. Although the doctrine of *foreign non conveniens* generally involves dismissing a lawsuit to allow for foreign litigation, the court's brief discussion of this issue suggests it was more concerned with adjudication of the case in state courts. "[W]e note that the foreign relations implications of this and other issues the district court will be required to adjudicate on remand underscores the wisdom of the First Congress in vesting jurisdiction over such claims in the federal district courts through the Alien Tort Statute. Questions of this nature are fraught with implications for the nation as a whole, and therefore should not be left to the potentially varying adjudications of the courts of the fifty states." *Id.* at 890.

mankind. Our holding today, giving effect to a jurisdictional provision enacted by our First Congress, is a small but important step
in the fulfillment of the ageless dream to free all people from brutal violence.[156]

For these reasons, the court reversed "the judgment of the district court
dismissing the complaint for want of federal jurisdiction."[157]

Five months after the *Filartiga* decision was released, Judge Kaufman
wrote an article about the case for *The New York Times Magazine*.[158] In the article, Judge Kaufman described the *Filartiga* case and then examined the
development of the international prohibition against torture. He traced the
use of torture throughout history, from its use during the Roman Empire,
through the Middle Ages, and even into the 20th century.[159] He also documented torture's lack of legitimacy, beginning in the Enlightenment and
culminating in the post-World War II movement to codify human rights
standards. Judge Kaufman viewed the *Filartiga* decision as an extension of
these developments. And yet, he also acknowledged the limits of ATS litigation and the *Filartiga* precedent. He noted, for example, that U.S. courts
could not redress all human rights abuses in the world and that the other
branches of government were better placed to resolve systematic abuses.
Nonetheless, the Judicial Branch had a role to play. Alluding to the role of
the federal courts in protecting civil rights in the United States, Judge
Kaufman argued that the courts could play a similar role in protecting
human rights in the world.

The obligation of our courts to identify egregious violations of
international law is in many ways analogous to the courts' traditional role in redressing deprivations of civil liberties that occur at
home. For the past 25 years, the Federal courts have condemned
unconstitutional denials of civil rights—in our schools, mental
hospitals and prisons. These judgments have often been condemned as politically naïve, even foolhardy. But the courts exist
to preserve our freedoms under the rule of law; the courts cannot

---

[156] *Id.*

[157] *Id.* at 878.

[158] Irving R. Kaufman, *A Legal Remedy for International Torture?*, N.Y. TIMES MAG., Nov.
9, 1980, at 44.

[159] Remarkably, Judge Kaufman criticized the U.S. government for extending military and economic assistance to foreign countries that abuse human rights, including
Paraguay. He then called on the President, Congress, and the courts to pursue a principled commitment to enforcing international human rights standards.

always resort to politically expedient solutions to difficult social problems. . . . The articulation of settled norms of international law by the Federal courts, much like their adherence to constitutional precepts, is an expression of this nation's commitment to the preservation of fundamental elements of human dignity throughout the world.[160]

Judge Kaufman also addressed the *Filartiga* decision in a 1984 article for the *Fordham Law Review*.[161] This article is particularly significant because Judge Kaufman offered details about his deliberations in the *Filartiga* case.

At the outset, my inclination was to announce that torture was certainly condemned by international law. As a judge, however, I was required to look beyond my own convictions. A Supreme Court case supplied us with an enumeration of the sources of the law of nations. Another Supreme Court precedent directed us to examine "customs and usages of civilized nations; and, as evidence of these, the works of jurists and commentators." Thus, in determining Dolly Filartiga's legal rights, we relied on cases and scholarly works. From there, we found our way to passages from the United Nations Charter and the Universal Declaration of Human Rights. Finally, we turned to the documentation underlying a variety of international treaties and accords. This examination reinforced my original inclination that official torture is universally condemned both by law and by custom, and that this prohibition "admits of no distinction between treatment of aliens and [of our own] citizens." In authoring the unanimous decision of the court, I was thus able to reject the trial court's narrow interpretation of the phrase "law of nations" that might have been read to preclude federal jurisdiction over Dolly Filartiga's suit.

As Cardozo wrote, a judge "is not a knight-errant roaming at will in pursuit of his own ideal of beauty or of goodness. He is to draw his inspiration from consecrated principles." The record, briefs and other sources turned to in analyzing the issues presented by *Filartiga* demonstrated that the court's intuitive response was not unique, but was widely shared and reflected in scholarly writings and legal documents. Thus, the controlling precedents, the views of the judges and the collective conscience of civilized

---

160 Kaufman, *supra* note 158, at 52.

161 Irving R. Kaufman, *The Anatomy of Decisionmaking*, 53 FORDHAM L. REV. 1 (1984). Judge Kaufman graduated from Fordham Law School in 1931.

society coalesced to form the court's holding: "[T]he right to be free from torture" is among those fundamental rights conferred upon all people by international law.

The cases we confront may concern human stories in our public schools, administrative agencies, the media, or any other sphere of social action. They may turn on an interpretation of the Constitution or of our contemporary laws. We may also face a legal dilemma generated by a tragedy played out in distant lands, the resolution of which turns on a statute almost two hundred years old. Whatever the genesis of the controversy, it is always my hope that my ultimate consideration will be not merely the avoidance of injustice, but what we might call the most just result not only for our place and time, but also for what lies before us.[162]

A few weeks after the Second Circuit's decision, Jose Emilio Gorostiaga notified Peña-Irala's U.S. attorneys that Peña-Irala was unable to pay for the legal services already provided and would be unable to pay for any further representation.[163] As a result, Peña-Irala's attorneys petitioned and received permission from Judge Nickerson to withdraw as counsel. Peña-Irala did not participate in further proceedings. Soon thereafter, the Filártigas filed a motion for judgment by default. On June 26, 1981, Judge Nickerson granted the motion, finding that Peña-Irala had failed to respond within the time requirements of the federal rules.[164] He then referred the issue of damages to federal magistrate John Caden.

On February 12, 1982, the damages hearing was held before Judge Caden at the federal courthouse in Brooklyn.[165] In their opening remarks, the Filártiga attorneys noted that financial compensation is the only available remedy for the injuries suffered by the Filártiga family. Accordingly, they sought compensatory and punitive damages in the amount of $10 million. This amount was not an evaluation of Joelito or an evaluation of the

---

[162] *Id.* at 21–22 (citations omitted).

[163] Affidavit of Murry D. Brochin in Support of Motion to Withdraw as Attorney, Filartiga v. Pena-Irala, 577 F. Supp. 860 (E.D.N.Y. 1984) (No. 79 C 917).

[164] Federal Rule of Civil Procedure 12(a)(1) provides that a responsive pleading must be filed within ten days of notice of the denial of a motion made pursuant to Rule 12.

[165] *See generally* Eric Nadler, *Paraguay Torture in U.S. Courts,* THE NATION, May 8, 1982, at 551; Beverly Beyette, *A 6-Year Quest for Justice: Paraguayan Dolly Filartiga Pursues a Killer,* L.A. TIMES, Apr. 28, 1982, at 1; Carla Hall, *In Paraguay, A Death in the Family; Dolly Filartiga's Crusade for Human Rights,* WASH. POST, Mar. 25, 1982, at B1; Larry Tell, *U.S. Court Hears of Torture: "A Death in Asuncion,"* NAT'L L.J., Mar. 1, 1982, at 6; Joseph P. Fried, *Brooklyn Court Told of Torture of Paraguayan,* N.Y. TIMES, Feb. 13, 1982, at 27.

family's suffering. Rather, it responded "to the wrong done in the only way possible, under our laws."[166]

Four witnesses testified at the hearing: Dolly Filártiga, Dr. Joel Filártiga, former U.S. Ambassador Robert White, and Jacobo Timerman. Dolly's testimony focused on her relationship with Joelito and the implications of his torture and murder. She expressed the intense psychological trauma of seeing her brother's mutilated corpse and being forced to carry it back to her home. She described the fear of being arrested and detained by Paraguayan authorities, and the constant threats made against her family. Dolly also described the family difficulties caused by Joelito's murder: "We couldn't emotionally help each other in the family because we were all going through the same [thing]."[167] Dolly indicated she came to the United States to seek justice for her brother and to escape the pressure of living in Paraguay.[168]

When Dr. Filártiga took the witness stand, he immediately pronounced his opposition to the dictatorial regime in Paraguay. He then described his relationship with Joelito. He indicated that he had spoken to Joelito about possible threats to the family: "I spoke about all this with my son and I told him to take care, that we were in danger."[169] If Joelito was detained by the police, he should state that he did not know anything. Dr. Filártiga then described his own experiences as a victim of torture.

> It is a sensation of being tremendously isolated. A sensation of sudden fear, of feeling prisoner. And thinking that almost all the people do not know what's going on in that place because one knows that people just walk in front of the building of the police and in that backyard I could count 70 or 80 of us and that night ten were tortured and they would do the same next night, another ten. And the people [weren't] conscious of the criminality of that regime.[170]

Dr. Filártiga also testified that he had seen many victims of torture. He had witnessed some acts of torture while he had been detained. In addition, he had treated numerous torture victims at his medical clinic, including individuals who had received electric shocks.

---

166 Transcript of Hearing, *supra* note 6, at 6.

167 *Id.* at 25.

168 Dolly broke down during her initial testimony and was escorted to Judge Caden's chambers to compose herself. She resumed her testimony at the end of the hearing after Dr. Filártiga, Jacobo Timerman, and Ambassador White finished their testimony.

169 Transcript of Hearing, *supra* note 6, at 35.

170 *Id.* at 32–33.

Dr. Filártiga then described what he believed happened to Joelito. He indicated that Joelito was probably tortured for 45 minutes and that he died of cardiac arrest. His body exhibited various signs of torture, such as bruises and electrical burns. In addition, the body had been stabbed after death with a knife in order to mask the signs of torture. When Dr. Filártiga saw the body, he knew immediately that Joelito had been tortured. Finally, Dr. Filártiga described the effects of Joelito's torture on him and his family. He felt terribly guilty about the death of his son and wondered whether his "militancy" in defending Paraguayan peasants had contributed to Joelito's death: "And for six months I just couldn't work. Afterwards I tried to rebuild my life. But evidently that life was abruptly changed and now here I am in this room trying to continue this struggle."[171]

Two other witnesses testified at the hearing. Jacobo Timerman, a former political prisoner from Argentina, was asked to testify about his experiences as a torture victim.[172] However, Judge Caden asked Timerman to provide his reflections on torture and not focus on the details of his torture: "I think we can only have so much of that one day."[173] Timerman noted that the consequences of torture extend beyond pain and humiliation: "[T]he moment you are tortured, and the days after torture, and the years after torture, they have changed your human condition. It is a biological change. Your feelings have difference, your feelings are different. Your relations with the rest of the people [are] different."[174] Timerman was then asked to describe the impact of torture on society. In response, he noted that torture facilitates the abuse of power. Torture is seen as a positive instrument by the torturer. "They act like God because they have the power not only to kill you, that is nothing, because to kill is a power that is in the hands of every human being. They have a bigger power to torture and to discover, find out and change everything they want to do. And this is the danger."[175] At the end of his testimony, Timerman recalled a conversation he had with Holocaust survivor Elie Wiesel.

> [H]e said to me, that my experience was much more painful than his because he was with thousands and thousands of people together. That is quite different; of being lonely, tortured, without any hope of nothing. There is more hope in a concentration camp, and Elie Wiesel saw his father going to the gas chambers,

---

[171] *Id.* at 51.

[172] *See* JACOBO TIMERMAN, PRISONER WITHOUT A NAME, CELL WITHOUT A NUMBER (1981).

[173] Transcript of Hearing, *supra* note 6, at 57.

[174] *Id.* at 59.

[175] *Id.* at 66.

but there is more hope in that collective experience than in the loneliness of the tortured man in which there is nothing, nothing left to you; not your body, not your mind, not your imagination, not your dreams, absolutely nothing.[176]

Finally, Robert White, the former U.S. Ambassador to Paraguay from 1977 to 1979, testified at the hearing. Ambassador White described the totalitarian and corrupt nature of the Paraguayan government. While political opposition exists in Paraguay, it is repressed, and dissidents are often arrested, detained, or exiled. He indicated that torture is an integral component of repression in Paraguay: "It's at the heart of the system that enables the Stroessner dictatorship to maintain itself in power."[177] As a result, torture and the threat of torture permeate Paraguayan society: "There is almost no one in Paraguay who hasn't been touched by torture, in the sense that either they or someone in their family . . . has been tortured. . . . The only people who would be immune would be the people who are part of the apparatus"[178] Ambassador White noted that international pressure, particularly from the Carter administration, helped to reduce human rights abuses in Paraguay. In addition, the *Filartiga* litigation had also affected Paraguayan leaders.

> After the case was decided in favor of Dr. Filartiga, a Paraguay official, one of the people closest to General Stroessner, told me that I just had to do everything possible to get this decision reversed. They don't really understand independence of the court system here. And he stressed to me that no Paraguayan government figure would feel free to travel to the United States if this judgment was upheld because, you know, they would feel that they would be liable to arrest for just even being in any state in the United States.[179]

Ambassador White concluded his testimony by noting that the Filártigas could not get justice in Paraguay.

In their posttrial memorandum to Judge Caden, the Filártigas addressed the issue of damages.[180] They argued that the determination of damages must be based on the dual character of the underlying injuries. "On the

---

[176] *Id.* at 68.

[177] *Id.* at 72.

[178] *Id.* at 75.

[179] *Id.* at 77–78.

[180] Plaintiffs' Post-Trial Memorandum of Law and Facts, Filartiga v. Pena-Irala, 577 F. Supp. 860 (E.D.N.Y. 1984) (No. 79 C 917).

one hand, all the acts committed against plaintiffs and their decedent, Joelito Filartiga, are torts under the relevant municipal law which prescribes the scope of damages recoverable. On the other, the torture-murder of Joelito also violates . . . customary international law."[181] As a result, the assessment of damages must incorporate both Paraguayan municipal law as well as customary international law.

> If this case involved a purely domestic offense then choice of law principles would point to the law of Paraguay. Given the international condemnation of torture, however, choice of law doctrine demands primary consideration of whether the domestic remedy provides just and full satisfaction as that is understood in international law. Alternatively, insofar as this case involves the customary international law which is incorporated into the federal common law, this court should apply international principles directly. In either case, the measure of damage must be sufficient to vindicate the interest of the community of nations in full reparation of the damage and vindication of the world's condemnation of torture.[182]

The Filártigas then presented a list of the physical and emotional pain and suffering inflicted on them as a result of Joelito's torture and death.

For Dolly Filartiga:

Apprehension at being awakened and called to Pena's house;

Confrontation with her brother's tortured, blood-soaked body;

Being harassed and forced to carry his body home;

Having to tell her younger sisters;

Being threatened by Pena and told to shut up, or it would happen again and that they got what they were looking for;

Having to endure the sight of her brother's body in their home during the wake;

Recurrent nightmares reenacting the discovery of her brother's body and expressing the wish that he were still alive;

---

[181] *Id.* at 29.

[182] *Id.* at 29–30.

Arrest and false imprisonment, without knowing for 6 hours whether she and her mother would ever be released;

Constant surveillance and threatening actions around her home by the police;

One year of frequent episodes of believing that her brother would reappear; and then no one came;

Loss of his friendship, society and her closest confidant;

Isolation within her family;

Anger and withdrawal;

Guilt that she blames her father; anger at her father;

Realization, one year later, that her brother would never return;

Severe depression, loss of appetite, ability to read, concentrate, study, mostly confined to bed;

Inability to sleep, and fear of attack during the night;

Contemplation of and attempt to commit suicide;

Loss of companionship of friends; people being afraid to associate with the Filartigas due to fear of reprisals;

Difficulty establishing personal relationships, apprehension at social occasions;

Constant feeling of being different;

Constant consciousness of the torture-murder and loss of her brother;

Inability to continue school in Paraguay;

Inability to maintain a job, to find work;

Worry about other family members, the kidnapping of her sister, whether she'd be found;

Personal harassment, rumors and slander; police agents pretending to be suitors, impugn her reputation;

Inability to obtain justice in Paraguay;

Apprehension at leaving Paraguay;

Separation from home, family and her country;

Inability to go home; to leave the United States;

Traumas of adjustment to a strange culture, new language, no job;

Apprehension at the filing of the lawsuit in this country; knowing she could never go back; fearing for her family;

Homelessness; waiting in limbo for three years for processing of political asylum;

Having to be strong.

For Dr. Filartiga:

Apprehension on hearing in Ybycui that something was wrong at home;

Reckless drive back to Asuncion;

Apprehension entering his home;

Confrontation with his son's tortured body;

Watching his wife's inconsolable hysteria; his children's suffering;

Experiencing his son's pain; reliving his own torture and the others he witnessed being tortured over and over;

Mourning at the wake; watching his family, anger;

Finding photographers, doctors to conduct second autopsy;

Exhuming his son's body for a third autopsy;

Blaming himself; feeling blamed by his family, and feeling fury;

Wishing it had been himself who had been tortured and died;

Constant police harassment; fear for himself and his family; paranoia;

Recklessness and anger; desire to destroy himself;

Missing his son, his companionship;

Anger and grief over his death; late nights all alone drawing, writing poems, imagining the instruments of torture, the screams, the taunts;

Loss of potential colleague, Joelito, who loved the rural people and would have carried on his work;

Preparing and trying to prosecute a lawsuit; constant surveillance; constant roadblocks; constant threats; losing lawyers; lawyer arrested;

Fearing Dolly and his wife would not be released from prison; fearing his youngest daughter would not be returned by her kidnappers;

Watching his wife's suffering—her loss of eyesight, memory, weight; her terrible pain with kidney stones;

Feeling responsible;

Experiencing the loss in her two miscarriages; her sadness;

Feeling numbness, pain and cramps in his limbs from circulatory problems;

Severe pains from ulcer; losing eyesight; borderline diabetes;

Inability to work; loss of half his capacity to work and anguish at being the only source of health care for the people of Ybycui;

Inability to obtain justice; persistence;

Isolation and aloneness;

Separation from Dolly; loss of her care of the younger children, her work in the clinic;

Feeling responsible for the upset of his younger daughters;

Separation from his family on trips to the United States;

Apprehension for his family's safety; threats against him on his return to Paraguay;

Facing death and torture;

Anger and responsibility;

Going on.[183]

The Filártigas submitted several supporting affidavits on the issue of damages. In her affidavit, Dolly Filártiga described the severe emotional toll she suffered as a result of Joelito's death.

> I don't think there is a moment in my life when I feel free of the torture of my brother's torture and death. I have always the memory of his tortured body and his death; always the weight of this experience, of my identity; always the great hole in my life left by his death. I used to want to be a doctor and I functioned like a nurse in my father's clinic. Today, I do not think I could bear the pain, just as I still cannot bear to read; or use my intellect; I am fearful of social situations and strangers. I always feel different, and like I will never know what it is like to live a relatively normal life.[184]

In his affidavit, Dr. Filártiga described the pain his family experienced as a result of Joelito's death. He also offered a detailed account of the expenses incurred by his family, including funeral and memorial expenses, medical expenses for the family, and lost earnings. He was deeply troubled, however, that he needed to quantify the family's suffering in financial terms: "To talk about this terrible suffering in terms of money is very difficult and very inadequate, but I realize I must do so to help the court in its job of trying to set a dollar amount on our damages."[185]

Four medical professionals submitted affidavits describing the psychological impact of Joelito's death on the family. Dr. Glenn Randall and Dr. Jose Quiroga, who had extensive experience working with torture survivors, submitted a joint affidavit.[186] They reviewed the oral and written testimony in the case and submitted a joint affidavit stating that the Filártigas were

---

[183] *Id.* at 70–73.

[184] Affidavit of Dolly Filartiga, *supra* note 14, at 5.

[185] Affidavit of Dr. Joel Filartiga, *supra* note 11, at 3.

[186] Dr. Randall was an internist and chairman of the San Francisco Medical Group of Amnesty International USA. Dr. Quiroga was a cardiologist and chairman of the Los Angeles Medical Group of Amnesty International USA. They both reviewed the affidavits and testimony of Joel Filártiga and Dolly Filártiga and examined the autopsy reports and photographs of Joelito's body.

suffering from severe psychological disturbances caused by the torture and murder of Joelito.

> [T]he whole family has suffered since 1976 following Joelito's death. From what we know, the suffering is characterized by recollection of traumatic events, disintegration of family ties, both geographically and emotionally, feelings of guilt, multipicsomatic complaints, reduced involvement with the external world, feelings of estrangement with other people, loss of interest in previously enjoyed social activities, sleep disorders and nightmares. These symptoms present in multiple members of the Filártiga family constitute the psychiatric diagnosis of Post-traumatic Stress Disorder.[187]

Two other affidavits submitted by a clinical psychologist and a psychiatrist described the psychological consequences of torture and its implications on family members.

Family friends submitted affidavits describing their perceptions of the trauma experienced by the Filártiga family. They noted the individual suffering of each family member as well as the damage caused to the entire family unit. They also described the family's goal of seeking justice for Joelito.

> Their suffering is a special suffering, because they lost a son and brother; because of the brutal manner in which they lost Joelito; because they lost a son without having had the opportunity to defend him; and because they lost him without having had an opportunity to look for and to bring the one who murdered him to justice. Their journey is one of righteousness. They would like to see the day when no man or woman has to suffer this, when no child has to be treated in such a way because of the ideals and dreams of one's parents. They look and hope for a day when all the campesinos will be able to live as normal human beings, free from the spying, the hateful oppression and the torture which they have so long felt and endured. Through an enormous gift of the spirit, they have also held onto a great faith and love even while they are themselves irreparably victims of the most vicious form of torture—the sacrifice of their only son.[188]

Finally, the Filártigas presented their claims for past and future pecuniary losses incurred as a consequence of Joelito's torture and death. They claimed $439,734 in pecuniary damages.

---

[187] Affidavits of Dr. Glenn Randall & Dr. Jose Quiroga, *supra* note 13, at 15.

[188] Partially Sealed Affidavit at 7–8, Filartiga v. Pena-Irala, 577 F. Supp. 860 (E.D.N.Y. 1984) (No. 79 C 917).

Table of Past Pecuniary Losses Suffered
As a Consequence of Joelito's Torture and Death[189]

Type of Expenses	Amount
1. Funeral Expenses	18,900
2. Memorial Services	5,810
3. Legal Costs (Paraguayan suit)	71,000
4. Legal Costs (U.S. lawsuit)	10,364
5. Medical Expenses (Dr. Filartiga)	4,100
6. Medical Expenses (Mrs. Filartiga)	19,340
7. Medical Expenses (Dolly Filartiga)	2,160
8. Lost Earnings	71,300
Total	**$202,974**

Table of Future Pecuniary Losses Suffered
As a Consequence of Joelito's Torture and Death[190]

Type of Expenses	Amount
1. Medical Expenses (Dr. Filartiga)	10,600
2. Medical Expenses (Mrs. Filartiga)	16,700
3. Medical Expenses (Dolly Filartiga's psychiatric care)	26,960
4. Future Lost Earnings (Dr. Filartiga)	162,500
5. Future Legal Expenses	20,000
Total	**$236,760**

The Filártigas did not identify a specific amount for their nonpecuniary losses. They noted, however, that punitive damages were warranted.

> The heinousness of the crime of torture, the virtually unparalleled brutality of the torture inflicted upon Joelito, the intentional and

---

[189] Plaintiffs' Post-Trial Memorandum of Law and Facts, *supra* note 180, at Appendix.

[190] *Id.*

enduring psychological torture and resulting physical suffering of Dr. Filartiga, Dolly, and their family, the systemic encouragement of torture and immunization of its perpetrators from both criminal and civil sanction in Paraguay—all these call for the harshest sanction of which this Court is capable.[191]

While the Filártigas presented evidence of monetary damages, they acknowledged the broader purposes of the litigation: "It is not in expectation of money that plaintiffs pursue this suit, but out of the conviction that this Court can, in a symbolic way, vindicate the enduring personal anguish of the victims of torture and take another 'small but important step in the fulfillment of the ageless dream to free all people from brutal violence.'"[192] Accordingly, Dr. Filártiga announced that all funds received would be placed in a foundation "devoted to protecting and advancing the health and welfare of the poor people of Paraguay."[193]

On May 13, 1983, Judge Caden issued his report and recommendation regarding damages and submitted it to Judge Nickerson.[194] After first summarizing the status of the litigation, he then listed the seven claims for damages raised in the proceedings:

(1) Dr. Filartiga, in his capacity under Paraguayan law as the personal representative of the decedent, claims an unspecified amount of damages for the bodily injuries, pain and suffering of the decedent caused by defendant's acts of torture;

(2) Dr. Filartiga and Dolly Filartiga each claim specific damages for his/her pecuniary losses and unspecified damages for emotional pain and suffering caused by decedent's wrongful death as a result of defendant's acts of torture;

(3) Dolly Filartiga claims an unspecified amount of damages for her emotional pain and suffering caused by being led to the mutilated and lifeless body of her brother, the decedent;

(4) Dolly Filartiga claims an unspecified amount of damages for being wrongfully charged in Paraguay with harassment of Pena's

---

191 Plaintiffs' Post-Trial Memorandum of Law and Facts, *supra* note 180, at 53.

192 *Id.* at 74 (quoting Filartiga v. Pena-Irala, 630 F.2d 876, 890 (2d Cir. 1980)). *See also* Beverly Beyette, *A 6-Year Quest for Justice*, L.A. TIMES, Apr. 28, 1982, at F1.

193 Affidavit of Dr. Joel Filartiga, *supra* note 11, at 15.

194 Magistrate's Report and Recommendation, Filartiga v. Pena-Irala, 577 F. Supp. 860 (E.D.N.Y. 1984) (No. 79 C 917).

house and battery on his stepson and for being sentenced to jail
without trial, and for being incarcerated for six hours;

(5) Dr. Filartiga seeks to recover court costs, attorneys fees and other
specified expenses incurred by him in prosecuting a criminal action
against the defendant in Paraguay, based upon the same acts of torture and murder as are alleged here, which prosecution was subverted by defendant's abuse of process, and false imprisonment of,
and physical threats to, Dr. Filartiga's Paraguayan attorney;

(6) Dr. Filartiga seeks to recover attorneys fees incurred and anticipated by him in defending a civil action brought against him by
the defendant herein and Jose Duarte in Paraguay, as well as the
amount of the damages claimed against him in that action; and

(7) Plaintiffs seek to recover court costs, attorneys fees and other
specified expenses incurred by them in pursuing the instant
litigation.[195]

Judge Caden rejected claims (4), (5), and (6) because there was no independent basis for federal jurisdiction.[196] Thus, the only eligible damages
claims were (1), (2), (3), and (7).[197]

Judge Caden first examined the *Lauritzen v. Larsen* factors, which would
determine the applicable law on the question of appropriate damages.[198]
These factors include: (1) the place of the injury; (2) the place of the conduct causing the injury; (3) the nationality and domicile of the respective
parties; (4) the place where the relationship between the parties is centered; (5) the relevant policies of the forum; and (6) the possibility of prejudice to the plaintiff in having the forum court apply a foreign nation's
law.[199] Based on these factors, Judge Caden determined that Paraguayan
tort law should apply to determine damages. In contrast, he declined to
consider claims "under the general international proscription of torture"

---

[195] *Id.* at 4–5.

[196] Judge Caden also found that claim (6) could not proceed because it had not been
mentioned in the complaint.

[197] Addendum to Report and Recommendation at 2, Filartiga v. Pena-Irala, 577 F.
Supp. 860 (E.D.N.Y. 1984) (No. 79 C 917). Judge Caden found no independent basis of
federal jurisdiction for Dolly Filártiga's claim for intentional infliction of emotional distress. Notwithstanding, the claim could still be considered under the doctrine of pendent jurisdiction. Magistrate's Report and Recommendation, *supra* note 194, at 6.

[198] *See* Lauritzen v. Larsen, 345 U.S. 571 (1954). In *Lauritzen v. Larsen*, the U.S.
Supreme Court identified several factors relevant for choice of law determinations.

[199] Magistrate's Report and Recommendation, *supra* note 194, at 7–8.

for purposes of determining damages.[200] According to Judge Caden, Paraguayan tort law recognized a variety of claims in cases of wrongful death.[201] Wrongful death actions can be instituted by a decedent's father and by those who have indirectly suffered a compensable injury as a result of the decedent's death.[202] Significantly, punitive damages are not recoverable under Paraguayan law because "punishment of the tortfeasor is a function of the criminal law."[203]

Judge Caden then identified three cognizable damage claims: (1) in his capacity under Paraguayan law as the personal representative of Joelito, Dr. Filártiga's claims to damages for the bodily injuries, pain and suffering of Joelito caused by Peña-Irala's acts of torture; (2) Dr. Filártiga and Dolly Filártiga's claims for pecuniary losses and unspecified damages for emotional pain and suffering caused by Joelito's wrongful death as a result of Peña-Irala's acts of torture; and (3) Dolly Filártiga's claims for damages for her emotional pain and suffering caused by being led to Joelito's mutilated and lifeless body.[204] In contrast, Judge Caden declined to award attorneys' fees or expenses because the Filártigas had not incurred such costs in pursuing the U.S. litigation. Judge Caden also found that such an award might encourage forum shopping. Based on his review of the testimony and supporting documents, Judge Caden recommended that Dr. Filártiga should receive $200,000 in compensatory damages and Dolly Filártiga should receive $175,000 in compensatory damages. He declined to award punitive damages.

On July 12, 1983, the Filártigas submitted their objections to Judge Caden's report and recommendations.[205] They raised three challenges. First, they argued that Judge Caden was incorrect in dismissing their claims under international law. While choice of law principles authorized refer-

---

[200] Addendum to Report and Recommendation, *supra* note 197, at 1.

[201] Judge Caden based his analysis of Paraguayan law on affidavits provided to the district court in 1979 by Alexandro Miguel Garro, Ramiro Rodriguez, and Emilio Gorostiaga.

[202] Magistrate's Report and Recommendation, *supra* note 194, at 10 (citing Paraguayan Civil Code).

[203] *Id.*

[204] *Id.* at 4.

[205] Plaintiff's Objections to Magistrate's Report, Filartiga v. Pena-Irala, 577 F. Supp. 860 (E.D.N.Y. 1984) (No. 79 C 917). The International Human Rights Law Group submitted an amicus brief supporting the Filártiga's objections. Brief of the International Human Rights Law Group as Amicus Curiae in Support of Plaintiffs' Objections to the Magistrate's Report, Filartiga v. Pena-Irala, 577 F. Supp. 860 (E.D.N.Y. 1984) (No. 79 C 917).

ence to Paraguayan law, this did not preclude a reference to international law. "A holding that the act of torture underlying this suit violates Paraguayan law in no way mandates a corollary holding that it does not simultaneously violate the law of nations."[206] Indeed, reference to international law was appropriate, because "an international tort requires an international remedy."[207] Second, they challenged Judge Caden's holding that awarding them litigation costs would somehow encourage forum shopping. They noted that Dolly came to the United States in order to escape persecution. Likewise, Peña-Irala did not come to the United States to be sued. "If Paraguay had an independent judiciary, Dr. Filartiga would by now have obtained redress from the courts of his country. The policy of this country is to maximize the international enforcement of human rights, not to relegate plaintiffs to fora in which the only consequences of an attempt to vindicate human rights is a further deprivation of such rights."[208] Third, they argued that punitive damages should be made available to them. While punitive damages were not available under Paraguayan law, they were, in fact, recognized by international law.

Having reviewed Judge Caden's report and the Filártigas' objections to the report, Judge Nickerson issued his decision on the matter of damages on January 19, 1984.[209] At the outset of his opinion, Judge Nickerson addressed, albeit briefly, two issues raised but not decided by the Second Circuit in its 1980 decision. He found that the act of state doctrine did not preclude the lawsuit. "Where the principle of international law is as clear and universal as the Court of Appeals has found it to be, there is no reason to suppose that this court's assumption of jurisdiction would give justifiable offense to Paraguay."[210] Indeed, Judge Nickerson noted that Paraguay had not submitted any expression of concern regarding the litigation. "Were the government of Paraguay concerned that a judgment by the court as to the propriety of Pena's conduct would so offend that government as to affect adversely its relations with the United States, presumably Paraguay would have had the means so to advise the court."[211] It was also significant that Paraguay had not ratified Peña-Irala's acts in any way. Judge Nickerson also found that the doctrine of *forum non conveniens* did not apply: "Pena

---

[206] Plaintiff's Objections to Magistrate's Report, *supra* note 205, at 2.

[207] *Id.* at 4.

[208] *Id.* at 5.

[209] Filartiga v. Pena-Irala, 577 F. Supp. 860 (E.D.N.Y. 1984).

[210] *Id.* at 862.

[211] *Id.*

submitted nothing to cast doubt on plaintiffs' evidence showing that further resort to Paraguayan courts would be futile."[212]

Judge Nickerson then addressed whether Paraguayan law or international law should inform the analysis of damages, an issue left unresolved by the Second Circuit. "Does the 'tort' to which the statute refers mean a wrong 'in violation of the law of nations' or merely a wrong actionable under the law of the appropriate sovereign state?"[213] Reviewing the meaning of the word "tort" and the history of the Alien Tort Statute, Judge Nickerson concluded that the purpose of the ATS would best be served by looking to international law, which "'became a part of the common law *of the United States* upon the adoption of the Constitution.'"[214] While international law did not provide for specific remedies in cases of torture, this should not preclude relief.

> The international law prohibiting torture established the standard and referred to the national states the task of enforcing it. By enacting Section 1350 Congress entrusted that task to the federal courts and gave them power to choose and develop federal remedies to effectuate the purposes of the international law incorporated into United States common law.[215]

In light of traditional choice of law principles, Judge Nickerson believed that Paraguayan law should be considered in determining damages. Reference to Paraguayan law was also appropriate, because all the pertinent individuals and events had a direct link to Paraguay: the torture took place in Paraguay and all the parties were Paraguayan.[216] While review of Paraguayan law was, therefore, appropriate, it should not inhibit the broader purposes of the ATS or international law: "[W]here the nations of the world have adopted a norm in terms so formal and unambiguous as to make it international 'law,' the interests of the global community transcend those of any one state."[217]

---

[212] *Id.*

[213] *Id.*

[214] *Id.* at 863 (citing Filartiga v. Pena-Irala, 630 F.2d 876, 886 (2d Cir. 1980) (emphasis in original)).

[215] *Id.* at 863.

[216] Judge Nickerson found it significant that Paraguayan law imposed criminal liability for acts of torture and that Paraguay had signed the American Convention on Human Rights, which proscribes the use of torture. "Where a nation's pronouncements form part of the consensus establishing an international law, it does not lie in the mouth of a citizen of that nation, though it professes one thing and does another, to claim that his country did not mean what it said." *Id.* at 864.

[217] *Id.* at 863.

In his Magistrate's Report and Recommendations, Judge Caden had recommended that punitive damages be denied because they were not recoverable under Paraguayan law.[218] Judge Nickerson did not dispute these findings but noted that "the objective of international law making torture punishable as a crime can only be vindicated by imposing punitive damages."[219] Thus, it was necessary to look beyond Paraguayan law. Even though punitive damages were rare in international law, they were not without precedent.[220] It was also relevant that Peña-Irala was the defendant in the case and not the Paraguayan government. "Where the defendant is an individual, the same diplomatic considerations that prompt reluctance to impose punitive damages are not present."[221]

In determining the appropriate amount of punitive damages, Judge Nickerson found that the nature of the underlying acts was relevant.[222] "Spread upon the records of this court is the evidence of wounds and of fractures, of burning and beating and of electric shock, of stabbing and whipping and of mutilation, and finally, perhaps mercifully, of death, in short, of the ultimate in human cruelty and brutality."[223] The fact that torture was condemned by the international community and should be deterred was particularly relevant. "To accomplish that purpose this court must make clear the depth of the international revulsion against torture and measure the award in accordance with the enormity of the offense."[224] After reviewing several cases involving punitive damages, Judge Nickerson concluded "than an award of punitive damages of no less than $5,000,000 to each plaintiff is appropriate to reflect adherence to the world community's proscription of torture and to attempt to deter its practice."[225] In

---

[218] Paraguayan law allows a court to consider the intensity and duration of suffering but only for purposes of calculating compensatory damages. *Id.* These damages are not designed to punish the defendant.

[219] *Id.* at 864.

[220] Judge Nickerson cited two cases where punitive damages were awarded against national governments. *See* I'm Alone (Can. v. U.S.), 3 R.I.A.A. 1609 (1933); Letelier v. Republic of Chile, 502 F. Supp. 259, 266 (D.D.C. 1980).

[221] Filartiga v. Pena-Irala, 577 F. Supp. 860, 865 (E.D.N.Y. 1984).

[222] Judge Nickerson also found that Peña-Irala's assets were a pertinent factor for determining the amount of punitive damages. The burden of offering such evidence in mitigation, however, was on the defendant and no such evidence was offered.

[223] Filartiga v. Pena-Irala, 577 F. Supp. 860, 866 (E.D.N.Y. 1984).

[224] *Id.*

[225] *Id.* at 867. Judge Nickerson noted, for example, that the plaintiffs in *Letelier v. Republic of Chile*, 502 F. Supp. 259 (D.D.C. 1980) had been awarded $2 million in punitive damages for the murder of the former Chilean Ambassador Orlando Letelier and Ronni Moffitt.

total, Judge Nickerson issued a judgment awarding Dolly Filártiga $5,175,000 and Dr. Filártiga $5,210,364 in compensatory and punitive damages.[226] The judgment was entered on February 2, 1984.

Efforts to collect the judgment were unsuccessful. Peña-Irala had no assets in the United States, and the Filártigas were unable to enforce the judgment in Paraguay. In February 2004, the Filártigas filed a complaint in federal district court for the Eastern District of New York seeking to renew their 1984 judgment.[227] Final judgment was entered in this action on July 13, 2006.[228] While the Filártiga family has been unable to collect the judgment, they still consider their case a success. For the Filártiga family, the lawsuit was never about money; it was about seeking justice for Joelito and keeping his memory alive.

---

[226] Filartiga v. Pena-Irala, 577 F. Supp. 860, 867 (E.D.N.Y. 1984).

[227] Complaint, Filartiga v. Pena-Irala, 04–0444 (E.D.N.Y. Feb. 2, 2004). The complaint was filed pursuant to Federal Rule of Civil Procedure 69(a) and New York Civil Practice Law and Rules 5014.

[228] Judgment, Filartiga v. Pena-Irala, 04–0444 (E.D.N.Y. July 13, 2006).

CHAPTER 3
FILARTIGA AND THE DEVELOPMENT OF TRANSNATIONAL LITIGATION

The *Filartiga* case established the viability of Alien Tort Statute (ATS) litigation and signaled the birth of transnational litigation in the United States. Federal courts now recognize jurisdiction under the ATS when three conditions are met: (1) an alien sues; (2) for a tort; (3) that alleges a violation of international law.

Since *Filartiga* was decided, it has been cited in approximately 1,100 law review articles and 180 published decisions in the United States.[1] It has also been cited and used in many foreign jurisdictions.[2] In 2004, the U.S. Supreme Court affirmed *Filartiga* and the Alien Tort Statute in its landmark ruling *Sosa v. Alvarez-Machain.*[3] Because of its prominence, the *Filartiga* case is used in every major international law and human rights law textbook as an example of the domestic application of international law.[4] As one set of scholars has noted, "[w]hen it first appeared, *Filartiga* seemed the answer to every international law teacher's dream of a first week case, and so it has

---

[1] These findings were calculated on July 1, 2006. *See generally* THE ALIEN TORT CLAIMS ACT: AN ANALYTICAL ANTHOLOGY (Ralph G. Steinhardt & Anthony D'Amato eds., 1999); BETH STEPHENS & MICHAEL RATNER, INTERNATIONAL HUMAN RIGHTS LITIGATION IN U.S. COURTS (1996); KENNETH RANDALL, FEDERAL COURTS AND THE INTERNATIONAL HUMAN RIGHTS PARADIGM (1990).

[2] *See, e.g.,* A and Others v. Secretary of State for the Home Department (No. 2), [2006] 1 All E.R. 575; Regina v. Bow Street Metropolitan Stipendiary Magistrate and Others, *Ex Parte* Pinochet Ugarte (No. 3), [2000] 1 A.C. 147. *See also* Beth Stephens, *Translating Filartiga: A Comparative and International Law Analysis of Domestic Remedies for International Human Rights Violations,* 27 YALE J. INT'L L. 1 (2002); TORTURE AS TORT: COMPARATIVE PERSPECTIVES ON THE DEVELOPMENT OF TRANSNATIONAL HUMAN RIGHTS LITIGATION (Craig Scott ed., 2001).

[3] Sosa v. Alvarez-Machain, 542 U.S. 692 (2004).

[4] *See, e.g.,* MARK W. JANIS & JOHN E. NOYES, INTERNATIONAL LAW 17 (3d ed. 2006); RICHARD B. LILLICH ET AL., INTERNATIONAL HUMAN RIGHTS: PROBLEMS OF LAW, POLICY, AND PRACTICE 479–84 (4th ed. 2006); JORDAN PAUST ET AL., INTERNATIONAL LAW AND LITIGATION IN THE U.S. 14–15, 229 (2d ed. 2003); LOUIS HENKIN ET AL., HUMAN RIGHTS 856 (1999); BARRY CARTER ET AL., INTERNATIONAL LAW 229–35 (4th ed. 2003); DAVID WEISSBRODT ET AL., INTERNATIONAL HUMAN RIGHTS: LAW, POLICY, AND PROCESS 764–67, 814–16 (3d ed. 2001); LORI F. DAMROSCH ET AL., INTERNATIONAL LAW: CASES AND MATERIALS 143 (4th ed. 2001); HENRY J. STEINER & PHILIP ALSTON, INTERNATIONAL HUMAN RIGHTS IN CONTEXT 1049 (2d ed. 2000).

remained."[5] And, as Harold Koh has noted, "[i]n *Filartiga*, transnational public law litigants finally found their *Brown v. Board of Education*."[6]

A. EXTENDING *FILARTIGA* THROUGH LEGISLATION

The Alien Tort Statute has been the principal mechanism for litigating human rights violations in U.S. courts. It is limited, however, to lawsuits filed by foreign nationals. In addition, it does not provide jurisdiction for lawsuits against foreign governments. In response to these jurisdictional limitations, Congress has adopted legislation to extend civil liability beyond the narrow parameters of the ATS. The adoption of the Torture Victim Protection Act (TVPA), the establishment of the Anti-Terrorism Act (ATA), and several amendments to the Foreign Sovereign Immunities Act (FSIA) have provided victims of human rights abuses with additional avenues for redress.

1. Torture Victim Protection Act

In 1991, Congress adopted the Torture Victim Protection Act to supplement the remedies available under the Alien Tort Statute and, presumably, to comply with the Convention against Torture and Other Cruel, Inhuman or Degrading Treatment or Punishment (Convention against Torture), which requires member states to establish remedies for victims of torture.[7]

According to the House Report accompanying the TVPA, torture violates standards of conduct accepted by virtually every nation, and its prohibition has attained the status of customary international law. "These universal principles provide scant comfort, however, to the thousands of vic-

---

[5] MARK W. JANIS & JOHN E. NOYES, TEACHER'S MANUAL, CASES AND COMMENTARY ON INTERNATIONAL LAW 3 (3d ed. 2006).

[6] Harold Hongju Koh, *Transnational Public Law Litigation*, 100 YALE L.J. 2347, 2366 (1991).

[7] Torture Victim Protection Act, Pub. L. No. 102-256, 106 Stat. 73 (1992). *See generally* Christopher W. Haffke, *Torture Victim Protection Act: More Symbol Than Substance*, 43 EMORY L.J. 1467 (1994); Rachel Schwartz, *"And Tomorrow?" The Torture Victim Protection Act*, 11 ARIZ. J. INT'L & COMP. L. 271 (1994); Yoav Gery, *The Torture Victim Protection Act: Raising Issues of Legitimacy*, 26 GEO. WASH. J. INT'L L. & ECON. 597 (1993). *Cf.* William J. Aceves, *Prosecuting Violations of Human Rights in U.S. Courts: A Primer for the Justice Department on the Convention against Torture, in* EFFECTIVE STRATEGIES FOR PROTECTING HUMAN RIGHTS 147 (David Barnhizer ed., 2000). For the Convention against Torture, see Convention against Torture and Other Cruel, Inhuman or Degrading Treatment or Punishment, Dec. 10, 1984, 1465 U.N.T.S. 85. A 1988 memorandum prepared by the State Department asserts that the negotiating history of the Convention against Torture does not indicate that a private right of action for torture is compelled by the treaty. *See* I CUMULATIVE DIGEST OF UNITED STATES PRACTICE IN INTERNATIONAL LAW 1981–1988, at 840 (Marian Nash (Leich) ed., 1993).

tims of torture and summary executions around the world. Despite universal condemnation of these abuses, many of the world's governments still engage in or tolerate torture of their citizens, and state authorities have killed hundreds of thousands of people in recent years."[8] The House Report acknowledges the role of the ATS and the *Filartiga* precedent in providing redress to victims. But it recognizes the limits of the ATS, which the TVPA was designed to alleviate.

> The TVPA would . . . enhance the remedy already available under section 1350 in an important respect: While the Alien Tort Claims Act provides a remedy to aliens only, the TVPA would extend a civil remedy also to U.S. citizens who may have been tortured abroad. Official torture and summary executions merit special attention in a statute expressly addressed to those practices. At the same time, claims based on torture or summary executions do not exhaust the list of actions that may appropriately be covered by section 1350. That statute should remain intact to permit suits based on other norms that already exist or may ripen in the future into rules of customary international law.[9]

The House Report then makes clear that the TVPA was not adopted to replace the ATS; rather, it was designed to work in conjunction with that statute.

> The TVPA would establish an unambiguous and modern basis for a cause of action that has been successfully maintained under an existing law, section 1350 of the Judiciary Act of 1789 (the Alien Tort Claims Act). . . . Section 1350 has other important uses and should not be replaced. There should also, however, be a clear and specific remedy, not limited to aliens, for torture and extrajudicial killing.[10]

The Senate Report accompanying the TVPA supports this interpretation.[11]

The TVPA establishes civil liability for acts of torture and extrajudicial killing committed abroad. The statute provides, in pertinent part, that "[a]n individual who, under actual or apparent authority, or color of law, of any foreign nation, (1) subjects an individual to torture shall, in a civil

---

[8] H.R. REP. NO. 102-367, at 3 (1991).

[9] *Id.* at 4.

[10] *Id.* at 3.

[11] *See* S. REP. NO. 102-249 (1991).

action, be liable for damages to that individual; or (2) subjects an individual to extrajudicial killing shall, in a civil action, be liable for damages to the individual's legal representative, or to any person who may be a claimant in an action for wrongful death."[12] For purposes of the TVPA, "extrajudicial killing" is defined as "a deliberated killing not authorized by a previous judgment pronounced by a regularly constituted court affording all the judicial guarantees which are recognized as indispensable by civilized peoples. Such term, however, does not include any such killing that, under international law, is lawfully carried out under the authority of a foreign nation."[13] The definition of torture is based upon the U.S. understanding of torture as submitted upon ratifying the Convention against Torture.

> (1) [T]he term 'torture' means any act, directed against an individual in the offender's custody or physical control, by which severe pain or suffering (other than pain or suffering arising only from or inherent in, or incidental to, lawful sanctions), whether physical or mental, is intentionally inflicted on that individual for such purposes as obtaining from that individual or a third person information or a confession, punishing that individual for an act that individual or a third person has committed or is suspected of having committed, intimidating or coercing that individual or a third person, or for any reason based on discrimination of any kind; and
>
> (2) mental pain or suffering refers to prolonged mental harm caused by or resulting from—
>
>> (A) the intentional infliction or threatened infliction of severe physical pain or suffering;
>>
>> (B) the administration or application, or threatened administration or application, of mind altering substances or other procedures calculated to disrupt profoundly the senses or the personality;
>>
>> (C) the threat of imminent death; or
>>
>> (D) the threat that another individual will imminently be subjected to death, severe physical pain or suffering, or the admi-

---

[12] 28 U.S.C. § 1350 (note), at § 2(a).

[13] *Id.* at § 3(a).

nistration or application of mind altering substances or other procedures calculated to disrupt profoundly the senses or personality.[14]

The TVPA's definition of torture differs from the definition of torture set forth in the Convention against Torture in one notable respect: it requires mental pain or suffering to be prolonged. In contrast, there is no temporal element to mental pain or suffering in the Convention against Torture or any other international instrument.[15]

The TVPA differs from the ATS in several respects. Unlike the ATS, the TVPA is not limited to plaintiffs who are foreign nationals; it allows U.S. citizens to pursue civil actions as well. The TVPA only allows civil actions for torture or extrajudicial killing; the ATS contains no such restriction. Whereas the ATS is a jurisdictional statute, the TVPA only provides a cause of action.[16] The TVPA also contains two additional restrictions not found in the ATS. First, a plaintiff must exhaust adequate and available remedies in the place where the conduct giving rise to the claim occurred.[17] Second, no action shall be maintained unless it is commenced within ten years after the cause of action arose.[18] This provision may be tolled, however, for good cause.

On signing the TVPA into law, President George Bush acknowledged the importance of providing a civil remedy to victims of torture.

> Today I am signing into law H.R. 2092, the "Torture Victim Protection Act of 1991," because of my strong and continuing commitment to advancing respect for and protection of human rights throughout the world. The United States must continue its vigorous efforts to bring the practice of torture and other gross abuses of human rights to an end wherever they occur.[19]

However, President Bush also expressed concern about the broad implications of the TVPA.

---

[14] *Id.* at § 3(b). *See also* 136 CONG. REC. S17486-01 (Oct. 27, 1990).

[15] Convention against Torture, *supra* note 7, at art. 1.

[16] Accordingly, plaintiffs must plead a jurisdictional statute such as 28 U.S.C. Section 1331 or 28 U.S.C. Section 1350 in order to establish subject matter jurisdiction.

[17] 28 U.S.C. § 1350 (note), at § 2(b).

[18] *Id.* at § 2(c).

[19] Statement on Signing the Torture Victim Protection Act of 1991, Mar. 12, 1992, 28 WEEKLY COMP. PRES. DOC. 465 (Mar. 16, 1992).

I note that H.R. 2092 does not help to implement the Torture Convention and does present a number of potential problems about which the Administration has expressed concern in the past. This legislation concerns acts of torture and extrajudicial killing committed overseas by foreign individuals. With rare exceptions, the victims of these acts will be foreign citizens. There is thus a danger that U.S. courts may become embroiled in difficult and sensitive disputes in other countries, and possibly ill-founded or politically motivated suits, which have nothing to do with the United States and which offer little prospect of successful recovery.

Such potential abuse of this statute undoubtedly would give rise to serious frictions in international relations and would also be a waste of our own limited and already overburdened judicial resources. As I have noted in connection with my own Civil Justice Reform Initiative, there is too much litigation at present even by Americans against Americans. The expansion of litigation by aliens against aliens is a matter that must be approached with prudence and restraint. It is to be hoped that U.S. courts will be able to avoid these dangers by sound construction of the statute and the wise application of relevant legal procedures and principles.

These potential dangers, however, do not concern the fundamental goals that this legislation seeks to advance. In this new era, in which countries throughout the world are turning to democratic institutions and the rule of law, we must maintain and strengthen our commitment to ensuring that human rights are respected everywhere. I again call upon the Congress to make a real contribution to the fight against torture by enacting the implementing legislation for the Torture Convention so that we can finally ratify that important treaty.

Finally, I must note that I am signing the bill based on my understanding that the Act does not permit suits for alleged human rights violations in the context of United States military operations abroad or law enforcement actions. Because the Act permits suits based only on actions "under actual or apparent authority, or color of law, of any foreign nation," I do not believe it is the Congress' intent that H.R. 2092 should apply to United States Armed Forces or law enforcement operations, which are always carried out under the authority of United States law.[20]

---

[20] *Id.* at 465–66. Similar concerns were expressed in 1988 when the Torture Victim Protection Act was originally introduced in Congress. I CUMULATIVE DIGEST OF UNITED

Several cases have been filed under the TVPA, and this litigation has clarified its scope and application. For example, courts have indicated that the TVPA is meant to complement the ATS and should not be used to restrict the scope of the ATS.[21] Courts have also determined that equitable tolling principles apply to the ten-year statute of limitations set forth in the ATS.[22] The ten-year statute of limitations has even been extended to ATS cases.[23] Finally, some courts have indicated that the TVPA does not extend liability to corporate defendants since the language of the statute refers to individuals.[24]

2. Anti-Terrorism Act

In 1985, Leon Klinghoffer, an American citizen, was murdered by Palestine Liberation Organization (PLO) terrorists who commandeered the Italian cruise ship, *Achille Lauro*, in the eastern Mediterranean. Klinghoffer's widow and estate subsequently filed a civil action in the United States against several defendants, including the PLO. Their lawsuit, *Klinghoffer v. S.N.C. Achille Lauro*, revealed the difficulties faced by U.S. citizens pursuing civil litigation in cases involving terrorism.[25] As noted in subsequent congressional hearings:

> [O]nly by virtue of the fact that the [Klinghoffer] attack violated certain Admiralty laws and the organization involved—the Palestinian Liberation Organization—had assets and carried on activities in New York, was the court able to establish jurisdiction over the case. A similar attack occurring on an airplane or in some other locale might not have been subject to civil action in the U.S.[26]

STATES PRACTICE IN INTERNATIONAL LAW 1981–1988, at 869–72 (Marian Nash (Leich) ed., 1993).

[21] *See, e.g.*, Flores v. S. Peru Copper Corp., 343 F.3d 140, 153 (2d Cir. 2003); Kadic v. Karadzic, 70 F.3d 232, 241 (2d Cir. 1996). *See generally* Ryan Goodman, *Congressional Support for Customary International Human Rights as Federal Common Law: Lessons of the Torture Victim Protection Act*, 4 ILSA J. INT'L & COMP. L. 455 (1998). *But see* Enahoro v. Abubakar, 408 F.3d 877 (7th Cir. 2005).

[22] *See, e.g.*, Arce v. Garcia, 434 F.3d 1254, 1264 (11th Cir. 2006); Cabello v. Fernandez-Larios, 402 F.3d 1148, 1155 (11th Cir. 2005).

[23] Papa v. United States, 281 F.3d 1004, 1012–13 (9th Cir. 2002).

[24] *See, e.g.*, Corrie v. Caterpillar, Inc., 403 F. Supp. 2d 1019, 1026 (W.D. Wash. 2006); Mujica v. Occidental Petroleum Corp., 381 F. Supp. 2d 1164 (C.D. Cal. 2005). *But see* Sinaltrainal v. Coca-Cola Co., 256 F. Supp. 2d 1345 (S.D. Fla. 2003).

[25] Klinghoffer v. S.N.C. Achille Lauro Ed Altri-Gestione Motonave Achille Lauto In Amministrazione Straordinaria, 739 F. Supp. 854 (S.D.N.Y. 1990), *vacated*, 937 F.2d 44 (2d Cir. 1991).

[26] 137 CONG. REC. S4511-04 (Apr. 16, 1991) (statement of Senator Grassley).

In response to these difficulties, Congress adopted the Anti-Terrorism Act in 1992.[27] The ATA authorizes civil lawsuits in cases of international terrorism.[28] It provides that "[a]ny national of the United States injured in his or her person, property, or business by reason of an act of international terrorism, or his or her estate, survivors, or heirs, may sue therefore in any appropriate district court of the United States and shall recover threefold the damages he or she sustains and the cost of the suit, including attorney's fees."[29] The term "international terrorism" is defined as any activities that:

(A) involve violent acts or acts dangerous to human life that are a violation of the criminal laws of the United States or of any State, or that would be a criminal violation if committed within the jurisdiction of the United States or of any State;

(B) appear to be intended—

(i) to intimidate or coerce a civilian population;

(ii) to influence the policy of a government by intimidation or coercion; or

(iii) to affect the conduct of a government by mass destruction, assassination or kidnapping; and

(C) occur primarily outside the territorial jurisdiction of the United States, or transcend national boundaries in terms of the means by which they are accomplished, the persons they appear intended to intimidate or coerce, or the locale in which their perpetrators operate or seek asylum.[30]

---

[27] Pub. L. No. 102-572, 106 Stat. 4522 (1992). The 1992 legislation is part of a broader legislative scheme addressing international terrorism. *See generally* JOHN NORTON MOORE, CIVIL LITIGATION AGAINST TERRORISM 60–62 (2004); Jennifer A. Rosenfeld, *The Antiterrorism Act of 1990: Bringing International Terrorists to Justice the American Way*, 15 SUFFOLK TRANSNAT'L L. REV. 726 (1992). There is also extensive federal legislation addressing criminal penalties for acts of international terrorism. *See* NORMAN ABRAMS, ANTI-TERRORISM AND CRIMINAL ENFORCEMENT (2003).

[28] *See Anti-Terrorism Act of 1990*, Hearing Before the Subcommittee on Courts and Administrative Practice of Committee on the Judiciary, United States Senate, 101st Cong., 2d Sess., July 25, 1990.

[29] 18 U.S.C. § 2333(a). *See* Boim v. Quranic Literacy Inst., 291 F.3d 1000, 1008 (7th Cir. 2002) ("Sections 2331 and 2333 [of the ATA] were initially enacted in 1990 as the Anti-Terrorism Act of 1990, Pub. L. No. 101-519, § 132, 104 Stat. 2250 (1990), but were repealed as the result of a technical deficiency. They were subsequently re-enacted as part of the Federal Courts Administration Act of 1992, Pub. L. No. 102-572, 106 Stat. 4506 (1992).").

[30] 18 U.S.C. § 2331(1).

The ATA allows litigants to use final judgments or decrees rendered in U.S. or foreign criminal proceedings as determinative evidence of the underlying offense.[31] It precludes dismissal on *forum non conveniens* grounds unless the foreign court has subject matter jurisdiction and personal jurisdiction over all the defendants, offers a remedy that is substantially the same as the ATA, and the foreign court is significantly more convenient and appropriate.[32] There is also a four-year statute of limitations for claims brought under the ATA.[33]

Since its adoption, several ATA lawsuits have been filed.[34] In *Estates of Ungar v. Palestinian Auth.*, for example, a U.S. citizen and his Israeli wife were killed in a terrorist attack in Israel by members of the Hamas Islamic Resistance Movement, which was subsequently designated a terrorist organization by the U.S. Department of State.[35] In 2000, the Ungar heirs and administrator of the Ungar estates brought a civil action pursuant to the ATA against several defendants, including Hamas, the Palestine Liberation Organization, and the Palestinian Authority. The complaint alleged various causes of action, including acts of international terrorism, wrongful death, negligence, intentional infliction of emotional distress, and negligent infliction of emotional distress. Several plaintiffs were dismissed because they were not U.S. nationals, a prerequisite for litigation under the ATA. In addition, several defendants were dismissed for lack of personal jurisdiction. However, the court refused to dismiss the case for lack of subject matter jurisdiction, insufficiency of service of process, improper venue, or *forum non conveniens*. After these defenses were rejected by the courts, the defendants refused to participate further in the litigation. Default judgments were then entered against the Palestine Liberation Organization and the Palestinian Authority in excess of $116,400,000 for each defendant.[36] Damages included lost earnings, pain and suffering of the decedent, mental anguish, loss of companionship, and loss of parental

---

[31] 18 U.S.C. § 2333(b) and (c).

[32] 18 U.S.C. § 2334(d).

[33] 18 U.S.C. § 2335. *See also* 18 U.S.C. § 2336.

[34] *See, e.g.*, Biton v. Palestinian Interim Self-Government Auth., 310 F. Supp. 2d 172 (D.D.C. 2004); Boim v. Quranic Literacy Inst., 291 F.3d 1000 (7th Cir. 2002).

[35] Estates of Ungar v. Palestinian Auth., 153 F. Supp. 2d 76 (D.R.I. 2001).

[36] The *Ungar* litigation resulted in numerous published opinions. *See* Estate of Ungar v. Palestinian Auth., 400 F. Supp. 2d 541 (S.D.N.Y. 2005); Estate of Ungar v. Palestinian Auth., 396 F. Supp. 2d 376 (S.D.N.Y. 2005); Estate of Ungar v. Palestinian Auth., 400 F. Supp. 2d 541 (S.D.N.Y. 2005); Estate of Yaron Ungar v. Palestinian Auth., 304 F. Supp. 2d 232 (D.R.I. 2004); The Estates of Ungar *ex rel.* Strachman v. The Palestinian Auth., 228 F. Supp. 2d 40 (D.R.I. 2002). *See generally* Debra M. Strauss, *Enlisting the U.S. Courts in a New Front: Dismantling the International Business Holdings of Terrorist Groups Through Federal Statutory and Common Law Suits*, 38 VAND. J. TRANSNAT'L L. 679 (2005).

services. The First Circuit rejected the defendants' subsequent efforts to set aside the default judgments on the grounds that they were entitled to sovereign immunity and that the case presented nonjusticiable political questions.[37] Subsequent litigation has addressed the efforts of the plaintiffs to collect the judgment.[38]

Most ATA lawsuits are filed in conjunction with other jurisdictional grants, including the ATS and the Foreign Sovereign Immunities Act. Thus, the myriad of lawsuits filed after the terrorist attacks of September 11, 2001, used the ATA and several other statutes to assert jurisdiction over a large number of defendants, including "al Qaeda and its members and associates; state sponsors of terrorism; and individuals and entities, including charities, banks, front organizations, terrorist organizations, and financiers who provided financial, logistical, and other support to al Qaeda."[39]

3. Foreign Sovereign Immunities Act

While the Alien Tort Statute, the Torture Victim Protection Act, and the Anti-Terrorism Act allow civil actions against public officials, private individuals, and even corporations in certain situations, they do not provide subject matter jurisdiction for actions against foreign governments. The Foreign Sovereign Immunities Act is the sole basis for obtaining jurisdiction over a foreign state in U.S. courts.[40] According to Congress:

> [T]he determination by United States courts of the claims of foreign states to immunity from the jurisdiction of such courts would serve the interests of justice and would protect the rights of both foreign states and litigants in United States courts. Under international law, states are not immune from the jurisdiction of foreign courts insofar as their commercial activities are concerned, and their commercial property may be levied upon for the satisfaction of judgments rendered against them in connection with their commercial activities. Claims of foreign states to immunity should henceforth be decided by courts of the United States and of the States in conformity with the principles set forth in this chapter.[41]

---

[37] Ungar v. The Palestine Liberation Organization, 402 F.3d 274 (1st Cir. 2005).

[38] *See, e.g.,* Estate of Ungar v. Palestinian Auth., 2006 U.S. Dist. LEXIS 27384 (D.D.C. 2006).

[39] *See, e.g., In re* Terrorist Attacks on September 11, 2001, 349 F. Supp. 2d 765, 780 (S.D.N.Y. 2005).

[40] Argentine Republic v. Amerada Hess Shipping Corp., 488 U.S. 428, 436–39 (1989).

[41] 28 U.S.C. § 1602.

Under the FSIA, a foreign state is presumed to be immune from suit unless one or more of the codified exceptions to immunity apply.[42] These exceptions include cases of waiver, commercial activity, and certain claims in tort and property.[43] Courts have construed these provisions narrowly, leading to relatively few successful lawsuits against foreign governments or their instrumentalities.[44]

In *Letelier v. Republic of Chile*, for example, a lawsuit was filed under the FSIA against the Republic of Chile in connection with the September 1976 assassination of Orlando Letelier, the former Chilean Ambassador to the United States, and his secretary, Ronni Moffitt.[45] The lawsuit was filed by the victims' families and the victims' personal representatives and alleged five causes of action, including conspiracy, assault and battery that caused death, negligent transportation and detonation of explosives, assassination, and assault on an internationally protected person. When the Chilean government failed to respond to the complaint, the district court ordered an entry of default. However, the court still considered whether Chile was subject to immunity under the FSIA. After reviewing the immunity exceptions offered by the FSIA, the court concluded that no immunity was available. Even though foreign states were subject to immunity for certain discretionary acts under the FSIA, the court held that no foreign country has discretion "to perpetrate conduct designed to result in the assassination of an individual or individuals, action that is clearly contrary to the precepts of humanity as recognized in both national and international law."[46] On November 5, 1980, the court found the Republic of Chile liable for the bombing and entered judgment in favor of the plaintiffs.[47] They were awarded $4,952,000 in compensatory and punitive damages, as well as $110,000 in attorney's fees and costs.[48] However, the plaintiffs were unable

---

[42] 28 U.S.C. § 1604.

[43] 28 U.S.C. § 1605. *See, e.g.*, Saudi Arabia v. Nelson, 507 U.S. 349 (1993).

[44] *See, e.g.*, Siderman v. Republic of Argentina, 965 F.2d 699 (9th Cir. 1992). *See generally* Patrick J. McDonnell, *A Long Battle for Vindication Pays Off*, L.A. TIMES, Sept. 16, 1996, at A1. Some of these lawsuits led to settlements between the parties. *See* Jerry Large, *A Life of Justice*, SEATTLE TIMES, Aug. 24, 1995, at A1 (describing $3 million settlement in *Domingo v. Republic of Philippines*, 808 F.2d 1349 (9th Cir. 1987)); *New Taiwanese Law May Free Journalist's Killer*, S.F. CHRON., Jan. 2, 1991, at A3 (describing $1.5 million settlement in *Liu v. Republic of China*, 892 F.2d 1419 (9th Cir. 1989)).

[45] A federal investigation led to the indictment of nine defendants and implicated DINA, the Chilean intelligence agency.

[46] Letelier v. Republic of Chile, 488 F. Supp. 665, 673 (D.D.C. 1980).

[47] Letelier v. Republic of Chile, 502 F. Supp. 259, 260 (D.D.C. 1980).

[48] *Id.* at 266–68.

to collect the judgment through domestic litigation.[49] Compensation was finally resolved through international arbitration, when the Chilean government was ordered to pay $2.6 million to the plaintiffs.[50]

In April 1996, Congress amended the FSIA to remove the immunity of foreign governments in lawsuits for personal injury or death caused by acts of state-sponsored terrorism, including torture, extrajudicial killing, hostage taking, aircraft sabotage, or the provision of material support or resources for such acts.[51] Several conditions were imposed on plaintiffs seeking to file such claims: (1) the plaintiff or victim must be a U.S. national at the time the act upon which the claim is based occurred; (2) the foreign state must have been designated as a state sponsor of terrorism by the State Department; and (3) the act or provision of material support is engaged in by an official, employee or agent of the foreign state while acting within the scope of his or her office.[52] If the act of terrorism occurred within the territory of the foreign state, that state must be offered a reasonable opportunity to arbitrate the claim. A statute of limitations was also imposed: no action can be maintained unless it is commenced within ten years from the date on which the cause of action arose. All principles of equitable tolling, however, apply in calculating this limitation period. In September 1996, Congress again revised the FSIA to establish liability for certain individuals or agents acting within the scope of their employment on behalf of a state designated as a state sponsor of terrorism.

> [A]n official, employee, or agent of a foreign state designated as a state sponsor of terrorism designated under section 6(j) of the Export Administration Act of 1979 while acting within the scope of his or her office, employment, or agency shall be liable to a United States national or the national's legal representative for personal

---

[49] Letelier v. Republic of Chile, 748 F.2d 790 (2d Cir. 1984).

[50] *See generally* Judith Hippler Bello, *Chile: Criminal Jurisdiction: Prosecution of Official of Secret Service for Assassination of Former Ambassador to United States,* 90 AM. J. INT'L L. 290 (1996), Jack I. Garvey, *Judicial Foreign Policy-Making in International Civil Litigation: Ending the Charade of Separation of Powers,* 24 LAW & POL'Y INT'L BUS. 461, 499 (1993), Marian Nash, *Claims for Wrongful Death,* 86 AM. J. INT'L L. 347 (1992), Barbara Crossette, *$2.6 Million Awarded Families in Letelier Case,* N.Y. TIMES, Jan. 13, 1992, at A11.

[51] Anti-Terrorism and Effective Death Penalty Act, Pub. L. No. 104–132, § 221, 110 Stat. 1214, 1241 (1996). *See generally* Joseph W. Glannon & Jeffery Atik, *Politics and Personal Jurisdiction: Suing State Sponsors of Terrorism Under the 1996 Amendments to the Foreign Sovereign Immunities Act,* 87 GEO. L.J. 675 (1999); John F. Murphy, *Civil Liability for the Commission of International Crimes as an Alternative to Criminal Prosecution,* 12 HARV. HUM. RTS. J. 1 (1999).

[52] 28 U.S.C. § 1605(a)(7).

injury or death caused by acts of that official, employee, or agent for which the courts of the United States may maintain jurisdiction under section 1605(a)(7) of title 28, United States Code for money damages which may include economic damages, solatium, pain, and suffering, and punitive damages if the acts were among those described in section 1605(a)(7).[53]

Prior to the 1996 FSIA amendments, lawsuits against foreign governments involving human rights abuses were generally unsuccessful. Few plaintiffs were able to meet the rigorous jurisdictional requirements for suing foreign governments. When Congress removed foreign sovereign immunity in cases of state-sponsored terrorism, it led to a flurry of lawsuits by victims and their families. Several of these cases resulted in significant damage awards, although plaintiffs were unable to collect due to the unavailability of the foreign assets.

In *Flatow v. Islamic Republic of Iran*, for example, a U.S. national, Alisa Flatow, was killed by a suicide bombing in Israel. Palestine Islamic Jihad, an organization funded by the Iranian government, claimed responsibility for the attack. In 1997, Alisa Flatow's father brought a lawsuit against the Iranian government and several Iranian officials in the federal district court for the District of Columbia. The lawsuit alleged that the Iranian government had provided financial assistance to Palestine Islamic Jihad and that Iran had been named a state sponsor of terrorism by the State Department, thereby fulfilling the core requirements of the Foreign Sovereign Immunities Act. Although the Iranian government was served with process, it refused to participate in the proceedings and default was entered. On March 11, 1998, the district court held that the plaintiff had met the requirements of the FSIA and awarded them approximately $22.5 million in compensatory damages and $225 million in punitive damages.[54] Initial efforts to satisfy the judgment by attaching Iranian government property in the United States were unsuccessful.

The inability of the *Flatow* plaintiffs to collect their judgment was not unique. Successful plaintiffs in other FSIA cases involving Iran and Cuba were unable to collect their judgments because the foreign government assets were either frozen or otherwise unavailable in the United States.[55] In

---

[53] Civil Liability for Victims of State Sponsored Terrorism, Pub. L. No. 104-208, 100 Stat. 3009–172 (1996), *reprinted in* 28 U.S.C. § 1605 note. This provision is also referred to as the Flatow Amendment, because it was adopted in response to the case of Alisa Flatow.

[54] Flatow v. Islamic Republic of Iran, 999 F. Supp. 1 (D.D.C. 1998).

[55] *See, e.g.,* Cicippio v. Islamic Republic of Iran, 18 F. Supp. 2d 62 (D.D.C. 1998); Alejandre v. Republic of Cuba, 996 F. Supp. 1239 (S.D. Fla. 1997). Other lawsuits were filed

response, Congress adopted the Victims of Trafficking and Violence Protection Act of 2000, which authorized the payment of certain FSIA judgments against Cuba and Iran from the U.S. Treasury.[56] The Act provided successful litigants with two options. Plaintiffs could choose to receive 110 percent of the compensatory damages awarded in their case but they would have to relinquish all claims to punitive damages against the defendant state.[57] Alternatively, plaintiffs could choose to receive 100 percent of the compensatory damages awarded in their case. While these plaintiffs would not relinquish their claims to punitive damages, they would relinquish all rights to execute against property: (1) that is at issue in claims against the United States before an international tribunal; (2) that is the subject of awards rendered by such tribunal; or (3) that is subject to 28 U.S.C. Section 1610(f)(1)(A).[58]

In response to the compensation scheme offered by Congress, several litigants, including the *Flatow* plaintiffs, accepted partial payment from the U.S. Treasury in satisfaction of their judgments.[59] The *Flatow* plaintiffs, for example, chose to collect compensatory damages from the U.S. Treasury and pursue their claims for punitive damages in U.S. courts. Over $300 million has been paid to victims of state-sponsored terrorism by the U.S. Treasury although these payments have been limited to a small group of plaintiffs with preexisting judgments against Cuba or Iran.[60]

Subsequent FSIA litigation reveals the continuing difficulties facing plaintiffs seeking to pursue lawsuits against foreign governments designated as state sponsors of terrorism. The Executive Branch has generally not supported the litigation, citing its interference with U.S. foreign policy interests. In addition, the federal courts have narrowly interpreted the FSIA, making these actions even more difficult to pursue.[61]

---

against Iraq and Libya. *See, e.g.*, Daliberti v. Republic of Iraq, 97 F. Supp. 2d 38 (D.D.C. 2000); Rein v. Socialist People's Libyan Arab Jamahiriya, 162 F.3d 748 (2d Cir. 1998).

56 *See* Victims of Trafficking and Violence Protection Act of 2000, Pub. L. No. 106-386, § 2002, 114 Stat. 1464. The Act only addressed judgments involving Cuba and Iran. It did not address judgments against other countries such as Iraq or Libya.

57 *Id.* at § 2002(a)(2)(C).

58 *Id.* at § 2002(a)(2)(D).

59 Michael L. Martinez & Stuart H. Newberger, *Combating State-Sponsored Terrorism with Civil Lawsuits*, VICTIM ADVOCATE 5, 7 (Spring/Summer 2002).

60 *See generally* Joseph Keller, *The Flatow Amendment and State-Sponsored Terrorism*, 28 SEATTLE U. L. REV. 1029 (2005); Ruthanne M. Deutsch, *Suing State Sponsors of Terrorism Under the Foreign Sovereign Immunities Act*, 38 INT'L LAW. 891 (2004).

61 *See, e.g.*, Acree v. Republic of Iraq, 370 F.3d 41 (D.C. Cir. 2004); Cicippio-Puleo v. Islamic Republic of Iran, 353 F.3d 1024 (D.C. Cir. 2004).

B. EXTENDING *FILARTIGA* THROUGH LITIGATION

The following six cases extended the *Filartiga* precedent and are representative of transnational litigation.[62] While the facts and legal issues vary, these cases share much in common. Like *Filartiga*, each case involves a country wracked by civil unrest, violence, and the systematic violation of basic human rights. Each case involves individuals who were unable to find justice in their own country and were forced to litigate their claims in the United States. The Alien Tort Statute is used in each case to establish subject matter jurisdiction, although other statutes are also referenced. And each case reveals the transnational advocacy network of public interest lawyers, nongovernmental organizations, and law professors that worked on behalf of victims.

1.   Argentina: *Forti v. Suarez-Mason*

In the early 1970s, political unrest plagued Argentina.[63] On November 6, 1974, President Isabel Perón declared a state of siege throughout the country, empowering the military to combat civil disturbances, including a purported left-wing insurgency. These efforts proved unsuccessful at repressing political opposition. On March 24, 1976, military officials staged a successful coup and replaced Perón's civilian government with a military junta. The new military regime extended the state of siege and imposed further limits on political activity and democratic opposition. Political opponents and other "undesirables" were targeted with threats and abuse by a regime intolerant of political dissent. Thousands of people were detained without charge. Many were killed; others simply disappeared while in government custody. This period of Argentine history is known as the Dirty War. According to the Report of the Argentine National Commission on the Disappeared, 8,900 people were victims of forced disappearance during the Dirty War, although some estimates place the num-

---

[62] Other notable ATS cases include: Wiwa v. Royal Dutch Petroleum Co., 226 F.3d 88 (2d Cir. 2000); Xuncax v. Gramajo, 886 F. Supp. 162 (D. Mass. 1995). Not all ATS cases end in judgments on behalf of the plaintiffs. *See, e.g.*, Flores v. S. Peru Copper Corp., 343 F.3d 140 (2d Cir. 2003); Tel-Oren v. Libyan Arab Republic, 726 F.2d 774 (D.C. Cir. 1984). And some ATS cases are properly dismissed because they fail to raise legitimate claims. *See, e.g.*, Zapata v. Quinn, 707 F.2d 691 (2d Cir. 1983) (ATS claim alleged that payment of lottery winnings in annuity rather than lump sum constituted a violation of the law of nations).

[63] *See generally* DEBORAH L. NORDEN, MILITARY REBELLION IN ARGENTINA (1996); II TRANSITIONAL JUSTICE: HOW EMERGING DEMOCRACIES RECKON WITH FORMER REGIMES 323 (Neil J. Kritz ed., 1995); JUAN MENDEZ, TRUTH AND PARTIAL JUSTICE IN ARGENTINA: AN UPDATE (1991); IAIN GUEST, BEHIND THE DISAPPEARANCES (1990); Alejandro M. Garro & Henry Dahl, *Legal Accountability for Human Rights Violations in Argentina: One Step Forward and Two Steps Backward*, 8 HUM. RTS. L.J. 283 (1987).

ber of victims at 30,000.[64] The *Forti* litigation involves two cases that arose from the Dirty War.

On February 18, 1977, Argentine military officials seized the Forti family, including Nelida Azucena Sosa de Forti, her 16-year-old son Alfredo, and four other children, as the family tried to leave the country on a commercial flight to Venezuela.[65] They were then escorted from the aircraft and taken to waiting vehicles.

> On an abandoned road the six were taken out of the cars and their eyes blindfolded. They then were taken to a kind of prison establishment, where they remained for seven days. At no time was any reason given for their incarceration, or was any authorization shown.
>
> On the seventh day, the children were taken from their mother and abandoned in the city of Buenos Aires, close to a house that they knew. As on the previous occasion, they were blindfolded. Before they were left, the person whom the others treated as their leader informed them that their mother would be taken to Tucumán and that she would be reunited with them in a week.
>
> No further news has been received of the mother's whereabouts since that time, nor of the reason for her detention, the causes behind it, nor of the authorities that ordered it and that still deprive her of her freedom. All the efforts of Cáritas in Venezuela and of the Venezuelan Embassy in Buenos Aires to ascertain her whereabouts have been fruitless.[66]

While the five Forti children were ultimately released, their mother was not. She was never seen again.

On July 25, 1977, 16-year-old Débora Benchoam and her 17-year-old brother were abducted from their home in Buenos Aires by military personnel. Her brother was tortured and summarily executed. His bruised and bullet-riddled body was returned to the Benchoam family the day after his

---

[64] COMISIÓN NACIONAL SOBRE LA DESAPARICIÓN DE PERSONAS, NUNCA MAS (1986). Other reports place the number of forced disappearances at 30,000. *See* RITA ARDITTI, SEARCHING FOR LIFE: THE GRANDMOTHERS OF THE PLAZA DE MAYO AND THE DISAPPEARED CHILDREN OF ARGENTINA 44 (1999); MARGUERITE GUZMAN BOUVARD, REVOLUTIONIZING MOTHERHOOD: THE MOTHERS OF THE PLAZA DE MAYO 31 (1994).

[65] *See* Nelida Azucena Sosa de Forti, Case No. 2271, 1978 Inter-Am. C.H.R. 29, OEA/ser. L/V/II.47, doc. 13 rev. 1 (1978).

[66] *Id.* at para. 5.

abduction. Initially, Débora was blindfolded and taken to a police station. She remained at the police station for a week, blindfolded and handcuffed. During her detention, one guard attempted to rape her. She was held at the police station for another three weeks before she was transferred to Devoto Prison in Buenos Aires. Débora was detained without charge for over four years. She was released on November 5, 1981, due to the intervention of U.S. Congressman William Lehman.[67] When she was released, Débora fled to the United States as a political refugee.

The state of siege in Argentina continued until 1983, when military rule ended with the election of President Raul Alfonsin.[68] Under President Alfonsin's administration, the National Commission on the Disappeared was created to investigate allegations of human rights abuses. The Commission confirmed that approximately 8,900 persons were subjected to forced disappearance in Argentina during the military rule. President Alfonsin decided to submit the responsible members of the military junta to the Argentine legal system for prosecution, although prosecution efforts were subsequently limited by amnesty grants.

In March 1984, General Carlos Guillermo Suarez-Mason was summoned to appear before the Argentine Supreme Council. Between 1976 and 1979, Suarez-Mason had commanded the First Army Corps, which was assigned to the Province of Buenos Aires and the national capital.[69] As the military commander of this region, he was implicated in numerous atrocities. Instead of appearing at trial, Suarez-Mason fled to the United States. In January 1987, he was arrested in California pursuant to an international arrest warrant issued at the request of the Argentine government. While in custody awaiting a decision on whether he should be extradited to Argentina, Suarez-Mason was served with the *Forti* complaint.

Alfredo Forti and Débora Benchoam filed their ATS lawsuit against Suarez-Mason in the federal district court for the Northern District of California in April 1987.[70] They sought compensatory and punitive damages for torture, prolonged arbitrary detention, cruel, inhuman, or degrad-

---

[67] During her detention, Débora obtained a writ of habeas corpus from an Argentine court but the writ was reversed on appeal.

[68] *See generally Annual Report of the Inter-American Commission on Human Rights 1983–1984, Situation of Human Rights in Several States: Argentina,* Inter-Am. C.H.R., OEA/Ser.L/V/II.63, doc. 10 (Sept. 24, 1984).

[69] Deposition of Carlos Guillermo Suarez-Mason, Forti v. Suarez-Mason, 672 F. Supp. 1531 (N.D. Cal. 1987) (No. C-87-2058 DLJ).

[70] Forti and Benchoam were represented by the Center for Constitutional Rights and several pro bono attorneys.

ing treatment, false imprisonment, assault and battery, intentional infliction of emotional distress, and conversion. In addition, Forti alleged damages for forced disappearance, and Benchoam asserted claims for murder,
wrongful death, and summary execution. In response, Suarez-Mason filed
a motion to dismiss that raised several challenges, including lack of subject
matter jurisdiction.

On October 6, 1987, the district court issued its ruling on the motion to
dismiss.[71] The court determined that the ATS establishes jurisdiction and a
cause of action for certain international common law torts. To be actionable
under the ATS, these norms must be universal, definable, and obligatory:
"The requirement of international consensus is of paramount importance,
for it is that consensus which evinces the willingness of nations to be bound
by the particular legal principle, and so can justify the court's exercise of
jurisdiction over the international tort claim."[72] As a separate jurisdictional
ground, the district court held that 28 U.S.C. Section 1331 would also apply
in cases presenting claims arising under customary international law.[73]

The district court then examined the substantive claims raised by the
plaintiffs. It held that torture, summary execution, and prolonged arbitrary
detention were each universal, definable, and obligatory. Accordingly, these
norms were actionable under the Alien Tort Statute.[74] In contrast, the district court held that the prohibitions against causing disappearance and
cruel, inhuman, or degrading treatment had not yet attained the requisite
degree of international consensus that demonstrates a customary international norm. Thus, the court dismissed the claim for causing disappearance
because the plaintiffs could "not cite the Court to any case finding that
causing the disappearance of an individual constitutes a violation of the law
of nations."[75] The claim for cruel, inhuman, or degrading treatment was
also dismissed because the court was not satisfied that this norm had the
necessary universal consensus to make it actionable under the ATS.[76]

The district court declined to dismiss the lawsuit under the act of
state doctrine. The court noted that official government action is not

---

[71] *See* Forti v. Suarez-Mason, 672 F. Supp. 1531 (N.D. Cal. 1987).

[72] *Id.* at 1540.

[73] *Id.* at 1544.

[74] While relying on the analysis in *Filartiga* to find the existence of an international
prohibition of official torture, the court ordered plaintiffs to amend the complaint to
more specifically allege the facts that formed the basis of their claims of official torture.

[75] Forti v. Suarez-Mason, 672 F. Supp. 1531, 1543 (N.D. Cal. 1987).

[76] *Id.*

automatically protected under this doctrine of judicial abstention. For example, acts that violate well-established principles of international law are not protected.

> That is, a police chief who tortures, or orders to be tortured, prisoners in his custody fulfills the requirement that his action be "official" simply by virtue of his position and the circumstances of the act; his conduct may be wholly unratified by his government and even proscribed by its constitution and criminal statutes. Thus, allegations of official action for purposes of § 1350 do not *necessarily* require application of the act of state doctrine. Indeed, since violations of the law of nations virtually all involve acts practiced, encouraged or condoned by states, defendant's argument would in effect preclude litigation under § 1350 for "tort[s] . . . committed in violation of the law of nations."[77]

Accordingly, the court denied Suarez-Mason's motion to dismiss based on the act of state doctrine. The court also denied Suarez-Mason's challenges based on the statute of limitations and the failure to join indispensable parties.

The plaintiffs subsequently filed a motion for reconsideration with the district court, asserting that the claims of causing disappearance and cruel, inhuman, or degrading treatment should not have been dismissed. They argued that there was an international consensus with respect to both norms. In support, they submitted affidavits from eight recognized legal scholars.[78] On July 6, 1988, the district court issued its ruling on the motion for reconsideration.[79] The court agreed with the plaintiffs that causing disappearance was a viable claim under international law. According to the court, "the submitted materials are sufficient to establish the existence of a universal and obligatory international proscription of the tort of 'causing disappearance.'"[80] In contrast, the court declined to reverse its prior ruling on cruel, inhuman, or degrading treatment, finding a lack of international consensus supporting the claim. Here, "[p]laintiffs' submissions fail to

---

[77] *Id.* at 1546 (citations omitted) (emphasis in original).

[78] Affidavits were submitted by Richard Falk (Princeton University), Thomas Franck (New York University), Louis Henkin (Columbia University), Richard B. Lillich (University of Virginia), Phillipe Sands (Cambridge University), Henry J. Steiner (Harvard Law School), David Weissbrodt (University of Minnesota), and Burns H. Weston (University of Iowa).

[79] Forti v. Suarez-Mason, 694 F. Supp. 707 (N.D. Cal. 1988).

[80] *Id.* at 711.

establish that there is anything even remotely approaching universal consensus as to what constitutes 'cruel, inhuman or degrading treatment.'"[81]

Before the case could be tried, Suarez-Mason was extradited to Argentina to face charges for multiple counts of murder.[82] He was never tried on these charges because of a blanket pardon subsequently issued by Argentine President Carlos Menem.[83] In the United States, the district court then entered a default judgment against Suarez-Mason in the ATS lawsuit.[84] After his extradition, Suarez-Mason did not participate further in the legal proceedings. In 1990, the plaintiffs were awarded $8 million in damages, although they never collected any money from the judgment.

Suarez-Mason was also sued in two other ATS lawsuits for human rights abuses committed under his military command. In 1988, a federal court awarded $11 million in compensatory damages and $10 million in punitive damages to Horacio Martinez-Baca, an Argentine citizen who suffered four years of detention and torture by police and military personnel.[85] In its Findings of Fact, the court described Suarez-Mason's role in the abuses.

> Defendant Suarez-Mason, as the Commander of the First Army Corps from 1976 to 1979, had direct operational control over the most populous region of Argentina during the height of the military repression in that country. The enterprise of terror that he oversaw in that region included: the kidnapping of thousands of persons from their homes, places of work, or off the streets; "disappearances" into a vast network of secret detention centers; arbitrary detention of political prisoners; subjugation of prisoners to routine torture, rape, and summary execution; and systematic theft of worldly possessions of the victims as tributary or "booty" to the military. . . . The allegations of the complaint and offered proof establish that defendant was directly responsible for the actions perpetrated against plaintiff, including repeated torture and pro-

---

[81] *Id.* at 712.

[82] Matter of Extradition of Suarez-Mason, 694 F. Supp. 676, 679 (N.D. Cal. 1988). The evidence used against Suarez-Mason was taken largely from the litigation documents submitted in the *Forti* case as well as two other ATS lawsuits filed against him. HUMAN RIGHTS WATCH, RELUCTANT PARTNER: THE ARGENTINE GOVERNMENT'S FAILURE TO BACK TRIALS OF HUMAN RIGHTS VIOLATORS (2001).

[83] Myrna Oliver, *G. Suarez Mason, 81; Ex-General Linked to Argentina's 'Dirty War,'* L.A. TIMES, June 22, 2005, at B10. *See generally* CARLOS SANTIAGO NINO, RADICAL EVIL ON TRIAL 103–04 (1996).

[84] *See* Forti v. Suarez-Mason, No. C-87-2058-DLJ, slip op. (N.D. Cal. Dec. 22, 1988).

[85] Judgment, Martinez-Baca v. Suarez-Mason, No. C-87-2057-SC, 1988 U.S. Dist. LEXIS 19470 at *9–10 (N.D. Cal. Apr. 22, 1988).

longed arbitrary detention. . . . Defendant did not personally apply the electric prods to the plaintiff's body. The persons who did, however, were acting under defendant's direct supervision and control, for defendant exercised operational control over all the prisons and clandestine detention centers within his jurisdiction, and over all the employees therein. The practice of torture and other human rights violations under defendant's command was widespread. The evidence shows that defendant was aware of all that went on below him.[86]

In 1989, a federal court found Suarez-Mason responsible for authorizing the torture and murder of two men in Argentina. The court awarded relatives of the two men $30 million in compensatory and punitive damages.[87]

Proceedings against Suarez-Mason were also instituted in other countries. In 1999, Suarez-Mason was arrested in Argentina to answer charges for the kidnapping and illegal adoption of over 200 children born to women who were held captive during the military dictatorship.[88] In 2000, an Italian court convicted Suarez-Mason *in absentia* for the kidnapping and murder of eight Italian nationals during the Dirty War, and he was sentenced to life imprisonment on those charges.[89] In 2001, a German court ordered Suarez-Mason's arrest and sought his extradition from Argentina to stand trial in Germany for the 1977 murder of a German citizen in Buenos Aires.[90] Argentina refused to extradite Suarez-Mason, asserting that foreign courts had no jurisdiction to prosecute him for human rights abuses committed in Argentina. In 2003, Suarez-Mason was convicted in Argentina of racial discrimination for making anti-Semitic comments.[91] At the sentencing hearing, the judge commented on Suarez-Mason's horrid legacy, stating the sentence was "[f]or having justified the crime, for having made an exaltation of the torture and of the activity that developed in the last genocidal dictatorship that terrorized the country and for the discrim-

---

[86] Findings of Fact and Conclusions of Law at 2–4, Martinez Baca v. Suarez-Mason, No. C-87-2057-SC (N.D. Cal. Apr. 22, 1988).

[87] *See* Quiros de Rapaport v. Suarez-Mason, No. C-87-2266, slip op. (N.D. Cal. Apr. 11, 1989).

[88] Oliver, *supra* note 83, at B10.

[89] *See* BBC News, *Argentina Generals Get Life* (Dec. 6, 2000), *at* http://news.bbc.co.uk/1/hi/world/americas/1058205.stm.

[90] *See* U.S. Dep't of State, Country Reports on Human Rights Practices 2001: Argentina (Mar. 4, 2002).

[91] *See* BBC News, *Argentine General Jailed for Racist Remarks* (June 25, 2003), *at* http://news.bbc.co.uk/1/hi/world/americas/3019090.stm.

ination in the Jewish community."[92] In June 2005, Suarez-Mason died in Buenos Aires of cardiac arrest at the age of 81.[93]

2. Burma: *Doe v. Unocal*

On September 18, 1988, a military coup took place in Burma. Upon seizing power, the State Law and Order Restoration Council (SLORC) imposed martial law and renamed the country Myanmar. In an effort to gain international legitimacy, SLORC held multiparty elections on May 27, 1990. The main opposition party, the National League for Democracy led by Tin Oo and 1991 Nobel Laureate Aung San Suu Kyi, captured 82 percent of the parliamentary seats. However, SLORC refused to recognize the election results and intensified its campaign against the pro-democracy movement.[94]

In October 1996, 15 Burmese villagers filed a lawsuit in federal district court for the Central District of California in connection with the development and construction of the Yadana gas pipeline project in Burma's Tenasserim region.[95] The complaint was brought against Unocal Corp., Total S.A., Myanmar Oil and Gas Enterprise (MOGE), SLORC, and two Unocal officials.[96] Jurisdiction was premised on several statutes, including the Alien Tort Statute.[97]

---

[92] *Id.*

[93] Oliver, *supra* note 83, at B10.

[94] Following the elections, representatives of the National League for Democracy formed a government-in-exile, the National Coalition Government of the Union of Burma.

[95] In September 1996, a lawsuit was also filed by the Federation of Trade Unions of Burma, the National Coalition Government of the Union of Burma, and four villagers from the Tenasserim region. *See* National Coalition Gov't of Burma v. Unocal, Inc., 176 F.R.D. 329 (C.D. Cal. 1997); Roe v. Unocal Corp., 70 F. Supp. 2d 1073 (C.D. Cal. 1999). This lawsuit was consolidated with *Doe v. Unocal* on appeal. In addition, two lawsuits were filed in September 2000 against Unocal Corporation, Union Oil Co. of California, and two Unocal officials in California state court.

Throughout these legal proceedings, the plaintiffs were represented by a large number of organizations and attorneys, including: Center for Constitutional Rights; Center for Human Rights and Constitutional Law; Earthrights International; International Labor Rights Fund; the National Center for Immigrants Rights; Schonbrun, DeSimone, Seplow, Harris & Hoffman; Hadsell & Stormer; and several private attorneys.

[96] Third Amended Complaint, Doe v. Unocal, No. 96-6959 RAP (C.D. Cal. Oct. 3, 1996).

[97] The complaint also cited 28 U.S.C. Sections 1331, 1367, and 18 U.S.C. Section 1964(c) in support of jurisdiction.

The complaint charged the defendants with numerous human rights violations perpetrated during the development and construction of the Yadana pipeline project. According to the complaint, several international oil companies, including Unocal and Total, began negotiating with SLORC for oil and gas exploration rights in 1991. In July 1992, Total signed a production-sharing contract with MOGE, a company owned and operated by SLORC, for the exploration and development of the Yadana natural gas field, located off the coast of Burma in the Andaman Sea. In early 1993, Unocal entered into a similar agreement with MOGE. The project included the exploration and development of the Yadana natural gas field and the construction of a pipeline from the Yadana field, through the Tenasserim region of Burma, to Thailand. Plaintiffs alleged that SLORC, Unocal, and Total also entered into an agreement by which SLORC undertook to clear the pipeline route and provide labor, materials, and security for the project in the Tenasserim region. As part of the agreement, Unocal and Total agreed to finance SLORC's activities in the region. Plaintiffs further alleged that SLORC soldiers committed a number of human rights violations against the local population in the development of the pipeline project. Whole villages were relocated. Homes, crops, livestock, and other property were confiscated and destroyed. Villagers were forced to clear tracts of forest, level the pipeline route, carry supplies and equipment, and construct buildings and military facilities. Those unwilling to cooperate were threatened, beaten, tortured, or killed. Women and young girls were victims of rape and other forms of sexual abuse perpetrated by SLORC soldiers. Plaintiffs further alleged that numerous actions in support of the joint venture took place in California, including the provision of funds and other resources, the assignment of personnel, and monitoring, advising, and auditing the project.

The complaint set forth 18 causes of action, including forced labor, crimes against humanity, torture, violence against women, arbitrary arrest and detention, and cruel, inhuman, or degrading treatment. The plaintiffs requested compensatory and punitive damages. They also sought injunctive and declaratory relief on behalf of themselves and a class of thousands of residents from the Tenasserim region seeking, in part, "an order directing defendants to cease payment to SLORC, and an order directing defendants to cease their participation in the joint enterprise until the resulting human rights violations in the Tenasserim region cease, and such other injunctive relief as this Court deems appropriate."[98]

---

[98] Third Amended Complaint, *supra* note 96, at 33–34.

On March 25, 1997, the district court issued an initial ruling on a motion to dismiss filed by the defendants.[99] The court first examined the application of the Foreign Sovereign Immunities Act to SLORC and MOGE, with specific reference to the commercial activity exception.[100] The court recognized that SLORC and MOGE had engaged in commercial activity by seeking to develop the Yadana project. However, the human rights abuses committed in connection with the project did not fall within the ambit of the commercial activity exception. Relying on the Supreme Court's rulings in *Saudi Arabia v. Nelson* and *Republic of Argentina v. Weltover, Inc.*, the court indicated that "because plaintiffs essentially allege that SLORC and MOGE abused their police power, the foreign sovereign defendants' acts that form the basis of plaintiffs' claims are 'peculiarly sovereign in nature' and do not come within the commercial activity exception to the FSIA."[101] Even if SLORC and MOGE's alleged human rights violations could be considered commercial activity, the court found that they had no direct effect in the United States within the meaning of the FSIA. The plaintiffs argued that the use of forced labor and other human rights violations reduced the cost of the Yadana pipeline project and decreased the defendants' labor and operational costs, providing the defendants with an unfair competitive advantage in the U.S. gas market. The court disagreed, finding that the legally significant acts giving rise to the plaintiffs' claims had occurred in Burma and not in the United States. Accordingly, SLORC and MOGE were entitled to sovereign immunity under the FSIA.

Second, the district court reviewed the application of the Alien Tort Statute. The court indicated that certain violations of international law— such as torture and summary execution—require state action. It recognized, however, that nonstate actors could be found liable for these violations

---

[99] Doe v. Unocal, 963 F. Supp. 880 (C.D. Cal. 1997). In addition to these issues, the court also addressed whether SLORC and MOGE were indispensable parties, jurisdictional questions regarding the Torture Victim Protection Act and the Racketeer Influenced and Corrupt Organizations Act, whether the plaintiffs had failed to state a claim pursuant to Federal Civil Procedure Rule 12(b)(6), whether the statute of limitations applied, and a claim under California Business and Professions Code Section 17200. *See generally* Richard L. Herz, *Doe v. Unocal and the Poverty of the Corporate Attack on the Alien Tort Statute*, 56 RUTGERS L. REV. 1005 (2004); Terry Collingsworth, *The Key Human Rights Challenge: Developing Enforcement Mechanisms*, 15 HARV. HUM. RTS. J. 183 (2002).

[100] 28 U.S.C. § 1605(a)(2) (1994).

[101] Doe v. Unocal, 963 F. Supp. 880, 888 (C.D. Cal. 1997). *See* Saudi Arabia v. Nelson, 507 U.S. 349 (1993); Republic of Argentina v. Weltover, Inc., 504 U.S. 607 (1992). In *Saudi Arabia v. Nelson* and *Republic of Argentina v. Weltover, Inc.*, the Supreme Court addressed the potential civil liability of foreign governments under the FSIA and the scope of exceptions to immunity.

of international law if they acted under color of law. "To the extent a state action requirement is incorporated into the ATCA [Alien Tort Claims Act], courts look to the standards developed under 42 U.S.C. § 1983."[102] The court then identified four distinct approaches used by the federal courts to establish state action in Section 1983 cases: public function, state compulsion, nexus, and joint action. Under the joint action test, for example, state action is present when there is a substantial degree of cooperative action between state officials and private parties. According to the court, the plaintiffs had alleged that SLORC and MOGE were agents of the private defendants; that the defendants were "joint venturers, working in concert with one another; and that the defendants have conspired to commit the violations of international law alleged in the complaint in order to further the interests of the Yadana gas pipeline project."[103] The court determined that these allegations were sufficient to establish state action. In addition, the court recognized that private actors may be found liable for certain violations of international law even in the absence of state action. Slave trading was one such violation. The court then analogized slave trading to the allegations of forced labor raised in the complaint.

> Although there is no allegation that SLORC is physically selling Burmese citizens to the private defendants, plaintiffs allege that, despite their knowledge of SLORC's practice of forced labor, both in general and with respect to the pipeline project, the private defendants have paid and continue to pay SLORC to provide labor and security for the pipeline, essentially treating SLORC as an overseer, accepting the benefit of and approving the use of forced labor. These allegations are sufficient to establish subject-matter jurisdiction under the ATCA.[104]

Third, the district court examined the application of the act of state doctrine. The court viewed the act of state doctrine as based upon separation of powers concerns. Therefore, application of the doctrine "is not appropriate unless it is 'apparent' that adjudication of the matter will bring the nation into hostile confrontation with the foreign state."[105] The court found that the coordinate branches of government had already denounced Burma's human rights record. Accordingly, "it is hard to imagine how judi-

---

[102] Doe v. Unocal, 963 F. Supp. 880, 890 (C.D. Cal. 1997). 42 U.S.C. Section 1983 imposes civil liability on an individual who, acting under color of law, deprives someone of any rights, privileges, or immunities secured by the U.S. Constitution and laws.

[103] *Id.* at 891.

[104] *Id.* at 892.

[105] *Id.* at 893.

cial consideration of the matter will so substantially exacerbate relations as to cause 'hostile confrontation.'"[106] The court also observed that it would be difficult to contend that SLORC and MOGE's alleged violations of international human rights were in the public interest, despite the fact that they were directly connected to decisions regarding allocation and profit from Burma's natural resources. It concluded that recognizing claims for violations of *jus cogens* norms would not undermine the policies behind the act of state doctrine.[107] "In the context of jus cogens violations of international law, which are, by definition, internationally denounced, the high degree of international consensus severely undermines defendants' argument that SLORC and MOGE's alleged activities should be treated as acts of state."[108]

On April 24, 1997, the district court issued an order clarifying its initial ruling. The clarification was based on issues raised in oral argument in the related action *National Coalition Gov't of Burma v. Unocal.*[109] The court reiterated that the act of state doctrine "does not preclude this Court from considering claims that are based on legal principles about which the international community has reached unambiguous agreement."[110] The plaintiffs' claims of torture and forced labor satisfied this requirement. In contrast, the court determined that the prudential concerns embodied in the act of state doctrine preclude consideration of the plaintiffs' claims based on expropriation of property.[111]

Subsequently, the district court requested an opinion from the U.S. Department of State concerning the ramifications of the litigation for U.S. foreign policy "as established by Congress and the Executive."[112] The

---

[106] *Id.*

[107] *Jus cogens* norms, or peremptory norms, apply to all states and do not allow derogation. *See* Siderman de Blake v. Republic of Argentina, 965 F.2d 699, 714 (9th Cir. 1992) (citing Vienna Convention on the Law of Treaties, art. 53, May 23, 1969, 1155 U.N.T.S. 332, 8 I.L.M. 679) ("As defined in the Vienna Convention on the Law of Treaties, a *jus cogens* norm, also known as a 'peremptory norm' of international law, 'is a norm accepted and recognized by the international community of states as a whole as a norm from which no derogation is permitted and which can be modified only by a subsequent norm of general international law having the same character.'").

[108] Doe v. Unocal, 963 F. Supp. 880, 894 (C.D. Cal. 1997).

[109] National Coalition Gov't of Burma v. Unocal, Inc., 176 F.R.D. 329 (C.D. Cal. 1997).

[110] Doe v. Unocal, 963 F. Supp. 880, 899 (C.D. Cal. 1997).

[111] *See* Banco Nacional de Cuba v. Sabbatino, 376 U.S. 398, 423 (1964). In *Sabbatino*, the Supreme Court held that U.S. courts should refrain from judging the acts of a foreign state when such acts are committed within that state's territory.

[112] Letter from Judge Richard Paez, to Michael Matheson, Acting Legal Adviser, U.S. Department of State (Apr. 24, 1997).

Department of State replied that it was not in a position "to express a view as to whether the act of state doctrine is necessarily implicated in the cases before the Court, nor would we want this letter to imply that we have reviewed or taken a position on any other legal issues in the litigation."[113] It added, however, that "at this time adjudication of the claims based on allegations of torture and slavery would not prejudice or impede the conduct of U.S. foreign relations with the current government of Burma."[114]

In 2000, Unocal and the other defendants filed four motions for summary judgment, asserting, *inter alia*, that Unocal could not be held liable for the actions of the Burmese government.[115] On August 31, 2000, the district court issued its ruling on this issue, holding that Unocal could not be held liable for alleged human rights abuses in the absence of its active participation in such abuses.[116] For the plaintiffs to prevail, the district court indicated they "must establish that Unocal is legally responsible for the Myanmar military's forced labor practices."[117] To establish the appropriate standard of liability, the court reviewed several cases involving issues of corporate complicity in human rights abuses, including three cases decided by U.S. military tribunals established after World War II and a more recent decision involving forced labor practices by Ford Motor Company.[118] It determined that these cases did not hold defendants liable for mere knowledge that someone else was committing acts of forced labor. Rather, liability required some participation or cooperation by the defendant. In *Doe v. Unocal*, the district court held there were no facts to suggest that Unocal

---

[113] Letter from Michael Matheson, Acting Legal Adviser, U.S. Department of State, to Frank Hunger, Assistant Attorney General, Department of Justice, at 2 (July 8, 1997).

[114] *Id.*

[115] Other issues were also litigated between the parties, including personal jurisdiction, discovery matters and class certification. *See, e.g.,* Doe v. Unocal, 67 F. Supp. 2d 1140 (C.D. Cal. 1999) (denying plaintiffs' motion for class certification); Doe v. Unocal, 27 F. Supp. 2d 1174 (C.D. Cal. 1998) (dismissing defendant Total S.A. for lack of personal jurisdiction).

[116] Doe v. Unocal, 110 F. Supp. 2d 1294 (C.D. Cal. 2000). This opinion was issued by Judge Ronald Lew, who had replaced Judge Paez on the case when he was elevated to the Ninth Circuit.

[117] *Id.* at 1308–09.

[118] *Id.* 1309–10. *See* United States of America v. Friedrich Flick, "The Flick Case," 6 Trials of War Criminals Before the Nuremberg Military Tribunals Under Control Council Law No. 10 (1952); United States of America v. Carl Krauch, "The Farben Case," 8 Trials of War Criminals Before the Nuremberg Military Tribunals Under Control Council Law No. 10 (1952); United States of America v. Alfried Felix Alwyn Krupp von Bohlen und Halbach, "The Krupp Case," 9 Trials of War Criminals Before the Nuremberg Military Tribunals Under Control Council Law No. 10 (1950). *See also* Iwanowa v. Ford Motor Co., 67 F. Supp. 2d 424 (D.N.J. 1999).

sought to use forced labor: "The evidence does suggest that Unocal knew that forced labor was being utilized and that the Joint Venturers benefitted from the practice. However, because such a showing is insufficient to establish liability under international law, Plaintiffs' claim against Unocal for forced labor under the Alien Tort Claims Act fails as a matter of law."[119] For these reasons, the district court dismissed the case.

On September 18, 2002, the Ninth Circuit overturned the district court's ruling.[120] The Court found that the alleged abuses—torture, murder, and slavery—are *jus cogens* norms and are, therefore, nonderogable. It noted that *jus cogens* norms can provide the basis for ATS lawsuits, because they involve norms that are specific, universal, and obligatory.[121] The court declined to apply the act of state doctrine, which precludes courts from sitting in judgment on the acts of a foreign government done within its own territory. It found that the high degree of international consensus against murder, torture, and slavery "severely undermines Unocal's argument that the alleged acts by the Myanmar Military and Myanmar Oil should be treated as acts of state."[122] It also noted that judicial review of the underlying claims would not substantially exacerbate relations with Myanmar. Finally, it determined that the alleged human rights abuses were not in the public interest and, therefore, they could not be designated as official acts of state.

The court then examined the issue of liability and whether Unocal could be held liable under the Alien Tort Statute for aiding and abetting in acts of forced labor, murder, and rape.[123] The court examined the liability standards set forth in international criminal law and, in particular, in the case law of the International Criminal Tribunals for the former Yugo-

---

[119] Doe v. Unocal, 110 F. Supp. 2d 1294, 1310 (C.D. Cal. 2000). *But see* Richard L. Herz, *Alien Tort Claims and Business Liability*, 95 AM. SOC'Y INT'L L. PROC. 47, 48 (2001).

[120] Doe v. Unocal, 395 F.3d 932 (9th Cir. 2002), *vacated, reh'g, en banc, granted*, Doe v. Unocal Corp., 395 F.3d 978 (9th Cir. 2003).

[121] The court noted, however, that ATS lawsuits do not require *jus cogens* violations but rather violations of international norms that are specific, universal, and obligatory. *Id.* at 945.

[122] *Id.* at 959.

[123] The court affirmed the dismissal of the torture claims, finding that the elements of torture had not been met. Doe v. Unocal, 395 F.3d 932, 955 (9th Cir. 2002) ("The record does not . . . contain sufficient evidence to establish a claim of torture (other than by means of rape) involving Plaintiffs. Although a number of witnesses described acts of extreme physical abuse that might give rise to a claim of torture, the allegations all involved victims other than Plaintiffs. As this is not a class action, such allegations cannot serve to establish the Plaintiffs' claims of torture here.").

slavia and Rwanda. One standard, used by the International Criminal Tribunal for the former Yugoslavia, provided that "aiding and abetting liability under international criminal law can be summarized as knowing practical assistance, encouragement, or moral support which has a substantial effect on the perpetration of the crime."[124] The court found this standard analogous to the standard for aiding and abetting under domestic tort law. Thus, the court held that the standard for aiding and abetting liability under the ATS is "knowing practical assistance or encouragement which has a substantial effect on the perpetration of the crime."[125] The *actus reus* requirement of aiding and abetting is "practical assistance or encouragement which has a substantial effect on the perpetration of the crime."[126] The *mens rea* requirement of aiding and abetting is "actual or constructive (i.e., reasonable) knowledge that the accomplice's actions will assist the perpetrator in the commission of the crime."[127] Applying these standards to the evidence offered, the court concluded "that there are genuine issues of material fact whether Unocal's conduct met the *actus reus* and *mens rea* requirements for liability under the ATCA for aiding and abetting forced labor."[128] The court made similar findings with respect to murder and rape, but not to other forms of torture.[129]

In a concurring opinion, Judge Stephen Reinhardt expressed his agreement with the majority opinion except for its analysis of the proper standard for establishing third party liability.

I do not agree that the question whether Unocal may be held liable in tort for the Myanmar military's alleged human rights violations should be resolved, as the majority holds, by applying a

---

[124] *Id.* at 951. The court's analysis on aiding and abetting under international criminal law was based primarily on *Prosecutor v. Furundzija*. Prosecutor v. Furundzija, IT-95-17/1-T (Dec. 10, 1998), *reprinted in* 38 I.L.M. 317 (1999). In *Furundzija*, the International Criminal Tribunal for the former Yugoslavia offered an extensive analysis of several international sources, including decisions of American, British, and German military courts and tribunals convened after the Second World War as well as more recent sources such as the 1996 Draft Code of Crimes against the Peace and Security of Mankind and the 1998 Rome Statute of the International Criminal Court.

[125] Doe v. Unocal, 395 F.3d 932, 951 (9th Cir. 2002).

[126] *Id.* at 952.

[127] *Id.* at 953.

[128] *Id.*

[129] *Id.* at 955 ("The record does not . . . contain sufficient evidence to establish a claim of torture (other than by means of rape) involving Plaintiffs. Although a number of witnesses described acts of extreme physical abuse that might give rise to a claim of torture, the allegations all involved victims other than Plaintiffs.").

recently-promulgated international criminal law aiding-and-abetting standard that permits imposition of liability for the lending of moral support. In fact, I do not agree that the question of Unocal's tort liability should be decided by applying any international law test at all. Rather, in my view, the ancillary legal question of Unocal's third-party tort liability should be resolved by applying general federal common law tort principles, such as agency, joint venture, or reckless disregard.[130]

The issue of the appropriate standard for establishing third-party liability was subsequently raised by Unocal in a motion for *en banc* review.

On February 14, 2003, the Ninth Circuit granted the motion for *en banc* review.[131] The primary issue on appeal involved whether federal courts should apply aiding and abetting standards under international law or general federal common law tort principles with respect to determining Unocal's liability.[132] Oral argument took place on June 17, 2003. The *en banc* panel subsequently withdrew the case from submission when the U.S. Supreme Court announced it would review the Alien Tort Statute in *Sosa v. Alvarez-Machain*. After the Supreme Court's June 2004 ruling in *Sosa*, the Ninth Circuit requested a new round of argument to address the implications of *Sosa* on the pending litigation.[133]

On December 8, 2004, the parties notified the Ninth Circuit that a settlement had been reached in principle. The case was subsequently dismissed when the settlement was finalized.[134] While the terms of the

---

[130] *Id.* at 963.

[131] Doe v. Unocal, 395 F.3d 978 (9th Cir. 2003). The Court indicated that the "three-judge panel opinion shall not be cited as precedent by or to this court or any district court of the Ninth Circuit, except to the extent adopted by the *en banc* court." *Id.* at 979.

[132] In May 2003, the United States submitted an amicus brief to the Ninth Circuit arguing that the ATS does not provide a cause of action, that it does not permit a court to infer a cause of action from unratified and non-self-executing documents, and that no cause of action may be implied for conduct occurring in other countries. Brief for the United States of Am. as Amicus Curiae, Doe v. Unocal, 403 F.3d 708 (9th Cir. 2005) (No. 00-56603).

[133] In August 2004, the United States submitted a supplemental amicus brief to the *en banc* panel, which argued that the factors set forth in the Supreme Court's ruling in *Sosa* counseled in favor of dismissing the aiding and abetting claims. Supplemental Brief for the United States of Am. as Amicus Curiae, Doe v. Unocal, 403 F.3d 708 (9th Cir. 2005) (No. 00-56603). "[A]ll of the cautionary admonitions articulated by the Sosa Court apply with full force to the claims in this case, and should lead the Court to affirm the district court's dismissal of the aiding and abetting counts of the complaint." *Id.* at 4.

[134] Doe I v. Unocal Corp., 403 F.3d 708 (9th Cir. 2005). The court also vacated the prior district court opinion, *Doe v. Unocal Corp.*, 110 F. Supp. 2d 1294 (C.D. Cal. 2000) based upon the plaintiffs' motion to vacate, which was joined by the defendants.

settlement were confidential, some reports suggest that the settlement reached $30 million.[135] According to a joint statement issued by the parties in March 2005:

> The parties to several lawsuits related to Unocal's energy investment in the Yadana gas pipeline project in Myanmar/Burma announced today that they have settled their suits. Although the terms are confidential, the settlement will compensate plaintiffs and provide funds enabling plaintiffs and their representatives to develop programs to improve living conditions, health care and education and protect the rights of people from the pipeline region. These initiatives will provide substantial assistance to people who may have suffered hardships in the region. Unocal reaffirms its principle that the company respects human rights in all of its activities and commits to enhance its educational programs to further this principle. Plaintiffs and their representatives reaffirm their commitment to protecting human rights.[136]

The legal team representing the plaintiffs issued a separate statement.

> The fifteen individuals who brought these cases suffered horribly at the hands of the Burmese military, with the complicity of Unocal. They risked their lives for the last eight years seeking justice through these suits. These villagers, ethnic minorities from a remote region, living under a brutal dictatorship, took on a major U.S. multinational oil company in court—and won. We are thrilled for our clients and gratified that the settlement will provide funds benefiting other victims of the Yadana pipeline.

> More generally, this is a historic victory for human rights and for the corporate accountability movement. Corporations can no longer fool themselves into thinking they can get away with human rights violations. This case will reverberate in corporate boardrooms around the world and will have a deterrent effect on the worst forms of corporate behavior.

> On behalf of the plaintiffs, we thank the many people and organizations working tirelessly to promote democracy in Burma. Our colleagues in the "Free Burma" movement have been instru-

---

[135] Paul Magnusson, *A Milestone for Human Rights*, BUSINESS WEEK, Jan. 24, 2005, at 63. *See also* Joshua Kurlantzick, *Pirates of the Corporation: Alien Tort Statute and Slave Labor Cases*, MOTHER JONES, July 2005, at 19; Marc Lifsher, *Unocal Settles Human Rights Lawsuit Over Alleged Abuses at Myanmar Pipeline*, L.A. TIMES, Mar. 22, 2005, at C1.

[136] Press Release, Unocal, Settlement Reached in Yadana Pipeline Lawsuit (Mar. 21, 2005).

mental in calling public attention to Unocal's complicity in the abuses suffered by so many in the pipeline region. We look forward to the day that freedom and democracy will come to Burma; a time when its citizens will live with hope rather than fear, under law rather than tyranny, and when the people of Burma will never again suffer egregious military abuses, whether in support of political repression or the corporate greed of companies like Unocal.[137]

In November 2005, the French oil company Total S.A., which had participated with Unocal on the Yadana pipeline project, announced it would pay $7.2 million to compensate victims of human rights abuses.[138] The settlement ended legal proceedings instituted in French courts by eight Burmese villagers.

3. Chile: *Cabello v. Fernandez-Larios*

On September 11, 1973, the Chilean military, led by General Augusto Pinochet, overthrew the democratically elected government of Salvador Allende.[139] Following the coup, military authorities launched a brutal and systematic repression of suspected political opponents. At the time, Winston Cabello worked as an economist for the Allende government and had been appointed the Director of the Regional Planning Office for the Atacama-Coquimbo region in northern Chile. On September 12, 1973, Cabello was detained by local military officials in his home town of Copiapó and accused of subversive activities. He was then imprisoned in the local military garrison.

On or about October 16, 1973, several officers of the Chilean military, acting with authorization from General Pinochet, arrived in Copiapó and ordered the elimination of 13 political prisoners being held there, including Winston Cabello.[140] Armando Fernández-Larios was a member of this

---

137 Press Release, Earthrights International, Historic Advance for Universal Human Rights: Unocal to Compensate Burmese Villagers (Apr. 2, 2005).

138 *See Total Settles Rights Case,* INT'L HERALD TRIB., Nov. 29, 2005, at 14. Total S.A. was dismissed as a defendant in *Doe v. Unocal* due to lack of personal jurisdiction. *See* Doe v. Unocal, 27 F. Supp. 2d 1174, 1190 (C.D. Cal. 1998).

139 *See generally* NAOMI ROHT-ARRIAZA, THE PINOCHET EFFECT: TRANSNATIONAL JUSTICE IN THE AGE OF HUMAN RIGHTS (2005); ARIEL DORFMAN, EXORCISING TERROR: THE INCREDIBLE UNENDING TRIAL OF AUGUSTO PINOCHET (2002).

140 This group and the surrounding atrocities attributed to them have been referred to as the "Caravan of Death." *See generally* HUGH O'SHAUGHNESSY, PINOCHET: THE POLITICS OF TORTURE 63 (2000); David Adams, *27 Years Later, Chile's Caravan of Death Touches U.S.,* ST. PETERSBURG TIMES, Mar. 13, 2000, at A1.

group of military officers.[141] Cabello and the other political prisoners were removed from the military garrison and taken to a secluded area. Some of the prisoners were executed immediately; others were slashed with knives before being shot. The military announced that the 13 prisoners had been killed while trying to escape. After the bodies were exhumed from a common grave in 1990, a Chilean government commission determined that the prisoners had been executed.[142]

In February 1987, Fernández-Larios entered the United States in connection with an agreement with U.S. officials to provide information concerning the 1976 assassination in Washington, D.C. of former Chilean Ambassador to the United States, Orlando Letelier, and his assistant Ronni Moffitt.[143] Fernández-Larios subsequently agreed to a plea bargain with U.S. prosecutors and pled guilty to being an "accessory after the fact" in the Letelier assassination. The agreement provided that Fernández-Larios would be placed in the federal Witness Security Program. Fernández-Larios moved to Florida, where he was eventually discovered.[144]

On February 18, 1999, the family of Winston Cabello filed a lawsuit against Fernández-Larios in federal district court for the Southern District of Florida.[145] The lawsuit was filed pursuant to the Alien Tort Statute and the Torture Victim Protection Act. The complaint raised several causes of action, including extrajudicial killing, torture, crimes against humanity, and cruel, inhuman, or degrading treatment. It alleged that "Chilean military officers, including defendant Armando Fernández Larios, conspiring together and acting in concert, counseled, procured, directed, ordered and caused Winston Cabello and twelve other prisoners who had been incar-

---

[141] *See generally* Second Amended Complaint, Cabello v. Fernandez-Larios, 157 F. Supp. 2d 1345 (S.D. Fla. 2001) (No. 99-0528-CIV-LENARD).

[142] *Id.* at 10–12.

[143] *See generally* Douglas Grant Mine, *The Assassin Next Door, Part 2*, MIAMI NEW TIMES, Oct. 12, 2000, at 25; Douglas Grant Mine, *The Assassin Next Door*, MIAMI NEW TIMES, Nov. 18, 1999, at 32.

[144] In November 1999, a Chilean judge investigating the "Caravan of Death" killings requested the extradition of Fernández-Larios. No official response was issued by the United States, although the Fernández-Larios' plea bargain with federal prosecutors may have barred his extradition to Chile. In April 2001, an Argentine court requested Fernández-Larios' extradition in connection with the assassination of former Chilean General Carlos Prats in Argentina.

[145] The complaint was subsequently amended on April 7, 1999, and September 17, 2001. The plaintiffs were represented by several organizations and attorneys, including: the Center for Justice & Accountability; Kerrigan, Estess, Rankin & McLeod; Wilson Sonsini Goodrich & Rosati; and several pro bono attorneys.

cerated by the Chilean Army to be tortured, abused and summarily executed in Copiapó, Chile."[146] The complaint further alleged that "the Chilean military government concealed the location of Winston Cabello's body from his family members, denied the Cabello family the ability to bury his corpse, and provided to the Cabello family death certificates listing three different and inconsistent causes of death."[147] The lawsuit sought compensatory and punitive damages on behalf of the Cabello estate as well as several surviving family members.

On August 10, 2001, the district court issued its ruling on Fernández-Larios's first motion to dismiss.[148] The court held that each individual plaintiff had standing to sue Fernández-Larios.[149] Citing *Filartiga* and other ATS cases, the district court indicated that the Alien Tort Statute establishes a federal forum where courts may fashion common law remedies to give effect to violations of customary international law.[150] The court then determined that customary international law prohibited extrajudicial killing, crimes against humanity, and cruel, inhuman, or degrading treatment.[151] Finally, the district court concluded that the Torture Victim Protection Act applied retroactively although both the TVPA and ATS were subject to a ten-year statute of limitations period. The limitations period was subject to equitable tolling, however, "because Chilean military authorities deliberately concealed the decedent's burial location from Plaintiffs, who were unable to view the decedent's body until 1990."[152]

On June 5, 2002, the district court denied Fernández-Larios' second motion to dismiss.[153] First, the district court upheld its prior ruling that equitable tolling principles applied to the statute of limitations. Second, the court concluded that Fernández-Larios could be held indirectly liable for

---

[146] Second Amended Complaint, *supra* note 141, at para. 1.

[147] *Id.*

[148] Estate of Winston Cabello v. Fernandez-Larios, 157 F. Supp. 2d 1345 (S.D. Fla. 2001).

[149] In contrast, the court dismissed all the claims brought by the estate of Winston Cabello because it did not have standing to bring such claims.

[150] Estate of Winston Cabello v. Fernandez-Larios, 157 F. Supp. 2d 1345, 1359 (S.D. Fla. 2001).

[151] The district court also upheld a separate claim for intentional infliction of emotional distress under Florida and Chilean law.

[152] Estate of Winston Cabello v. Fernandez-Larios, 157 F. Supp. 2d 1345, 1368 (S.D. Fla. 2001).

[153] *See* Barrett v. Larios, 205 F. Supp. 2d 1325 (S.D. Fla. 2001).

participating in the torture and murder of Cabello, citing several international sources in support, including the Convention against Torture and case law for the International Criminal Tribunals for the former Yugoslavia and Rwanda.

> The Court agrees that principles of conspiracy and accomplice liability are well established in customary international law, set forth in all of the sources discussed above. The ATCA is the legal means by which individuals who violate well-established international law may be held liable in United States courts. Congress has clearly indicated its intent to provide federal courts as a forum to bring to justice individuals who contribute directly to human rights abuses, even where it cannot be shown that an individual actually committed the acts of abuse. Accordingly, the Court determines as a matter of law that Defendant may be held liable under the ATCA for conspiring in or aiding and abetting the actions taken by other Chilean military officials, contrary to international law, with respect to Plaintiffs' decedent.[154]

Finally, the district court determined that Zita Cabello Barrett, Winston's sister, had legal standing as the legal representative of the Cabello estate to bring the claims alleged in her representative capacity.[155]

One month prior to trial, Fernández-Larios filed yet another motion to dismiss, asserting that the plaintiffs had failed to exhaust domestic remedies in Chile. In response, the plaintiffs argued that any purported domestic remedies available in Chile would be ineffective and futile. The district court acknowledged that the Torture Victim Protection Act contains an exhaustion requirement.[156] It determined, however, that the requirement is not jurisdictional in nature and, therefore, it must be properly pled as an affirmative defense. Since Fernández-Larios had not raised the defense in a timely manner, the district court refused to consider it.

The jury trial took place in Fall 2003. It lasted three weeks and encompassed extensive documentary evidence and witness testimony. At the conclusion of the trial, the jury was asked to consider whether Fernández-Larios should be held liable for extrajudicial killing, torture, cruel, inhu-

---

[154] *Id.* at 1333.

[155] *Id.* at 1335.

[156] Estate of Winston Cabello v. Fernandez-Larios, 291 F. Supp. 2d 1360 (S.D. Fla. 2003).

man, or degrading treatment, or crimes against humanity.[157] Liability could be established under three separate theories: (1) that he personally committed the violations; (2) that he aided and abetted the person or persons who committed the violations; or (3) that he entered into a conspiracy to commit the violations. On October 13, 2003, the jury found Fernández-Larios liable and issued a verdict in favor of the plaintiffs. The estate of Winston Cabello was awarded $2 million in compensatory damages with respect to the claims of extrajudicial killing and crimes against humanity, and $1 million in punitive damages. In addition, the surviving family members were jointly awarded $1 million in compensatory damages with respect to their claims for extrajudicial killing. The judgment was entered on October 31, 2003.

Fernández-Larios appealed the trial court judgment on several grounds, raising arguments that had been previously rejected by the district court.[158] On March 14, 2005, the Eleventh Circuit Court of Appeals dismissed the appeal and affirmed the judgment. The court of appeals found that the Alien Tort Statute was governed by a ten-year statute of limitations. It determined, however, that equitable tolling principles applied.

> The district court determined that the Cabello survivors knew that Cabello was killed in October 1973 and that unknown military officers were involved. However, it was not until 1990 that they obtained knowledge of Cabello's manner of death and information about the harm suffered by him before his death. Until Cabello's unmarked grave was located, his family did not know that he and the other prisoners had been tortured before being massacred. Although Victor Bravo, a local official called upon by the military authorities to identify the bodies of the dead, had seen the prisoners' bodies shortly after they were killed, he never spoke of their conditions to the families.

> The Chilean government, with whom Fernández conspired, concealed both the manner in which Cabello died and his place of burial. The Chilean government also created great confusion by

---

[157] Court's Instructions to the Jury, Cabello v. Fernandez-Larios, 402 F.3d 1148 (11th Cir. 2005) (No. 99-0528-CIV-LENARD).

[158] Cabello v. Fernandez-Larios, 402 F.3d 1148 (11th Cir. 2005). Fernandez raised four issues on appeal: "(1) that the Cabello survivors' claims are barred by the statute of limitations; (2) that neither the TVPA, nor the ATCA provide private causes of action such as this one; (3) that he did not have any command responsibility and did not personally participate in the alleged human rights violations, and, as a result, he is not liable under the TVPA or the ATCA; (4) that the trial court erred in admitting certain depositions into evidence and denying his pretrial motion in limine to restrict evidence as to the treatment of Cabello." *Id.* at 1151–52.

sending three conflicting death certificates to the Cabello family. Until the first post-*junta* civilian president was elected in 1990, the Chilean political climate prevented the Cabello family from pursuing any efforts to learn of the incidents surrounding Cabello's murder. The district court decided that Cabello's family could not possibly have pursued their claims until Cabello's body was exhumed.[159]

Because the Pinochet regime covered up the events surrounding Cabello's death, it prevented the plaintiffs from discovering the abuses perpetrated by Fernández-Larios. Accordingly, the court agreed that equitable tolling was appropriate.

The court of appeals also determined that the ATS and TVPA are not limited to cases of direct liability but also apply to cases of indirect liability. The court noted that several ATS cases extended liability to cases of conspiracy and accomplice liability. Furthermore, an examination of the legislative history of the TVPA revealed that it was also "intended to reach beyond the person who actually committed the acts, to those ordering, abetting, or assisting in the violation."[160] The court found that there was sufficient evidence available for the jury to find Fernández-Larios responsible under a direct liability theory. In addition, there was overwhelming evidence that he was indirectly liable. Furthermore, the court of appeals accepted the district court's characterization of the two theories of indirect liability.

> In assessing "active participation," the jury was instructed to consider if (1) one or more of the wrongful acts that comprise the claim were committed, (2) Fernandez substantially assisted some person or persons who personally committed or caused one or more of the wrongful acts that comprise the claim, and (3) Fernandez knew that his actions would assist in the illegal or wrongful activity at the time he provided the assistance.[161] . . . For the jury to find Fernandez indirectly liable by means of conspiracy, the Cabello survivors needed to prove by a preponderance of the evidence that (1) two or more persons agreed to commit a wrongful act, (2) Fernandez joined the conspiracy knowing of at least one of the goals of the conspiracy and intending to help accomplish it, and (3) one or more of the violations was committed by someone who was a member of the conspiracy and acted in furtherance of the conspiracy.[162]

---

[159] *Id.* at 1155.

[160] *Id.* at 1157.

[161] *Id.* at 1158.

[162] *Id.* at 1159.

Finally, the court of appeals found it was relevant for the plaintiffs to introduce evidence at trial of other abuses perpetrated in Chile. The court concluded that evidence concerning other victims at Copiapó and at other locations was relevant for determining "whether Fernández knowingly participated in crimes against humanity and to whether he conspired to commit or aided and abetted the commission of other offenses."[163]

Despite the judgment, Fernández-Larios remained in the United States, and efforts to collect the judgment proved unsuccessful. But for the Cabello family, the litigation was not about compensation or revenge. In 2002, Zita Cabello-Barrett explained why her family brought the lawsuit on behalf of her brother, Winston Cabello.

> We recognize our responsibility in the construction of the world we live in, and our actions since the 17th of October 1973 are directed toward helping build a world that celebrates human dignity. We understand the value of the search for justice and truth in the construction of that better world. Justice will not change past events, but it can help prevent in other fathers, brothers, sons and spouses the magnitude of pain that many like us have had to endure.[164]

4. Ethiopia: *Abebe-Jiri v. Negewo*

From 1974 to 1991, Ethiopia was ruled by a military government that threatened, tortured, and summarily executed political opponents.[165] Thousands were killed by military and paramilitary groups. Students were specifically targeted by the government. Violence in urban areas was mirrored by a different kind of violence in rural areas: famine. Through indifference and the incompetence of the Ethiopian government, over two million people died of starvation. This period of Ethiopian history is known as the Red Terror.

In 1978, Edgegayehu Taye was 21 years old and worked at the Ministry of Agriculture in Addis Ababa. Her father had been a prominent government official under the prior regime of Haile Selassie. On February 13, 1978, Taye was arrested and taken to the local detention facility controlled by Kelbessa Negewo, a government official.[166] At the detention facility, she was ordered to remove her clothes. Her arms and legs were then bound,

---

163   *Id.* at 1161.

164   Zita Cabello-Barrett, Address at the University of Santiago, Chile (Oct. 20, 2002).

165   *See generally* AFRICA WATCH, ETHIOPIA: RECKONING UNDER THE LAW (1994); ALEXANDER DE WAAL, EVIL DAYS: THIRTY YEARS OF WAR AND FAMINE IN ETHIOPIA (1991).

166   *See generally* Findings of Fact, Abebe-Jiri v. Negewo, 1993 U.S. Dist. LEXIS 21158 (N.D. Ga. 1993) (No. 1:90-cv-2010-GET).

and she was suspended from a pole. She was repeatedly threatened with death if she did not cooperate and disclose her membership in an opposition group. She was then severely beaten by Negewo and several guards. Water was poured on her wounds to increase her pain. Taye was interrogated and tortured in Negewo's presence for several hours. When Negewo grew tired of the interrogation, he ordered the guards to cut Taye loose from the pole and take her to a prison cell. She received no medical care for her wounds. Taye was subsequently transferred to other prison facilities in Addis Ababa. After three years of detention, she was finally released without ever being charged or brought before a court.

After escaping to Canada and receiving Canadian citizenship, Taye moved to Atlanta, Georgia. While working in an Atlanta hotel, she discovered that Negewo had not only entered the United States as a refugee but was also working at the same hotel. When Taye first saw Negewo at the Atlanta hotel, she became nauseous and then felt incomprehension that he was now in the United States: "He made my life so miserable. He's the person who snatched away my happiness, my youth, my laugh at that age. I didn't want to leave him alone. I didn't want to let it go. Knowing that he is living here, after he did so many crimes. I had to do something, even if it was a small thing. I hadn't any idea about the magnitude of this case. For me it is a simple case."[167] In September 1990, Taye, along with two other Ethiopian women, Hirut Abebe-Jiri and Elizabeth Demissie, filed an ATS lawsuit against Negewo in the federal district court for the Northern District of Georgia.[168] Each plaintiff alleged that Negewo had ordered and participated in numerous acts of torture and other cruel, inhuman, or degrading treatment against them when they lived in Ethiopia. Jurisdiction was premised on the Alien Tort Statute, and the complaint raised seven causes of action: torture; prolonged arbitrary detention; cruel, inhuman, or degrading treatment; assault and battery; false imprisonment; summary execution; and disappearance. The trial was held in May 1993 before Judge Ernest Tidwell and without a jury. Negewo represented himself during the two-day trial.

In *Abebe-Jiri v. Negewo*, the federal district court for the Northern District of Georgia found Negewo liable for human rights violations.[169] The district court made the following findings of fact.

---

[167] Andrew Rice, *The Long Interrogation*, N.Y. TIMES MAG, June 4, 2006, at 50, 54. *See also* Ronald Smothers, *Nightmare of Torture in Ethiopia is Relived in an Atlanta Court*, N.Y. TIMES, May 22, 1993, at A6.

[168] Complaint, Abebe-Jiri v. Negewo, 1993 U.S. Dist. LEXIS 21158 (N.D. Ga. 1993) (No. 1:90-cv-2010-GET). The plaintiffs were represented by the Center for Constitutional Rights, the law firm of Kilpatrick & Cody, and several other pro bono attorneys.

[169] Abebe-Jiri v. Negewo, 1993 U.S. Dist. LEXIS 21158 (N.D. Ga. 1993).

7. On January 6, 1978, plaintiff Abebe-Jiri was arrested again along with her 16 year old sister Yesharge. She was taken to the same prison. At the prison in Subzone 10, she was interrogated and tortured in the presence of defendant Negewo and several other men for a period of several hours. She was told to take off her clothes. Her arms and legs were then bound and she was whipped with a wire on her legs and her back. She suffered severe pain. She was repeatedly threatened with death if she did not reveal the location of a gun. At all times, the interrogation and torture of plaintiff Abebe-Jiri was conducted in a humiliating and degrading manner.

8. Defendant Negewo personally supervised at least some part of the interrogation and torture of plaintiff Abebe-Jiri. He also personally interrogated her and participated directly in some of the acts of torture of plaintiff Abebe-Jiri. . . .

11. Plaintiff Edgegayehu Taye is a citizen of Canada who is currently living in Atlanta, Georgia. On or about February 13, 1978, while living in Addis Ababa, she was "arrested" by armed personnel of the Revolutionary Squad and taken to the jail for Higher Zone 9, Subzone 9. She was 21 years old at the time, working in the Ministry of Agriculture.

12. Shortly after her arrival at Higher Zone 9, Subzone 9, plaintiff Taye was interrogated and tortured for a period of several hours. She was told to remove her clothes and her arms and legs were bound together. She was hung from a pole and severely beaten by defendant Negewo and several other men. Water was poured on her wounds to increase the amount of her pain. She suffered severe pain and after several hours, she became unconscious. At all times the interrogation and torture were conducted in a way that humiliated and degraded plaintiff Taye. . . .

19. On or about March 17, 1978, plaintiff Demissie and her sister were taken from Kirchele Jail to Higher Zone 9, Subzone 10 which was controlled by defendant Negewo. At first they were kept in an unlit cell by themselves. Then, plaintiff Demissie's sister was taken to an interrogation room and tortured for approximately two hours. When her sister was brought back to their room, plaintiff Demissie was immediately taken to the torture room. There plaintiff Demissie was interrogated and tortured for approximately two hours.

20. Plaintiff Demissie was told to undress when she entered the torture chamber. She was then bound by her arms and her feet. A

wooden pole was put under her legs and she was lifted into the air and beaten severely. She suffered severe pain during this session and nearly passed out. The interrogation and torture of Demissie were conducted in a humiliating, degrading and insulting manner. Defendant Negewo personally supervised at least some part of the interrogation and torture of Demissie.

21. After her torture, plaintiff Demissie was returned to her cell with her sister. She was not provided with any medical attention. Two days later her sister was taken from the cell and "transferred" to another location. Shortly thereafter, plaintiff Demissie's sister "disappeared" and has never been seen or heard from.[170]

The district court determined that Negewo was responsible for the abuses perpetrated on the defendants: "Defendant Negewo was directly involved in the interrogation and torture of each of the plaintiffs in this case. He was personally present during part of the time they were tortured and supervised at least part of the torture."[171] The court then indicated that torture and cruel, inhuman, or degrading treatment constituted violations of international law. The court also noted that international law recognizes both compensatory damages and punitive damages. Accordingly, the court awarded each plaintiff $200,000 in compensatory damages and $300,000 in punitive damages for a total award of $1.5 million.[172] But as Edgegayehu Taye noted, the lawsuit "was not [about] collecting money. It was about collecting justice."[173]

Negewo appealed the judgment to the Eleventh Circuit. While his appeal was pending, Negewo filed an application for naturalization with the Immigration and Naturalization Service. His application was subsequently granted, and he took the oath of allegiance on July 28, 1995.

In *Abebe-Jira v. Negewo*, the Eleventh Circuit affirmed the district court's ruling.[174] The court of appeals rejected Negewo's contention that subject matter jurisdiction was lacking because the ATS did not establish a private

---

[170] *Id.* at *3–*8.

[171] *Id.* at *8.

[172] The plaintiffs ultimately collected $798 and donated the amount to charity. Rice, *supra* note 167, at 55.

[173] *Clinton in Africa: Ethiopia's Uglier Past Recalled Closer to Home*, CNN MORNING NEWS, Mar. 31, 1998.

[174] Abebe-Jira v. Negewo, 72 F.3d 844 (11th Cir. 1996). The court of appeals misspelled the plaintiff's name as "Abebe-Jira."

right of action. A review of ATS case law—including *Filartiga v. Pena-Irala, Forti v. Suarez-Mason, Hilao v. Estate of Marcos,* and *Kadic v. Karadzic*—indicated that the ATS provides both a private cause of action and a federal forum to redress violations of international law. The court read the ATS as "requiring no more than an allegation of a violation of the law of nations in order to invoke section 1350."[175] The court found that the language of the ATS suggests "that Congress did not intend to require an alien plaintiff to invoke a separate enabling statute as precondition for relief."[176] The court also found support for its findings in the legislative history of the Torture Victim Protection Act, which provides that the Alien Tort Statute "confers both a forum and a private right of action to aliens alleging a violation of international law."[177] Accordingly, the court held that the ATS "establishes a federal forum where courts may fashion domestic common law remedies to give effect to violations of customary international law."[178] Finally, the court rejected the assertion that the political question doctrine barred adjudication of the case.

In May 2001, the Justice Department filed a civil action to revoke Negewo's naturalization.[179] The complaint alleged two counts: illegal procurement of U.S. citizenship and material misrepresentation. Specifically, it alleged that Negewo was initially ineligible for refugee status when he entered the United States because he "had ordered, incited, assisted, or otherwise participated in the persecution of a person on account of political opinion."[180] Since he was not a valid refugee, he was ineligible for asylum, adjustment of status, permanent residence, and naturalization. Negewo's citizenship was revoked in October 2004, and he was subsequently ordered deported.[181]

---

[175] *Id.* at 847.

[176] *Id.*

[177] *Id.* at 848.

[178] *Id.*

[179] *See generally Federal Efforts Related to the Exclusion, Removal and Prosecution of Aliens and Naturalized U.S. Citizens Who Have Committed War Crimes or Human Rights Abuses Outside the U.S. Testimony: Hearing Before the Committee on Appropriations,* 109th Cong. (Dec. 8, 2005) (statement of Eli M. Rosenbaum, Director, Office of Special Investigations Criminal Division Department of Justice).

[180] 8 U.S.C. § 1101(a)(42).

[181] *See* Mike Morris, *Ethiopian to be Deported,* ATLANTA J. CONST., Aug. 2, 2005, at B5. In May 2002, Negewo was convicted *in absentia* by an Ethiopian court for human rights abuses. He was sentenced to life imprisonment. Rice, *supra* note 167, at 57.

5. The Philippines: *In re Marcos Human Rights Litigation*

Ferdinand Marcos was elected president of the Philippines in 1965 and re-elected in 1969. As the end of his second term neared, Marcos imposed martial law to suspend constitutional protections and, thereby, perpetuate his rule over the country. Inevitably, human rights abuses followed. Political opponents were routinely tortured and summarily executed by military and paramilitary groups. Detainees were subjected to extraordinary abuse, including:

1. Beatings while blindfolded by punching, kicking and hitting with the butts of rifles;

2. The "telephone" where a detainee's ears were clapped simultaneously, producing a ringing sound in the head;

3. Insertion of bullets between the fingers of a detainee and squeezing the hand;

4. The "wet submarine," where a detainee's head was submerged in a toilet bowl full of excrement;

5. The "water cure," where a cloth was placed over the detainee's mouth and nose, and water poured over it producing a drowning sensation;

6. The "dry submarine," where a plastic bag was placed over the detainee's head producing suffocation;

7. Use of a detainee's hands for putting out lighted cigarettes;

8. Use of flat-irons on the soles of a detainee's feet;

9. Forcing a detainee while wet and naked to sit before an air conditioner often while sitting on a block of ice;

10. Injection of a clear substance into the body a detainee believed to be truth serum;

11. Stripping, sexually molesting and raping female detainees; one male plaintiff testified he was threatened with rape;

12. Electric shock where one electrode is attached to the genitals of males or the breast of females and another electrode to some

other part of the body, usually a finger, and electrical energy produced from a military field telephone is sent through the body;

13. Russian roulette; and

14. Solitary confinement while hand-cuffed or tied to a bed.[182]

Thousands of people fell victim to the brutality of the Marcos regime. These atrocities were condemned by opposition groups in the Philippines and throughout the world. Protests against the Marcos regime culminated in his resignation and forced exile on February 25, 1986.

Upon exile, Marcos established residence in Hawaii. His arrival spawned a number of class action and individual lawsuits alleging massive human rights violations.[183] The plaintiffs sought relief under the Alien Tort Statute.[184] One lawsuit, *Hilao v. Marcos*, was a class action lawsuit filed "by the alleged victims or personal representatives of victims of torture perpetrated by Marcos. The complaint alleged that the plaintiffs were university students and labor organizers who were detained and routinely subjected to electric shock, beatings, Russian roulette, gang rapes, and in some cases murder."[185] Another lawsuit, *Trajano v. Marcos*, was filed by Agapita Trajano, whose son Archimedes Trajano, was kidnapped, tortured, and murdered by Philippine military intelligence. "Trajano alleged false imprisonment, wrongful death, kidnapping, and violation of international law on behalf of Archimedes' estate, and the intentional infliction of emotional distress for her own suffering on being shown the tortured body of her son."[186] Other complaints alleged similar human rights abuses.[187] Marcos passed

---

[182] *In re* Estate of Ferdinand E. Marcos Human Rights Litig., 910 F. Supp. 1460, 1463 (D. Haw. 1995).

[183] *See generally* Ralph G. Steinhardt, *Fulfilling the Promise of Filartiga: Litigating Human Rights Claims Against the Estate of Ferdinand Marcos*, 20 YALE J. INT'L L. 65 (1995); Anita Ramasastry, *Secrets and Lies? Swiss Banks and International Human Rights*, 31 VAND. J. TRANSNAT'L L. 325 (1998); Ellen Lutz, *The Marcos Human Rights Litigation: Can Justice Be Achieved in U.S. Courts for Abuses that Occurred Abroad?*, 14 B.C. THIRD WORLD L.J. 43 (1994); Joan Fitzpatrick, *The Future of the Alien Tort Claims Act of 1789: Lessons from In Re Marcos Human Rights Litigation*, 67 ST. JOHN'S L. REV. 491 (1993).

[184] Lawsuits against Marcos were also filed in state courts. *See, e.g.*, Roxas v. Marcos, 969 P.2d 1209 (Haw. 1998).

[185] Trajano v. Marcos, 878 F.2d 1439, *1 (9th Cir. 1989) (unpublished disposition).

[186] *Id.*

[187] In addition to lawsuits by private litigants, Ferdinand Marcos and his wife were also sued in a separate civil lawsuit by the Philippine government for illegal activities, including mail fraud, wire fraud, and transportation of stolen property. *See* Republic of

away in 1989 during the pendency of the litigation. His wife and son were substituted as defendants on behalf of the Marcos Estate.

Originally, the district courts in Hawaii and California dismissed the lawsuits, holding that the act of state doctrine precluded the litigation. According to one district court ruling, "it is clear that this case would require examination of official policies of the Marcos administration. Regardless of the semantics, these cases would still involve judicial review of the acts of the duly recognized head of a foreign sovereign committed under authority of law. Such cases have long been considered non-justiciable under the act of state doctrine."[188] The cases were then appealed in a consolidated action to the Ninth Circuit Court of Appeals.[189] In 1986, the Ninth Circuit reversed the district court rulings, finding that the act of state doctrine was inapplicable in these cases: "Without needing extensive analysis of whether the alleged acts constituted acts of state, we found the doctrine to be of 'little or no applicability' to the situation of a deposed ruler from whom his former domain seeks an accounting. 'Once deposed, [a] dictator will find it difficult to deploy the [act of state doctrine] successfully.'"[190] In addition, "[n]either the present government of the Republic of the Philippines nor the United States government objects to judicial resolution of these claims, or sees any resulting potential embarrassment to

---

the Philippines v. Marcos, 862 F.2d 1355 (9th Cir. 1988). Claims were asserted under the Racketeer Influenced and Corrupt Organizations Act (RICO) and several other federal statutes.

[188] Trajano v. Marcos, 1986 U.S. Dist. LEXIS 22541, *21 (D. Haw. 1986).

[189] After hearing oral argument, the Ninth Circuit requested an amicus brief from the U.S. Justice Department addressing three issues: "(1) Does the Alien Tort Statute provide a cause of action for wrongful death, wrongful arrest or torture committed by a foreign governmental official against a foreign national in a foreign nation? (2) Does the act of state doctrine remove wrongful death, wrongful arrest or torture from the federal courts' jurisdiction or is the doctrine inapplicable as a matter of law because those actions can never be 'acts of state' or because the 'balance of relevant considerations' favors a hearing? (3) Is the possibility of potential embarrassment to the United States sufficient reason for the federal courts to abstain from hearing these cases?" David Cole et al., *Interpreting the Alien Tort Statute: Amicus Curiae Memorandum of International Law Scholars and Practitioners in Trajano v. Marcos*, 12 HASTINGS INT'L & COMP. L. REV. 1, 2 (1988). In response, the United States submitted a brief to the Ninth Circuit arguing for a restrictive interpretation of the ATS. *See* Brief for the United States of America as Amicus Curiae, Trajano v. Marcos, 9th Cir. 1989 (No. 86-2448). A group of 19 international law scholars and practitioners then submitted their own amicus brief addressing the U.S. submission. *See* Amicus Curiae Memorandum on Behalf of International Law Scholars and Practitioners in Support of Plaintiffs in Trajano v. Marcos, Trajano v. Marcos, 9th Cir. 1989 (No. 86-2448), *reprinted in* Cole et al., *supra*, note 189, at 4–33.

[190] Trajano v. Marcos, 878 F.2d 1439, *2 (9th Cir. 1989) (citing Republic of the Philippines v. Marcos, 862 F.2d 1355, 1360–61 (9th Cir. 1988)).

any government. The issues raised, although extraordinarily complex, are within the capacity of the courts to resolve."[191] Thereafter, the Judicial Panel on Multidistrict Litigation consolidated all of the actions in the District of Hawaii, and the case was certified as a class action.[192] The class included "[a]ll current civilian citizens of the Republic of the Philippines, their heirs and beneficiaries, who between 1972 and 1986 were tortured, summarily executed or disappeared while in the custody of military or paramilitary groups."[193] Survivors of deceased class members were also permitted to join as plaintiffs in the litigation. Over 10,000 plaintiffs opted into the class. Some plaintiffs, however, opted out of the class and pursued direct actions against the Marcos Estate. These 23 direct actions were tried as part of the same consolidated case.

The jury trial took place in Hawaii and was bifurcated into two separate issues: liability and damages. In September 1992, the liability portion of the case was tried. The district court instructed the jury that it could find the Marcos Estate liable if it determined either that "(1) Marcos directed, ordered, conspired with, or aided the military in torture, summary execution, and 'disappearance' or (2) if Marcos knew of such conduct by the military and failed to use his power to prevent it."[194] After three days of deliberations, the jury reached verdicts in favor of the class plaintiffs and 22 direct plaintiffs. It also reached a verdict in favor of the Marcos Estate and against one direct plaintiff. The damages portion of the case was itself bifurcated into two separate proceedings: one trial on exemplary damages and one trial on compensatory damages. In February 1994, the jury returned a verdict against the Estate in the amount of $1.2 billion for exemplary damages. In January 1995, the jury returned a verdict against the Estate for approximately $766 million in compensatory damages.[195] The district court entered final judgment in the class action on February 3, 1995. The judgments were upheld on appeal.

---

[191] *Id.* at *2.

[192] The five consolidated cases were: Clemente v. Marcos, Ortigas v. Marcos, Sison v. Marcos, Hilao v. Marcos, and Trajano v. Marcos.

[193] Hilao v. Estate of Marcos, 103 F.3d 767, 774 (9th Cir. 1996).

[194] *Id.* at 776.

[195] Pursuant to Federal Rule of Evidence 706, the district court appointed a special master to consider the issue of damages. In the cases of torture victims, the special master considered several factors in calculating damages, including: "(1) physical torture, including what methods were used and/or abuses were suffered; (2) mental abuse, including fright and anguish; (3) amount of time torture lasted; (4) length of detention, if any; (5) physical and/or mental injuries; (6) victim's age; and (7) actual losses, including medical bills." Hilao v. Estate of Marcos, 103 F.3d 767, 783 (9th Cir. 1996). In the cases of summary execution and disappearance, the special master considered: "(1) [the

During the litigation, the Ninth Circuit issued several rulings on the Alien Tort Statute as well as the status of torture and other human rights abuses under international law. The court indicated that "[a]ctionable violations of international law must be of a norm that is specific, universal, and obligatory."[196] It then determined that the prohibition against torture was a universal, definable, and obligatory norm.

> The right to be free from official torture is fundamental and universal, a right deserving of the highest stature under international law, a norm of *jus cogens.* The crack of the whip, the clamp of the thumb screw, the crush of the iron maiden, and, in these more efficient modern times, the shock of the electric cattle prod are forms of torture that the international order will not tolerate. To subject a person to such horrors is to commit one of the most egregious violations of the personal security and dignity of a human being.[197]

The court made similar findings with respect to the prohibition against summary execution and forced disappearance.[198] Citing *Filartiga*, the Ninth Circuit concluded that the Alien Tort Statute "creates a cause of action for violations of specific, universal and obligatory international human rights standards which 'confer fundamental rights upon all people vis-à-vis their own governments.'"[199]

The federal courts also rejected claims that Marcos was immune from civil liability based on sovereign immunity or due to his status as a former head of state.[200] Significantly, the Ninth Circuit found that acts of torture,

---

presence or absence of] torture prior to death or disappearance; (2) the actual killing or disappearance; . . . (3) the victim's family's mental anguish[;] and (4) lost earnings [computed according to a formula established by the Philippine Supreme Court and converted into U.S. dollars]." *Id. See generally* Sol Schreiber & Laura D. Weissbach, *In re Estate of Ferdinand E. Marcos Human Rights Litigation: A Personal Account of the Role of the Special Master,* 31 LOY. L.A. L. REV. 475 (1998).

[196] *In re* Estate of Marcos Human Rights Litigation, 25 F.3d 1467, 1475 (9th Cir. 1994).

[197] *Id.*

[198] *Id.*

[199] *Id.* at 1475–76 (citing Filartiga v. Pena-Irala, 630 F.2d 876, 885–87 (2d Cir. 1980)). For purposes of ATS litigation, international law need not offer an explicit cause of action for human rights violations. "International law 'does not require any particular reaction to violations of law. . . . Whether and how the United States wished to react to such violations are domestic questions.'" *Id.* at 1475 (citing Tel-Oren v. Libyan Arab Republic, 726 F.2d 774, 777–78 (D.C. Cir. 1984) (Edwards, J., concurring)).

[200] Trajano v. Marcos, 978 F.2d 493, 498 (9th Cir. 1992).

summary execution, and disappearance could not be considered official acts leading to immunity from civil proceedings. The Ninth Circuit also declined to dismiss the litigation under the political question doctrine, finding that the underlying claims were, in fact, justiciable.

> Although sometimes criticized as a ruler and at times invested with extraordinary powers, Ferdinand Marcos does not appear to have had the authority of an absolute autocrat. He was not the state, but the head of the state, bound by the laws that applied to him. Our courts have had no difficulty in distinguishing the legal acts of a deposed ruler from his acts for personal profit that lack a basis in law. As in the case of the deposed Venezuelan ruler, Marcos Perez Jimenez, the latter acts are as adjudicable and redressable as would be a dictator's act of rape.[201]

For several reasons, efforts to enforce the Marcos judgment proved difficult. The Marcos Estate agreed to transfer the bulk of its U.S.-based assets to the Philippine government to settle a separate lawsuit brought by the Philippine Presidential Commission on Good Governance. Other U.S.-based assets were subject to extensive litigation.[202] The Estate's assets in Switzerland were frozen at the request of the Philippine government in August 1995. While the federal district court for the District of Hawaii issued several orders to enjoin foreign banks from transferring assets that could be used to fund the settlement, these efforts generally proved unsuccessful.[203] In June 2006, the federal district court issued yet another order in the litigation, authorizing partial compensation of $2,500 each to 7,500 victims of human rights abuses.[204] The plaintiffs have also pursued other avenues for redress, including additional domestic litigation as well as proceedings before international bodies.[205]

---

[201] Republic of the Philippines, 862 F.2d 1355, 1361 (9th Cir. 1988) (*en banc*). *See also In re* Estate of Ferdinand Marcos Human Rights Litigation, 25 F.3d 1467, 1471 (9th Cir. 1994).

[202] *See, e.g.*, Merrill Lynch, Pierce, Fenner and Smith v. ENC Corp., 446 F.3d 1019 (9th Cir. 2006); *In re* Republic of the Philippines, 309 F.3d 1143 (9th Cir. 2002).

[203] Hilao v. Estate of Ferdinand Marcos, 393 F.3d 987 (9th Cir. 2004).

[204] *See* Oliver Teves, *Filipino Victims Left Waiting for Cash*, SOUTH FLORIDA SUN-SENTINEL, June 29, 2006, at 14A.

[205] Jon M. Van Dyke, *Promoting Accountability for Human Rights Abuses*, 8 CHAP. L. REV. 153, 159–64 (2005). *See also* Gregg Jones, *Marcos Wealth Remains Elusive*, DALLAS MORNING NEWS, Feb. 22, 2001, at 1A; Arleen Jacobius, *Collection Next Step for Marcos Victims: Getting Money for Human Rights Abuse is Hardest Part of International Cases*, 81 ABA J. 24 (Apr. 1995).

Despite these difficulties, the Marcos litigation is viewed as a milestone. Its significance stems from its unique role in the history of ATS litigation.

First, Marcos was the first human rights case brought under the ATCA to be fully contested in a trial on the merits, illustrating the numerous obstacles that plaintiffs must overcome in proving human rights allegations. Second, Marcos was the first human rights case under the ATCA to be decided by a jury, testing the ability and willingness of ordinary Americans to provide redress for violations of fundamental human rights committed abroad. Third, Marcos was the first human rights case under the ATCA to be brought as a class action, presenting unique issues of proof, damages, and potential divergence of priorities among victims, non-governmental organizations and counsel.[206]

6. Former Yugoslavia: *Kadic v. Karadzic*

In 1989, the fall of the Soviet Union created a power vacuum throughout Eastern Europe, and Yugoslavia was one of the first states to implode.[207] In the former Yugoslav territory of Bosnia-Herzegovina, Radovan Karadzic began using ethnicity as a weapon in his efforts to establish a Bosnian Serb state, the *Republika Srpska.* Torture and mass executions became rampant. Rape and sexual violence were used as weapons of war against men, women, and children. Concentration camps were built to house prisoners segregated by ethnicity and religion. By the summer of 1992, it became evident that Bosnian Serb leaders were conducting a campaign of ethnic cleansing, seeking to eliminate all traces of the non-Serb population from Bosnia-Herzegovina.

In 1993, several Bosnian women and men filed two lawsuits against Karadzic in federal district court for the Southern District of New York.[208] The

---

[206] Fitzpatrick, *supra* note 183, at 491.

[207] *See generally* NOEL MALCOLM, BOSNIA: A SHORT HISTORY (1994); ROBERT KAPLAN, BALKAN GHOSTS: A JOURNEY THROUGH HISTORY (1993); ALEX N. DRAGNICH, SERBS & CROATS: THE STRUGGLE IN YUGOSLAVIA (1992).

[208] The two lawsuits were *Kadic v. Karadzic,* No. 93 Civ 1163 (S.D.N.Y. 1993) and *Doe v. Karadzic,* No. 93 Civ 0878 (S.D.N.Y. 1993). The complaints were served on Karadzic while he was visiting the United Nations in New York. The plaintiffs were represented by a large group of organizations and attorneys, including: Center for Constitutional Rights; International Women's Human Rights Clinic; Allard K. Lowenstein International Human Rights Clinic; NOW Legal Defense and Education Fund; and several pro bono attorneys.

Doe v. Karadzic was filed as a class action lawsuit. On December 2, 1997, the district court granted certification of the class, which consisted of "all people who suffered injury as a result of rape, genocide, summary execution, arbitrary detention, disappearance,

complaints alleged numerous violations of international law, including genocide, war crimes, and crimes against humanity.[209] The allegations mirrored the
countless human tragedies that had scarred the Yugoslav landscape.

> Plaintiff Jane Doe IX is a Bosniak woman and a former resident of
> Bosnia-Herzegovina. She is a citizen of Bosnia-Herzegovina. In the
> summer of 1992, Jane Doe IX, then 17 years old, was taken away
> from her home by Bosnian-Serb Forces. She and two other girls in
> the apartment were told that they would be taken to the police
> department, but instead were taken to another location. Jane Doe
> IX was separated from the two other girls, interrogated and repeat-
> edly raped by a paramilitary officer. She was also threatened with
> death and gang rape. Other officers threatened to strip her naked
> and force her to walk through town. During her detention, she
> heard one of the girls screaming and asking for her; she has never
> seen or heard from either of the girls since. She files anonymously
> out of fear for her safety if her identity were known. . . .

> Plaintiff John Doe I, a Bosniak man and former resident of
> Bosanski Samac, was arbitrarily detained by Bosnian-Serb police for
> six to seven months in 1992. While in police custody, John Doe was
> periodically beaten by Bosnian-Serb military commanders, repeat-
> edly interrogated and tortured by the police, and forced to per-
> form sexual acts on other prisoners. John Doe I was then detained
> at the Batkovic concentration camp for approximately a year and
> a half. During that time, Bosnian-Serb Forces running the camp
> made him perform forced labor, including the digging of trenches
> and removal of corpses at the front lines of fighting. John Doe I

---

torture or other cruel, inhuman or degrading treatment inflicted by Bosnian-Serb Forces
under the command and control of defendant between April 1992 and the present."
Doe v. Karadzic, 176 F.R.D. 458, 461 (S.D.N.Y. 1997). On March 27, 2000, however, the
district court granted a motion to decertify the class. Doe v. Karadzic, 192 F.R.D. 133
(S.D.N.Y. 2000). *See generally* Catherine A. MacKinnon, *Collective Harms Under the Alien
Tort Statute: A Cautionary Note on Class Actions*, 6 ILSA J. INT'L & COMP. L. 567 (2000).

[209] Several articles have examined the *Karadzic* litigation. *See* Michele Brandt, *Doe v.
Karadzic: Redressing Non-State Acts of Gender-Specific Abuse Under the Alien Tort Statute*, 79
MINN. L. REV. 1413 (1995); Yolanda Wu, *Genocidal Rape in Bosnia: Redress in U.S. Courts
Under the Alien Tort Claims Act*, 4 UCLA WOMEN'S L.J. 101 (1993). In addition, several
publications have examined the broader issue of mass rape in the former Yugoslavia. *See*
Elizabeth Kohn, *Rape as a Weapon of War: Women's Human Rights During the Dissolution of
Yugoslavia*, 24 GOLDEN GATE U. L. REV. 199 (1994); THE ENTRENCHMENT OF SYSTEMATIC
ABUSE: MASS RAPE IN FORMER YUGOSLAVIA (Alexandra Stiglmayer ed., 1994); Krishna R.
Patel, *Recognizing the Rape of Bosnian Women as Gender-Based Persecution*, 60 BROOK. L. REV.
929 (1994).

files this action on his own behalf. He files anonymously out of fear for his safety if his identity were known.[210]

On September 7, 1994, the district court granted Karadzic's motion to dismiss both cases.[211] As a preliminary matter, the district court indicated that Karadzic's status as a potential head of state counseled against the exercise of jurisdiction. According to the court, "[w]ere the Executive Branch to declare defendant a head-of-state, this Court would be stripped of jurisdiction. This consideration, while not dispositive at this point in the litigation, militates against this Court exercising jurisdiction over the instant action."[212]

The district court then proceeded to examine whether it had subject matter jurisdiction under the Alien Tort Statute. While this issue was not raised by Karadzic, the court indicated that it could raise the issue *sua sponte*.[213] The district court examined whether the ATS provides jurisdiction and "whether the actions of defendant, alleged herein, constitute an actionable violation of the law of nations under the statute."[214] The district court began its analysis of the ATS by noting that the Second Circuit "has found that only conduct which rises to the level of an 'international common law tort' by violating universally accepted standards of human rights is within the law of nations, and thus within the subject-matter jurisdiction of the Act."[215] The court recognized that international law applied primarily to conduct between states. It then examined the Second Circuit's earlier decision in *Filartiga v. Pena-Irala* and the D.C. Circuit's decision in *Tel-Oren v. Libyan Arab Republic*.[216] The district court argued that both *Filartiga* and

---

[210] Consolidated Complaint at 4, 6, Doe v. Karadzic, 866 F. Supp. 734 (S.D.N.Y. 1993) (No. 93 Civ. 878).

[211] Doe v. Karadzic, 866 F. Supp. 734 (S.D.N.Y. 1994).

[212] *Id.* at 738.

[213] The district court examined three jurisdictional claims asserted by the plaintiffs: (1) the Alien Tort Statute; (2) the Torture Victim Protection Act; and (3) the federal question statute (28 U.S.C. § 1331).

[214] Doe v. Karadzic, 866 F. Supp. 734, 738 (S.D.N.Y. 1994).

[215] *Id.* at 738–39.

[216] In *Tel-Oren v. Libyan Arab Republic*, the D.C. Circuit Court of Appeals affirmed the dismissal of an ATS lawsuit filed by survivors and representatives of persons killed by the Palestine Liberation Organization (PLO) in several terrorist attacks committed in Israel. Tel-Oren v. Libyan Arab Republic, 726 F.2d 774 (D.C. Cir. 1984). The court issued a *per curiam* decision, with each judge submitting a separate concurring opinion affirming the district court dismissal. Judge Edwards proclaimed his adherence to the legal principles established in *Filartiga* but distinguished that case on factual grounds. He indicated that the PLO was not a state actor and that neither the ATS nor *Filartiga* extended potential

Tel-Oren reinforce the conclusion that "acts committed by non-state actors do not violate the law of nations."[217] The district court cited several other cases, which also indicated that the ATS does not cover the conduct of non-state actors.[218] Indeed, the district court stated that courts have only found causes of action under the ATS when "state actors violated the law of nations."[219] The district court then examined the legal status of the Bosnian Serbs and the *Republika Srpska* to determine whether they could be considered state actors.[220] It concluded that the Bosnian-Serbs did not constitute a recognized state. Indeed, the Bosnian-Serbs had not even reached the level of political organization or international recognition achieved by the PLO at the time of the *Tel-Oren* decision. Thus, the court concluded that Karadzic's faction was not acting under the color of any recognized state.[221] The district court held that since the Bosnian Serbs were not acting under the color of any recognized state, the actions of Karadzic could not be remedied through the ATS. In addition, the court refused to extend the ATS to redress acts of torture committed by private individuals.[222]

---

civil liability to nonstate actors. According to Judge Edwards, such an extension "would require this court to venture out of the comfortable realm of established international law—within which Filartiga firmly sat—in which states are the actors. It would require an assessment of the extent to which international law imposes not only rights but also obligations on individuals." *Id.* at 792. Judge Robb declined jurisdiction on the grounds that the court was presented with a nonjusticiable political question. Judge Bork took a different approach. He stated that the ATS was merely a jurisdictional statute and could not be considered a grant of a cause of action. While the *Tel-Oren* decision generated much controversy and debate in academic circles, it failed to generate judicial support. Judge Bork's opinion was subject to particular criticism. *See, e.g.,* Anthony D'Amato, *What Does Tel-Oren Tell Lawyers? Judge Bork's Concept of the Law of Nations is Seriously Mistaken,* 79 AM. J. INT'L L. 92 (1985). *But see* Alfred P. Rubin, *What Does Tel-Oren Tell Lawyers? D'Amato Concept of American Jurisdiction is Seriously Mistaken,* 79 AM. J. INT'L L. 105 (1985). It received only minimal support in subsequent ATS decisions. *See* Al Odah v. United States, 321 F.3d 1134, 1146–48 (D.C. Cir. 2003) (Randolph, J., concurring), *rev'd sub nom.* Rasul v. Bush, 542 U.S. 466 (2004).

217 Doe v. Karadzic, 866 F. Supp. 734, 739 (S.D.N.Y. 1994).

218 *See* Linder v. Calero Portocarrero, 747 F. Supp. 1452 (S.D. Fla. 1990); Carmichael v. United Technologies Corp., 835 F.2d 109 (5th Cir. 1988); Forti v. Suarez-Mason, 672 F. Supp. 1531 (N.D. Cal. 1987).

219 Doe v. Karadzic, 866 F. Supp. 734, 740 (S.D.N.Y. 1994).

220 In 1992, the *Republika Srpska* was established by Bosnian Serbs in Bosnia-Herzegovina with Radovan Karadzic as its purported leader. *See generally* RICHARD HOLBROOK, TO END A WAR (1998). *See also* Mehinovic v. Vuckovic, 198 F. Supp. 2d 1322 (N.D. Ga. 2002).

221 Doe v. Karadzic, 866 F. Supp. 734, 741 (S.D.N.Y. 1994).

222 *Id.*

Since the district court found no basis for subject matter jurisdiction, it granted Karadzic's motion to dismiss. The plaintiffs immediately appealed the district court's ruling to the Second Circuit Court of Appeals. Several human rights organizations filed amicus briefs urging the Second Circuit to reverse the district court's ruling.[223] At the request of the Second Circuit, the U.S. government also submitted a Statement of Interest urging reversal of the district court's ruling.[224] The United States maintained that Karadzic was not entitled to immunity and that the case was justiciable. It also contended that the district court's analysis of international law and its purported inapplicability to nonstate actors was incorrect. "Customary international law does not bind exclusively state actors. Depending upon the violation alleged, acts committed by non-state actors may indeed violate international law."[225] The case was argued before the Second Circuit on June 20, 1995.

On October 13, 1995, the Second Circuit issued its ruling, reversing the district court's dismissal. At the outset of its opinion, the court acknowledged the unique quality of the litigation.

> Most Americans would probably be surprised to learn that victims of atrocities committed in Bosnia are suing the leader of the insurgent Bosnian-Serb forces in a United States District Court in Manhattan. Their claims seek to build upon the foundation of this Court's decision in *Filartiga v. Pena-Irala*, which recognized the important principle that the venerable Alien Tort Act, 28 U.S.C. § 1350 (1988), enacted in 1789 but rarely invoked since then, validly creates federal court jurisdiction for suits alleging torts committed anywhere in the world against aliens in violation of the law of nations.[226]

The Second Circuit identified three requirements for establishing subject matter jurisdiction under the ATS: (1) an alien sues; (2) for a tort; (3)

---

[223] Amicus briefs were filed by several groups, including Human Rights Watch, the International Human Rights Law Group, and several international law professors.

[224] Statement of Interest of the United States, Kadic v. Karadzic, 70 F.3d 232 (2d Cir. 1995) (No. 94-9069). The U.S. Statement represents one of the few occasions where the U.S. government has filed a brief in support of plaintiffs in ATS litigation. *See generally* Beth Stephens, *Upsetting Checks and Balances: The Bush Administration's Efforts to Limit Human Rights Litigation*, 17 HARV. HUM. RTS. J. 169 (2004); Brian C. Free, *Comment: Awaiting Doe v. Exxon Mobil Corp.: Advocating the Cautious Use of Executive Opinions in Alien Tort Claims Act Litigation*, 12 PAC. RIM L. & POL'Y J. 467 (2003).

[225] Statement of Interest of the United States, *supra* note 224, at 5.

[226] *See* Kadic v. Karadzic, 70 F.3d 232, 236 (2d Cir. 1995) (citations omitted).

committed in violation of the law of nations.[227] Since the first two conditions were clearly satisfied, "the only disputed issue is whether plaintiffs have pleaded violations of international law."[228] In determining the application of the Alien Tort Statute, the Second Circuit considered three issues. First, it examined whether nonstate actors could violate international law. Second, it examined whether the specific allegations made by the plaintiffs—genocide, war crimes, and torture—were violations of international law when committed by nonstate actors. Third, it examined whether the *Republika Srpska*, the Bosnian-Serb entity headed by Karadzic, constituted a state under international law or, alternatively, whether Karadzic was acting under the color of Yugoslav law.[229]

The Second Circuit first examined whether nonstate actors could violate international law. On this point, it immediately challenged the district court's contention that "the law of nations, as understood in the modern era, confines its reach to state action."[230] The Court indicated that piracy, for example, was traditionally viewed as a violation of international law even though it was committed by private individuals. In addition, slave trading and certain war crimes were also violations of international law even when committed by private individuals. The court noted that the Executive Branch had long recognized the liability of private individuals for violations of international law and the availability of the Alien Tort Statute as a remedy in such matters. The court also referred to the Statement of Interest filed by the United States, which indicated the government's position was that private individuals may be sued under the ATS for certain violations of international law. In contrast to the district court's interpretation of *Filartiga* and *Tel-Oren*, the Second Circuit ruled that these decisions do not support the contention that the actions of nonstate actors do not violate the law of nations. *Filartiga* involved allegations of torture committed by a public official. "We had no occasion to consider whether international law violations other than torture are actionable against private individuals, and

---

[227] The Second Circuit addressed two other jurisdictional arguments. It determined that the Torture Victim Protection Act is not a jurisdictional statute and only provides a cause of action for official torture. It then declined to address whether the federal question statute authorized the assertion of jurisdiction in the case.

[228] Kadic v. Karadzic, 70 F.3d 232, 236 (2d Cir. 1995).

[229] The Court noted that "because the Alien Tort Act requires that plaintiffs plead a 'violation of the law of nations' at the jurisdictional threshold, this statute requires a more searching review of the merits to establish jurisdiction than is required under the more flexible 'arising under formula of section 1331.'" *Id.* The Court indicated that it was not enough to plead a colorable violation of the law of nations. Rather, the complaint must adequately plead a violation of the law of nations or a treaty of the United States.

[230] *Id.* at 239.

nothing in *Filartiga* purports to preclude such a result."[231] Similarly, Judge Edwards' concurring opinion in *Tel-Oren* was limited to the specific allegation of torture. He did not suggest a similar result for other human rights violations. Indeed, Judge Edwards acknowledged that there exists a "handful of crimes to which the law of nations attributes individual responsibility," including piracy and slave-trading.[232] Thus, the court concluded that "certain forms of conduct violate the law of nations whether undertaken by those acting under the auspices of a state or only as private individuals."[233]

The Second Circuit then examined whether the specific allegations made by the plaintiffs—genocide, war crimes, and torture—were violations of international law when such acts were committed by non-state actors. In reviewing these allegations, the court recognized that "evolving standards of international law govern who is within the [Alien Tort Statute's] jurisdictional grant."[234]

The court first considered the status of genocide under international law and considered whether nonstate actors could be held accountable for such acts. On several occasions, the U.N. General Assembly had declared that genocide is a violation of international law regardless of whether committed by state or nonstate actors.[235] Similarly, the Convention on the Prevention and Punishment of the Crime of Genocide provides that "persons committing genocide . . . shall be punished, whether they are constitutionally responsible rulers, public officials or private individuals."[236] The court also noted that the Genocide Convention Implementation Act of 1987 criminalizes the crime of genocide without regard to whether the offender is acting under color of law.[237] Thus, the court concluded that the proscription against genocide under international law is applied equally to state and nonstate actors.[238] According to the complaint, Karadzic had allegedly "personally planned and ordered a campaign of murder, rape,

---

[231] *Id.* at 240.

[232] *Id.*

[233] *Id.* at 239.

[234] *Id.* at 241 (quoting Amerada Hess Shipping Corp. v. Argentine Republic, 830 F.2d 421, 425 (2d Cir. 1987), *rev'd on other grounds*, 488 U.S. 428 (1989)).

[235] *See* G.A. Res. 95(I), 1 U.N. GAOR, U.N. Doc. A/64/Add.1, at 188 (1946); G.A. Res. 96(I), 1 U.N. GAOR, U.N. Doc. A/64/Add.1, at 188–89 (1946).

[236] Convention on the Prevention and Punishment of the Crime of Genocide, art. IV, Jan. 12, 1951, 78 U.N.T.S. 277.

[237] 18 U.S.C. § 1091 (1988).

[238] Kadic v. Karadzic, 70 F.3d 232, 242 (2d Cir. 1995).

forced impregnation, and other forms of torture designed to destroy the religious and ethnic groups of Bosnian Muslims and Bosnian Croats."[239] Since the complaint clearly stated a violation of the international norm against genocide, the court held that subject matter jurisdiction existed over these claims.

The court then examined the status of war crimes under international law and whether nonstate actors could be held accountable for such acts. The court noted that acts, such as murder, rape, torture and arbitrary detention of civilians, have long been recognized as violations of the laws of war. Indeed, "[t]he liability of private individuals for committing war crimes has been recognized since World War I and was confirmed at Nuremberg after World War II."[240] These prohibitions are now codified in the four Geneva Conventions of 1949. Common Article 3, which appears in each of the Geneva Conventions, applies specifically to armed conflicts that are not of an international nature. The court indicated that "under the law of war as codified in the Geneva Conventions, all 'parties' to a conflict—which includes insurgent military groups—are obliged to adhere to these most fundamental requirements of the law of war."[241] Thus, the court concluded that private individuals could be held liable for war crimes. According to the court, "the offenses alleged by the appellants, if proved, would violate the most fundamental norms of the law of war embodied in Common Article 3, which binds parties to internal conflicts regardless of whether they are recognized nations or roving hordes of insurgents."[242] Since these offenses were clearly war crimes, the court held that subject matter jurisdiction existed over these claims.

Finally, the court examined whether nonstate actors can be held accountable for torture and summary execution. The court recognized that official torture and summary execution are prohibited by international law. However, it could not identify an international prohibition when these acts are committed by nonstate actors. The Convention against Torture requires that acts of torture must be "inflicted by or at the instigation of or with the consent or acquiescence of a public official or other person acting in an official capacity."[243] Similarly, the Torture Victim Protection Act only imposes liability for acts of torture or summary execution committed by individuals acting "under actual or apparent authority, or color of law, of

---

[239]   *Id.*

[240]   *Id.* at 243.

[241]   *Id.*

[242]   *Id.*

[243]   Convention against Torture, *supra* note 7, at art. 1.

any foreign nation."[244] Thus, the court held that torture and summary execution are prohibited by international law only when such acts are committed by state officials.[245]

Having determined that torture and summary execution require state action, the court then examined whether the plaintiffs could establish the existence of state action. Specifically, the court examined the plaintiffs' contention that they were entitled to prove that the Bosnian Serb entity of *Republika Srpska* "satisfies the definition of a state for purposes of international law violations and, alternatively, that Karadzic acted in concert with the recognized state of the former Yugoslavia and its constituent republic, Serbia."[246] As the court recognized, formal recognition is not a condition of statehood. Indeed, international humanitarian law applies to states regardless of their status as recognized or unrecognized states. "It would be anomalous indeed if non-recognition by the United States, which typically reflects disfavor with a foreign regime—sometimes due to human rights abuses—had the perverse effect of shielding officials of the unrecognized regime from liability for those violations of international law norms that apply only to state actors."[247] In addition, the court suggested that the state actor requirement merely requires a semblance of official authority: "The inquiry, after all, is whether a person purporting to wield official power has exceeded internationally recognized standards of civilized conduct, not whether statehood in all its formal aspects exists."[248] Alternatively, the court recognized that the plaintiffs were entitled to prove that Karadzic was acting under color of law in cooperation with the former Yugoslavia. The court referred to the "color of law" jurisprudence of 42 U.S.C. Section 1983 as a relevant guide to determine "whether a defendant has engaged in official action for purposes of jurisdiction under the Alien Tort Act."[249] Established case law under 42 U.S.C. Section 1983 recognized that an individual acts under color of law when he acts in cooperation with state officials or with significant state aid.[250] Thus, the plaintiffs were entitled to

---

[244] 28 U.S.C. § 1350 (note), at § 2(a).

[245] The Court noted, however, that torture and summary execution may be encompassed within the claims of genocide and war crimes.

[246] Kadic v. Karadzic, 70 F.3d 232, 243 (2d Cir. 1995).

[247] *Id.* at 245.

[248] *Id.*

[249] *Id.*

[250] *See generally* Lugar v. Edmondson Oil Co., 457 U.S. 922, 937 (1982); Monroe v. Pape, 365 U.S. 167, 172–90 (1961).

prove that "Karadzic acted under color of law of Yugoslavia by acting in concert with Yugoslav officials or with significant Yugoslavian aid."[251]

The last portion of the court's opinion addressed justiciability. The court recognized that "cases of this nature might pose special questions concerning the judiciary's proper role when adjudication might have implications in the conduct of this nation's foreign relations."[252] It rejected, however, any attempt to invoke doctrines of justiciability in a categorical fashion: "[A] preferable approach is to weigh carefully the relevant considerations on a case-by-case basis."[253] The court then examined whether the political question doctrine or the act of state doctrine should bar justiciability of the case.

On the political question doctrine, the court indicated that "although these cases present issues that arise in a politically charged context, that does not transform them into cases involving nonjusticiable political questions."[254] The court then reviewed the political question factors identified by the Supreme Court in *Baker v. Carr*.[255] It recognized that the Judicial Branch is the appropriate branch of government to examine these claims. It also recognized that international law provides judicially discoverable and manageable standards for adjudicating claims brought under the ATS. The court noted that its decision would not interfere with important government interests, since the U.S. government had indicated that it was not opposed to the lawsuit. Finally, the court recognized that while disputes involving for-

---

[251] Kadic v. Karadzic, 70 F.3d 232, 245 (2d Cir. 1995).

[252] *Id.* at 248.

[253] *Id.* at 249.

[254] *Id.*

[255] Baker v. Carr, 369 U.S. 186 (1962). In *Baker v. Carr*, the Supreme Court indicated that "it is error to suppose that every case or controversy which touches foreign relations lies beyond judicial cognizance." *Id.* at 211. The Court then identified several factors to consider when determining whether a particular case constitutes a political question.

> Prominent on the surface of any case held to involve a political question is found a textually demonstrable constitutional commitment of the issue to a coordinate political department; or a lack of judicially discoverable and manageable standards for resolving it; or the impossibility of deciding without an initial policy determination of a kind clearly for nonjudicial discretion; or the impossibility of a court's undertaking independent resolution without expressing lack of the respect due coordinate branches of government; or an unusual need for unquestioning adherence to a political decision already made; or the potentiality of embarrassment from multifarious pronouncements by various departments on one question.

Id. at 217.

eign policy have the potential to raise political question issues, "it is 'error to suppose that every case or controversy which touches foreign relations lies beyond judicial cognizance.'"[256] Thus, the court concluded that the *Karadzic* litigation did not present a nonjusticiable political question.

The court also considered whether the act of state doctrine barred adjudication. It recognized that the act of state doctrine might be applicable to some cases brought under the Alien Tort Statute. However, the court doubted "that the acts of even a state official, taken in violation of a nation's fundamental law and wholly unratified by that nation's government, could properly be characterized as an act of state."[257] In addition, the court noted that the act of state doctrine had been previously applied in those cases that lacked unambiguous agreements regarding controlling legal principles. In the *Karadzic* case, however, there was universal agreement regarding the legal principles underlying international human rights.

For these reasons, the court of appeals reversed the judgment of the district court, and remanded both cases back to the district court. Karadzic's subsequent petitions for rehearing and certiorari were denied.[258] Karadzic then announced he would no longer participate in the litigation, and default was entered. In Fall 2000, two separate juries awarded the plaintiffs verdicts of $745 million and $4.5 billion in damages.[259] As Judge Peter Leisure noted to jurors in one of the cases, "[i]t's of historical significance what you participated in. It's very important that the United States of America rise to the challenge and that we just don't wait for the United Nations war-crimes trial."[260] The jury foreman echoed these concerns: "I hope the world gets the message. What happened was reprehensible."[261]

---

[256] Kadic v. Karadzic, 70 F.3d 232, 250 (2d Cir. 1995) (quoting Japan Whaling Ass'n v. Am. Cetacean Soc'y, 478 U.S. 221, 229–30 (1986)).

[257] *Id.*

[258] Karadzic filed a petition for rehearing on October 27, 1995. Thomas Scheffey, *Bosnian Serb Leader on Trial*, LEGAL TIMES, Nov. 13, 1995, at 2. The Second Circuit denied Karadzic's request to review the decision *en banc*. Kadic v. Karadzic 74 F.3d 377 (2d Cir. 1996). Karadzic then filed a petition for *certiorari* with the Supreme Court, which was denied on June 17, 1996. Linda Greenhouse, *Supreme Court Roundup*, N.Y. TIMES, June 18, 1996, at A20.

[259] David Rohde, *Jury in New York Orders Bosnian Serb to Pay Billions*, N.Y. TIMES, Sept. 26, 2000, at A10.

[260] Greg B. Smith, *N.Y.C. Jury Orders Serb Leader to Pay 4B for War Crimes*, DAILY NEWS (New York), Sept. 28, 2000, at 8.

[261] Rohde, *supra* note 259, at A10.

In these six cases, the plaintiffs won their lawsuits. But not all ATS cases end in favorable judgments for plaintiffs. In fact, most ATS cases end in the dismissal of the complaint.[262] Most cases are dismissed for lack of subject matter jurisdiction. In some cases, courts concluded that the alleged tort is not a violation of international law.[263] In other cases, courts determined that the case should be dismissed on justiciability grounds, including the political question doctrine or the act of state doctrine.[264] Some cases have been dismissed on immunity grounds.[265] While ATS cases are high-profile and often controversial, the judicial record reveals that few cases are ever brought to trial or result in a successful judgment for the plaintiffs.

C. HOLOCAUST LITIGATION

In the 1990s, numerous lawsuits were filed in the United States and Europe by Holocaust survivors and heirs seeking compensation for human rights violations committed during the Holocaust.[266] Defendants included foreign governments, banks, insurance companies, and multinational corporations.[267] Claims ranged from the use of slave labor to summary execution.[268] Property claims involving stolen bank accounts, unpaid insurance

---

[262] *See generally* Jeffrey Davis, *Justice Without Borders: Human Rights Cases in U.S. Courts*, 28 LAW & POL'Y 60 (2006); Kathryn Lee Boyd, *Universal Jurisdiction and Structural Reasonableness*, 40 TEX. INT'L L.J. 1 (2004).

[263] *See, e.g.*, Flores v. S. Peru Copper Corp., 343 F.3d 140, 161 (2d Cir. 2003); Beanal v. Freeport-McMoran, Inc., 197 F.3d 161, 166–67 (5th Cir. 1999).

[264] *See, e.g.*, Tel-Oren v. Libyan Arab Republic, 726 F.2d 774, 823 (D.C. Cir. 1984) (Robb, J., concurring); Greenham Women Against Cruise Missiles v. Reagan, 591 F. Supp. 1332 (S.D.N.Y. 1984).

[265] *See, e.g.*, Tachiona v. United States, 386 F.3d 205 (2d Cir. 2004); Hwang Geum Joo v. Japan, 332 F.3d 679 (D.C. Cir. 2003).

[266] *See generally* MICHAEL BAZYLER, HOLOCAUST JUSTICE: THE BATTLE FOR RESTITUTION IN AMERICA'S COURTS (2003); STUART E. EIZENSTAT, IMPERFECT JUSTICE: LOOTED ASSETS, SLAVE LABOR, AND THE UNFINISHED BUSINESS OF WORLD WAR II (2003); JANE SCHAPIRO, INSIDE A CLASS ACTION: THE HOLOCAUST AND THE SWISS BANKS (2003).

[267] There was even a lawsuit filed against the United States for mishandling looted assets captured by the U.S. Army at the end of the World War II. The assets included gold, jewelry, and artwork taken from Hungarian Jews by the Nazis. *See* Rosner v. United States, 231 F. Supp. 2d 1202 (S.D. Fla. 2002). In January 2005, the United States agreed to settle the case. Henry Weinstein, *U.S. Settles Suit with Holocaust Survivors*, L.A. TIMES, Mar. 12, 2005, at A1.

[268] *See, e.g.*, *In re* Holocaust Victim Assets Litig., 1998 U.S. Dist. LEXIS 18014 (E.D.N.Y. Oct. 7, 1998) (Swiss banks); Burger-Fischer v. Degussa AG, 65 F. Supp. 2d 248 (D.N.J. 1999) (German corporations); *In re* Austrian & German Bank Holocaust Litig., 80 F. Supp. 2d 164 (S.D.N.Y. 2000) (German and Austrian banks); In re Assicurazioni Generali S.P.A. Holocaust Ins. Litig., Judicial Panel on Multi District Litig., 2000 U.S.

policies, and confiscated real and personal property were also raised.[269] Most of these lawsuits were settled or dismissed. However, this litigation led several public and private actors to provide significant restitution to resolve these claims and settle historical wrongs.[270]

In *Iwanowa v. Ford Motor Co.*, for example, a victim of forced labor filed a lawsuit against Ford Motor Co. and its German subsidiary, Ford Werke A.G.[271] The lawsuit was filed in the federal district court for the District of New Jersey. The plaintiff, Elsa Iwanowa, alleged that Ford Motor Co., through its German subsidiary, had profited from the use of slave labor in Nazi Germany during the Second World War.

> On October 6, 1942, Nazi troops abducted [16-year-old] Iwanowa and transported her to Germany with approximately 2,000 other adolescents. When Iwanowa arrived in Wuppertal, Germany, a representative of Ford Werke purchased her, along with thirty-eight (38) other adolescents from Rostov. Ford Werke's representative had Iwanowa, and the other adolescents, transported to Ford Werke's plant in Cologne. Once in Cologne, Ford Werke placed Iwanowa with approximately sixty-five Ukrainian deportees in a wooden hut, without heat, running water or sewage facilities. They slept in three-tiered bunks without bedding and were locked in at night.

> From 1942–1945, Ford Werke required Iwanowa to perform heavy labor at its Cologne plant. Iwanowa's assignment consisted of drilling holes into the motor blocks of engines for military trucks. Ford Werke security officials supervised the forced laborers, at times using rubber truncheons to beat those who failed to meet production quotas.

Dist. LEXIS 17853 (insurance companies); Bodner v. Bank Paribas, 114 F. Supp. 2d 117 (E.D.N.Y. 2000) (French banks); Abrams v. Societe Nationale Des Chemins De Fer Francais, 389 F.3d 61 (2d Cir. 2004) (French railroad).

[269] Lawsuits were also filed by other victims of human rights abuses committed during World War II, including U.S. prisoners of war as well as Chinese and Korean women who were victims of sexual violence. *See, e.g.*, Hwang Geum Joo v. Japan, 332 F.3d 679 (D.C. Cir. 2003); *In re* World War II Era Japanese Forced Labor Litig., 164 F. Supp. 2d 1153 (N.D. Cal. 2001).

[270] *See, e.g.*, Testimony of Edward B. O'Donnell, Jr., U.S. Special Envoy for Holocaust Issues, Bureau of International Information Programs, U.S. Department of State (Nov. 11, 2004); Morris A. Ratner, *The Settlement of Nazi-era Litigation Through the Executive and Judicial Branches*, 20 BERKELEY J. INT'L L. 212 (2002).

[271] Iwanowa v. Ford Motor Co., 67 F. Supp. 2d 424 (D.N.J. 1999).

Iwanowa continued to perform forced labor for Ford Werke until 1945, when the victorious Allied Powers liberated her, and thousands of other slave laborers, in 1945. After the War, she became a citizen of Belgium, where she presently resides. Ford Werke's forced laborers, including Iwanowa, have never received compensation for their years of forced labor.[272]

Iwanowa filed the lawsuit as a class action on behalf of thousands of people who were forced to work for Ford Werke from 1941–1945. The complaint sought the disgorgement of all economic benefits received by the defendants as a result of forced labor, compensation for the reasonable value of services, and damages.

The district court found that the Alien Tort Statute provided subject matter jurisdiction because the case involved an alien suing for torts that were alleged to violate the law of nations. The court found that Ford's "use of unpaid, forced labor during World War II violated clearly established norms of customary international law."[273]

First, the Nuremberg Tribunals held that the enslavement and deportation of civilian populations during World War II constitutes a crime against humanity in violation of customary international law. The Nuremberg trials "for the first time made explicit and unambiguous what was theretofore, as the tribunal has declared, implicit in International Law, namely, that . . . to exterminate, enslave or deport civilian populations, is an international crime." Further, Nuremberg Principle IV(b) provides that the "deportation to slave labor . . . of civilian populations of or in occupied territory" constitutes both a "war crime" and a "crime against humanity."

Second, courts have repeatedly held that "deportation to slave labor" violates the law of nations. Thus, the case law and statements of the Nuremberg Tribunals unequivocally establish that forced labor violates customary international law.[274]

While the district court recognized subject matter jurisdiction under the ATS, the court found the plaintiff's claims were ultimately barred by the statute of limitations and the London Debt Agreement, and were otherwise nonjusticiable.[275] Despite the dismissal, Ford and other corporate defen-

---

[272] *Id.* at 433–34 (citations omitted).

[273] *Id.* at 440.

[274] *Id.* at 440–41 (citations omitted).

[275] *Id.* at 491. *See generally* Allyn Lite, *Another Attempt to Heal the Wounds of the*

dants negotiated with several Jewish organizations and agreed to settle the German slave labor claims in December 1999. The total payout from the German slave labor settlement was approximately $5 billion.

Most Holocaust-era litigation met the same judicial fate as the *Iwanowa* case. Other efforts to facilitate this litigation were also thwarted. In 1999, for example, California adopted the Holocaust Victim Insurance Relief Act to facilitate efforts by Holocaust survivors to track down outstanding insurance claims.[276] The legislation required insurance companies doing business in California to provide a list of all policies they issued to persons living in Europe between 1920 and 1945. According to the California legislature, "[i]nsurance companies doing business in the State of California have a responsibility to ensure that any involvement they or their related companies may have had with insurance policies of Holocaust victims are disclosed to the state and to ensure the rapid resolution of these questions, eliminating the further victimization of these policyholders and their families."[277] Significantly, the legislature acknowledged that "[t]he international Jewish community is in active negotiations with responsible insurance companies through the International Commission on Holocaust Era Insurance Claims to resolve all outstanding insurance claims issues."[278] Nonetheless, the legislature felt that its actions were "necessary to protect the claims and interests of California residents, as well as to encourage the development of a resolution to these issues through the international process or through direct action by the State of California, as necessary."[279] Several insurance companies then challenged the California legislation in federal court. In *American Insurance Association v. Garamendi*, the U.S. Supreme Court struck down the statute, holding that California's legislation interfered with the federal government's exclusive role in foreign affairs and was, therefore, preempted.[280]

> The basic fact is that California seeks to use an iron fist where the President has consistently chosen kid gloves. We have heard powerful arguments that the iron fist would work better, and it may be that if the matter of compensation were considered in isolation

---

Holocaust, 27 HUM. RTS. 12 (Spring 2000). The London Debt Agreement was signed by 21 countries in 1953. Its purpose was to settle the external debts of the Federal Republic of Germany and establish normal economic relations between Germany and other countries.

[276] CAL. CODE CIV. PROC. § 354.6.

[277] CAL. INS. CODE § 13801(e).

[278] *Id.* at § 13801(f).

[279] *Id.*

[280] Am. Ins. Ass'n v. Garamendi, 539 U.S. 396 (2003).

from all other issues involving the European allies, the iron fist would be the preferable policy. But our thoughts on the efficacy of the one approach versus the other are beside the point, since our business is not to judge the wisdom of the National Government's policy; dissatisfaction should be addressed to the President or, perhaps, Congress. The question relevant to preemption in this case is conflict, and the evidence here is "more than sufficient to demonstrate that the state Act stands in the way of [the President's] diplomatic objectives."[281]

One Holocaust-era lawsuit with a successful judicial outcome for the plaintiffs is *Republic of Austria v. Altmann*, which was decided by the U.S. Supreme Court in 2003.[282] During the Second World War, Nazi officials seized several valuable paintings owned by Ferdinand Bloch-Bauer and transferred them to the Austrian National Gallery.[283] Despite numerous requests by Bloch-Bauer and his descendants, the Austrian government refused to return the paintings. In 1998, Maria Altmann, Bloch-Bauer's niece, filed a federal lawsuit against the Republic of Austria and the Austrian National Gallery, raising eight causes of action based on alleged violations of Austrian law, California law, and international law. Both the district court and the Ninth Circuit Court of Appeals held that the Foreign Sovereign Immunities Act applied to the lawsuit even though the statute had been adopted well after the Second World War. The lower courts also held that the FSIA expropriation exception precluded Austria from claiming immunity.[284] The Supreme Court affirmed the applicability of the FSIA, holding that the presumption against retroactive application of federal statutes did not extend to the FSIA because Congress had expressed an unambiguous desire for it to apply to conduct that occurred prior to the FSIA's adoption.[285] The Supreme Court's ruling did not end the *Altmann* litigation, however. Both parties subsequently agreed to binding arbitration in Austria to resolve the dispute. In January 2006, an arbitration panel

---

[281] *Id.* at 427 (citations omitted).

[282] Republic of Austria v. Altmann, 541 U.S. 677 (2003).

[283] The paintings were the work of Gustav Klimt and were valued at $150–200 million.

[284] The FSIA provides an exception to sovereign immunity in cases where a foreign government has taken property in violation of international law, provided the property has a commercial connection to the United States or the agency or instrumentality that owns the property is engaged in commercial activity in the United States. *See* 28 U.S.C. § 1605(a)(3).

[285] The Supreme Court declined to address the applicability of the FSIA expropriation exception. Republic of Austria v. Altmann, 541 U.S. 677, 688 (2003).

ruled that the paintings belonged to the descendants of Bloch-Bauer.[286] As a result, Austria returned the five paintings to Altmann, who then sold one of the paintings for $135 million.[287]

While most Holocaust-era lawsuits were dismissed, this litigation played a significant role in promoting the search for justice by Holocaust survivors and other victims of atrocities committed during World War II.[288] As a result of these lawsuits, several foreign governments and multinational corporations entered negotiations with victims and survivor groups to address the underlying merits of the claims. These negotiations led to significant financial settlements, which occurred, in part, because of the threat of continued litigation. As noted by the Supreme Court in *American Insurance Association v. Garamendi,* the willingness of defendants to settle these claims "was conditioned on some expectation of security from lawsuits in United States courts."[289] The settlements were not limited to financial matters; they also addressed responsibility for atrocities committed during World War II. In dismissing a consolidated class action brought against numerous German companies, Judge William Bassler acknowledged the significance of the litigation and the eventual settlement, which was formalized in a Joint Statement signed by all the parties as well as several countries.[290]

> The allegations in the Complaints personalize the belief of Omer Bartov that "the Holocaust is indeed a crucial event for Western civilization, and that however much we learn about other instances of inhumanity, we cannot avoid the fact that this genocide, in the heart of our civilization, perpetrated by one of its most important nations (with the collaboration or complicity of many others), can never be relegated to a secondary place."

---

[286] *See* Anne-Marie O'Connor, *Attorney's Perseverance Yields a Legal Masterpiece,* L.A. TIMES, Jan. 23, 2006, at A1; Diane Haithman & Christopher Reynolds, *Court Awards Nazi-Looted Artworks to L.A. Woman,* L.A. TIMES, Jan. 17, 2006, at A1.

[287] *See* Alan G. Artner, *All That Glitters Is Golden,* CHI. TRIB., June 22, 2006, at C3; Sharon Waxman, *A Homecoming, in Los Angeles, for Looted Klimts,* N.Y. TIMES, Apr. 6, 2006, at E1; Suzanne Muchnic, *LACMA to Show Klimts,* L.A. TIMES, Mar. 16, 2006, at E4.

[288] *See* Burt Neuborne, *Preliminary Reflections on Aspects of Holocaust-era Litigation in American Courts,* 80 WASH. U. L.Q. 795 (2002).

[289] Am. Ins. Ass'n v. Garamendi, 539 U.S. 396, 405 (2003).

[290] In July 2000, the German government established the Foundation "Remembrance, Responsibility and the Future," which was designed to provide compensation to victims of the Nazi era who had made claims against German industry. A Joint Statement expressing support for the Foundation was subsequently signed by German industrial groups and lawyers representing plaintiffs involved in U.S. litigation and was supported by the United States and Germany. *See* Agreement Concerning the Foundation "Remembrance, Responsibility and the Future," 39 I.L.M. 1298 (2000).

As Bartov observes, "the carnage and genocide of World War II that followed did more than shatter the dreams of military and national greatness, it dealt a lethal blow to the very idea of shared humanity. Half a century later we are still groping for a way to come to terms with the belated effects of this trauma, even as its last witnesses are leaving the stage."

While the Complaints and Bartov's comments look to the past, the Joint Statement looks to the past and the future. This historic document is signed not only by the parties to the litigation but by the Republic of Belarus, the Czech Republic, the State of Israel, the Republic of Poland, the Russian Federation, and Ukraine, together with the Government of the United States of America and the Federal Republic of Germany as well as the Conference on Jewish Material Claims against Germany.

The Joint Statement acknowledges "the intention of both the Government of the Federal Republic of Germany and German companies to accept moral and historical responsibility arising from the use of slave laborers, and from property damage suffered as a consequence of racial persecution and from other injustices of the National Socialist era and World War II," and notes "with appreciation the December 17, 1999, statement of the President of the Federal Republic of Germany paying tribute to those who were subjected to slave and forced labor under German rule, recognizing their suffering and the injustices done to them, and begging forgiveness in the name of the German people."[291]

The *Filartiga* case played a subtle but significant role in promoting the Holocaust litigation. When these cases were filed in the mid-1990s, *Filartiga* was firmly established, and ATS litigation was increasing in the United States.

American judges were familiar with the suits being presented to them involving acts committed on foreign soil against foreign defendants. Moreover, they were amenable to finding that U.S. courts had jurisdiction over such suits when the acts consisted of gross violations of human rights law committed by foreign defendants who were present in the United States. That was all that was

---

[291] *In re* Nazi Era Cases against German Defendants Litig., 198 F.R.D. 429, 447–48 (D.N.J. 2000) (citations omitted). *See also In re* Holocaust Victim Asset Litig., 105 F. Supp. 2d 139 (E.D.N.Y. 2000) (approving a $1.25 billion settlement involving Swiss banks and Holocaust victims).

needed for the lawyers representing the Holocaust survivors to fit their allegations into the existing *hostis humani generis* principle.[292]

Without the ATS and the *Filartiga* precedent, the Holocaust litigation would have faced even more difficulties. At the same time, the Holocaust litigation has influenced ATS litigation. It gave legitimacy to efforts seeking to promote corporate accountability for human rights violations.[293] It also promoted other efforts to seek reparations and redress for historical wrongs.[294]

D. *SOSA V. ALVAREZ-MACHAIN:* THE SUPREME COURT SPEAKS

In 2004, the U.S. Supreme Court examined the Alien Tort Statute and addressed the *Filartiga* precedent in *Sosa v. Alvarez-Machain.* The case arose from the notorious transborder kidnapping of a Mexican doctor by individuals acting at the behest of U.S. government officials.

The early 1980s saw a significant increase in drug trafficking operations by Mexican cartels.[295] The Guadalajara narcotics cartel in Mexico was responsible for the cultivation and distribution of large quantities of marijuana as well as the importation of cocaine to the United States. As a result, the United States began extensive drug interdiction operations in cooperation with the Mexican government. Indeed, the U.S. Drug Enforcement Administration (D.E.A.) conducted numerous operations in Mexican territory. D.E.A. Special Agent Enrique Camarena was assigned to these operations. On February 7, 1985, Camarena was kidnapped outside the

---

[292] BAZYLER, *supra* note 266, at 56. *See also* Sandra Coliver, *Bringing Human Rights Abusers to Justice in U.S. Courts: Carrying Forward the Legacy of the Nuremberg Trials,* 27 CARDOZO L. REV. 1689 (2006); RICHARD ALLEN WHITE, BREAKING SILENCE: THE CASE THAT CHANGED THE FACE OF HUMAN RIGHTS 286 (2004).

[293] BAZYLER, *supra* note 266, at 57–58. *See also* Robert A. Swift, *Holocaust Litigation and Human Rights Jurisprudence, in* HOLOCAUST RESTITUTION: PERSPECTIVES ON THE LITIGATION AND ITS LEGACY 50 (Michael J. Bazyler & Roger Alford eds., 2006); Owen Pell, *Historical Reparation Claims: The Defense Perspective, in* Bazyler & Alford, *supra* note 293, at 330, 332–33.

[294] *See generally* Pierre d'Argent, *Wrongs of the Past, History of the Future?,* 17 EUR. J. INT'L L. 279 (2006); Morris Ratner & Caryn Becker, *The Legacy of Holocaust Class Action Suits: Have They Broken Ground for Other Cases of Historical Wrongs?, in* Bazyler & Alford, *supra* note 293, at 345, 346; BAZYLER, *supra* note 266, at 307.

[295] *See generally* William J. Aceves, *The Legality of Transborder Abductions: A Study of United States v. Alvarez-Machain,* 3 SW. J. L. & TRADE 101 (1996); John Quigley, *Our Men in Guadalajara and the Abduction of Suspects Abroad: A Comment on United States v. Alvarez-Machain,* 68 NOTRE DAME L. REV. 723 (1993); Jonathan A. Bush, *How Did We Get Here? Foreign Abduction After Alvarez-Machain,* 45 STAN. L. REV. 939 (1993); Aimee Lee, *United States v. Alvarez-Machain: The Deleterious Ramifications of Illegal Abductions,* 17 FORDHAM INT'L L.J. 126 (1993).

American consulate in Guadalajara, Mexico, by Mexican drug traffickers. Camarena was tortured for approximately 36 hours, during which he was repeatedly revived so that his torture and interrogation could continue. His mutilated and lifeless body was found one month later alongside that of Alfredo Zavala-Avela, a Mexican pilot who had assisted Camarena in aerial reconnaissance of marijuana plantations in Mexico. The D.E.A. eventually suspected Dr. Humberto Alvarez-Machain, a Mexican gynecologist who lived and worked in Guadalajara, Mexico, of participating in the torture of Camarena. When the Mexican government refused to transfer Alvarez-Machain to the United States, U.S. government officials developed a plan with several Mexican nationals to abduct Alvarez-Machain and bring him to the United States.

On April 2, 1990, Alvarez-Machain was taken by masked gunmen from his medical offices in Guadalajara, Mexico. He was held in Mexico for approximately 20 hours and was then transported by aircraft to El Paso, Texas, where he was taken into custody by U.S. federal officials. Alvarez-Machain remained in federal custody in El Paso from April 3 through April 10. During his detention, he was interrogated by D.E.A. agents. He was also taken to a local hospital for observation after complaining of chest pains. On April 10, Alvarez-Machain was transferred to Los Angeles, California, and brought before the federal district court for the Central District of California. Alvarez-Machain was charged with violating federal law in connection with the kidnapping and murder of D.E.A. agent Camarena and his pilot Zavala-Avela. Alvarez-Machain challenged his indictment on several grounds. He argued that his abduction from Mexico violated the U.S.-Mexico Extradition Treaty and that the circumstances of his abduction constituted a denial of due process. On August 14, 1990, the district court held that the abduction did, in fact, violate the Extradition Treaty and that the appropriate remedy was to return Alvarez-Machain to Mexico.[296] On appeal, the Ninth Circuit concurred.[297] In a 6-3 ruling, however, the U.S. Supreme Court reversed. It held that a criminal defendant abducted from a country that has an extradition treaty with the United States may still be tried in a federal court for violations of U.S. criminal law.[298] On remand, the Ninth Circuit denied Alvarez-Machain's additional claim that customary international law precluded his prosecution.[299] The court also denied

---

[296] United States v. Caro-Quintero, 745 F. Supp. 599 (C.D. Cal. 1990). *See* Ker v. State of Illinois, 119 U.S. 436 (1886). The district rejected Alvarez-Machain's claims of physical mistreatment, finding them "not worthy of belief." United States v. Caro-Quintero, 745 F. Supp. 599, 605 (C.D. Cal. 1990).

[297] United States v. Alvarez-Machain, 946 F.2d 1466 (9th Cir. 1991).

[298] United States v. Alvarez-Machain, 504 U.S. 655 (1992).

[299] United States v. Alvarez-Machain, 1992 U.S. App. LEXIS 28367 (9th Cir. 1992).

Alvarez-Machain's assertion that the circumstances of his abduction were so shocking that they constituted a denial of due process.[300]

The criminal trial of Alvarez-Machain began on December 1, 1992, before Judge Edward Rafeedie in Los Angeles. The prosecution concluded its case on December 10, 1992. Alvarez-Machain then submitted a motion for judgment of acquittal, pursuant to Rule 29 of the Federal Rules of Criminal Procedure.[301] The motion charged that the "government has failed to provide sufficient evidence from which a rational jury could find the defendant guilty beyond a reasonable doubt on each of the essential elements of the crimes charged."[302] On December 14, Judge Edward Rafeedie granted Alvarez-Machain's motion for acquittal, holding there was insufficient evidence to prosecute him. Specifically, Judge Rafeedie stated that the evidence presented against Alvarez-Machain had been based on "hunches" and the "wildest speculation" and had failed to support the government's allegations. Despite last-minute attempts by the U.S. government to detain him in Los Angeles, Alvarez-Machain returned to Mexico on December 14, 1992, ending an odyssey that lasted 987 days.[303]

In July 1993, Alvarez-Machain filed a federal lawsuit against the United States, various U.S. government officials, and several Mexican nationals, including Jose Francisco Sosa. The lawsuit claimed subject matter jurisdiction, in part, on the Alien Tort Statute. It raised several claims, including kidnapping, torture, cruel and inhuman and degrading treatment or punishment, prolonged arbitrary detention, assault and battery, false imprisonment, intentional infliction of emotional distress, false arrest, negligent employment of public employees and agents, negligent infliction of emotional distress, and violations of the Fourth, Fifth, and Eighth Amendments to the U.S. Constitution.

Most of Alvarez-Machain's claims, including those against the U.S. government, were dismissed after a series of pretrial motions and an interlocutory appeal by the defendants.[304] Thereafter, only Jose Francisco Sosa,

---

[300] *Id.* at *3. *See* United States v. Toscanino, 500 F.2d 267 (2d Cir. 1974).

[301] Federal Rule of Criminal Procedure 29(a) provides that a court "must enter a judgment of acquittal of any offense for which the evidence is insufficient to sustain a conviction." FED. R. CRIM. P. 29(a).

[302] Defendant Alvarez-Machain's Motion for Acquittal at 24, United States v. Alvarez-Machain, No. CR-87-422-(G)-ER (C.D. Cal. 1992).

[303] *See generally Mexico Hails Man's Acquittal,* DALLAS MORNING NEWS, Dec. 16, 1992, at A13.

[304] Alvarez-Machain v. United States, 1999 U.S. Dist. LEXIS 23304 (C.D. Cal. 1999). *See also* Alvarez-Machain v. United States, 107 F.3d 696 (9th Cir. 1997).

a Mexican national implicated in the kidnapping, remained as a defendant in the case. After a bench trial, the district court entered a $25,000 judgment against Sosa for arbitrary arrest and detention under the ATS.[305] The court found Sosa liable for the kidnapping in Mexico, but his liability stopped once Alvarez-Machain was transferred to U.S. custody in El Paso, Texas. In 2001, a three-judge panel of the Ninth Circuit affirmed the ATS judgment against Sosa but reinstated the claims against the U.S. government.[306] In 2003, an *en banc* panel of the Ninth Circuit affirmed the panel decision in a 6-5 ruling.[307] The Court indicated that ATS claims should be limited to international norms that are specific, universal, and obligatory: "This formulation, which lays the foundation for our approach to international norms, is in keeping with the narrow scope of ATCA jurisdiction and the general practice of limiting judicial review to those areas of international law that have achieved sufficient consensus to merit application by a domestic tribunal."[308] While the court found that arbitrary arrest and detention violate clear and universally recognized norms, it determined that transborder abductions did not: "Because a human rights norm recognizing an individual's right to be free from transborder abductions has not reached a status of international accord sufficient to render it 'obligatory' or 'universal,' it cannot qualify as an actionable norm under the ATCA. This is a case where aspiration has not yet ripened into obligation."[309] The dissent did not challenge the permissibility of ATS litigation in all cases.[310] It also found that Alvarez-Machain had stated a justiciable claim under the ATS. It concluded, however, that Alvarez-Machain was not entitled to relief for his claim of arbitrary arrest.

Subsequently, the U.S. Supreme Court granted Sosa's petition for *certiorari* in the case. It accepted three questions for review.[311]

---

[305] Alvarez-Machain v. United States, 1999 U.S. Dist. LEXIS 23433 (C.D. Cal. 1999). The district court found no evidence that Alvarez-Machain was tortured or abused during his detention. *Id.* at *10. Accordingly, it limited the award to compensatory damages and declined to award punitive damages.

[306] Alvarez-Machain v. United States, 266 F.3d 1045 (9th Cir. 2001).

[307] Alvarez-Machain v. United States, 331 F.3d 604 (9th Cir. 2003) (*en banc*).

[308] *Id.* at 612 (citations omitted).

[309] *Id.* at 620.

[310] Four judges argued that the arbitrary detention did not constitute an actionable norm under the ATS in this case. One judge argued that the case should be dismissed because of the political question doctrine.

[311] The Supreme Court also considered a separate appeal filed by the United States that addressed the scope of the Federal Tort Claims Act. The appeals were consolidated by the Court for oral argument.

1. Whether the ATA [Alien Tort Statute], is simply a grant of jurisdiction, or whether, in addition to granting jurisdiction, it provides a cause of action upon which aliens may sue for torts in violation of the law of nations or treaties of the United States.

2. If the ATA provides a cause of action, whether the actions it authorizes are limited to suits for violations of jus cogens norms of international law.

3. Whether a detention that lasts less than 24 hours, results in no physical harm to the detainee, and is undertaken by a private individual under instructions from senior United States law enforcement officials, constitutes a tort in violation of the law of nations actionable under the ATA.

Numerous individuals and organizations submitted amicus briefs to the Court. Several former ATS plaintiffs, including Dolly Filártiga, submitted an amicus brief in support of Alvarez-Machain, urging the Court to maintain the ATS as a redress mechanism for victims of torture.[312] "ATCA cases have provided a judicial remedy consistent with international law principles that enables survivors to break the silence surrounding their abuses, to restore their dignity and sense of control over their lives by securing judicial acknowledgement of the horrors they endured, and to achieve a measure of justice against those responsible for their suffering."[313] Other organizations representing human rights victims as well as the broader human rights movement also submitted briefs in support of the ATS and the *Filartiga* precedent.[314] In addition, several briefs were filed by legal scholars that

---

[312] Brief for the Center for Justice and Accountability et al., Sosa v. Alvarez-Machain, 542 U.S. 692 (2004) (No. 03-339). Other ATS plaintiffs who participated on the brief included: Elizabeth Demissie (*Abebe-Jira v. Negewo*); Juan Romagoza Arce, Neris Gonzalez, and Carlos Mauricio (*Romagoza v. Garcia*); Zita Cabello-Barrett (*Cabello v. Fernandez-Larios*); Alma Vilogorac (*Doe v. Karadzic*); Kemal Mehinovic (*Mehinovic v. Vuckovic*); Oscar Reyes, Gloria Reyes, and Zenaida Velásquez (*Reyes v. Grijalba*); John Roe VIII, John Doe V, and John Doe XI (*Doe v. Unocal, Roe v. Unocal*); Jose Domingo Flores (*Sinaltrainal v. Coca-Cola Co.*).

[313] *Id.* at 2.

[314] The following amicus briefs were filed in support of Alvarez-Machain: Center for Justice and Accountability, National Consortium of Torture Treatment Programs, and Individual ATCA Plaintiffs; National and Foreign Legal Scholars; Alien Friends Representing Hungarian Jews and Bougainvilleans Interests; Professors of Federal Jurisdiction and Legal History; Corporate Social Responsibility; Presbyterian Church of Sudan and Clifton Kirkpatrick as Stated Clerk of the General Assembly of the Presbyterian Church (U.S.A.); Career Foreign Service Diplomats; Women's Human Rights Organizations; International Human Rights Organizations and Religious

reviewed the legislative history of the ATS and urged the Court to uphold *Filartiga* as consistent with the understanding of the First Congress.

The United States submitted a brief in support of Sosa.[315] It argued that the ATS was only a jurisdictional statute and did not confer a private right of action to litigants. It then asserted that federal courts could not identify a cause of action through the law of nations. The United States also expressed concern over the foreign policy implications of ATS litigation.

> Section 1350 litigation may implicate and inflame international tensions or disagreements over highly sensitive matters in several different respects. First, courts may be required to resolve factual disputes over the responsibility for alleged human rights abuses, a task complicated by the fact that most Section 1350 action involve events that allegedly occurred in foreign countries. Second, the entry of judgment (or even dismissal of actions) may create the impression to the citizens of other nations—who are not familiar with the American constitutional system or Section 1350—that the United States Government has taken sides in an internal dispute, even where the Executive Branch has not spoken directly on a question. Third, and perhaps most fundamentally, in resolving such disputes, federal courts have construed and made pronouncement on the consensus that has developed with respect to particular international agreements or the scope and application of those agreements.[316]

Several other briefs were submitted on behalf of Sosa.[317] They raised a number of arguments, addressing the legislative history of the ATS and

---

Organizations; International Jurists; Surviving Family Members of the Victims of the September 11, 2001 Terrorist Attacks; World Jewish Congress and American Jewish Committee.

[315] Brief for the United States as Respondent Supporting Petitioner, Sosa v. Alvarez-Machain, 542 U.S. 692 (2004) (No. 03-339). The United States also submitted a second brief to the Court in its capacity as petitioner, raising issues pertaining to the Federal Tort Claims Act.

[316] *Id.* at 42–43.

[317] The following amicus briefs were filed in support of Sosa: Governments of Australia, Switzerland, and the United Kingdom of Great Britain and Northern Ireland; Pacific Legal Foundation; Professors of International Law, Federal Jurisdiction and the Foreign Relations Law of the United States; Washington Legal Foundation, National Fraternal Order of Police, and Allied Educational Foundation; National Association of Manufacturers; National Foreign Trade Council, USAEngage, the Chamber of Commerce of the United States of America, the United States Council for Organization in International Investment, the International Chamber of Commerce, the Organization

expressing concern with the foreign investment and foreign relations implications of ATS litigation.

Finally, the European Commission submitted an amicus brief in support of neither party.[318] It urged the Court to consider international law when examining what actors and what conduct could be liable under the ATS. It also asked the Court to recognize any applicable international limitations on U.S. jurisdiction. While the principle of universal jurisdiction was recognized under international law, the European Commission argued that its application in civil proceedings was less developed. Only some claims could conceivably give rise then to universal jurisdiction in civil proceedings. In addition, any application of universal jurisdiction in civil proceedings should be limited to those cases where a plaintiff was unable to pursue justice in a state that could exercise a more traditional form of jurisdiction, such as nationality or territory. According to the European Commission, such an approach would be consistent with international law.

> Simply put, assuming that Congress intended to create a cause of action when it enacted the Alien Tort Statute, the European Commission respectfully suggests that Congress intended federal courts not to breach the law of nations but to rigorously apply it. This Court would honor that intent by defining the scope of the cause of action created by the statute to incorporate the substantive content and jurisdictional limits imposed by international law.[319]

Oral argument was heard by the Supreme Court on March 30, 2004, which marked the 28-year anniversary of Joelito Filártiga's murder.[320]

On June 29, 2004, the Supreme Court issued its decision in *Sosa v. Alvarez-Machain*.[321] In a 6-3 ruling written by Justice Souter, the Court held

---

for International Investment, the Business Roundtable, the American Petroleum Institute, and the US-ASEAN Business Council.

[318] Brief of Amicus Curiae the European Commission in Support of Neither Party, Sosa v. Alvarez-Machain, 542 U.S. 692 (2004) (No. 03-339).

[319] *Id.* at 5.

[320] Paul Hoffman argued on behalf of Alvarez-Machain. Carter Phillips argued on behalf of Sosa. The United States was represented by Deputy Solicitor General Paul Clement. *See generally* Charles Lane, *Court Hears Cases on Agents' Actions Abroad*, WASH. POST, Mar. 31, 2004, at A6; Linda Greenhouse, *Justices Hear Case About Foreigners' Use of Federal Courts*, N.Y. TIMES, Mar. 31, 2004, at A16; Warren Richey, *When Can Foreigners Sue in U.S. Courts?*, CHRISTIAN SCI. MONITOR, Mar. 30, 2004, at 2.

[321] The Court was unanimous in finding that Alvarez-Machain could not pursue his claim for arbitrary detention. It split 6-3, however, on the status of the ATS.

that the ATS is a jurisdictional statute and does not provide an independent cause of action for violations of international law.[322] The Court found that the historical record did not support the assertion that the ATS created a cause of action.[323] This did not end the Court's analysis, however. While the ATS was a jurisdictional statute, the Court went on to find that the historical record did support the proposition that the ATS would allow some actions to proceed through the power of the federal courts to recognize certain claims under the common law.

> First, there is every reason to suppose that the First Congress did not pass the ATS as a jurisdictional convenience to be placed on the shelf for use by a future Congress or state legislature that might, some day, authorize the creation of causes of action or itself decide to make some element of the law of nations actionable for the benefit of foreigners. The anxieties of the preconstitutional period cannot be ignored easily enough to think that the statute was not meant to have a practical effect. . . . There is too much in the historical record to believe that Congress would have enacted the ATS only to leave it lying fallow indefinitely.

> The second inference to be drawn from the history is that Congress intended the ATS to furnish jurisdiction for a relatively modest set of actions alleging violations of the law of nations.[324]

According to the Court, the First Congress would have considered the law of nations a part of the common law. The First Congress would also have recognized the power of the federal courts to "recognize private causes of action for certain torts in violation of the law of nations."[325] This

---

[322] With respect to Alvarez-Machain's claim against the United States under the Federal Tort Claims Act, the Court held that he was not entitled to relief. "We hold that the FTCA's foreign country exception bars all claims based on any injury suffered in a foreign country, regardless of where the tortuous act or omission occurred." Sosa v. Alvarez-Machain, 542 U.S. 692, 712 (2004).

[323] *Id.* at 713 ("As enacted in 1789, the ATS gave the district courts 'cognizance' of certain causes of action, and the term bespoke a grant of jurisdiction, not power to mold substantive law. The fact that the ATS was placed in § 9 of the Judiciary Act, a statute otherwise exclusively concerned with federal-court jurisdiction, is itself support for its strictly jurisdictional nature. Nor would the distinction between jurisdiction and cause of action have been elided by the drafters of the Act or those who voted on it."). *See generally* William Casto, *The Federal Courts' Protective Jurisdiction over Torts Committed in Violation of the Law of Nations*, 18 CONN. L. REV. 467 (1986). *Cf.* William S. Dodge, *The Constitutionality of the Alien Tort Statute: Some Observations on Text and Context*, 42 VA. J. INT'L L. 687 (2002).

[324] Sosa v. Alvarez-Machain, 542 U.S. 692, 719 (2004).

[325] *Id.* at 724.

principle was established at the time of the First Judiciary Act and continued in force when the Second Circuit issued its ruling in *Filartiga.*[326]

> [N]o development in the two centuries from the enactment of §
> 1350 to the birth of the modern line of cases beginning with
> *Filartiga v. Pena-Irala,* has categorically precluded federal courts
> from recognizing a claim under the law of nations as an element
> of common law; Congress has not in any relevant way amended §
> 1350 or limited civil common law power by another statute.[327]

Not all claims alleging violations of international law are actionable under the common law, however. To determine whether violations of international law are actionable under the Alien Tort Statute the Court indicated that such claims must "rest on a norm of international character accepted by the civilized world and defined with a specificity comparable to the features of the 18th-century paradigms we have recognized."[328] Indeed, "federal courts should not recognize private claims under federal common law for violations of any international law norm with less definite content and acceptance among civilized nations than the historical paradigms familiar when § 1350 was enacted."[329] According to the Court, the three historical paradigms that were probably considered by the ATS drafters were: violation of safe conduct, infringement of the rights of ambassadors, and piracy.[330]

To recognize private claims under the law of nations, therefore, *Sosa* requires the existence of international norms that are clear and accepted by the international community. In fact, this cautious approach "is gener-

---

[326] As the Court noted, "[t]he position we take today has been assumed by some federal courts for 24 years, ever since the Second Circuit decided *Filartiga* v. *Pena-Irala,* and for practical purposes the point of today's disagreement has been focused since the exchange between Judge Edwards and Judge Bork in *Tel-Oren* v. *Libyan Arab Republic,* Congress, however, has not only expressed no disagreement with our view of the proper exercise of the judicial power, but has responded to its most notable instance by enacting legislation supplementing the judicial determination in some detail." *Id.* at 731 (citations omitted).

[327] *Id.* at 724–25 (citations omitted).

[328] *Id.* at 725.

[329] *Id.* at 732.

[330] *Id.* at 724. *See also* 4 William Blackstone, *Commentaries on the Laws of England* 68 (1769). *But see* Eugene Kontorovich, *Implementing Sosa v. Alvarez-Machain: What Piracy Reveals About the Limits of the Alien Tort Statute,* 80 NOTRE DAME L. REV. 111 (2004); Eugene Kontorovich, *The Piracy Analogy: Modern Universal Jurisdiction's Hollow Foundation,* 45 HARV. INT'L L.J. 183 (2004).

ally consistent with the reasoning of many of the courts and judges who faced the issue before it reached" the Supreme Court.[331] Significantly, the Court cited *Filartiga* and its analysis of torture as an example of how this standard should be applied.[332]

In addition to requiring the existence of a norm that is clear and accepted by the international community, the Court noted that other factors might also serve as limiting principles in ATS litigation. For example, the Court suggested that the exhaustion of remedies in other domestic legal systems and even international tribunals may be appropriate.[333] The Court also indicated the possible application of "a policy of case-specific deference to the political branches."[334] Finally, the Court noted that some international norms may not apply to all defendants. Thus, it may be necessary to consider "whether international law extends the scope of liability for a violation of a given norm to the perpetrator being sued, if the defendant is a private actor such as a corporation or an individual."[335]

While acknowledging that courts could recognize certain private claims under the law of nations, the Supreme Court indicated such cases should proceed with caution. It then offered five reasons why federal courts should be cautious when formulating common law principles and creating private rights of action.

> First, the prevailing conception of the common law has changed since 1789 in a way that counsels restraint in judicially applying internationally generated norms. . . . Second, along with, and in part driven by, that conceptual development in understanding

---

[331] Sosa v. Alvarez-Machain, 542 U.S. 692, 732 (2004).

[332] In addition to *Filartiga v. Pena-Irala*, the Supreme Court also cited *In re Estate of Marcos Human Rights Litigation* and Judge Edwards' concurring opinion in *Tel-Oren v. Libyan Arab Republic* as examples of how courts should apply this standard.

[333] Sosa v. Alvarez-Machain, 542 U.S. 692, 733 (2004). In support, the Court referenced the exhaustion requirement set forth in the Torture Victim Protection Act.

[334] *Id.* The Court offered the example of the pending litigation involving human rights abuses perpetrated in South Africa during the apartheid era. *See In re South African Apartheid Litigation*, 238 F. Supp. 2d 1379 (S.D.N.Y. 2002). In these cases, both South Africa and the United States had submitted statements expressing their concerns with the litigation. "In such cases, there is a strong argument that federal courts should give serious weight to the Executive Branch's view of the case's impact on foreign policy." Sosa v. Alvarez-Machain, 542 U.S. 692, 733 (2004).

[335] Sosa v. Alvarez-Machain, 542 U.S. 692, 732 (2004) (citing Tel-Oren v. Libyan Arab Republic, 726 F.2d 774, 791–95 (D.C. Cir. 1984) and Kadic v. Karadzic, 70 F.3d 232, 239–41 (2d Cir. 1996)).

common law has come an equally significant rethinking of the role of the federal courts in making it. . . . Third, this Court has recently and repeatedly said that a decision to create a private right of action is one better left to legislative judgment in the great majority of cases. . . . While the absence of congressional action addressing private rights of action under an international norm is more equivocal than its failure to provide such a right when it creates a statute, the possible collateral consequences of making international rules privately actionable argue for judicial caution. Fourth, the subject of those collateral consequences is itself a reason for a high bar to new private causes of action for violating international law, for the potential implications for the foreign relations of the United States of recognizing such causes should make courts particularly wary of impinging on the discretion of the Legislative and Executive Branches in managing foreign affairs. . . . The fifth reason is particularly important in light of the first four. We have no congressional mandate to seek out and define new and debatable violations of the law of nations, and modern indications of congressional understanding of the judicial role in the field have not affirmatively encouraged greater judicial creativity.[336]

For these reasons, the Court recognized that federal courts could formulate private rights of action under the ATS but that such power compels judicial restraint and "the understanding that the door is still ajar subject to vigilant doorkeeping."[337] Because of these concerns, the Court added that the power to establish private rights of action is best exercised by the legislative branches in most cases.

> While we agree with Justice Scalia to the point that we would welcome any congressional guidance in exercising jurisdiction with such obvious potential to affect foreign relations, nothing Congress has done is a reason for us to shut the door to the law of nations entirely. It is enough to say that Congress may do that at any time (explicitly, or implicitly by treaties or statutes that occupy

---

[336] Sosa v. Alvarez-Machain, 542 U.S. 692, 725–28 (2004).

[337] *Id.* at 729. Unlike Justice Scalia, the Court did not believe that prudential considerations should divest federal courts of their power to recognize actionable international norms, particularly in light of the historical record. "For two centuries we have affirmed that the domestic law of the United States recognizes the law of nations. It would take some explaining to say now that federal courts must avert their gaze entirely from any international norm intended to protect individuals." *Id.* at 729–30 (citations omitted).

the field) just as it may modify or cancel any judicial decision so far as it rests on recognizing an international norm as such.[338]

Applying the foregoing analysis, the Court then held that Alvarez-Machain's allegations of arbitrary detention failed to meet the requisite standards for ATS litigation. The Court found that neither the Universal Declaration of Human Rights nor the International Covenant on Civil and Political Rights endowed Alvarez-Machain with judicially enforceable rights. The Universal Declaration was a U.N. General Assembly resolution and not a treaty and, therefore, it did not create international obligations. While the United States had ratified the International Covenant on Civil and Political Rights, the treaty was not self-executing "and so did not itself create obligations enforceable in the federal courts."[339] The Court also rejected Alvarez-Machain's efforts to pursue his claim under customary international law. In particular, the Court rejected Alvarez-Machain's claim that "officially sanctioned action exceeding positive authorization" constitutes a violation of customary international law, particularly when such action involves a relatively brief detention.[340] "It is enough to hold that a single illegal detention of less than a day, followed by the transfer of custody to lawful authorities and a prompt arraignment, violates no norm of customary international law so well defined as to support the creation of a federal remedy."[341] Thus, the Court did not hold that all claims of arbitrary detention were impermissible under the ATS. Rather, the Court implied that it was Alvarez-Machain's specific claim of arbitrary detention that failed. For these reasons, the Court reversed the Ninth Circuit's decision.

In a concurring opinion, Justice Scalia, joined by Justice Thomas and Chief Justice Rehnquist, accepted most of the majority opinion but criticized it for extending federal common law-making powers to the federal courts through the Alien Tort Statute.[342] Such an extension of judicial power was neither authorized nor appropriate: "In Benthamite terms, creating a federal command (federal common law) out of 'international norms,' and then constructing a cause of action to enforce that command through the purely jurisdictional grant of the ATS, is nonsense upon

---

[338] *Id.* at 731.

[339] *Id.* at 735.

[340] *Id.* at 736.

[341] *Id.* at 738.

[342] Justice Scalia joined Parts I, II, and III of the Court's opinion but declined to join Part IV, which addressed the power of the federal courts to recognize causes of action under the ATS.

stilts."[343] Justice Scalia found it inconsistent that the majority would allow federal courts the power to formulate common law principles and create private rights of action and yet express serious reservations about such a development. Finally, Justice Scalia expressed concern about the law-making role granted to federal courts through ATS litigation: "For over two decades now, unelected federal judges have been usurping this lawmaking power by converting what they regard as norms of international law into American law."[344] Allowing federal courts to identify and apply international norms through ATS litigation would perpetuate this trend at the expense of democratic principles.

In a separate concurring opinion, Justice Breyer agreed with the majority opinion, recognizing the legitimacy of ATS litigation for norms with definite content and widespread acceptance. He acknowledged that there were some limitations on ATS litigation, however, including an exhaustion of domestic remedies requirement and the need to defer to Executive Branch views regarding the foreign policy implications of such litigation. He also recognized that Congress could act to limit ATS litigation, "through a direct or indirect command or by occupying the field."[345] Justice Breyer suggested that principles of comity might place additional restrictions on ATS litigation.

> Since enforcement of an international norm by one nation's courts implies that other nations' courts may do the same, I would ask whether the exercise of jurisdiction under the ATS is consistent with those notions of comity that lead each nation to respect the sovereign rights of other nations by limiting the reach of its laws and their enforcement. In applying those principles, courts help assure that "the potentially conflicting laws of different nations" will "work together in harmony," a matter of increasing importance in an ever more interdependent world. Such consideration is necessary to ensure that ATS litigation does not undermine the very harmony that it was intended to promote.[346]

On remand, the district court entered judgment for Sosa, thereby ending the 11-year odyssey of the litigation.[347]

---

[343] Sosa v. Alvarez-Machain, 542 U.S. 692, 743 (2004) (Scalia, J., concurring in part and concurring in the judgment).

[344] *Id.* at 750.

[345] *Id.* at 760 (Breyer, J., concurring in part and concurring in the judgment).

[346] *Id.* at 761 (citations omitted).

[347] Alvarez-Machain v. United States, 2004 U.S. Dist. LEXIS 28528 (C.D. Cal. 2004).

The *Sosa* decision is viewed as a success by both advocates and critics of ATS litigation.[348] Advocates of ATS litigation view the decision as an affirmation of the *Filartiga* precedent. They argue that the Supreme Court's decision rejected the assertion that policy considerations should compel dismissal of all ATS litigation. In contrast, critics of ATS litigation assert that the decision would make it harder to bring ATS lawsuits. They argue that the Supreme Court's decision instructed courts to carefully consider the foreign policy implications of these cases and that such rigorous review would result in the dismissal of most cases. In practice, the long-term implications of the *Sosa* decision are difficult to measure. Since the decision was released, some cases have been dismissed for their failure to meet the *Sosa* standards.[349] Other cases have been allowed to proceed.[350]

Four months after the *Sosa* decision, Senator Dianne Feinstein introduced a legislative proposal in Congress to restructure the ATS. Senate Bill 1874 was drafted in response to *Sosa* and would have placed significant restrictions on ATS litigation. According to Senator Feinstein, "courts are essentially adrift in terms of being able to pinpoint the underlying meaning, scope and intent of the Alien Tort Statute. I hope this legislation will settle the questions that surround this 200-year-old law by providing a reasonable legal means that both plaintiffs and defendants can rely on to liti-

---

[348] *See, e.g.*, Lisa Girion, *Court OKs Foreign-Abuse Suits*, L.A. TIMES, June 30, 2004, at C1; Warren Richey, *Ruling Makes it Harder for Foreigners to Sue in U.S. Courts*, CHRISTIAN SCI. MONITOR, June 30, 2004, at 3; Robert S. Greenberger & Pui-Wing Tam, *Human Rights Suits Against U.S. Firms Curbed*, WALL ST. J., June 30, 2004, at A3; Reni Gertner, *Human Rights Claims Against Corporations May Go Forward*, LAW. WKLY. USA, July 19, 2004, at 1. The scholarly response was equally significant. *See generally* Igor Fuks, *Sosa v. Alvarez-Machain and the Future of ATCA Litigation*, 106 COLUM. L. REV. 112 (2006); Virginia Monken Gomez, *The Sosa Standard: What Does it Mean for Future ATS Litigation?*, 33 PEPP. L. REV. 469 (2006); Carolyn A. D'Amore, *Sosa v. Alvarez-Machain and the Alien Tort Statute: How Wide Has the Door to Human Rights Litigation Been Left Open?*, 39 AKRON L. REV. 593 (2006); John K. Setear, *A Forest with No Trees: The Supreme Court and International Law in the 2003 Term*, 91 VA. L. REV. 579 (2005); Ehren J. Brav, *Opening the Courtroom Doors to Non-Citizens: Cautiously Affirming Filartiga for the Alien Tort Statute*, 46 HARV. INT'L L.J. 265 (2005); Benjamin Berkowitz, *Sosa v. Alvarez-Machain: United States Courts as Forums for Human Rights Cases and the New Incorporation Debate*, 40 HARV. C.R.-C.L. L. REV. 289 (2005); Beth Stephens, *Sosa v. Alvarez-Machain: "The Door Is Still Ajar" For Human Rights Litigation in U.S. Courts*, 70 BROOK. L. REV. 533 (2004); Brad R. Roth, *International Decision: Sosa v. Alvarez-Machain*, 98 AM. J. INT'L L. 798 (2004).

[349] *See, e.g.*, Doe v. Exxon Mobil Corp., 393 F. Supp. 2d 20 (D.D.C. 2005); *In re* S. African Apartheid Litig., 346 F. Supp. 2d 538 (S.D.N.Y. 2004).

[350] *See, e.g.*, Jogi v. Voges, 425 F.3d 367 (7th Cir. 2005); Odilla Mutaka Mwani v. Bin Laden, 417 F.3d 1 (D.C. Cir. 2005).

gate their differences. It is time for Congress to bring clarity to the law and I believe this legislation does so."[351] Specifically, the bill would have limited ATS cases to six enumerated claims—torture, extrajudicial killing, genocide, piracy, slavery, or slave trading—but only if the defendant was a direct participant acting with specific intent to commit the alleged tort.[352] District courts would not have jurisdiction "if a foreign state is responsible for committing the tort in question within its sovereign territory."[353] Other provisions would have placed further restrictions on ATS litigation. For example, district courts would have been precluded from proceeding with ATS cases "if the President, or a designee of the President, adequately certifies to the court in writing that such exercise of jurisdiction will have a negative impact on the foreign policy interests of the United States."[354] Anonymous complaints would have been precluded except in narrow circumstances. Contingency fee arrangements would have been prohibited.[355] Not surprisingly, the announcement of the bill was met with strong criticism by the human rights community, which urged Congress to take no action on the proposed legislation.[356] Eight days after the bill was submitted, Senator Feinstein sent a letter to Senate Judiciary Chairman Arlen Specter asking that he not schedule a hearing on the proposal. In her letter, Senator Feinstein indicated "that the legislation in its present form calls for refinement in light of concerns raised by human rights advocates, and thus a hearing or other action by the Committee on this bill would be premature."[357]

Because it can expose public and private actors to civil liability for human rights abuses, the ATS and the *Filartiga* precedent will continue to generate controversy in the United States and abroad. Moreover, several issues remain unresolved despite the Supreme Court's decision in *Sosa v. Alvarez-Machain*. What norms give rise to actionable claims under the ATS? How should choice of law issues be resolved in these cases? Is there an exhaustion of remedies requirement? Can defendants be held liable under the ATS through theories of accomplice liability? How much deference

---

[351] 151 CONG. REC. S 11423, 11433 (Oct. 17, 2005) (statement of Senator Feinstein).

[352] S. 1874, 109th Cong. § 2(a) (2005).

[353] *Id.*

[354] *Id.* at § 2(e).

[355] *Id.* at § 2(f) and (g).

[356] *See generally* Eliza Strickland, *Was DiFi Batting for Big Oil?*, EAST BAY EXPRESS, Nov. 9, 2005, at 9; Press Release, Human Rights First, Human Rights First Welcomes Senator's About Face on Bill Limiting Human Rights Accountability (Nov. 3, 2005).

[357] Letter from Senator Dianne Feinstein, to Senator Arlen Specter (Oct. 25, 2005).

should be accorded to U.S. government filings on behalf of litigants in ATS cases? The possibility of congressional revisions to the Alien Tort Statute or even Supreme Court reconsideration of the *Filartiga* precedent will likely depend on how the federal courts address these remaining issues.[358]

---

[358] *See, e.g.,* Julian G. Ku, *The Third Wave: The Alien Tort Statute and the War on Terrorism,* 19 EMORY INT'L L. REV. 105 (2005); Ralph G. Steinhardt, *Laying One Bankrupt Critique to Rest: Sosa v. Alvarez-Machain and the Future of International Human Rights Litigation in U.S. Courts,* 57 VAND. L. REV. 2241 (2004).

CHAPTER 4
CONCLUSION

The establishment of the *Filartiga* precedent and the subsequent development of transnational litigation in the United States have not occurred without criticism. In a 1995 letter to the federal district court for the Southern District of New York, Radovan Karadzic expressed disdain for the ongoing litigation against him and announced he would no longer participate in the proceedings. His comments to the district court are representative of the many criticisms made about transnational litigation in the United States: "[c]an you really hope to find truth or do justice or protect rights for people in distant nations? Do you really believe that attaching a U.S. dollar sign to human tragedy around the world by empty judgments in uncontested lawsuits is a step toward peace or justice?"[1]

Karadzic is not alone in his criticism of transnational litigation.[2] Indeed, several challenges have been raised.[3]

---

[1] David Rohde, *Jury in New York Orders Bosnian Serb to Pay Billions*, N.Y. TIMES, Sept. 26, 2000, at A10.

[2] The debate on transnational litigation extends well beyond the *Filartiga* case. *See, e.g.*, NAOMI ROHT-ARRIAZA, THE PINOCHET EFFECT: TRANSNATIONAL JUSTICE IN THE AGE OF HUMAN RIGHTS 211 (2005); Beth Stephens, *Translating Filartiga: A Comparative and International Law Analysis of Domestic Remedies for International Human Rights Violations*, 27 YALE J. INT'L L. 1 (2002); William J. Aceves, *Liberalism and International Legal Scholarship: The Pinochet Case and the Move Toward a Universal System of Transnational Law Litigation*, 41 HARV. INT'L L.J. 129 (2000); Harold Hongju Koh, *Transnational Public Law Litigation*, 100 YALE L.J. 2372, 2364–68 (1991).

[3] *See, e.g.*, ROBERT H. BORK, COERCING VIRTUE: THE WORLDWIDE RULE OF JUDGES 25 (2003) ("These suits do not really seek recompense; rather, they aspire to make a propaganda point appear more morally compelling by the decision of a U.S. court."); JEREMY RABKIN, WHY SOVEREIGNTY MATTERS 52 (1998) ("Cases like *Filartiga* are no longer about providing a remedy to a distinct victim under well-established law. They can promise little more than moral satisfaction to the actual victims, since the perpetrators of human rights abuses in other countries are typically beyond the actual reach of U.S. courts. . . . The ultimate target is not the practice of other countries but the policy of the United States."). *See also* GARY CLYDE HUFBAUER & NICHOLAS K. MITROKOSTAS, AWAKENING MONSTER: THE ALIEN TORT STATUTE OF 1789 (2003); Curtis A. Bradley, *The Costs of International Human Rights Litigation*, 2 CHI. J. INT'L L. 457 (2001); William Glaberson, *U.S. Courts Become Arbiters of Global Rights and Wrongs*, N.Y. TIMES, June 21, 2001, at A1. These criticisms of the ATS are part of a broader challenge against the principle of universal jurisdiction. *See, e.g.*, HENRY KISSINGER, DOES AMERICA NEED A FOREIGN POLICY? TOWARD A DIPLOMACY FOR THE 21ST CENTURY 273–82 (2001).

One criticism of transnational litigation is that these lawsuits could affect U.S. foreign policy.[4] Certainly, lawsuits alleging human rights violations in foreign countries can raise sensitive diplomatic issues. For example, some lawsuits allege foreign government complicity in human rights atrocities. Some of these lawsuits even implicate the U.S. government. As a result, the United States has argued in several cases that continued adjudication of these cases could have an adverse impact on the conduct of U.S. foreign policy.[5] In arguments before the U.S. Supreme Court in *Sosa v. Alvarez-Machain*, the Bush administration took the position that transnational litigation "embroiled United States courts in difficult and politically sensitive disputes that, in many instances, are confined to foreign nations."[6] Indeed, "the mere filing of such litigation can raise serious international relations issues and difficulties for the governments of the foreign countries or officials involved in such suits, as well as the United States Government."[7] The United States has repeated this argument in other cases.[8]

While foreign policy concerns may arise in some cases, the federal courts have developed several approaches for addressing cases that implicate U.S. foreign policy interests. Courts can use doctrines of judicial abstention, including the political question doctrine or the act of state doctrine, to dismiss lawsuits that infringe on the constitutional powers of the President or Congress.[9] While these doctrines may not apply in all or even

---

4 *See* David B. Rivkin, Jr. & Lee Casey, *Crimes Outside the World's Jurisdiction*, N.Y. TIMES, July 22, 2003, at A19; Anne-Marie Slaughter & David Bosco, *Plaintiff's Diplomacy*, FOREIGN AFF., Sept.–Oct., 2000, at 102. *But see* Arlen Specter, *The Court of Last Resort*, N.Y. TIMES, Aug. 7, 2003, at A23.

5 *See, e.g.*, Sarei v. Rio Tinto PLC, 221 F. Supp. 2d 1116 (C.D. Cal. 2002). In *Sarei*, the United States submitted a Statement of Interest to the district court stating that "continued adjudication of this lawsuit 'would risk a potentially serious adverse impact on the [Bougainville] peace process, and hence on the conduct of [United States] foreign relations.'" *Id.* at 1181 (quoting U.S. Statement of Interest). On appeal, a three-judge panel of the Ninth Circuit Court of Appeals reversed the district court's dismissal of the lawsuit. Sarei v. Rio Tinto, PLC, 2006 U.S. App. LEXIS 21074 (9th Cir. 2006). The Ninth Circuit found that the U.S. Statement of Interest, while entitled to serious weight, did not control the judicial analysis.

6 Brief for the United States as Respondent Supporting Petitioner at 47, Sosa v. Alvarez-Machain, 542 U.S. 692 (2004) (No. 03-339).

7 *Id.* at 42.

8 *See* Brief for the United States of America as Amicus Curiae, Doe v. Unocal Corp., 403 F.3d 708 (9th Cir. 2003) (Nos. 00-56603).

9 *See, e.g.*, Tel-Oren v. Libyan Arab Republic, 726 F.2d 774, 823 (D.C. Cir. 1984) (Robb, J., concurring); Greenham Women Against Cruise Missiles v. Reagan, 591 F. Supp. 1332 (S.D.N.Y. 1984). *See generally* Julian Ku & John Yoo, *Beyond Formalism in Foreign Affairs: A Functional Approach to the Alien Tort Statute*, 2004 SUP. CT. REV. 153.

most ATS cases, U.S. courts can use them to address legitimate foreign policy concerns in appropriate cases. Indeed, the Supreme Court acknowledged the possibility of "case-specific deference to the political branches" in *Sosa v. Alvarez-Machain*.[10]

For example, the political question doctrine allows courts to dismiss lawsuits that require them to consider matters that extend beyond the recognized realm of judicial competence.[11] According to the Supreme Court, the political question doctrine incorporates three elements: "(i) Does the issue involve resolution of questions committed by the text of the Constitution to a coordinate branch of Government? (ii) Would resolution of the question demand that a court move beyond areas of judicial expertise? (iii) Do prudential considerations counsel against judicial intervention?"[12] Several ATS cases have been dismissed, in whole or in part, based on the political question doctrine.[13] However, most courts have been cautious about using the political question doctrine to categorically dismiss ATS litigation. They have been mindful of disregarding their judicial responsibility even in cases involving foreign affairs absent serious concerns that rise to the level of constitutional significance. As the Supreme Court set forth in *Baker v. Carr*, not all questions touching foreign relations are political questions, and "it is error to suppose that every case or controversy which touches foreign relations lies beyond judicial cognizance."[14] Efforts to adopt a blanket political question doctrine exception that would apply to all ATS litigation are, therefore, misplaced.[15] A more measured case-by-case approach is appropriate. The Supreme Court acknowledged such an approach in *Sosa v. Alvarez-Machain*, when it found that the door remained ajar to ATS litigation but that such cases were subject to vigilant doorkeeping.[16]

---

[10] Sosa v. Alvarez-Machain, 542 U.S. 692, 733 (2004).

[11] *See generally* Jack L. Goldsmith, *The New Formalism in United States Foreign Relations Law*, 70 U. COLO. L. REV. 1395 (1999); Anne-Marie Slaughter (Burley), *Are Foreign Affairs Different?*, 106 HARV. L. REV. 1980 (1993); THOMAS M. FRANCK, POLITICAL QUESTIONS/JUDICIAL ANSWERS (1992); Michael J. Glennon, *Foreign Affairs and the Political Question Doctrine*, 83 AM. J. INT'L L. 814 (1989).

[12] Goldwater v. Carter, 444 U.S. 996, 998 (1979) (Powell, J., concurring).

[13] *See, e.g.*, Joo v. Japan, 413 F.3d 45 (D.C. Cir. 2005); Iwanowa v. Ford Motor Co., 67 F. Supp. 2d 424 (D.N.J. 1999).

[14] Baker v. Carr, 369 U.S. 186, 211 (1962).

[15] *See* K. Lee Boyd, *Are Human Rights Political Questions?*, 53 RUTGERS L. REV. 277 (2001); Michael Glennon, *Foreign Affairs and the Political Question Doctrine*, 83 AM. J. INT'L L. 814 (1989); Louis Henkin, *Lexical Priority or "Political Question": A Response*, 101 HARV. L. REV. 524 (1987).

[16] Sosa v. Alvarez-Machain, 542 U.S. 692, 729 (2004).

Likewise, the act of state doctrine provides that courts should refrain from judging the acts of a foreign state when such acts are committed within that state's territory.[17] The Supreme Court has indicated that the act of state doctrine has constitutional underpinnings founded on separation of powers concerns.[18] It applies when U.S. courts must declare invalid "and thus ineffective as 'a rule of decision for the courts of this country,' the official act of a foreign sovereign."[19] While available, the act of state doctrine may not always apply in ATS cases. It is inapplicable, for example, in cases that involve an unambiguous international agreement regarding controlling legal principles.[20] Several federal courts have indicated that ATS cases often involve such principles.[21] Thus, it "would be a rare case in which the act of state doctrine precluded suit under section 1350."[22]

A separation of powers argument also counsels against summary dismissal of ATS cases on judicial abstention grounds. Through the adoption of the ATS and related mechanisms, Congress has indicated that the violation of international human rights norms is "our business" and that perpetrators of these atrocities should be held accountable.[23] Indeed, Congress placed its imprimatur on the *Filartiga* precedent and the ATS when it adopted the TVPA in 1992.[24] It would be inconsistent with this congressional mandate to dismiss ATS litigation (and other cases of transnational litigation) without careful analysis and a firm belief that such

---

[17] Banco Nacional de Cuba v. Sabbatino, 376 U.S. 398 (1964).

[18] W.S. Kirkpatrick v. Environmental Tectonics, 493 U.S. 400, 404 (1990).

[19] *Id.* at 405 (citing Ricaud v. Am. Metal Co., 246 U.S. 304, 310 (1918)).

[20] Banco Nacional de Cuba v. Sabbatino, 376 U.S. at 428.

[21] *See* Mujica v. Occidental Petroleum Corp., 381 F. Supp. 2d 1164, 1190 (C.D. Cal. 2005); Presbyterian Church of Sudan v. Talisman Energy, Inc., 244 F. Supp. 2d 289, 345 (S.D.N.Y. 2003).

[22] Kadic v. Karadzic, 70 F.3d 232, 250 (2d Cir. 1995).

[23] *See* Wiwa v. Royal Dutch Petroleum Co., 226 F.3d 88, 106 (2d Cir. 2000) ("The new formulations of the Torture Victim Protection Act convey the message that torture committed under color of law of a foreign nation in violation of international law is 'our business,' as such conduct not only violates the standards of international law but also as a consequence violates our domestic law."). *Cf.* WALTER RUSSELL MEAD, SPECIAL PROVIDENCE: AMERICAN FOREIGN POLICY AND HOW IT CHANGED THE WORLD (2001).

[24] H.R. REP. NO. 102-367, pt. 1, at 4 (1991); S. REP. NO. 102-249, at 4 (1991). *See also* Wiwa v. Royal Dutch Petroleum Co., 226 F.3d 88, 104 (2d Cir. 2000); Abebe-Jira v. Negewo, 72 F.3d 844, 848 (11th Cir. 1996); Hilao v. Marcos, 25 F.3d 1467, 1475–76 (9th Cir. 1994); Tel-Oren v. Libyan Arab Republic, 726 F.2d 774, 797 (D.C. Cir. 1984) (Edwards, J., concurring) ("[I]n implementing section 1350, courts merely carry out the existing view of the legislature that federal courts should entertain certain actions that implicate the law of nations.").

litigation adversely affects U.S. foreign policy and infringes on the constitutional separation of powers.

If a foreign government has a functioning legal system capable of addressing transnational claims in a fair and efficient manner, U.S. courts may also use the doctrine of *forum non conveniens* to dismiss these lawsuits.[25] The Carter administration alluded to this option in its amicus submission in *Filartiga*.[26] The Supreme Court appeared to recognize this option in *Sosa* by suggesting the applicability of an exhaustion of domestic remedies requirement for ATS litigation.[27] Of course, U.S. courts should not take such drastic action in the absence of compelling evidence that foreign governments have the ability and inclination to punish serious violations of international law. U.S. courts should be particularly wary of *forum non conveniens* claims when the alternate forum is a country that has a history of promoting impunity.

A second criticism of transnational litigation is that it constitutes judicial imperialism. This challenge asserts that the United States is improperly intervening in the affairs of other countries and seeking to extend its own values to these countries through ATS litigation.[28] Such criticisms, however, are misplaced.

For example, only foreign nationals can bring lawsuits under the Alien Tort Statute. It is difficult to characterize Joel and Dolly Filártiga as evinc-

---

[25] *See* Aric K. Short, *Is the Alien Tort Statute Sacrosanct? Retaining Forum Non Conveniens in Human Rights Litigation,* 33 N.Y.U. J. INT'L L. & POL. 1001 (2001). *But see* Kathryn Lee Boyd, *The Inconvenience of Victims: Abolishing Forum Non Conveniens in Human Rights Litigation,* 39 VA. J. INT'L L. 41 (1998).

[26] Memorandum for the United States as Amicus Curiae at 25, Filartiga v. Pena-Irala, 630 F.2d 876 (2d Cir. 1980) (No. 79 C 917).

[27] Sosa v. Alvarez-Machain, 542 U.S. 692, 733 (2004).

[28] *See, e.g.,* M.O. Chibundu, *Making Customary International Law Through Municipal Adjudication: A Structural Inquiry,* 39 VA. J. INT'L L. 1069, 1148–49 (1999) ("[W]hen domestic courts insist that all disputes must be resolved under our laws and in our courts, they do not only evince morally deplorable parochialism, but consequentially, they retard the cross-cultural convergence and internalization of the very human rights norms that they assert as uniformly applicable to the global community."); Slaughter & Bosco, *supra* note 4, at 115 ("[T]he expansion of plaintiffs' power in U.S. courts looks quite different from the perspective of other countries. . . . [T]he successful lawsuits against the Cuban and Iranian governments, Swiss banks, and German corporations suggest that the world's sole superpower is arming itself with superpower courts. This picture understandably may threaten those uncomfortable with U.S. hegemony."). Even Judge Kaufman, who wrote the majority opinion in *Filartiga,* acknowledged that ATS litigation could be subject to a judicial imperialism claim. *See* Irving R. Kaufman, *A Legal Remedy for International Torture?,* N.Y. TIMES MAG., Nov. 9, 1980, at 44.

ing imperialist motives when they filed their civil lawsuit. They sued Peña-Irala so they could hold him accountable for Joelito's death. Victims from other countries are similarly situated. While U.S. citizens can pursue transnational litigation through the Torture Victim Protection Act and other statutes, they are also motivated to find justice through accountability. The victim-centered approach of transnational litigation undermines claims of imperialist bias because victims (and not states) are the principal advocates. While victims may seek political change and the promotion of human rights abroad, their interests are distinct from, and at times contrary to, the interests of the United States.

More significantly, transnational litigation has a strong foundation in international law, which further undermines claims of imperialist bias. For example, the International Covenant on Civil and Political Rights provides that any person whose rights are violated is entitled to an effective remedy.[29] The Convention against Torture and Other Cruel, Inhuman or Degrading Treatment or Punishment requires member states to provide torture victims with redress and an enforceable right to fair and adequate compensation.[30] There are 155 states parties to the International Covenant on Civil and Political Rights and 141 states parties to the Convention against Torture.[31] Customary international law also recognizes the obligation of states to provide remedies to victims of human rights abuses. Thus, states shall, "with respect to claims by victims, enforce domestic judgments for reparation against individuals or entities liable for the harm suffered and endeavor to enforce valid foreign legal judgments for reparation in accordance with domestic law and international legal obligations. To that end, states should provide under their domestic laws effective mechanisms for the enforcement of reparation judgments."[32]

Transnational litigation also finds support in the principle of universal jurisdiction, which authorizes the assertion of state jurisdiction even in the absence of an explicit relationship between the state and the perpetrator

---

[29] International Covenant on Civil and Political Rights, art. 3, Mar. 23, 1976, 999 U.N.T.S. 171.

[30] Convention against Torture and Other Cruel, Inhuman or Degrading Treatment or Punishment, art. 14, Dec. 10, 1984, 1465 U.N.T.S. 85.

[31] These statistics were compiled on July 1, 2006.

[32] U.N. General Assembly, Basic Principles and Guidelines on the Right to a Remedy and Reparation for Victims of Gross Violations of International Human Rights Law and Serious Violations of International Humanitarian Law, U.N. Doc. A/C.3/60/L.24 (2005), at para. 17. *See also* ILARIA BOTTIGLIERO, REDRESS FOR VICTIMS OF CRIMES UNDER INTERNATIONAL LAW (2004); RESTATEMENT (THIRD) OF THE FOREIGN RELATIONS LAW OF THE UNITED STATES § 404 (1987).

or the victim.[33] Universal jurisdiction is premised upon the notion that certain violations of international law are condemned by all states. Accordingly, all states have the authority and, in some cases, the obligation to punish such acts regardless of where they took place. The principle of universal jurisdiction is well established in criminal proceedings and now extends to civil proceedings.[34] It is codified in several treaties and is recognized under customary international law.[35] Justice Breyer discussed the role of universal jurisdiction in ATS litigation in his concurring opinion in *Sosa v. Alvarez-Machain*.

> Today international law will sometimes similarly reflect not only substantive agreement as to certain universally condemned behavior but also procedural agreement that universal jurisdiction exists to prosecute a subset of that behavior. That subset includes torture, genocide, crimes against humanity, and war crimes.

> The fact that this procedural consensus exists suggests that recognition of universal jurisdiction in respect to a limited set of norms is consistent with principles of international comity. That is, allowing every nation's courts to adjudicate foreign conduct involving foreign parties in such cases will not significantly threaten the practical harmony that comity principles seek to protect. That con-

---

[33] *See generally* Cedric Ryngaert, *Universal Criminal Jurisdiction Over Torture*, 23 NETHERLANDS Q. HUM. RTS. 571 (2005); UNIVERSAL JURISDICTION: NATIONAL COURTS AND THE PROSECUTION OF SERIOUS CRIMES UNDER INTERNATIONAL LAW (Stephen Macedo ed., 2003); LUC REYDAMS, UNIVERSAL JURISDICTION: INTERNATIONAL AND MUNICIPAL LEGAL PERSPECTIVES (2003); M. Cherif Bassiouni, *Universal Jurisdiction for International Crimes: Historical Perspectives and Contemporary Practice*, 42 VA. J. INT'L L. 81 (2001).

[34] *See generally* Donald Francis Donovan & Anthea Roberts, *The Emerging Recognition of Universal Civil Jurisdiction*, 100 AM. J. INT'L L. 142 (2006); Beth Van Schaack, *In Defense of Civil Redress: The Domestic Enforcement of Human Rights Norms in the Context of the Proposed Hague Judgments Convention*, 42 HARV. INT'L L.J. 141, 159–65 (2001); Curtis A. Bradley, *Universal Jurisdiction and U.S. Law*, 2001 U. CHI. LEGAL F. 323; David Bederman et al., *The Enforcement of Human Rights and Humanitarian Law by Civil Suits in Municipal Courts: The Civil Dimension of Universal Jurisdiction, in* CONTEMPORARY INTERNATIONAL LAW ISSUES: NEW FORMS, NEW APPLICATIONS 156 (Wybo P. Heere ed., 1998).

[35] *See* Convention against Torture, *supra* note 30, at arts. 5, 7; International Convention against the Taking of Hostages, Dec. 17, 1979, art. 5, T.I.A.S. No. 11,081, 1316 U.N.T.S. 205; Convention on the Prevention and Punishment of Crimes Against Internationally Protected Persons, Including Diplomatic Agents, Dec. 14, 1973, art. 3, T.I.A.S. No. 8532, 1035 U.N.T.S. 167; Convention for the Suppression of Unlawful Acts against the Safety of Civil Aviation, Sept. 23, 1971, art. 5, 564 T.I.A.S. No. 564, 974 U.N.T.S. 177; Convention for the Suppression of Unlawful Seizure of Aircraft, Dec. 16, 1970, art. 4, T.I.A.S. No. 7192, 860 U.N.T.S. 105; Geneva Convention Relative to the Treatment of Prisoners of War, Aug. 12, 1949, art. 129, 75 U.N.T.S. 135, 6 U.S.T. 3316.

sensus concerns criminal jurisdiction, but consensus as to universal criminal jurisdiction itself suggests that universal tort jurisdiction would be no more threatening. That is because the criminal courts of many nations combine civil and criminal proceedings, allowing those injured by criminal conduct to be represented, and to recover damages, in the criminal proceeding itself. Thus, universal criminal jurisdiction necessarily contemplates a significant degree of civil tort recovery as well.[36]

Claims of judicial imperialism are even less meaningful when made by countries that have accepted treaties authorizing remedies for victims of human rights abuses or treaties that authorize the assertion of universal jurisdiction for these abuses. Many of the countries where atrocities have occurred have ratified the International Covenant on Civil and Political Rights and the Convention against Torture, treaties that establish a state's obligation to provide reparations for victims of human rights violations. The Convention against Torture also establishes universal jurisdiction for acts of torture, albeit in the criminal context. But even if states have not ratified these treaties, they typically acknowledge the wrongfulness of torture and other human rights abuses in their domestic legislation. In *Filartiga*, for example, the Second Circuit acknowledged that Paraguay had prohibited torture and other cruel treatment in its national constitution.[37]

A related criticism of transnational litigation is that violations of international law should be addressed at the international level and not through domestic litigation. Some commentators have argued that international proceedings are generally preferable to domestic litigation in cases of serious human rights abuses. Because these abuses often implicate state actors, they argue it should be the responsibility of the international community to respond.[38] An international response would also be appropriate because human rights abuses violate international norms.

---

[36] Sosa v. Alvarez-Machain, 542 U.S. 692, 762–63 (2004) (Breyer, J., concurring) (citations omitted).

[37] Filartiga v. Pena-Irala, 630 F.2d 876, 884 (2d Cir. 1980). The Second Circuit noted "[t]he fact that the prohibition of torture is often honored in the breach does not diminish its binding effect as a norm of international law." *Id.* In support, the court then cited the work of J.L. Brierly, who indicated that "[t]he best evidence for the existence of international law is that every actual State recognizes that it does exist and that it is itself under an obligation to observe it. States often violate international law, just as individuals often violate municipal law; but no more than individuals do States defend their violations by claiming that they are above the law." *Id.* (quoting J.L. BRIERLY, THE OUTLOOK FOR INTERNATIONAL LAW 4–5 (1944)). *See also* Sosa v. Alvarez-Machain, 542 U.S. 692, 738 (2004) ("It is not that violations of a rule logically foreclose the existence of that rule as international law.").

[38] *See, e.g.,* Saul Mendlovitz & John Fousek, *The Prevention and Punishment of the Crime*

Despite their prominence, however, international tribunals are seldom given exclusive jurisdiction to redress violations of international law. And some international tribunals are designed to function in cooperation with domestic tribunals. The Rome Statute of the International Criminal Court, for example, is based on the principle of complementarity, which evinces a preference for domestic prosecution. Complementarity is a central feature of the Rome Statute and was a critical issue during the negotiating process for the Statute.[39] Thus, a case is considered inadmissible by the International Criminal Court if the case is being investigated or prosecuted by a state that has jurisdiction.[40] Other international tribunals, such as the International Criminal Tribunals for the former Yugoslavia or Rwanda, have even greater restrictions on their jurisdiction.

Alternatively, it is argued that violations of international law should only be punished in the country where these acts occurred.[41] For example, the Genocide Convention authorizes prosecution for acts of genocide by an international penal tribunal or a tribunal in the state where such acts were committed.[42] It does not explicitly authorize universal jurisdiction or even civil remedies in third countries. The only country authorized to prosecute acts of genocide is the country where the acts were committed. The Convention against Torture, which does authorize universal jurisdiction for

---

of Genocide, in GENOCIDE, WAR, AND HUMAN SURVIVAL 137, 141–42 (Charles B. Strozier & Michael Flynn eds., 1996); Farooq Hassan, *A Conflict of Philosophies: The Filartiga Jurisprudence*, 32 INT'L & COMP. L.Q. 250 (1983).

[39] For commentary on the relationship between national and international tribunals, see LEILA NADYA SADAT, THE INTERNATIONAL CRIMINAL COURT AND THE TRANSFORMATION OF INTERNATIONAL LAW: JUSTICE FOR THE NEW MILLENNIUM 119 (2002); Mahnoush H. Arsanjani, *The Rome Statute of the International Criminal Court*, 93 AM. J. INT'L L. 22 (1999); Richard Dicker & Helen Duffy, *National Courts and the ICC*, 6 BROWN J. WORLD AFF. 53 (1999); Bartram S. Brown, *Primacy or Complementarity: Reconciling the Jurisdiction of National Courts and International Criminal Tribunals*, 23 YALE J. INT'L L. 383 (1998); LAWYERS COMMITTEE FOR HUMAN RIGHTS, PROSECUTING GENOCIDE IN RWANDA: THE ICTR AND NATIONAL TRIALS (1997).

[40] *See* Rome Statute of the International Criminal Court, art. 17(1), July 17, 1998, 2187 U.N.T.S. 90. *See generally* John T. Holmes, *Complementarity: National Courts versus the ICC, in* I THE ROME STATUTE OF THE INTERNATIONAL CRIMINAL COURT: A COMMENTARY 667 (Antonio Cassese et al. eds., 2002); COMMENTARY ON THE ROME STATUTE OF THE INTERNATIONAL CRIMINAL COURT 383–94 (Otto Triffterer ed., 1999).

[41] This concern was raised by Lord Lloyd in the first decision by the House of Lords in the Pinochet litigation. R v. Bow Street Metro. Stipendiary Magistrate, *ex parte* Pinochet Ugarte, 4 All E.R. 897, 934–35 (H.L. 1998) ("For an English court to investigate and pronounce on the validity of the amnesty in Chile would be to assert jurisdiction over the internal affairs of that state at the very time when the Supreme Court in Chile is itself performing the same task.").

[42] *See* Convention on the Prevention and Punishment of the Crime of Genocide, art. VI, Jan. 12, 1951, 78 U.N.T.S. 277.

torture, implies that acts of torture should first be prosecuted in the country where these acts were committed.[43]

While it may be preferable to punish crimes in the country where the acts occurred, such a preference should not preclude transnational litigation. In the context of traditional tort litigation, "domestic courts are increasingly less content (if they ever were) to allow national boundaries to frustrate the efficacy of the civil justice process."[44] This observation is equally applicable in the context of human rights litigation. The principle of transitory torts, which forms the jurisdictional basis for transnational litigation, is not a uniquely American legal principle.[45] As the Second Circuit indicated in *Filartiga v. Pena-Irala*, "[i]t is not extraordinary for a court to adjudicate a tort claim arising outside of its territorial jurisdiction. A state or nation has a legitimate interest in the orderly resolution of disputes among those within its borders, and where the *lex loci delicti commissi* is applied, it is an expression of comity to give effect to the laws of the state where the wrong occurred."[46]

There is, perhaps, an even more fundamental response to the argument that human rights violations should be resolved exclusively at the international level or in the countries where these atrocities were committed. Quite simply, these fora have yet to show they are fully capable of addressing these cases in an efficient and effective manner. The *ad hoc* international criminal tribunals have limited mandates, and political considerations continue to hamper their effectiveness. The International Criminal Court will undoubtedly face similar obstacles. In addition, countries where atrocities have been committed are generally unwilling or

---

[43] Convention against Torture, *supra* note 30, at art. 5. *See generally* J. HERMAN BURGERS & HANS DANELIUS, THE UNITED NATIONS CONVENTION AGAINST TORTURE: A HANDBOOK ON THE CONVENTION AGAINST TORTURE AND OTHER CRUEL, INHUMAN OR DEGRADING TREATMENT OR PUNISHMENT 130–33 (1988).

[44] Campbell McLachlan, *Transnational Tort Litigation: An Overview*, in TRANSNATIONAL TORT LITIGATION: JURISDICTIONAL PRINCIPLES 1, 2 (Campbell McLachlan & Peter Nygh eds., 1996). The doctrine of transitory torts has a long history in English and American jurisprudence. *See, e.g.*, McKenna v. Fisk, 42 U.S. (1 How.) 241 (1843); Mostyn v. Fabrigas, 1 Cowp. 161 (1774).

[45] *See, e.g.*, Jeffrey M. Blum & Ralph G. Steinhardt, *Federal Jurisdiction over International Human Rights Claims: The Alien Tort Claims Act After Filartiga v. Pena-Irala*, 22 HARV. INT'L L.J. 53, 63 (1981).

[46] Filartiga v. Pena-Irala, 630 F.2d 876, 885 (2d Cir. 1980). *See also* McKenna v. Fisk, 42 U.S. 241, 248 (1843); Dennick v. R.R. Co., 103 U.S. 11 (1881); Slater v. Mexican Nat'l R.R. Co., 194 U.S. 120 (1904).

unable to punish perpetrators. For these reasons, transnational litigation may offer the only effective response to human rights violations.[47]

Finally, transnational litigation has been criticized because it might upset the delicate balance within emerging democracies and deter the peaceful transition of authoritarian regimes.[48] For example, dictators may refuse to relinquish power if they fear foreign prosecution. Alternatively, forcing countries that have already experienced democratic transition to address past atrocities may threaten a fragile peace. This critique of transnational litigation suggests that efforts to punish perpetrators of abuse may not be appropriate in all cases.[49] The South African government made this point in *Khulumani v. Barclays Nat'l Bank Ltd.*, an ATS lawsuit filed by South African nationals against several multinational corporations that did business in South Africa during the apartheid era.

> In the context of the Government's fundamental commitment to broad programs of reconstruction and transformation, . . . South Africa has chosen a policy of promoting economic growth, including by encouraging business investment, both foreign and domestic, rather than demanding reparations or seeking punishment from corporations that may have profited from or cooperated with the apartheid regime. Further, it is the Government's view that these lit-

---

[47] *See* Beth Van Schaack, *With All Deliberate Speed: Civil Human Rights Litigation as a Tool for Social Change*, 57 VAND. L. REV. 2305 (2004); John F. Murphy, *Civil Liability for the Commission of International Crimes as an Alternative to Criminal Prosecution*, 12 HARV. HUM. RTS. J. 1 (1999). *See also* Slaughter & Bosco, *supra* note 4, at 115 ("When traditional diplomacy proves inadequate to the task of enforcing international law and justice, plaintiffs should be able to carve out new diplomatic channels, bypassing the uncertainty of political negotiations and compensating for the weakness of international tribunals by turning to effective national courts.").

[48] *See generally* Eric Posner & Adrian Vermeule, *Transitional Justice as Ordinary Justice*, 117 HARV. L. REV. 761 (2004); Michael Warder, *Let Chileans Handle Their Own Tyrant*, L.A. TIMES, Jan. 5, 1999, at B7; Oscar Alzaga Villamil, *Es Espana un buen juez de la transicion Chilena?*, ABC (Madrid), Dec. 1, 1998. For a general discussion on transitional justice, see BURYING THE PAST: MAKING PEACE AND DOING JUSTICE AFTER CIVIL CONFLICT (Nigel Biggar ed., 2001); RUTI TEITEL, TRANSITIONAL JUSTICE (2000); Heraldo Munoz & Ricardo Lagos, *The Pinochet Dilemma*, FOREIGN POL'Y, Spring 1999, at 26; Luc Huyse, *Justice After Transition: On the Choices Successor Elites Make in Dealing with the Past*, 20 L. & SOC. INQUIRY 51 (1995); SARA STEINMETZ, DEMOCRATIC TRANSITION AND HUMAN RIGHTS: PERSPECTIVES ON U.S. FOREIGN POLICY (1994); GUILLERMO O'DONNELL & PHILIPPE C. SCHMITTER, TRANSITIONS FROM AUTHORITARIAN RULE: TENTATIVE CONCLUSIONS ABOUT UNCERTAIN DEMOCRACIES (1986).

[49] *See, e.g.*, Elazar Barkan, *Between Restitution and International Morality*, 25 FORDHAM INT'L L.J. 46 (2001).

igations may disrupt the growth of the South African economy "by deterring foreign direct investment and undermining economic stability." With due respect, these are decisions for the sovereign, democratic Republic of South Africa, not foreign courts.[50]

The Bush administration echoed these concerns in its own filing submitted on behalf of the corporate defendants in the *Khulumani* case.

> [A]djudication of these aiding and abetting claims would interfere with South Africa's own reconciliation and redress efforts. Notably, the South Africa Government opposes this case being allowed to proceed and deems these actions incompatible with South Africa's own internal reconciliation process. More generally, recognition of an aiding and abetting claim as a matter of federal common law would hamper the policy of encouraging positive change in developing countries via economic investment.[51]

Even the U.S. Supreme Court referenced the South African apartheid litigation in *Sosa v. Alvarez-Machain*. The Court cited the statements of the South African government and the United States, suggesting that in such cases the "federal courts should give serious weight to the Executive Branch's view of the case's impact on foreign policy."[52]

In response to these concerns, the Chairperson of South Africa's Truth and Reconciliation Commission (TRC), Archbishop Desmond Tutu, and several former TRC members filed their own amicus brief in the *Khulumani* case challenging the statements of the South African government and the United States. They argued that ATS litigation would not undermine the democratic transition in South Africa.

> In our collective opinion, formed of years of intimate experience in shaping and carrying out the mission of the TRC, litigation seeking individual compensation against multinational corporations for aiding and abetting the commission of gross human rights abuses during apartheid does not conflict, in any manner, with the

---

50 Brief of Amicus Curiae Republic of South Africa in Support of Affirmance at 3–4, Khulumani v. Barclays Nat'l Bank Ltd., No. 05-2141-CV (2d Cir. 2005) (citations omitted).

51 Brief for the United States of America as Amicus Curiae at 4, Khulumani v. Barclays Nat'l Bank Ltd., No. 05-2141-CV (2d Cir. 2005). The United States made a similar argument in *Sosa. See* Brief for the United States as Respondent Supporting Petitioner at 44–45, Sosa v. Alvarez-Machain, 542 U.S. 692 (2004) (No. 03-339).

52 Sosa v. Alvarez-Machain, 542 U.S. 692, 733 (2004).

policies of the South African government, or the goals of the South African people, as embodied in the TRC. To the contrary, such litigation is entirely consistent with these policies and with the findings of the TRC.[53]

The South African experience suggests that transnational litigation would not necessarily undermine democratic transitions. And so transnational litigation (and the principle of universal jurisdiction) present a paradox: "In theory, at least, its exercise may threaten to displace democratic deliberations in societies that have endured atrocious crimes. In practice, however, it has fortified and energized those processes."[54]

There are other reasons why transnational litigation need not impede democratic transitions.[55] Grants of amnesty will continue to protect perpetrators of human rights abuses who remain in their home countries. Transnational litigation only functions if perpetrators leave their territory.[56] If Pinochet had remained in Chile, for example, he would never have faced extradition from England or prosecution in Spain. Once he left Chile, however, there was no justification for this amnesty to immunize him from foreign prosecutions. A similar dynamic existed in the *Filartiga* case. If Peña-Irala had remained in Paraguay, he would never have been subject to the federal court's jurisdiction in the United States.[57]

Similarly, transnational litigation need not impede economic development. Despite the concerns of the South African government and the

---

[53] Brief of Amici Curiae Commissioners and Committee Members of South Africa's Truth and Reconciliation Commission in Support of Appellants at 1–2, Khulumani v. Barclays Nat'l Bank Ltd., No. 05-2141-CV (2d Cir. 2005).

[54] Diane Orentlicher, *Whose Justice? Reconciling Universal Jurisdiction with Democratic Principles*, 92 GEO. L.J. 1057, 1066–67 (2004).

[55] *Cf.* David Gray, *An Excuse-Centered Approach to Transitional Justice*, 74 FORDHAM L. REV. 2621 (2006); Ruti Teitel, *Transitional Jurisprudence: The Role of Law in Political Transformation*, 106 YALE L.J. 2009 (1997).

[56] *See* Amanda L. Morgan, *U.S. Officials' Vulnerability to "Global Justice": Will Universal Jurisdiction over War Crimes Make Traveling for Pleasure Less Pleasurable?*, 57 HAST. L.J. 423 (2005).

[57] Ironically, Paraguayan dictator Alfredo Stroessner understood the implications of the *Filartiga* precedent. While living in exile in Brazil, Stroessner wrote to former U.S. Ambassador to Paraguay, George Landau, inquiring about the possibility of visiting the United States for gallbladder surgery. "The ambassador advised the general to stay way, warning that he could become the target for a lawsuit by Paraguayans. General Stroessner ended up having the operation in São Paulo." *See* Diana Jean Schemo, *Gen. Alfredo Stroessner, Colorful Dictator of Paraguay for 35 Years, Dies in Exile at 93*, N.Y. TIMES, Aug. 17, 2006, at A25.

United States in the *Khulumani* case, the apartheid litigation was not inherently antithetical to corporate interests in South Africa. "The payment of compensatory damages to satisfy *past* liability should not affect a business's decision to make investment in the future. If there are sound investments in South Africa, if there are opportunities for profit, businesses will take advantage of them."[58] Moreover, litigation that promotes human rights and respect for the rule of law can promote transparency and political legitimacy in developing countries, thereby providing incentives for investment and economic development.

There is also a broader and more fundamental response to the democratic transition critique. International law generally prohibits the use of amnesties or grants of immunity in cases of serious human rights abuses such as torture, genocide, war crimes, or crimes against humanity.[59] Even diplomats and heads of state are not entitled to absolute immunity in all cases.[60] In this context, the International Court of Justice (ICJ) has distinguished between immunity and impunity: "Jurisdictional immunity may well bar prosecution for a certain period or for certain offences; it cannot exonerate the person to whom it applies from all criminal responsibility."[61] The ICJ identified at least four scenarios where even high-ranking government officials could be held liable for human rights abuses.

---

[58] Brief of Amici Curiae Commissioners and Committee Members of South Africa's Truth and Reconciliation Commission in Support of Appellants, *supra* note 53, at 15.

[59] Human Rights Committee, General Comment 20 (1992), Compilation of General Comments and General Recommendations Adopted by Human Rights Treaty Bodies, U.N. Doc. HRI/GEN/1/Rev.7 at 150, 153 (2004) ("Amnesties are generally incompatible with the duty of States to investigate such acts; to guarantee freedom from such acts within their jurisdiction; and to ensure that they do not occur in the future."). *See also* Leila Nadya Sadat, *Exile, Amnesty and International Law*, 81 NOTRE DAME L. REV. 955 (2006); ANDREAS O'SHEA, AMNESTY FOR CRIME IN INTERNATIONAL LAW AND PRACTICE (2002); Roman Boed, *The Effect of a Domestic Amnesty on the Ability of Foreign States to Prosecute Alleged Perpetrators of Serious Human Rights Violations*, 33 CORNELL INT'L L.J. 297 (2000); Steven R. Ratner, *The Schizophrenias of International Criminal Law*, 33 TEX. INT'L L.J. 237 (1998); IMPUNITY IN INTERNATIONAL HUMAN RIGHTS LAW AND PRACTICE (Naomi Roht-Arriaza ed., 1995); Adam C. Belsky et al., *Implied Waiver Under the FSIA: A Proposed Exception to Immunity for Violations of Peremptory Norms of International Law*, 77 CAL. L. REV. 365 (1989).

[60] *See generally* Hazel Fox, *State Immunity and the International Crime of Torture*, 2006 EUR. HUM. RTS. L. REV. 142; Salvatore Zappala, *Do Heads of State in Office Enjoy Immunity from Jurisdiction for International Crimes? The Ghaddafi Case Before the French Cour de Cassation*, 12 EUR. J. INT'L L. 595 (2001); Amber Fitzgerald, *The Pinochet Case: Head of State Immunity Within the United States*, 22 WHITTIER L. REV. 987 (2001); Peter Evan Bass, *Ex-Head of State Immunity: A Proposed Statutory Tool of Foreign Policy*, 97 YALE L.J. 299 (1987).

[61] Arrest Warrant of 11 April 2000 (Dem. Rep. Congo v. Belg.) 2002 I.C.J. 1 (Feb. 14), at para. 60.

First, such persons enjoy no criminal immunity under international law in their own countries, and may thus be tried by those countries' courts in accordance with the relevant rules of domestic law. Secondly, they will cease to enjoy immunity from foreign jurisdiction if the State which they represent or have represented decides to waive that immunity. Thirdly, after a person ceases to hold the office of Minister for Foreign Affairs, he or she will no longer enjoy all of the immunities accorded by international law in other States. Provided that it has jurisdiction under international law, a court of one State may try a former Minister for Foreign Affairs of another State in respect of acts committed prior or subsequent to his or her period of office, as well as in respect of acts committed during that period of office in a private capacity. Fourthly, an incumbent or former Minister for Foreign Affairs may be subject to criminal proceedings before certain international criminal courts, where they have jurisdiction. Examples include the International Criminal Tribunal for the former Yugoslavia, and the International Criminal Tribunal for Rwanda, established pursuant to Security Council resolutions under Chapter VII of the United Nations Charter, and the future International Criminal Court created by the 1998 Rome Convention. The latter's Statute expressly provides, in Article 27, paragraph 2, that "[i]mmunities or special procedural rules which may attach to the official capacity of a person, whether under national or international law, shall not bar the Court from exercising its jurisdiction over such a person."[62]

Thus, countries that use amnesty decrees or grants of immunity to insulate perpetrators from accountability are already on notice that such acts are not always consistent with international law. It should not be surprising then if other countries do not automatically accept the validity of foreign amnesty decrees or grants of immunity.[63]

---

[62] *Id.* at para. 61. *See also* THE REDRESS TRUST, IMMUNITY V. ACCOUNTABILITY: CONSIDERING THE RELATIONSHIP BETWEEN STATE IMMUNITY AND ACCOUNTABILITY FOR TORTURE AND OTHER SERIOUS INTERNATIONAL CRIMES (2005).

[63] *See generally* Kate Parlett, *Immunity in Civil Proceedings for Torture: The Emerging Exception*, 2006 EUR. HUM. RTS. L. REV. 49; Kathryn Lee Boyd, *Universal Jurisdiction and Structural Reasonableness*, 40 TEX. INT'L L.J. 1 (2004); Antonio Cassese, *When May Senior State Officials Be Tried for International Crimes? Some Comments on the Congo v. Belgium Case*, 13 EUR. J. INT'L L. 853 (2002); Steffen Wirth, *Immunity for Core Crimes?*, 13 EUR. J. INT'L L. 877 (2002); Andrea Bianchi, *Denying State Immunity to Violators of Human Rights*, 46 AUSTRIAN J. PUB. & INT'L L. 195 (1994). *But see* Jones v. Ministry of Interior Al-Mamlaka Al-Arabiya AS Saudiya, [2006] U.K.H.L. 26; Wei Ye v. Zemin, 383 F.3d 620 (7th Cir. 2004); Tachiona v. United States, 386 F.3d 205 (2d Cir. 2004); Al-Adsani v. United Kingdom, 34 EUR. HUM. RTS. REP. 273 (2001).

Apart from these considerations, situations may arise where transnational litigation is necessary to promote democratic transition. The move to democracy may not succeed if countries disregard past atrocities.[64]

As societies attempt to recover from these periods of lawlessness, one of the first opportunities to reestablish the primacy of law over individuals comes in the treatment of the former rulers, torturers, and jailers. If such people are treated summarily, extracting an eye for an eye, the transition to a society of laws is set back immeasurably. On the other hand, a blanket amnesty and silence from the new government perpetuate the existence of a separate class to whom the rule of law does not apply.[65]

In these cases, transnational litigation may be necessary to promote reconciliation. Similarly, it may encourage countries to accelerate the process of democratic transition in order to facilitate their integration into the international community.[66]

In sum, transnational litigation remains a vibrant and viable mechanism for promoting justice and the rule of law. Indeed, the *Filartiga* case is a testament to the influence that transnational litigation can have, both in the United States and abroad.

---

[64] *See also* David Crocker, *Reckoning with Past Wrongs: A Normative Framework,* 13 ETHICS & INT'L AFF. 43 (1999); Susan Dwyer, *Reconciliation for Realists,* 13 ETHICS & INT'L AFF. 81 (1999); David Little, *A Different Kind of Justice: Dealing with Human Rights Violations in Transitional Societies,* 13 ETHICS & INT'L AFF. 65 (1999); Margaret Popkin & Nehal Bhuta, *Latin American Amnesties in Comparative Perspective: Can the Past Be Buried?,* 13 ETHICS & INT'L AFF. 99 (1999); Steven R. Ratner, *New Democracies, Old Atrocities: An Inquiry in International Law,* 87 GEO. L.J. 707 (1999); Naomi Roht-Arriaza & Lauren Gibson, *The Developing Jurisprudence on Amnesty,* 20 HUM. RTS. Q. 843 (1998); CARLOS SANTIAGO NINO, RADICAL EVIL ON TRIAL 127–34 (1996); David Pion-Berlin, *To Prosecute or to Pardon? Human Rights Decisions in the Latin American Southern Cone,* 16 HUM. RTS. Q. 105 (1993); Jamal Benomar, *Justice After Transitions,* 4 J. DEMOCRACY 3 (1993); Jose Zalaquett, *Confronting Human Rights Violations Committed by Former Governments: Principles Applicable and Political Constraints, in* STATE CRIMES: PUNISHMENT OR PARDON 23 (The Aspen Inst. ed., 1989); FROM DICTATORSHIP TO DEMOCRACY: COPING WITH THE LEGACIES OF AUTHORITARIANISM AND TOTALITARIANISM (John H. Herz ed., 1982); JUAN J. LINZ & ALFRED STEPAN, THE BREAKDOWN OF DEMOCRATIC REGIMES: CRISIS, BREAKDOWN & REEQUILIBRIUM (1978).

[65] Naomi Roht-Arriaza, *Introduction, in* IMPUNITY AND HUMAN RIGHTS IN INTERNATIONAL LAW AND PRACTICE 3, 4 (Naomi Roht-Arriaza ed., 1995).

[66] *See generally* Thomas M. Franck, *The Emerging Right to Democratic Governance,* 86 AM. J. INT'L L. 46 (1992).

While it cannot function in isolation from other justice mechanisms, transnational litigation serves several purposes.[67] Human rights are universal in nature. They attach value to each human life and accept the inherent dignity of each individual. Impunity undermines the legitimacy of these claims.

> Human rights imply the obligation of society to satisfy those claims. The state must develop institutions and procedures, must plan, must mobilize resources as necessary to meet those claims. . . . The idea of human rights implies also that society must provide some system of remedies to which individuals may resort to obtain the benefits to which they are entitled or be compensated for their loss. Together, the affirmation of entitlement, the recognition by society of an obligation to mobilize itself to discharge it, and the implication of a remedy, all enhance the likelihood that the right will be realized, that individuals will actually enjoy the benefits to which they are entitled.[68]

Punishing human rights violations, even if only through civil judgments, serves to affirm these values and voice condemnation for such acts of violence.

Efforts to combat impunity also affirm the rule of law.[69] Human rights abuses violate national and international law. Thus, the failure to punish violations undermines the legitimacy of the challenged norms as well as the broader rule of law.

> [T]he case for prosecutions turns on the consequences of failing to punish atrocious crimes committed by a prior regime on a sweeping scale. If law is unavailable to punish widespread brutality

---

[67] *See generally* AMNESTY INTERNATIONAL USA, USA: A SAFE HAVEN FOR TORTURERS (2002). *See also* Sandra Coliver, *Bringing Human Rights Abusers to Justice in U.S. Courts: Carrying Forward the Legacy of the Nuremberg Trials*, 27 CARDOZO L. REV. 1689 (2006); Sandra Coliver et al., *Holding Human Rights Violators Accountable by Using International Law in U.S. Courts: Advocacy Efforts and Complementary Strategies*, 19 EMORY INT'L L. REV. 169 (2005). For different perspectives on international justice efforts, see Helena Cobban, *International Courts*, FOREIGN POL'Y, Mar.–Apr. 2006, at 22; ACCOUNTABILITY FOR ATROCITIES: NATIONAL AND INTERNATIONAL RESPONSES (Jane E. Stromseth ed., 2003); MARTHA MINOW, BETWEEN VENGEANCE AND FORGIVENESS: FACING HISTORY AFTER GENOCIDE AND MASS VIOLENCE (1998).

[68] LOUIS HENKIN, THE AGE OF RIGHTS 3 (1990).

[69] *See generally* IMPUNITY AND HUMAN RIGHTS IN INTERNATIONAL LAW AND PRACTICE (Naomi Roht-Arriaza ed., 1995); BRUCE BROOMHALL, INTERNATIONAL JUSTICE AND THE INTERNATIONAL CRIMINAL COURT: BETWEEN SOVEREIGNTY AND THE RULE OF LAW (2002).

of the recent past, what lesson can be offered for the future? A complete failure of enforcement vitiates the authority of law itself, sapping its power to deter proscribed conduct. This may be tolerable when the law or the crime is of marginal consequence, but there can be no scope for eviscerating wholesale laws that forbid violence and that have been violated on a massive scale. Societies recently scourged by lawlessness need look no farther than their own past to discover the costs of impunity. Their history provides sobering cause to believe, with William Pitt, that tyranny begins where law ends.[70]

And, as stated by the International Military Tribunal at Nuremberg, "[c]rimes against international law are committed by men, not by abstract entities, and only by punishing individuals who commit such crimes can the provisions of international law be enforced."[71]

Transnational litigation can help promote the search for truth.[72] Human rights abuses are often committed in private by perpetrators who subsequently deny their complicity in the atrocities. Military and political leaders perpetuate the subterfuge by failing to investigate or even acknowledge atrocities. In many cases, victims simply disappear. By pursuing these cases, a public record is created that describes the human rights abuses committed by the perpetrators and the injustices suffered by the victims.

Litigation that alleges violations of international law and pursues tort claims for damages and equitable relief on behalf of groups victimized by genocide, ethnic cleansing, and other atrocities fulfills a unique role in creating and sustaining an official record of crimes against humanity. As with the case of the gypsy victims of the Nazi regime, it is all too easy for history to omit, and the public to forget, the details, or even the existence, of egregious genocidal episodes. The record created by published opinions, transcripts, and clerk's dockets assures, at the least, that there will be a per-

---

[70] Diane F. Orentlicher, *Settling Accounts: The Duty to Prosecute Human Rights Violations of a Prior Regime*, 100 YALE L.J. 2537, 2542 (1991).

[71] TRIAL OF THE MAJOR WAR CRIMINALS BEFORE THE INTERNATIONAL MILITARY TRIBUNAL, NUREMBERG, 14 NOVEMBER 1945–1 OCTOBER 1946, 1 OFFICIAL DOCUMENTS 223 (1947).

[72] *See generally* Jose E. Mendez, *In Defense of Transitional Justice, in* TRANSITIONAL JUSTICE AND THE RULE OF LAW IN NEW DEMOCRACIES 1 (A. James McAdams ed., 1997); LAWRENCE WESCHLER, A MIRACLE, A UNIVERSE: SETTLING ACCOUNTS WITH TORTURERS (1990).

manent record—immune from expungement, spoliation, or revision by interested or implicated governments or perpetrators—of these events.[73]

Through depositions and interrogatories, defendants are forced to disclose their role in abuses. Plaintiffs also participate in the process, telling their stories to the judge and jury. These developments can further advance social and political reconciliation in countries traumatized by periods of repression and persecution.[74]

Promoting accountability through transnational litigation can serve as a deterrent against future atrocities.[75] In many countries, human rights violations often go unpunished. Lack of individual accountability encourages human rights abuses and promotes further disintegration of the rule of law. "Impunity sends the message to torturers that they will get away with it."[76] In contrast, civil litigation sends a message to perpetrators that they may be subject to liability for their actions. The deterrent effect of civil litigation may be particularly significant on foreign governments, corporations, and other nongovernmental organizations that have significant

---

[73] Elizabeth J. Cabraser, *Human Rights Violations as Mass Torts: Compensation as a Proxy for Justice in the United States Civil Litigation System*, 57 VAND. L. REV. 2211, 2236 (2004) (citations omitted).

[74] *See, e.g.*, MY NEIGHBOR, MY ENEMY: JUSTICE AND COMMUNITY IN THE AFTERMATH OF MASS ATROCITY (Eric Stover & Harvey M. Weinstein eds., 2004); Laurel F. Fletcher & Harvey M. Weinstein, *Violence and Social Repair: Rethinking the Contribution of Justice to Reconciliation*, 24 HUM. RTS. Q. 573 (2002); Nora Sveaass & Nils Johan Lavik, *Psychological Aspects of Human Rights Violations: The Importance of Justice & Reconciliation*, 69 NORDIC J. INT'L L. 35 (2000); Naomi Roht-Arriaza, *Punishment, Redress, and Pardon: Theoretical and Psychological Approaches, in* IMPUNITY AND HUMAN RIGHTS IN INTERNATIONAL LAW AND PRACTICE (Naomi Roht-Arriaza ed., 1995).

[75] *See, e.g., Foreign Torture, American Justice*, N.Y. TIMES, Aug. 20, 1980, at A18 ("American courts, long a haven for citizens whose civil rights are violated, used to look the other way when foreigners asked for relief on matters of human rights and political violence abroad. But now, as the global pattern of terrorism infects the United States also, that attitude is changing. . . . To critics of judicial imperialism, that may seem a presumptuous assertion of judicial power. . . . But if American courts rejected such suits, they would only encourage malefactors, hoping to avoid accountability, to come here. It is to the opposed that America should wish to give refuge."). *See generally* Payam Akhavan, *Beyond Impunity: Can International Criminal Justice Prevent Future Atrocities?*, 95 AM. J. INT'L L. 7 (2001). *But see* David Wippman, *Atrocities, Deterrence, and the Limits of International Justice*, 23 FORDHAM INT'L L.J. 473, 476–77 (1999); MARTHA MINOW, BETWEEN VENGEANCE & FORGIVENESS: FACING HISTORY AFTER GENOCIDE AND MASS VIOLENCE (1998).

[76] AMNESTY INTERNATIONAL, END IMPUNITY: JUSTICE FOR THE VICTIMS OF TORTURE 6 (2001). *See also* Kenneth Roth, *The Case for Universal Jurisdiction*, FOREIGN AFF., Sept.–Oct. 2001, at 150.

financial assets subject to attachment in a successful judgment. Civil liability may also deter future abuses in other ways. For example, financial sanctions can limit funding opportunities for perpetrators of human rights abuses.[77] A successful lawsuit that imposes financial sanctions on a foreign government or terrorist organization may affect the ability of these actors to fund future activities.

Transnational litigation also performs the crucial function of distinguishing individual liability from group responsibility.[78] Groups identified by certain shared characteristics often receive public blame, both at home and abroad, for the crimes of relatively few offenders. Judge Richard Goldstone, the first prosecutor of the International Criminal Tribunal for the former Yugoslavia, explained this phenomenon in the context of regional human rights abuses: "Too many people in the former Yugoslavia still blame Serbs or Croats or Muslims for their suffering. The tribunal's mandate is to help reverse this destructive legacy."[79] Legal proceedings focus blame where it belongs, calling individuals to account for their crimes and absolving communal blame.

More broadly, efforts to hold perpetrators accountable can reinforce human rights in other parts of the world.[80] Publicity generated by these cases helps to educate the public about the importance of human rights. These cases can also provide support for human rights activists throughout the world. Efforts to hold perpetrators accountable demonstrate that judicial systems are capable of adjudicating human rights cases and combating impunity. "Through focusing world attention, through forcing the government to defend its judiciary, through empowering and strengthening domestic human rights lawyers and activists, transnational prosecutions time and time again have jump-started stalled or non-existent processes of accountability."[81] This phenomenon is found in the case of Augusto Pinochet. Upon his return to Chile in 2000, Pinochet's claims of immunity were successfully challenged in numerous proceedings, something that had not occurred prior to the Spanish and English proceed-

---

[77] *See, e.g.*, COUNCIL ON FOREIGN RELATIONS, TERRORIST FINANCING (2002).

[78] *See generally* David A. Crocker, *Punishment, Reconciliation, and Democratic Deliberation*, 5 BUFF. CRIM. L. REV. 509, 521–22, 544–46 (2002). *But see* GARY JONATHAN BASS, STAY THE HAND OF VENGEANCE: THE POLITICS OF WAR CRIMES TRIBUNALS (2000).

[79] Richard J. Goldstone, *Ethnic Reconciliation Needs the Help of a Truth Commission*, INT'L HERALD TRIB., Oct. 24, 1998, at 6.

[80] *See, e.g.*, Elliot Schrage, *Judging Corporate Accountability in the Global Economy*, 42 COLUM. J. TRANSNAT'L L. 153, 157 (2003).

[81] ROHT-ARRIAZA, *supra* note 2, at 223.

ings.[82] The Pinochet precedent soon extended beyond Chile, however, as other former heads of states became subject to prosecution for acts they committed while in office.[83]

The struggle against impunity, however, is not limited to punishing perpetrators. It can also benefit victims by assuaging their feelings of helplessness and defeat, emotions that often permeate victims of abuse.[84] Proceedings can empower victims and facilitate their recovery.[85] They can provide victims with an opportunity to tell their stories in public, and a full and fair hearing can help restore their sense of justice.[86] Juan Romagoza,

---

[82] *See, e.g.*, Patrick J. McDonnell, *Pinochet Loses Immunity in Abuse Case*, L.A. TIMES, Jan. 21, 2006, at A3; Larry Rohter, *A Web of Investigations Increasingly Entangles Pinochet*, INT'L HERALD TRIB., Feb. 8, 2005, at 3; Larry Rohter, *Judge Finds Pinochet Fit for Trial*, INT'L HERALD TRIB., Dec. 5, 2004, at 7; Ariel Dorfman, *Why Chile Is Hopeful*, N.Y. TIMES, Sept. 11, 2004, at A15.

[83] *See generally* Sarah C. Rispin, *Implications of Democratic Republic of the Congo v. Belgium on the Pinochet Precedent: A Setback for International Human Rights Litigation?*, 3 CHI. J. INT'L L. 527 (2002); Naomi Roht-Arriaza, *The Pinochet Precedent and Universal Jurisdiction*, 35 NEW ENG. L. REV. 311 (2001); Inbal Sansani, *The Pinochet Precedent in Africa: Prosecution of Hissene Habre*, 8 HUM. RTS. BR. 32 (2001); TORTURE AS TORT: COMPARATIVE PERSPECTIVES ON THE DEVELOPMENT OF TRANSNATIONAL HUMAN RIGHTS LITIGATION (Craig Scott ed., 2001); Ellen Lutz & Kathryn Sikkink, *The Justice Cascade: The Evolution and Impact of Foreign Human Rights Trials in Latin America*, 2 CHI. J. INT'L L. 1 (2001); Jodi Thorp, *Welcome Ex-Dictators, Torturers, and Tyrants: Comparative Approaches to Handling Ex-Dictators and Past Human Rights Abuses*, 37 GONZ. L. REV. 167 (2001/2002).

[84] *See generally* Jamie O'Connell, *Gambling with the Psyche: Does Prosecuting Human Rights Violators Console Their Victims?* 46 HARV. INT'L L.J. 295 (2005); DANIEL W. SCHUMAN & ALEXANDER MCCALL SMITH, JUSTICE AND THE PROSECUTION OF OLD CRIMES: BALANCING LEGAL, PSYCHOLOGICAL, AND MORAL CONCERNS (2000); DEALING WITH THE PAST: TRUTH AND RECONCILIATION IN SOUTH AFRICA (Alex Boraine et al. eds., 1994); THE BREAKING OF BODIES AND MINDS: TORTURE, PSYCHIATRIC ABUSE, AND THE HEALTH PROFESSIONS (Eric Stover & Elena O. Nightingale eds., 1985); William J. Curran, *Official Torture and Human Rights: The American Courts and International Law*, 304 NEW ENG. J. MED. 1342 (May 28, 1981).

[85] *See generally* E. Allan Lind et al., *In the Eye of the Beholder: Tort Litigants' Evaluations of Their Experiences in the Civil Justice System*, 24 L. & SOC'Y REV. 953 (1990).

[86] Accountability can even serve as a rehabilitative mechanism for perpetrators. *See* Prosecutor v. Nikolic, Case No. IT-02-60/1-S (Dec. 2, 2003), at para. 93 ("Particularly in cases where the crime was committed on a discriminatory basis, . . . the process of coming face-to-face with the statements of victims, if not the victims themselves, can inspire—if not reawaken—tolerance and understanding of 'the other,' thereby making it less likely that if given an opportunity to act in a discriminatory manner again, an accused would do so. Reconciliation and peace would thereby be promoted."). *See generally* Mark Andrew Sherman, *Some Thoughts on Restoration, Reintegration, and Justice in the Transnational Context*, 23 FORDHAM INT'L L.J. 1397 (2000); William A. Schabas, *Sentencing by International Tribunals: A Human Rights Approach*, 7 DUKE J. COMP. & INT'L L. 461 (1997).

a torture survivor who sued two former Salvadoran government officials in *Romagoza v. Garcia*, described the cathartic experience of testifying at trial.[87]

> When I testified, a strength came over me. I felt like I was in the prow of a boat and that there were many, many people rowing behind. I felt that if I looked back, I'd weep because I'd see them again: wounded, tortured, raped, naked, torn, bleeding. So, I didn't look back, but I felt their support, their strength, their energy. Being involved in this case, confronting the generals with these terrible facts—that's the best possible therapy a torture survivor could have.[88]

Medical professionals have also recognized the benefits of civil litigation for victims of human rights abuses.

> This legal recourse presents the opportunity for torture survivors living in the United States to seek justice and confront impunity. The few who are able to take their cases to court create a collective voice for all torture victims, bringing the issue of human rights atrocities into the public eye. This opportunity also presents a means for psychological healing of torture's wounds by breaking the silence, confronting perpetrators and refuting impunity.[89]

Legal professionals share a similar view about the benefits of litigation.

> [C]ivil suits, controlled by plaintiff/victims and their chosen attorneys, and not prosecutors responsive to other agendas, may also be more effective in preserving a collective memory that is more sensitive to victims than some judicial accounts rendered in the course of criminal trials. Indeed, if studies about litigants' relative satisfactions with adversarial versus inquisitorial methods of criminal procedure are an accurate guide, it may be that having greater control of the process, including the selection of attorneys and the ability to discover and present one's own evidence and develop one's own strategy, is itself a value for victims, and one that is better met through civil suits such as those now occurring in United States courts.[90]

---

[87] *See* Arce v. Garcia, 434 F.3d 1254 (11th Cir. 2006).

[88] Statement of Juan Romagoza, quoted in Coliver et al., *supra* note 67, at 180–81.

[89] Statement of Dr. Mary Fabri, quoted in Coliver et al., *supra* note 67, at 181–82.

[90] Jose Alvarez, *Rush to Closure: Lessons of the Tadic Judgment*, 96 MICH. L. REV. 2031, 2102 (1998). *Cf.* Stephens, *supra* note 2, at 52 ("[C]riminal prosecutions locate control over such actions in the hands of governments, rather than private citizens, thus avoiding diplomatic turmoil.").

Anti-impunity efforts can also promote reparations for victims of human rights abuses, including rehabilitation, restitution, compensation, and guarantees of nonrepetition.[91] These concerns are particularly relevant in the United States, where hundreds of thousands of torture survivors live and search for a renewed life.

The advantages of transnational litigation must be tempered by the reality that litigation cannot heal all wounds. Victims of human rights abuses often suffer serious physical injuries.[92]

> Physicians regularly document paralysis, fractured bones, severed limbs, burned skin, organ damage, and countless other physical ailments caused by torture. Musculoskeletal injuries are common. Victims of cranial trauma suffer from impaired vision, loss of hearing, and neurological damage. Victims of sexual assault often suffer sterility and impotence. Few victims of torture escape without a permanent, physical reminder of their ordeal. Others share a different fate, however, when torture becomes murder.[93]

These injuries are exacerbated by psychological trauma, including post-traumatic stress disorder.

> Victims of torture often suffer anxiety, depression, and guilt. Suicidal thoughts are common. Many survivors experience post-traumatic stress disorder, where they persistently re-experience the trauma of torture in flashbacks and nightmares. The past can break into the present at any time—a painful and disorienting phenomenon triggered by the sight of someone wearing a uniform, a small enclosed area, or numerous other reminders of torture. To avoid nightmares, many survivors avoid sleeping. For a survivor repeatedly pushed into a vat of water and nearly drowned, the sight of rain can be unbearable. For others, uncertainties involved in waiting

---

[91] *See generally* DINAH SHELTON, REMEDIES IN INTERNATIONAL HUMAN RIGHTS LAW (2d ed. 2006); MARSHALL SHAPO, COMPENSATION FOR VICTIMS OF TERRORISM (2005); THE REDRESS TRUST, REPARATION: A SOURCEBOOK FOR VICTIMS OF TORTURE AND OTHER VIOLATIONS OF HUMAN RIGHTS AND INTERNATIONAL HUMANITARIAN LAW (2003).

[92] *See generally* Derrick Silove et al., *The Psychological Effects of Torture, Mass Human Rights Violations, and Refugee Trauma: Toward an Integrated Conceptual Framework*, 187 J. NERVOUS & MENTAL DISEASES 200 (1999); Yael Danieli, *Preliminary Reflections from a Psychological Perspective, in* TRANSITIONAL JUSTICE: HOW EMERGING DEMOCRACIES RECKON WITH FORMER REGIMES 572 (Neil J. Kritz ed., 1995); BEYOND TRAUMA: CULTURAL AND SOCIETAL DYNAMICS (Rolf J. Kleber et al. eds., 1995).

[93] AMNESTY INTERNATIONAL USA, *supra* note 67, at 74 (citations omitted).

for an appointment to begin can be traumatic. A survivor of electric shock torture may not be able to tolerate the sight of electrical equipment. Common activities, such as reading a newspaper or watching television, may appear threatening as potential reminders of the violence suffered. In attempting to avoid painful memories or extreme stress, survivors may isolate themselves from familiar people and situations. An emotional numbing can occur. At the same time, survivors often carry out daily activities in an "emergency mode," constantly on their guard. Hyperalertness and exaggerated responses to startling sounds or sights continue to plague many survivors. A general lack of trust and a sense of extreme vulnerability may characterize a survivor's experience of the surrounding world in the aftermath of torture. . . . Alcoholism and drug abuse often complicate this clinical picture as survivors try to numb their pain.[94]

While physical scars may fade over time, the psychological scars that victims carry can remain for decades and legal proceedings may not provide closure and comfort in all cases.

Dr. Joel Filártiga and Dolly Filártiga still carry these scars with them, and they will continue to do so for the rest of their lives. In this respect, *Filartiga v. Pena-Irala* represents both the promise and limits of transnational litigation. The Filártiga family was given the opportunity to confront Peña-Irala and tell Joelito's story in court. They won their lawsuit and found redemption in the Second Circuit's judgment. Though her family did not collect the financial judgment, Dolly Filártiga recognized that financial redress was not the only measure of success.

Although Mr. Peña-Irala was sent back to Paraguay and none of the $10 million judgment has yet been paid, our case established a remarkable precedent: from Ethiopia's Red Terror to Argentina's Dirty War to the Philippines' dictatorship under Ferdinand Marcos, in 19 instances survivors or victims' relatives have used this law to obtain a measure of justice. . . . I came to this country in 1978 hoping simply to look a killer in the eye. With the help of American law, I got so much more. Eventually I received political asylum, then became a citizen. I am proud to live in a country where human rights are respected, where there is a way to bring to justice people who have committed horrible atrocities.[95]

---

94 *Id.* at 74–75 (citations omitted).

95 Dolly Filartiga, *American Courts, Global Justice*, N.Y. TIMES, Mar. 30, 2004, at A21.

But this legal victory must be balanced against the less noticeable but no less significant limits of the *Filartiga* litigation. While the *Filartiga* case led to a groundbreaking decision in the United States and promoted transnational litigation as a viable response to human rights abuses, its implications for Paraguay are less clear.[96] The litigation highlighted human rights abuses in Paraguay and caused significant consternation within the Paraguayan government. It led to several conversations between Paraguayan officials and U.S. diplomats about Paraguay's treatment of the Filártiga family as well as its broader human rights record. The litigation and resulting publicity also offered some protection to the Filártiga family in Paraguay. According to Dolly Filártiga, "[f]or my family, the court decision put us at risk but also gave protection—the Paraguayan government threatened us but wouldn't risk retaliating once we had the American legal system on our side. In Paraguay, the case remains a symbol of the injustice of the Stroessner dictatorship, and my brother is considered a martyr for human rights."[97] And yet, the litigation did not significantly improve Paraguay's human rights record and Stroessner remained in power until 1989.[98] Moreover, Peña-Irala was never prosecuted for his role in Joelito Filártiga's murder. Even Hugo Duarte, who was charged with the murder and allegedly confessed to the crime, was released from prison after only five years of detention. He also successfully sued the Filártiga family for slander and defamation in Paraguay.

In *Filartiga v. Pena-Irala*, the anatomy of torture reveals the legacy of this terrible crime. The litigation documents describe the excruciating injuries suffered by Joelito Filártiga in the last moments of his life. They chronicle the pain suffered by Joel and Dolly Filártiga, both in the immediate aftermath of Joelito's murder and in subsequent years. But the litigation documents also reveal the courage and resilience of the Filártiga family. They describe how the Filártiga family persisted in its search for justice, both in Paraguay and the United States. And, the documents chronicle hope in the face of adversity. Finally, the litigation documents reveal how a group of lawyers and activists crafted a legal strategy that would leave a lasting legacy for the human rights movement. Through the Alien Tort Statute and the *Filartiga* precedent, victims of human rights abuses now have a voice to call out for justice and a forum to hear their cries.

---

[96] *See also* Lutz & Sikkink, *supra* note 83, at 19–20.

[97] Filartiga, *supra* note 95, at A21.

[98] Alfredo Stroessner died in exile in Brazil on August 16, 2006. *See* Reed Johnson, *Alfredo Stoessner, 93: Ruled Paraguay for 3 Decades With Repression and Paternalism*, L.A. TIMES, Aug. 17, 2006, at B6.

LITIGATION DOCUMENTS AND RELATED MATERIALS

The following documents describe the history of the *Filartiga* litigation. These documents include litigation filings from *Filartiga v. Pena-Irala*. They also include communications between the U.S. Embassy in Asunción, Paraguay and the U.S. Department of State. The documents were compiled from various sources, including the Center for Constitutional Rights, the *Centro de Documentacion y Archivo* in Asunción, Paraguay, the Special Collections Department of the University of Virginia Law Library, the Special Collections Division of the University of Washington Libraries, and the U.S. National Archives and Records Administration. Several documents were acquired through Freedom of Information Act petitions to the U.S. Department of State and the U.S. Department of Justice. The documents have been formatted for consistency, and obvious errors have been corrected. Spanish language documents were translated.

.

MARCH 30, 1976: PARAGUAY

Police Summary of Crime Scene

DERLIS HUGO DUARTE ARREDONDO*

Paraguayan, married, 25 years old, incarcerated at the moment in the National Prison, charged in this Capital with an alleged murder, born in Asuncion on November 23, 1953, son of PEDRO BONIFACIO DUARTE, Attorney at Law, and of SARA ARREDONDO DE DUARTE, Pharmacist, all domiciled in Carlos Antonio Lopez Avenue, between 25 and 26 (Sajonia).

EDUCATION: Elementary: Escuela Dante Alighieri of this Capital; Secondary: Colegio Cristo Rey of this Capital from 1965 to 1972; University: From 1973 to 1975, Third Course of Medicine.

MARRIAGE: Married in 1974 with a local girl from Barrio Sajonia named MARIA DEL ROSARIO VILLALBA FERNANDEZ (then 15 years old). They have a five year old son: DERLIS HUGO DUARTE (m), who ended up in the custody of the paternal grandparents.

PARENTS-IN-LAW: NERY FELIPE VILLALBA, Paraguayan, carpenter, domiciled at the moment behind a school known as Escuela de Cuatro Nojon, and JUANA MANUELA FERNANDEZ, divorced before DERLIS became their daughter's boyfriend. They have four children: Three boys and a girl. The mother-in-law is in a common-law marriage with Principal Inspector AMERICO PENA since a long time ago, the date of which DERLIS does not know.

BACKGROUND: At the end of 1975, in order to continue with his studies in this Capital and to look after his wife and son who were under the care of Derlis' parents at that time, that he immediately looked for employment to not depend on his parents anymore, and that he managed to get a job as a cashier of the Hotel Guarani where he remained until the day of the perpetration of the crime (March 30, 1976).

JOEL FILARTIGA: who lived with his sister DOLLY since a long time ago, being supported with the help of his father and Captain SPERATTI, who provided them with supplies and other sorts of help. He was 17 years old at the time of his death.

---

* Document located in the *Centro de Documentacion y Archivo*, Asunción, Paraguay. Translated from Spanish by author.

EDUCATION: Elementary: DERLIS does not know very well, but he believes JOEL FILARTIGA attended a religious boarding school in San Juan Bautista de las Misiones. He also believes that he accomplished several secondary education courses in Colegio Nacional de Ybycui, and later on he might have completed some courses in this Capital after peregrinating from school to school.

MORTAL NIGHT: That, he was at his work working the nightshift because he was completing a course in the evening in order to be admitted to the Capital's Faculty. That he had to apply the following day and he needed his personal documents. That he went to his residence at two o'clock in the morning after his labor activities had calmed down at the Hotel, and for that, he took a bus to his residence in Barrio Sajonia. He then entered his home normally with all the attendant sounds that occur upon opening the door and entering his home and when he entered to his bedroom and turned the light on, he found JOEL FILARTIGA intimately close to his wife, who was punched in the face by him. That they got into a hand-to-hand fight for several minutes, and during the fighting Derlis had taken possession of a knife located on a small table in the bedroom, with which he stabbed [Filartiga] in the back running through his chest, the consequences of which Filartiga fell in a faint. Taking advantage of this and while being blinded by his nerves, Duarte stabbed him in the back and sides on many occasions. With only the desire to kill and realizing that nothing could be done, he hit him several times with a thick cable from a bedside lamp, leaving him dead.

OCTOBER 21, 1976: PARAGUAY

Memorandum from American Embassy, Asunción to File

Subject: Filartiga Case—Visit by Dr. Horacio Galeano Perrone

CONFIDENTIAL

MEMORANDUM FOR THE FILES

From: POL-Philip C. Gill

Date: October 21, 1976

Subj: Filartiga Case: Visit by Dr. Horacio Galeano Perrone.

1. On October 12, Dr. Galeano wrote a letter to Ambassador Landau (see copy attached) setting forth his version of the facts in the celebrated Filartiga murder case. He alleges that young Filartiga died after being tortured by the police who believed, mistakenly, that he had been engaged in subversive activities. The letter calls for Embassy investigation of the case as an example of a "human rights" violation, and the publication of the results of the investigation.

2. Dr. Galeano, who represents the Filartiga family in the case, came to my office on October 19, in response to my invitation to discuss his letter to the Ambassador. Emphasizing the deep Embassy and USG interest in promoting respect for human rights in Paraguay, I thanked him for bringing this matter to our attention. I told him that as a diplomatic mission in a foreign country, it would be improper for the Embassy to make a full scale investigation of the murder of Joel Filartiga, even if we had the capacity to do so—which we do not. I said that we had to depend very much on people of good will, such as himself, with knowledge of the facts, to provide us with information. I said that his letter and this meeting were valuable in giving the Embassy a more complete picture of the respect or lack of respect for human rights in Paraguay. Dr. Galeano replied that he had great respect for the United States and its democratic institutions. He said he was aware of our interest in promoting respect for human rights in Paraguay, and his motive in bringing the case to our attention was to inform the Embassy of this tragic incident in the hope that we would be able to do something to prevent this type of thing happening again. He promised to send the Embassy a more detailed report in writing of the case.

Attachment

FEBRUARY 15, 1977: UNITED STATES

Telegram from U.S. Department of State to American Embassy, Asunción

[Excised]
n/a
[Excised]

PAGE 01   STATE 034542
ORIGIN ARA-10

INFO OCT-0 ISO-00 DHA-02 H-01 SS-15 NSC-05 INR-07 PRS-01
      A-01   /043 R

DRAFTED BY ARA/ECA:RCGRAHAM:RC
APPROVED BY ARA/ECA:RWZIMMERMANN

P 152237Z   FEB   77
FM SECSTATE WASHDC
TO AMEMBASSY ASUNCION PRIORITY

C [Excised]   STATE 034542

E.O. 11652:   GDS

TAGS: SHUM, PA

SUBJECT: FILARTIGA STORY INSERTED IN CONGRESSIONAL RECORD
REF: ASUNCION 466.

1. SENATOR KENNEDY, ON FEBRUARY 1, AND CONGRESSMAN
KOCH, ON FEBRUARY 9, INSERTED IN CONGRESSIONAL RECORD
AN ARTICLE ON THE FILARTIGA INCIDENT WHICH APPEARED IN A
PUBLICATION CALLED "AMERICA." THE ARTICLE WAS WRITTEN BY
ALBERTO CABRAL, A PSEUDONYM. AS THE AMBASSADOR IS AWARE,
THE REAL AUTHOR ASKED THAT HIS IDENTITY BE PROTECTED.

2. THE ARTICLE IS A VIVID DESCRIPTION OF THE ALLEGED TOR-
TURE AND DEATH OF JOELITO FILARTIGA, ORGANIZED BY A
PARAGUAYAN POLICE INSPECTOR. COPIES OF THE ARTICLE, TOO
LONG TO SEND TELEGRAPHICALLY, ARE BEING POUCHED.

3. THE ARTICLE CONTAINS THE FOLLOWING REFERENCE TO THE
EMBASSY: QUOTE EVEN THE UNITED STATES EMBASSY EVIDENTLY

HAS BEEN MOVED TO BREAK WITH ITS LONG ESTABLISHED POLICY OF IGNORING THE CONSTANT VIOLATIONS OF HUMAN RIGHTS THAT HAVE CHARACTERIZED THE TWENTY-TWO YEAR LONG RULE OF GENERAL ALFREDO STROESSNER. IN A CLEAR DISPLAY OF THEIR DISAPPROVAL OF THIS PARTICULARLY CLUMSY JOB BY THE DICTATOR'S SECRET POLICE, IN LATE SEPTEMBER IT SPONSORED A WIDELY PUBLICIZED EXHIBITION OF DR. FILARTIGA'S ART WORK AT THE USIS PARAGUAYAN AMERICAN CULTURAL CENTER. IF THE PHOTOGRAPH OF AMBASSADOR GEORGE LANDAU SHAKING HANDS WITH DR. FILARTIGA THAT WAS CARRIED IN THE NEWSPAPERS THE MORNING AFTER OPENING NIGHT DID NOT GET THE MESSAGE ACROSS TO STROESSNER, THE FACT THAT THE EXHIBITION'S BROCHURE DEDICATED THE EVENT TO JOELITO LEFT LITTLE DOUBT AS TO THE EMBASSY'S DISPLEASURE. UNQUOTE.

4. WE ARE GENERALLY AWARE THAT THERE ARE VARIOUS INTERPRETATIONS OF THE FILARTIGA INCIDENT BUT THERE IS LITTLE INFORMATION OF RECORD AVAILABLE TO US HERE. CONGRESSMAN KOCH MADE THE FOLLOWING STATEMENT, WHEN INSERTING THE ARTICLE IN THE CONGRESSIONAL RECORD: QUOTE. I DO NOT UNDERSTAND WHY THE UNITED STATES CONTINUES TO PROVIDE MILITARY AND ECONOMIC AID TO THE STROESSNER REGIME IN THE FACE OF OVERWHELMING EVIDENCE OF A "CONSISTENT PATTERN OF GROSS VIOLATIONS OF INTERNATIONALLY RECOGNIZED HUMAN RIGHTS." AS A MEMBER OF THE FOREIGN OPERATIONS SUBCOMMITTEE OF THE APPROPRIATIONS COMMITTEE, I INTEND TO SCRUTINIZE ANY REQUESTS THAT ARE MADE IN THE FISCAL YEAR 1978 BUDGET FOR PARAGUAY, AND ALL OTHER COUNTRIES WHICH SHOW NO REGARD FOR THE HUMAN RIGHTS OF THEIR PEOPLE. UNQUOTE.

5. ANY INFORMATION WHICH THE EMBASSY CAN PROVIDE REGARDING THE FILARTIGA CASE WOULD BE USEFUL.

HARTMAN

[Excised]

[Excised]

FEBRUARY 18, 1977: PARAGUAY

Telegram from American Embassy, Asunción to U.S. Department of State

Subject: Filartiga Case

[EXCISED]

PAGE 01   ASUNCI   00713   01   OF   02   191052Z
ACTION ARA-10

INFO   OCT-01 ISO-00 DHA-02 H-01   SS-15   NSC-05 CIAE-00INR-07
         NSAE-00   PRS-01   /042 W

-----------------------------191103 111912 /125

P 182005Z FEB   77
FM AMEMBASSY ASUNCION
TO SECSTATE WASHDC PRIORITY 9465

[EXCISED] SECTION 1 OF 2 ASUNCION 0713

E.O. 11652: N/A
TAGS: SHUM, PA
SUBJ: FILARTIGA CASE

REF: STATE 34542

SUMMARY. JOEL FILARTIGA, 16 YEAR OLD SON OF PROMINENT
PHYSICIAN AND ARTIST, WAS MURDERED LAST MARCH. IT IS
UNCLEAR WHO COMMITTED THE CRIME; TRIAL OF THE ACCUSED
IS STILL IN PROCESS. ALTHOUGH THERE ARE RUMORS OF SEX,
DRUGS AND/OR POLITICAL MOTIVES AND THAT FILARTIGA WAS
ACTUALLY KILLED BY POLICE, GOP OFFICIALS AND OPPOSITION
LEADERS (INCLUDING CHAIRMAN OF PARAGUAYAN HUMAN
RIGHTS COMMISSION) AS WELL AS HIGH CHURCH OFFICIALS TO
DATE DO NOT RPT NOT BELIEVE CASE INVOLVES A HUMAN
RIGHTS VIOLATION, BUT RATHER WAS A COMMON CRIME. IN
VIEW OF ALLEGATIONS OF HR VIOLATIONS IN US, HOWEVER,
EMBASSY HAS URGED GOP TO INVESTIGATE FULLY AND TAKE
APPROPRIATE MEASURES IF WARRANTED. END SUMMARY.

1. EMBASSY'S OFFICIAL INFORMAL LETTER TO RICHARD GRAHAM
(ARA/ECA) DATED JANUARY 7, AND ENCLOSURES, SET FOR THE

EMBASSY'S KNOWLEDGE (AS OF THAT TIME) OF THE BACK-GROUND OF THE FILARTIGA CASE IN ANTICIPATION THAT THE MATTER WOULD SURFACE IN THE U.S. IN SUMMARY, ON MARCH 30, 1976, THE BODY OF JOEL FILARTIGA, THE 16 YEAR OLD SON OF DR. JOEL FILARTIGA, MEDICAL DOCTOR AND ONE OF PARAGUAY'S LEADING PAINTERS, WAS FOUND AT THE HOME OF A YOUNG MARRIED WOMAN. THAT THE BODY WAS BADLY MUTILATED IS ATTESTED TO BY THE MANY PHOTOS OF IT PUBLISHED IN THE LOCAL PRESS. THE WOMAN'S HUSBAND WAS SUBSEQUENTLY CHARGED WITH THE MURDER AND BROUGHT TO TRIAL. THE TRIAL HAS NOT YET BEEN COMPLETED. (SUCH A DELAY IS NOT UNUSUAL IN THE PARAGUAYAN LEGAL SYSTEM).

2. BEYOND THIS, THERE IS NO GENERALLY AGREED UPON VERSION OF WHAT TRANSPIRED. BECAUSE OF SOME OBVIOUS DISCREPANCIES, SUCH AS THE CONDITION OF THE BODY AND THAT FACT THAT THE YOUNG WOMAN REPORTEDLY WAS STILL IN BED WITH THE CORPSE WHEN THE POLICE ALLEGEDLY ARRIVED, AND SHORTLY THEREAFTER DISAPPEARED NEVER TO GIVE TESTIMONY IN THE CASE, CREATED SERIOUS DOUBTS REGARDING THE MURDER CHARGES.

3. DR. FILARTIGA HIRED A WELL-KNOWN LOCAL LAWYER, DR. HORACIO GALEANO PERRONE, TO INVESTIGATE THE CASE AND TO REPRESENT HIS INTERESTS AT THE MURDER TRIAL. IN A LETTER TO THE EMBASSY DATED 12 OCTOBER 1976, (A COPY OF WHICH WAS TRANSMITTED TO THE DEPARTMENT WITH THE LETTER OF JANUARY 7), DR. GALEANO PERRONE STATED THAT THIS INVESTIGATION ESTABLISHED THAT JOEL FILARTIGA WAS DETAINED BY THE POLICE THE EVENING OF MARCH 29, HAVING BEEN DENOUNCED AS A SUBVERSIVE BY THE MAN LATER ACCUSED OF HIS MURDER. DR. GALEANO PERRONE FURTHER STATED THAT THE MAN'S MOTIVE IN DENOUNCING YOUNG FILARTIGA WAS BECAUSE HE BELIEVED THE LATTER WAS HAVING SEXUAL RELATIONS WITH HIS WIFE, NOT THAT HE WAS A SUBVERSIVE. FOLLOWING TWO HOURS OF TORTURE IN A POLICE STATION, JOEL FILARTIGA UNEXPECTEDLY DIED, ACCORDING TO THE LAWYER, WHO ADDED THAT IN ORDER TO COVER UP THE CIRCUMSTANCES OF YOUNG FILARTIGA'S DEATH, THE POLICE TOOK FILARTIGA'S BODY TO THE HOUSE OF THE MAN WHO HAD DENOUNCED HIM AND FORCED THE LATTER TO TAKE RESPONSIBILITY FOR THE CRIME.

4. THE PRESUMED AUTHOR OF THE ARTICLE PUBLISHED IN THE CONGRESSIONAL RECORD (SEE REFTEL) TOLD THE EMBASSY

THAT HIS KNOWLEDGE OF THE CASE WAS LARGELY BASED ON THE RESULTS OF DR. GALEANO PERRONE'S INVESTIGATION, ALTHOUGH HIS VERSION OF THE FACTS AS RELATED TO THE EMBASSY ON SEVERAL OCCASIONS DIFFERED FROM THAT OF DR. GALEANO IN SOME IMPORTANT RESPECTS. HE SAID THE CRIME WAS COMMITTED BY OFF DUTY POLICEMEN ACTING ON PRIVATE MOTIVES AND IT TOOK PLACE AT THE HOUSE WHERE THE BODY WAS "DISCOVERED", NOT IN A POLICE STATION.

5. THE LOCAL PRESS HAS OPENLY QUESTIONED THE VALIDITY OF THE MURDER PROSECUTION, AND OTHER VERSIONS OF THE CASE HAVE BEEN WIDELY RUMORED, INCLUDING REPORTS THAT YOUNG FILARTIGA WAS INVOLVED WITH HOMOSEXUALS AND DRUGS. ALL VERSIONS ATTRIBUTE THE DEATH TO POLICEMEN. THE EMBASSY HAS NO INDEPENDENT KNOWLEDGE OF THE FACTS IN THIS CASE AND IS NOT ABLE TO CONDUCT ITS OWN INVESTIGATION. CONSEQUENTLY, WE ARE UNABLE TO DISCRIMINATE AMONG THE VARIOUS VERSIONS OF THE CASE THAT ARE CIRCULATING.

6. THE AMBASSADOR DISCUSSED THE CASE ON FEBRUARY 17 WITH THE PRESIDENT OF THE PARAGUAYAN HUMAN RIGHTS COMMISSION (A PROMINENT LEADER OF THE OPPOSITION) WHO CONFIRMED HER BELIEF, EXPRESSED TO HIM LAST FALL, THAT THIS CASE DID NOT HAVE POLITICAL OVERTONES, BUT IF ANYTHING WAS A MATTER OF ORDINARY POLICE BRUTALITY THAT COULD HAVE HAPPENED ANYWHERE. SHE FELT THE COMMISSION WOULD BE BETTER ADVISED TO CONFINE ITS EFFORTS TO HELPING THOSE WHO WERE BEING DETAINED FOR THEIR SUSPECTED SUBVERSIVE POLITICAL BELIEFS OR ACTIVITIES, RATHER THAN WASTE THEIR AMMUNITION ON A DUBIOUS AFFAIR LIKE THE FILARTIGA CASE. SHE OBSERVED THAT A NUMBER OF PEOPLE HAD DISAPPEARED WHILE IN THE HANDS OF THE POLICE BUT THE POLICE HAD NEVER BEFORE FELT THE NEED TO CONCOCT AN ELABORATE COVER UP.

7. OTHER OPPOSITION LEADERS AND HIGH CHURCH OFFICIALS HAVE EXPRESSED THE SAME VIEWS TO EMBASSY OFFICERS. THE EMBASSY HAS ALSO NOTED THAT NEITHER EL RADICAL, THE PRINCIPAL ORGAN OF THE OPPOSITION LIBERAL PARTY, NOR SENDERO, A CATHOLIC CHURCH PUBLICATION, BOTH OF WHICH REGULARLY COMMENT ON HUMAN RIGHTS ISSUES IN A WAY OPENLY CRITICAL OF THE GOVERNMENT AND THE POLICE, HAS EVER MENTIONED THE FILARTIGA CASE.

8. SINCE RECEIPT OF REFTEL, AMBASSADOR LANDAU HAS CALLED ATTENTION TO THE PUBLICATION OF THE ARTICLE ON THE FILAR-TIGA CASE IN THE CONGRESSIONAL RECORD TO SEVERAL HIGH-RANKING GOP OFFICIALS, INCLUDING PRESIDENT STROESSNER, FOREIGN MINISTER NOGUES, AND INTERIOR MINISTER MONTA-NARO. THE AMBASSADOR HAS URGED THAT THE ACCUSATION OF POLICE INVOLVEMENT BE THOROUGHLY INVESTIGATED AND THE GUILTY, IF THERE IS A FINDING OF GUILT, BE TRIED AND PUNISHED.

9. DEPARTMENT MAY DRAW ON FOREGOING IN REPLYING TO INQUIRIES STIMULATED BY FEBRUARY 1 CONGRESSIONAL RECORD ACCOUNT OF THE FILARTIGA CASE.

LANDAU

[EXCISED]

MARCH 29, 1977: PARAGUAY

Correspondence from American Embassy, Asunción to U.S. Department of State

Asuncion, Paraguay
March 29, 1977

OFFICIAL-INFORMAL
LIMITED OFFICIAL USE

Richard C. Graham, Esquire
ARA/ECA
Room 4906
Department of State
Washington, DC

Dear Dick:

There has been a further development in the Filartiga case that you should know about. Last Friday the Ambassador received a letter from Galeano Perrone, the lawyer for the Filartiga family, in which he, in effect, retracted statements made to the Ambassador last October. His most recent letter, a copy of which is attached, says that the police were not responsible for the death of Joel Filartiga, and that there have been no irregularities in the murder trial. Denying that the case has political overtones, he ends the letter by praising President Stroessner for promoting high respect for human rights. He asks that all this be conveyed to Senator Kennedy.

At my request, lawyer Galeano came to the Embassy on March 25 to discuss the letter. He reported that several weeks ago Lopez Escobar, Paraguayan Ambassador-designate to Washington mentioned on a local television show the remarks Senator Kennedy had inserted in the Congressional record regarding the Filartiga case. Ever since, Galeano said he had been harassed by the police at his home and office, and that a few days before his brother-in-law, an officer, had been thrown out of the army, allegedly because of Galeano's activities. He disclosed that he was now fearful of his own future in Paraguay, and had written this letter solely for the purpose of "covering his back". He assured me that it did not represent the truth, which remains as set forth in his letter of last October. He said to tear up the letter or file it away.

At the moment, this is all we know. I will keep you posted on any further news of importance. Have you heard any more about the case at your end, or has interest died down (I hope).

Sincerely yours,

Philip C. Gill

Enclosure: As stated

APRIL 6, 1977: UNITED STATES

Correspondence from U.S. Department of State to American Embassy, Asunción

DEPARTMENT OF STATE
Washington, DC 20520

April 6, 1977

OFFICIAL-INFORMAL
LIMITED OFFICIAL USE

Mr. Philip C. Gill
Chief, Political Section
American Embassy
Asuncion, Paraguay

Dear Phil:

I appreciate your letter of March 29 on the Filartiga case. My instinct warns me that this case may end up causing us some damage. It has not gone away.

As you know, we sent the basic telegram on the Filartiga case (ASUNCION 713) to staff officers of Senator Kennedy and Congressmen Koch and Fraser.

On March 30, I talked for almost one hour by telephone to a reporter representing the Los Angeles Free Press. He had the entire story, probably directly from Richard White. I followed up this conversation with a letter to the reporter, Jerry Helfiend. I felt this was necessary in that he is going ahead with an article for his newspaper, which sounded heavily slanted. A copy of my letter is enclosed.

In your current letter you report that Galeano Perrone asked that his disavowal letter be torn up or filed. I assume by this that the disavowal letter was for local consumption, and not really intended to be conveyed to Senator Kennedy.

What we need to know in the Department is whether the new development changes in any way the interpretation we are now giving to the Filartiga case. Is it still considered, at worst, a case of police brutality? The Helfiend article, when and if it appears, will probably generate new inquiries, some of which will probably come through Congress.

As you can see, I have not tried to gloss over the details as we know them in my letter to the reporter. So, many thanks for your report, and let us know quickly of any more developments. I just wish that the GOP would take the Ambassador's advice and carry out a formal investigation.

Sincerely,

Richard C. Graham

Enclosure: As stated.

LIMITED OFFICIAL USE

APRIL 21, 1977: UNITED STATES

Memorandum from U.S. Department of State to Files

Subject: Filartiga and Related Matters

MEMORANDUM

TO: The Files

FROM: DCM—Everett F. Briggs

DATE: April 21, 1977

SUBJECT: Filartiga and Related Matters

In the course of a conversation covering a variety of topics, new Paraguayan Ambassador to Washington Mario Lopez Escobar commented at length on the Filartiga case.

He said that he was very close to the young lawyer engaged by the Filartigas, Galeano Perrone, whom he had thought to invite to serve as his Minister Counselor in Washington. He said Galeano Perrone is a close personal friend of Gustavo Stroessner, as well as of Conrado Pappalardo. That there seemed to be a plot to discredit Galeano Perrone—on several fronts simultaneously—he attributed to enemies of Pappalardo's who hoped thereby to destroy a man who at present probably is closer to the President than anyone in Paraguay. He said he could not identify who might be behind these maneuvers; it was all very puzzling.

According to Dr. Lopez Escobar, the woman involved (the person with whom young Filartiga's body was found) had a reputation as having many lovers. At all hours of the day and night men were seen to arrive and leave her house, and even before the murder of Filartiga a neighbor is alleged to have remarked that there was bound to be trouble when the young husband found out what was going on. Among her lovers were said to be police officers.

As far as the legal aspects of the case are concerned, he said Galeano Perrone had explained the Filartiga case to him in detail and they are very clear. He said there is a large stack of evidence (testimony, declarations) now being studied, which *inter alia* shows that the husband was responsible for the youth's bizarre death. Until someone proves differently, his confession and supporting testimony and evidence seem conclusive.

cc: AMB, POL

MAY 10, 1977: PARAGUAY

Memorandum from American Embassy, Asunción

Subject: The Filartiga Case

CONFIDENTIAL
MEMORANDUM OF CONVERSATION

PARTICIPANTS:	Dr. Joel Filartiga
	Mr. Jose Alfredo Fornos
	Mr. Philip C. Gill, Chief, Political Section
	Mr. Bruce G. Burton, Political Officer
DATE AND PLACE:	May 10, 1977-Mr. Gill's Office
SUBJECT:	The Filartiga Case
REF:	Memorandum of Conversation, March 31, 1977
DISTRIBUTION:	AMB, DCM, POL, POL/R, ARA/ECA

Dr. Filartiga came to the Embassy accompanied by Mr. Fornos, an American research assistant who has been living in the Filartiga home. During the course of an hour-long meeting, Dr. Filartiga reviewed problems in the investigation of his son's murder and other matters.

He expressed doubts about his ability to pursue the investigation since the attorney handling the case, Dr. Horacio Galeano Perrone, formally withdrew from the case (on May 10). Dr. Filartiga said that while he had some reservations about Galeano in matters unrelated to the Filartiga case, he felt Galeano had done an excellent job representing him; the attorney's withdrawal resulted from the Supreme Court's refusal to renew his law license and not because of a falling out between Filartiga and the lawyer. Filartiga said he would search for a new attorney but doubted that he could find anyone of prominence to take the case.

Filartiga complained of reprisals and harassment against himself, members of his family, and anyone associated with the case. However, Mr. Fornos noted that threatening phone calls had abated somewhat and that he believed the overall situation had improved. He attributed this in part to the presence of an American in the household, which he believed gave the Filartigas a measure of protection. However, Fornos said he was planning to leave Asuncion in June and that he did not know if he could find a replacement to stay with the family.

Dr. Filartiga complained that he had not received the police protection which he felt had been promised by the GOP as a result of the Embassy's representations. He also said he had received no letter or other communication from the Minister of the Interior, who he believed was to have gotten in touch with him. However, he said a policeman who is a friend of the family regularly patrols in front of the house.

Filartiga remarked that he had begun to question whether he could safely remain in Paraguay, and inquired about going to the U.S. As before, he said the GOP had not issued him a passport (he did not say whether he had made new efforts to obtain one).

[EXCISED]

POL:BGBurton:ms

CONFIDENTIAL

JANUARY 23, 1978: PARAGUAY

Memorandum from American Embassy, Asunción

Subject: Filartiga Case

UNITED STATES GOVERNMENT
MEMORANDUM

TO: See Distribution Below

DATE: January 23, 1978

FROM: The Files of the American Embassy ASUNCION

SUBJECT: Filartiga Case

CURRENT STATUS OF CASE

Hugo Duarte Arredondo, accused of killing 17-year old Joelito Filartiga, is in prison while the case continues its judicial course. The Appeals Court is currently reviewing a defense claim that the coroner's report was incorrect as to the time of death.

The prosecution case is that Duarte caught Filartiga in bed with his 17-year old wife Maria de Rosario Villalba de Duarte, the night of March 29, 1976. In a crime of passion he killed Filartiga—knifing him repeatedly. In his first declaration to the judge, Duarte admits committing the crime.

ALTERNATE THEORIES

Professor White: In early 1977, Professor Richard White, who was living with the Filartigas at the time of the incident, published the following account in the U.S. under a pseudonym.

Dr. Filartiga, because of his reputation as a maverick, his philanthropic work with peasants in Ybycui, and frequent visits to Posadas, Argentina (where his wife's family lives), was suspected of being involved in the Organizacion Politico-Militar (OPM) subversive movement. Because of his health and prominence, the authorities felt they couldn't "question" the elder Filartiga so they zeroed in on the son. The son was vulnerable also because he had become involved in the neighboring family's squabble between Maria de Rosario Villalba and her step-father, police inspector Americo Pena, who had tried to rape her in January 1976.

This combination of personal and political factors caused Pena to obtain permission for Joelito's "kidnapping" from Pastor Coronel and Interior Minister Montanaro. Young Filartiga was then tortured to obtain a confession of his father's and his complicity in the OPM. When Joelito had nothing to confess, electric torture was increased to the point where he suffered cardiac arrest. The police panicked, decided to pass it off as a crime of passion and severed the major arteries so that the body could not be embalmed.

They brought the body to Pena's house and threw it into Rosario Villalba's room. Her husband agreed to take the rap after a beating and a promise he would be out of jail in a week. Filartiga's sister was then summoned by two police officers who took her to the Pena house where she found her brother's body.

The coroner made out a false report and the judge who would try the case legalized the false death certificate. Duarte was arrested and Rosario held as a witness but disappeared five days later after sending the Filartigas a note that she wanted to see them. Two motions to dismiss the case have been denied, a judge has removed himself from the case because he was clearly involved in the cover-up. Pena threatened to kill Filartiga's lawyer when he was arrested September 30, 1976 and also threatened to kill Filartiga and his daughter if they continued to push the case.

Filartiga, Sr.: Dr. Filartiga tells the same story except the beginning. He sees his son's death as the result of a personal vendetta against him and his family by a Dr. Roque Vallejo, who was involved in a bounced check legal case with Dr. Filartiga's mother. He says Vallejo has connections with Presidential Secretary Mario Abdo Benitez and Police Inspector Americo Pena.

Filartiga's lawyer, Galeano Perone: Galeano sent a letter to Ambassador Landau in October 1976 in which he pointed out several discrepancies in the case based on an investigation by his detectives and lawyers.
- The death of young Filartiga could not have occurred when the police claimed.
- The alleged scene of the crime did not fit the physical evidence.
- Duarte had denounced Joelito to Pena as an OPM subversive for reasons of sexual jealousy.
- They detained Filartiga at 11:00 p.m. on March 29 and tortured him for about two hours in the First Comisaria.
- They did not want to torture him to death.

— After an hour they decided to pin the rap on Duarte, as an injured husband is not liable to criminal punishment in crimes of passion.
— The law suit against Galeano Perone was merely part of an effort to get the case against Duarte dismissed.

EVIDENCE

Evidence of an erroneous coroner's report has been presented but seems peripheral. The coroner said Filartiga died of a knife wound in the chest. Doctors who examined the body following exhumation said he died of multiple knife wounds. Otherwise there has been no sworn testimony to support the White thesis. Galeano Perone's letter to Ambassador Landau supports the White story in some aspects but he formally denounced the letter in March 1977 as well as withdrawing as defense lawyer because his license had not been renewed.

GALEANO PERONE AFFAIR

Galeano Perone was taken into police custody September 30, 1976, but quickly released. He claims it was because of the Filartiga case. Officially it was in connection with a suit against Galeano by the mother of two young men whose case he had been handling. Galeano had allegedly advised them to flee to Buenos Aires and when they were murdered there some time later, their land in Paraguay was found to be in the name of Galeano Perone. The case was settled out of court but the Supreme Court did not renew Galeano's license in January 1977.

PERSECUTION OF DR. FILARTIGA

Friends of Dr. Filartiga especially in the U.S., report he has become the object of a campaign of official harassment and persecution by the Paraguayan authorities, that his life is in danger, and that his work at Yoicui will be interfered with. There may well be a cause and effect relationship between the international campaign to brand the Filartiga Case a major example of a human rights violation in Paraguay and a discernible coolness towards Dr. Filartiga by Paraguayan authorities, but this coolness falls far short of being persecution.

The passport issuing authority (Investigations Police) did not respond to Dr. Filartiga's request in 1977 to extend the validity of his passport, presumably to inhibit his ability to keep foreign interest in the case alive. Whatever the intention, the effect was the opposite: Filartiga traveled abroad anyway, and although his return was uneventful his friends raised the possibility that he might be arrested on arrival home and stimulated a concerted campaign to bring their fears to the attention of members of the U.S. Congress, the Department of state, and the American Embassy in Asuncion.

While some of the peculiar circumstances of the case may similarly be reactions to the international furor rather than reasons for it (e.g., the interrogation of two Americans working at Dr. Filartiga's clinic on January 16), this does not explain the reported brief detention of Mrs. Filartiga a week after her son's murder; and there is no question that Dr. Filartiga has earned a considerable amount of enmity on the part of those whom he has accused of complicity in the murder, and may be courting personal retaliation.

Meanwhile, however, his clinic is operating normally, he is free to come and go as he wishes, and to hold well-publicized, periodic exhibits of his art work.

HUMAN RIGHTS ASPECTS

1. If the police, under orders of Pastor Coronel and/or his superiors, [REDACTED] had tortured and killed Joel Filartiga as part of the OPM investigation, there is certainly a human rights violation. There is no evidence to support this charge, however, and there are important flaws in the thesis.

2. If police officers, acting unofficially, had tortured or murdered Filartiga, as part of a scheme of revenge, they should certainly be brought to justice if there is evidence to this effect. But this does not seem a human rights violation unless the GOP has connived in protecting the police officials. There is no proof of this and, in fact, the press gave full play to the story at the time.

3. If Duarte was forced to confess to a crime committed by others, there would be a human rights violation. However, he has not disavowed his confession and Galeano claimed to have evidence that he had murdered six other persons.

4. If Galeano Perone has been deprived of his license because he handled the Filartiga case, this would be a human rights violation. However, the Supreme Court would seem to be on solid ground in denying his license on ethical grounds if his clients' property ended up in Galeano's name, a charge never denied.

5. For what it is worth, those who follow human rights cases most closely in Paraguay (i.e., the inter-faith church group, the opposition parties, the Paraguayan Human Rights Commission, and academic circles) do not consider the Filartiga case to be a prime example of a human rights violation, but seem to subscribe to [the] theory it was a crime of passion "which could have happened anywhere." Some have told us they believe that all the

attention focused on the Filartiga case detracts from the "real" human rights problems here—the fate of political prisoners in particular.

AN EDUCATED GUESS

— There was an adulterous relationship between Duarte's wife and Filartiga.
— Police officials were involved in a scheme of personal revenge through torture but not premeditated murder.
— Either the torture or Duarte killed Filartiga.
— Unless the missing Rosario Villalba de Duarte is found and will talk, it will be impossible to find out what actually happened.

POL: ARKay:ms

DISTRIBUTION: AMB, DOM, POL, POL/R, USIS, ECON, CONS, ARA/ ECA, ARA-Mr. Glister, INR/RAR, D/HA

APRIL 5, 1979: UNITED STATES

Telegram from U.S. Department of State to American Embassy, Asunción

Subject: NIV Case

[LIMITED OFFICIAL USE]
n/a

[REDACTED]

STATE 084980
ORIGIN VO-05

INFO   OCT-01   CA-01   ADS-00   ARA-11   INSE-00   (ADS) R

DRAFTED BY CA/VO: ERAVEN: MK
APPROVED BY CA: HHORAN
CA/VO/L: CUDSCULLY
ARA/ECA: TBROWN   (SUBS)

088842 060317Z / 62

O 052350Z APR 79
FM SECSTATE WASHDC
TO AMEMBASSY ASUNCION IMMEDIATE

[REDACTED] STATE 084980

VISAS

E.O. 12065   N/A
TAGS: CVIS, PINT (PENA, AMERICO)

SUBJECT: NIV   CASE

REF: ASUNCION 1150

1. CASE OF AMERICO PENA HAS BEEN REPORTED IN NEW YORK TIMES AND WASHINGTON POST TODAY. TIMES HAS REPORTED STATEMENT ATTRIBUTED TO COHA AND REPEATED BY INS THAT PENA HAS BEEN INDICTED FOR MURDER IN PARAGUAY AND THAT HE WAS A MEMBER OF A POLICE "DEATH SQUAD". IS THIS TRUE? DEPARTMENT HAD BEEN UNDER IMPRESSION THAT NO LEGAL

CHARGES WERE PENDING AGAINST PENA AND THAT DEROGATORY INFORMATION AGAINST HIM RELATED PRIMARILY TO FILARTIGA CASE WITH ITS PERSONAL OVERTONES. POST IS ASKED TO CLARIFY BY IMMEDIATE CABLE.

2. DEPARTMENT IS ATTEMPTING TO HAVE TEXT OF ARTICLES TRANSMITTED SEPARATELY.

VANCE

[LIMITED OFFICIAL USE]

APRIL 6, 1979: UNITED STATES

Correspondence from Congressman Robert F. Drinan to Barbara Watson, Assistant Secretary of State

Congress of the United States
House of Representatives
Washington, D.C. 20515

April 6, 1979

Ms. Barbara Watson
Assistant Secretary
Bureau of Consular Affairs
Department of State
Room 6811
Washington, D.C. 20520

Dear Ms. Watson:

I write to express my deep concern about the issuance of a visitor's visa to Mr. Americo Pena, the ex-Paraguayan police officer who has, we understand, been charged with murder in his country. He is currently being held in New York City by the U.S. Immigration and Naturalization Service because of the expiration of his visa some months ago.

There is a question as to whether Mr. Pena has been indicted on this alleged charge and I recognize that in the absence of an indictment there may have been no legal basis upon which the Consulate Office in Asuncion, Paraguay could deny him a visa. However, I am familiar with the Immigration law governing the issuance of nonimmigrant visas and wonder what evidence Mr. Pena provided the Embassy of his intention to return to Paraguay following his visit to the United States. I would assume that with a murder charge outstanding against him, the Consular Office would have been quite circumspect in the matter of his visa request.

I would like to know where the decision to issue this visa was made and what consideration was given to the charges pending against Mr. Pena.

Given the notoriety of Mr. Pena's activities in Paraguay as has been reported in the press, I would like to know if the Undersecretary for Human Rights was consulted in this matter.

I would appreciate hearing from you at the earliest time. With every best wish, I am

Cordially yours,

Robert F. Drinan
Member of Congress

RFD/dc

Civil Complaint Filed in U.S. District Court for the Eastern District of New York; Exhibits; Affidavit of Richard Arens

UNITED STATES DISTRICT COURT
EASTERN DISTRICT OF NEW YORK

DOLLY M.E. FILARTIGA and DR. JOEL FILARTIGA,	**VERIFIED COMPLAINT** **JURY TRIAL REQUESTED**

Plaintiffs,

— against —

AMERICO NORBERTO PENA-
IRALA, LEONEL CASTILLO, as
Commissioner of the United States
Immigration and Naturalization
Service and GEORGE VICIAN, as
District Director, Immigration and
Naturalization Service, New York.

Defendants.

PRELIMINARY STATEMENT

Plaintiffs, for their Verified Complaint, say and allege:

1. This is an action for damages for violation of human rights for the wrongful torture and murder of the decedent, Joel (Joelito) Filartiga, under the treaties of the United States, the law of nations and the laws of the states of the United States.

JURISDICTION

2. The jurisdiction of this Court arises under 28 U.S.C. §§ 1331, 1350, 1651, 2201 and 2202 and the doctrine of pendent jurisdiction.

3. The amount in controversy exceeds $10,000 exclusive of interest and costs, in that the value of the rights of which plaintiffs have been deprived is in excess of $10,000.

4. Plaintiffs' causes of action arise under Article 2, §2, Clause 1 and Article 6, Clause 2 of the Constitution of the United States; 28 U.S.C. §§ 1350, 2201-2202; 8 U.S.C. § 1252(c); the wrongful death statutes; the U.N. Charter; the Universal Declaration on Human Rights; the U.N. Declaration Against Torture; the American Declaration of the Rights and Duties of Man; and other pertinent declarations, documents, and practices constituting the customary international law of human rights and the law of nations.

PARTIES

PLAINTIFFS

5. Plaintiff Dr. Joel Filartiga is the father of the decedent and resides in Ybycui, Paraguay. He sues on his own behalf and as personal representative of the decedent.

6. Plaintiff Dolly M. E. Filartiga is the sister of the decedent and resides in Washington, D.C. She arrived in the United States on April 28, 1978 with a visitor's visa. On April 5, 1979 she filed with the Immigration and Naturalization Service an application for political asylum in the United States.

DEFENDANTS

7. Defendant Americo Norberto Pena-Irala is a former Inspector General of Police of Asuncion, Paraguay. He is presently in the United States as an illegal alien and subject to a deportation order entered April 5, 1979 by Immigration Judge Anthony M. DeGaeto. He is being held in custody of the U.S. Immigration and Naturalization Service at the Brooklyn Navy Yard.

8. Defendant Leonel Castillo is the Commissioner of the Immigration and Naturalization Service, U.S. Department of Justice.

9. Defendant George Vician is the District Director of the Immigration and Naturalization Service, U.S. Department of Justice.

10. All defendants are sued in their official and individual capacities.

STATEMENT OF FACTS

11. On information and belief, on March 29, 1976, the decedent, seventeen-year old Joel (Joelito) Filartiga was kidnapped and tortured to death by defendant Americo Norberto Pena-Irala and others.

12. Approximately four hours later, plaintiff Dolly Filartiga was awakened by Paraguayan police officials who summoned her to the defendant Pena-Irala's home. There she was led to the mutilated body of her brother. A photograph of his whipped, slashed and electric-shocked corpse is attached hereto as Exhibit A.

13. As Dolly Filartiga was running screaming from the house where her brother lay, Pena approached her, yelling and gesticulating and said: "Here you have what you have been looking for for so long and what you deserve. Now shut up."

14. Joelito Filartiga was the son of plaintiff Dr. Joel Filartiga, a noted medical philanthropist, and artist of international reputation, whose paintings depict the oppression and suffering of the people of Paraguay. Dr. Filartiga is a leading political opponent of General Stroessner, the dictator-President of Paraguay. He has been arrested three times for his political opposition and tortured in 1966.

15. On information and belief, Joelito Filartiga was tortured and murdered by the defendant and others in retaliation for the political activities and opinions of his father.

16. On April 28, 1976, plaintiff Dolly Filartiga, and her mother were wrongfully summoned to the Criminal Court in Asuncion where they were charged with harassment of Pena's house ("Atropellio a Domicilio"), and battery on Jorge Villalba, Pena's stepson, and sentenced without trial, to jail. They were released after six hours.

17. Dr. Filartiga filed a lawsuit against the defendant Pena and the Paraguayan police for the murder of his son. On September 30, 1976, Dr. Filartiga's attorney, Horacio Galeano Perrone, was arrested and shackled to a wall in the central police headquarters. The defendant Pena arrived and threatened to kill Dr. Galeano, Dr. Filartiga, and Dr. Filartiga's thirteen-year-old daughter if they continued to press the lawsuit against him and the police for Joelito's murder.

18. Judge Rojas Via has unduly delayed the Filartiga case in the courts, and no relief can be obtained, as the Paraguayan judiciary is an appendage of the executive branch.

19. On behalf of Joelito Filartiga and Dr. Joel Filartiga, a complaint has been filed with the Chairman of the Inter-American Commission on Human Rights, Organization of American States, (attached hereto as Exhibit B).

20. On information and belief, defendant Pena has been living in Brooklyn, New York for the last nine months. On April 4, 1979, he was arrested by agents of the U.S. Immigration and Naturalization Service. He was ordered deported on April 5, 1979 (Attached hereto are Exhibits C and D, articles from the New York Times reporting on his discovery and detention.) Prior to September, 1978, the whereabouts of defendant Pena were unknown to plaintiffs.

FIRST CAUSE OF ACTION AGAINST
AMERICO NORBERTO PENA-IRALA

21. Plaintiffs repeat and reallege each and every allegation above as if fully set forth herein.

22. As a result of the acts of defendant Pena, the deceased sustained pain and suffering and bodily injuries causing death.

23. At the time of these acts, the deceased was in good health and physical condition.

24. As a result of these acts, plaintiffs incurred damages by reason of decedent's wrongful death.

25. As a result of the deliberate confrontation of plaintiff Dolly Filartiga with the tortured body of her brother, she suffered emotional pain and suffering.

26. As a result of the unlawful sentencing and jailing of Dolly Filartiga, she suffered deprivation of liberty and emotional pain and suffering.

27. The aforesaid acts of the defendant Pena constitute violations of the treaties of the United States and the law of nations.

SECOND CAUSE OF ACTION AGAINST
AMERICO NORBERTO PENA-IRALA

28. Plaintiffs repeat and reallege each and every allegation above as if fully set forth herein.

29. As a result of the acts of defendant Pena, the deceased sustained pain and suffering and bodily injuries causing death.

30. At the time of these acts, the deceased was in good health and physical condition.

31. As a result of these acts, plaintiffs incurred damages by reason of decedent's wrongful death.

32. As a result of the deliberate confrontation of plaintiff Dolly Filartiga with the tortured body of her brother, she suffered emotional pain and suffering.

33. As a result of the unlawful sentencing and jailing of Dolly Filartiga, she suffered deprivation of liberty and emotional pain and suffering.

34. The aforesaid acts of the defendant Pena constitute violations of the wrongful death statutes.

PRAYER FOR RELIEF

WHEREFORE, plaintiffs pray that this Court

1. Assume jurisdiction of this cause;

2. Enter a judgment awarding compensatory and punitive damages to be paid by the defendant Pena to plaintiff Joel Filartiga as personal representative of Joelito Filartiga, deceased, and to Dolly Filartiga, in the sum of $10,000,000 plus interest, costs and disbursements;

3. Enter an order prohibiting defendant Castillo, his agents, employees and assigns, and all persons acting in concert or participation with him, from deporting defendant Americo Norberto Pena-Irala;

4. Award plaintiffs reasonable attorneys fees and costs;

5. Award plaintiffs such other and further relief as to this Court seems just and reasonable.

Respectfully submitted,

PETER WEISS
RHONDA COPELON
JOHN W. CORWIN
JOSE ANTONIO LUGO
c/o Center for Constitutional Rights
853 Broadway
New York, New York 10003
(212) 674-3303

MICHAEL MAGGIO
Goren and Maggio
1801 Columbia Road, N.W.
Suite 100
Washington, D.C.
(202) 483-8055

Attorneys for Plaintiffs

Dated: New York, New York
      April 6, 1979

Exhibit A

[Images omitted]

Exhibit B

Chairman
Inter-American Commission on Human Rights
Organization of American States
Washington, D.C. 20006

RE: Case 2158
Joel Filártiga

Name: Harold R. Berk
Nationality: United States of America
Address: 405 S. 12th Street
              Philadelphia, PA 19147
              United States of America

wishes to supplement his communication to the Inter-American Commission on Human Rights concerning the case of Joelito Filártiga and Dr. Joel Filártiga of Asunción, Paraguay, as follows:

Rejection of the Response of the Government of Paraguay:

The Response of the Government of Paraguay to the communications filed on this case is totally unacceptable and does not represent the true facts of the events surrounding the murder of Joelito Filártiga.

Supplemental Information on the Violations:

The attached three page statement by Dr. Joel Filártiga is submitted to supplement the communication previously filed by Harold R. Berk concerning the murder of Joelito Filártiga. The events and circumstances outlined in the attached statement are filed as a rebuttal to the Response of the Government of Paraguay.

As further rebuttal to the Response of the Government of Paraguay, Harold R. Berk states the following:

1. The Paraguayan Government stated that the alleged murderer, Duarte Arrendondo, confessed to the killing of Joelito Filártiga during judicial proceedings of the Regular Courts. However, at the time that Duarte supposedly confessed, Dr. Joel Filártiga, father of the victim, was barred from the proceedings. Dr. Filártiga's own lawyer was also barred from the judicial proceedings during the supposed confession.

2. There was no cross-examination or other questioning of Duarte at the time he entered his confession. Thus, there was no inquiry surrounding the circumstances of the murder to learn if the confession was true.

3. On information and belief, Duarte was not questioned by the Court or any lawyer to determine if his confession was voluntary and freely given or whether it was coerced.

4. Dr. Filártiga and I submit that Duarte's confession was physically and psychologically coerced by the authorities.

5. Though Duarte was prosecuted on charges brought by the Government of Paraguay, and though he "confessed" to the killing of Joelito Filartiga over a year ago, he has not been sentenced for his crime. In fact, Duarte was seen freely walking on the streets between Christmas 1976 and August 1977. He is now confined in jail, but he is a trustee in the jail which gives him special privileges.

6. The failure to sentence Duarte even though twenty-two months has elapsed since the killing, indicates that the Government does not intend to accept his confession and sentence him to prison for the murder. This failure to sentence Duarte is an indication that the Government of Paraguay believes his confession to be false, as it is.

7. Dr. Filártiga has submitted to the Commission photographs of the body of his son taken shortly after his death. These photographs show that Duarte could not have been the killer. The body has evidence of numerous deep burns which could not have been inflicted by Duarte in his supposed rage. The photographs also show the penis to be erect since the wire used to inflict electroshock through his penis was still inside the penis causing it be extended. Duarte did not admit inserting this electrical probe into the penis, and he did not, the police officers performed this act during the torture of Joelito.

Request for Investigation in Paraguay:

Based upon the original complaints filed in this case, the unacceptable response of the Government of Paraguay, the attached statement of Dr. Joel Filártiga, the supplemental information provided herein, and the other evidence and communications sent to the Commission on this case, we ask that the Commission conduct an investigation of this case through a direct and personal investigation conducted within Paraguay. We understand that the Government of Paraguay has agreed to a site visit by the Commission in March 1978; we ask that this case be included in that investigation.

Harold R. Berk
Attorney at Law
Member of Amnesty International
(USA) Legal Committee

January 16, 1978
Philadelphia, Pennsylvania
United States of America

Exhibit C

The New York Times, **April 5, 1979**

Paraguay Alien Tied to Murders in Native Land

Ex-Police Official Seized by the U.S. in Brooklyn

By: Selwyn Raab

A former Paraguayan police official who has been accused by international and refugee organizations of being involved in political murders in his South American country was arrested yesterday by Federal agents in Brooklyn for illegally entering the United States.

The former official, Américo Norberto Peña-Irala, is believed to have been living quietly under his real name for the last nine months in a largely Hasidic Jewish neighborhood in Borough Park. Mr. Peña, who is 45 years old and was a chief inspector of police in Paraguay until last July, was arrested with a woman companion by agents of the Federal Immigration and Naturalization Service as he left an apartment building at 1865 52d Street in the morning.

Attached to a special police unit in Asuncion, the capital of Paraguay, Mr. Peña had been sought by Federal agents since October, when he was recognized in Brooklyn by a political refugee from Paraguay. According to the Immigration and Naturalization Service, Mr. Peña has been formally accused in Paraguay on a murder charge.

Two Held Pending Deportation

Frank DiConstanzo, the Federal agent in charge of the case, said Mr. Peña was being held in $75,000 bond and his companion, Juana Villalba, 41, in $25,000 bond in detention facilities in Brooklyn pending deportation hearings. Their 3-year-old son and the niece of Miss Villalba are being sheltered by social-service agencies, the Immigration Service said.

Political groups opposed to the current government in Paraguay have identified Mr. Peña as a member of a police "death squad" that investigated and tortured opponents of the government of Gen. Alfred Stroessner. The general has ruled the country as President since a coup d'etat in 1954.

In addition Amnesty International and a human-rights committee of the Organization of American States have asserted that Mr. Peña was chiefly responsible for the torture-murder in 1976 of Joel Filártiga Speratti, the 17-year-old son of a political opponent of General Stroessner.

Richard D. White, a senior research fellow with the Council on Hemispheric Affairs, who has lived in Paraguay, said that Mr. Peña was "among the most detested and feared government officials in his nation." The council, a nonprofit research organization specializing in Latin-American affairs, had pressed the Immigration and Naturalization Service to locate Mr. Peña after he was seen here last October.

The Immigration Service said that Mr. Peña, with his woman companion, their son and the woman's 16-year-old niece, arrived in Miami as tourists last July 21 with entry permits that expired August 3. The four, according to neighbors in Borough Park, have lived since July in a modest ground-floor apartment in the middle-income neighborhood.

The death of the Filártiga youth led to international publicity and investigations by human-rights groups. It also eventually attracted attention to Mr. Peña's alleged role in the case.

A confidential report prepared by the Inter-American Commission on Human Rights of the Organization of American States, contended that Mr. Peña and three other policemen kidnapped the Filártiga youth on March 29, 1976 with the intent of forcing him to incriminate his father falsely in sedition charges. The report, obtained by The New York Times, asserted that the boy had died of a heart attack after being beaten and receiving high-voltage electric shocks.

Dr. Filártiga, who is a physician and a painter, started an international campaign to bring charges against the "death squad," and the case was investigated by Amnesty International and the Organization of American States.

Mr. White of the Council on Hemispheric Affairs said that Dr. Filártiga was successful in getting a criminal court judge in Paraguay to file murder charges last year against Mr. Peña.

"The scandal got so big that Peña had to leave the country for a while," Mr. White said.

Gilberto Olmedo-Sanchez, a Paraguayan economist and journalist who is living in exile in Queens, said that Mr. Peña, after being recognized here last fall, had told another Paraguayan that he was in New York "to let the situation cool off in Paraguay."

Exhibit D

The New York Times, **April 6, 1979**

Paraguayan Tied to Murders Is Ordered Deported

By: Selwyn Raab

A former Paraguayan police official who has been accused by human-rights groups of political torture-murders in his country was ordered deported yesterday after he admitted overstaying a tourist visa and living illegally for nine months in Brooklyn.

The Council on Hemispheric Affairs, a human-rights organization specializing in Latin American affairs, however, urged that Federal authorities detain the man, Américo Peña-Irala until it could be determined how he was granted a visa by United States Embassy officials in Paraguay although his alleged role as a member of a political "death squad" had become an international controversy.

Laurance Birns, director of the council, called for a Congressional inquiry "into a number of disturbing aspects" of the Peña case, including whether State Department officials may have been bribed to give him a visa last July.

Both Ask to Be Deported

Mr. Peña and Juana Fernandez-Gonzales, a Paraguayan woman friend with whom he was arrested in a Borough Park apartment Wednesday, both asked to be deported at a hearing before an immigration judge in Manhattan. "All we want is to be sent back to our country as quickly as possible," said the 45-year-old Mr. Peña, who was a chief inspector in Asuncion, the capital of Paraguay, until last summer.

At the hearing before Judge Anthony M. DeGaeto, the 2-year-old son of Mr. Peña and his companion crawled on the courtroom floor and drank milk from a bottle.

Agents of the Federal Immigration and Naturalization Service said Mr. Peña had been charged with the torture-murder of the 17-year-old son of a political opponent of the government in Paraguay. International human-rights organizations and Paraguayan refugee groups have accused Mr. Peña of participating in the torture and murder of political opponents.

Mr. Peña was arrested by Federal agents after he was recognized in Brooklyn by a political refugee from his country.

A spokesman for the State Department said it was looking into the visa matter but that it was unclear whether Mr. Peña had been formally accused of any crime in Paraguay.

AFFIDAVIT

RICHARD ARENS, being duly sworn, deposes and says:

1. I have been a member of the District of Columbia Bar since 1950 and of the Bar of the Supreme Court of the United States since 1955, engaged in both practice and teaching.

2. I am Professor of Law at Temple University in Philadelphia, Pennsylvania. I have specialized in the teaching and research of the law of international human rights, particularly in the last ten years. I am author, among other works, of *Genocide in Paraguay* (Temple Univ. Press) 1976.

3. It is my professional judgment, particularly in the light of the customary phase of international law exemplified by U.N. covenants, conventions, the U.N. Declaration Against Torture and authoritative scholarly interpretations thereof that the torture of a human being, resulting in death, is a tort committed in violation of the law of nations.

4. I have further consulted in this matter with Professor Albert Blaustein of the Rutgers University Law School at Camden, New Jersey. Professor Blaustein, the author of a 15-volume work on world constitutions, and the President of the Human Rights Advocates International Center at 230 Park Avenue, Suite 460, New York, New York 10017, asked me to transmit his identical view to this Court.

RICHARD ARENS
Professor of Law, Temple Univeristy
Member, American Committee, Inter-
American Association of Democracy And Freedom
Member, Human Rights Advocates Int'l
New York, New York

Sworn to before me this 6th day of April, 1979.

Notary Public

APRIL 6, 1979: UNITED STATES

Telegram from U.S. Department of State to American Embassy, Asunción

VV   ESB020BRA517
RR RUESAS
DE RUEHFO   0200/02   0960657
ZNR UUUUU ZYN
R 06065 1Z APR 79
FM: USINFO WASHDC
TO: AMEMBASSY ASUNCION
BT
UNCLAS SECTION 02 OF 02

USINFO

EO 12065 N/A

PARAGUAY.

INITIALLY, PENA WAS NOT CHARGED WITH THE KIDNAPING, TOR-
TURE OR MURDER OF JOELITO FILARTIGA. PENA HELD THE RANK
OF INSPECTOR AT THE TIME OF THE KILLING, AND THE GOVERN-
MENT OF GEN. ALFREDO STROESSNER DECLARED THAT NO
POLICE PARTICIPATED IN THE CRIME.

PENA WAS PROMOTED TO CHIEF INSPECTOR, BUT THE INTERNA-
TIONAL PUBLICITY ORGANIZED BY THE DEAD YOUTH'S WELL-
KNOWN FATHER APPARENTLY LED TO PENA'S BEING CHARGED
AND FORCED TO LEAVE PARAGUAY.

A JAN. 31, 1978, ORGANIZATION OF AMERICAN STATES REPORT ON
HUMAN RIGHTS IN PARAGUAY MENTIONED THE CASE, AND
DESCRIBED PENA AS THE MAN ALLEGED TO HAVE PLANNED THE
KIDNAPING AND TORTURE. THE REPORT SAID THE OAS HAS PHO-
TOGRAPHS OF THE MUTILATED BODY OF JOELITO FILARTIGA.

SOURCES SAID THERE HAD BEEN PERSONAL ANIMOSITY BETWEEN
PENA AND THE FILARTIGA FAMILY FOR SOME TIME BEFORE THE
MURDER. THE VICTIM'S FATHER WAS KNOWN AS A DISSIDENT IN A
COUNTRY WHERE LITTLE DISSENT IS TOLERATED. PENA AND
FILARTIGA LIVED TWO HOUSES APART IN ASUNCION.

SOURCES SAID PENA IS BELIEVED TO HAVE CONTINUED TO DRAW HIS POLICE SALARY WHILE LIVING IN THE UNITED STATES, AND THEY ACCUSE HIM OF HELPING TO TRANSPORT YOUNG PARAGUAYAN WOMEN TO NEW YORK TO WORK AS PROSTITUTES.

AN IMMIGRATION OFFICIAL SAID PENA DID NOT DENY HIS IDENTITY WHEN HE WAS APPREHENDED BY INVESTIGATORS THIS MORNING WHILE ON HIS WAY TO A JOB HE HAD TAKEN AS A WOOD FINISHER IN DOWNTOWN BROOKLYN. THE OFFICIAL ADDED THAT VILLALBA WAS EMPLOYED AS A SEWING MACHINE OPERATOR AND THAT THE NIECE APPARENTLY WAS BROUGHT TO THE UNITED STATES AS A BABYSITTER FOR THE 3-YEAR-OLD BOY. (END TEXT)

REGARDS DAVIS

ITEM

BT

0220

APRIL 6, 1979: UNITED STATES

Telegram from U.S. Department of State to American Embassy, Asunción

Subject: NIV Case

LEE ELMER E
79 STATE 85759

LIMITED OFFICIAL USE

PAGE 01   STATE   025759
ORIGIN VO-05
INFO OCT-01 ADS-00 /006 R
DRAFTED BY VO/F/P:RNCHIPERFIELD:VAB
APPROVED BY CA:HHORAN
VO/L:CDSCULLY

--- 100682 0E2_32Z /56

0 062243Z APR 79 ZFF4
FM SECSTATE WASHDC
TO AMEMBASSY ASUNCION NIACT IMMEDIATE
LIMITED OFFICIAL USE STATE 085759
VISAS
E.O. 12065 N/A
TAGS: CVIS, PA (PENA, AMERICO)
SUBJECT: NIV CASE
REFERENCE: ASUNCION 2378 AND PREVIOUS

1. DEPT (VO) REQUESTS EMBASSY TO SUBMIT IMMEDIATELY ORIGINALS OF ALL NONIMMIGRANT VISA APPLICATIONS (OF-155) FOR AMERICO NORBERTO PENA-IRALA. DPOB 7/12/33. LUQUE, PARAGUAY AND JUANA BAUTISTA FERNANDEZ-GONZALEZ. DPOB 6/24/36. LAMBARE, PARAGUAY BY REGISTERED POUCH ATTN: ANTI-FRAUD COORDINATOR, POST LIAISON DIVISION, OFFICE OF FIELD SUPPORT AND LIAISON, VISA SERVICES DIRECTORATE. ACCORDING TO ASUNCION 1265 AND 1328 PENA RECEIVED HIS VISAS ON JULY 11, 1977 AND JULY 11, 1978 AND FERNANDEZ ON JULY 11, 1978. AUTHENTICATED COPIES OF THESE VISA APPLICATIONS SHOULD BE RETAINED BY POST.

2. EMBASSY ALSO REQUESTED TO PROVIDE BY IMMEDIATE CABLE TEXT OF INFORMATION PROVIDED ON VISA APPLICATIONS FOR

PENA AND FERNANDEZ. POST SHOULD KEY INFORMATION TO NUMBERS ON VISA APPLICATION.

3. PENA WILL BE DEPORTED TUESDAY, APRIL 10, UNDER INS ESCORT TO ASUNCION. TWO MINOR CHILDREN WILL ACCOMPANY BUT THEY [WERE] GRANTED VOLUNTARY DEPARTURE RATHER THAN ORDERED DEPORTED. DEPT WILL SEND EXACT TRAVEL PLACES WHEN RECEIVED.

VANCE

LIMITED OFFICIAL USE.

APRIL 7, 1979: PARAGUAY

Telegram from American Embassy, Asunción to U.S. Department of State

Subject: Americo Peña Case

UNCLASSIFIED
(REDACTED)
n/a

Page 01   ASUNCI   01560   071711z
Action vo-05

INFO   OCT-01 ARA-11 ADS-00 CA-01   INSE-00 SSO-00 /018 W

----------------------------------109210   071719z /64

0 07163OZ   APR 79
FM: AMEMBASSY ASUNCION
TO: SECSTATE WASHDC IMMEDIATE 5732

(REDACTED)   ASUNCION 1560

E.O. 12065: GDS 4/7/85 (WHITE, ROBERT E.) OR-M
TAGS: CVIS SHUM PA (PENA, AMERICO)
SUBJECT: AMERICO PENA CASE

REF: STATE 84980

1. (REDACTED) (WHOLE TEXT)

2. JOEL HUGO FILARTIGA, SEVENTEEN YEARS OLD WAS BEATEN, TORTURED AND KILLED MARCH 30, 1976. THE OFFICIAL VERSION IS THAT AN OUTRAGED HUSBAND HUGO DUARTE COMMITTED THIS BRUTAL SLAYING. DUARTE HAS CONFESSED TO BEING THE SOLE AUTHOR OF THE CRIME AND IS DETAINED IN PRISON AWAITING FINAL DISPOSITION OF THE CASE. THE UNFAITHFUL COMPANION OF DUARTE IN WHOSE BED JOEL FILARTIGA WAS ALLEGEDLY FOUND DISAPPEARED FIVE DAYS AFTER THE MURDER. THERE ARE REPORTS SHE LIVES IN BUENOS AIRES. JOEL HUGO FILARTIGA WAS THE SON OF DR. JOEL FILARTIGA, A WELL KNOWN PHYSICIAN, ARTIST AND CRITIC OF THE STROESSNER REGIME.

3. IT IS PROBABLE THAT DUARTE IS GUILTY. IT IS ALMOST CERTAINLY NOT POSSIBLE THAT HE COMMITTED THE BARBARIC ACTS

ALONE AND IN A FIT OF PASSION. IT IS PROBABLE THAT HE HAS CONFESSED AND SHIELDED OTHERS OUT OF FEAR OF CONSEQUENCES SIMILAR TO THOSE VISITED ON YOUNG FILARTIGA IF HE DID NOT COOPERATE. THERE ARE LEGITIMATE, SOLID REASONS TO SUSPECT POLICE INVOLVEMENT. THE POSSIBILITY ALSO EXISTS OF POLITICAL PERSECUTION BUT IT APPEARS TO BE BASED MORE ON INHERENT SUSPICION OF THIS GOVERNMENT RATHER THAN ANY REAL EVIDENCE.

4. THE FATHER OF THE MURDERED BOY ACCUSED AMERICO PENA, A POLICE INSPECTOR AND STEP FATHER OF DUARTE'S COMMON LAW WIFE, OF CO-RESPONSIBILITY FOR THE CRIME. THE JUDGE IN THE CASE HAS IN EFFECT EXONERATED PENA OF THE ACCUSATION. THERE ARE NO CHARGES AGAINST PENA. A HIGH OFFICIAL OF THE INTERIOR MINISTRY TOLD AN EMBASSY OFFICER YESTERDAY THAT TECHNICALLY, PENA IS STILL A CO-ACCUSED AND WILL REMAIN SO UNTIL THE CASE IS DECIDED BY A JUDGE, IF IT EVER IS. THE COURT OF APPEALS IS PRESENTLY REVIEWING A DEFENSE CLAIM THAT THE CORONER'S REPORT WAS INCORRECT AS TO TIME OF THE BOY'S DEATH. THE COURT HAS PLACED NO RESTRICTIONS ON PENA'S TRAVEL.

5. REGARDING THE GRANTING OF THE VISA BY THE CONSUL, THE ONLY POSSIBLE CRITICISM OF HIS ACTION WOULD BE THAT HE DID NOT INVESTIGATE SUFFICIENTLY THE NON-IMMIGRANT BONA FIDES OF AMERICO PENA. THIS WOULD SEEM TO BE A SHALLOW CHARGE, HOWEVER. A MAN FORTY PLUS YEARS OLD WITH HIS ENTIRE FAMILY LIVING IN PARAGUAY, OF SOME ECONOMIC MEANS WHO HAD PAID FOR A ROUND TRIP TICKET FOR A TOUR OF DISNEY WORLD POSSESSES MOST OF THE OBVIOUS REQUISITES TO BE CLASSIFIED AS A NON-IMMIGRANT. THE TOUR COMPANY WAS A REPUTABLE ONE. IT PROMPTLY REPORTED PENA'S FAILURE TO RETURN TO INS IN MIAMI.

6. AS FAR AS WE KNOW AMERICO PENA IS NOT AMONG THAT GROUP OF POLICE OFFICIALS WHO ROUTINELY TORTURE SUSPECTS. HE WAS NOT EMPLOYED IN INVESTIGACIONES BUT AS A MUNICIPAL POLICE OFFICER WHOSE JOB WAS TO MANAGE THE POLICE PX. NO ONE WE KNOW HERE ACCUSES PENA OF DEATH SQUAD ASSOCIATION. THEREFORE HE COULD NOT BE HELD INELIGIBLE FOR A VISA UNDER 212 A 27 1.4 AS AN ALIEN "NOTORIOUS FOR ALLEGEDLY ENGAGING IN EXCESSES, INCLUDING PHYSICAL BRUTALITY WHILE IN POLITICAL POWER." IN MY OPINION, THE IMPORTANT POINT TO UNDERLINE IS THAT IF AMERICO PENA

WAS PLANNING HIS TRIP TO THE US NEXT WEEK INSTEAD OF IN JULY 1978 AND EVEN IF WE HAD GOOD REASON TO BELIEVE THAT IT WAS HE WHO PARTICIPATED IN THE FILARTIGA MURDER WE WOULD HAVE NO LEGAL MEANS TO WITHHOLD THE VISA ON THAT GROUND. IT SEEMS TO ME THAT IT WOULD BE DESIRABLE TO MAKE THAT FACT KNOWN AND THEREBY PUBLICLY CLEAR THE NAME OF THE CONSULAR OFFICER WHOM COHA HAS SO COWARDLY AND WRONGLY MALIGNED.

n/a

(REDACTED)

UNCLASSIFIED

APRIL 7, 1979: PARAGUAY

Telegram from American Embassy, Asunción to U.S. Department of State

UNCLASSIFIED
n/a

UNCLASSIFIED

PAGE 01   ASUNCI   01559   071514Z
ACTION VO-03

INFO   OCT-01   ARA-15   ADS-00   HA-05 SSO-00 INSE-00
                  CA-01/025 W

                ---------------------------------108523   071634Z / 62

O 071540Z APR 79
FM: AMEMBASSY ASUNCION
TO: SECSTATE WASHDC IMMEDIATE 5731

UNCLAS ASUNCION 1559

E.O. 12065: N/A
TAGS: SHUM, CVIS, (PENA, AMERICO)

REF: STATE 84980

1. THE GOP'S OFFICIAL POSITION REGARDING THE FILARTIGA CASE WAS PROVIDED IN ITS RESPONSE TO THE INTER-AMERICAN HUMAN RIGHTS COMMISSION'S REQUEST FOR INFORMATION ON ALLEGED HUMAN RIGHTS VIOLATIONS IN PARAGUAY. A FREE TRANSLATION OF THE GOP RESPONSE IS PROVIDED BELOW FOR THE DEPT'S INFORMATION.

2. CASE 2158:

JOEL FILARTIGA WAS MURDERED IN A CRIME OF PASSION BY A HUSBAND WHO DISCOVERED FILARTIGA IN THE ACT OF ADULTERY WITH HIS WIFE. THE MURDERER DUARTE ARREDONDO HAS CONFESSED HIS GUILT IN THE TRIAL WHICH IS BEING HEARD IN THE COMMON COURTS. ALL OF THE FACTS OF THIS CASE ARE KNOWN TO THE PUBLIC AND THE PROCESS IS BEING FOLLOWED BY THE PUBLIC THROUGH THE NEWSPAPERS BECAUSE OF THE

FASCINATION THIS TYPE OF CASE HOLDS FOR THE GENERAL PUB-
LIC. IT IS ABSOLUTELY UNTRUE THAT THE POLICE PARTICIPATED
IN THIS CRIME THE DETAILS OF WHICH ARE BEING CLARIFIED IN
THE CASE WHICH IS UNDER THE JURISDICTION OF THE COURTS.

WHITE

UNCLASSIFIED

APRIL 9, 1979: UNITED STATES

Plaintiffs' Memorandum of Points and Authorities in Support of Order to Show Cause for Stay of Deportation and for Order Permitting Depositions of the Prisoners; Affidavit of Dolly Filártiga

UNITED STATES DISTRICT COURT
EASTERN DISTRICT OF NEW YORK

DOLLY M.E. FILARTIGA and DR. JOEL FILARTIGA,	**MEMORANDUM OF POINTS AND AUTHORITIES IN SUPPORT OF ORDER TO SHOW CAUSE FOR STAY OF DEPORTATION AND FOR ORDER PERMITTING DEPOSITIONS OF THE PRISONERS**
Plaintiffs,	
— against —	
AMERICO NORBERTO PENA-IRALA, et al.,	
Defendant.	

PRELIMINARY STATEMENT

This civil action for damages for the wrongful torture and death of Joelito Filartiga was commenced by the filing of a complaint on Friday, April 6, 1979, just a few days ago. Defendant Pena-Irala, who is accused of the murder, was ordered deported by the federal defendants on April 5, 1979 by Immigration Judge Anthony M. DeGaeto. So was Juana Villalba, a material witness to the torture-murder. They are presently in the custody of the federal defendants at the Brooklyn Navy Yard. Plaintiffs need to take their depositions and seek a court order to authorize the depositions and to stay their deportations so as to preserve plaintiffs' ability to pursue this lawsuit and the capacity of the Court to adjudicate it.

ARGUMENT

I. PLAINTIFFS SHOULD BE PERMITTED TO TAKE THE DEPOSITION OF DEFENDANT PENA-IRALA AND JUANA VILLALBA, A MATERIAL WITNESS.

Plaintiffs are required to seek this Court's permission to take the deposition of Pena-Irala and Juana Villalba solely because they are in custody.

F.R.C.P. 30(a).[1] The need for these depositions is manifest. Pena-Irala is not only a party but is accused of the torture-murder upon which this action is based. He is uniquely in possession of many of the facts which plaintiffs will need to prove their case, facts highly relevant to his liability in this action and to recovery against him. Juana Villalba is a crucial material witness to the alleged tort and crime against human rights as she shares the same house with Pena-Irala, the house where the body of Joelito Filartiga was tortured or brought after his torture-murder. The mere fact of their incarceration presents no basis for denying plaintiffs their opportunity to depose him. Thus, an order permitting the taking of these depositions should be granted.

II. THIS COURT HAS POWER TO STAY THE DEPORTATIONS PENDING THE TAKING OF THE DEPOSITIONS.

This Court's power to stay the deportations pending depositions flows from the inherent power and duty of the federal courts, codified in 28 U.S.C. §1651, to issue all orders "necessary or appropriate in aid of their respective jurisdictions and agreeable to the usages and principles of law."

There is no doubt of the Court's power to order that Pena Irala and Juana Villalba be available to testify in this action. See *United States v. Hayman*, 342 U.S. 205, 72 S. Ct. 263, 273 (1952). To achieve this, both the Federal Rules of Civil Procedure 30(a) and 28 U.S.C. §1651 give the Court the power to issue the writ of habeas corpus ad testificandum to assure their presence for the deposition already noticed, and for other proceedings as they become necessary. 4A Moore's *Federal Practice*, ¶ 30.56. This writ is clearly necessary and appropriate in aid of this Court's jurisdiction to entertain plaintiffs' civil action. *Price v. Johnston*, 334 U.S. 266, 68 S. Ct. 1049, 1057 (1948); *United States v. Hayman, supra.* Such a writ is also "agreeable to the usages and principles of law" founded as it is on common principles. *Price v. Johnston, supra.* Blackstone describes this writ as one "which issuer[s] when it is necessary to remove a prisoner, in order to . . . bear testimony in any court." 3 Blackstone's *Commentaries*, 129-130. *United States v. Hayman, supra* at 273, n. 35. This writ necessarily takes precedence over any other order of custody.

Here it is likewise clear that orders to testify in a deposition would be meaningless if Pena-Irala and Juana Villalba were to be deported from the

---

[1] The Court's permission in not sought or required on the basis that plaintiffs seek to take the depositions prior to the expiration of 30 days from the filing of the complaint since defendant Pena-Irala is about to go out of the United States. F.R.C.P. 30(b)(a)(A); Affidavit of Dolly M.E. Filartiga, ¶¶.

United States immediately or in the very near future as is intended by the federal defendants. Returning them to Paraguay, where they would be inaccessible to plaintiffs and free to disappear, would frustrate the Court's intention that the depositions be taken and effectively defeat the jurisdiction of this Court to adjudicate plaintiffs' claims. Therefore, the All Writs Act likewise recognizes this Court's inherent power to stay their deportations to permit the depositions and other matters related to the civil action to go forward. In this respect, the stay of deportation is in the nature of the common law writ *ne exeat. In re Lipke*, 98 F. 970 (S.D.N.Y. 1900); *In re Cohen*, 136 F. 999 (S.D. Ill. 1905), and is "agreeable to the usages and principles of law" as that phrase is used in 28 U.S.C. § 1651. As the Court held in *Price v. Johnston, supra*, federal courts are not "confined to the precise forms of . . . writ[s] in vogue at the common law." Rather, the concept of "law" and the inherent power to issue writs recognized in §1651 "is a legislatively approved source of procedural instruments designed to achieve 'the rational ends of justice' (cite omitted)." *supra* at 282.

Indeed, the inherent authority of the federal district courts to stay deportation orders to permit pursuit of pending litigation has been explicitly recognized. In *Hong v. Agency for International Development*, 470 F. 2d 507 (9th Cir. 1972), the court affirmed the authority of the district court in which an alien's action for breach of contract was pending to stay the alien's deportation pending prosecution of his civil proceeding.

The federal courts have also recognized that losing the presence of a deportable alien can raise constitutional problems. In *United States v. Takamatsu*, 500 F. 2d 420 (9th Cir. 1974) and *United States v. Mendez-Rodriguez*, 450 F. 2d 1 (9th Cir. 1971), the courts dismissed indictments against aliens who were deprived of their Sixth Amendment right to confrontation by virtue of the deportation of otherwise validly deportable potential witnesses for the defense. In this case, deportation of Pena-Irala and Juana Villalba will deprive plaintiffs of their right under the Fifth Amendment to prosecute this civil action against Pena-Irala. The stay of deportation is here the necessary and, indeed, the only available remedy to ensure plaintiffs this right and to preserve the jurisdiction of this Court.

III. THIS COURT SHOULD EXERCISE ITS POWER TO STAY PENA-IRALA'S DEPORTATION PENDING THE TAKING OF HIS DEPOSITION AND CONSIDERATION OF PLAINTIFFS' MOTION FOR A STAY OF DEPORTATION PENDING THE ADJUDICATION OF THIS LAWSUIT.

The stay of deportation requested herein is temporary to preserve the *status quo* and thereby permit the taking of the depositions to which plaintiffs are entitled under Rule 30(a). Preserving the *status quo* is also necessary to permit the Court to consider issuance of a longer-term stay of deportation pending the adjudication of this lawsuit. It is equitable in nature and is authorized by the Federal Rules of Civil Procedure, 65(b). Here, the temporary stay should be granted because if Pena Irala or Juana Villalba leave the country immediately, plaintiffs will suffer immediate and irreparable injury. In addition, plaintiffs meet the tests which make issuance of a stay in the nature of a preliminary injunction likely—i.e., the balance of hardships tips in their favor, they have raised serious questions on the merits, and there is a strong public interest in maintaining them here pending resolution of this dispute. *Pride v. Community School Board of Brooklyn, New York*, 482 F. 2d 257, 264 (2d Cir. 1973).

A. *Plaintiffs Will Be Irreparably Harmed If A Stay Is Not Granted.*

It is plain that the opportunity of the plaintiffs to obtain justice through this civil action will be irreparably lost if Pena-Irala and Juana Villalba are allowed to leave this country before their deposition can be taken, and consideration of maintaining them here for further proceedings can be had. There is no assurance whatsoever that plaintiffs will ever have the opportunity to depose them again if they leave.

Although the Federal Rules of Civil Procedure provide a variety of mechanisms for securing testimony of a witness abroad, Rule 28, the efficacy of these methods depends on the recognition thereof and the cooperation of the government of Paraguay, which has acted in every respect to shield Pena-Irala from investigation and blocked efforts to have civil redress against him there. Reports of international investigating tribunals also affirm that the judiciary is merely an appendage of the executive. (Exhs. 1-3 to D.M.E. Filartiga Affidavit). More importantly, upon return to Paraguay, Pena-Irala could and is likely simply to disappear, with the connivance of the Paraguayan government. This would completely frustrate pursuit of this action against him. Thus, the planned, immediate deportations will spell the effective end of plaintiffs' ability to pursue their claims.

B. *Defendants Will Not Be Prejudiced By The Issuance Of A Stay.*

The federal defendants can point to no interest whatsoever which requires that Pena-Irala or Juana Villalba be deported immediately. Nor can they be in any way harmed by the taking of their deposition by the plaintiffs in this civil action.

Indeed, the public interest and stated commitment of this country to halting gross human rights violations such as those alleged herein warrants that Pena-Irala's deportation be stayed, both to preserve this action and to permit thorough investigation of his activities in Paraguay and here.

Neither defendant Pena-Irala nor Juana Villalba can complain of this effort to take their depositions. Depositions are explicitly authorized under the Federal Rules of Civil Procedure and are automatically permitted immediately following the filing of a complaint where the witnesses are about to leave the jurisdiction. F.R.Civ. P. 30(a).

C. *The Complaint Raises Substantial Questions On The Merits.*

For the purposes of issuing the temporary stay sought herein, the Court need not decide whether the complaint states a valid cause of action. The power to issue a temporary injunction and maintain the *status quo* may be exercised even to permit the Court to determine whether it has jurisdiction over the action. *United States v. United Mine Workers of America*, 330 U.S. 258, 293, 67 S. Ct. 677, 695 (1947). It needs no argument to sustain the proposition that an action for the wrongful death by torture of their son and brother, as well as the pain and suffering inflicted upon the plaintiffs in connection there with, constitutes a substantial claim.

However, since the use of 28 U.S.C. §1350 jurisdiction to redress violations of human rights appears to be one of first impression, plaintiffs will briefly outline here their theory of jurisdiction.

This Court has jurisdiction over the subject matter. Diversity jurisdiction, per se, under 28 U.S.C. §1332, does not apply to a case in which both plaintiff and defendant are aliens. 1 Moore's *Federal Practice*, ¶O.75 at 709.6-7 (1974). No such prohibition, however, exists in a case brought under 28 U.S.C. §1350, which confers jurisdiction over "any civil action by an alien for a tort only, committed in violation of the law of nations or a treaty of the United States. II." *IIT v. Vencap, Ltd.*, 519 F. 2d 1001, 1015 (2d Cir. 1975); *Dreyfus v. Von Finck*, 534 F. 2d 24 (2d Cir. 1976).

In *IIT*, the parties were, respectively, a Luxemburg corporation and a Bahamian corporation. In *Dreyfus*, they were a citizen of Switzerland and a citizen of West Germany. In the former case, one sounding in fraud and conversion, jurisdiction, although present in principle, was ultimately held to be absent because the court could not "subscribe to plaintiff's view that the Eighth Commandment 'Thou Shalt not steal' is part of the law of nations." 519 F. 2d 1001, 1015. Here, the gravamen of the complaint is death by torture, a violation of the law of nations if ever there was one in this age of human rights. (See Affidavit of Professor Richard Arens, attached to Complaint.)

In *Dreyfus*, the tort alleged was defendant's purchase from plaintiff of plaintiff's interest in a banking firm, at far less than its real value, under duress caused by the confiscation of plaintiff's assets by the Nazi government. Based on these facts, the court held that "for purposes of this lawsuit, violations of international law do not occur when the aggrieved parties are nationals of the acting state." In support of this highly dubious proposition, the court, at 534 F. 2d 24, 31, cites only a dictum by Mr. Justice White in *Banco Nacional de Cuba v. Sabbatino*, 376 U.S. 398, 441-442 (1964), and an old opinion by the New York Court of Appeals in *Salinoff & Co. v. Standard Oil Co.*, 262 N.Y. 220, 186 N.E. 679 (1933).

In fact, particularly in the area of human rights, there has in recent years been a marked shift away from the old doctrine of international law as applicable only between states, toward the recognition of individuals as both subjects and objects of international law. According to Louis Henkin, Hamilton Fish Professor of International Law and Diplomacy at Columbia University and President of the U.S. Institute of Human Rights, "The new law buried the old dogma that the individual is not a 'subject' of international politics and law and that a governments behavior toward its own nationals is a matter of domestic, not international concern. It penetrated national frontiers and the veil of sovereignty." Henkin, *The Right of Man Today*, Westview Press, 1978, p. 94.[2]

Indeed, as early as 1955, Professor Lauterpacht added the following crucial revision to his 8th Edition of Oppenheim, *International Law*, the leading treatise in the field:

> . . . the quality of individuals as subjects of International Law is apparent from the fact that, in various spheres, they are, as such, bound by duties which International Law imposes directly upon them. The various developments since the two World Wars no longer countenance the view that, as a matter of positive law, States are the only subjects of International law. In proportion as the realisation of that fact gains ground, there must be an increasing disposition to treat individuals, within a limited sphere, as subjects of International Law. Quoted at, p. 6, Sohn & Buergenthal, *International Protection of Human Rights*, Babbs-Merrill, 1973.

Furthermore, since no government could lawfully have authorized the monstrous actions of the defendant described in Complaint, the tort for

---

[2] For a number of views generally supportive of this thesis, see *International Human Rights Law and Practice*, a Professional Education Publication prepared in cooperation with the Section of International Law, American Bar Association, 1978. Thus, Prof. Virginia Leary, at p. 21: "In summary, it appears clear that gross violations of human rights can no longer be considered a matter essentially within the domestic jurisdiction of the offending state under the U.N. Chapter."

which redress is sought here was committed by the defendant in his individual capacity, as well as in his capacity as an agent of the government of Paraguay.

In *IIT v. Vencap, Ltd., supra* at 1001, Judge Friendly described 28 U.S.C. §1350 as "a kind of legal Lohengrin; although it has been with us since the first judiciary . . . (1789), no one seems know whence it came." Although we cannot trace its ancestry with precision, we know from its birth date that it must have come out of a legal-philosophical environment in which the inalienable rights of humankind counted for a great deal more than in the positivist era of the late nineteenth and early twentieth century. Now, after Nuremberg, after the U.N. Charter, after the multitude of treaties, conventions and solemn declarations dealing with all aspects of fundamental human rights, § 1350 may be ready, after 200-year wait, to come into its own. This case may be the vehicle for its rebirth.

For all these reasons, plaintiffs' motion for a temporary restraining order to stay the deportations of Pena-Irala and Juan Villalba and to permit the taking of their depositions while in the custody of the Immigration and Naturalization Service should be granted.

Respectfully submitted,

PETER WEISS
RHONDA COPELON
JOHN W. CORWIN
JOSE ANTONIO LUGO
c/o Center for Constitution Rights
853 Broadway 14th floor
New York, New York 10003
(212) 674- 3303

MICHAEL MAGGIO
Goren and Maggio
1801 Columbia Road, N.W.
Suite 100
Washington, D.C.
(202) 483-8055

Attorneys for Plaintiffs

Dated: New York, New York
April 9, 1979

**UNITED STATES DISTRICT COURT
EASTERN DISTRICT OF NEW YORK**

DOLLY M.E. FILARTIGA and
DR. JOEL FILARTIGA,

        Plaintiffs,

    — against —

AMERICO NORBERTO PENA-
IRALA, et al.,

    Defendants.

**AFFIDAVIT OF DOLLY
FILARTIGA**

79 Civ. 917

DOLLY M.E. FILARTIGA, being duly sworn deposes and says:

1. I am one of the plaintiffs in this action, I am fully familiar with the facts and proceedings in this case, and I make this affidavit in support of plaintiffs' application to take the depositions of defendants AMERICO NORBERTO PENA-IRALA and JUANA BAUTISTA FERNANDEZ VIL-LALBA and prohibiting defendants CASTILLO and VICIAN from deporting them pending the taking said depositions and further proceedings in this Court.

2. On information and belief, defendant Pena-Irala kidnapped and tortured to death my brother JOELITO FILARTIGA, on or about March 29, 1976 in retaliation for my brother's opposition to the Stroessner regime. On or about March 30, 1976, PENA-IRALA intentionally inflicted emotional distress on me, on or about April 28, 1976 he wrongfully caused me to be arrested and imprisoned. I was forced to leave Paraguay in October, 1978 because PENA's actions resulted in my being denied all educational and job opportunities.

3. Defendant PENA-IRALA and JUANA VILLALBA are presently in custody of the federal defendant at Brooklyn Navy Yard and are awaiting immediate deportation pursuant to the April 5, 1979 order of Immigration Judge Anthony M. Gaeto.

4. PENA-IRALA left Paraguay on or about July, 1978 in the midst of public furor created by the evidence of his having been responsible for the torture-murder of my brother and by the government's unsuccessful attempts to create an alternative explanation for my brother's death.

5. On information and belief JUANA VILLALBA accompanied him here. She is a material witness to the facts surrounding the torture-murder of my brother and the harassment against me because she lived with Mr. PENA in Paraguay in the house where my brother's body was shown to me following his murder.

6. On information and belief defendant PENA-IRALA entered the United States on or about July 21, 1978 with a B-2 (tourist) visa which he had obtained from the U.S. Consulate at Asuncion, Paraguay. Before leaving Paraguay he sold his home and in the approximately nine months following the expiration of his tourist visa he has lived here as an illegal alien. On information and belief the same is true for Juana Villalba.

7. Mr. PENA's presence in the United States was made known to me on or about March 1, 1979 by Paraguayans who live in Brooklyn, New York. They informed me that PENA-IRALA and JUANA BAUTISTA FERNANDEZ VILLALBA were living at 1865 52nd Street in Brooklyn. On or about March 8, 1979, my attorney and others alerted the Immigration and Naturalization Service (INS) to PENA-IRALA presence in Brooklyn and of the fact that a Paraguayan ship was anchored in New York harbor, providing a possible base for illegal activity and a means of escape.

8. On or about April 1, 1979 an INS investigator came to Washington, D.C. to show me photos of persons they had photographed in Brooklyn. I positively identified a woman as Juana Villalba and also identified albeit not positively, a photograph of a man as PENA-IRALA.

9. On April 4, 1979, PENA-IRALA and JUANA VILLALBA were arrested by INS agents at 1865 52d Street, Brooklyn, New York. On April 5, 1979 PENA-IRALA, a deportation hearing was held before Immigration Judge Anthony M. DeGaeto in Manhattan, when, according to the New York Times PENA-IRALA said "All we want is to be sent back to our country as quickly as possible," and PENA-IRALA and VILLALBA were ordered deported.

10. PENA was personally served with a copy of the summons and complaint in this lawsuit on April 6, 1979 at the Brooklyn Navy Yard where he is detained pending deportation.

11. The defendant PENA is a high-ranking police inspector in the investigaciones (anti-subversive squad) in Asuncion and is nationally and internationally known and dreaded as one of Paraguay's chief torturers. In Paraguay the police are considered more powerful than the military, are

the chief arm of repression by the Stroessner regime and are commonly held to be involved in smuggling contraband, drugs and an international trade in child prostitutes.

12. To provide the Court background on these matters, I am attaching the following documents:

Exhibit 1:   International League for Human Rights
"Report of Commission of Enquiry into Human Rights In Paraguay," September, 1976.

Exhibit 2:   Amnesty International Briefing, Paraguay July, 1976.

Exhibit 3:   Death Under Torture and Disappearance of Political Prisoners in Paraguay, 1977

13. This suit seeks damages for the wrongful torture and murder of my brother, Joel (Joelito) Filartiga as well as PENA-IRALA's infliction of emotional stress upon me and my false imprisonment by PENA-IRALA. Because the defendant PENA will never be brought to justice in Paraguay, this lawsuit presents a crucial and the only means by which I can seek justice for my brother's death and my injuries

14. The International League for Human Rights, Amnesty International, and the Inter-American Human Right Commission of the O.A.S. have all noted that the Paraguayan judiciary is no more than an appendage of the executive branch, in particular General Stroessner and his dreaded police of which PENA is a noted member. In the words of Dr. Ben Stephansky, former Secretary of State for Latin America and Professor Robert Alexander of Rutgers University, "The rule of law does not exist in Paraguay" as "[T]here is no independence of the judiciary." *Report of the Commission of Enquiry into Human Rights in Paraguay of The International League for Human Rights.* (September 1976). The Report by the State Department to the Senate Committee on Foreign Relations entitled "Report on Human Rights Practices In Countries Receiving U.S. Aid" February 8, 1979 notes that "executive influence is excessive and often appears paramount, in judicial proceedings." (p. 318).

15. The impossibility of redress of my brother's torture and murder is also evidenced by the frightening obstruction of my father's attempt to seek justice in the Paraguayan courts. When he tried to bring Mr. PENA's responsibility for my brother's death to the attention of a Paraguayan criminal court, his lawyer, Horacio Galeano Perrone was arrested, thrown in jail,

shackled to a wall, and threatened with death by Mr. PENA. Nothing has been done to investigate Mr. PENA'S responsibility. Instead the regime has tried to perpetrate a patently false story that Joelito's death was a crime of passion. Three independent autopsies which I will submit to the Court as soon as I get them made clear that Joelito's death was the result of professional methods of torture common to police practices in Paraguay.

16. In April, 1978 Mr. PENA initiated harassing proceedings against my mother and me and had us arrested and jailed without trial.

17. It is because of these events that I am certain that if defendant PENA is allowed to leave the United States to return to Paraguay before I have even begun to proceed with my lawsuit, that neither I nor my father will ever be able to obtain redress as guaranteed to us by the laws of New York and of the United States. It is also for these reasons that discovery in Paraguay is no alternative as PENA's availability would be most unlikely. In addition, the cost of even trying to locate and compel his attendance would be an insurmountable financial barrier to my family as my father is still attempting to raise funds to cover the legal expenses incurred in his efforts to have criminal charges lodged against PENA in Paraguay.

18. In addition, as a result of these events and the filing of this lawsuit, I fear that my father's life will be in immediate danger if PENA is allowed to leave the United States and effectively escape the process of this Court. Mr. PENA is a man of very violent character and the major thing that has protected my father despite his outspoken opposition to the Stroessner regime and his brave efforts to expose PENA's responsibility for my brother's torture-murder has been international scrutiny and outrage. If this Court allows PENA to return without investigation of and accountability for his violation of the most fundamental principles of human rights, it will be touted in Paraguay as an endorsement of PENA's innocence. Already, I am told that the Paraguayan papers are reporting that PENA has been released in this country.

19. My father and I have taken a substantial risk in invoking the jurisdiction of this Court because we see it as the only opportunity to see PENA brought to justice and to warn other human rights' violators that they cannot enter this country with impunity.

20. I have not sought this relief from those or any other Court and have no other remedy at law.

DOLLY M. E. FILARTIGA

April 9, 1979

APRIL 9, 1979: UNITED STATES

U.S. District Court for the Eastern District of New York: Order to Show Cause and to Stay Deportation

UNITED STATES DISTRICT COURT
EASTERN DISTRICT OF NEW YORK

DOLLY M.E. FILARTIGA and DR. JOEL FILARTIGA,	**ORDER TO SHOW CAUSE AND STAY OF DEPORTATION**
Plaintiffs,	
	79 Civ 917
— against —	
AMERICO NORBERTO PENA-IRALA, et al.	
Defendants.	

Upon the annexed affidavit of plaintiff DOLLY M. FILARTIGA, executed the 9th day of April, 1979, the Memorandum of Points and Authorities attached hereto, and the Complaint and affidavits and exhibits attached thereto,

LET THE DEFENDANT show cause before this Court at 9:30 o'clock in the a.m. on the 30th day of April, 1979, why an Order should not be entered

1) permitting plaintiffs to take the deposition of defendant AMERICO NORBERTO PENA-IRALA and JUANA BAUTISTA FERNANDEZ VILLALBA, a material witness both being in the custody of the United States;
2) staying their deportations pending the taking of said depositions and further proceedings in the Court;

SUFFICIENT CAUSE HAVING BEEN SHOWN, it is hereby ORDERED that pending the return date of this Order, defendants CASTILLO and VICIAN or their agents, servants and employees shall refrain from deporting defendants PENA-IRALA and JUANA VILLALBA from the United States, and it further ORDERED that service of copy of this Order upon defendant PENA-IRALA or his attorney, and upon JUANA VILLALBA or her attorney and upon the federal defendants by delivering a copy to the United States Attorney for this District an authorized assistant by 12 o'clock a.m. on April 9, 1979, shall be deemed good and sufficient service.

Eugene H. Nickerson
U.S.D.J.

Dated: Brooklyn, New York

April 9, 1979

APRIL 10, 1979: PARAGUAY

Criminal Investigation Report

CAPITAL POLICE*
DEPARTMENT OF INVESTIGATIONS
DIRECTOR OF POLITICS

Asunción, April 10, 1979

D.P.A. No.: 239
Purpose: To present a report

TO: Mr. Chief of the Department of Investigations
       Mr. PASTOR MILCIADES CORONEL
       E.S.D.

It is my honor to address these authorities, with the objective of informing you of the following report:

It is known, according to the report, that yesterday, Dr. JOEL FILARTIGA, accompanied by his wife, NIDIA SPERATTI and the journalist MIGUEL ANGEL CABALLERO FIGUN, were interviewed by the American AMBASSADOR ROBERT WHITE, in order to solicit his intervention so that the Principal Inspector (S.R) AMERICO PENA, may be tried by an American court. The American diplomat pointed out to them that this would be a difficult trial in their country because of the characteristics of the case, but that he would do everything possible for PENA to be tried, because, at the same time, much of the behind-the-scenes repressive politics of the Department of Investigations would come out, and consequently, its discrediting would be inevitable and that Mr. ROBERT WHITE is convinced that the aforementioned Police Department had ample participation in the notorious case of the death of JOEL FILARTIGA JR.

Inspector General ALBERTO B. CANTERO
DIRECTOR OF POLITICS

Asunción, April 10, 1979
Attention: the Chief of Police

Pastor M. Coronel
Third Chief, Department of Investigations

---

* Document located in the *Centro de Documentacion y Archivo*, Asunción, Paraguay. Translated from Spanish by author.

APRIL 10, 1979: UNITED STATES

Plaintiffs' Petition for Writ of Habeas Corpus Testificandum

UNITED STATES DISTRICT COURT
EASTERN DISTRICT OF NEW YORK

DOLLY M.E. FILARTIGA and DR. JOEL FILARTIGA, Plaintiffs, — against — AMERICO NORBERTO PENA-IRALA, LEONEL CASTILLO, as Commissioner of the United States Immigration and Naturalization Service and GEORGE VICIAN, as District Director, Immigration and Naturalization Service, New York. Defendants.	PETITION FOR WRIT OF HABEAS CORPUS AD TESTIFICANDUM 79 Civ. 917

Upon the annexed affidavit of Jose Antonio Lugo, Esq., and all the proceedings heretofore plaintiffs respectfully petition this Court pursuant to Rules 26(a) and 30(a) of the Federal Rules of Civil Procedure for a writ of *habeas corpus ad testificandum* directing defendants Leonel Castillo and George Vician to have the bodies of defendant Americo Norberto Pena-Irala and of Juana Bautista Fernandez Villalba, a material witness, both being in the custody of the United States, at Room 130 of the United States District Courthouse for the Eastern District of New York at 10:30 A.M. on the 12th day of April, 1979 for purposes of taking their deposition pursuant to this Court's Order entered April 9, 1979 by the Hon. Eugene H. Nickerson U.S.D.J., and for such further relief as may be just and proper in the premises.

WHEREFORE

Plaintiffs respectfully request that a Writ for Habeas Corpus Ad Testificandum be granted directing defendants Leonel Castillo, as Commissioner of the United States Immigration and Naturalization Service and George

Vician, as District Director, Immigration and Naturalization Service, New York, to have the bodies of Americo Norberto Pena Irala and of Juana Bautista Fernandez Villalba at the United States District Courthouse for the Eastern District of New York at 10:30 A.M. on the 12th day of April, 1979 and from day to day thereafter until the oral examination is completed.

Respectfully submitted,

JOSE ANTONIO LUGO
PETER WEISS
RHONDA COPELON
JOHN W. CORWIN
c/o Center for Constitutional Rights
853 Broadway, Suite 1401
New York, New York 10003
(212) 674-3303

MICHAEL MAGGIO
Goren and Maggio
1801 Columbia Road, N.W.
Suite 100
Washington, D.C.
(202) 483-8055

Attorneys for Plaintiffs

Dated: New York, New York
April 10, 1979

UNITED STATES DISTRICT COURT
EASTERN DISTRICT OF NEW YORK

DOLLY M.E. FILARTIGA and DR. JOEL FILARTIGA, Plaintiffs, – against – AMERICO NORBERTO PENA-IRALA, LEONEL CASTILLO, as Commissioner of the United States Immigration and Naturalization Service and GEORGE VICIAN, as District Director, Immigration and Naturalization Service, New York. Defendants.	**AFFIDAVIT IN SUPPORT OF PETITION FOR WRIT OF HABEAS CORPUS AD TESTIFICANDUM**

State of New York

County of New York

JOSE ANTONIO LUGO being duly sworn deposes and says:

1. I am a staff attorney at the Center for Constitutional Rights, one of the attorneys for Plaintiffs Dolly M.E. and Dr. Joel Filartiga and make this affidavit in support of their petition for Writ of Habeas Corpus ad Testificandum.

2. By this Writ plaintiffs seek to take the deposition of defendant Americo Norberto Pena-Irala and of material witness Juana Bautista Fernandez Villalba at a room to be designated in the Federal District Courthouse for the Eastern District of New York and not at the Flushing Detention Facility of the Immigration and Naturalization Services at the Brooklyn Navy Yard in Brooklyn (hereinafter referred to as the "Flushing Facility") where defendant Pena-Irala and witness Fernandez-Villalba are presently in custody.

3. This request is based on the following reasons:

a) Taking the deposition in the Courthouse will ensure the possibility of immediate access to the Court should objections arise regarding the depositions. Given the particular importance of expediting these depositions in this matter, such access is essential. Substantial periods of time could be lost if it were necessary even for the attorneys to get from the Brooklyn Navy Yard to the Court during the process of the deposition. Moreover, the deponents would be entitled likewise to appear before the Court which would require the issuance of the very writ we seek here as well as on-the-spot arrangements for their transportation here. Given these problems, it is clear that the progress of the deposition could be unnecessarily and indeed irresponsibly obstructed simply by creating the need to come before the Court for resolution of issues arising in its course.

b) Based on information obtained from Richard Emery, Esq. of the ACLU, an attorney challenging the decency of existing conditions at the Brooklyn Navy Yard "Flushing Facility" where deponents are being held, we have learned that not only are the physical conditions deplorable but that it is unlikely that facilities exist to accommodate the attorneys, plaintiffs, the deponents, their advisors, experts and other persons who should attend this deposition.

c) Mr. Emery further advised me that there is only one room large enough for a deposition such as this one at the "Flushing Facility." This room is the "hearing room," or "courtroom" and he further advised that hearings are scheduled there almost every day at approximately 1:00 P.M. and that the other rooms are totally inadequate.

d) We are concerned too about the potentially delaying interruptions, distractions and logistical problems created by taking this deposition in the jail. The setting of the Courthouse is necessary to guarantee an expeditious, uninterrupted and dignified examination.

WHEREFORE your deponent respectfully requests that the relief requested in this Petition for Writ of Habeas Corpus Ad Testificandum be granted in all aspects.

JOSE ANTONIO LUGO

Sworn before me this
10th day of April, 1979.

NOTARY PUBLIC

APRIL 12, 1979: PARAGUAY

Telegram from American Embassy, Asunción to U.S. Department of State

Subject: Filartiga Case Press Reaction

UNCLASSIFIED
(REDACTED)
n/a

PAGE 01   ASUNCI 01614   121530Z
ACTION ARA-15

INFO   OCT-01 ADS-00 HA-05   SR-05   CIAE-00DODE-00   PM-05
       H-01   INR-10 L-03   NSAE-00   NSC-05 PA-01   SP-02
       SS-15   ICA-11 TRSE-00   /079 W

--046666 121739Z/47

P 121500Z APR 79
FM AMEMBASSY ASUNCION
TO SECSTATE WASHDC PRIORITY 5760

(REDACTED) ASUNCION 1614

E.O. 12065: GDS 4/12/85 (WHITE, ROBERT E.) OR-M

TAGS: PGOV, SHUM, PA

SUBJECT: FILARTIGA CASE PRESS REACTION

1. (U) THE ASUNCION PRESS IS REPORTING EXTENSIVELY ON THE
DETENTION IN NEW YORK OF AMERICO PENA. MOST OF THE ARTI-
CLES SEEM TO BE TRANSLATIONS OF NEWS ITEMS THAT HAVE
APPEARED IN VARIOUS NEW YORK AND WASHINGTON NEWSPA-
PERS. PARAGUAY'S SECOND MOST IMPORTANT MORNING NEWS-
PAPER HOY IS RUNNING A BACKGROUND SERIES ON THE
FILARTIGA CASE. THE HOY ARTICLES ASSUME THAT THE TRUTH
ABOUT THE FILARTIGA MURDER HAS NOT YET COME TO LIGHT
AND THAT THE OFFICIAL VERSION, IF NOT TOTALLY UNTRUE, IS
FAR FROM THE COMPLETE STORY.

2. (C) COMMENT: A GOOD DEAL OF THE INFORMATION IN THE
HOY SERIES WAS EVIDENTLY DEVELOPED AT THE TIME OF THE

FILARTIGA MURDER BUT COULD NOT BE PUBLISHED THEN. THE ARTICLES ARE BEING WRITTEN BY JOEL FILARTIGA'S FORMER LAWYER WHO WAS DETAINED BRIEFLY AND DISBARRED FROM HIS PROFESSION, SUPPOSEDLY FOR INFRACTIONS OF THE LEGAL CODE BUT ALMOST CERTAINLY FOR PURSUING THE TRUTH IN THIS CASE. FBIS IS CABLING EXTRACTS FROM THE HOY SERIES.

WHITE

APRIL 12, 1979: UNITED STATES

Deposition of Americo Peña-Irala

UNITED STATES DISTRICT COURT
EASTERN DISTRICT OF NEW YORK

DOLLY M.E. FILARTIGA and DR. JOEL FILARTIGA,	**DEPOSITION OF AMERICO NORBERTO PENA-IRALA**
Plaintiffs,	**79 Civ. 917**
– against –	

AMERICO NORBERTO PENA-
IRALA, LEONEL CASTILLO, as
Commissioner of the United States
Immigration and Naturalization
Service, and GEORGE VICIAN, as
District Director, Immigration and
Naturalization Service, New York,

Defendants.

Deposition of AMERICO NORBERTO PENA-IRALA, a Defendant herein, taken by the Plaintiffs, pursuant to Order of Hon. Judge Eugene H. Nickerson, at the Brooklyn Navy Yard, Immigration and Naturalization Service, Flushing Avenue, Brooklyn, New York, at 10:40 a.m., on Thursday, 12 April 1979, before Barbara Dachman, a Shorthand Reporter and a Notary Public for the State of New York.

APPEARANCES:

        GOREN AND MAGGIO, ESQS.,
            Attorneys for the Plaintiffs
            1801 Columbia Road, N.W.
            Washington, D.C.

BY: MICHAEL MAGGIO, ESQ.

            – and –

PETER WEISS, ESQ.,
JOSE ANTONIO LUGO, ESQ.,
    Attorneys for the Center for Constitutional Rights
    853 Broadway
    New York, New York 10003

– and –

HAROLD A. MAYERSON, ESQ.,
    Attorney for AMICI
    36 West 44th Street
    New York, New York 10036

ALSO PRESENT:

    DOLLY M.E. FILARTIGA
    ANA RODRIGUEZ/Consultant

INTERPRETER:

    HALINA S. BASTIANELLO

MR. MAGGIO: My name is Michael Maggio, and I am here with these other attorneys, and we are here today with a court order to ask you various questions. You will recall that the other day, when I was here with you, I asked you about a lawyer. We want you to know that we have discussed this matter with you about a lawyer previously. You have nothing to be afraid of here. The warden, Mr. Schmidt, has provided two security people for you here on your request. All we want is the truth from you, and we are very interested in what you have to say. First, Mr. Weiss is going to ask you some questions, simple questions about your background, where you were born, where you have lived and what you have done for a living in Paraguay.

(The interpreter was sworn in.)

(AMERICO NORBERTO PENA-IRALA, the witness herein, was attempted to be first duly sworn by the reporter.)

THE WITNESS: First I want to state that I have nothing to say. I have no lawyer. I have no lawyer. In due time I shall speak, when I have properly a lawyer. That is all I have to say now.

MR. WEISS: Have you made an effort to obtain a lawyer?

THE WITNESS: I am looking.

MR. WEISS: When do you think you will have a lawyer?

THE WITNESS: I don't know about that.

MR. WEISS: We would like to explain to you that this proceeding is taking place under the jurisdiction of the Federal Court of the United States and the judge has the authority to order you to reply to your questions under penalty of contempt of court. Now, the judge also has the authority to allow you more time to find a lawyer.

THE WITNESS: Perfect.

MR. WEISS: If you have nothing else to say at this point, we will bring you before the judge so that he may make a ruling.

THE WITNESS: I don't understand.

MR. WEISS: We will arrange to have you taken before the judge, who is in charge of this case, so that he may decide whether you should be kept in this country for an additional reasonable time until you can find a lawyer, or whether you should be compelled to answer without a lawyer.

THE WITNESS: I, in court—I shall speak in the court. I shall speak in the court, yes. But here I do not feel it is appropriate for me to say anything. I feel it a little strange, a little peculiar, that they should have assigned a place which is outside the court where I would have to speak.

MR. WEISS: Well, you may be interested to know that we asked to have this deposition taken in the court, but the judge ruled that it should be taken here.

THE WITNESS: Here I shall answer nothing.

MR. WEISS: If you have nothing further to say, I think the record should show that Mr. Pena-Irala refused to be sworn.

THE WITNESS: I said that I will answer absolutely nothing. They cannot make me take the oath since I consider that this is not an appropriate place for the proceeding. In the court, yes; here, no.

MR. WEISS: Then let the record show that when the reporter and the translator asked Mr. Pena to raise his right hand to be sworn, he refused to raise his right hand.

THE WITNESS: They cannot make me do anything and I have my rights. Why should I raise my hand to swear when I am not going to answer any questions.

MR. WEISS: I understand. We cannot make you do anything. Only the judge. Only the judge can make you do anything. That will be all for now.

(Adjourned at 10:55 a.m.)

APRIL 13, 1979: UNITED STATES

Brief Amicus Curiae in Support of Plaintiffs' Motion to Restrain Defendant Immigration and Naturalization Service from Enforcing Defendant Pena-Irala's Departure from the United States

UNITED STATES DISTRICT COURT
EASTERN DISTRICT OF NEW YORK

DOLLY M.E. FILARTIGA and DR. JOEL FILARTIGA, Plaintiffs, – against – AMERICO NORBERTO PENA-IRALA, et al., Defendant.	**BRIEF AMICUS CURIAE IN SUPPORT OF PLAINTIFFS' MOTION TO RESTRAIN DEFENDANT IMMIGRATION AND NATURALIZATION SERVICE FROM ENFORCING DEFENDANT PENA-IRALA'S DEPARTURE FROM THE UNITED STATES** **79 Civ. 917**

Amici are organizations and individuals concerned about re-dressing and halting violations of human rights. Paraguay has been identified internationally as a prime violator, ruled by a regime which uses torture and political assassination to eliminate and silence its political opponents. The brutal torture and murder of seventeen-year-old Joelito Filartiga in retaliation for his father's opposition to the 25-year-old Stroessner dictatorship is a notorious example of Paraguay's use of official terror for political ends. Americo Norberto Pena-Irala is a notorious torturer.

This case has been brought to international attention primarily because of the unusual courage of the Filartiga family and their refusal to suffer in silence. But all their efforts to achieve justice in Paraguay have been to no avail. Instead of receiving justice, they and their attorney have been jailed and harassed.

The presence of Americo Pena-Irala in this country provides a unique and historic opportunity to place our legal institutions at the service of our traditional commitment to human rights. As a first step, the impending deportation of the defendant Pena-Irala and of Juana Villalba should be stayed to permit this civil action to proceed, and also to permit investigations by United States authorities of possible violations of U.S. criminal statutes by Pena-Irala.

The case at bar may prove to be historic. A U.S. statute passed in the wake of our nation's struggle for independence may be awakened from dormancy to assure significance in our renewed dedication to the achievement of a basic and universal standard of human justice. It raises important questions about the extent of our nation's commitment to acting in accord with its professed ideals, as well as the role of the judiciary in a society committed to international human rights. Possibly for the first time, a U.S. court is being asked to exercise its authority to hear claims by aliens, based on gross violations of the human rights standards which now form part of the law of nations. This case must be understood in the context of the Paraguayan reality. Paraguay is a land-locked police state devoid of profitable natural resources. For 25 years the Paraguayan people have struggled to free themselves from the iron hand of dictator President Alfredo Stroessner. He has proclaimed states of emergency resulting in the suspension of all individual liberties at three-month intervals ever since he seized power in 1954, lifting them only on election days.

While members of the Army are used "to build expensive houses for high figures in and friends of the regime, . . . the police are virtually all-pervasive in Stroessner's Paraguay." Stephansky and Alexander, *Report of the Commission of Enquiry Into Human Rights in Paraguay of the International League for Human Rights*, September, 1976, New York, p. 4 (hereinafter, Stephansky and Alexander). The police are particularly engaged in "keeping track of the opposition and potential opposition, in harassing and persecuting its members." Stephansky and Alexander, p.4.

Amnesty International and other human rights organizations report that the "Investigaciones" branch of the Paraguayan police, of which defendant Pena-Irala is a well-known member, specializes in the torture of political opponents, both real and imagined. (See also, Affidavit of *amicus* Ada Rodriguez, attached hereto.) They are known to seize individuals from their homes at will, jail them without charge, and to subject them to sexual assault, mock drownings, and other monstrous acts. *Id.* They act with apparent impunity because

> the rule of law does not exist in Paraguay. There is no independence of the judiciary. All judges must be members of the Colorado party, and are appointed by the Executive. They must do what the Executive indicates that it wants done. We have heard of cases where the mere accusation by the police that a person has

been guilty of some illegal act has been sufficient to bring about a conviction. Alexander and Stephansky, p. 27.

President Stroessner's personal control over the police is said to be so complete that no political prisoner can be released without his approval. Stephansky and Alexander, p. 7.

Plaintiffs' suit charges that defendant Pena-Irala, both in his individual capacity and in his official capacity as a member of the dreaded "Investigaciones" torture team, kidnapped, tortured and murdered Joelito Filartiga and wrongfully imprisoned plaintiff Dolly Filartiga. These horrible acts were apparently designed to retaliate against plaintiff Dr. Filartiga for his nationally and internationally known opposition to the Stroessner dictatorship.

Despite the grave injustices plaintiffs have endured, it is clear that they have no remedy at law in Paraguay. The United States Department of State recently confirmed Stephansky and Alexander's finding that the Paraguayan judiciary is subservient to the Executive. (Paragraph 14 of D.M.E. Filartiga Affidavit). This fact is underscored by the jailing of plaintiffs' Paraguayan counsel simply for pressing the Filartiga family's claim against Pena-Irala in a Paraguayan "court of law." Clearly, plaintiffs only remedy for the injuries suffered at Pena-Irala's hands lies with this Court.

The statute in question, 28 U.S.C. § 1350, confers jurisdiction on this Court if a tort was committed by the defendant "in violation of the law of nations." What the law of nations is "may be ascertained by consulting the works of jurists, writing professedly on public laws; or by the general usage and practice of nations; or by judicial decisions recognizing and enforcing that law." *United States v. Smith*, 18 U.S. 71, 74 (1820). Any examination of the phrase "law of nations" must consider the words used as part of an "organic growth." See *Romero v. International Term. Operating Co.*, 358 U.S. 354 (1959).

In recent years, President Carter has made human rights a cornerstone of U.S. foreign policy. At the United Nations he has proclaimed that "no member of the United Nations can claim that mistreatment of its citizens is solely its own business." This concern for human rights has prompted the President to publicly decry human rights violations around the globe.

Congress too, has responded to changing international norms of conduct by enacting legislation which places limits on U.S. military and economic aid to countries which engage in "a consistent pattern of gross violations of human rights." 502B(b) of the Foreign Assistance Act of 1961, as amended.

Our country's treaty obligations and other international commitments, taken in conjunction with our pronouncements and legislation regarding human rights, lead to the conclusion that U.S. courts must regard the U.N. Universal Declaration of Human Rights and other such accords as part of the law of nations. With all our talk of Helsinki Accord violations by others, would we not rightfully be subject to ridicule if our courts held that kidnapping, murder and torture do not constitute "tort[s] in violation of the law of nations?"

Assistant Secretary of State for Human Rights Patricia Derian observed last year in a speech before the D.C. Bar Association that

> The law is as critical an element in shaping and carrying out our human rights policy as it was in forging our civil rights program. In dealings with other governments on human rights, it is the law that provides a solid point of departure.

Amici respectfully submit that U.S. courts should participate "in shaping and carrying out" our nation's human rights policy. 28 U.S.C. § 1350 provides a ready vehicle for that noble but difficult effort. By assuming jurisdiction over this important case, this Court announces to those who flagrantly disregard accepted norms of the international law of human rights not to expect refuge from justice in the United States and that, in appropriate cases, the doors of our courts are open to the persecuted who find themselves shut out in their homeland.

WHEREFORE, the relief requested by plaintiffs should be granted.

Respectfully submitted,

HAROLD A. MAYERSON
36 West 44th Street
New York, New York
(212) 661-1886

Attorney for *Amici Curiae*

Dated: New York, New York
April 13, 1979

APRIL 14, 1979: UNITED STATES

Telegram from American Embassy, Asunción to U.S. Department of State

Subject: NIV Case; Legal Status

UNCLASSIFIED
(REDACTED)
n/a

(REDACTED)
PAGE 01   ASUNCI 01619   141620Z
ACTION VO-05

INFO   OCT-01 ARA-11 ADS-00 CA-01 INSE-00 SSO-00 HA-05
      SR-05 L-03 SIG-03   PA-01 SS-15 /050 W

-------------------------------------071040   141626Z   /70

O 141545Z APR 79
FM AMEMBASSY ASUNCION
TO SECSTATE WASHDC IMMEDIATE 5762

(REDACTED) ASUNCION 1619

EO 12065: GDS 4/14/85 (WHITE, ROBERT E.) OR-M
TAGS: CVIS, SHUM (PENA, AMERICO)
SUBJECT: (C) NIV CASE; LEGAL STATUS

REF STATE 91799

1. (C—ENTIRE TEXT)

2. IMMEDIATELY FOLLOWING THE MURDER OF JOELITO FILAR-TIGA, THE STATE BROUGHT CHARGES AGAINST DUARTE ARRE-DONDO WHO WAS ARRESTED AND PLACED UNDER PREVENTIVE DETENTION PENDING TRIAL AND SENTENCING. HE CONFESSED TO BEING THE SOLE AUTHOR OF THE CRIME; HE IS STILL DETAINED; THERE HAS BEEN NO TRIAL OR SENTENCING. THE JUDGE DISMISSED ANY CASE AGAINST AMERICO PENA WHEN HE REFUSED TO PLACE HIM UNDER PREVENTATIVE DETENTION. THE JUDGE DID NOT FIND THE EVIDENCE OF COMPLICITY AGAINST AMERICO PENA CONVINCING AND, IN EFFECT, EXONERATED HIM BY SETTING HIM FREE. UNDER PARAGUAYAN LAW WHEN FILAR-

TIGA GAVE A STATEMENT ACCUSING AMERICO PENA THE JUDGE
EITHER CREDITED THE STATEMENT AND BINDS PENA OVER OR HE
FINDS THE CHARGE WITHOUT MERIT AND DEMONSTRATES THIS
BY REFUSING TO BIND HIM OVER AND ALLOWING THE ACCUSED
TO GO FREE.

3. SOME TEN DAYS AFTER THE MURDER, THE BOY'S FATHER, DR.
JOEL FILARTIGA, CHARGED THAT THE CORONER'S REPORT WAS
FRAUDULENT AND HE BROUGHT A SEPARATE CASE AGAINST
DUARTE ARREDONDO AND AMERICO PENA AS CO-ACCUSED IN
THE MURDER OF JOELITO FILARTIGA. THIS IS A SEPARATE CASE
THAT WAS NOT HEARD AT THE LOWER CRIMINAL LEVEL AND IS
PRESENTLY BEFORE THE APPEALS COURT WHERE IT HAS LAN-
GUISHED FOR SEVERAL YEARS. DR. FILARTIGA HAS PRESSED THE
CASE ON THE SUPREME COURT, DEMANDING THAT IT INSTRUCT
THE APPEALS COURT TO MAKE A DECISION AND OVERRULE THE
LOWER COURT'S INITIAL REFUSAL TO CONSIDER THIS SEPARATE,
PRIVATE CASE AGAINST TWO DEFENDANTS. MEANWHILE, AMERICO
PENA HAS NO RESTRICTIONS ON HIS FREEDOM OF MOVEMENT
AND, WHILE HE IS ACCUSED IN A PENDING CASE, HE WAS EXON-
ERATED BY THE INITIAL REFUSAL OF THE JUDGE TO PUT HIM
UNDER PREVENTATIVE DETENTION AND THE SUBSEQUENT DECI-
SION OF THE JUDGE TO REFUSE TO HEAR DR. FILARTIGA'S CASE
ALSO LEAVES HIM WITHOUT ANY INDICTMENT AGAINST HIM. TO
PUT IT ANOTHER WAY, FILARTIGA'S CHARGES AGAINST PENA IN
THE COURT OF APPEALS AND HIS SUBSEQUENT REQUEST TO THE
SUPREME COURT HAVE NO STATUS UNTIL THE COURT PRO-
NOUNCES THAT IT FINDS SOME EVIDENCE INVOLVING PENA.

4. THIS IS THE LEGAL STATUS OF AMERICO PENA IN PARAGUAY. AS
WE REPORTED IN ASUNCION 1560, PARAGUAYAN JUSTICE IS SERI-
OUSLY FLAWED AND THERE IS CERTAINLY A GOOD POSSIBILITY
THAT PENA DID TAKE PART IN THE MURDER. AS PART OF THE
POLICE ESTABLISHMENT, IT IS HIGHLY UNLIKELY THAT HE WILL
EVER BE TRIED OR SENTENCED IN PARAGUAY. THIS DOES NOT
MEAN HOWEVER THAT THE CONSUL HAS THE RIGHT TO SET
ASIDE PARAGUAYAN JUSTICE, REACHING THE DETERMINATION
THAT WE KNOW BETTER AND SAYING THAT PENA SHOULD HAVE
BEEN BARRED FROM A VISA AS A "NOTORIOUS" OFFENDER
AGAINST HUMAN RIGHTS. HIS LEGAL STATUS AND PREVIOUS
RECORD HERE DO NOT ALLOW FOR THAT INTERPRETATION.
THAT PENA SUCCESSFULLY DECEIVED THE CONSULAR OFFICER AS
TO HIS NON-IMMIGRANT STATUS IN NO WAY JUSTIFIES THE MALI-

CIOUS CHARGE BEING MADE IN WASHINGTON THAT PENA BRIBED THE CONSUL WHO KNEW OF HIS PART IN THE FILARTIGA CASE AND GAVE HIM A VISA ALTHOUGH HE WAS INELIGIBLE ON GROUNDS OF MORAL TURPITUDE. UNDER THE LAW, PENA WAS NOT INELIGIBLE ON THAT GROUND AND I BELIEVE THE DEPART-MENT SHOULD CLEARLY REJECT THE IMPUTATION OF WRONG-DOING BY THE FORMER CONSUL.

WHITE

(REDACTED)

APRIL 14, 1979: UNITED STATES

Telegram from American Embassy, Asunción to U.S. Department of State

Subject: NIV Case

UNCLASSIFIED
n/a

PAGE 01
ACTION VO-03 ASUNCI   01621   1416322

INFO   OCT-01   ARA-15   ADS-00   CA-01   HA-05   H-02   INSE-00
        SSO-00   /027   W

---071154   141642Z   /40

O 141605Z APR 79
FM AMEMBASSY ASUNCION
TO SECSTATE WASHDC IMMEDIATE 5764
UNCLAS ASUNCION 1621

EO   12065:   NA
TAGS: CVIS (PENA, AMERICO)
SUBJECT: NIV CASE

REFS   A) STATE 93188   B) ASUNCION 1619

1. STATE 91388 JUST RECEIVED ASKS FOR EMBASSY'S PREFERRED LANGUAGE TO USE IN ANSWERING CONGRESSIONAL INQUIRIES. I SUGGEST SOMETHING ALONG FOLLOWING LINES: THE U.S. EMBASSY IN ASUNCION GRANTED A TOURIST VISA TO AMERICO PENA ON JULY 11, 1978 AS A MEMBER OF A LARGE GROUP TAKING AN EXCURSION TRIP TO THE UNITED STATES ORGANIZED BY A REPUTABLE LOCAL TRAVEL FIRM AND ON PRESENTATION OF EVIDENCE REQUIRED BY U.S. VISA LAW TO DEMONSTRATE HIS BONA FIDES AS A NON-IMMIGRANT. PENA IS ONE OF THE MOST COMMON PARAGUAYAN NAMES; HIS FINANCIAL STATUS, THE FACT THAT HIS FAMILY WAS REMAINING BEHIND AND HIS POSITION IN THE FAMILY FIRM SATISFIED THE CONSUL. PENA WAS NOT INTERVIEWED. WHEN HE DID NOT JOIN THE EXCURSION ON ITS RETURN FROM THE UNITED STATES, THE TOUR OPERATOR REPORTED THIS TO INS IN MIAMI; A WOMAN AND CHILD TRAVELING ON THE SAME EXCURSION ALSO FAILED TO RETURN. THE

EMBASSY'S FIRST NOTIFICATION OF THE PENA GROUP'S FAILURE TO RETURN CAME IN A VISA OFFICE INQUIRY OF MARCH 7, 1979.

2. AMERICO PENA WAS DETAINED BRIEFLY FOLLOWING THE BRUTAL MURDER OF 17-YEAR-OLD JOELITO FILARTIGA IN MARCH OF 1976. ANOTHER PARAGUAYAN, DUARTE ARREDONDO, WAS ALSO ARRESTED WITHOUT CHARGE. THE CRIME: HE CONFESSED AND HAS BEEN DETAINED EVER SINCE, WITHOUT TRIAL OR SENTENCING. AMERICO PENA WAS RELEASED WITHOUT CHARGE. SEVERAL WEEKS LATER, DR. JOEL FILARTIGA, FATHER OF THE MURDERED BOY, BROUGHT A SEPARATE ACTION AGAINST PENA AND DUARTE, ACCUSING THEM OF COMPLICITY IN THE MURDER AND CHARGING THAT THE CORONER'S REPORT FALSIFIED THE TIME AND PLACE OF DEATH. DR. FILARTIGA HAS BEEN FRUSTRATED IN HIS LEGAL EFFORT TO BRING PENA AND DUARTE TO TRIAL. THE LOWER COURT REFUSED TO HEAR HIS CASE; THE COURT OF APPEALS HAS TAKEN NO ACTION ON HIS APPEAL; THE SUPREME COURT HAS NOT TAKEN COGNIZANCE OF HIS DEMAND THAT THE APPEALS COURT OVERRULE THE INITIAL REJECTION. THUS NO LEGAL CHARGES STAND AGAINST AMERICO PENA IN PARAGUAY. HE IS NOT UNDER INDICTMENT. ACCORDING TO U.S. IMMIGRATION LAW HE IS NOT INELIGIBLE FOR A VISA EXCEPT AS TO HIS NON-IMMIGRANT BONA FIDES.

3. SERIOUS DOUBTS CAN CERTAINLY BE ENTERTAINED ABOUT THE QUALITY OF PARAGUAYAN JUSTICE, ESPECIALLY WHEN A POLICE OFFICER IS ONE OF THE ACCUSED. BUT THE DEPARTMENT OF STATE AND THE EMBASSY IN ASUNCION HAVE NO ALTERNATIVE BUT TO ADMINISTER THE LAW AS IT IS WRITTEN. AMERICO PENA MAY BE SUSPECTED OF DECIDING TO ACCEPT OR REJECT THE VERDICT OF PARAGUAYAN JUSTICE. ACCORDING TO THE LAWS OF PARAGUAY, HE IS NOT GUILTY SO FAR AND BY U.S. LAW, HE IS NOT INELIGIBLE FOR A VISA ON GROUNDS OF MORAL TURPITUDE.

WHITE

UNCLASSIFIED

APRIL 16, 1979: PARAGUAY

Telegram from American Embassy, Asunción to U.S. Department of State

Subject: Filartiga Case Press Reaction

UNCLASSIFIED
n/a

UNCLASSIFIED

PAGE 01   ASUNCI   01642   162101Z
ACTION VOE-00

INFO   OCT-01   ARA-15   ADS-00   HA-05   CA-01   INSE-00   CIAE-00
        INR-10   NSAE-00   PA-02   ICA-20   SP-02   L-03   JUSE-00
        FBIE-00 NSC-05 H-02   / 066 W

--086781   162116Z / 15

P 162030Z APR 79
FM AMEMBASSY ASUNCION
TO SECSTATE WASHDC PRIORITY 5775

UNCLAS ASUNCION 1642

E.O. 12065: N/A
TAGS: CVIS, SHUM, PA
SUBJECT: FILARTIGA CASE PRESS REACTION

1. ASUNCION PRESS, PARTICULARLY THE DAILY "HOY" WHICH IS SENDING A REPORTER AND PHOTOGRAPHER TO THE U.S. TO COVER THE CASE, CONTINUES TO REPORT EXTENSIVELY ON AMERICO PENA'S DETENTION IN NEW YORK. APRIL 14 A "HOY" REPORTER INTERVIEWED THE LAWYER DR. JOSE EMILIO GOROS-TIAGA, WHO HAD PREPARED 1976 COURT TESTIMONY FOR PENA IN THE FILARTIGA CASE. WIRE SERVICE STORIES CARRIES HERE QUOTED PENA AS DECLARING HE WOULD NOT MAKE ANY STATE-MENTS ON THE FILARTIGA CASE IN THE U.S. UNTIL HE WAS REP-RESENTED BY GOROSTIAGA. HOWEVER, GOROSTIAGA, WHO WAS ON VACATION AT A RESORT TOWN OUTSIDE ASUNCION, DIS-CLAIMED ANY KNOWLEDGE OF THE LEGAL PROCEEDINGS IN NEW YORK. HE REPORTEDLY SAID HE HAD NOT BEEN APPROACHED BY ANYONE TO REPRESENT PENA IN NEW YORK AND ADDED THAT, IF ASKED, HE WOULD FIRST HAVE TO LOOK INTO THE MATTER CLOSELY AND CONSULT WITH THE FOREIGN MINISTRY.

2. "HOY" ALSO CARRIED LOCAL LEGAL OPINIONS ON VARIOUS ASPECTS OF THE NEW YORK LEGAL PROCEEDINGS AGAINST PENA. ONE PARAGUAYAN LAWYER REPORTEDLY NOTED THE ACCUSED (PENA) COULD EASILY BECOME THE ACCUSER. THIS SOURCE SAID THAT PENA MIGHT LATER SEEK DAMAGES FROM THE U.S. GOVERNMENT IF HE HAD BEEN SUBJECTED TO UNCALLED FOR DETENTION AND ILLEGAL PRESSURES.

3. "HOY" ALSO QUOTED A NATIONAL PENITENTIARY OFFICIAL AS SAYING THAT DERLIS DUARTE ARREDONDO, WHO CONFESSED TO JOEL FILARTIGA'S MURDER, IS THE ONLY PENITENT INMATE WHO MAINTAINS HE IS THE SOLE AUTHOR OF THE CRIME. THIS IN CONTRAST TO ALL OTHER INMATES WHO STAUNCHLY DENY COMMITTING THE CRIMES THEY ARE ACCUSED OF.

4. THE OFFICIAL COLORADO PARTY'S DAILY "PATRIA" CARRIED A COLUMN APRIL 16 WHICH CONTAINS THE ONLY REACTION SO FAR TO THE PENA CASE FROM OFFICIAL OR SEMI-OFFICIAL CIRCLES. "PATRIA" CHARGES THAT ANTI-PARAGUAYAN INDIVIDUALS AND HUMAN RIGHTS GROUPS IN THE U.S. ARE ATTEMPTING TO USE THE 10 MILLION DAMAGE SUIT AGAINST PENA AS A MEANS TO ATTACK THE PARAGUAYAN GOVERNMENT RATHER THAN TO SEEK JUSTICE. THREE PARAGUAYANS MENTIONED ARE EPIFANIO MENDEZ FLEITAS, GILBERTO OLMEDO SANCHEZ AND JORGE LARA CASTRO.

WHITE

UNCLASSIFIED

APRIL 20, 1979: PARAGUAY

Memorandum from American Embassy, Asunción to Files

Subject: Statement by Mother of the Accused Murderer of Dr. Filartiga's Son

UNITED STATES GOVERNMENT
MEMORANDUM

Date: April 20, 1979

Reply to Attn. Of: Andrew R. Kay, Jr.—POL

Subject: Statement by Mother of the Accused Murderer of Dr. Filartiga's Son

To: The Files

Sra. Arredondo de Duarte came to the Embassy on April 20. She related to me the following information regarding her son (Derlis Duarte) and the circumstances surrounding the murder of Joel Filartiga by her son in 1976.

Sra. de Duarte said that she had refused to give her son permission to marry his wife but he had obtained his father's consent to marry her even though he was underage. On the night of the murder she was called by neighbors who said that her son was fighting with someone in his house. She ran to the house which she said was approximately one-half block from her own residence, paid a taxi driver who was in front who had brought her son to the house and then entered the house. Coming out of the house were some men who were physically restraining her son who she said appeared to be acting like a madman with disheveled hair and a look of hatred on his face. She said her son was screaming that the woman (his wife) had to be killed because she had disgraced him. She also said that her son cried out to her that he (presumably young Filartiga) had insulted him, had hit him and that he (Derlis Duarte Arredondo) had killed him. The mother said that she ran into the bedroom where she discovered her daughter-in-law on the bed naked with the body of Filartiga on top of her. The girl was crying. She called to the girl asking what had happened and the girl responded "I think he is dead." The mother said that there was no appearance from the back of any wounds and so she lifted Filartiga's body up noticing a slash mark on his face and shortly thereafter noticed a deep knife wound in the area of the heart from which blood was flowing freely. The body was warm. Sra. de Duarte said there were marks on young Filartiga's back, perhaps four or five, similar to marks which would be raised when one hits a child with a belt or switch. However, other than this and the cut on Filartiga's face and the knife wound in his chest, there were no other marks on his body when she moved it. She said that when she saw the pictures in the newspaper of the body with marks allover it, she scarcely believed her eyes because that must mean that someone had defaced the body after the boy's death.

Sra. de Duarte said that she then went to the police station from where she took her son under escort to a hospital for a physical examination to determine the extent of her son's injuries. She said he had a contusion near the eye, a chipped tooth and a broken bone in his hand.

She said it appeared to her that these had come from a fight. During all this time her son kept saying to her "That woman has to die; she has disgraced me" over and over again. She claimed she would never have recognized her son because of his disheveled and demented manner.

Sra. de Duarte said that she had gone to the Filartiga house the following day to give her condolences to the family which she did to relatives of Dr. Filartiga. They then advised her to leave before the doctor appeared because of his distraught manner. A few days later, Dr. Filartiga arranged a meeting through a mutual friend with Sra. de Duarte and her husband. At this meeting she said Dr. Filartiga told her that her son was not responsible for the murder, that it was an act committed by the police and that they should unify their forces in order to obtain justice. Sra. de Duarte told Dr. Filartiga that they could not do so because they knew that their son was guilty. Sra. de Duarte said that she had kept silent in the matter because she and her family do not want to become involved in the controversy which surrounded and presently surrounds the Filartiga case. However, she said she is absolutely convinced that her son was the murderer and that he still maintains a homicidal impulse against his wife. Sra. de Duarte said she believes the wife is now living outside of Paraguay but she does not know where. However, she said the wife had sent a letter to Duarte in Tacumbu Prison about six months ago in which she begged his forgiveness, said that she realized that all the trouble was her fault and that she had named their latest child after Duarte Arredondo's father. Sra. de Duarte said that when her son read the contents of the letter he again exclaimed in a demented fashion that "this woman who has disgraced me must die."

Sra. de Duarte said that she had come to the Embassy to tell someone her story because she had read in the newspapers about the charges which were being leveled against former police inspector Americo Pena in the U.S. in which he is being accused of the murder of the young Filartiga. She said that she could not in good conscience allow a person (Pena) to be convicted of the murder when she was completely convinced that he was not responsible for it.

COMMENT: [**REDACTED**] find it difficult to believe a Paraguayan mother should testify against her son in this manner if it was not true. She presented her story in a manner which indicated she had lived through the experience and at times became somewhat agitated when relating some of the more horrible aspects of the murder. However, her comments about the marks on Filartiga's back could indicate that the boy had been mistreated before the murder occurred.

ARKay: mkn

CONFIDENTIAL

APRIL 23, 1979: PARAGUAY

Telegram from American Embassy, Asunción to U.S. Department of State

Subject: Press Reaction to Pena/Filartiga Case

DECONTROLLED/UNCLASSIFIED

(REDACTED)
n/a

(REDACTED)USE

PAGE 01   ASUNCI   01749   232106Z
ACTION ARA-15

INFO   OCT-01   ADS-00   HA-05   VO-05   CA-01   INSE-00   CIAE-00
        INR-10   NSAE-00   PA-01   ICA-11   SP-02   L-03   JUSE-00
        FBIE-00 NSC-05 /059 W

-------------------------------------052853   232116Z /64

P 232029Z APR 79
FM AMEMBASSY ASUNCION
TO SECSTATE WASHDC PRIORITY 5825

(REDACTED) ASUNCION 1749

E.O. 12065: N/A
TAGS: CVIS, SHUM, PA
SUBJECT: PRESS REACTION TO PENA/FILARTIGA CASE

REF: ASUNCION 1642

1. ASUNCION DAILY PRESS CONTINUES TO PROVIDE PROMINENT COVERAGE TO THE AMERICO PENA CASE AND ITS REPERCUSSIONS ON THE FILARTIGA MURDER CASE WHICH IS AT A STANDSTILL HERE. NOW THAT THE PRESS HAS PUBLISHED MOST OF THE PREVIOUSLY UNPUBLISHED INCONSISTENCIES IN THE FILARTIGA CASE, PENA'S LAWYER TRIP TO THE U.S. HAS BECOME THE CENTER OF ATTENTION.

2. DEPARTING FOR THE U.S. APRIL 19 THE LAWYER, DR. JOSE EMILIO GOROSTIAGA, TOLD THE PRESS HE WAS NOT GOING THERE TO

DEFEND PENA IN THE FILARTIGA CASE BUT RATHER TO ARGUE THE INADMISSIBILITY OF THE FILARTIGA FAMILY'S $10 MILLION SUIT AGAINST PENA. GOROSTIAGA REPORTEDLY REMARKED THAT TO TRY A PERSON IN A THIRD COUNTRY FOR AN ALLEGED CRIME COMMITTED IN THE HOME COUNTRY OF TWO NATIONALS WOULD INFRINGE NATIONAL SOVEREIGNTY AND THAT THE PROCEDURE HAS NO BASIS IN INTERNATIONAL LAW. HE DESCRIBED AS "BARBARIC" THE U.S. COURT'S CONTINUED DETENTION OF PENA.

3. NEWSPAPERS ALSO PROMINENTLY PLAYED LAST WEEK'S WASHINGTON PRESS CONFERENCE BY FILARTIGA'S LAWYER MICHAEL MAGGIO IN WHICH HE ACCUSED PENA, IN ADDITION TO THE FILARTIGA MURDER, OF OTHER CRIMES, I.E., INVOLVEMENT IN ORGANIZED PROSTITUTION AND NARCOTICS SMUGGLING. MENTION OF DR. RICHARD ARENS' (AUTHOR OF "GENOCIDE IN PARAGUAY") PRESENCE AT THE PRESS CONFERENCE FINALLY AROUSED COMMENT FROM OFFICIAL CIRCLES. THE OFFICIAL COLORADO PARTY DAILY "PATRIA" BEGAN TO CHARGE THAT SINISTER PARAGUAYAN OPPOSITION FIGURES IN THE U.S., AIDED AND ABETTED BY IRRESPONSIBLE U.S. HUMAN RIGHTS ZEALOTS WERE ATTEMPTING TO USE THE PENA/FILARTIGA CASE AS THE MEANS TO MOUNT A POLITICAL ASSAULT ON THE PARAGUAYAN GOVERNMENT.

4. IN AN APRIL 22 EDITORIAL ENTITLED "JUSTICE AND SOVEREIGNTY", "PATRIA" FORMALLY ADDRESSED THE PENA/FILARTIGA CASE. "PATRIA" MAINTAINED THERE WERE TWO CASES INVOLVED. ONE, THE PENA CASE, WAS A QUESTION OF PENA OVERSTAYING HIS AUTHORIZED PERIOD IN THE U.S. AND THIS THE U.S. COURTS QUITE CORRECTLY HAD DECIDED BY ORDERING DEPORTATION. THE OTHER, THE FILARTIGA CASE, PARAGUAYAN COURTS ARE HANDLING IN ACCORDANCE WITH LEGAL NORMS AS A COMMON CRIMINAL CASE. HOWEVER, "PATRIA" CHARGES THAT CERTAIN ELEMENTS ARE ATTEMPTING TO TURN A COMMON CRIMINAL CASE UNDER PARAGUAYAN JURISDICTION INTO AN INTERNATIONAL POLITICAL ISSUE. CLOSING, THE EDITORIAL WRITER STATES HE DOES NOT KNOW THE MOTIVATION OF THOSE ATTEMPTING TO TWIST THE ISSUE BUT THAT THEY ARE CREATING LEGAL "MONSTROSITIES" WHICH DAMAGE PARAGUAY'S SOVEREIGNTY AND ENDANGER ALL PARAGUAYANS WHO APPARENTLY COULD BE TRIED ABROAD FOR ALLEGED CRIMES COMMITTED IN PARAGUAY.

5. THE INDEPENDENT DAILY "ABC" CARRIED A STRONG EDITORIAL ALSO ON APRIL 22 WHICH CRITICIZED THE FEW WHO NEGATE

THE MAJORITY'S EFFORTS TO PROTECT PARAGUAY'S INTERNA-
TIONAL IMAGE. "ABC" LAMENTS THAT BECAUSE OF IRREGULARI-
TIES SUCH AS THE DOMINGO LAINO KIDNAPPING AND THE
PROCEEDINGS AGAINST CARME DE LARA CASTRO, A FEW PEOPLE
ARE MAKING IT IMPOSSIBLE FOR PARAGUAY TO DENY THAT
ABUSES HAVE OCCURRED OR PROMISE THEY WILL NOT BE
REPEATED. THE EDITORIAL SEES THE SOLUTION IN A RULE OF
LAW UNDER WHICH AMERICO PENA'S ROLE IN THE FILARTIGA
CASE WOULD BE HEARD IN A PARAGUAYAN COURT OF LAW WHICH
WOULD SEEK TRUTH AND JUSTICE, LETTING THE CHIPS FALL
WHERE THEY MAY.

WHITE

(REDACTED) USE

APRIL 25, 1979: PARAGUAY

Telegram from American Embassy, Asunción to U.S. Department of State

Subject: Meeting with President Stroessner

UNCLASSIFIED

(REDACTED)

n/a

(PAGE 01   ASUNCI   01799   261741Z
ACTION ARA-15

INFO   OCT-01   ADS-00   SS-15   NSC-05   SP-02   CIAE-00   INR-10
       NSAE-00   HA-05   / 053 W

---------------------------------------088748   270609Z /10

R 251659Z APR 79
FM AMEMBASSY ASUNCION
TO SECSTATE WASHDC 5852
INFO AMEMBASSY LA PAZ

(REDACTED)   ASUNCION 1799

LA PAZ FOR DAS BUSHNELL

E.O. 12065: GDS 4/25/85 (WHITE, ROBERT E.) OR-M
TAGS: PGOV, PA
SUBJECT: MEETING WITH PRESIDENT STROESSNER

REF: ASUNCION 1686

1. C—ENTIRE TEXT

2. DEPUTY ASSISTANT SECRETARY JOHN BUSHNELL AND I CALLED
ON PRESIDENT STROESSNER THE MORNING OF APRIL 20. THE
MEETING WAS ARRANGED AT THE INITIATIVE OF DR. CONRADO
PAPPALARDO, CONFIDENTIAL ASSISTANT TO THE PRESIDENT, FOL-
LOWING MY EARLIER CALL ON PRESIDENT STROESSNER APRIL 17
(REFTEL).

3. THE PRESIDENT CARRIED ON A MONOLOGUE FOR PRACTICALLY
THE ENTIRE MEETING, TELLING ANECDOTES ABOUT AMERICAN

PRESIDENTS HE HAD KNOWN AND REFERRING AGAIN TO THE TER-
RIBLE MISTAKES WE ARE ALLEGEDLY COMMITTING IN NICARAGUA.
IN THE FEW INTERVENTIONS WE SUCCEEDED IN MAKING, MR.
BUSHNELL REMARKED ON THE EVIDENT ECONOMIC PROGRESS
VISIBLE IN PARAGUAY, AND SUGGESTED THAT POLITICAL DEVEL-
OPMENT WAS ALSO IMPORTANT FOR THE FUTURE OF THE COUN-
TRY. THE ONLY POINT OF REAL INTEREST TO COME OUT OF THE
CONVERSATION WAS WHEN THE PRESIDENT VOLUNTEERED THAT
HE HAD NO INTENTION OF RUNNING FOR ANOTHER TERM OF
OFFICE IN 1983. HE SAID, "NO MORE. I WALKED IN THROUGH THE
FRONT DOOR AND I WANT TO WALK BACK OUT THE SAME WAY."

4. COMMENT: CLEARLY THE GOVERNMENT WISHED TO GIVE THE
IMPRESSION TO THE PUBLIC THAT IT CONSIDERED MR. BUSH-
NELL A HIGH LEVEL VISITOR WHOSE PRESENCE HERE SIGNIFIED
IMPROVEMENT IN ITS RELATIONS WITH THE U.S. THE GOP PROB-
ABLY ALSO LOOKED UPON THE HIGHLY PUBLICIZED CALL AS
SOMETHING OF AN ANTIDOTE TO THE AMERICO PENA CASE
WHICH CONTINUES TO DOMINATE LOCAL NEWSPAPERS. PHO-
TOGRAPHS OF OUR MEETING APPEARED THE NEXT DAY ON
FRONT PAGES AND WAS CARRIED ON LOCAL TV.

WHITE

(REDACTED)

APRIL 26, 1979: UNITED STATES

Correspondence from Defense Counsel Robert Rebollo to U.S. District Court Judge Nickerson

Fragano, Rebollo & Barone
Counselors-at-Law

Vincent F. Fragano
Robert G. Rebollo
Michael A. Barone

POST OFFICE BOX 'D'
ELTINGVILLE STATION
STATEN ISLAND, N.Y. 10312

GREAT KILLS OFFICE
4059 HYLAN BOULEVARD
STATEN ISLAND, N.Y. 10308
(212) 356-2662

April 26, 1979

U.S. District Court
Eastern District of New York
Emanuel Celler Fed. Bldg.
225 Cadman Plaza East
Brooklyn, N.Y. 11201

Honorable Eugene H. Nickerson

   Re: Dolly M.E. Filartiga and Dr. Joel Filartiga
       v. Americo Norberto Pena-Irala, et.al.
       79 Civ. 917 (EHN)

Dear Honorable Judge Nickerson:

  This letter will be presented to you by Mr. Jose Emilio Gorosdiaga, an attorney of Paraguay with respect to two affirmations submitted in our application for an adjournment, since Paraguayan counsel is laboring under a severe handicap with respect to conversing with the Court.

  It is respectfully requested that the Court take the opportunity to review these short affirmations and to afford us the adjournment requested even peremptorily, if necessary.

  Thank you for your kind attention and consideration.

           Very truly yours,

RGR/eb
Enc.

           Robert G. Rebollo
           For the Firm

UNITED STATES DISTRICT COURT
EASTERN DISTRICT OF NEW YORK

DOLLY M.E. FILARTIGA and DR. JOEL FILARTIGA,	**AFFIRMATION** **79 Civ. 917 (EHN)**

Plaintiffs,

– against –

AMERICO NORBERTO PENA-
IRALA, et al.,

Defendants.

Jose Emilio Gorosdiaga, an attorney-at-law, hereby affirms the following under penalties of perjury:

That I am an attorney, duly licensed to practice in the sovereign country of Paraguay.

That I have presently been retained by the Defendant, AMERICO NORBERTO PENA-IRALA, to represent him in the criminal proceeding presently pending against him in such country. That, at the time of Mr. Pena's detention in this country, I was still in my native land, and did not arrive at these shores until April 20, 1979. I attempted, on that day, to obtain permission to visit my client, but [he] was incarcerated in the Immigration Detention Center. Permission for such visitation was refused me, and the first time I saw my client in this country was on Monday, April 23, 1979. I saw both Defendants, Pena and nominated Defendant, Villalba on that day. I spent Tuesday and Wednesday of that week attempting to obtain translations of materials which I brought with me from Paraguay. I have not yet received translations of such documents and only expect to receive the same this afternoon, April 26, 1979 at 5 P.M. Owing to the obvious existing language difficulty, I have requested that an explanation of all documents in this matter be afforded me by a proper translation.

I am sorely afraid that my client will be tempted to enlist the aid of anyone around him who offers help in this matter. As a case in point, when I interviewed Mr. Pena on Monday, April 23, 1979, he informed my client that he had been visited by a Spanish speaking priest who informed my client that he would be able to obtain proper counsel for him, if he so desired. My client, although it may seem to the Court naïve, but undoubtedly, through fear of his present situation, told the priest then instituted a phone call to a fictitious attorney with the surname, Cohen, and obtained from my client the sum of $1,000.00 as and for a retainer in this matter. When I arrived at these shores, I questioned Mr. Pena concerning the same and was given an address in Manhattan where this attorney was supposed to maintain offices. I was not surprised to find that no such law offices existed, and I fear that in desperation, Mr. Pena may again accept the aid of those who seek only to profit thereby. I can only state to this Honorable Court that I am faced with a most difficult and trying situation. It would be entirely impossible for me, as a foreigner to these shores, to present a satisfactory proposal and competent case in opposition to this requested relief. I have been informed by New York Counsel that many questions of law, both procedural and substantive, are raised in this matter, and that time and time alone will afford us the opportunity to properly oppose this motion.

I respectfully request that the Court grant to these Defendants, Respondents, in this order to show cause, an adjournment.

UNITED STATES DISTRICT COURT
EASTERN DISTRICT OF NEW YORK

DOLLY M.E. FILARTIGA and   **AFFIRMATION**
DR. JOEL FILARTIGA,
                                      79 Civ. 917 (EHN)

Plaintiffs,

– against –

AMERICO NORBERTO PENA-
IRALA, et al.,

Defendants.

ROBERT G. REBOLLO, an attorney-at-law, hereby affirms the following under penalties of perjury:

That on April 26, 1979, your affirmant, conferred with Jose Emilio Gorosdiaga, an attorney-at-law, of the sovereign country of Paraguay. That Mr. Jose Emilio Gorosdiaga informed your affirmant at such conference that he was the attorney for Americo Norberto Pena-Irala with respect to a certain pending criminal indictment and prosecution against him in the country of Paraguay.

Such conference was brought about at the insistence of Mr. Pena's attorneys in order that he may seek information relative to the Federal Statutory Law of the United States concerning the above-captioned Civil action. This conference as hereinbefore stated occurred at your affirmant's office and took the greater part of the day because your affirmant was not familiar with the Spanish language and was unable to express himself colloquially with respect to nuances and vernacular. It was necessary that a translator be present. Your affirmant was presented with a copy of the order to show cause to said deportation herein and even at the time of the making of this affirmation has not had sufficient opportunity to review the same, much less provide Paraguayan counsel with proper directives in establishing and preparing papers in opposition to such motion. Your affirmant verily believes that a severe jurisdictional problem appears and cries out from the very face of the papers, and to permit this motion to be heard without availing the Defendants of a proper opportunity to prepare papers in opposition and even a cross motion for dismissal on the basis of a lack of jurisdiction, would cause the Defendants an irreparable harm and deny these Defendants of their right to a proper hearing before this honorable tribunal. Your affirmant verily believes that, in order to prepare papers in opposition hereto, it will be necessary to further confer with Paraguayan counsel, to interview the Defendant, Americo Norberto Pena-Irala, who is presently in the custody of Defendants Castillo and Vician, who upon information and belief, are Agents of the United States Immigration Service, to interview Defendants, Villalba with respect to any of her knowledge in this action, if any, and to permit a reasonable time within which to research the points of law involved in this proceeding, especially, including but not limited to questions of conflicts of law, and comity.

In all likelihood, this affirmation will be presented to the Court by Paraguayan counsel, inasmuch as scheduling and calendar practice would not permit any member of our office to be present on the return date of this order to show cause. With the further understanding that undoubtedly the Court as well as counsel appearing before it will be presented with a difficult language problem, I have taken this opportunity to prepare a statement for Paraguayan counsel to use and to present before the Court. I ask that the Court consider this affirmation together with the affirmation of Paraguayan counsel and the written statement as a formal request for granting an adjournment in this matter for a period of no less than two and, hopefully, as much as three weeks. It is understood that the Court, in consideration of this application for adjournment would, in all likelihood, continue to retain Mr. Pena in custody with the United States Immigration Service. In any event, however, to fail to have a proper in opposition hereto would cause a grave injustice to these Defendants, and your affirmant reiterates his request for the adjournment as aforesaid.

Robert G. Rebollo, Esq.

Dated: April 26, 1979
       Staten Island, N.Y.

MAY 3, 1979: PARAGUAY

Telegram from American Embassy, Asunción to U.S. Department of State

Subject: Filartiga Case

UNCLASSIFIED

[Excised]

n/a

[Excised]

PAGE 01   ASUNCI 01938 031428Z
ACTION ARA-15

INFO   OCT-01   ADS-00   HA-05   CIAE-00   INR-10   NSAE-00   L-03
        SY-05   SYE-00   MCT-02   /041W

--034881   041845Z   /50

R 031500Z MAY 79
FM AMEMBASSY ASUNCION
TO SECSTATE WASHDC 5924

[Excised]   ASUNCION 1938
E.O. 12065:   XDS 5/2/99 (KAY, ANDREW R.) OR-P
TAGS: SHUM, PA

SUBJECT: FILARTIGA CASE: ALLEGED THREAT TO DR FILARTIGA'S LIFE

1. DURING MEETING WITH EMBOFF ON MAY 2, DR. JOEL FILAR-
TIGA, THE COMPLAINANT IN THE AMERICO PENA CASE CUR-
RENTLY BEFORE THE NEW YORK COURT, CLAIMED THAT DURING
A MEETING ON APRIL 27 AMONG PRESIDENT STROESSNER, INTE-
RIOR MINISTER MONTANARO, FOREIGN MINISTER NOGUES AND
INTERIOR DEPUTY SECRETARY BESTARD THE PENA/FILARTIGA
CASE WAS DISCUSSED. ACCORDING TO DR FILARTIGA, PRESIDENT
STROESSNER EXPRESSED DISGUST WITH THE WAY THE CASE WAS
GOING AND SAID THAT ONE MORE DEATH WOULD NOT BE A MAT-
TER OF ANY CONSEQUENCE. DR. FILARTIGA SAID HE HAD
LEARNED OF THE ALLEGED STATEMENT THROUGH [EXCISED]
AND THAT THE IMPLICATION WAS MADE THAT THE PRESIDENT'S
STATEMENT REFERRED TO HIM, DR. FILARTIGA.

2. COMMENT: ALTHOUGH ANYTHING IS POSSIBLE IN PARAGUAY, THE EMBASSY FINDS IT VERY DIFFICULT TO BELIEVE THAT SUCH A THREAT AGAINST DR. FILARTIGA'S LIFE WOULD BE CARRIED OUT GIVEN THE CURRENT WORLDWIDE PUBLICITY OVER THE CASE AND THE PREVAILING BELIEF HERE THAT FILARTIGA DOES WHAT HE DOES BECAUSE HE IS MENTALLY UNBALANCED. HOWEVER, THE PRESIDENT MAY WELL HAVE MADE SOME VERY STRONG COMMENT REGARDING THIS CASE WHICH DEMONSTRATES THE DEGREE TO WHICH ANIMOSITIES HAVE BEEN AROUSED HERE BY THE LAWSUIT IN THE UNITED STATES.

WHITE

MAY 7, 1979: UNITED STATES

Defendant Pena-Irala's Notice Memorandum of Law in Support of Motion to Dismiss Complaint and Vacate Stay

UNITED STATES DISTRICT COURT
EASTERN DISTRICT OF NEW YORK

DOLLY M.E. FILARTIGA and
DR. JOEL FILARTIGA,

Plaintiffs,

– against –

AMERICO NORBERTO PENA-
IRALA, LEONEL CASTILLO, as
Commissioner of the United States
Immigration and Naturalization
Service and GEORGE VICIAN, as
District Director, Immigration and
Naturalization Service, New York,

Defendants.

**DEFENDANT PENA-IRALA'S
MEMORANDUM OF LAW IN
SUPPORT OF MOTION TO
DISMISS COMPLAINT AND
VACATE STAY**

79 Civ. 917

ROBERT G. REBOLLO, ESQ.
FRAGANO, REBOLLO & BARONE
4044 Hylan Boulevard
Staten Island, New York 10308
(212) 356-2662

–AND–

MATTHEW P. BOYLAN, ESQ., and
MURRY D. BROCHIN, ESQ.
LOWENSTEIN, SANDLER, BROCHIN, KOHL,
FISHER & BOYLAN
A Professional Corporation
744 Broad Street
Newark, New Jersey 07102
(201) 624-4600

Attorneys for Defendant Pena-Irala

TABLE OF CONTENTS

PRELIMINARY STATEMENT

This is a brief on behalf of defendant Americo Norberto Pena-Irala in support of his application for the following relief:

1. To dismiss this suit for lack of federal jurisdiction;
2. To vacate the pending stay of deportation on the ground that this court has no authority either to stay deportation or to detain the defendant for the purpose of compelling his deposition; and
3. To dismiss this suit on the grounds of *forum non conveniens.*

The only substantial question of civil rights raised by this case is the question of the civil rights of defendant Pena-Irala, a foreign national who must be presumed innocent by the standards of American law, and who, with his companion and young child, is being unlawfully detained in custody so that plaintiffs may make this court a theater for the display of political propaganda. To anyone concerned with civil rights in the United States, the proposition that a man, woman, and their child can be kept in federal confinement against their will as the result of a civil case so that they may participate in a show-trial should be shocking indeed! Our laws will not sustain so egregious a violation of due process!

There is a second fundamental issue of policy also present in this case. The premise of plaintiffs' action is that this court is the proper tribunal before which to try the culpability of defendant Pena-Irala for a homicide, allegedly politically motivated, which is said to have taken place three years ago in Paraguay. In a case such as this, where the alleged tortfeasor and the complainants are all Paraguayan nationals, it would be an unwarranted intrusion into the affairs of a foreign state for this court to take cognizance of plaintiff's claim.

Even if this court possessed jurisdiction—and it does not—it should seek to avoid a precedent which would encourage every Kurdish rebel, every West Bank Palestinian, every Soviet dissident—the list is endless in a turbulent world—to appeal to our courts for redress of politically motivated injuries which he claims to have sustained in his own country. Consider what a justifiable outcry would be aroused in the United States if one of our citizens were detained and tried in Moscow—or in Paraguay—upon the allegation that he was responsible for a racially motivated killing perpetrated against another American in the United States! Fortunately, our laws do not compel this court to act the role of Don Quixote seeking to cure the ills of the world. In fact, our laws prohibit this court from undertaking such an adventure and we are confident that the court will reject the proffered role.

STATEMENT OF FACTS

Defendant Pena-Irala, his companion Juana Villalba and their two year old child are being held in the custody of Immigration and Naturalization Service solely pursuant to order of this Court issued on application of the plaintiff. All three of the detainees are Paraguayan citizens who entered this country legally on tourist visas, but then remained beyond their expiration date without obtaining their renewals. Pena-Irala, Villalba and their child were apprehended and confined by the federal authorities pending immediate deportation. All three have agreed to, and in fact request, immediate deportation. This Court's order, therefore, is the only bar to their liberty.

Plaintiffs are also Paraguayan nationals. According to the complaint plaintiff Joel Filartiga is a resident of Paraguay. Dolly Filartiga claims to be a resident of Washington, D.C. Her complaint alleges that she arrived in the United States more than a year ago on a visitor's visa and has filed an application for political asylum. There is no indication in the papers before the Court what the present status of that application is. It may be that one of her purposes for coming here was to institute this lawsuit. (See paragraph 13 of Dolly M. E. Filartiga's affidavit sworn to and subscribed April 9, 1979.)

The lawsuit which plaintiffs have commenced in this Court alleges that defendant Pena-Irala wrongfully killed and tortured Joelito Filartiga who was plaintiff Joel Filartiga's son and plaintiff Dolly M. E. Filartiga's brother. The alleged killing and torture is said to have occurred 3 years ago in Paraguay. These allegations concerning the circumstances of the alleged killing and torture are expressly set forth on information and belief.

The papers filed by plaintiffs themselves and an affidavit submitted on behalf of defendant Pena-Irala show that the alleged killing is currently the subject of a criminal proceeding in Paraguay against Pena-Irala and a co-defendant, Hugo Duarte. Duarte has made a written statement admitting that he was solely responsible for the death of Joelito Filartiga, although he contends that the homicide was justifiable. As appears from the affidavit of Jose Emilio Gorostiaga a Paraguayan attorney who has represented Pena-Irala in Paraguay (annexed hereto as Exhibit A*), the decedent's father has the right to file a civil suit in a Paraguayan Court under Paraguayan law for the recovery of civil damages for the wrongful death of his son and he has not yet done so although the period in which he may file such a suit has not yet expired. (See, also, Statement of Dr. Ramon Rodriguez Alcala, Professor of Law, National University of Asuncion, Paraguay, and Certification, Supreme Court of Justice of Paraguay, annexed hereto as

Exhibits B* and C*, respectively).[1]

The plaintiffs have attached to their complaint various newspaper articles and reports purporting to describe the political, legal and juridical situation in Paraguay in highly disparaging terms. Plaintiffs' prayer for relief asks ten million dollars compensatory and punitive damages and, apparently as interim relief, the continued detention of Pena-Irala.

POINT I

THIS COURT LACKS FEDERAL JURISDICTION TO
ENTERTAIN PLAINTIFFS' SUIT

It is fundamental that a plaintiff in a federal court must allege and must carry the burden of establishing the basis for the court's jurisdiction. *Thomson v. Gaskill*, 315 U.S. 442, 86 L.Ed. 951 (1941); *Gibbs v. Buck*, 307 U.S. 66, 83 L.Ed. 111 (1939); *Tubeco Inc. v. Crippen Pipe Fabrication Corp.*, 1402 F.Supp. 838 (S.D.N.Y. 1975), *aff'd without opinion*, 538 F.2d 314 (2d Cir. 1976); 5 *Wright & Miller, Federal Practice and Procedure* § 1350 at fn. 91. In the instant case, plaintiffs have implicitly conceded that that is their burden by undertaking to allege the grounds upon which they seek to establish federal jurisdiction.

Paragraph 2 of plaintiffs' complaint alleges, "The jurisdiction of this court arises under 28 U.S.C. §§ 1331, 1350, 1651, 2201 and 2202 and the doctrine of pendent jurisdiction." Paragraph 4 states, "Plaintiffs' causes of action arise under Article II, Section 2, clause 1 and Article 6, clause 2 of the Constitution of the United States; 28 U.S.C. §§ 1350, 2201-2202; 8 U.S.C. § 1252(c); the wrongful death statutes; the U.N. Charter; the Universal Declaration on Human Rights; the U.N. Declaration Against Torture; the American Declaration of the Rights and Duties of Man; and other pertinent declarations, documents and practices constituting the customary international law of human rights and law of nations."

Fortunately, an exegesis of the statute, constitutional provisions and treaties to which plaintiffs have referred is unnecessary because plaintiffs themselves have chosen to argue only 28 U.S.C. § 1350 as the basis upon which they seek to sustain this Court's jurisdiction. That section reads as follows: "The District Court shall have original jurisdiction of any civil action by an alien for a tort only, committed in violation of the law of

---

[1] A translation of Exhibits A and B from the original Spanish into English, together with an affidavit of translation, are annexed hereto as Exhibit D. Exhibit C has an English translation included as part of exhibit.

nations or a treaty of the United States." Plaintiffs have not explained how any treaties have created a cause of action which they may assert, and we know of no treaty which makes a Paraguayan's wrongful killing of another in Paraguay into an offense covered by American law. (See *Dreyfus v. Von Finck*, 534 F.2d 24, 29 (2d Cir.) *cert. denied*, 429 U.S. 835 (1976) ("Rarely is the relationship between a private claim and a general treaty sufficiently direct so that it may be said to 'arise under' the treaty as required by Article III, Section 2, Cl. 1 of the Constitution.").

Rather, plaintiffs' brief indicates that their argument is that murder, wherever and by whom it may have been committed, is contrary to the "law of nations" within the meaning of 28 U.S.C. § 1350, at least when it is politically motivated and accompanied by torture. The critical question upon which the jurisdiction of this court depends, therefore, is the meaning of the statutory phrase "in violation of the law of nations" in 28 U.S.C. § 1350.

In this instance, the process of statutory construction will be facilitated by starting with first principles. The language of 28 U.S.C. § 1350 which purports to confer jurisdiction upon this Court must, of course, be construed in a manner consistent with Section 2 of Article III of the United States' Constitution:

> Section 2. The judicial power shall extend to all Cases in Law and Equity, arising under this Constitution, the Laws of the United States, and Treaties made, or which shall be made, under their Authority; to all Cases affecting Ambassadors, other public Ministers and Consuls; to all Cases of Admiralty and maritime Jurisdiction; to Controversies in which the United States shall be a Party; to Controversies between two or more States; between a State and Citizens of another State; between Citizens of different States; between citizens of the same State claiming Lands under Grants of different States; and between a State, or the Citizens thereof, and foreign States, Citizens or Subjects.

Plaintiffs themselves have admitted, as they must, that jurisdiction in this case cannot be sustained upon the basis of the citizenship of the parties. Their concession is inevitable because the United States Supreme Court has held that Congress may not constitutionally confer jurisdiction upon District Courts predicated solely upon the alienage of all of the parties. *Jackson v. Twentyman*, 2 Pet. (27 U.S.) 136, 7 L.Ed. 374 (1829); *Hodgson v. Bower Bank*, 5 Cranch (9 U.S.) 303, 3 L.Ed. 108 (1809); *Montlet v. Murray*, 4 Cranch (9 U.S.) 303, 3 L.Ed. 545 (1807); *Mossman v. Higginson*, 4 Dall. (4 U.S.) 12, 1 L.Ed. 720 (1800). See 13 *Wright-Miller-Cooper, Federal Practice and Procedure* §3604.

Where in this grant is the authority of Congress to confer upon the United States District Courts jurisdiction over "any civil action by an alien for a tort only, committed in violation of the law of nations?" The only language of Article III which appears relevant is that which extends the judicial power "to all cases affecting ambassadors, or other public ministers and counsels," "to all cases of admiralty and maritime jurisdiction," and perhaps the phrase "between a state or the citizens thereof and foreign states, citizens or subjects." An additional possible source of constitutional authority for the "in violation of the law of nations" provision of 28 U.S.C. § 1350 may be the federal government's implied power over international relations. See *Banco Nacional de Cuba v. Sabbatino*, 376 U.S. 398, 427, 11 L. Ed. 2d 804, 823 n.25 (1964).

Consider the implication for our case of the very limited scope of the definition of jurisdiction found in Article III, Section 2. Congress has no delegated authority to make even the wrongful killing of one New Yorker by another a tort or crime (except within the narrow range of circumstances dealt with by the Thirteenth and Fourteenth Amendments or some other specific constitutional provision). Certainly, therefore, the Constitution does not authorize Congress to empower the federal district courts to try civil damage cases by one foreigner against another for acts committed abroad!

The "alien's action for tort" statute, 28 U.S.C. § 1350, the predecessor of which was first enacted as part of the Judiciary Act of 1789 (see *Annot.*, 34 ALR Fed. 388, 390 (1977)), could not have had such an expansive purpose. Rather its purpose was to grant to the Federal Courts jurisdiction over violations of those aspects of the "law of nations" with which the constitution authorizes them to deal, i.e., cases affecting diplomatic representatives of foreign states, that part of admiralty and maritime law which is part of the law of nations such as the law of prizes (privateering), matters directly affecting the conduct of foreign relations, and, of course, treaties.

The decided cases have been entirely consistent with such a construction of 28 U.S.C. § 1350 and have restricted the phrase "law of nations" to relations between states rather than among individuals. In *Lopes v. Reederei Richard Schroder*, 225 F. Supp. 292 (E.D. Pa. 1963), the Court discussed the meaning of the phrase "in violation of the law of nations" within the meaning of 28 U.S.C. § 1350 as follows:

This phrase has been held to include acts such as the unlawful seizure of a vessel and its disposition as a prize, the seizure of neutral property upon the ship of a belligerent, unjustified seizure of an alien's property in a foreign country by a United States officer, failure to accord comity to ships of foreign countries, and concealment of a child's true nationality coupled with the wrongful inclusion of that child on another's passport. The other cases arising under this section do not elucidate the meaning of this phrase.

Article I, Section 8, Clause 10, of the Constitution also contains the phrase "Law of Nations." Cases discussing this phrase have held the following to be "Offences against the Law of Nations": violation of slave trade, acts tending to incriminate, coerce, harass or bring into public disrepute any diplomatic or consular representative of a foreign government, and counterfeiting notes of foreign countries.

After consideration of the above authorities, the conclusion of this court is that the phrase "in violation of the law of nations," for the purpose of deciding this issue, means, *inter alia*, at least a violation by one or more *individuals* of those standards, rules or customs (a) affecting the relationship between states or between an individual and a foreign state, and (b) used by those states for their common good and/or in dealings *inter se* . . . . (225 F. Supp. at pp. 296-97.)

See also Valanga v. Metropolitan Life Insurance Company, 259 F. Supp. 324 (E.D. Pa. 1966).

In only two reported cases have United States courts sustained jurisdiction on the basis of 28 U.S.C. § 1350 or its predecessors. One such case appears to be *Bolchos v. Darrell,* Fed. Cas. No. 1607 (D.C. S.C. 1795), where the issue was a contest between citizens of two foreign countries over the right to neutral property seized as a prize of war. The court found jurisdiction based upon admiralty and also based upon the predecessor to 28 U.S.C. § 1350. The only modern case in which jurisdiction has been sustained based upon the "law of nations" provision of 28 U.S.C. § 1350 is *Abdul-Rahman Omar Adra v. Clift,* 195 F. Supp. 857 (D. Md. 1961), a suit by a divorced husband against his former wife, both foreign nationals, seeking custody of his daughter. The court held that the conduct of the mother in taking the daughter from country to country under a foreign passport obtained by concealing the daughter's name and nationality and in withholding the daughter from her husband's custody constituted a tort "in violation of the law of nations" within the meaning of the statute. The court explained its rationale as follows:

In the instant case, despite the fact that the child Najwa was a Lebanese national, not entitled to be admitted to the United States under an Iraqi passport, defendant concealed Najwa's name and nationality, caused her to be included in defendant's Iraqi passport, and succeeded in having her admitted to the United States thereby. These were wrongful acts not only against the United States, 8 U.S.C.A. 1182, 18 U.S.C.A. 1546, but against the Lebanese Republic, which is entitled to control the issuance of passports to its nationals. See *Kent v. Dulles*, 357 U.S. 116, 121, 78 S.Ct. 1113, 2 L.Ed.3d 1204, where the Court quoted from *Urtetiqui v. D'Arbel*, 9 Pet. 692, 699, 9 L.Ed. 276, as follows: "[A passport] is a document, which, from its nature and object, is addressed to foreign powers; purporting only to be a request that the bearer of it may pass safely and freely; and is to be considered rather in the character of a political document, by which the bearer is recognized, in foreign countries, as an American citizen; and which, by usage and the law of nations, is received as evidence of the fact." See also Hackworth, Digest of International Law, vol. III. ch. X, 1942.

The wrongful acts were therefore committed in violation of the law of nations. And since they caused direct and special injury to the plaintiff, he may bring an action in tort therefor.

In *IIT v. Vencap, Ltd*, 519 F.2d 1001 (2d Cir. 1975), the Court refused to find federal jurisdiction under the "law of nations" provisions of § 1350. The Court summarized the applicable law as follows:

This leaves 28 U.S.C. § 1350 which confers jurisdiction over "any civil action by an alien for a tort only, committed in violation of the law of nations or a treaty of the United States." This old but little used section is a kind of legal Lohengrin; although it has been with us since the first Judiciary Act, § 9, 1 Stat. 73, 77 (1789), no one seems to know whence it came. We dealt with its some years ago in *Khedivial Line, S. A. v. Seafarers' Union*, 278 F.2d 49, 52 (2 Cir. 1960) (per curiam). At that time we could find only one case where jurisdiction under it had been sustained, in that instance violation of a treaty, *Bolchos v. Darrell*, 3 Fed.Cas. No. 1,607, p. 810 (D.S.C. 1795); there is now one more. See *Abdul Rahman Omar Adra v. Clift*, 195 F. Supp. 857, 863-65 (D. Md. 1961). Here there is no allegation of anyone's violating a treaty. The reference to the law of nations must be narrowly read if the section is to be kept within the confines of Article III. We cannot subscribe to plaintiffs' view that the Eighth Commandment "Thou shall not steal" is part of the law of nations. While every civilized nation doubtless has this as a part of its legal system, a violation of the law of nations arises only when there has been "a violation by one or more individuals of those standards, rules or customs (a) affecting the relationship between states or between an individual and a foreign state, and (b) used

by those states for their common good and/or in dealings *inter se.*"
Lopes v. Reederei Richard Schroder, 225 F. Supp. 292, 297 (E.D. Pa.
1963). See also *Damaskinos v. Societa Navigacion Interamericana, S.A.,
Pan.*, 255 F. Supp. 919, 923 (S.D.N.Y. 1966); *Valanga v. Metropolitan
Life Insurance Co.*, 259 F. Supp. 324, 328 (E.D. Pa., 1966). We there-
fore turn to the two sections of the securities laws.

Since defendant Pena-Irala's alleged wrongful killing of a Paraguayan
in Paraguay is not a violation of a standard, rule or custom which both (a)
affects the relationship between states or between an individual and a foreign state and (b) is used by those states for their common good or in dealing with one another, such a wrongful killing is not a tort in violation of the
law of nations within the meaning of § 1350.

If any question remains, that question is disposed of by the decision of
the Second Circuit Court of Appeals in *Dreyfus v. Von Finck*, 534 F.2d 24 (2d
Cir.), *cert. denied*, 429 U.S. 835 (1976). The underlying tort complained of
in that case was an "Aryan" German's acquisition of a German Jew's property for less than its value in a coerced sale. On the issue of the availability
of federal jurisdiction under the "law of nations" provision of 28 U.S.C. §
1350, the court said:

> More importantly for purposes of this lawsuit, violations of inter-
> national law do not occur when the aggrieved parties are nationals
> of the acting state. This was pointed out by Mr. Justice White in his
> dissenting opinion in *Banco Nacional de Cuba v. Sabbatino* [citations
> omitted] and it is the clear holding in *Salimoff & Co. v. Standard
> Oil Co.*, 262 N.Y. 220, 186 N.E. 679 (1933) cited by both the major-
> ity and dissenting opinions.

> In the instant case, plaintiff was a citizen and resident of Germany
> at the time of defendants alleged wrong doing. Moreover his com-
> plaint did not allege that defendants played any role in the policy
> making decision of the German government. Defendants conduct,
> tortious though it may have been, was not a violation of the law of
> nations, which governs civilized states in their dealings with each
> other. (534 F.2d at 31.)

This clear holding of *Dreyfus v. Von Finck, supra*, is dispositive of the
instant case and requires its dismissal for lack of jurisdiction. Plaintiffs and
defendant Pena-Irala are all Paraguayan nationals. Tortious acts by one
against the other within the territory of Paraguay do not constitute violations of the "law of nations" within the meaning of 28 U.S.C. § 1350.
Indeed, that statute could not be construed to confer jurisdiction over a

case such as this, because, if it were, it would be beyond the authority granted to Congress by Article III of the Federal Constitution.

POINT II

THE DETENTION OF DEFENDANT PENA-IRALA IN THE CUSTODY OF THE UNITED STATES FOR PLAINTIFFS' PURPOSES HAS NO FOUNDATION IN LAW.

A. *The notion that an American Court should detain a man, a woman and their child in custody to compel one or more of them to testify in a civil case is mind-boggling!*

The power to detain a defendant or a witness under federal law exists only in criminal cases. Pursuant to 28 U.S.C. § 3149, a material witness can be held against his will in order to guarantee his testimony at trial, but only upon a showing that the anticipated testimony is indeed material and that it is potentially impracticable to obtain such testimony by subpoena. *United States v. Feingold*, 416 F. Supp. 627 (E.D.N.Y. 1976). The foundation for such a provision is the strong public policy for disclosure of knowledge of criminal activity, a need "so vital that one known to be innocent may be detained, in the absence of bail, as a material witness." *Stein v. State of New York*, 346 U.S. 156, 184, *reh. denied*, 346 U.S. 842 (1953). Neither the strong public policy nor the specific grant of statutory authority exists with respect to civil actions.

The stay of deportation here at issue constitutes in effect a writ *ne exeat* or its modern equivalent, civil arrest. Defendant is a foreign national subject to a valid order of deportation. As such, he has been entirely deprived of any freedom of movement until and unless he is deported. Only after his deportation will he be permitted his right to liberty, if not in the United States, then at least in his homeland of Paraguay. In every respect, his confinement is due solely to the intervention of the District Court, at plaintiffs' behest. He is, in substance if not in form, under civil arrest. His person has been seized as a prejudgment remedy.

Both federal common law and the Federal Rules of Civil Procedure provide expressly that civil arrests are to be governed by the law of the State in which the District Court is sitting. *See, eg., Granny Goose Foods, Inc. v. Brotherhood of Teamsters*, 415 U.S. 423, 436 n.10 (1974) ("in all cases in federal courts . . . state law is incorporated to determine the availability of prejudgment remedies for the seizure of person or property . . . ."). *See also*, F.R.Civ.P. 64.

The sole basis, then, upon which the Court could base its stay of deportation would be New York law, and civil arrest is wholly impermissible under New York law in an action for wrongful death. Effective January 1, 1979, the only basis for pre-judgment civil arrest in New York law is the following:

> "An order of arrest as a provisional remedy may be granted only when the Court finds it probable that the plaintiff will succeed on the merits, and where the plaintiff has demanded and would be entitled to a judgment or order requiring the performance of an act, the neglect or refusal to perform which would be punishable by the court as a contempt and where the defendant is about to depart from the state with the intent to render the judgment or order ineffectual." N.Y. C.P.L.R. § 6101.

The memorandum of the Office of the Court Administrator explains as follows the purpose and effect of the amendment which gave the statute its quoted form:

> This is one of the series of measures recommended by the Judicial Conference to amend the C.P.L.R.

> This measure would amend several provisions of C.P.L.R. Article 61 governing civil arrest: (1) to abolish the provisional remedy of arrest in actions at law, and (2) to safeguard the rights of defendants in respect to arrest in equity actions alone.

Plaintiffs fail to meet these standards in several respects. First of all they have detained two persons who are not even defendants! Secondly, they have not demonstrated probability that they will prevail. Thirdly, plaintiffs have not demanded and would not be entitled to a "judgment or order requiring the performance of an act" disobedience of which is punishable by contempt (such as an order for specific performance). Finally, this suit would be an action at law under New York procedure—and the purpose and effect of the most recent amendment to the New York law of civil arrest is to make that remedy unavailable in any action at law.

It should also be noted that even when a case appears to fall within § 6101, New York courts are loath to impose civil arrest. *See e.g., Pan American World Airways v. Premier Tours,* 52 App. Div.2d 807, 383 N.Y.S.2d 338 (1st Dept. 1976); *Repetti v. Gill,* 83 Misc.2d 75, 372 N.Y.S.2d 840 (Sup. Ct. 1975); *Gould v. Gould,* 82 Misc.2d 835, 371 N.Y.S.2d 267 (Sup. Ct. 1975) (quoting § 6101.02, Weinstein-Korn-Miller: "Most commentators would agree . . . that civil arrest . . . is an 'anachronistic survival of imprisonment for debt and has no place in a modern jurisprudence.'").

B. *Plaintiffs have no standing or authority to interfere with the orderly execution of the immigration and naturalization laws of the United States.*

A reading of Title 8 of the United States Code demonstrates clearly that the Attorney General and Commissioner of Immigration and Naturalization are obligated to enforce the immigration laws (8 U.S.C. § 1103), that an alien who, as did defendant, outstays his welcome "shall, upon order of the Attorney General, be deported" (8 U.S.C. § 1251(a)), that determinations of deportability and entry of deportations orders are final judgments (8 U.S.C. § 1252), and that the alien himself is the only person with standing to challenge such orders. *See* 8 U.S.C. § 1105a.

The child of a deportable alien, although a United States citizen whose right to live in the country of his citizenship would be effectively negated by his mother's deportation, was held to have no right to attempt to interfere with the deportation proceedings. *Enciso-Cardozo v. Immigration and Naturalization Service*, 504 F.2d 1252 (2d Cir. 1974). The relatives in general of deportable aliens cannot intervene. *Agosto v. Boyd*, 443 F.2d 917 (9th Cir. 1971). Even employers have no standing to challenge orders barring the entry of aliens under temporary work permits. *Braude v. Wirtz*, 350 F.2d 702 (9th Cir. 1965). What possible claim to standing can these plaintiffs have to seek to interfere with the immigration laws in the face of the case law?

Even the alien himself can obtain a stay of deportation only under the most narrow circumstances. Fear of physical persecution and job loss resulting from his desertion from a Hungarian vessel were not enough to win a stay for a Hungarian seaman in *Blagaic v. Flagg*, 304 F.2d 623 (7th Cir. 1962). Severe hardship to his family did not help the applicant in *Giaimo v. Pederson*, 289 F.2d 483 (6th Cir. 1961). Even where the alien seeking a stay had as his reason a desire to bring legal proceedings to clear his good name, and added economic hardship to his family and an apparently good moral character to his side of the scale, the Court tipped the scales in favor of deportation in *United States ex rel. Weddeke v. Watkins*, 166 F.2d 369 (2d Cir.), *cert. denied*, 333 U.S. 876 (1948). Indeed, the only case in which an alien's stay was granted to permit a suit to proceed was a case in which the foreign national was attempting to pursue a legal action which, if successful, would have affected his status as a deportable alien. *Hong v. Agency for International Development*, 470 F.2d 507 (9th Cir. 1972). On what basis, then, can a stay be granted at the behest of some entirely unaffected third party? If an alien who has admittedly outstayed his welcome does not wish to contest the order, and is perfectly ready to go home, neither plaintiffs nor this Court may interfere.

POINT III

EVEN WERE FEDERAL JURISDICTION TO BE ASSUMED *ARGUENDO*, JURISDICTION SHOULD BE DECLINED PURSUANT TO THE DOC-TRINE OF *FORUM NON CONVENIENS.*

More than 30 years ago, in the case of *Gulf Oil Corporation v. Gilbert*, 330 U.S. 501, 508 (1947), the Supreme Court set forth the factors to be considered by the courts in deciding whether or not to exercise jurisdiction:

> Important considerations are the relative ease of access to sources of proof; availability of compulsory process for attendance of unwilling, and the cost of obtaining attendance of willing witnesses; possibility of view of premises, if view would be appropriate to the action; and all other practical problems that make trial of a case easy, expeditious and inexpensive. There may also be questions as to the enforceability of a judgment if one is obtained . . . . It is often said that the plaintiff may not, by choice of an inconvenient forum, "vex," "harass," or "oppress" the defendant by inflicting upon him expense or trouble not necessary to his own right to pursue his remedy.

Two other factors were set forth in the case: the inadvisability of requiring a court to learn and apply to the case a body of law which is foreign to the jurisdiction in which the court sits (*id.* at 509) and the lack of either residency in the district by the plaintiff or of any clear convenience to him of the chosen forum (*id.* at 509-510).

Each of these factors is clearly present here. All of the witnesses and all of the real evidence involved in the trial of this matter are in Paraguay. There is absolutely no way for a United States court to compel the attendance of unwilling witnesses from Paraguay. The cost of producing willing witnesses from a South American nation would be staggering. The location of the death scene may make a view of the premises advisable, and such a view is entirely impossible for an American court. Any judgment obtained against defendant in the United States would be valueless, as any assets defendant may have are in Paraguay.

A federal court sitting in New York and attempting to decide a tort case would, under the conflicts of laws doctrine, apply the law of the place where the tort occurred. *Vanity Fair Mills, Inc. v. T. Eaton Co.*, 234 F.2d 633, 645 n.17 (2d Cir.), *cert. denied*, 352 U.S. 871, *reh. denied*, 352 U.S. 913 (1956). It is unrealistic to ask an American court to determine rights and remedies under Paraguayan law.

Neither of the plaintiffs is a resident of the chosen district. Both are Paraguayan citizens, free to enter into and depart from that nation. Their right to pursue their remedy for wrongful death exists in Paraguay, has been in no way infringed by Paraguayan courts, and does not require the infliction of expense or trouble upon the defendant.

Perhaps most significant to this question is the existence of an admission to the killing of the decedent by a Paraguayan national now in custody in Paraguay. While plaintiffs allege that the confession may have been coerced, or may be otherwise ineffective, the testimony of this man, Hugo Duarte, is absolutely essential to the resolution of the issues raised by plaintiffs' complaint. This witness cannot be produced by compulsory process in a United States court.

The fact that the forum to which plaintiffs would have to bring their action is that of a foreign nation, rather than another district court under 28 U.S.C. § 1404, does not affect the applicability of the doctrine of *forum non conveniens*. Three times the Second Circuit has been faced with this problem, and three times it has held that the doctrine remains applicable.

In *Vanity Fair Mills, Inc., supra*, allegations of trademark infringements in the United States and Canada were raised. Because the law to be applied to the case under the applicable conflicts-of-law choice was the law of the place where the tort occurred—Canada—the district court declined jurisdiction under *forum non conveniens*. The Second Circuit held such declination entirely appropriate (234 F.2d at 645).

Ten years later, in *Fitzgerald v. Westland Marine Corp*, 369 F.2d 499 (2d Cir. 1966), the Court faced the question again with respect to the owner of a vessel alleged to have been negligently operated and unseaworthy and two additional Japanese defendants. The Court applied precisely the formula set forth in *Gulf v. Gilbert, supra*, and concluded that the district court was correct in declining jurisdiction. In doing so, it noted (369 F.2d at 501 n.3): "The doctrine [of *forum non conveniens*] is . . . still vital in federal law and is applicable to a case which cannot be saved by [28 U.S.C.] § 1404(a) transfer because no other district court would have jurisdiction over the action and, indeed, which should have been brought in a *foreign* jurisdiction in any event." (Emphasis in original.)

On facts nearly identical with those of *Fitzgerald v. Westland Marine Corp, supra*, declination of jurisdiction was held appropriate in *Fitzgerald v. Texaco. Inc.*, 521 F.2d 448 (2d Cir. 1975), *cert. denied*, 423 U.S. 1052 (1976). As in the earlier *Fitzgerald* case, the complaint alleged negligence and unseaworthiness of a vessel. English companies, however, rather than Japanese, were named as defendants. The Second Circuit again cited the *Gulf v. Gilbert* criteria for the doctrine of *forum non conveniens*. It then noted its applicability in cases where a foreign jurisdiction is the more practical forum, and proceeded to affirm the decision not to accept jurisdiction even though English law would severely limit the recovery of the plaintiffs: "A district court has discretion to dismiss an action under the doctrine of *forum non conveniens* . . . even though the law applicable in the alternative forum may be less favorable to the plaintiff's chances of recovery." *Id.* at 453. Any other holding, the Court noted, would be an invitation to forum-shoppers.

On the facts of the instant case and under the applicable law, it is clear that New York is a wholly inappropriate forum for resolution of the issues being presented. Paraguay provides a cause of action for plaintiffs and an appropriate remedy. Thus, application of the doctrine of *forum non conveniens* to this case is proper because plaintiffs' rights can be vindicated in Paraguay without the undue delay, expense and difficulty that would be involved in a trial here.

CONCLUSION

For the foregoing reasons, defendant Pena-Irala respectfully urges the Court to grant the requested relief.

Respectfully submitted,
ROBERT G. REBOLLO, ESQ.
SANGIORGIO, FRANGANO,
REBOLLO & BARONE

— AND —

MATTHEW P. BOYLAN, ESQ., and
MURRY D. BROCHIN, ESQ.
LOWENSTEIN, SANDLER, BROCHIN,
KOHL, FISHER & BOYLAN
A Professional Corporation
Attorneys for defendant Pena-Irala.

By: _____
ROBERT G. REBOLLO

Dated: May 7, 1979

UNITED STATES DISTRICT COURT
EASTERN DISTRICT OF NEW YORK

DOLLY M.E. FILARTIGA and   **AFFIDAVIT**
DR. JOEL FILARTIGA,   **(TRANSLATION)**

Plaintiffs,

– against –

AMERICO NORBERTO PENA-
IRALA, LEONEL CASTILLO, as
Commissioner of the United States
Immigration and Naturalization
Service and GEORGE VICIAN, as
District Director Immigration and
Naturalization Service, New York.

Defendants.

JOSE EMILIO GOROSTIAGA, of full age, being duly sworn according to law upon his oath deposes and says:

1. I reside at 150 Catorce de Mayo Street, Asuncion, Paraguay and I am a resident and citizen of Paraguay.

2. I am a lawyer practicing in the City of Asuncion, Paraguay. I have practiced law for the past twenty years. I am a graduate of the Faculty of Law of the National University of Asuncion and I am now a Professor at the Law School teaching Criminology and Criminal Procedure.

3. On June 26, 1976, Mr. Americo Norberto Pena-Irala put me in charge of his defense in a criminal proceeding in Paraguay wherein he was accused by plaintiff Joel Filartiga as one of the persons responsible for the death of Joelito Filartiga. Since July 1, 1976, I have been representing Mr. Pena-Irala as his attorney in that proceeding. As the result of my representation of Mr. Pena-Irala, I became familiar with the proceedings against him and against his co-defendant, Hugo Duarte.

4. In Paraguay, a criminal proceeding may be commenced by the accusation of the alleged victim of the crime or by his close relatives. The accusing party may then participate in the criminal proceedings, as one of the plaintiffs together with the representative of the state (the prosecutor).

5. As previously stated, the proceedings against Mr. Pena-Irala were commenced upon the accusation of Joel Filartiga. Mr. Filartiga also accused another person, Hugo Duarte, of the responsibility for the death of Joelito Filartiga and as a result, the criminal case is now proceeding against both Mr. Pena-Irala and Mr. Duarte. As is his right under Paraguayan law, Mr. Filartiga has been participating actively as a plaintiff in that criminal proceeding.

6. I am informed that in the United States, a criminal case is decided after a trial in open court before a judge and jury during which the witnesses appear and testify one after the other without substantial interruptions until the case is completed. In Paraguay, as in most other countries of Europe and South America, that is not the procedure. In Paraguay, each witness testifies before the judge, his testimony is transcribed and signed and the signed transcript is added to the file. This process of receiving evidence may continue over a period of many months or years and is not necessarily continuous. The scheduling of witnesses depends upon the judge's convenience, upon the number of other cases which he has to decide, upon the diligence of the attorneys for the parties and upon whether interlocutory appeals are taken during the course of the proceeding.

7. The criminal case against Messrs. Duarte and Pena-Irala has been prolonged by a number of interlocutory appeals taken on behalf of Mr. Duarte. Mr. Duarte has admitted in a writing signed by him before the judge that he is the person alone who killed Joelito Filartiga. However, Mr. Duarte claims that the homicide was justifiable because he committed it when he found his wife in the course of committing adultery and was moved by a strong moral pain. Moreover, Mr. Duarte alleged that on the occasion of the offense, in the preceding struggle with Joelito Filartiga, he suffered injuries caused by the deceased, which injuries were described on the medical certificates presented and added to the proceedings. In view of it, Mr. Duarte's attorneys presented an appeal for an exception of action asking the judge of the proceeding to cancel the intervention of Mr. Filartiga in his role of a particular plaintiff. This exception was resolved by the judge of first trial, who did not rule in its favor. This decision was appealed by Mr. Duarte's attorneys and the record of the proceeding was submitted to the Criminal Tribunal in charge of appeals. In this second instance, the decision was reversed, and the Tribunal in this instance made room for the exception in favor of Mr. Duarte. Mr. Filartiga's attorneys appealed this decision of second instance and the proceeding was submitted to the Supreme Court of Justice to study the appeal. This appeal has not yet been decided upon. Mr. Pena-Irala has not initiated any of these appeals of the aforementioned interlocutory writs. In actuality, these delays, instead of benefiting him, have prejudiced him since the decision of the case has been postponed in reference to his person in the same proceeding.

8. Under Paraguayan law a father whose son has been wrongfully killed may in addition to commencing a criminal proceeding bring a civil action for damages against the person responsible. Accordingly, Mr. Filartiga has the right to commence a civil action against both Mr. Duarte and Mr. Pena-Irala since he accuses both of them of responsibility for his son's death. He may commence such a civil action either simultaneously with the commencement of the criminal proceeding, during the time that the criminal proceeding lasts, or within a year after the criminal proceeding has terminated. In either event, however, the civil action may not proceed to judgment until the criminal proceeding has been disposed of. If the defendant is found not guilty because he was not the author of the case under investigation in the criminal proceeding, no civil action for indemnity for damages based upon the same deed investigated in the criminal proceeding, can prosper or succeed.

9. I reiterate that although Mr. Filartiga initiated the criminal proceeding against Mr. Pena-Irala and has been participating actively therein, Mr. Filartiga has not commenced a civil action against Mr. Pena-Irala although he had and still has the right to do so in a Paraguayan court under Paraguayan law.

10. Under Paraguayan law, the father of the deceased is the person indicated by law to have the right to promote a civil action for damages from the violent death of his son. The compensable amount in this type of claim depends upon the damages as a result of the death and on the contingent future earnings of the murdered (loss of profits). In the case of violent death, the sufferings which the deceased may have gone through before his death are not compensable. The Paraguayan legislation does not foresee, as part of the compensable amount fixed by the judge at the time of the verdict, any type of fine or monetary penalty [punitive damages] in a civil action for damages. The losing party, however, must bear the payment of the trial costs. Likewise, in the civil trial for damages, the testimony of the defendant before or during trial is not permitted.

JOSE EMILIO GOROSTIAGA

Witnessed at this General Consulate
of Paraguay, in the United States of North America,
New York, May 3rd, 1979.
(Signature) Consul General
of Paraguay

STATEMENT
(TRANSLATION)

I, RAMIRO RODRIGUEZ ALCALA, an incumbent professor in the Faculty of Law at the National University of Asuncion, consulted by my colleague, Dr. Jose Emilio Gorostiaga, testify under oath as follows:

1st) That I am informed through newspaper publications about the existence of a judicial claim promoted in the City of New York (U.S.A.) before Judge E. Nickerson, by Dr. Joel Filartiga and his daughter Dolly Filartiga against Americo Pena, for the death of Joel Filartiga (son) in the Republic of Paraguay, being completely ignorant of its terms as well as plaintiffs and defendant.

2nd) That according to the law in force in Paraguay, the persons directly or indirectly damaged for an offense committed in the national territory could claim the corresponding indemnity before the Tribunals of Justice of the Republic. I am ignorant of whether or not said action was brought.

> Asuncion, May 2nd, 1979.
> (Signature) DR. RAMIRO RODRIGUEZ ALCALA, ATTORNEY
>
> Stated: The foregoing signature corresponds to that one of Doctor RAMIRO RODRIGUEZ ALCALA.
> Asuncion, May 3rd, 1979.
>
> (Signature and Seal of Notary Public Carlos Alberto Alfieri
> Asuncion, Paraguay)

MAY 8, 1979: PARAGUAY

Telegram from American Embassy, Asunción to U.S. Department of State

Subject: Pena/Filartiga Case

UNCLASSIFIED
n/a

UNCLASSIFIED

PAGE 01   ASUNCI 02047   082042Z

ACTION VOE-00

INFO   OCT-01   ARA-15   ADS-00   CA-01   INSE-00   HA-05   PA-02
       SSO-00   NSCE-00   /024 W

---101793   082047Z   /21
O 082019Z MAY 79
FM AMEMBASSY ASUNCION
TO SECSTATE WASHDC IMMEDIATE 5980

UNCLAS ASUNCION 02047

E.O. 12065: N/A
TAGS: SHUM, PA
SUBJECT: PENA/FILARTIGA CASE

REF: ASUNCION 1619

1. THE PARAGUAYAN SUPREME COURT MAY 8 FINALLY ISSUED A JUDGMENT ON THE FILARTIGA FAMILY'S APPEAL TO THE SUPREME COURT THAT THE LOWER COURT SHOULD INVESTIGATE UNEXPLAINED CIRCUMSTANCES SURROUNDING THE MURDER OF JOEL FILARTIGA, JR. IN A JUDGMENT WRITTEN BY JUDGE GARAY AND CONCURRED IN THE OTHER FOUR MEMBERS OF THE COURT, THE SUPREME COURT SAID THAT THE UNCERTAINTIES, DOUBT AND UNEXPLAINED CIRCUMSTANCES WHICH SURROUND THE CASE PARTICULARLY IN REGARD TO THE PLACE AND THE HOUR AT WHICH THE MURDER OCCURRED SHOULD BE INVESTIGATED.

2. COMMENT: WE CAN ONLY ATTRIBUTE THIS SUDDEN ACTION BY THE SUPREME COURT TO ISSUE A JUDGMENT ON THE FILARTIGA APPEAL TO THE LEGAL PROCEEDINGS AGAINST AMERICO PENA IN

NEW YORK. THE SUPREME COURT HAD NOT TAKEN ANY ACTION ON THE APPEAL FOR MORE THAN A YEAR AND LEGAL CIRCLES HERE HAD CONSIDERED THAT THE MATTER WAS LIKELY TO BE KEPT IN LIMBO FOREVER. APPARENTLY PENA'S LAWYER, DR. GOROS-TIAGA, HAS BEEN ABLE TO CONVINCE THE GOP THAT UNLESS THE FILARTIGA APPEAL HERE WAS ALLOWED TO PROCEED IN A NORMAL MANNER THAT HIS EFFORTS TO DEFEND PENA, AND INDI-RECTLY THE HONOR OF PARAGUAY, COULD RUN INTO DIFFI-CULTIES IN THE U.S. THE SUPREME COURT'S DECISION DOES NOT HAVE ANY PARTICULAR SIGNIFICANCE AS TO WHAT THE FINAL JUDICIAL OUTCOME OF THE JOEL FILARTIGA MURDER CASE WILL BE IN THE LOWER COURT.

WHITE

UNCLASSIFIED

MAY 9, 1979: UNITED STATES

Correspondence from United States Attorney Edward R. Korman to U.S. District Court Judge Nickerson

United States Department of Justice

United States Attorney
Eastern District of New York
Federal Building
Brooklyn, N.Y. 11201

JCJ: jd
F#792061

May 9, 1979

Honorable Eugene H. Nickerson
United States District Judge
Eastern District of New York
225 Cadman Plaza East
Brooklyn, New York 11201

Re: Dolly M.E. Filartiga, et al. v.
Americo Norberto Pena-Irala,
et al. - 79 C 917

Dear Judge Nickerson:

We have received a copy of the motion papers submitted by counsel for the defendant Americo Norberto Pena-Irala in the above action and we write to advise the Court that we join in this motion to the extent that it seeks to vacate the preliminary injunction order that prohibits the federal defendants from proceeding with the deportation of Mr. Pena-Irala, Ms. Juana Villalba and their infant child.

It is clearly established that an alien who seeks to enjoin his own deportation in order to prosecute a civil action has no right to do so, absent a showing that the District Director of the Immigration and Naturalization Service is "motivated by an invidious factor" in denying the alien's application for a stay of deportation. *Bolanos v. Kiley*, 509 F.2d 1023, 1026 (2d Cir. 1975); *Ladd v. United States*, 539 F.2d 808, 809 (1st Cir. 1976); *Adame v. INS*, 349 F.Supp. 313 (N.D. Ill. 1972); *Pressinos v. District Director*, 193 F.Supp. 416 (N.D. Ohio 1960); *aff'd per curiam*, 289 F.2d 490, *cert. denied*, 366 U.S. 966. *A fortiori*, un-related individuals who seek to enjoin the deportation of a defendant in a civil action that does not involve the government may not do so.

Although in certain extraordinary circumstances a federal court has jurisdiction under the All Writs Act. 28 U.S.C. §1651, to grant a writ *ne exeat* to prohibit a defendant in a civil case from leaving the country, 9 *Moores Federal Practice*, §110.29, the underlying action must be one for equitable relief or for a liquidated claim. A general unliquidated claim for damages, such as the plaintiff's wrongful death claim herein, will not support issuance of such a writ. In this regard, the United States Supreme Court has quoted with approval the explanation by the Wisconsin Supreme Court in *Davidor v. Rosenberg*, 130 Wis. 22, 24, 109 N.W. 925 (1906) that:

> At common law it was simply a writ to obtain equitable bail. It was issued by a court of equity on application of the complainant against the defendant when it appeared that there was a debt positively due, certain in amount or capable of being made certain . . . and that the defendant was about to leave the jurisdiction, having conveyed away his property, or under other circumstances which would render any decree ineffectual.

quoted in *D. Ginsberg & Sons v. Popkin*, 285 U.S. 204, 208 (1932).

An unliquidated claim for civil tort damages does not satisfy the requirements for issuance of the writ *ne exeat* under the All Writs Act, 28 U.S.C. §1651, in aid of this Court's jurisdiction. *See also* New York CPLR §6101.

This Court plainly lacks jurisdiction to enjoin the defendant, Mr. Pena-Irala, himself from leaving the United States much less enjoin the Immigration Service from proceeding with a deportation that is mandated by congressional statutes. 8 U.S.C. §1251(a). Since Ms. Villalba and the child are not even parties to this litigation, it is unreasonable to continue an injunction against their deportation which they do not themselves oppose.

For all of these reasons, we respectfully request this Court to vacate its order of April 9, 1979 and to dismiss this action against the federal defendants for lack of any conceivable subject matter jurisdiction.

Respectfully yours,

EDWARD R. KORMAN
United States Attorney

BY: J. CHRISTOPHER JENSEN
Chief, Civil Division

cc: Robert G. Rebollo, Esq.
       Fraqano, Rebollo & Barone
       4044 Hylan Boulevard
       Staten Island, New York 10308

       Matthew P. Boylan, Esq. and
       Murry D. Brochin, Esq.
       Lowenstein, Sandler, Brochin,
       Kohl, Fisher & Boylan
       744 Broad Street
       Newark, New Jersey 07102

MAY 11, 1979: UNITED STATES

Plaintiffs' Memorandum of Law in Opposition to Defendant Peña-Irala's Motion to Dismiss Complaint and Vacate Stay; Affidavits of Myres MacDougal, Richard Lillich, Thomas Franck, and Richard Falk

UNITED STATES DISTRICT COURT
EASTERN DISTRICT OF NEW YORK

DOLLY M.E. FILARTIGA and DR. JOEL FILARTIGA, Plaintiffs, – against – AMERICO N. PENA-IRALA, et al., Defendants.	**PLAINTIFFS' MEMORANDUM OF LAW IN OPPOSITION TO DEFENDANT PENA-IRALA'S MOTION TO DISMISS COMPLAINT AND VACATE STAY** **79 Civ. 917**

POINT I

THIS COURT CLEARLY HAS JURISDICTION TO ENTERTAIN PLAINTIFFS' SUIT UNDER 28 U.S.C. SEC. 1350

It is somewhat difficult to follow defendant Pena's argument on this point. On p. 6 of his brief, defendant, referring to Sec. 2 Article III of the Constitution, asks

Where in this grant is the authority of Congress to confer upon the United States District Courts jurisdiction over "any civil action by an alien for a tort only, committed in violation of the law of nations. . . .?"

The answer is simple: The authority lies in the grant conferred upon the judicial power, in the first clause of Sec. 2 of Article III, to deal with "all cases . . . arising under the laws of the United States."

In the words of Judge Lord, in *Valanqa v. Metropolitan Life Insurance Company* (E.D. Pa. 1966) 259 F. Supp. 324, 327

Once a tort can be considered to be in violation of the law of nations, Sec. 1350 allows immediate access to a federal court. It thus functions as an independent grant of federal jurisdiction in situations where the conduct of the parties so offends the standards of conduct underpinning international relations that it can be considered to be a violation of the law of nations. In such a capacity and unencumbered with minimal requisite jurisdictional amounts as found in the diversity of citizenship grant of jurisdiction (28 U.S.C. Sec. 1332), Sec. 1350 serves as an extraordinary channel of federal jurisdiction.

If defendant's query is intended to impugn the constitutionality of Sec. 1350, he might have chosen a more forthright way to do so. An examination of the relatively few cases decided under Sec. 1350 in its long but desultory career fails to reveal a single case raising a question as to whether the Alien Tort Claims Act, as Sec. 1350 is sometimes called, comes within the purview of Sec. 2 Article III of the Constitution, nor has defendant cited any such case. Professor Moore lists Sec. 1350 as one of many statutes conferring statutory jurisdiction upon the federal courts based on "special federal questions." 1 Moore's Federal Practice Sec. 8.09(2) fn 14.

If, then, there is no inherent defect in Sec. 1350, it remains only to examine whether plaintiffs' complaint meets the two requirements of the section, i.e., that it allege (1) a tort only, (2) in violation of the law of nations. As to the first, there is no controversy between the parties. As to the second, defendant includes, on p. 12 of his brief, a long citation from *Abdul-Rahman Omar Adra v. Clift*, 195 F. Supp. 857 (D. Md. 1961), which he correctly describes as the only modern case in which 1350 jurisdiction has been sustained based on the law of nations.

This, followed by the defendant's excerpt at pp. 12 and 13, of the Second Circuit's decision in *ITT v. Vencap, Ltd.*, 519 F.2d 1001 (2d Cir. 1975), is intended to pave the way for defendant's conclusion, at p.13, that since the

alleged wrongful killing of a Paraguayan in Paraguay is not a violation of a standard, rule or custom which both (a) affects the relationship between states or between an individual and a foreign state and (b) is used by those states for their common good or in dealing with one another, such a wrongful killing is not a tort in violation of the law of nations within the meaning of Sec. 1350.

It is doubtful whether the two-part definition of the phrase "in violation of the law of nations," enunciated by Judge Van Dusen in *Lopes v.*

Reederei Richard Schroder, 225 F. Supp. 292, 297 (E.D. Pa. 1963) and adopted by the Second Circuit in *ITT v. Vencap, Ltd.* is a complete statement of the law on the subject. Judge Van Dusen's conclusion is based on one eighteenth century commentator (Burlamaqui) and two from the nineteenth century (Kent and Story). As will be shown below, international law, which is but another name for "the law of nations," has undergone an explosive development in the decades following World War II, particularly in the area of individual rights and the relationship between individual rights and duties and international law.

It is noteworthy that Judge Van Dusen himself, on p. 295 of *Lopes,* had this to say:

> The court's examination of the phrase "the law of nations" must consider the words used as part of an "organic growth." see *Romero v. International Term, Operating Co.,* 358 U.S. 354, 360, 79 S.Ct. 468, 3 L.Ed.2d 368 (1959).

However, even the *Lopes/Vencap* standard is easily met by the facts alleged in the complaint.

For as long as human beings have been in contact with each other on this earth, they have sought to formulate a set of principles or norms, which, depending upon the level of ambition of the framers, would be regarded as the minimum acceptable, or the maximum desirable, standard of human behavior. Following the rise and fall of Nazism and Fascism, the Allied powers organized a series of war crimes trials, of which the Nuremberg trials were only the most spectacular part. These trials introduced into the law of nations new principles of personal accountability and of collective international responsibility for and jurisdiction over the grossest kinds of human rights violations. Shortly thereafter, these principles made their way into the United Nations Charter and, primarily under the impetus of Mrs. Eleanor Roosevelt, into the Universal Declaration of Human Rights. In the last three decades, a veritable flurry of conventions, treaties and declarations has firmly enshrined in international law the prohibition against inhuman and degrading treatment. These include:

The International Covenant on Civil and Political Rights
General Assembly Resolution 2200(XI), 16 December 1966
The Proclamation of Teheran
UN Doc. A/Conf.32/41, UN Publ. E.68.XIV.2, endorsed by General Assembly Resolution 2442 (XXIII) 19 December 1968
The American Declaration of the Rights and Duties of Man

Resolution XXX, Ninth International Conference of American States, Bogota, Colombia 30 March—2 May 1948.
The American Convention on Human Rights
OAS Treaty Series No. 36, at 1-21, 1969
The European Convention for the Protection of Human Rights and Fundamental Freedoms, and Protocols Thereunder
Council of Europe, European Convention on Human Rights: Collected Texts, Section 1, Doc.1 (1971)

As a result, it is now generally accepted by the United States and the vast majority of other member nations of the United Nations that gross violations of human rights are, as a matter of international law, a legitimate concern of the World community.

A natural consequence of this development is that the level of domestic performance in the field of human rights has become one of the touchstones of relations between nations.

The notion that human rights should serve as a central tenet of U.S. foreign policy was first espoused by President Carter in his inaugural address. Since then, the treatment of foreign nationals by their own governments has emerged as an important factor in U.S. foreign policy formulation and practice. See *Human Rights and U.S. Policy Issue*, No. IB77056, Foreign Affairs and National Defense Division, Congressional Research Service, Library of Congress, Dec. 9, 1977.

International law serves as the source of this policy. This view was lucidly expressed by Deputy Assistant Secretary of State for Human Rights Schneider, in testimony before Congress in October 1977:

We have based our actions on our obligations under the United Nations Charter and other international commitments, on our responsibilities under domestic law, and on our belief that the people of this country want a foreign policy that is in accord with our values. We believe that a foreign policy that fails to reflect those values will not receive, nor deserve, the support of the American people.

To those who argue that our concern for the human rights of people in other lands constitutes intervention, we say look to the Charter of the United Nations, to the Universal Declaration of Human Rights, to the Helsinki Final Act, to the Declaration Against Torture adopted by the United Nations in 1975, and to similar regional instruments and resolutions. No nation in the world today can hide torture, apartheid, arbitrary imprisonment,

censorship, or other such violations of human rights behind assertions of sovereignty. The denial of internationally recognized
human rights and fundamental freedoms is a matter of international concern.

*Human Rights and U.S. Foreign Policy: A Review of the Administration
Record,* Hearings before the Subcommittee on International Organizations, 95th Congress, 1st Session, October 25, 1977.

Thus, it is clear that the human rights component of our foreign policy is
based upon the emergence of a norm of customary international conduct
which prohibits violations of basic human rights.

During the past few years Congress has passed legislation to limit economic and military assistance to countries which violate internationally recognized human rights standards. Sec. 32 of the Foreign Assistance Act of
1973 (P.L. 93-189); Sec. 46 of the Foreign Assistance Act of 1974 (P.L. 93-
559); Sec. 310 of the International Development and Food Assistance Act
of 1975 (P.L. 94-161); Sec. 301 of the International Security Assistance and
Arms Export Control Act (P.L. 94-329). See also Weissbrodt, Human Rights
Legislation and U.S. Foreign Policy, Georgia Journal of Int. & Comp. Law,
v. 7, summer 1977; 231-287.

While Congress has not come forward with a specific definition of
human rights, the legislation it has enacted relies on language that is frequently used in United Nations resolutions:

Consistent pattern of gross violations of internationally recognized
human rights, including torture or cruel, inhuman, or degrading
treatment or punishment, prolonged detention without charges,
or other flagrant denial of the right to life, liberty, and the security
of person. . . .

Sec. 310 of the International Development and Food Assistance
Act of 1975 (P.L. 94-161).

The International Security Assistance and Arms Control Act of 1976
also relies on criteria and standards that have been established by the international community. This act also declares that it

is the policy of the United States . . . to promote and encourage
increased respect for human rights and fundamental freedoms for
all . . . . To this end, a principal goal of the foreign policy of the
United States is to promote the increased observance of internationally recognized human rights by all countries.

Relations between the United States and numerous other nations have been directly affected by the incorporation of international standards of human rights into our foreign policy. For example, in February of 1977, Secretary of State Vance announced that the Carter Administration had decided to reduce the Security Assistant Program budget for Argentina for FY 1978 from the $32 million recommended by the Ford Administration to $15.7 million, explicitly linking the decision to violations of human rights by the Argentine regime. The military junta responded by announcing that it considered this action an interference in Argentina's internal affairs, and rejected the $15 million left in the Security Assistance Program for FY 1978. *Human Rights Conditions for Selected Countries and the U.S. Responses,* Prepared for the Subcommittee on International Organizations of the Committee on International Relations, U.S. House of Representatives, by the Foreign Affairs and National Defense Division, Congressional Research Service, Library of Congress, 95th Congress, 2d Session, July 25, 1978.

Relations between the United States and a host of other nations, including Brazil, Chile, the Soviet Union, Rhodesia (Zimbabwe), South Africa and the Philippines have also been affected by what has become a "standard rule and custom" in both U.S. foreign policy and the international community: respect for the right of the person, which includes the right to freedom from torture; from arbitrary arrest and imprisonment; and from invasion of the home. Id. All of these rights were, according to the complaint, violated by defendant Pena-Irala.

Indeed, as this case proceeds, plaintiffs are confident that the developing record will show that the murder of Joelito Filartiga and its consequences have directly and seriously affected relations between Paraguay and the United States and are continuing to do so.

For confirmation of the proposition that torture, which is the central tort alleged by plaintiffs, is a violation of the law of nations, they respectfully refer this Court to the respective affidavits of Professors Richard Anderson Falk, Thomas M. Franck, Richard B. Lillich and Myres S. MacDougal, all eminent authorities in the field of international law. See also Note, "Torture Under the European Convention on Human Rights," 73 American Journal of International Law 267; Special Issue, "The Prevention and Suppression of Torture," 1977 Revue Internationale de Droit Penal, nos. 3 and 4; and John G. Humphrey, "The International Law of Human Rights in the Middle Twentieth Century," in "The Present State of International Law and Other Essays Written in Honor of the Centenary Celebration of The International Law Association," Kluwer, The Netherlands, 1973.

POINT II

IF THIS COURT WERE TO DECLINE JURISDICTION UNDER THE DOCTRINE OF FORUM NON CONVENIENS, IT WOULD LEAVE PLAINTIFFS WITHOUT ANY REMEDY WHATSOEVER

Defendant's assertion that this Court should decline jurisdiction pursuant to the doctrine of *forum non conveniens* is without merit. The Supreme Court has described the doctrine as

". . . the dismissal of a case because the forum chosen by the plaintiff is so *completely inappropriate and inconvenient* that it is better to stop the litigation in the place where it is brought and let it start all over again somewhere else . . . ."

Norwood v. Kirkpatrick, 349 U.S. 29, 31 (1955) quoting *All States Freight v. Modarelli*, 196 F.2. at 1011 (3rd Cir. 1952) (emphasis added). Its application should be limited to those "rare cases" in which a plaintiff misuses general venue statutes, succumbing to the "temptation to resort to a strategy of forcing the trial at a most inconvenient place for an adversary, even at some inconvenience to himself. *Gulf Oil Corporation v. Gilbert*, 330 U.S. 501, 507, 509 (1947). It would be completely inappropriate for this court to decline jurisdiction on the ground of *forum non conveniens* when plaintiffs have moved forward in this Court because it alone offers the opportunity of a fair and just hearing of the merits of their complaint.

There is no precise formula for the Court to determine whether to grant or deny dismissal under *forum non conveniens*. While issues of convenience, such as ease of access to sources of proof are relevant, "the more important question is whether the relinquishment of jurisdiction would best serve the ends of justice." *Mobil Tankers Co. v. Mene Grande Oil Company*, 363 F.2d 611 (3rd Cir. 1966). In that case the Court of Appeals reversed a District Court's dismissal on the ground of *forum non conveniens*, despite the fact that the balance of convenience favored the defendant, because the alternative forum, a Venezuelan court, followed more restrictive rules pertaining to discovery and presentation of expert testimony than would be available in United States Courts. The Court noted that

the relinquishment of jurisdiction could result in serious detriment to (plaintiffs') causes of action. It would relegate the (plaintiffs) to a foreign forum in which the procedural remedies are far less conducive to the fair administration of justice than those available under our admiralty rules. The mode of trial, the lack of adequate pre-trial procedures, and the limitation on the manner in which expert testimony may be offered do not comport with our concepts of fairness.

363 F.2d. at 614.

Plaintiffs will suffer similar detriment if they are forced to pursue their action under the procedures available under Paraguayan law. See Affidavit of Jose Antonio Lugo.

Moreover, the consequences of the Filartiga's prior attempt to initiate proceedings against the defendant in Paraguay—the arrest of plaintiff Dolly Filartiga and her mother; the arrest, beating and disbarment of their attorney; and the continuing death threats against the plaintiffs—make it evident that relinquishment of jurisdiction by this court would be an egregious act of injustice.

The political realities facing plaintiffs in foreign countries have been recognized by other courts in similar circumstances.

In *Flota Maritima Browning v. The Ciudad de La Habana*, 181 F. Supp. (D. Md. 1960), the court was asked to renounce its jurisdiction over suits in admiralty between Cuban corporations, based on contracts executed in Cuba and Canada pertaining to ships which were or had become part of the Cuban Merchant Marine and containing clauses assenting to the jurisdiction of the Havana courts and waiving all other jurisdictions. Recognizing that "these facts would ordinarily weigh heavily in favor of this court's refusing jurisdiction," the Court retained jurisdiction because it questioned the capacity of the Cuban courts to deal with the matter fairly. The Court observed that

> the situation in Cuba today, however, is very far from ordinary; it is very doubtful whether Libelant (sic) can hope to receive justice in Cuba. This is *the dominant factor to be considered in every case when such doubt exists.* At 311 (emphasis added).

The most closely analogous recent case is *Phoenix Canada Oil Co. Ltd. v. Texaco, Inc.*, 78 F.R.D. 445 (D.Del. 1978). In that case, a Canadian corporation sued a number of international oil companies and their Ecuadorian subsidiaries for alleged tortious conduct involving oil exploration in Ecuador. In discussing defendants' *forum non conveniens* motion to dismiss, the court quoted as follows from *Mobil Tankers*, supra, at 614:

"(T)he relinquishment of jurisdiction could result in serious detriment to (plaintiffs') causes of action. It would relegate the libellants to a foreign forum (Venezuela) in which the procedural remedies are far less conducive to the fair administration of justice than those available under our admiralty rules. The mode of trial, the lack of adequate pre-trial procedures, and the limitation on the manner in which expert testimony may be offered do not comport with our concepts of fairness."

and went on to state the law of *forum non conveniens* as follows:

"(N)ot only must an alternate forum exist, and not only must that forum provide relief for the actions alleged to violate United States law, but the alternate forum must also provide comparable procedural protections to those in the United States."

Applying this principle to the facts of the case, the court rejected the *forum non conveniens* motion both because of a number of procedural weaknesses inherent in the Ecuadorian procedure which would be applicable to the case at bar and because

Plaintiff has represented by affidavit that Ecuador is presently controlled by a military government which has "assumed the power of the executive and legislative branches and rules by fiat," "has specifically retained the right to veto or intervene in any judicial matter which the Military Government deems to involve matters of national concern," and "has absolute power over all branches of government." At 455.

That the above quoted language could be used, almost word for word, to describe the lack of independence of the judiciary in Paraguay will appear from the following excerpts from Exhibit I to the affidavit of plaintiff Dolly Filartiga's attached to plaintiffs' Order To Show Cause And To Stay Deportation (Exhibit I being the report on an inquiry into human rights in Paraguay, conducted in September 1976 by Dr. Ben Stephansky, Deputy Assistant, former Secretary of State for Latin America, and Professor Robert Alexander of Rutgers University, on behalf of the International League for Human Rights):

One of the principal instruments of the Stroessner dictatorship has been the perpetual State of Siege. . . (U)nder Stroessner, the State of Siege has been a permanent feature of the regime, not an emergency one.

(T)he state of siege permits the regime to hold people under arrest "at the pleasure of the President" for an indefinite period of time.

The fact is that the rule of law does not exist in Paraguay. There is no independence of the judiciary. All judges must be members of the Colorado party, and are appointed by the Executive.

A year after the above report was written, Dr. Stephansky, together with Professor David Helfeld, former Dean of the School of Law, University of Puerto Rico, made another trip to Paraguay on behalf of the International League for Human Rights. Their report on this second mission, one of the principal purposes of which was to evaluate the legal system of Paraguay, has been submitted as an Exhibit in response to defendant Pena's Motion to Dismiss. The Court's attention is respectfully directed to the sections entitled "Independence of the Judiciary" beginning on p. 29, and "Human Rights and the Legal Profession" beginning at p. 33, as well as to the following statement appearing on p. 35:

(N)either is a single case known of any governmental official who has been held responsible for Constitutional violations or in which the State has voluntarily indemnified persons or their families for deprivation of Constitutional rights.

In the light of these authoritative findings as to complete subservience of the Paraguayan judiciary to the military dictatorship ruling the country, and the highly political nature of this case, defendant's statements, at p. 23, that plaintiffs' "right to pursue their remedy for wrongful death exists in Paraguay" and "has been in no way infringed by Paraguayan courts," can only be described as an excursion into the wild blue yonder of free-wheeling fantasy.

As to the alleged "confession" of Hugo Duarte—which leaves the torture wounds totally unexplained—and his immunity to compulsory process, this should present no problem at all. Compulsory process is not the only way to obtain testimony from a witness residing in a foreign country, and all indications are that Mr. Duarte is most anxious to assist his step-father-in-law, Mr. Pena, in this matter.

In sum, if the allegedly more convenient forum were Canada, Japan or England, as in the *Vanity Fair* and *Fitzgerald* cases cited by defendant at pp. 23-25, plaintiffs would not be in this Court today. Had they lived in any of these countries, their son and brother would not have died as he did, and they would have no reason to seek the aid of the courts of this country for the redress of any wrongs which they might have suffered in their own.

CONCLUSION

For the foregoing reasons, plaintiffs respectfully urge this Court to deny defendant Pena-Irala's Motion to dismiss the complaint and vacate the stay.

Respectfully submitted,

PETER WEISS
RHONDA COPELON
JOHN W. CORWIN
JOSE ANTONIO LUGO
c/o Center for Constitutional Rights
853 Broadway
New York, New York 10003

MICHAEL MAGGIO
GOREN AND MAGGIO
1801 Columbia Rd. N.W.
Suite 100
Washington, D.C.

Attorneys for Plaintiffs

Dated: New York, New York
        May 11, 1979

UNITED STATES DISTRICT COURT
EASTERN DISTRICT OF NEW YORK

DOLLY M.E. FILARTIGA and DR. JOEL FILARTIGA,	**AFFIDAVIT OF MYRES S. MACDOUGAL**
Plaintiffs,	
– against –	
AMERICO NORBERTO PENA-IRALA, et al.	
Defendants.	

I, Myres S. MacDougal, of 401A Yale Station, New Haven, Connecticut, 06520, being duly sworn, depose and say:

1. I have been a professor of international law since 1947, occupying the chair of Sterling Professor of Law at Yale Law School from 1958 to 1975. I am a former President of the American Society of International Law and the author of many books and articles in the field of international law, including (with Harold Lasswell and Lung-chu Chen), "Human Rights and World Public Order," to be published shortly by Yale University Press.

2. In the above book, we demonstrate that the Universal Declaration of Human Rights and associated covenants on human rights, including the International Covenant on Civil and Political Rights, have become customary international law and thus a part of the Law of Nations.

3. By virtue of, *inter alia,* article 5 of the Universal Declaration and Article 7 of the Covenant, torture is an offense against the Law of Nations.

4. While the real party in interest in these offenses against human rights is the individual, it has long been recognized that such offenses vitally affect relations between states.

MYRES S. MACDOUGAL

Dated: May 10, 1979

UNITED STATES DISTRICT COURT
EASTERN DISTRICT OF NEW YORK

DOLLY M.E. FILARTIGA and   **AFFIDAVIT OF RICHARD B.**
DR. JOEL FILARTIGA,   **LILLICH**

Plaintiffs,

– against –

AMERICO NORBERTO PENA-
IRALA, et al.

Defendants.

RICHARD B. LILLICH, being duly sworn, deposes and says:

1. Since 1969, I have been a member of the faculty of the University of Virginia School of Law, Charlottesville, Virginia, where I am Howard W. Smith Professor of Law. I also serve as President of the Procedural Aspects of International Law Institute, and am an international legal consultant to government and the private sector.

2. I have an A.B. from Oberlin College (1954), an L.L.B. with Specialization in International Affairs from the Cornell Law School (1957), and an LL.M. in International Law and J.S.D. from the New York University School of Law (1960).

3. In 1957, I was admitted to the Bar of the State of New York where I engaged in private practice until 1960.

4. From 1960 to 1969, I was a member of the faculty of the Syracuse University College of Law. During this period of time I spent two years in England as a Ford Foundation Law Faculty Fellow (1963) and a John Simon Guggenheim Memorial Fellow (1966-67). From 1968 to 1969, I held the Charles H. Stockton Chair of International Law at the United States Naval War College.

5. I served as Editor of the Procedural Aspects of International Law Series from 1962 to 1977 and am the author of four of its titles, the most recent being *International Claims: Their Settlement by Lump Sum Agreements* (1975) (two volumes). I have also edited and contributed to *Economic Coercion and the New International Economic Order* (1976), *The Valuation of*

Nationalized Property (1972-75) (three volumes), *Humanitarian Intervention and the United Nations* (1973), and *International Human Rights: Problems of Law and Policy*. I am also the author of over 50 book chapters, law review articles and other legal studies.

6. In addition to the foregoing, I was a member of the Executive Council of the American Society of International Law (1966-72; 1973-76) and presently serve as the Rapporteur of its Panel on State Responsibility, and as an Editor of its *Journal*. I am a member of the British Institute on International and Comparative Law and of the International Law Association, where I currently serve as Rapporteur of the International Committee on Human Rights and Chairman of the American Branch's Committee on Human Rights. I am also the Chairman of the Advisory Board of the International Human Rights Law Group, and a member of the Advisory Council of the United States Institute on Human Rights.

7. I have been asked by the plaintiffs, Dolly M.E. Filartiga and Dr. Joel Filartiga, to comment upon whether the act of torture committed by an official of Paraguay constitutes, in addition to being an offense under the law of that country, a violation of international law (formerly called the law of nations). I have duly examined the international precedents and scholarly writing in this area and have come to the conclusion that it is.

8. Initially, torture is proscribed by the following international instruments:

a. The Universal Declaration of Human Rights, adopted by the United Nations General Assembly on December 10, 1948, (G.A. Res. 217A (III), U.N. Doc. A/810 at 710 (1948)) states in Article 5: No one shall be subjected to torture or to cruel, inhuman or degrading treatment or punishment.

b. The International Covenant on Civil and Political Rights, (*adopted* December 16, 1966, *entered into force* March 23, 1976, G.A. Res. 2200(XXI), 21 U.N. GAOR, Supp. (No. 16) 52, U.N. Doc. A/6316 (1966)), similarly provides in Article 7: No one shall be subjected to torture or to cruel, inhuman or degrading treatment or punishment . . . .

c. The American Convention on Human Rights (*signed* Nov. 22, 1969, *entered into force* July 18, 1978, O.A.S. T.S. No. 36, at 1. OAS. Off. Rec. OEA/Ser. L/V/II.23, doc. 21, rev. 2 (English 1975)) provides in Article 5: No one shall be subjected to torture or to cruel, inhuman or degrading punishment or treatment. . . .

d. Finally, The European Convention for the Protection of Human Rights and Fundamental Freedoms (*signed* Nov. 4, 1950, *entered into force*

Sept. 3, 1953, Council of Europe, Collected Texts 1-19 (9th ed. 1974)), states in Article 3: No one shall be subjected to torture or to inhuman or degrading treatment or punishment.

9. These almost identical and unequivocal statements endorsed by nearly all of the states in the international community reflect the emergence of a norm of customary international law condemning torture. Thus, like piracy, slavery and genocide before it, the prohibition against torture is now a peremptory norm of international law.

10. Additionally, the recently adopted General Assembly resolution on the Protection of All Persons From Being Subjected to Torture and Other Cruel, Inhuman or Degrading Treatment or Punishment ("Declaration"), *adopted* Dec. 9, 1975, G.A. RES. 3452 (XXX), 30 U.N. GAOR Supp. (No. 34) 91, U.N. Doc. A/I034 (1975), further reinforces the international community's affirmation of the prohibition against torture as a peremptory norm of international law. The Declaration specifies in Article 2:

> Any act or torture or other cruel, inhuman or degrading treatment or punishment is an offence to human dignity and shall be condemned as a denial of the purposes of the Charter of the United Nations as a violation of the human rights and fundamental freedoms proclaimed in the Universal Declaration of Human Rights.

It should also be noted that, acting upon a request from the General Assembly, the U.N. Commission on Human Rights currently is drawing up a draft convention against torture, thus codifying the customary international law norms expressed in the above Declaration and providing for procedures to implement its prohibition of torture.

11. Since torture is proscribed by customary international law, which is part of the substantive law to be applied by courts in the United States, this court should not be hesitant in invoking and applying it in the present case. As the Supreme Court stated in *The Paquete Habana*, 175 U.S. 677, 708 (1900),

> International law is part of our law, and must be ascertained and administered by the courts of justice of appropriate jurisdiction as often as questions of right depending upon it are duly presented for their determination. For this purpose, where there is no treaty and no controlling executive or legislative act or judicial decision, resort must be had to the customs and usages of civilized nations, and as evidence of these, to the works of jurists and commentators who by years of labor, research, and experience have made themselves peculiarly well acquainted with the subjects of which they treat.

12. Confirming my above opinion that torture, through the development of the entire Universal Declaration into a norm of customary international law, is now prohibited by international law, are the following two significant pronouncements:

a. Montreal Statement of the Assembly for Human Rights 2 (1968), *reprinted in* 9 Journal of the International Commission of Jurists 94, 95 (1968).

b. Declaration of Teheran, Final Act of the International Conference on Human Rights 3, at 4, para. 2 (UN Doc. A/CONF./32/41 (1968)).

13. Further confirming my above opinion that torture now violates customary international law are the following two commentators:

a. O'Boyle, "Torture and Emergency Powers Under the European Convention on Human Rights: Ireland v. The United Kingdom," 71 Amer. J. Int'l L. 674, 687 (1977).

b. Dinstein, "The Human Rights to Life, Physical Liberty and Integrity," in *The International Bill of Rights: A Guide to Interpretation* (L. Henkin ed. forthcoming).

Richard B. Lillich

Date: May 10, 1979

UNITED STATES DISTRICT COURT
EASTERN DISTRICT OF NEW YORK

DOLLY M.E. FILARTIGA and
DR. JOEL FILARTIGA,

Plaintiffs,

– against –

AMERICO NORBERTO PENA-
IRALA, et al.

Defendants.

**STATUTORY DECLARATION
OF THOMAS M. FRANCK**

I, THOMAS M. FRANCK, residing at 15 Charlton Street, New York, New York, do hereby solemnly and sincerely declare as follows:

1) I am professor of international law at New York University, a staff associate for international law for the Carnegie Endowment for International Peace, Director of the New York University Center for International Studies, author of various books on aspects of international law, and, periodically, consultant to the Government of the United States and various foreign governments.

2) Customary International Law holds torture to be a violation of fundamental human rights and makes the use of torture by governments or individuals illegal.

3) Evidence of this is to be found in article 5 of the Universal Declaration of Human Rights approved overwhelmingly by the General Assembly of the United Nations which states that "No one shall be subjected to torture or to cruel, in human or degrading treatment or punishment." Similarly, article 5 of the American Convention on Human Rights states in section 2 that "No one shall be subjected to torture or to cruel, inhuman or degrading punishment or treatment. All persons deprived of their liberty shall be treated with respect for the inherent dignity of the human person." Article 7 of the International Covenant on Civil and Political Rights, adopted by resolution of the General Assembly, provides that "No one shall be subjected to torture or to cruel, inhuman or degrading treatment or punishment."

4) A recent study of the International Association of Penal Law ("The Prevention and Suppression of Torture," Revue Internationale de Droit

Penal, 1977, pg. 28) has found that "torture to extract confessions was at one time a part of most legal systems in the world, but now has been rejected by virtually all nations." In my opinion this is a correct summary of practice.

5) Practice is evidence of law. Article 38 of the Statute of the International Court of Justice confirms that international law embraces "b. international custom, as evidence of a general practice accepted as law" and "c. the general principles of law recognized by civilized nations." The prohibition of torture is of this normative character, made illegal in international law regardless of its status in the domestic law of a particular state which chooses to engage in the practice of torture.

AND I MAKE THIS SOLEMN DECLARATION conscientiously believing the same to be true.

Thomas M. Franck

Dated: May 9, 1979

UNITED STATES DISTRICT COURT
EASTERN DISTRICT OF NEW YORK

DOLLY M.E. FILARTIGA and DR. JOEL FILARTIGA,	**AFFIDAVIT OF RICHARD FALK**

Plaintiffs,

– against –

AMERICO NORBERTO PENA-IRALA, et al.

Defendants.

I, Richard Anderson Falk, residing at 168 Prospect Avenue, Princeton, New Jersey, do hereby solemnly and sincerely declare as follows:

I, Richard Anderson Falk, possess various qualifications to act as an expert in matters of international law or the law of nations. I studied law at Yale Law School receiving a LL.B. degree in 1955 and, subsequently, at Harvard Law School receiving a J.S.D. degree in 1962. Between 1955 and 1961 I taught at the College of Law of the Ohio State University and was responsible for the course offerings in international law during this period. Since 1961 I have been a member of the faculty at Princeton University and since 1965 have been the Albert G. Milbank Professor of International Law and Practice. I was admitted to the New York Bar in 1956 and have testified as an international law expert in numerous trials in the last twenty years on various subjects. I have written various books on international law and served as editor of the four volume series *The Vietnam War and International Law*. I have also written extensively on the international law of human rights. Among other professional affiliations I have served as Vice President of the American Society of International Law for a period of four years (see attached resume for more detailed description of qualifications).

In my judgment it is now beyond reasonable doubt that torture of a person held in detention that results in severe harm or death is a violation of the law of nations. This conclusion is based on an assessment of the evolving customary law of nations bearing on human rights. Article 5 of the Universal Declaration of Human Rights declares that "no one shall be subjected to torture or to cruel, inhuman or degrading treatment or punishment." This Declaration was unanimously endorsed by the Members of the United Nations in 1948, including the United States. Article 7 of the unratified International Covenant on Civil and Political Rights of 1966 carries forward the prohibition on torture contained in the Universal Declaration, as do subsequent widely endorsed resolutions of the General Assembly of the United Nations.

At this stage in international history a consensus of states can generate new norms of customary international law through the formal procedures of the United Nations. Given the numbers of states and the complexity of international life this is a practical necessity. With respect to torture, the law-forming attitudes of governments has been manifest over a long period of time. No state claims a right to engage in torture. The duty to refrain is not merely a matter of habit, but of obligation acknowledged as such by leaders of the principal countries in the world.

The domestic courts of the United States have long made it clear that a rule of international law should be applied whenever relevant even if it is not embodied in a duly ratified treaty. There are numerous judicial authorities to this effect in cases involving oceans and investment disputes, as well as concerning human rights. On this basis the international law prohibition on torture is part of the law of nations and should be applied by this court.

Respectfully submitted,

Richard Anderson Falk

Dated: May 8, 1979

MAY 14, 1979: UNITED STATES

Plaintiffs' Opposition to Point II of Defendant's Memorandum Urging Vacatur of the Stay of Deportation

UNITED STATES DISTRICT COURT
EASTERN DISTRICT OF NEW YORK

DR. JOEL FILARTIGA and
DOLLY FILARTIGA,

          Plaintiffs,

   – against –

AMERICO PENA-IRALA,

        Defendant.

PLAINTIFFS' OPPOSITION TO POINT II OF DEFENDANTS' MEMORANDUM URGING VACATUR OF THE STAY OF DEPORTATION

Defendant's contention in Point II of his memorandum that this Court has no power to stay his deportation and thereby prolong his custody here is legally without merit. Before addressing the legal question of this Court's power, however, it is essential to look at the background which demonstrates that his continued custody in this country and that of his companion, are due to their acts and to delays sought by the defendant and more significantly by his attorneys.

First, Pena and Villalba are in custody because they are adjudicated illegal aliens subject to deportation and to detention pending deportation as ordered by the INS magistrate. The effect of this Court's stay is inevitably to continue the pre-existing custody. It is being prolonged, however, because of delays sought by the defendant and his attorneys.

Indeed, plaintiffs have no desire to maintain either Pena or Villalba here beyond that brief period necessary to permit the taking of their depositions and, thereafter, the fashioning of the undertaking necessary to assure that the Court can continue meaningfully to exercise its jurisdiction and effectuate its judgment. Had the defendant allowed the depositions originally scheduled for April 12, 1979 to go forward, these matters might well have been resolved within one week of the Court's original order staying the deposition. Had this occurred, it is possible that this Court's intervention would not even have occasioned a delay in their actual deportation given the difficulty of obtaining flights to Paraguay.

But defendant sought on April 12 a two-week delay to obtain counsel, as is his right. Plaintiffs made clear they were prepared to go ahead with the depositions as soon as Pena's counsel should arrive and indicate that he was ready. The Assistant United States Attorney undertook to notify plaintiffs. On about April 23, plaintiffs learned unofficially that Jose Emilio Gorostiaga had arrived in this country to represent Pena. When we appeared in Court on May 30, we were informed that Staten Island counsel had been contacted the preceding Friday and was unable to do any preparation over the weekend because of a scheduled trip to Vermont. Defendant's lawyers asked for a further two-week adjournment of the return date and continuation of the stay until today.

Throughout this period, plaintiffs have stood ready to depose Pena and Villalba in order to expedite this stage of the proceeding. Defendant's attorney still remains unwilling to set a date.

Defendant's assertion that this Court has no power to restrain him and his companion from leaving the jurisdiction until plaintiffs can depose them and until the Court has assured the defendant's accountability is based upon a misstatement of the governing law. He asserts that Rule 64 of the Federal Rules Civil Procedure limits plaintiffs to only those prejudgment remedies presently available at state law and that the remedy of civil arrest would not be available in this case. Defendant ignores the clear proviso of Rule 64 that federal law applies to broaden the available state remedies and that, in this case, the Federal All Writs Act, 28 U.S.C. § 1651, provides ample authority to this Court to stay the deportations of Pena and Villalba and thereby briefly prolong his detention because the stay is "necessary or appropriate in and of . . . [its] jurisdiction and agreeable to the usages of law."

The relevant provisions of Rule 64 are:

At the commencement of and during the course of an action, all remedies providing for seizure of person or property . . . are available under the circumstances and in the manner provided by the law of the state in which the district court is held, existing at the time the remedy is sought, *subject to the following qualifications: (1) any existing statute of the United States governs to the extent to which it is applicable . . . .* The remedies thus available include arrest, attachment . . . sequestration, and other corresponding or equivalent remedies . . . . (emphasis supplied).

As stated in *Brown v. Beckham*, Rule 64 "undoubtedly means that if there is any existing applicable federal statute that modifies the manner provided by the state in making the remedy . . . available, the . . . [federal] court is bound thereby." *Brown v. Beckham*, 137 F.2d 644 (6th Cir. 1943).[1]

There is no question that § 1651, the "All Writs Statute," qualifies as a governing statute under Rule 64, enabling this Court to issue those orders necessary to preserve its jurisdiction in this lawsuit, regardless of what remedies are available under state law. The principle that the All Writs Act takes precedence over clear limitations in federal rules of procedure is illustrated by *Harris v. Nelson*, 394 U.S. 286, 89 S.Ct. 1082, reh. denied 394 U.S. 1025, 89 S.Ct. 1623 (1969). *Harris* concerned the power of the district court in *habeas corpus* proceedings to answer interrogatories for the purpose of discovery. The Supreme Court held F.R. Civ. P. 8l(a)(2) excludes use of Rule 33 interrogatories in *habeas corpus* proceedings. Despite this limitation the Court held that § 1651 provides the district courts with authority to permit *habeas corpus* petitioners to use interrogatories to prepare for a hearing "when necessary . . . order that a fair and meaningful evidentiary hearing may be held so that the court may properly 'dispose of the matter as law and justice require.'" *Harris v. Nelson, supra* at 300. The court emphasized the affirmative and expansive nature of the "All Writs" power:

> [W]here specific allegations before the court show reason to believe that the petitioner may, if the facts are fully developed, be . . . entitled to relief, it is the *duty* of the court to provide for an adequate inquiry. Obviously, in exercising this power, the court may utilize familiar procedures, as appropriate, whether these are found in the civil or criminal rules or elsewhere in the "usages and principles of law." (*Ibid*) (emphasis supplied)

Neither state law nor the nature and scope of writs available at common law limit the federal power under § 1651. As the Supreme Court held in *Price v. Johnston*, federal courts are not "confined to the precise forms of . . . writ[s] in vogue at the common law." Rather, the concept of "law" and the inherent power to issue writs recognized in § 1651 is a "legislatively approved source of procedural instruments designed to achieve 'the rational ends of justice.'" (citation omitted). 334 U.S. 266, 282, 88 S.Ct. 11049 (1948).

---

[1] We note that the footnote in *Granny Goose Foods Inc. v. Brotherhood of Teamsters*, which is, curiously, the only authority cited by defendant for the proposition that state law limits federal remedies, is also consistent with the proviso of Rule 64. There the court held that once removed to federal court, the durational limitations of Rule 65 (b) govern notwithstanding state law to the contrary. 415 U.S. 423, 436, n. 10 (1974).

Analogously, the absence of explicit authority in the immigration and naturalization laws also does not limit the Court's power to stay a deportation, whether upon the deportee's motion or upon that of a third party. Defendant glides over the significance of *Hong v. Agency for International Development*, 420 F.2d 507 (9th Cir. 1972). It was not because his lawsuit might affect his deportation status but because his presence in the country was necessary to pursuing the claim that the Court stayed Hong's deportation. And while not explicitly invoking section 1651, this section was the implicit fount of authority.

The power confined by § 1651 extends not simply to the defendant Pena but also to the material witness Villalba. The Supreme Court recently approved exercise of the all writs power against a non-party in *United States v. New York Telephone Co.*, 434 U.S. 159, 98 S.Ct. 364 (1977), sustaining the power of the district courts to order the telephone company to assist the FBI in installing a pen register. In so doing the Court applied the principle that:

> The power conferred by the Act extends, under appropriate circumstances, to persons who though not parties to the original action or engaged in wrong doing are in a position to frustrate the implementation of a court order or the proper administration of justice, and encompasses even those who have not taken any affirmative action to hinder justice. (citations and note omitted). *Supra* at 372-373.

For all these reasons this Court is fully empowered under section 1651 to stay Pena's and Villalba's deportation to secure their testimony and such undertaking from the defendant as will assure the Court's ability to exercise jurisdiction and effectuate its judgment.

It is furthermore notable here that, notwithstanding the power to do so, this court did not order, nor did plaintiffs seek the arrests of Pena and Villalba. When this suit was filed they were already in custody pursuant to the INS magistrate's order. This court's order had the effect simply of prolonging their detention here subject to the conditions previously imposed. It is their status as adjudicated deportable aliens that is responsible for their detention. And, as such, they can be held pending deportation for six months on the authority of the Attorney General. See 8 U.S.C. § 1252(c) for far less cause than is shown here.

But beyond that, plaintiffs do not seek to stay their deportation in excess of the brief period necessary to assure the jurisdiction of this Court and to "achieve the rational ends of justice." What could have been no more than a week's delay has been extended, not by any act of plaintiffs but by virtue of adjournments sought by the defendant and his attorneys.

Finally, this Court's authority to issue and maintain the stay of deportation is not affected by the fact that defendant now interposes jurisdictional questions in his motion to dismiss. The issuance of orders designed to preserve the *status quo* while the court determines the scope of its jurisdiction is clearly appropriate in aid of jurisdiction. *United States v. United Mine Workers*, 330 U.S. 258, 293, 67 S.Ct. 677, 695, (1947). Commenting on such 'status quo orders' the Court of Appeals for the Fifth Circuit stated:

> A federal court has the power under the All Writs to issue injunctive orders in a case even before the Court's jurisdiction has been established. When potential jurisdiction exists, a federal court may issue status quo orders to ensure that once its jurisdiction is shown to exist, the court will be in a position to exercise it. *See e.g., F.T.C. v. Dean Foods Co.*, 384 U.S. 597, 603-05 (1966).

ITT Community Development Corp v. Barton, 569 F.2d 1351, 1359 n.19 (1978). *See also United States v. Western Pennsylvania Sand and Gravel Ass'n*, 114 F.Supp. 158 (W.D. Pa. 1953).

Plaintiffs are asking this Court to issue orders restraining defendants from leaving this Court's jurisdiction only until plaintiffs can depose Pena and Villalba concerning the brutal murder of Joelito Filartiga and Pena's ability to satisfy any judgment which might be rendered against them. Plaintiffs do not seek to have defendants incarcerated pending the outcome of this litigation, but merely to have this Court issue those writs "necessary or appropriate in aid of . . . [its] jurisdiction in order to prevent defendant's flight from justice and the complete frustration of the power of this Court."

Respectfully submitted,

PETER WEISS
RHONDA COPELON
JOHN W. CORWIN
JOSE ANTONIO LUGO
c/o Center for Constitutional Rights
853 Broadway
New York, New York 10003

MICHAEL MAGGIO
Goren & Maggio
1801 Columbia Road N.W.
Washington, D.C. 20009
Attorneys for Plaintiffs

Dated: New York, New York
May 14, 1979

MAY 15, 1979: UNITED STATES

U.S. District Court for the Eastern District of New York: Memorandum and Order

UNITED STATES DISTRICT COURT
EASTERN DISTRICT OF NEW YORK

DOLLY M.E. FILARTIGA and DR. JOEL FILARTIGA,	**MEMORANDUM AND ORDER**
	79 Civ 917
Plaintiffs,	
– against –	
AMERICO NORBERTO PENA-IRALA, et al., Defendants.	

NICKERSON, District Judge

Plaintiff brought this action "for damages for violation of human rights for the wrongful torture and murder of the decedent Joel Filartiga." The action is brought by the decedent's father, a resident of Paraguay, and the decedent's sister who resides in Washington, D.C., having arrived on a visitor's visa and applied for political asylum in the United States. The defendant Pena-Irala is former Inspector General of Police of Asuncion, Paraguay, and is presently in the United States as an illegal alien and subject to a deportation order entered April 5, 1979 by an Immigration judge. Pena-Irala is being held in custody by the Immigration and Naturalization Service. The other defendants are officials of the Immigration and Naturalization Service.

In substance the complaint alleges that on March 29, 1979 the decedent was kidnapped and tortured to death by Pena-Irala and others. Allegedly the decedent was tortured and murdered in retaliation for the political activities and opinions of his father who is a leading political opponent of General Stroessner, the dictator-president of Paraguay. The complaint also alleges that the decedent's sister was deliberately led to the mutilated body of her brother and thereby suffered emotional pain and suffering and was wrongfully charged in Paraguay with harassment of Pena-Irala's house and battery on his stepson and sentenced to jail without trial, although released after six hours.

The court previously signed an order to show cause as to why an order should not be entered permitting plaintiffs to take the depositions of Pena-Irala and one Juan Bautista Fernandez Villalba, a female companion of Pena-Irala, as material witnesses, both being in the custody of the Immigration and Naturalization Service, and staying their deportation pending the taking of the depositions. Pending decision of the motion the Immigration and Naturalization officials have been ordered to refrain from deporting the witnesses.

Defendant Pena-Irala has now moved to dismiss the complaint and to vacate the stay.

Jurisdiction of the court is invoked under 28 U.S.C. § 1350 which reads "the district courts shall have original jurisdiction of any civil action by an alien for a tort only, committed in violation of the Law of Nations or a treaty of the United States."

Plaintiffs contend that the court has jurisdiction because the torture and murder of the decedent was "in violation of the Law of Nations." Plaintiffs do not contend that Pena-Irala committed a tort in violation of a treaty of the United States.

This court is bound by the decision in *IIT v. Vencap, Ltd.*, 519 F.2d 1001 (2d Cir. 1975) and *Dreyfus v. von Finck*, 534 F.2d 24 (2d Cir. 1976). Those decisions held that conduct, though tortious, is not in violation of "the Law of Nations", as those words are used in 28 U.S.C. §1350, unless the conduct is in violation of those standards, rules or customs affecting the relationship between states and between an individual and a foreign state, and used by those states for their common good and/or in dealings *inter se. IIT v. Vencap, Ltd., supra*, 519 F.2d at 1015.

Plaintiffs argue cogently that 28 U.S.C. § 1350 should not be so narrowly read and that the proscription of torture in numerous international instruments accepted by nearly all the states in the international community reflects the emergence of a norm of customary international law condemning torture.

Despite the strength of these arguments this court feels bound by the Second Circuit decisions cited above. Accordingly the complaint will be dismissed.

The stay will be continued for 48 hours after entry of this order to enable plaintiff to apply to the Court of Appeals for a further stay. The motion of the *Amici* for leave to file a brief *amicus curiae* is granted. So ordered.

Eugene H. Nickerson, U.S.D.J.

Dated: Brooklyn, New York
     May 15, 1979

The Clerk shall make copies of this Memorandum and Order and serve them upon the parties.

MAY 15, 1979: UNITED STATES

Plaintiffs' Notice of Appeal

UNITED STATES DISTRICT COURT
EASTERN DISTRICT OF NEW YORK

DOLLY M.E. FILARTIGA and DR. JOEL FILARTIGA,	**NOTICE OF APPEAL**
Plaintiffs,	**79 Civ 917**
– against –	
AMERICO N. PENA-IRALA,	
Defendant.	

DOLLY M.E. FILARTIGA and DR. JOEL FILARTIGA by their under-signed counsel, hereby appeal from the order of United States District Judge Eugene H. Nickerson entered May 15, 1979 dismissing their complaint.

Respectfully submitted,

Peter Weiss
Rhonda Copelon
John Corwin
Jose Antonio Lugo
c/o CENTER FOR CONSTITUTIONAL RIGHTS
853 Broadway
New York, New York 10003
(202) 674-3303

Michael Maggio
GOREN and MAGGIO
1801 Columbia Road, N.W.
Washington, D.C. 20009
(202) 483-8055

Dated: New York, New York
May 15, 1979

MAY 16, 1979: UNITED STATES

Plaintiffs' Notice of Motion and Motion for Interim Relief Pending Appeal

UNITED STATES COURT OF APPEALS
FOR THE SECOND CIRCUIT

DOLLY M.E. FILARTIGA and
DR. JOEL FILARTIGA,

        Appellants,

    – against –

AMERICO NORBERTO PENA-
IRALA, et al.,

        Appellees.

**NOTICE OF MOTION AND
MOTION FOR INTERIM
RELIEF PENDING APPEAL**

TO THE DEFENDANTS:

PLEASE TAKE NOTICE that, upon the annexed affidavit of Rhonda Copelon, the Certificate of Attorney and affidavit of Peter Weiss and Exhibits in support thereof, plaintiffs DOLLY M.E. FILARTIGA and DR. JOEL FILAR-TIGA shall move this Court on May ___, 1979, at ___ o'clock __.m., pursuant to Rule 62(g) of the Federal Rules of Civil Procedure, Rule 8 of the Federal Rules of Appellate Procedure, and 28 U.S.C. § 1651, for an order:

(1) Permitting plaintiffs to take the immediate depositions of the defendant Pena-Irala and Juana Bautista Fernandez Villalba, a material witness, both of whom are in the custody of the Immigration and Naturalization Service at the Brooklyn Navy Yard;

(2) Staying their deportations, in the event that should necessitate, until 24 hours following the completion of the deposition; and

(3) Returning this matter to the District Court simply for the purpose of facilitating the supervision of this relief.

The grounds for this application are as follows:

I. *The District Court Denied The Relief Sought on Jurisdictional Grounds.*

1. The relief requested herein was denied by the District Court Judge on May 15, 1979.

2. The ground for the denial was that, having dismissed the complaint for want of jurisdiction, the District Court considered that it had no power to grant the relief requested (see ¶11 of Copelon affidavit).

II. *The Appeal Has Substantial Merit.*

3. District Court Judge Nickerson indicated in his Memorandum and Order, dated May 15, 1979 (Exhibit B submitted herewith), that he found great merit in plaintiffs' contention that torture, as alleged in the complaint, constitutes a tort which violates the law of nations, as that concept is internationally understood today, but that this Court's decisions bind him to a narrower construction of the "law of nations."

4. As explained in the accompanying certificate of attorney and affidavit of Peter Weiss, the jurisdictional question presented on this appeal is substantial and meritorious and the appeal is not taken for the purposes of delay.

III. *The Equities Favor Granting Interim Relief.*

5. The background of proceedings before the Immigration and Naturalization Service and the District Court is set forth in the accompanying affidavit of Rhonda Copelon, and is incorporated as if set forth herein. The facts as set forth therein are not disputed.

6. Plaintiffs' prayer for interim relief meets the tests articulated by this Court which make issuance of a stay in the nature of a preliminary injunction proper—i.e., the balance of hardships tips in their favor, they have raised serious questions on the merits, and there is a strong public interest in assuring that this Court and the District Court are able potentially to exercise effective and meaningful jurisdiction over this case after resolution of this appeal. *Pride v. Community School Board of Brooklyn, New York,* 482 F.2d 257, 264 (2d Cir. 1973).

7. The relief requested is unusual but also unusually simple. It is the minimal necessary to safeguard the interests of plaintiffs effectively to pursue, and the capacity of the Court meaningfully to adjudicate, the complaint should this Court find jurisdiction on appeal. The relief is designed to minimize any burden on the rights of the defendant and Ms. Villalba, the material witness.

a. Granting this relief will not prolong their detention here, unless further delay is sought by their counsel. Since their deportation is now scheduled for May 23, an order to permit the immediate taking of the depositions could be satisfied well in advance of the scheduled departure. Indeed, had defendant's counsel sought initially to facilitate rather than delay the taking of depositions, the witnesses could have been returned to Paraguay several weeks ago.

b. The obligation, to respond to a deposition is the ordinary duty of every person subject to the court's jurisdiction, whether citizen or alien, whether detained or at liberty. The law recognizes no special burden in such proceeding.

c. Indeed, but for the fact that the witnesses are in custody here, Rule 30(b)(2) of the Federal Rules of Civil Procedure grants an automatic right to plaintiff to take the immediate deposition of a defendant or any person prior even to the interposition of jurisdictional or other dismissal claims where, as here, the witness "is about to go out of the . . . United States, and will be unavailable for examination unless his deposition is taken before expiration of the 30-day period."

8. Taking these depositions is necessary to prevent irreparable harm to the plaintiffs.

9. These witnesses are uniquely in possession of facts which go to the heart of plaintiffs' claim.

a. Pena-Irala is accused of the torture-murder on which this action is based. Ms. Villalba is a crucial material witness to the alleged tort and crime against human rights as she lives with Pena-Irala and shares the house where the body of Joelito Filartiga was tortured or brought after the torture-murder.

b. The witnesses are also uniquely in possession of facts concerning the assets of the defendant Pena-Irala and, therefore, the means by which this Court can attempt to assure this accountability to the continuing process of our courts and to the potential judgment for plaintiffs.

10. Once the witnesses are returned to Paraguay, there is no assurance whatsoever that they will be amenable to any process of our courts.

a. The defendant Pena-Irala disappeared from Paraguay at a time when his involvement and that of the Stroessner regime in the torture-murder of Joelito Filartiga and the effort to cover up this deliberate wrongdoing was becoming increasingly notorious and embarrassing to the regime. For nine months he succeeded in overstaying his visitor's visa here and escaping identification by U.S. Immigration and Naturalization Service officials. Given this history, there is no reason to assume that he or his companion, Ms. Villalba, will remain in Paraguay and that plaintiffs will be able even to locate him after this appeal has been resolved. Given this background, it is particularly likely that he would deliberately seek to escape the future process of our courts and probably be encouraged in so doing by the Stroessner regime.

b. Even assuming knowledge of the whereabouts of the witnesses, the cost to plaintiffs, who have minimal resources, of going to Paraguay to seek to take the needed depositions is virtually prohibitive. The round trip airfare from New York to Asuncion is approximately $1,000. Plaintiffs may be required to pay not only for their counsel but for the defendant's U.S. counsel as well. The recognition in Federal Rules of Civil Procedure 30(b)(2) of the need for immediate depositions where potential witnesses are simply about to go out of the district or 100 miles beyond the trial court attests to the concern of our laws to facilitate discovery and avoid unnecessary expense. The clear policy of Rule 30(b)(2) to avoid even lesser burdens than would be imposed here, notwithstanding potentially decisive jurisdictional problems, applies with particular force where the underlying action is for violation of civil and human rights and not a garden-variety commercial case.

c. Even if the witnesses are ultimately located in Paraguay and the money necessary to go there is raised, it is virtually certain that the Paraguayan courts will not be amenable to facilitating the process of the court in this case.

(i) Although Rule 28(b) of the Federal Rules of Civil Procedure (28 U.S.C.) permits the taking of depositions in foreign countries, that authorization is subject to the law of the country in which the deponent is located. In most instances, especially in non-common law countries, parties to actions in the United States must utilize the process of local courts through letters rogatory, in order to proceed with a deposition. Even the most friendly of non-common law countries, such as France and Switzerland, place severe restrictions on the method of deposition to be used (only written interrogatories are permitted) and often will not compel unwilling witnesses to answer. 4 Moore's Federal Practice, ¶28.05 (2nd ed.).

(ii) Moreover, the defendant Pena-Irala was, at the time of the torture-murder, a high-ranking police inspector in the Investigaciones (anti-subversive squad) and is known as one of Paraguay's chief torturers (Dolly M.E. Filartiga affidavit, ¶11). Numerous international reports, as well as our own State Department, have officially documented the absence of the rule of law in Paraguay and the control of the judiciary by the executive branch, particularly by the most powerful police (see authorities noted in affidavit of Dolly M.E. Filartiga., ¶¶ 12-14, Exhibit D). Given the previous responses of the courts in Paraguay to the plaintiffs' prosecution of Pena-Irala, it is all but certain that the Paraguayan courts will effectively insulate defendants from any process which might issue from the United States (see affidavit of Dolly M.E. Filartiga, ¶¶ 15-l9, Exhibit D). Indeed, to defer the taking of testimony until the witnesses are returned to Paraguay unnecessarily invites diplomatic confrontations such as that which is presently occurring between this country and Chile over the latter's refusal to extradite persons charged in the murder of Orlando Letelier and Ronnie Moffitt.

11. The paramount public interest of this country would be served by granting the interim relief sought.

a. The construction of § 1350 sought by plaintiffs on appeal is consistent with and supportive of the public policy commitment of this country - through its administration and laws - to concern itself with and deter violations of fundamental human rights abroad. See Certificate of Attorney and authorities cited in Exhibit F, submitted herewith. Plaintiffs have invoked the jurisdiction of this Court at great risk to their lives and safety, given the previous retaliation against them and their Paraguayan attorney by the Stroessner regime and its courts, and given threats made, even in this country, toward the person who identified Pena-Irala to the Immigration and Naturalization Service (see affidavits of Dolly M.E. Filartiga, Exhibit D, ¶¶ 15-19, and of Gilberto Olmedo Sanchez, Exhibit G).

b. In light of the substantial legal questions presented in this appeal, the absence of burden to the witnesses and the overwhelming hardship to plaintiffs of not permitting the depositions to go forward while the witnesses remain necessarily in custody in Brooklyn and fully accessible to plaintiffs, it is both necessary and appropriate, in the interest also of the public policy of this nation, to issue an order permitting the taking of these depositions and protecting plaintiffs' ability to pursue this action in the future.

12. The District Court did not rule on the merits of the need and appropriateness of this deposition because it considered itself without jurisdiction. This Court, which must consider the jurisdictional question, has authority under Rule 62(g) of the Federal Rules of Civil Procedure to grant the interim relief requested here. In particular, Rule 62(g) empowers the Court to make any order appropriate to preserve the status quo or the effectiveness of the judgment subsequently to be entered. In addition, 28 U.S.C. § 1651, the "All Writs Act," gives this Court further power to aid its ability, and ultimately that of the District Court, to exercise meaningful jurisdiction over this civil action. Three cases bear special mention in this

regard. *Price v. Johnson*, 334 U.S. 266, 282, 88 S. Ct. 1049 (1948), affirms the authority of the federal courts under 28 U.S.C. § 1651 to fashion "procedural instruments designed to achieve the rational ends of justice." The Supreme Court's decision in *Harris v. Nelson*, 394 U.S. 286, 300, 89 S. Ct. 1082, reh. denied 394 U.S. 1025, 89 S. Ct. 1623 (1969), affirms that § 1651 power authorizes the issuance of discovery orders even where the Federal Rules of Civil Procedure explicitly makes them unavailable "when necessary. . . in order that a fair and meaningful evidentiary hearing may be held so that the court may properly 'dispose of the matter as law and justice require.'" Finally, the Court has construed 28 U.S.C. § 1651 to provide even broader power than that given by Rule 62(g). In *F.T.C. v. Dean Foods*, 384 U.S. 597, 86 S. Ct. 1738 (1966), the Court affirmed the power to issue writs in anticipation of future appeals being filed. Here, the appeal is pending, and the authority of Rule 62(g) is sufficient basis for the relief requested.

WHEREFORE, movants pray for an order permitting them to take the depositions of Pena-Irala and Fernandez Villalba forthwith and for such other and further relief as to this Court may seem just and proper.

Respectfully submitted,

PETER WEISS
RHONDA COPELON
JOHN W. CORWIN
JOSE ANTONIO LUGO
c/o Center for Constitutional Rights
853 Broadway
New York, New York 10003
(212) 674-3303

MICHAEL MAGGIO
Goren and Maggio
1801 Columbia Road, N.W.
Washington, D.C.
(202) 483-8055

Attorneys for Plaintiffs

Dated: New York, New York
      May 16, 1979

UNITED STATES COURT OF APPEALS
FOR THE SECOND CIRCUIT

DOLLY M.E. FILARTIGA
DR. JOEL FILARTIGA,

**AFFIDAVIT IN SUPPORT OF
MOTION FOR INTERIM
RELIEF**

Appellants,

– against –

AMERICO NORBERTO PENA-
IRALA, et al.,

Appellees.

RHONDA COPELON hereby affirms under the penalties of perjury:

1. I am one of the attorneys for Dolly M.E. Filartiga and Dr. Joel Filartiga and am fully familiar with all the facts and circumstances of their case.

2. On April 4, 1979, defendant Pena-Irala and his companion Ms. Fernandez Villalba, were arrested by agents of the United States Immigration and Naturalization Service (hereinafter, "INS") in Brooklyn, New York. On April 5, 1979, they were ordered deported as illegal aliens, after admitting that they had overstayed their tourist visas and had been living here illegally for nine months. They were ordered detained in the custody of INS at the Brooklyn Navy Yard subject to $75,000 bail and they remain in such custody.

3. On April 6, 1979, plaintiffs filed this civil action for wrongful death, submitted herewith as Exhibit C. The gravaman of the complaint is that Pena-Irala, a former Inspector General of the Paraguayan police intelligence force, tortured and murdered Joelito Filartiga in retaliation for the political activities and opinions of his father, Dr. Joel Filartiga, a leading opponent of the dictator president of Paraguay. Jurisdiction was premised upon 28 U.S.C. § 1350 and on the principle that this torture constitutes a violation of the law of nations. The plaintiff Dr. Filartiga presently resides in Washington, D.C. as an alien and has an application pending for political asylum.

4. On information and belief, the reason that the defendant came to this country and secreted himself here was to escape increasingly adverse

publicity surrounding his responsibility and that of the Stroessner regime for the torture-murder of Joelito Filartiga. (See Affidavit of D.M.E. Filartiga, ¶4, Exhibit D and Exhibit B to Complaint, Exhibit C hereto.)

5. The torture and murder of Joelito Filartiga has become a case of major international concern. (See Affidavit of Dolly M.E. Filartiga, submitted herewith as Exhibit D.)

6. Upon order to show cause, the District Court on April 9, 1979 stayed the deportation of Pena-Irala and Fernandez Villalba a material witness to the alleged torts, and issued an order permitting plaintiffs to take their depositions while in custody. The Court order was required under F.R.C.P. 30, simply because the witnesses were in custody. The deposition was arranged between plaintiffs and the U.S. Attorney for Thursday morning, April 12, 1979.

7. On April 12, 1979, the witnesses appeared without counsel and stated that they would not answer questions until their attorney arrived from Paraguay. Upon application of the plaintiffs, Judge Nickerson ordered that the witnesses be brought to court. In response to the Court's queries, they stated both that they were invoking the Fifth Amendment privilege, and that they would call their Paraguayan counsel and would speak upon his arrival to the United States. Accordingly, the Court advanced the return date on the order to show cause to April 30, 1979 and continued the stay of deportation. Plaintiffs indicated that they were ready to proceed with the deposition at defense counsel's earliest convenience.

8. On information and belief, attorney Gorostiaga arrived from Paraguay on or about April 23 but did not contact plaintiffs.

9. On April 30, 1979, defendants were represented by Mr. Gorostiaga from Paraguay and Mr. Rebollo from Staten Island. Mr. Rebollo indicated that he had been contacted the preceding Friday and requested a two-week extension of the stay to respond to the complaint. The Court then advanced the return date to May 14. On May 7, the defendant served his motion to dismiss on jurisdictional grounds and to vacate the stay of deportation. Plaintiffs served responding papers and a hearing was had on May 14, 1979. After hearing argument, the Court reserved decision on the jurisdictional questions and on the motion to take the depositions and continued the stay.

10. In the early afternoon of May 15, 1979, the Judge's chambers notified plaintiffs that he had completed his opinion. The Memorandum and Order (submitted herewith as Exhibit B), explains that, notwithstanding

the cogency of plaintiffs' argument that § 1350 jurisdiction should be read to embrace the almost universally approved modern norm of international law proscribing torture, he felt bound by rulings of this Circuit in other contexts which appear to approve a narrower interpretation of the concept of the "law of nations." He continued the stay of deportation to permit plaintiffs to apply to this Court for interim relief pending appeal.

11. In the late afternoon of May 15, the undersigned counsel called the Chambers of Judge Nickerson to ask him to reconsider and/or clarify whether, notwithstanding his order dismissing the complaint, he would permit plaintiffs to take the necessary depositions. The law clerk informed me that Judge Nickerson would not order the depositions on the ground that he believed that his dismissal for want of jurisdiction deprived him of the power to order the taking of the depositions, and that he had accordingly stayed his order to permit application to this Court.

12. Judge Nickerson, stayed the deportations for 48 hours to permit application to this Court for the relief sought herein.

13. Plaintiffs' Notice of Appeal was filed on May 16, 1979 (submitted herewith as Exhibit A).

14. I am informed that the government cannot lawfully deport the witnesses until 9:45 a.m. Wednesday, May 23, 1979. The government attorney cannot, however, guarantee their continuing presence in this country should they make application to INS to leave the country voluntarily.

15. Accordingly, it is essential that this matter be heard by a judge or panel of this Court prior to the expiration on May 17, 1979 of Judge Nickerson's 48 hour stay. Emergency determination is necessary because otherwise the witnesses' departure could moot this application and defeat the intention of the District Court that a court with the requisite jurisdiction, here provided particularly by F.R.A.P. 62(g) (see Plaintiffs' Motion for Interim Relief, ¶12) consider the appropriateness of an order permitting immediate depositions.)

16. Plaintiffs will be irreparably harmed, and the future capacity of this Court to meaningfully exercise its jurisdiction and adjudicate this complaint will be irreparably undermined if the defendant and a material witness to the torture and death charged are deported to Paraguay without first being required to submit to depositions. (See Plaintiffs' Application for Interim Relief.)

17. The essential relief sought herein is an order permitting the taking of the depositions forthwith. Given that the witnesses' deportation is presently not contemplated for a week, such an order should not delay their departure. The stay of deportation is requested herein simply to ensure plaintiffs against any change of plans by INS or delays attributable to the actions of defendant's counsel.

18. No prior application for the relief requested by this motion has been made to this or any other appellate court.

———————————————————

RHONDA COPELON

Dated: New York, New York
       May 16, 1979

UNITED STATES COURT OF APPEALS
FOR THE SECOND CIRCUIT

DOLLY M. E. FILARTIGA and DR. JOEL FILARTIGA,	**CERTIFICATE OF ATTORNEY AND AFFIDAVIT IN SUPPORT OF MOTION FOR INTERIM RELIEF**

Appellants,

– against –

AMERICO NORBERTO PENA-IRALA, et al.,

Appellees.

PETER WEISS affirms under penalty of perjury:

1. I am one of the attorneys for plaintiffs in this matter.

2. I certify that this appeal is not being taken for delay and that, for the reasons stated below and set out more fully in Point I of Plaintiffs' Memorandum of Law in Opposition to Defendant Pena-Irala's Motion to Dismiss, submitted herewith as Exhibit F, the questions on appeal are substantial and meritorious.

3. This case, which alleges a tort consisting of torture resulting in death, was brought under 28 U.S.C. § 1350, sometimes referred to as the Alien Tort Claims Act, which provides that the district courts shall have original jurisdiction of any civil action by an alien for a tort only, committed in violation of the law of nations or a treaty of the United States.

4. In his Memorandum and Order dated May 15, 1979, submitted herewith as Exhibit B, Judge Nickerson dismissed the complaint for want of jurisdiction over the subject matter. In doing so, he stated that plaintiffs "argue cogently" in favor of "a norm of customary international law condemning torture" but that, "despite the strength of these arguments" he felt bound by the decisions of this Court in *IIT v. Vencap, Ltd.*, 519 F. 2d 1001 (1975) and *Dreyfus v. von Finck*, 534 F. 2d 24 (1976). Those cases hold that conduct, though tortious, is not in violation of the law of nations unless it also violates "those standards, rules or customs affecting the relationship between states or between an individual and a foreign state, and used by those states for their common good and/or in dealings *inter se*."

5. It is plaintiffs' position that this definition of international law is too narrow but that, even taken on its face, it supports their claim that torture is a violation of the law of nations and therefore confers jurisdiction under 28 U.S.C. § 1350. They contend that, although *Vencap* and *Dreyfus* reached correct results, this was so only because the torts alleged—fraud in one case, confiscation of property on racial grounds in the other—were not violative of international law standards at the time the acts were committed.

6. In the instant case, plaintiffs have placed in the record affidavits from eminent authorities in international law, submitted herewith as Exhibit E, to the effect that torture is a violation of the law of nations and that "offenses against human rights . . . vitally affect relations between nations." These affidavits, which represent a standard method of proof of international law, are incontroverted by contrary evidence.

7. If the evidence of these experts, and of the texts and commentaries cited by plaintiffs, is accepted, the conclusion is inescapable that, however the law of nations is defined in previous decisions of this Court, the tort alleged here is a violation of the law of nations giving rise to § 1350 jurisdiction, either because it fits the definition mentioned in paragraph 4 above, or because that definition is too narrow, considering the current state of international law.

PETER WEISS

Dated: New York, New York
        May 16, 1979

MAY 18, 1979: UNITED STATES

U.S. District Court for the Eastern District of New York: Judgment

**UNITED STATES DISTRICT COURT
EASTERN DISTRICT OF NEW YORK**

DOLLY M.E. FILARTIGA and   **JUDGMENT**
DR. JOEL FILARTIGA,

         Plaintiffs,

     – against –

AMERICO NORBERTO PENA-
IRALA, et al.,

         Defendants.

A memorandum and order of Honorable Eugene H. Nickerson, United States District Judge, having been filed on May 16, 1979, dismissing the complaint, it is

ORDERED and ADJUDGED that the plaintiffs take nothing of the defendants; and that the complaint is dismissed.

                  Clerk

Dated: Brooklyn, New York
        May 18, 1979

MAY 18, 1979: UNITED STATES

Federal Appellees Affirmation in Opposition to Motion for Interim Relief Pending Appeal

UNITED STATES COURT OF APPEALS
FOR THE SECOND CIRCUIT

DOLLY M.E. FILARTIGA and
DR. JOEL FILARTIGA,

    Appellants,

 – against –

AMERICO NORBERTO PENA-
IRALA, et al.

    Appellees.

**FEDERAL APPELLEES
AFFIRMATION IN OPPOSITION
TO MOTION FOR INTERIM
RELIEF PENDING APPEAL**

Docket No. 79-6090

I, CYRIL HYMAN, hereby affirm under penalty of perjury that:

1. I am an Assistant United States Attorney on the staff of EDWARD R. KORMAN, United States Attorney for the Eastern District of New York, and am responsible for the defense of this appeal on behalf of the federal appellees. As such, I am fully familiar with the facts underlying the present motion for interim relief pending the outcome of this appeal.

2. I submit this affirmation in opposition to the appellants' motion for interim relief to the extent that such relief would stay the deportation of the appellee Americo Pena-Irala or his companion Juana Bautista Fernandez Villalba. Both of these individuals are currently detained by the United States Immigration and Naturalization Service at their detention center in Brooklyn and are scheduled to be deported to Paraguay on Wednesday, May 23, 1979.

3. Mr. Pena-Irala and Ms. Villalba were ordered deported on April 5, 1979, as persons who had overstayed their original tourist visas in violation of the Immigration and Nationality Act, § 241(a) (2), 8 U.S.C. § 1251(a) (2). Neither individual contested his deportation and neither individual has ever requested a stay of that deportation nor has appealed the deportation order.

4. On April 9, 1979, plaintiffs-appellants obtained a temporary restraining order directing the Immigration and Naturalization Service not to deport Mr. Pena-Irala and Ms. Villalba and to retain custody of these persons pending the return date of plaintiffs' motion to enjoin deportation of the defendants. On April 12, this order was extended by the District Court until April 30 at the request of Mr. Pena-Irala and Ms. Villalba so that they could obtain counsel. At a hearing on April 30, counsel appeared for Mr. Pena-Irala and Ms. Villalba and requested another two week adjournment of the plaintiffs' motion so that they could prepare an appropriate response. The government opposed all of these extensions of the temporary restraining order on the grounds that the district court had no jurisdiction to enjoin the deportation of these aliens at the request of parties who had a private civil action against the aliens.

The district court did modify its order, in response to the government's argument, on April 12, to strike that provision of the order requiring the Immigration Service to keep Mr. Pena-Irala and Ms. Villalba incarcerated. They remain incarcerated, however, as the result of their failure to post the appearance bond administratively imposed by the Immigration Service to secure their appearance for deportation.

5. After a final hearing on May 14, the district court dismissed the entire action for lack of jurisdiction under 28 U.S.C. § 1350 because of its view that the tortious conduct alleged by plaintiffs was not in violation of the "law of nations" as that phrase has been interpreted by this Court in *IIT v. Vencap, Ltd.*, 519 F.2d 1001 (2d Cir. 1975) and *Dreyfus v. Von Finck*, 534 F.2d 24 (2d Cir. 1976).

Although the district court did not reach the issue of its jurisdiction to enjoin the United States Immigration and Naturalization Service from deporting the appellees, it is clear that the district court would, at the very least, have abused its discretion in granting a preliminary injunction against the deportations in question and probably lacked any subject matter jurisdiction to award such relief. Aliens who themselves have sought to obtain an injunction against their deportation so that they could pursue civil litigation in this country have been consistently denied such relief by this Court and other courts. *Bolanos v. Kiley*, 509 F.2d 1023, 1026 (2d Cir. 1975); *Lad v. Immigration and Naturalization Service*, 539 F.2d 808, 809 (1st Cir. 1976), *Adame v. INS*, 349 F. Supp. 313 (N.D. Ill. 1972), *Prassinos v. District Director*, 193 F. Supp. 416 (N.D. Ohio 1960); *aff'd per curiam*, 289 F.2d 490 (6th Cir. 1961), *cert. denied*, 366 U.S. 966. *A fortiori*, an injunction may not issue against the deportation of defendants in a private civil case at the request of plaintiffs in that action. The only case cited by appellants on this issue in their brief below, *Hong v. Agency for International Development*, 470

F.2d 507 (9th Cir. 1972), simply does not apply. In *Hong*, the civil lawsuit was brought by the alien against a federal agency for breach of its contract to allow the alien to remain in the United States to complete his studies. As such, the validity of the deportation order itself was the subject of the suit. Here, the subject of this suit is not the validity of the government's deportation of the appellees. Appellants do not question the lawfulness of the deportation order. Rather, they seek to stay deportation for reasons totally unconnected with the validity of the order. As such, the standards set forth in Bolanos v. Kiley, supra, apply. In that case, the alien sought to restrain his deportation so that he could pursue a tort action against the law enforcement officers who had apprehended him and taken him into custody. The Court held that an alien was not entitled to a judicial stay of his deportation unless there was evidence indicating that the Immigration Service was "motivated by an invidious factor" in denying the stay of deportation. Here there is no allegation of any "invidious factors" by INS relating to their deportation.

6. Appellants invoke this Court's jurisdiction under the All-Writs Act, 28 U.S.C. § 1651. Yet it is clear that the most analogous writ to that sought by appellants is the writ *ne exeat* and that issuance of such a writ is never justified unless the underlying action is for equitable relief or a liquidated claim for damages. 9 *Moore's Federal Practice*, § 110.29. *See also D. Ginsberg & Sons v. Popkin*, 285 U.S. 204, 208 (1932). Since appellants, in a tort action such as this, are not entitled to a writ *ne exeat* prohibiting Mr. Pena-Irala or Ms. Villalba from departing the United States, they can hardly be said to be entitled to a writ against the Immigration and Naturalization Service prohibiting it from discharging its obligations under the deportation laws.

WHEREFORE, it is respectfully requested that this Court deny the appellants' motion to the extent that it seeks to enjoin the deportation of Mr. Pena-Irala or Ms. Villalba beyond Wednesday, May 23, 1979.

CYRIL HYMAN

Dated: Brooklyn, New York
      May 18, 1979

MAY 18, 1979: UNITED STATES

Correspondence from Defense Counsel Murry Brochin to Second Circuit Court of Appeals

Lowenstein, Sandler, Brochin, Kohl, Fisher & Boylan
A Professional Corporation

744 Broad Street
Newark, N.J. 07102

Refer to File No.
P 4136

May 18, 1979

Honorable Judges of the United States
   Court of Appeals for the Second Circuit
c/o Edward J. Guardaro Clerk,
Second Cir. Ct. of Appeals
17th Floor
U.S. Courthouse
Foley Square (40 Center Street)
New York City, New York

   Re: Motion of Appellants Filartiga

My dear Judges:

   This letter is submitted on behalf of defendant Pena-Irala and a non-party, Juana Villalba, both of whom are now being held in federal detention awaiting deportation. The stay which previously prevented their detention is no longer in effect. They and their infant child seek their release and return to Paraguay. Plaintiffs are seeking to detain them in custody to take their depositions in a civil suit over which the Court below found it had no subject matter jurisdiction.

   In the District Court defendant Pena-Irala moved to dismiss the complaint and vacate the stay upon three grounds; i.e. for lack of federal jurisdiction, because their detention in the custody of the United States was without legal justification and under the doctrine of *forum non conveniens*. On May 15, 1979, the District Court issued its memorandum and order dismissing the complaint for lack of federal jurisdiction, but continued the stay of deportation for an additional forty-eight hours to enable plaintiffs to apply to this court for a further stay.

The United States Attorney for the Eastern District of New York, representing the federal defendants, submitted a letter dated May 9, 1979, to Judge Nickerson setting forth the Government's position in this matter. The United States attorney argued that "unrelated individuals who seek to enjoin the deportation of a defendant in a civil action that does not involve the Government may not do so," that "a general unliquidated claim for damages, such as the plaintiff's wrongful death claim herein will not support issuance of a writ of *ne exeat*", that the court "plainly lacks jurisdiction to enjoin the defendant Mr. Pena Irala . . . from leaving the United States, much less enjoining the Immigration Service from proceeding with the deportation that is mandated by Congressional statutes", and that "since Ms. Villalba and the child are not even parties to this litigation, it is unreasonable to continue an injunction against their deportation which they do not themselves oppose." The United States attorney asked the court to "dismiss this action against the federal defendants for lack of any conceivable subject matter jurisdiction." We urge this Court to deny the extraordinary relief sought by Appellants. We rely primarily upon the affidavit and brief submitted to the Court below and we respectfully direct the Court's attention to those papers. In addition, however, we wish briefly to supplement our previous argument by this letter.

First of all the hearsay documents which plaintiffs have filed in the Court below purporting to describe the political and legal situation in Paraguay are inflammatory, scandalous and improper. They are entitled to consideration for only one purpose—to demonstrate incontrovertibly that plaintiffs' purpose in instituting this suit in the United States District Court for the Eastern District of New York was to stage a political trial in the guise of a private lawsuit, perverting the processes of that court in order to wage a propaganda war against the government of a foreign state. If any confirmation was needed of plaintiffs' purpose to abuse the processes of our courts, that confirmation was supplied by a "Notice of Taking Deposition" —which plaintiffs' counsel distributed during the course of the argument before Judge Nickerson purporting to notice the deposition of "the Secretary of State, the Assistant Secretary of State for Latin American affairs or other persons designated by them and demanding that the deponents bring with them all cables, memoranda and other communications between the United States Embassy at Asuncion, Paraguay and the Department of State . . . ." and "all information regarding visas granted to Paraguayan police officials or other agents of the Paraguayan government in the last years." For this Court to authorize the continuation of Appellants' campaign despite the District Court's dismissal of the suit for lack of jurisdiction would be to countenance a totally unwarranted intrusion into the diplomatic relations of the United States.

The court below held that it was bound by two recent decisions of this Court interpreting 28 U.S.C. §1350, the statute which plaintiffs have seized upon to support their notion that a District Court of the United States should exercise subject matter jurisdiction over two Paraguayans' civil suit against a third Paraguayan for the wrongful death of another Paraguayan which occurred in Paraguay and which Appellants claim (and Appellee denies) was a politically motivated torture-murder resulting from quarrels between supporters and opponents of the Paraguayan regime. Those two decisions of this court are *Dreyfus v. Von Finck*, 534 F.2d 24 (2d Cir.) *cert. den.*, 429 U.S. 335 (1976) and *IIT v. Vencap, Ltd.*, 519 F.2d 1001 (2d Cir. 1975). It is the teaching of those cases, followed by the court below, that 28 U.S.C. §1350's reference to the "law of nations" must be narrowly read if the section "is to be kept within the confines of Article III of the Constitution." We respectfully urge that this Court should remain equally faithful to the limitations which the Constitution places upon the jurisdiction of the Federal Courts as well as upon their power to detain persons in custody to testify in a civil suit.

We emphasize that Appellee Pena-Irala is a co-defendant in a criminal case now pending in the courts of Paraguay. He is about to be deported to that country. Although Villalba is not now a party to a criminal proceeding, plaintiffs allege in their initial brief to the court below that she "is a crucial material witness to the . . . crime . . . as she shares the same house with Pena-Irala, the house where the body of [the victim] was tortured or brought after his torture-murder." On the basis of Appellants' allegations, it thus appears that Villalba could also reasonably apprehend being named as a defendant in a criminal case. Neither Pena nor Villalba could be compelled to testify against themselves under Paraguayan law. Significantly for this case, the reasonable apprehension of prosecution under the laws of a foreign country is sufficient justification for Pena's and Villalba's invoking the constitutional privilege against self-incrimination in a court of the United States. *In re Letters Rogatory*, 448 F.Supp. 786 (S.D. Fla. 1978). See *Zicarelli v. Investigation Commission*, 406 U.S. 472, 478 (1972); *In Re Grand Jury Proceedings*, 532 F. 2d 404, 406 (5th Cir. 1976), *cert. denied* 429 U.S. 940 (1976). To detain them for the purpose of compelling their testimony would therefore be a futile act as well as an oppressive one.

For all of these reasons and for the reasons argued in the brief submitted to the court below, Appellee Pena-Irala respectfully requests that Appellants' motion to take their depositions and to stay deportation be denied, that the dismissal of this suit for lack of federal jurisdiction be permitted to stand and that Pena, Villalba and their child be deported to their own country.

Respectfully yours,

LOWENSTEIN, SANDLER, BROCHIN,
    KOHL, FISHER & BOYLAN
A Professional Corporation
Attorneys for defendant Pena-Irala

By: _____
    Murry D. Brochin

MAY 22, 1979: UNITED STATES

Second Circuit Court of Appeals: Order

UNITED STATES COURT OF APPEALS
FOR THE SECOND CIRCUIT

DOLLY M.E. FILARTIGA and DR. JOEL FILARTIGA,	**ORDER** **Docket No. 79-6090**
Appellants,	
– against –	
AMERICO NORBERTO PENA-IRALA, et al.	
Appellees.	

Upon this appeal from an order of the District Court for the Eastern District of New York dismissing for lack of jurisdiction this action for damages for wrongful death in which federal jurisdiction has been invoked under Title 28 U.S.C. § 1350, the motion of plaintiffs-appellants for an order (1) authorizing them to take the depositions of defendant and Juana Bautista Fernandez Villalba, (2) staying their deportation, and (3) remanding the case to the district court to oversee the deposition proceedings is

DENIED.

J. Edward Lumbard, U.S.C.J.

Walter R. Mansfield, U.S.C.J.

Murray I. Gurfein, U.S.C.J.

MAY 23, 1979: UNITED STATES

Application to United States Supreme Court for a Stay of Deportation to Permit Taking Immediate Depositions Pending Appeal

IN THE
SUPREME COURT OF THE UNITED STATES

October Term, 1979

No. ___

DOLLY M.E. FILARTIGA and
DR. JOEL FILARTIGA,
Petitioners,

– against –

AMERICO NORBERTO PENA-IRALA, LEONEL CASTILLO, as
Commissioner of the United States Immigration and Naturalization
Service and GEORGE VICIAN, as District Director Thereof,

Respondents.

APPLICATION FOR A STAY OF DEPORTATION
TO PERMIT TAKING IMMEDIATE DEPOSITIONS PENDING APPEAL.

TO: ASSOCIATE JUSTICE THURGOOD MARSHALL,
       CIRCUIT JUSTICE FOR THE SECOND CIRCUIT

DOLLY M.E. FILARTIGA and DR. JOEL FILARTIGA, by their under-signed counsel, hereby move, pursuant to Rules 50 and 51 of this Court, for an order

1) staying the deportation scheduled for this evening of Americo N. Pena-Irala and Juana Villalba to permit the immediate taking of their depositions; and

2) permitting petitioners immediately to take the deposition of defendant Pena-Irala and Juana Villalba, a material witness in connection with petitioners' civil action filed under 28 U.S.C. § 1350; and

3) returning this matter to the District Court for the purpose of supervising this relief; and

4) staying the impending deportation of Pena-Irala and Juana Villalba pending receipt of opposing papers and disposition of the instant Application.

INTRODUCTORY STATEMENT

1. Pena-Irala is the defendant and Juana Villalba is a material witness in connection with petitioners' lawsuit filed under 28 U.S.C. § 1350, charging Pena-Irala with having caused the death of Joelito Filartiga, petitioners' brother and son, by torture, a universally recognized violation of fundamental human rights under the "law of nations."

2. Pena-Irala and Juana Villalba are scheduled to be deported at 9:45 p.m. this evening, May 23, 1979, and preparations for their departure will begin no later than 5:00 p.m. this afternoon.

3. A very brief stay of deportation and an order permitting the immediate taking of their depositions is necessary because this is the last time petitioners will be able to compel their testimony in connection with the civil action now pending on appeal on the issue of the scope of federal jurisdiction under 28 U.S.C. § 1350.

4. The relief is authorized under F.R.C.P. 62(g), since it is "appropriate to preserve the status quo or the effectiveness of the judgment subsequently to be entered."

5. The relief sought is unusual but also unusually simple. It is the minimum necessary to safeguard the interests of the petitioners effectively to pursue, and the capacity of the United States courts meaningfully to adjudicate the complaint, should federal jurisdiction under § 1350 be sustained on appeal. The relief sought was designed in light of the fact that the respondent and Ms. Villalba are presently in custody and in the spirit of minimizing any burden on their rights.

6. Petitioners stand ready to commence these depositions as soon as Your Honor rules on this application. As explained hereinafter, the depositions should be able to be completed expeditiously and should necessitate only the briefest delay in the deportation of respondents.

7. Given the substantial jurisdictional question raised on this appeal, the irreparable injury to petitioners should the witnesses be returned to

Paraguay before being deposed, the minimal burden to the witnesses and the consistency of the relief sought with the paramount public policy of the United States to encourage and implement concrete deterrents to violations of fundamental human rights, petitioners respectfully urge that the interests of justice overwhelmingly justify the limited relief requested herein.

I.
PROCEEDINGS BELOW

8. On April 4, 1979, defendant Pena-Irala and his companion were arrested by agents of the United States Immigration and Naturalization Service (hereinafter "INS") in Brooklyn, New York. On April 5, 1979, they were ordered deported as illegal aliens after admitting that they had been living here illegally for nine months. They were ordered detained in the custody of INS at the Brooklyn Navy Yard subject to extraordinarily high bonds of $75,000 and $25,000 respectively, and they remain in such custody.

9. On April 6, 1979, plaintiffs filed this civil action for wrongful death, submitted herewith as Exhibit A. The gravamen of the complaint is that Pena-Irala, individually and in his official capacity as Inspector General of the Paraguayan police force, tortured and murdered Joelito Filartiga in retaliation for the political activities and opinions of his father, Dr. Joel Filartiga, a leading Paraguayan human rights advocate. Jurisdiction was premised upon 28 U.S.C. § 1350 and on the principle that torture constitutes a violation of the "law of nations." The plaintiff Dr. Filartiga presently resides in Paraguay. The plaintiff Dolly M.E. Filartiga resides in Washington, D.C. as an alien and has an application pending for political asylum. Defendant Pena-Irala has been charged by international human rights organizations as being a well-known member of a police "death squad" that tortures and murders political opponents of Paraguay's dictator President, General Alfredo Stroessner. (See Affidavit of Dolly M.E. Filartiga, attached hereto as Exhibit B.)

10. Upon order to show cause, the District Court on April 9, 1979 stayed the deportation of Pena-Irala and Fernandez Villalba, a material witness to the alleged torts, and issued an order permitting plaintiffs to take their depositions while in custody pursuant to F.R.C.P. 30(a). The depositions were arranged between plaintiffs and the United States Attorney for Thursday morning, April 12, 1979.

11. On April 12, 1979, the witnesses appeared without counsel and upon being advised of their right to counsel by plaintiffs, they stated that

they would not answer questions until their attorney arrived from Paraguay. Upon application of the plaintiffs, Judge Nickerson ordered that the witnesses be brought to court where they stated both that they were invoking the Fifth Amendment privilege, and that they would speak upon arrival of their Paraguayan counsel to the United States. Accordingly, the court advanced the return date on the order to show cause why the depositions should not proceed to April 30, 1979 and continued the stay of deportation. Plaintiffs indicated that they were ready to proceed with the depositions at defense counsel's earliest convenience.

12. On information and belief, defendant Pena-Irala's attorney Jose Emilio Gorostiaga arrived from Paraguay on or about April 23, but did not contact plaintiffs.

13. On April 30, 1979, defendants were represented by Mr. Gorostiaga from Paraguay and Mr. Rebollo from Staten Island. Mr. Rebollo requested a two-week adjournment of the show cause order and extension of the stay to respond to the complaint. The court then advanced the return date to May 14. On May 7, the defendant served his motion to dismiss on jurisdictional grounds and to vacate the stay of deportation. Plaintiffs served responding papers and a hearing was had on May 14, 1979.

14. On May 10, plaintiffs' counsel called defendants' counsel to try to arrange for the depositions following the May 14 hearing. Counsel refused to agree to a schedule without a court order and, at the hearing on May 14, Judge Nickerson reserved decision both on the jurisdictional question and on re-ordering the depositions.

15. In the early afternoon of May 15, 1979, the Judge's chambers notified plaintiffs that he had completed his opinion. The Memorandum and Order (submitted herewith as Exhibit C), explains that, notwithstanding the cogency of plaintiffs' argument that § 1350 jurisdiction should be read to embrace the almost universally approved modern norm of international law proscribing torture, he felt bound by rulings of the United States Court of Appeals for the Second Circuit in other contexts which appear to approve a narrower interpretation of the concept of the "law of nations."

16. In the late afternoon of May 15, the undersigned counsel called the chambers of Judge Nickerson to ask him to reconsider and/or clarify whether, notwithstanding his order dismissing the complaint, he would permit plaintiffs to take the necessary depositions. The law clerk informed me that Judge Nickerson would not order the depositions on the ground that he believed that his dismissal for want of jurisdiction deprived him of the power to order the taking of the depositions, and that he had accordingly

stayed his order to permit application to the United States Court of Appeals for the Second Circuit.

17. Judge Nickerson stayed the deportations for 48 hours to permit application to the Second Circuit Court of Appeals for the relief sought herein. (See Exhibit C.)

18. Plaintiffs' notice of appeal to the Second Circuit was filed on May 16, 1979 (submitted herewith as Exhibit D.)

19. The same day, plaintiffs filed an emergency motion for interim relief seeking the same relief requested herein. The motion was calendared for oral argument at 10:30 a.m. May 22, 1979, approximately 36 hours before the scheduled deportation.

20. At oral argument before a panel of three judges, defendant Pena-Irala's counsel once again objected to an order compelling depositions as well as any stay of deportation. In his opposing papers, he took the position that a deposition would be futile as well as oppressive, claiming that the witnesses would plead the Fifth Amendment. (See Exhibit E hereto.)

21. The Assistant United States Attorney informed the Court that, although the government was taking no position on the jurisdictional question, a number of executive departments had expressed interest in the merits of this appeal. He further indicated that the government did not oppose and stands ready to facilitate the taking of immediate depositions. However, he opposed any stay of the deportations on the ground that the Court lacked power to issue such an order in these circumstances. (See Exhibit F hereto.)

22. The Circuit Court reserved decision on the motion.

23. Following the oral argument, plaintiffs' counsel asked defendant Pena-Irala's counsel to agree to immediate depositions in light of the government's expressed willingness to facilitate them and to avoid delaying his clients' scheduled deportation. He refused, reiterating that he would not allow his clients to be deposed without a court order.

24. At approximately 4:00 p.m. on May 22, 1979, the Clerk of the Second Circuit advised counsel that their motion had been denied without explanation. Counsel will forward a copy of the Court's order as soon as it is obtained.

25. In sum, petitioners are before this Court at this juncture because of the non-cooperation and adjournments sought by counsel for respon-

dent Pena-Irala and the witness Villalba. If their counsel had been truly interested in expediting his clients' return, rather than avoiding the process of the United States courts, the depositions would have been completed weeks ago.

II.
REASONS WHY THE STAY AND THE ORDER PERMITTING DEPOSITIONS SHOULD BE GRANTED

26. The relief sought herein is authorized both by F.R.C.P. 62(g), F.R.A.P. 8(a) and 28 U.S.C. § 1651, the All Writs Act.

27. The applicable standard for relief "appropriate to preserve the status quo or the effectiveness of the judgment subsequently to be entered." F.R.C.P. 62(g) is set forth in *Reserve Mining Co. v. United States*, 498 F.2d 1073, 1076-1077 (8th Cir. 1974), application to vacate stay denied 419 U.S. 802, 95 S.Ct. 287 (1974).

28. In seeking this stay we must make

(1) a strong showing that he is likely to succeed on the merits of the appeal; (2) a showing that, unless a stay is granted, he will suffer irreparable injury; (3) a showing that no substantial harm will come to other interested parties; and (4) a showing that a stay will do no harm to the public interest. Id. at 1076-1077.

29. However, in assessing whether we have met our burden, "factor[s] can [not] be isolated . . . [the] 'court should not and perhaps cannot erect an artificial absolute standard; there are degrees of irreparable injury and probability of a successful appeal. The duty of this Court is to weigh the strength of these showings against each other and [being that it is an equitable test] balance them against the potential harm to the interest of the plaintiff and the public.'" *Evans v. Buchanan*, 455 F. Supp. 705, 708 (D. Del. 1978).

A. *The Appeal Raises Substantial Questions on the Merits as to Which Petitioners Have a Strong Likelihood of Success*

30. The merits of this appeal—the Court's power under 28 U.S.C. § 1350, to entertain this civil action alleging a tort consisting of torture resulting in death—present a substantial and weighty question of the scope of federal jurisdiction. Section 1350 provides that

the district courts shall have original jurisdiction of any civil action by an alien for a tort only, committed in violation of the law of nations or a treaty of the United States.

31. In his Memorandum and Order dismissing the complaint for want of jurisdiction over the subject matter, Judge Nickerson stated that plaintiffs "argue cogently" in favor of "a norm of customary international law condemning torture" but that, "despite the strength of these arguments," he felt bound by the decisions of Second Circuit in *IIT v. Vencap, Ltd.*, 519 F.2d 1001 (1975) and *Dreyfus v. von Finck*, 534 F.2d 24 (1976). Those cases hold that tortious conduct does not violate the "law of nations" unless it also violates "those standards, rules or customs affecting the relationship between states or between an individual and a foreign state, and used by those states for their common good and/or in dealings *inter se.*"

32. It is petitioners' position that this definition of international law is too narrow but that, nonetheless, torture meets the articulated test.

33. First, petitioners have placed in the record affidavits from eminent authorities in international law (submitted herewith as Exhibit G) to the effect that torture is particularly and universally recognized as a violation of the "law of nations."

34. Second, judicially noticeable evidence abounds demonstrating that severe violations of human rights affect the relationship between states.

35. For example, during the past few years Congress has passed legislation to limit economic and military assistance to countries which violate internationally recognized human rights standards. *See, e.g.*, § 32 of the Foreign Assistance Act of 1973 (P.L. 93-189); § 46 of the Foreign Assistance Act of 1974 (P.L. 93-559); § 310 of the International Development and Food Assistance Act of 1975 (P.L. 94-161); §301 of the International Security Assistance and Arms Export Control Act (P.L. 94-329). See also Weissbrodt, Human Rights Legislation and U.S. Foreign Policy, Georgia Journal of Int. & Comp. Law, V. 7, summer 1977, 231-287. Since his inaugural address, President Carter has made human rights violations a central tenet of this Nation's foreign policy. (See authorities cited in Plaintiffs' Memorandum, submitted herewith as Exhibit H.)

36. Third, violations of human rights, in fact, have severely affected state-to-state relationships including that between the United States and Paraguay. Military and economic aid has, in recent years, been eliminated or, substantially reduced based on human rights violations, among which is the very torture-assassination which is the subject of this lawsuit. Approximately

two weeks ago, the Senate Foreign Relations Committee recommended to the Senate that economic aid be denied to Paraguay and eight other countries which are notorious for human rights violations.

37. In addition, petitioners will demonstrate on appeal that although *Vencap* and *Dreyfus* reached correct results, this was so only because the torts alleged—fraud in one case, confiscation of property on racial grounds in the other—were not violative of international law standard at the time the acts were committed.

38. Finally, petitioners will suggest that the dicta in *Vencap* and *Dreyfus* should be revised, since it is based solely on eighteenth and nineteenth century international law authorities and ignores the significant developments in the past three decades introducing the principle that gross violations of human rights are, as a matter of international law, a legitimate and central concern of the world community. *See, e.g., The International Covenant on Civil and Political Rights*, General Assembly Resolution 2200 (XI) 12/16/66; *The Proclamation of Teheran*, U.N. Doc. A/Conf 32/41, U.N. Publ. E.68.XIV.2, endorsed by General Assembly Resolution 2442 (XXIII), 12/19/68; *The American Declaration of the Rights and Duties of Man*, Resolution XXX, Ninth Inter. Conference of American States, Bogota, Columbia, 3/30/-5/2/488; *The American Convention on Human Rights*, OAS Treaty Series No. 36, at 1-21, 1969 OAS; and *The European Convention for the Protection of Human Rights and Fundamental Freedoms, and Protocols Thereunder*, Council of Europe, European Convention on Human Rights: Collected Texts Section 1, Doc. 1 (1971).

39. The undisputed opinion of the experts, the texts and commentaries cited by petitioners and this country's conduct of foreign relations leads, we submit to the inescapable conclusion that the particular tort alleged here is clearly a violation of the "law of nations" giving rise to § 1350 jurisdiction, either because it fits the definition previously articulated by the Second Circuit, or because that definition is too narrow, considering the current state of international law.

40. Pena-Irala's counsel argues vigorously that to recognize § 1350 jurisdiction in this case would do terrible damage to the state-to-state relations between the United States and Paraguay. In this regard, we think it significant to note that the United States Ambassador to Paraguay, in an interview with the Paraguayan press, expressed no such concern. Indeed, he criticized the uproar over the case created by the Paraguayan press, stating:

> I believe that the outrage which Pena's detention has caused has been misplaced. According to the majority of international law attorneys, international law is in a constant state of evolution. One

of the principal roads of that evolution is traced by daring and imaginative decisions of judges who explore new areas. I believe that as international laws condemning human rights violations become stronger, the issue of territoriality loses importance.

Ambassador White likened the right to sue a torturer to the right, which was originally protected by § 1350, of an alien to sue for piracy irrespective of where the tort occurred or of the nationality of the perpetrator, so long as he is found in this country. (The reported interview with Ambassador White with the pertinent portions translated is submitted herewith as Exhibit I.) As we have already noted, the recognition of §1350 jurisdiction in this case is, far from an interference, but rather fully consistent with, this Nation's policy commitments.

B. *Petitioners will Suffer Irreparable Injury In That This Is Their Last Opportunity To Compel These Examinations*

41. Pena-Irala is accused of the torture-murder on which this action is based. Ms. Villalba is a crucial material witness to the alleged tort and crime against human rights as she lives with Pena-Irala and shares the house where Joelito Filartiga was tortured and/or died. She is reported to have stated that she was home at the time of Joelito's death and that she heard his screams. She has also participated in fabrication of a false account of the circumstances of Joelito's death. (See D.M.E. Filartiga Affidavit, ¶¶4, 15.)

42. The witnesses are also uniquely in possession of facts concerning the assets of the respondent Pena-Irala and, therefore, the means by which this Court can attempt to assure his accountability to the continuing process of our courts and to the potential judgment for petitioners.

43. Once the witnesses are returned to Paraguay, there is no assurance whatsoever that they will be amendable to any process of our courts.

44. The respondent Pena-Irala disappeared from Paraguay when his involvement in the torture-murder of Joelito Filartiga and the effort to cover up this deliberate wrongdoing was becoming increasingly notorious and embarrassing to the regime. For nine months he escaped identification by United States Immigration and Naturalization Service officials here. Given this history, it is more than likely that he and his companion Ms. Villalba will likewise seek to escape the future process of our courts and probably be encouraged in so doing by the Stroessner regime.

45. Indeed, it is virtually certain that the Paraguayan Courts will not be amendable to facilitating the process of the Court in this case.

46. Under Rule 28(b), the taking of depositions in foreign countries depends upon the cooperation of local Courts through letters rogatory, and even the most friendly of non-common law countries often will not compel unwilling witnesses to answer. 4 Moore's *Federal Practices*, ¶28.05 (2d ed.). Here, numerous reports, as well as the State Department, have documented the absence of the rule of law in Paraguay and the control of the judiciary by the executive branch, particularly by the police in which the respondent was a high official. (See authorities noted in affidavit of Dolly M.E. Filartiga, ¶¶12-14, Exhibit B.) This means that to defer the taking of testimony until the witnesses are returned to Paraguay unnecessarily invites diplomatic confrontations such as that which is presently occurring between this country and Chile over the latter's refusal to extradite persons charged in the murder of Orlando Letelier and Ronnie Moffitt.

47. The Suggestion of defense counsel in the court below, that Mr. Pena and Ms. Villalba intend to plead the Fifth Amendment at the deposition, unsuccessfully seeks to obviate the harm to petitioners of allowing the witnesses to be deported and thereby escape the future proceedings of our courts.

48. First, a lawyer's statement of intention to plead the Fifth Amendment is without legal significance. The privilege is a personal one and must therefore be personally asserted by the witnesses. Further, it must be asserted in relation to specific questions and cannot be blanketly asserted in advance of the depositions.

49. Thus there is no assurance that the witnesses will assert the Fifth Amendment to all questions to be posed by petitioners and they have previously indicated that they would testify. (See ¶11, p. 4-5, *supra.*) Petitioners are entitled to seek their information. Furthermore, until the questions are posed, it cannot be determined whether the privilege is rightfully asserted, as, for example, respecting questions concerning respondents' assets or official employment. If issues of the validity of any plea should arise, they can be expeditiously resolved by the District Court concurrent with the taking of the depositions. Even to the extent that the respondent and the witness might validly interpose the Fifth Amendment plea, however, petitioners are entitled to have the plea formalized and to proceed following favorable disposition of the appeal on the basis of the preclusionary and other applicable sanctions of the Federal Rules of Civil Procedure.

50. In sum, without permission to take the depositions before deportation, petitioners will lose forever the power to compel their testimony and their submission to judicial process. This is likely to unduly complicate and obstruct petitioners' ability to proceed on the merits of their claim and to

entail prohibitive expense. The policy of F.R.C.P. 30(b)(2) to avoid unnecessary and burdensome procedures and expense when a witness is about to leave the jurisdiction applies with particular force where the underlying action is for violation of civil and human rights and not a garden-variety commercial case.

C. *To Permit These Depositions And Briefly Stay The Deportation Will Not Harm The Defendant-Respondent Or The Witness*

51. The obligation to respond to a deposition is the ordinary duty of every person subject to the Court's jurisdiction, whether citizen or alien, whether detained or at liberty. The law recognizes no special burden in such proceeding.

52. Taking the deposition necessitates only the briefest delay in their deportation, unless further delay is sought by their counsel. Indeed, had respondents' counsel agreed, at any time, to facilitate rather than delay the depositions, they could have been completed weeks ago and most certainly prior to the scheduled deportation this evening.

D. *The Paramount Public Interest Of This Country Would Be Served By Granting The Interim Relief Sought*

53. The construction of § 1350 sought by petitioners on appeal is consistent with and supportive of the public policy commitment of this country—through its administration and laws—to concern itself with and deter violations of fundamental human rights abroad.

54. This case has drawn enormous attention in the Paraguayan press and has been consistently distorted to favor Pena and the Stroessner regime and cast petitioners in a bad light. It is clear that the denial of the relief sought here will likewise be presented as vindicating the respondent and thereby weakening our stated public policy commitment to human rights.

55. Moreover, petitioners here, like the domestic civil rights plaintiffs who courageously expanded federal jurisdiction, have invoked the jurisdiction of the federal courts to redress violations of human rights at great risk to their lives and safety. The risks are revealed in the previous retaliation against them and their Paraguayan attorney by the Stroessner regime and its courts, and in the threats made, even in this country, toward the person who identified Pena-Irala to the INS. (See affidavits of Dolly M.E. Filartiga, Exhibit B, ¶¶15-19, and of Gilberto Olmedo Sanchez, Exhibit J.) The Paraguayan press reports the statements by Pena-Irala's attorney Gorostiaga that he is contemplating action against the petitioners in retaliation for their having commenced this lawsuit here. (Exhibit K hereto).

56. The United States courts are ultimately powerless to protect the Filartiga family against legal and extra-legal retaliation abroad. However, to grant the relief sought here would contribute to vindicating their courageous effort by explicitly recognizing the substantiality of the jurisdictional question presented. This explicit recognition is essential if aliens are not to be chilled from rightfully invoking the jurisdiction of the federal courts under § 1350, which jurisdiction should properly be recognized on appeal.

E. *This Court Has Power To Grant The Relief Requested.*

57. Respondents erroneously assert that the Court lacks power to stay the deportation. They rely on a series of inapposite immigration cases which refused to overturn administrative determinations by INS that the alien-plaintiff should be deported despite the pendency of a civil action. (See Exhibits E and F.) *Bolanos v. Kiley*, 509 F.2d 1023, 1026 (2d Cir. 1975); *Lad v. Immigration and Naturalization Service*, 539 F.2d 808, 809 (1st Cir. 1976); *Adam v. INS*, 349 F. Supp. 313 (N.D. Ill. 1972); *Prassinos v. District Director*, 193 F. Supp. 416 (N.D. Ohio, 1960); *aff'd per curiam* 289 F. 2d 490 (6th Cir. 1961), *cert. denied* 366 U.S. 966.

58. The citation to *Bolanos* is particularly curious since a brief stay was granted there to assure that the defendant in the alien's lawsuit could complete pretrial discovery. The inherent power of the court to stay a deportation in appropriate circumstances where the substantiality of the civil claim and need to remain is shown was also recognized in *Hong v. Agency for Int'l Development*, 470 F.2d 507 (9th Cir. 1972).

59. The power to grant the brief stay sought here to permit the depositions is, indubitably, found in F.R.C.P. 62(g) and 28 U.S.C. § 1651, the "All Writs Act," which give this Court power to aid its ability, and ultimately that of the lower federal courts, to exercise meaningful jurisdiction over this civil action and preserve the effectiveness of future judgments. Three cases bear special mention in this regard. *Price v. Johnson*, 334 U.S. 266, 282, 88 S. Ct. 1049 (1948), affirms the authority of the federal courts under 28 U.S.C. § 1651 to fashion "procedural instruments designed to achieve 'the rational ends of justice.'" The Supreme Court's decision in *Harris v. Nelson*, 394 U.S. 286, 300, 89 S. Ct. 1082, *reh. denied* 394 U.S. 1025, 89 S. Ct. 1623 (1969), affirms that § 1651 power authorizes the issuance of discovery orders even where the Federal Rules of Civil Procedure explicitly makes them unavailable "when necessary . . . in order that a fair and meaningful evidentiary hearing may be held so that the court may properly 'dispose of the matter as law and justice require.'"

60. Finally, the Court has construed 28 U.S.C. § 1651 to provide even broader power than that given by Rule 62(g). In *F.T.C. v. Dean Foods*, 384

U.S. 597, 86 S. Ct. 1738 (1966), the Court affirmed the power to issue writs in anticipation of future appeals being filed. Here, the appeal is pending, and the authority of Rule 62(g) is sufficient basis for the relief requested.

WHEREFORE, in view of the weighty jurisdictional question presented on appeal and the decided balance of the equities in favor of the relief requested, petitioners pray for an order permitting them to take the depositions of Pena-Irala and Fernandez Villalba forthwith and staying the deportations for the brief period necessary to accomplish this relief.

Respectfully submitted,

PETER WEISS
RHONDA COPELON
JOHN W. CORWIN
JOSE ANTONIO LUGO
c/o Center for Constitutional Rights
853 Broadway
New York, New York 10003

MICHAEL MAGGIO
Goren and Maggio
1801 Columbia Road, N.W.
Washington, D.C. 20009
(202) 483-8055

Attorneys for Petitioners

Dated: New York, N.Y.
      May 23, 1979

MAY 24, 1979: UNITED STATES

United States Supreme Court: Order

OFFICE OF THE CLERK
SUPREME COURT OF THE UNITED STATES
WASHINGTON, D.C. 20543

May 24, 1979

Rhonda Copelon, Esquire
Center for Constitutional Rights
853 Broadway, 14th Floor
New York, NY 10003

      Re: Dolly M.E. Filartiga et al. v. Americo Norberto Pena-Irala, et al.
      A-1017

Dear Ms. Copelon:

Your application for stay of deportation, presented to Mr. Justice Marshall and by him referred to the Court, is denied.

A copy of the order of the Court is enclosed.

                   Very truly yours,

                   MICHAEL RODAK, JR., Clerk

cc: The Honorable Wade H. McCree, Jr.
    Solicitor General of the United States
    Department of Justice
    Washington, D.C. 20530

    Murray Brochin, Esquire
    744 Broad Street
    Newark. New Jersey 07102

    Daniel Fusaro, Esquire
    Clerk, U.S. Court of Appeals for the Second Circuit
    Room 1702—U.S. Courthouse
    Foley Square
    New York, New York 10007

THURSDAY, MAY 24, 1979

ORDERS IN PENDING CASES

A-1016 JOHN A. SPINKELLINK V. LOUIE WAINWRIGHT ET AL.

The application for stay of execution, presented to Mr. Justice Marshall and by him referred to the Court, is denied.

Mr. Justice Brennan and Mr. Justice Marshall would grant the application for a stay of execution. Furthermore, they object because the Court announces its action without first affording them an opportunity to prepare, circulate and file a statement in support of their view.

A-1020 LOUIE WAINWRIGHT ET AL. V. JOHN A. SPINKELLINK.

The motion of the Attorney General of Florida to vacate the order entered by Hon. Elbert Parr Tuttle, Senior Judge of the United States Court of Appeals for the Fifth Circuit on May 22, 1979 is denied.

Mr. Justice Rehnquist reserves the right to file a written statement at a future date.

A-1017 DOLLY M.E. FILARTIGA ET AL. V. AMERICO NORBERTO PENA-IRALA, ET AL.

The application for stay of deportation, presented to Mr. Justice Marshall and by him referred to the Court, is denied.

JULY 3, 1979: UNITED STATES

Brief of Amici Curiae (Amnesty International USA, International League for Human Rights, and Lawyers Committee for International Human Rights) on Behalf of Appellants

In The United States Court of Appeals
For The Second Circuit

No. 79-6090

Dolly M.E. Filartiga and Dr. Joel Filartiga,

Plaintiffs-Appellants,

v.

Americo N. Pena-Irala, et al.,
Defendant-Appellee.

On Appeal from the United States District Court
for the Eastern District of New York

Brief for Amnesty International-U.S.A., the International League
for Human Rights, and the Lawyers' Committee for International
Human Rights,
as Amici Curiae

Donald L. Doernberg
17 Franklin Avenue
Croton-on-Hudson, New York 10520
(914) 682-7258

David Weissbrodt*
Professor of Law
University of Minnesota
Law School
285 Law Building
229 19th Avenue South
Minneapolis, Minnesota 55455
(612) 373-2724

Attorneys for Amici Curiae

* Professor Weissbrodt was assisted by Dianne Isaacson, a student at the University of Minnesota Law School. The University of Minnesota Law School is Professor Weissbrodt's place of business. The University of Minnesota takes no part in these proceedings.

TABLE OF CONTENTS

QUESTIONS PRESENTED

1. Whether the District Court should accept jurisdiction of a case under 28 U.S.C. § 1350 for torture "committed in violation of the law of nations or a treaty of the United States."

2. Whether the District Court has "arising under" jurisdiction pursuant to 28 U.S.C. § 1331.

3. Whether the District Court is the only forum where the plaintiffs-appellants can obtain justice.

INTEREST OF AMICI CURIAE

Torture is a gross violation of international human rights laws. Amici Curiae believe that the civil jurisdiction of U.S. courts should be available to torture victims and/or their families when torturers are found within the United States. This country should not offer safe haven for torturers by refusing to consider tort suits arising under customary international law and treaties of the United States, which forbid torture.

This case involves a single innocent victim of a single infamous torturer in a distant nation, Paraguay. But this court's decision will determine whether vicious torturers will be permitted safe haven in the United States and whether this country is serious in its public, statutory, and treaty commitment to international human rights law. This brief is intended to place the present case in that larger context and to afford an international perspective upon the grim world problem of torture.

Amici Curiae are three human rights organizations: Amnesty International-U.S.A., the International League for Human Rights, and the Lawyers' Committee for International Human Rights.

Amnesty International is a worldwide organization, centered in London and established in 1961. Amnesty International-U.S.A. is one of 38 national sections and has over 100,000 U.S. members and/or contributors. Amnesty International is concerned with the protection of human rights around the world, with particular interest in the release of prisoners of conscience, the prevention of torture, and the abolition of capital punishment. In recent years, Amnesty International has made a considerable number of diplomatic, as well as public, appeals in regard to serious violations of human rights in Paraguay. The last few annual reports of Amnesty International indicate the organization's considerable activities in regard to Paraguay. In addition, Amnesty International has issued a briefing paper on the situation in Paraguay, which is mentioned several times and reproduced in the record. *Amnesty International Briefing: Paraguay* (July 1976).

Furthermore, Amnesty International has been very concerned about the problem of torture and the establishment of international norms to proscribe and prevent torture.

The International League for Human Rights was formed in 1942 and comprises 38 affiliates, with hundreds of thousands of members throughout the world. Altogether, the League has affiliates and correspondents in 60 countries. One of the League's affiliates is the Paraguayan Commission for the Defense of Human Rights. The International League for Human Rights deals with a wide variety of human rights issues, and enjoys consultative status with the United Nations, UNESCO, the Council of Europe, and the I.L.O. The League has shown particular interest in Paraguay by sending two investigatory missions for the purpose of studying the status of human rights. See, for example, Stephansky and Alexander, *Report of Commission on Enquiry Into Human Rights in Paraguay of the International League for Human Rights* (Sept. 1976). In addition, the League has been the author of several communications to the United Nations on behalf of human rights victims in Paraguay.

The Lawyers' Committee for International Human Rights is also an organization concerned with human rights. The Lawyers' Committee, which was founded in 1975 by the International League for Human Rights and the Council of New York Law Associates, was established as a legal resource center for human rights organizations. The Lawyers' Committee is supported by a grant from the Ford Foundation and works on specific cases where legal assistance may contribute to the redress of international human rights violations.

PRELIMINARY STATEMENT

The plaintiffs have instituted this lawsuit to recover damages for the brutal torture and murder of Joelito Filartiga, who was plaintiff Joel Filartiga's son and plaintiff Dolly Filartiga's brother.

As alleged in their complaint, on March 29, 1976, 17 year-old Joelito Filartiga was kidnapped, tortured, and viciously murdered by the defendant Americo Norberto Pena-Irala. The senseless murder of this young boy was in retaliation for his father's political beliefs and resistance to the dictatorship of General Stroessner. Following the execution, Paraguayan police ordered plaintiff Dolly Filartiga to defendant Pena-Irala's home, where she saw the mutilated body of her brother and was harassed by the defendant. As a result, she has experienced intense emotional distress and pain.

As amici curiae, we urge the court to accept jurisdiction of the present case. There is no dispute that the court has personal jurisdiction over the defendant, as he was found in New York and served process while in custody for immigration-related offenses. There is a question of whether the court has subject-matter jurisdiction. In this brief, we will show that 28

U.S.C. § 1331 and § 1350 establish the basis for the court's jurisdiction and that there is no other place where the plaintiffs can obtain a remedy for this grievous harm.

ARGUMENT

I.
THE DISTRICT COURT HAS JURISDICTION UNDER 28 U.S.C. § 1350

28 U.S.C. § 1350 states: "The District Court shall have original jurisdiction of any civil action by an alien for a tort only, committed in violation of the law of nations or a treaty of the United States." The parties have agreed that the plaintiffs' claim is "for a tort only." We will show that the torture and murder of Joelito Filartiga violated a treaty of the United States. In addition, the "law of nations," as incorporated into United States law, proscribes all torture or cruel and inhuman treatment. Accordingly, § 1350 affords the district court jurisdiction over this matter.

A. *Torture is Prohibited by a Treaty of the United States*

1. *The United Nations Charter is a Treaty of the United States and Paraguay, Promoting Respect for and Observance of Human Rights*

Article 55 of the Charter of the United Nations states: "With a view to the creation of conditions of stability and well being which are necessary for peaceful and friendly relations among nations . . . the United Nations shall promote . . . universal respect for, and observance of, human rights and fundamental freedoms for all without distinction as to race, sex, language, or religion." Article 56 goes on to state: "All Members pledge themselves to take joint and separate action in cooperation with the Organization for the achievement of the purposes set forth in Article 55."

The Universal Declaration of Human Rights,[1] the International Covenant on Economic, Social and Cultural Rights,[2] and the International Covenant on Civil and Political Rights,[3] give authoritative definition to and make specific the meaning of human rights as set forth in the Charter.[4] Article 5 of the Universal Declaration states: "No one shall be subjected to

---

[1] Universal Declaration of Human Rights, adopted by the United Nations General Assembly on December 10, 1948 (G.A. Res. 217A (III), U.N. Doc. A/810 at 71 (1948)). [hereinafter cited as Universal Declaration].

[2] International Covenant on Economic, Social and Cultural Rights, entered into force January 3, 1976, G.A. Res. 2200A, 21 U.N. GAOR, Supp. (No. 16) 49, U.N. Doc.

torture or to cruel, inhuman or degrading treatment or punishment." Similarly, Article 7 of the Covenant on Civil and Political Rights proscribes torture and cruel, inhuman or degrading treatment or punishment. The United States and Paraguay are bound further, in the language of the Covenants, "to ensure that any person whose rights or freedoms . . . are violated shall have an effective remedy,"[5] to be "determined by competent judicial, administrative, or legislative authorities."[6]

More recently, the United Nations General Assembly has further elaborated the meaning of Articles 55 and 56 in adopting the Declaration on the Protection of All Persons from Torture and other Cruel, Inhuman or Degrading Treatment or Punishment.[7] The Declaration Against Torture condemns torture "as a denial of the purposes of the Charter of the United Nations . . ."[8] As such, all members of the United Nations are bound to "take effective measures to prevent torture."[9] Paraguay is thus in violation of the Charter of the United Nations by torturing its citizens.

Since the Charter is also a treaty of the United States, Paraguay is "in violation of . . . a treaty of the United States" according to 28 U.S.C. § 1350. Therefore, the United States is empowered to "take . . . separate action . . . for the achievement of the purposes set forth in Article 55" of the Charter.[10] If the district court fails to take jurisdiction of the present case,

---

A/6316 (1967). [hereinafter cited as Covenant on Economic, Social and Cultural Rights].

[3] International Covenant on Civil and Political Rights, entered into force March 23, 1976, G.A. Res. 2200A, 21 U.N. GAOR, Supp. (No. 16) 49, 52, U.N. Doc. A/6316 (1967). [hereinafter cited as Covenant on Civil and Political Rights].

[4] The International Bill of Human Rights is a United Nations General Assembly document composed of the Universal Declaration, the two Human Rights Covenants, and the Optional Protocol. Secretary-General Kurt Waldheim observed: "These historic international instruments will furnish the United Nations and its Members important tools for the achievement of one of the main objectives of the Charter . . . the promotion of human rights for all. . ." United Nations, The International Bill of Human Rights 3 (1978); *see also* Weissbrodt, *United States Ratification of the Human Rights Covenants*, 63 Minn. L. Rev. 35, 35-42 (1978).

[5] Covenant on Civil and Political Rights, Art. 2(3) (a).

[6] *Id.* Art. 2(3) (b).

[7] Declaration on the Protection of All Persons from Torture and other Cruel, Inhuman or Degrading Treatment or Punishment, adopted December 9, 1975, G.A. Res. 3452 (XXX), 30 U.N. GAOR Supp. (No. 34) 91, U.N. Doc. A/1034 (1975). [hereinafter cited as Declaration Against Torture].

[8] Declaration Against Torture, Art. 2.

[9] *Id.* Art. 4

the United States may also be in violation of the Charter.

2. *Case Law Interpreting the Language of Section 1350: "in Violation of a Treaty of the United States"*

The defense attempts to use the case of *Dreyfus v. Von Finck*, 534 F.2d 24 (2d Cir.), *cert. denied*, 429 U.S. 835 (1976), to argue that the plaintiffs' cause of action is not "in violation of a treaty of the United States." The *Dreyfus* case is, however, easily distinguishable from the present situation. In that case, it was not clear to the court that there was a violation of a treaty. Consequently, they indicated that the confiscation of property in Nazi Germany in 1938 was merely associated indirectly with the Hague Convention, the Kellogg-Briand Pact, the Versailles Treaty, and the Four Power Occupation Agreement. *Dreyfus*, 534 F.2d at 26-27. The *Dreyfus* court went on to declare that only when a treaty prescribes rules by which private rights may be determined, can a court rely upon it for the enforcement of those rights. *Dreyfus*, 534 F.2d at 20. *See also*, Crandall, *Treaties: Their Making and Enforcement*, 160-61 (2d Ed. 1916).

In the present case, the relationship between the Charter of the United Nations, the Covenant on Civil and Political Rights, the Declaration Against Torture, and the plaintiffs' claim is sufficiently direct to "arise under" the treaties of the United States, as required by Article III, Section 2, clause 1, of the Constitution. The essential purpose of these documents is to prevent human rights violations and to furnish effective remedies to persons whose rights have been violated. The plaintiffs' complaint alleges such violations and seeks a remedy so as to directly arise under these treaties of the United States.

B. *Torture is Prohibited by the Law of Nations and Customary International Law*

At the time of its adoption in 1789, the Constitution accepted the law of nations (presently called international law) as part of the country's national law.[11] Since that historic date, the federal courts have been determining international law as constituting federal law.[12] As early as 1820, in *United States v. Smith*, 18 U.S. (5 Wheat.) 153, 160 (1820), Justice Story stated that the "law of nations . . . may be ascertained by consulting the works of jurists . . . or by the general usage and practice of nations; or by

---

[10] Charter of the United Nations, Art. 56.

[11] Dickinson, *The Law of Nations as Part of the National Law of the United States*, 101 Pa. L. Rev. 26, 48 (1952).

[12] Henkin, *Foreign Affairs and the Constitution* 223 (1972).

judicial decisions recognizing and enforcing that law." Justice Gray developed this principle further by asserting that judicial tribunals resort to the works of jurists "not for the speculations of their authors concerning what the law ought to be, but for trustworthy evidence of what the law really is." *The Paquete Habana*, 175 U.S. 677, 700 (1900).

Torture is proscribed by conventional, customary, and general principles of international law.[13] Its prohibition is embodied in the Universal Declaration (Art. 5) and the Covenant on Civil and Political Rights (Art. 7). The Universal Declaration has become part of the customary law of nations because of judicial consensus resulting in its invocation as law on countless occasions.[14] Likewise, the United States has signed the Covenant on Civil and Political Rights. Under customary international law, by signing the Covenant, the United States is obligated to avoid violating the treaty.[15]

Further evidence of worldwide condemnation of torture is found in U.N. Resolution 3059[16] and in the declaration pronounced at the Amnesty International Conference for the Abolition of Torture.[17] The Declaration stated in part:

The use of torture is a violation of all principles of human freedom and of the life and dignity of the human person, and as such must be identified as a crime against humanity.

1. *U.S. Foreign Policy Objectives Require That the Court Assume Jurisdiction of This Case*

Several weeks before his election, President Carter outlined his intentions for this nation's foreign policy:

---

[13] Association Internationale de Droit Penal, *The Prevention and Suppression of Torture* 280 (1977).

[14] Humphrey, *The Implementation of International Human Rights Law*, 24 N.Y.L.S. L. Rev. 31, 32-33 (1978).

[15] Vienna Convention on the Law of Treaties, Art. 18, U.N. Doc. A/CONF. 39/27 (1969), reprinted in United Nations Conference on the Law of Treaties 291, U.N. Doc. A/CONF. 39/ II/Add. 2 (1971) ("A State is obliged to refrain from acts which would defeat the object and purpose of a treaty when . . . it has signed the treaty or . . . expressed its consent to be bound by the treaty. . .").

[16] Resolution 3059, adopted by the United Nations General Assembly on November 2, 1973, G.A. Res. 3059, 28 U.N. GAOR, Supp. (No. 30) 74, *U.N.* Doc. A/9030 (1973). The Resolution rejects torture and implores all States "to become parties to existing international instruments which contain provisions relating to the prohibition of torture . . . ."

[17] The Conference met in Paris on December 10-11, 1973.

We should begin by having it understood that if any nation, what-ever its political system, deprives its people of basic human rights, that fact will help shape our people's attitude toward that nation's government. If other nations want our friendship and support, they must understand that we want to see basic human rights respected.[18]

President Carter repeated these thoughts at a speech to the United Nations General Assembly when he asserted that "no member of the U.N. can claim that mistreatment of its citizens is solely its own business. Equally no member can avoid its responsibilities to review and to speak when torture or unwarranted deprivation of freedom occurs in any part of the world."[19]

Even before President Carter's election, the Congress had enacted legislation addressed to human rights problems throughout the world. Section 502B of the Foreign Assistance Act has created a statutory obligation for the United States to "promote the increased observance of internationally recognized human rights by all countries."[20] This provision establishes an affirmative duty for the United States to take action to prevent and halt violations of human rights. Hence, the United States must accept jurisdiction of this case to be consistent with this nation's human rights policy.

Congress has enacted a considerable body of specific legislation in an effort to promote international human rights. Under Section 502B, Congress has provided for the termination or restriction of military aid "to any country which engages in a consistent pattern of gross violations of internationally recognized human rights."[21] Similar limitations have been attached to bilateral economic aid[22] and food aid.[23] "Gross violations" are statutorily defined to include torture.[24]

All of these statutory provisions lead to the conclusion that human rights violations affect United States relations with foreign countries. Therefore, the present case presents a violation of the law of nations under

---

[18] Address by Jimmy Carter, B'nai B'rith Convention (Sept. 8, 1976).

[19] Address by President Carter, United Nations, 76 Dep't. State Bull. 332 (1977); reprinted in New York Times, March 18, 1977, at 10, col. 1.

[20] 22 U.S.C.A. § 2304(a) (1) (1979).

[21] 22 U.S.C.A. § 2304(a) (2) (1979).

[22] 22 U.S.C.A. § 2151n (1979).

[23] 7 U.S.C.A. § 1712 (Supp. 1979).

[24] 22 U.S.C.A. §§ 2304(d) (1), 2151n(a), 7 .U.S.C.A. § 1712(a).

28 U.S.C. § 1350 according to the two criteria established in *Lopes v. Reederei Richard Schroeder*, 225 F. Supp. 292 (E.D. Pa. 1963)—one of only a handful of reported cases construing Section 1350. The *Lopes* court defined the phrase "in violation of the law of nations" to mean a violation by one or more individuals of those standards, rules, or customs (a) affecting the relationship between states or between an individual and a foreign state, and (b) used by those states for their common good and/or in dealings inter se. *Lopes*, 225 F. Supp. at 297. The Second Circuit echoed these same criteria in *IIT v. Vencap, Ltd.*, 519 F.2d 1001, 1015 (2d Cir. 1975).

As already demonstrated by Section 502B, similar statutory provisions, this Administration's public statements, and the conduct of this nation's foreign policy, human rights violations do affect the relationships between states.[25] To be consistent with the United States' human rights objectives and policies, the district court must construe 28 U.S.C. § 1350 broadly. Section 1350 functions as an independent grant of federal jurisdiction in situations where the conduct of the parties so offends the standards of conduct underpinning international relations that it can be considered a violation of the law of nations. *Valanga v. Metropolitan Life Insurance Co.*, 259 F. Supp. 324, 327-328 (E.D. Pa. 1966). The torture and murder of young Joelito Filartiga is such a gross violation of human rights as to be a violation of the "law of nations."

2. *Recent Developments Make Individuals a Subject of International Human Rights Law*

International human rights law has injected a new dimension into traditional international law, which only concerned the relations between states. Under the new international law of human rights which has developed since 1948, individual men and women are subjects possessing inter-

---

[25] There are numerous historical instances when human rights violations caused a disruption or termination of friendly relations among states. For example, in 1902, the Unites States protested against persecution of Jews in Romania in violation of the International Treaty of Berlin of 1878.

Even though the United States was not a party to the treaty, it protested because of "principles of law and eternal justice." A further example is illustrated by the adoption of a resolution by the United Nations General Assembly on December 8, 1946. The resolution stated that because of the treatment of Indians in South Africa, "friendly relations between two member states (India and South Africa) have been impaired, and unless a satisfactory settlement is reached, these relations are likely to be further impaired." *See* Jessup, *A Modern Law of Nations* 88 (1948). Many more historical and recent examples of how human rights violations have affected U.S. relations with other countries may be found in Weissbrodt, *Human Rights Legislation and United States Foreign Policy*, 7 Ga. J. Int'l and Comp. L. 231, 232-240, 278-281 (1977).

national legal personalities.[26] Past decisions, like *Dreyfus v. Von Finck*, 534 F.2d 24, 31, fail to take into account the recent development of international human rights law within international law. It is now clear that if a nation commits gross violations of human rights upon its own citizens, those violations can become a subject of international concern and may be the basis for complaints by individuals to international organizations, other nations, and to the world community at large.[27] It is now generally accepted that the welfare of all societies is jeopardized by failure to recognize human rights.[28] Recognition of human rights is necessary for continued friendly relations with all nations of the world. It is already the law, at least for members of the United Nations, that respect for human dignity and fundamental human rights is obligatory.[29] See also 22 U.S.C.A. § 2304(a) (1) (1979).

Inherent in the concept of fundamental human rights is that those rights inhere in the individual and are not derived from the State. International human rights law applies to the individual and does not disappear when he enters the territory of his own State or of any other State.[30] The Charter of the United Nations, customary international law (as embodied in the Universal Declaration of Human Rights), and numerous human rights treaties place human rights under international guarantee.[31] Hence, a State may not ignore international concern about violations of those rights on the ground that the victims were its citizens and that international law leaves a State free to deal with its own as it wills.[32] The treatment by a State of its own citizens is no longer a matter essentially within the domestic jurisdiction. [33]

---

[26] Humphrey, *The Implementation of International Human Rights Law*, 24 N.Y.L.S. L. Rev. 31, 33 (1978).

[27] *See* 1 Hyde, *International Law* 33-36, § 11A (2d rev. ed. 1945); *see generally*, Weissbrodt, *The Role of International Nongovernmental Organizations in the Implementation of Human Rights*, 12 Tex. Int'l L.J. 293 (1977). *See also Human Rights in Uruguay and Paraguay: Hearings Before the Subcomm. on International Organizations of the House Comm. on International Relations*, 94th Cong., 2d Sess. (1976).

[28] 1 Hyde, *International Law* 38-39, § 11C (2d rev. ed. 1945).

[29] United Nations Charter, Art. 55 and 56; Universal Declaration, *supra*, note 1 at 2; Jessup, *A Modern Law of Nations* 91 (1948).

[30] *See* 1 Hyde, *International Law* 34, § 11A (2d rev. ed. 1945); *see also* Weissbrodt, *United States Ratification of the Human Rights Covenants*, 63 Minn. L. Rev. 35, 47 n. 82 (1978).

[31] 1 Hyde, *International Law* 38, § 11C.

[32] Jessup, *A Modern Law of Nations* 87 (1948).

[33] *Id.*

In conclusion, in light of new developments, the decisions in *Dreyfus v. Von Finck*, 534 F.2d 24, 30-31, and *Salimoff & Co. v. Standard Oil Co.*, 262 N.Y. 220, 186 N.E. 679 (1933), that violations of international law do not occur when the aggrieved parties are nationals of the acting state, are no longer good law—at least insofar as human rights violations are concerned. Even if the court should uphold *Dreyfus*, the present case is easily distinguishable. The underlying tort in *Dreyfus* was the wrongful acquisition of property. In the present case, torture and murder are universally condemned by international law no matter where they occur (*supra* at 6-8). In contrast, there unfortunately exists no internationally accepted norm about the taking of property.[34]

3. *Torture is so Heinous as to Give Courts Universal Jurisdiction at International Law*

The commission of particular acts may be so detrimental to the welfare of the international community as to be declared violations of international law. Piracy and the slave trade have long been regarded as these types of offenses.[35] Piracy, for example, has been considered an offense "against the law of nations" and the offender has been subject to punishment by any nation capturing him.[36] As declared in *In re Piracy Jure Gentium* [1934]A.C. 586, "A person guilty of such piracy has placed himself beyond the protection of any state. He is no longer a national but hostes humani generis and as such he is justiciable by any State anywhere. . . ." In addition, slave trading was made punishable as piracy.[37]

The phrase "hostes humani generic" has traditionally been applied to pirates and slave traders to mean "enemies to all mankind" and thus to identify the enormity and odiousness of those offenses.[38] Hostes humani generis are, therefore, subjects of universal criminal jurisdiction.[39] Section 1350 essentially adopts this same approach for universal civil jurisdiction over those who commit torts which are the subject of international disapproval.

Recently it has been suggested that international law declare torture to be an international crime and adopt universal criminal jurisdiction over torturers.[40] An international treaty against torture is now in the drafting

---

[34] *See* Weissbrodt, *United States Ratification of the Human Rights Covenants*, 63 Minn. L. Rev. 35, 46 n. 77 (1978).

[35] Borchard, *The Diplomatic Protection of Citizens Abroad* 738 (1915); Dickinson, *Is the Crime of Piracy Obsolete?*, 38 Harv. L. Rev. 334, 338 (1925).

[36] *See United States v. Smith*, 18 U.S. (5 Wheat.) 153, 161-162 (1820).

[37] *See* 18 U.S.C. § 1585; F.C.A. 18, § 1585.

[38] Dickinson, *Is the Crime of Piracy Obsolete?*, 38 Harv. L. Rev. 334, 351 (1925).

[39] *Id.*; Dickinson, *The Law of Nations as Part of the National Law of the United States*, 101 Pa. L. Rev. 26, 29 (1952).

process at the United Nations Human Rights Commission and the present working document establishes such universal criminal jurisdiction for torturers. This court, however, need not reach that issue, as the plaintiffs in the present case merely seek civil jurisdiction for a tort.

As has been the case with piracy and the slave trade, torture must be considered an offense against the law of nations. The offense is considered so heinous, torturers are so difficult to apprehend, and the interest in prompt determination of torture claims has become so universally recognized,[41] that torturers should be considered hostes humani generis at least for purposes of universal civil jurisdiction under Section 1350.

II.
THE CONSTITUTION PERMITS THE COURT TO OBTAIN JURISDICTION UNDER ARTICLE III, SECTION 2

Article III, Section 2, of the Constitution states in part:

Section 2. The judicial power shall extend to all Cases in Law and Equity, *arising under* this Constitution, *the Laws of the United States, and Treaties* made, or which shall be made, under their authority; to all cases affecting Ambassadors, other public Ministers and Consuls; to all Cases of Admiralty and maritime Jurisdiction; . . . and between a State, or the Citizens thereof, and foreign States, Citizens or Subjects. (Emphasis added.)

Section 1350, which authorizes the district court to assume jurisdiction over acts committed in violation of the law of nations or a treaty of the United States, is constitutional because it establishes jurisdiction under the language "arising under this Constitution, the Laws of the United States, and Treaties. . . ." A tort action for the torture and murder of Joelito Filartiga "arises under" treaties of the United States (*supra* at 5-8) and "the laws of the United States" (*supra* at 9-10), as the law of nations is a law of the United States.[42] Given the venerable age of Section 1350, which originated in the Judiciary Act of 1789, it is very doubtful that a serious argument can now be sustained that this provision is inconsistent with the Constitution.

---

[40] Association Internationale de Droit Penal, *The Prevention and Suppression of Torture* 289-290 (1977).

[41] Universal Declaration (Art. 5), *supra*, note 1, at p. 7; Covenant on Civil and Political Rights (Art. 7), *supra*, note 3, at p. 7.

[42] Dickinson, *The Law of Nations as Part of the National Law of the United States*, 101 Pa. L. Rev. 26, 48 (1952).

Finally, plaintiff Dolly Filartiga came to the United States seeking asylum and is presently a resident of Washington, D.C. She seeks permanent residence here in the United States. This situation differs from that of *Dreyfus v. Von Finck*, 534 F.2d 24, where the plaintiff was a resident of Switzerland and the defendant was a resident of Germany. Therefore, the district court has a far greater interest in accepting jurisdiction over this case to afford the resident plaintiff an impartial tribunal.

III.
THE DISTRICT COURT HAS "ARISING UNDER" JURISDICTION UNDER 28 U.S.C. § 1331

28 U.S.C. § 1331(a) states: "The district courts shall have original jurisdiction of all civil actions wherein the matter in controversy exceeds the sum or value of $10,000, exclusive of interest and costs, and arises under the Constitution, laws, or treaties of the United States. . . ."

This language is similar to that of Article III, Section 2. Both treaties and customary international law are "laws of the United States."[43] Since it has already been demonstrated that the torture of Joelito Filartiga was in violation of both treaties of the United States and customary international law, the present situation creates a substantial federal question. The rule is that mere assertion of such a claim is sufficient to give the court jurisdiction to determine it, unless the claim is plainly unsubstantial. *Spiesel v. City of New York*, 239 F. Supp. 106, 108 (S.D.N.Y. 1964). Therefore, even if the court refuses to accept jurisdiction under § 1350, the District Court must accept jurisdiction of the present case under § 1331.

IV.
THE DISTRICT COURT WILL PROVIDE THE ONLY FAIR AND IMPARTIAL FORUM AVAILABLE TO THESE PLAINTIFFS

It would be entirely improper for this court to deny jurisdiction under the doctrine of forum non conveniens as the plaintiffs will not be able to receive justice in Paraguay.

Under the Stroessner Regime, the judiciary is controlled by the executive.[44] There is no independence of the judiciary when all the judges serve

---

[43] *The Paquete Habana*, 175 U.S. 677, 700 (1900); *Dreyfus v. Von Finck*, 534 F.2d 24, 29 (2nd Cir. 1976).

[44] Stephansky and Alexander, *Report of Commission of Enquiry into Human Rights in Paraguay*, International League for Human Rights, 27 September 1976. [hereinafter cited as Stephansky and Alexander].

at the will of the executive.[45] In addition, the police, of which defendant Pena-Irala is a high-ranking member, are Stroessner's principal protectors and enforcers of repression.[46] Hence, the only conclusion that may be drawn is that a Paraguayan court would not provide the plaintiffs with a just and impartial remedy, as required by Article 2 of the Covenant on Civil and Political Rights.[47] In fact, on September 30, 1976, after Dr. Filartiga had filed a lawsuit in Paraguay against the defendant Pena-Irala and the Paraguayan police, Filartiga's Paraguayan attorney was arrested and threatened with death if the suit was not abandoned.[48] Recently, it was learned that Mario Melgarejo, the Filartiga's attorney, was kidnapped on June 19, 1979, and was being held at the Paraguayan police headquarters.[49]

The cases of *Flota Maritime Browning v. The Ciudad de La Habana*, 181 F. Supp. 301 (D. Md. 1960), and *Mobil Tankers Co. v. Mene Grande Oil Company*, 363 F.2d 611 (3d Cir. 1966), support this court's assuming jurisdiction. In both cases, a motion to dismiss on the ground of forum non conveniens was denied. In *Flota Maritime*, 181 F. Supp. at 311, the court based its action on the doubtful attainment of justice in the foreign tribunal. In *Mobil Tankers Co.*, 363 F.2d at 614, the basis of the court's decision was that the foreign court provided fewer procedural remedies which were "far less conducive to the fair administration of justice . . . ."

In conclusion, due to the nature of General Stroessner's regime in Paraguay, the plaintiffs have no other impartial forum to make a judgment as to what happened to Joelito Filartiga. The District Court cannot deny them this opportunity on the spurious argument of forum non conveniens. In accepting jurisdiction of this case, the District Court will make it possible for an impartial tribunal to do justice and to make findings of fact concerning human rights violations, when no other court is capable of accepting this task.

CONCLUSION

For the reasons stated above, the District Court should assume jurisdiction under Art. III, Section 2, of the Constitution, 28 U.S.C. § 1331, and 28 U.S.C. § 1350.

---

[45] *Id.*

[46] *Id.* at 4-5.

[47] Article 2(3) (a) states: "any person whose rights or freedoms as herein recognized are violated shall have an effective remedy . . . ." Article 2(3) (b) states: "any person claiming such a remedy shall have his right thereto determined by competent . . . authorities . . . ."

[48] Filartiga Complaint, para. 17.

[49] Letter from Washington Office on Latin America to Friends of Paraguay (June 23, 1979).

Respectfully submitted,

Donald L. Doernberg	David Weissbrodt
17 Franklin Avenue	Professor of Law
Croton-on-Hudson, New York 10520	University of Minnesota Law
(914) 682-7258	School
	285 Law Building
	229 19th Avenue South
	Minneapolis, Minnesota 55455
	(612) 373-2724
	Attorneys for Amici Curiae

JULY 23, 1979: UNITED STATES

Appellants' Brief

UNITED STATES COURT OF APPEALS
IN THE SECOND CIRCUIT

No. 79-6090

DOLLY M.E. FILARTIGA and
DR. JOEL FILARTIGA,

Plaintiffs-Appellants,

– against –

AMERICO NORBERTO PENA-IRALA

Defendant-Appellee.

On Appeal From Judgment From New York District Court
Eastern District of New York

Appellants' Brief

PETER WEISS
RHONDA COPELON
JOHN CORWIN
JOSE ANTONIO LUGO
c/o Center for Constitutional Rights
853 Broadway
New York, New York 10003
(212) 674-3303

MICHAEL MAGGIO
GOREN and MAGGIO
1801 Columbia Road, Washington, D.C. 20009
(202) 483-8055

Attorneys for Appellants

INDEX TO APPELLANTS' BRIEF

PRELIMINARY STATEMENT

This is an appeal from the judgment of Hon. Eugene H. Nickerson of the Eastern District of New York. His opinion is contained in the Joint Appendix (JA. pp. 105-108).

ISSUE PRESENTED

Whether the torture-murder alleged in the Complaint is a tort in violation of the Law of Nations or the treaties of the United States giving rise to concurrent federal jurisdiction under 28 U.S.C. § 1350.

STATEMENT OF THE CASE

This is an action for damages against the defendant Americo Norberto Pena-Irala, for the wrongful torture and death at the age of 17, of the decedent, Joelito Filartiga. Plaintiffs allege that the acts complained of are a tort under the laws of the states and violate the law of nations and treaties of the United States. It is this two-fold character of the alleged wrongdoing which gives rise to federal jurisdiction pursuant to 28 U.S.C. §§ 1331 and 1350.

The decedent's sister, plaintiff Dolly Filartiga, has resided since October 1978[1] in Washington, D.C. pursuant to a visitors' visa. She came to this country as a consequence of the acts complained of because Pena's actions resulted in her being denied all educational and job opportunities. (JA. 17). Her application for political asylum here is pending with INS. (JA. 5).

The second plaintiff is the decedent's father, Dr. Joel Filartiga, a noted doctor residing in Ybycui, Paraguay where he operates a free clinic for the poor. (JA. 5). Dr. Filartiga is also an artist of international repute and a leading political opponent of General Stroessner, the Dictator President of Paraguay since 1954. For this political opposition, Dr. Filartiga has been arrested three times and was himself tortured in 1966. (JA. 6).

Defendant Pena came to this country under pretense of visitor's visa in July, 1978 in the midst of a public furor over his responsibility for the torture-murder of Joelito and the Paraguayan government's unsuccessful attempts to create an alternative explanation for his death. (JA. 17). He resided illegally in Brooklyn until April 4, 1979 when he was arrested by agents of the U.S. Immigration and Naturalization Service (INS). At the deportation hearing, he asked to be sent back to Paraguay and was ordered

---

[1] In paragraph 6 of the Complaint, "April 28, 1978" should read "October. . ." (JA. 5)

deported on April 5. (JA. 18). On April 6, 1979, personal jurisdiction was obtained through service of the Complaint on him at the Brooklyn Navy Yard where he was being held on bond pending deportation. (JA. 19).

Prior to any evidentiary hearings, defendant moved to dismiss the action for want of jurisdiction and under the doctrine of *forum non conveniens*. (JA. 47). The District Court recognized that "the proscription of torture in numerous international instruments accepted by nearly all the states in the international community reflected the emergence of a norm of customary international law condemning torture." (JA. 108). It dismissed the action, however, based upon narrowly construed dicta in this Circuit's decision in *IIT v. Vencap Ltd.*, 519 F.2d 1001 (2d Cir. 1975) and *Dreyfus v. von Finck*, 534 F.2d 24 (2d Cir. 1976) which defined the "Law of Nations" in § 1350 as "Those standards, rules or customs affecting the relationship between states and between an individual and a foreign state, and used by those states for their common good and/or in dealings *inter se*." (JA. 107-108).[2]

The decision dismissing this action was issued May 15, 1979 and filed May 16, 1979. The District Court properly did not address the question of *forum non conveniens*, nor hold evidentiary hearings thereon since the question of subject-matter jurisdiction is separate and prior. Thus *forum non conveniens* is not before this Court on this appeal. The notice of appeal was filed by plaintiffs on May 16, 1979. (JA. 109).

Ancillary to the merits of the complaint and this appeal, plaintiffs sought to stay the deportation of the defendant in order to take his deposition in this country.[3] On April 9, the District Judge issued an order staying Pena's deportation to permit the taking of his deposition and that of his traveling companion, a material witness, but the depositions were delayed at defendant's request until the filing and disposition of the motion to dismiss.

In his order dismissing the action, Judge Nickerson granted a 48 hour stay of deportation to permit application to a higher court. (JA. 108). Plaintiffs' application to a panel of this Court was denied without explanation on May 22. Application was made the next day to Justice Marshall in his capacity as Circuit Justice. The defendant's scheduled departure was vol-

---

[2] The Standard cited to *IIT v. Vencap, supra*, was incorrectly cited in part. It should read "affecting the relationship between states *or* between an individual and a foreign state . . . ." (Emphasis added for clarification.).

[3] For the purpose of such temporary relief only, officials of the United States Immigration and Naturalization Service were originally joined as defendants. They are accordingly not appellees in this court.

untarily delayed by the Justice Department in response to Justice Marshall's request to allow the entire Court to rule on the stay application. On May 24, the Supreme Court issued an order denying the stay and on or about May 25 the defendant was deported to Paraguay.

The Complaint alleges that on March 29, 1976, Joelito Filartiga was kidnapped and tortured to death by Pena and others in retaliation for the political activities and opinions of his father. (JA. 6).

At the time of the torture-murder, defendant Pena was a member of the Paraguayan police, holding the rank of Inspector General in "Investigaciones," the political police squad in Asuncion. (JA. 19). His unit has been identified by Amnesty International as the site of "the more brutal forms of torture." (JA. 42)

Amnesty International USA has identified torture as one of the three "main human rights violations committed under General Stroessner's regime." (JA. 41) Pena himself is reputed to be one of the most dreaded torturers. (JA. 19).

The torture-murder of Joelito Filartiga is not an isolated incident in Paraguay. Prestigious international human rights organizations have noted the unchecked use of torture by the police in Paraguay. Former Assistant Secretary of State for Latin America, Dr. Ben S. Stephansky and Professor Robert J. Alexander of Rutgers University who, in 1976, conducted a study of Paraguay for the International League for Human Rights, reported:

> Torture has undoubtedly been used. . . . The purpose of torture does not seem to have been, in general, to acquire information, but rather to force those being submitted to it to confess to things to which the police wanted them to confess, regardless of whether these confessions represented realities or fiction. As some Paraguayans pointed out to us, the technique bears certain similarities to that described in *Gulag Archipelago*. . . . The real motivation is to terrorize the population. Arrests, tortures, murders have been perpetrated in random fashion. Stephansky & Alexander, "Report of Commission of Inquiry into Human Rights in Paraguay of the International League for Human Rights." (JA. 22-28)

The Amnesty International "Briefing on Paraguay" describes the political use of torture:

> Although the use of torture appears to be general, it is not necessarily applied systematically. It may depend on the place and

length of detention and personality of the jailers involved . . . . It is not clear what purpose such torture serves, since the extraction of false confessions does not seem relevant, as political prisoners are rarely brought to trial. . . . It has been argued that torture is applied primarily as a punishment for and deterrent to opposition activities. (JA. 34).

Paraguay did not initiate any official investigation of Pena's responsibility for Joelito's torture and death.[4] Under the laws of Paraguay, however, victims of crime are entitled to act as private prosecutors (JA. 50) and Dr. Filartiga filed a lawsuit against the defendant and others for the torture-murder of his son. (JA. 7). Following the filing of these charges, there began a systematic campaign of harassment against Dr. Filartiga, his family, friends, and the attorney representing the family, to dissuade and prevent them from pursuing the lawsuit. (JA. 72). This included the arrest and detention, without trial, of the plaintiff Dolly Filartiga and her mother (JA. 6, 20, 72), and death threats by Pena himself against the family and the attorney. (JA. 7). The attorney was arrested, shackled to a wall, charged with plotting murder and was illegally disbarred by a Supreme Court Justice who is also alleged to have instigated the murder complaint against him. (JA. 7, 74). The case has been unduly delayed by the Paraguayan courts and there is no prospect of relief therein.[5] (JA. 7).

Various reports, both governmental and non-governmental, illuminate the futility which the Filartigas are experiencing with respect to the criminal charges they have filed against Pena in Paraguay. The Inter-American Human Rights Commission, an agency of the Organization of American States,[6] the international League for Human Rights and Amnesty International have all noted that the Paraguayan judiciary is an appendage

---

[4] The Paraguayan police purport to have the confession of Pena's son-in-law to the killing of Joelito and characterize it as a "crime of passion." (JA. 10, 20). This is viewed as a fabrication both by the plaintiffs and by international investigators (JA. 44, 10-12 and OAS Complaint attached to Complaint).

[5] Several days before argument of the motion to dismiss, the Supreme Court of Paraguay, in an action completely unprecedented in the annals of the Stroessner regime, reversed the lower court decision barring Dr. Filartiga from prosecuting the criminal charges against Pena. The transparency of this maneuver in aid of defendant's *forum non conveniens* argument, which is not before this Court on this appeal, merely demonstrates the dependence of the Paraguayan judiciary on the executive.

[6] OAS "Annual Report for 1976 of the Inter-American Commission on Human Rights to General Assembly," OEA/Ser/G/CP/doc. 652/77 Corr. 1, 3 Mar, 1977; OAS, Inter-American Commission on Human Rights, "Report on the Situation of Human Rights in Paraguay," DEA/Ser/P/AG/doc. 920/78, 27 April 1978.

of the executive branch controlled by General Stroessner and the police of which the defendant here was a ranking official. (JA. 19-20, 24, 36). The U.S. State Department's "Report on Human Rights Practices in Countries Receiving U.S. Aid" dated February 8, 1979 likewise notes that "Executive influence is excessive and often appears paramount in judicial proceedings."

Torture and human rights violation in Paraguay have been specifically condemned by the OAS[7] and have been the basis for denying U.S. foreign aid. (Addendum I, CRS 18-19). In this connection, the Senate Foreign Relations Committee recently placed Paraguay among the most intractable human right's violators and cut all development assistance.[8]

SUMMARY OF ARGUMENT

This Court has jurisdiction of this civil action under 28 U.S.C. § 1350, the Alien Tort Claims Act, which provides that an alien may sue in federal court "for a tort only, committed in violation of the law of nations or a treaty of the United States." Jurisdiction is likewise afforded by § 1331.

The issue in this case is *not* whether torture committed by one alien against another on foreign soil can be actionable in courts within the territorial boundaries of the United States. It is settled that American state courts have jurisdiction over personal injury torts committed abroad because such torts are "transitory" and follow the wrongdoer across national borders. The question is whether federal courts have concurrent jurisdiction when the tort involved also violates international law.

The Alien Tort Claims Act was included as part of the Federal Judiciary Act of 1789 to implement the framers' preference for federal jurisdiction in cases of potential international significance. Settled principles of federalism support the appropriateness, and indeed the preferability, of adjudicating these cases in courts which, by their structure and experience, are more likely to be sensitive to matters of national policy and international law.

There is no doubt that torture by government officials violates the contemporary law of nations. Torture is the grossest, most universally recognized human rights violation. The District Judge would have sustained jurisdiction had he not narrowly read dicta in *IIT v. Vencap* and *Dreyfus v.*

---

[7] *Ibid.*

[8] Senate Committee on Foreign Relations, Report to Accompany The International Development Assistance Act of 1979, No. 96-137 (96th Cong. 1st Sess, May 11, 1979) pp. 12-13 (Addendum II, hereto).

von Finck as limiting the phrase "law of nations" to rules directly affecting relations between states.

If so read, however, the *Vencap* standard would be too narrow and inconsistent with the framers' intent. In 1789, as well as today, the law of nations included proscription of individual conduct viewed as an offense against humanity. Moreover, the entire development of modern international law, which since Nuremberg has elevated protection of basic human rights to a central concern of the world community, compels recognition of torture as a violation of international law.

But beyond that, the international proscription of torture does meet the test set forth in *Vencap*. The condemnation of torture is designed to serve the common good of all nations, and the practice of torture necessarily affects relations between states. Indeed, the commitment to eradicate torture and other gross human rights violations has become one of the touchstones of U.S. foreign policy, affecting our relations with many nations, not the least of which is Paraguay itself.

It is, therefore, fully consistent with the intent of the first judiciary act, with the proscriptions and obligations of international law, and with the settled policy favoring federal jurisdiction in cases of international dimension, that this Court recognize its concurrent jurisdiction under Section 1350 to entertain this tort action.

I. 28 U.S.C. 1350 PROVIDES CONCURRENT JURISDICTION TO FEDERAL COURTS OVER FOREIGN TORTS INVOLVING ALIENS WHICH ALSO VIOLATE INTERNATIONAL LAW AND THEREFORE HAVE POTENTIAL INTERNATIONAL IMPLICATIONS.

A. *Wrongful Death By Torture Is A Transitory Tort Over Which State Courts Have Universal Civil Jurisdiction Under The Principles Of Private International Law And Anglo-American Jurisprudence*

It is a settled principle of private international law that injuries to the person or personal property of another are transitory. In such cases, the plaintiff's right to redress follows the defendant even to foreign lands. Kuhn, *Comparative Commentaries on Private International Law*, New York, 1937 at 304. The principle was stated by Mr. Justice Holmes:

> The theory of the foreign suit is that although the act complained of was subject to no law having force in the forum, it gave rise to an obligation, an *obligation*, which like other obligations, follows the person and may be enforced wherever the person may be

found. *Slater v. Mexican National Railway Co.*, 194 U.S. 120, 24 S.Ct. 582, 583 (1904).

The rationale for this principle is that "justice demands that wrongs be redressed even if they occur outside the jurisdiction. If this were not so, the guilty party could easily escape liability because of the facility of movement in modern life, and the increase in the number of sovereign jurisdictions." Kuhn, op. cit. at 304.

Three criteria must be met for a state court to take jurisdiction over an alien's foreign tort: (1) there must be personal jurisdiction over the defendant alien; (2) the defendant's actions must be actionable under the relevant foreign law, the *lex loci delicti commissi*; and (3) the cause of action must not be repugnant to the policies of the forum state, in the sense of violating local principles of justice or morality. *Cheshire's Private International Law*, 8th Ed., (London, 1970) at 257-261; *Westlake's Private International Law*, 6th Ed., (London, 1922) at 267-272; Phillimore, *Commentaries Upon International Law*, 3rd Ed. Vol. 4, (London, 1889); *2 Corpus Juris Secondum* 47-48.

All three criteria are met in the instant case. Pena was personally served within the jurisdiction of the district court. Indeed he had been residing there for approximately nine months and, but for his apprehension by federal agents as an illegal alien, would have continued his illegal residence. The tort alleged—torture and death by torture—are, at least in theory, both criminally and civilly punishable under the laws of Paraguay. (Gorostiaga Affid., JA 50-52). Indeed, the Paraguayan Constitution contains a complete catalogue of human rights, among which is Article 65, the right to life and to be free from torture. (Stephansky II (19), JA 80). Finally, torture, which is an aggravated form of assault and battery, and wrongful death, is a tort under the domestic law of New York State as, indeed, of probably every jurisdiction in the world.

In *McKenna v. Fisk*, 1 How. 31, 42 U.S. 241 (1843), the Supreme Court adopted and applied the principle of the transitory foreign tort to establish the jurisdiction of the several states over out-of-state torts:

It then appears from our books that the courts in England have been open in cases of trespass other than trespass upon real property, to foreigners as well as to subjects, *and to foreigners against foreigners when found in England for trespass committed* within the realm and *out of the realm*, or within or without the king's foreign dominions. The courts in the District of Columbia have a like jurisdiction. 42 U.S. 248-249 (emphasis supplied).

McKenna relies on several British cases, among them, *Mostyn v. Fabrigas,* 1 Cowp. 162 (1774), which explain the rule in its purest form:

> If A becomes indebted to B, or commits a tort upon his person or upon his personal property in Paris, an action in either case may be maintained against A in England, if he is there found. . . [A]s to transitory actions, there is not a colour of doubt but that any action which is transitory may be laid in any county in England, though the matter arises beyond the seas. *Mostyn v. Fabrigas,* 1 Cowp. 161.

Mostyn has been cited in a number of American decisions including *Denick v. Railroad Co.,* which holds, appropriately here, that wrongful death is a transitory action. 103 U.S. 11 (1880).

State courts in this country clearly have jurisdiction to entertain foreign tort actions between aliens although jurisdiction may be discretionary rather than compulsory in accordance with *forum non conveniens* principles.[9]

The issue of *forum non conveniens* is not present on appeal because it was never reached by the district court below. The district court correctly recognized that before *forum non conveniens* could even be considered there first had to be subject-matter jurisdiction. *Gulf Oil Corp. v Gilbert,* 330 U.S. 501, 504 (1947); *See also DeCendendor Arosa Mercanttile S.A.,* 91 Misc. 2d 577, 398 NYS 2d 250, 252 (Sup. Ct. 1977). It is clear, however, that application of the doctrine of *forum non conveniens* turns in this case on a factual finding concerning the neutrality, and accessibility to these plaintiffs, of a Paraguayan forum. This case could not be dismissed if, as would be shown

---

[9] *See, e.g., Eingartner v. Illinois Steel Co.,* 94 Wisc. 70, 76 (Sup. Ct. 1896); *Great Western Railway Co. v. Miller,* 19 Mich. 309, 310-311 (Sup. Ct. 1896); *Mexican Railway Co. v. Jackson,* 89 Tex. 107, 116 (Sup. Ct. 1896); *Gardener v. Thomas,* 14 Johns. 134, 137 (N.Y. Sup. Ct. 1817). Prior to the mid-twentieth century, New York courts tended to be closed to tort actions between non-residents to avoid overburdening their courts which consistently entertained foreign contract actions. Nonetheless they developed a "special circumstances" exception for foreign torts which included *e.g.,* cases where a foreigner flees to this country. *DeWitt v. Buchanan,* 54 Barb. 31 (NY Sup. Ct. 1868). *See also, Ferguson v. Nielson,* 11 NYS 524 (Sup. Ct. 1890); *Johnson v. Dalton,* 1 Cowen 548 (NY Marine Ct. 1823); *Pugh v. Gillam,* 1 Cal. 485 (Sup. Ct. 1861). But since *Gulf Oil Corporation v. Gilbert,* 330 U.S. 501 (1947), New York courts have abandoned the more rigid approach and followed the general rules of *forum non conveniens* in foreign torts, rejecting the doctrine where an alternative forum was not readily available. *See, e.g., Trujillo v. Bank of Nova Scotia,* 51 Misc. 2d, 680, 273 NYS 2d 700 (NY Sup. Ct. 1966), aff'd 29 App. Div. 2d 847, 289 NYS 2d 389; *Varkonyi v. Varig,* 22 NY 2d 333, 239 N.E. 2d 542 (1968). *See* Note, "The Convenient Forum Abroad", 20 Stanford Law Review 57 (1967) at 66-67.

on remand, there is no adequate forum in Paraguay. See *Gulf Oil Corp. v. Gilbert*, 330 U.S. at 506-07, 67 S. Ct. at 842; *Schertenlieb v. Traum*, 589 F. 2d 1156 (2d Cir. 1978); *Mobil Tankers Co. v. Mene Grande Oil Co.*, 363 F. 2d 611 (3d Cir. 1966); *Phoenix Canada Oil Co. Ltd. v. Texaco Inc.*, 78 F.R.D. 445 (D. Del. 1978).

B. *Section 1350 Was Enacted To Implement The Framers' Preference For Federal Adjudication Of Cases Of Concern To The Nation As A Whole, And Particularly Of Potential Impact On International Relations*

The necessity of establishing federal control over matters involving international law and foreign relations was one of the predominant themes of the period in which Section 9 of the First Judiciary Act, now Section 1350, was adopted. Section 1350 is the product of this concern which is no less vital today.

That the need to centralize federal control over foreign relations and to end the confusion created by divergent state interpretations of international laws and treaties was a principal concern to the framers of the Constitution and drafters of the Judiciary Act need not be belabored. Let Max Farrand, the chronicler of the Constitutional Convention, state the case, even though the passage quoted contains an unseemingly racial slur by today's standards:

> If it was exasperating to find themselves overreached in matters of international trade, it was humiliating to find themselves [the delegates] too weak to force the British to live up to the terms of the Treaty of Paris of 1783, and it was positively disgraceful to be unable to compel the individual states to observe the provisions of that or any other treaty that might be made. Without authority to require the states to regard the principles of international law and incompetent even to punish piracy or felony on the high seas, it was truly a pitiable spectacle that the United States presented, when a contemporary who had traded with various countries could say that he found "this country held in the same light by foreign nations as a well-behaved negro is in a gentleman's family," there need be little wonder that this newly independent and sensitive people should demand reforms that would tend to dispel some of the contempt inspired abroad. The least that could be done was to establish a strong central government which should have control of all foreign relations. Max Farrand, *The Framing of the Constitution of the United States*, Yale University Press New Haven), pp. 46-47 (footnotes omitted).

The need for federal supremacy in international matters was not limited to the executive, but as shown in the following passage describing the mood of the delegates, extended to the judiciary as well:

> There ought . . . to be a separate executive . . . which should be capable of action in foreign relations . . . . There ought to be an organized federal judiciary which should have, in addition to that developed under the articles of confederation, jurisdiction in matters relating to foreigners or people of other states. *Id.* at 50.

In arguing for federal jurisdiction over all cases involving aliens, Hamilton made clear that the need for such jurisdiction over alien claims arising upon treaties and the law of nations was obvious to all and forcefully explained the reasons for broad federal jurisdiction in these cases:

> As the denial or perversion of justice by the sentences or courts, as well as in any other manner, is with reason classed among the just causes of war, it will follow that the federal judiciary ought to have cognizance of all causes in which the citizens of other countries are concerned. This is not less essential to the preservation of the public faith, than to the security of the public tranquility. *A distinction may perhaps be imagined between cases arising upon treaties and the laws of nations, and those which may stand merely on the footing of the municipal law. The former kind may be supposed proper for the federal jurisdiction, the latter for that of the states.* But it is at least problematical whether an unjust sentence against a foreigner, where the subject of controversy was wholly relative to the *lex loci*, would not, if unredressed, be an aggression upon his sovereign, as well as one which violated the stipulations in a treaty or the general laws of nations. And a still greater objection to the distinction would result from the immense difficulty, if not impossibility, of a practical discrimination between the cases of one complexion and those of the other. So great a proportion of the cases in which foreigners are parties involve national questions, that it is by far most safe and most expedient to refer all those in which they are concerned to the national tribunals. *The Federalist*, No. 80, Jacob E. Cooke, *The Federalist* (1961 Ed.) at 536 (emphasis supplied).

The consensus at the Convention on this point is confirmed by a leading historian of the period:

> Thus, notwithstanding a cleavage foreshadowed between defenders of states' rights and proponents of national power with respect to the structure of a national judiciary, there appears to have been

an impressive measure of agreement at the outset that the Law of Nations and treaties must be the subjects, immediately or ultimately, of a paramount national concern. Edwin D. Dickinson, "The Law of Nations as Part of the National Law of the United States," 101 U. Pa. L. Rev. 26, 37 (1952).

Despite opposition by anti-nationalist forces which prevented authorization of general federal question jurisdiction, the consensus concerning a federal forum in cases with international implications survived in the First Judiciary Act. Dickinson, *supra*. Hamilton's concern about cases involving foreigners was largely implemented. All cases in which an alien was a party, were made cognizable in federal circuit as well as state courts, under diversity and removal provisions. 1 Stat. 73 §11 (1789). And the unquestioned need for federal jurisdiction over alien claims raising international law issues discussed by Hamilton was given special treatment by the drafters of the First Judiciary Act. Section 9 gave the federal district as well as the circuit courts concurrent jurisdiction over such alien tort claims. See Dickinson, *supra*, at 47. It should be noted that diversity jurisdiction was unavailable as a constitutional matter where aliens were on both sides of a non-federal question, *Hodgson & Thompson v. Bowerbank*, 5 Cranch 304, 3 L. Ed. 109 (1809), but that it was available where an alien sued a non-alien. Thus, the original § 1350 was not necessary to provide federal jurisdiction over alien tort claims except as to those claims where both the plaintiff and the wrongdoer were aliens.

As Hamilton urged, concurrent federal jurisdiction was seen as particularly necessary in cases which combined alienage with violation of the law of nations or the treaties. Hamilton's concern has been echoed by the courts. In *Banco Nacional de Cuba v. Sabbatino*, the Supreme Court recognized that the origins of § 1350 arise from the interest in placing the power over foreign affairs in the federal government, describing § 1350 as one of several statutes:

> reflecting a concern for uniformity in this country's dealings with foreign nations and . . . a desire to give matters of international significance to the jurisdiction of federal institutions. 376 U.S. 398, 428, 84 S.Ct. 923, 240 note 25 (1964).

In *Abdul-Rahman Omar Adra v. Clift*, 195 F. Supp. 857, at 865 (D. Md. 1961), the most recent case recognizing § 1350 jurisdiction,[10] the court noted the framers' concern over foreign policy implications of these cases:

---

[10] *Abdul-Rahman* premises jurisdiction on passport fraud against Lebanon and the United States, which was the vehicle by which defendant committed the alleged tort of

An alien, understandably but unjustifiably, may prefer to bring an action for a tort in a federal court rather than in a local court, and Congress has authorized him to do so in this limited class of cases. The importance of foreign relations to our country today cautions federal courts to give weight to such considerations and not to decline jurisdiction given by an Act of Congress unless required to do so by dominant considerations.

And, in *Valanga v. Metropolitan Life Insurance Co.*, 259 F. Supp. 324 (E.D. Pa., 1966), the court likewise explained that § 1350 was designed to embrace cases "with international overtones" and presenting issues of "international import":

> [T]he type of conduct considered to be within the ambit of § 1350 . . . transcends the violation of local norms embodied in . . . personal injury actions since it is injected with overtones which impinge upon the standards which nations have established to control their relationship. [Such] conduct immediately raises issues of international import and conceivably could constitute an affront to the power and dignity of the nations involved. *Supra* at 328.

In Point II we will demonstrate that the framers understood the law of nations to include rules pertaining to conduct by individuals as well as by states, and that this facet of the law of nations has been strengthened by the post-World War II developments of modern international law. Finally, we will show in Point III that the preference of Hamilton and the framers for federal jurisdiction in cases with potential international ramifications remains a tenet of our federal system and compels recognition of jurisdiction in this case.

II. THE WRONGFUL DEATH BY TORTURE ALLEGED HEREIN IS A TORT WHICH VIOLATES THE LAW OF NATIONS AND THE TREATIES OF THE UNITED STATES AND OVER WHICH FEDERAL JURISDICTION IS CONFERRED BY 28 U.S.C. § 1350

In order for the federal courts to exercise concurrent jurisdiction under § 1350, the act complained of must be both a tort under domestic law and a violation of international law. As Section A will demonstrate, torture preeminently meets the dual test. Jurisdiction under 1350 thus turns

---

unlawfully transporting her child in violation of the father's rights under Muslim law. Likewise, here, Pena committed visa fraud, which is an affront to this nation, and which was the vehicle by which he came to this country to escape public embarrassment in Paraguay.

on how the concept of the law of nations is defined. Dicta in *Vencap* and *Dreyfus*, suggesting that it is limited to rules affecting the relationship between states, must be supplemented or liberally construed to encompass prevailing international law principles both in the late eighteenth century (Section B) and today (Section C).

Indeed, today, torture is the kind of conduct which, when visited even upon a state's own nationals, incurs international condemnation and affects the foreign relations of that state generally and with the United States in particular (Section D).

A. *Torture Is A Violation Of International Law*

It is well settled that our courts have a constitutional obligation to interpret and apply the guarantees of international laws. In *The Paquete Habana*, 175 U.S. 677, 708 (1900), the Supreme Court held

International law is part of our law, and must be ascertained and administered by the courts of justice of appropriate jurisdiction as often as questions of right depending upon it are duly presented for their determination.

See also, The Nereide, 13 U.S. (9 Cranch) 423 (1853); *U.S. v. Toscanino*, 500 F.2d 278 (2d. Cir. 1974).

It is undisputed that torture[11] is a violation of international law. The Supreme Court has held that the content of the law of nations:

"may be ascertained by consulting the works of jurists, writing professedly on public laws; or by the general usage and practice of nations; or by judicial decisions recognizing and enforcing that law." *United States v. Smith*, 18 U.S. 71, 74 [153], 5 Wheat, 71, 74 (1820).

---

[11] By consensus, the UN General Assembly adopted the following definition of torture on December 9, 1975:

[T]orture means any act by which severe pain or suffering, whether physical or mental, is intentionally inflicted by or at the instigation of a public official or a person for such purposes as obtaining from him or a third person information or confession, punishing him for an act he has committed or is suspected of having committed, or intimidating him or other persons. It does not include pain or suffering arising only from, inherent in or incidental to lawful sanctions to the extent consistent with the Standard Minimum Rules for the Treatment of Prisoner. Article 1, Declaration on the Protection of All Person From Being Subjected To Torture and Other Cruel, Inhuman or Degrading Treatment or Punishment, (G.A. Res. 3452 (XXX), 30 U.N. GAOR Supp. (No. 34) 91, UN Doc. A/1034 (1975)). (Addendum III hereto).

In *The Paquete Habana*, the Court explained further that

> [W]here there is no treaty and no controlling executive or legisla-
> tive act or judicial decision, resort must be had to the customs and
> usages of civilized nations, and as evidence of these, to the works
> of jurists and commentators who by years of labor, and experience
> have made themselves well acquainted with the subject of they
> treat. *Supra* at 708.

Here, international treaties,[12] declarations, conventions, customs and
the general principles of international law all unequivocally proscribe tor-
ture. UN Charter, Article 55; The Universal Declaration of Human Rights
Article 5 (UN G.A. Res. 217A (III), U.N. Doc. A1810 at 710 (1948));
International Covenant on Civil and Political Rights, Article 7, (UN G.A.
Res. 2200 (XXI), 21 GAOR, Supp. (No. 16) 52, U.N. Doc. A/6316 (1966);
Declaration on the Protection of all Persons From Being Subjected to
Torture and Other Cruel, Inhuman, or Degrading Treatment or Punishment, *supra*; American Convention on Human Rights, Article 5, OASTS
No. 36 at 1, OAS Off. Rec. OEA/Ser. L/V/II. 23, doc. 21, rev. 2 (English
1975); European Convention for the Protection of Human Rights and
Fundamental Freedoms, Article 3, Council of Europe, Collected Texts, 1-
19 (19*th* ed. 1974) and other authorities cited by Lillich, R. (JA. 67-69). The
five eminent international law authorities whose affidavits are in the record
of this case, Professor Arens, Falk, Franck, Lillich and McDougal, affirm,
with a unanimous voice, that torture today is universally regarded as a violation of international law.

Defendants made no argument and put in no evidence to the contrary.
The district court agreed that:

> the proscription of torture in numerous international instruments
> accepted by nearly all the states in the international community
> reflects the emergence of a norm of customary international law
> condemning torture. (JA. 108).

---

[12] The Complaint alleges that the tort committed by Pena was in violation of both
the treaties of the United States and the Law of Nations. (JA. 4). Plaintiffs did not separately brief the treaty claim below and do not do so here as those treaties relevant here
are merely one of the sources of the applicable law of nations. See *U.S. v. Toscanino,*
supra where this Court recognized the right of individuals to relief based on the UN
Charter and enactments which are analogous in status to the Declarations and
Resolutions condemning torture here. The briefs of the *amici curiae* ably argue the treaty
point as distinct from the Law of Nations. Plaintiffs associate themselves with those arguments, but emphasize the law of nations aspect of the case.

The clear proscription of torture in international law distinguishes, this case from prior 1350 cases where the act complained of failed to qualify as a violation of the law of nations.[13] This was the holding of *IIT v. Vencap, supra*, referred to by Justice White dissenting in *Banco Nacional de Cuba v. Sabbatino*, 376 U.S. 398, 441-442, confiscation of the property of one's nationals is not a legal wrong according to the law of nations. *Dreyfus v. von Finck, supra* at 31 n.10.[14] By contrast, it should be stressed that torture is in international law today what piracy was in 1789, i.e., the grossest, most universally recognized international violation, the international crime *par excellence*. We agree with Judge Friendly that for a tort to provide 1350 jurisdiction, there must be no doubt that it is an international law violation, unequivocal in nature, and satisfying all the traditional tests laid down by the doctrine of "sources of international law."

It is difficult, nay, impossible, to find a practice which more completely meets these tests. Even such almost universally condemned practices as terrorism or aerial hijacking have their defenders in the parliament of nations. Detention without trial, though widely assailed, is also widely excused. The world loathes apartheid, but the government of South Africa manages to justify it on the authority of, *inter alia*, the Bible. Censorship, alas, has as many proponents as detractors, if not more, not to mention the lack of unanimity on such issues as the right to work, the right to compensation for expropriation, or the right to a safe and healthy environment.

---

[13] See *Aboidun v. Martin Oil Service*, 475 F. 2d 142 (7th Cir., 1973), *cert. denied* 414 U.S. 866 (1974) (transporting people to work against their will and fraud); *Khedivial Line S.A.E. v. Seafarers' International Union*, 278 F.2d 49, 52, n.1 (access of foreign vessels to friendly ports usually matter of treaty); *Metropolitan Life Ins. Co.*, 259 F. Supp. 324 (E.D. Pa., 1966) (refusal to pay proceeds of life insurance company); *Lopes v. Reederei Richard Schroeder*, 225 F. Supp. 292 (E.D. Pa., 1963) (doctrine of unseaworthiness unique to domestic law). See also, *Damaskinos v. Societa Navigacion Interamericana, S.A.*, 225 F. Supp. 919, 923 (S.D.N.Y., 1966). But see *Nguyen Da Yen v. Kissinger*, 528 F. 2d 1194 (9th Cir. 1975), on remand 70 F.R.D. 656 (N. Cal.) (suggesting that illegal seizure, removal and detention of an alien against his will may be an international tort); *O'Reilly De Camara v. Brooke*, 209 U.S. 45 (1908) (implies coverage of unjustified seizure of alien's property in a foreign country); see *Khedival Line S.A.E. v. Seafarers' International Union, supra* at 278 (abductions by one state of persons located within territory of another state). And see generally Petovich, "Construction and Application of 28 U.S.C. § 1350 giving United States District Courts Jurisdiction of Actions By Alien for Tort Only, committed in violation of Law of Nations or Treaty of United States," 34 ALR Fed. 388.

[14] The District Court correctly did not rely here on the language of *Dreyfus* which states that "violations of international law do not occur when the aggrieved parties are nationals of the acting state." That is undoubtedly a correct statement of international law as applied to the confiscations of property, the tort alleged in *Dreyfus*. It cannot, however, as defendant suggested below, be elevated to a general rule of international law. Obviously if international law were to condemn confiscations of the property of one's nationals, the seizure would violate the law of nations.

But no government on earth today, no matter how brutal or dictatorial, would dare take issue with the condemnation of torture as a universally shared value. Accusations of torture leveled against such governments are either denied, as here, or written off as "regrettable excesses;" they are *never* justified on moral, philosophical, or legal grounds.

The international sources also make clear that there are no circumstances under which torture will be viewed as legitimate. The UN General Assembly has declared by consensus that "Exceptional circumstances such as state of war or a threat of war, internal political instability or any other public emergency may not be invoked as justification of torture . . . ." Article 3, Declaration on the Protection of All Persons From Being Subjected to Torture and Other Cruel, Inhuman or Degrading Treatment or Punishment. *Supra.* (Addendum III).

We do not say that torture is the only human rights violation that is also a violation of international law, since *absolute* unanimity is not a criterion for such a finding. We do say, however, that, in order of indisputability, torture heads the list and, therefore, unquestionably satisfies the strict construction standard enunciated by this court in *Vencap.*

B. *The Law Of Nations, Both As Understood By The Framers And As Accepted Today, Brings Individual Conduct Viewed As Offenses To Humanity Within The Purview Of Section 1350*

The narrow construction of the law of nations in *Vencap* and *Dreyfus* as dealing with "the relationship among nations rather than among individuals," *Dreyfus, supra,* at 30-21, and as "affecting the relationship between states . . . ." *Vencap, supra,* at 1015, was adopted from *Lopes v. Reederei Richard Schroeder,* 225 F. Supp. 292, 296 297 (E.D. Pa. 1963). In developing that definition, *Lopes* relies principally on those portions of the writings of eighteenth century international jurists and commentators which focused on the state-to-state aspect of international law. But, these same jurists also recognized, as did the framers and the early decisions of the courts, the aspect of international law which addressed its rules directly to individual conduct. Thus, in *Dreyfus,* Judge van Graafeiland was careful to define the law of nations as concerned "*primarily* with the relationship among nations," as it would be patently incorrect to say that the law of nations (or international law) imposes no duties on individuals or on nations to provide redress for the conduct of individuals abroad.

1. *The Framers Intended § 1350 to Provide Redress For Individual Conduct Condemned by the Law of Nations*

Even before 1789, the law of nations had included a doctrine of *hostes humani generis* (enemies of all humanity), which holds that certain tortious acts are so reprehensible and universally condemned that universal jurisdiction is accorded to insure that the perpetrators are brought to justice. This doctrine is recognized in the writings of Kent, Story and Burlamaqui, the same jurists relied upon in *Lopes* for the more limited definition of the law of nations, *supra*, at 296-297. For example, Kent writes that among the "rights and . . . duties of nations in their intercourse with each other," *Dreyfus v. von Finck, supra*, at 31, are the right to try the common enemies of humanity wherever they were found, and the duty to ensure that such common enemies did not escape accountability for their acts. See 1 Kent *Commentaries* 181-87 (2nd ed. 1823). The doctrine was most commonly applied to pirates, about whom Kent wrote:

> Pirates have been regarded by all civilized nations as the enemies of the human race, and the most atrocious violators of the universal law of society . . . It is of no importance, for the purpose of giving jurisdiction, on *whom* or *where* a piratical offence has been committed. A pirate, who is one by the law of nations, may be tried and punished in any country where he may be found, for he is reputed to be out of the protection of all laws and privileges. (1832 ed., pp. 182-83, 186). *Commentaries on American Law* (vol. I).

In *United States v. Smith, supra*, Justice Story reported the agreement of international jurists on this point. He quoted Burlamaqui's description of pirates as "robbers and enemies of mankind, and consequently, persons whose acts of violence are manifestly unjust, which authorizes all nations to treat them as enemies." *Supra*, at 175. Similarly, he found Blackstone to say:

> "The crime of piracy, or robbery and depradation upon the high seas, is an offense against the universal law of society, a pirate being, according to Sir Edward Coke, *hostis humani generis*." He [Blackstone] goes on to remark that every community hath a right to punish it, for it is a war against all mankind. *Supra*, at 182.

The United States Supreme Court adopted the doctrine of *hostes humani generis* in interpreting a Congressional statute against "piracy under the law of nations." 18 U.S.C. § 1651. In *United States v. Pirates*, the Court declared that:

> when embarked on a piratical cruise, every individual becomes equally punishable under the law of 1790, whatever may be his national character, or whatever may have been that of the vessel in which he sailed, or of the vessel attacked . . . The moment that ship was taken from her officers, and proceeded on a piratical cruise,

the crew lost all claim to national character, and whether citizens or foreigners became equally punishable under the act. 5 Wheat 184, 193 (1820).

Similarly, in the *United States v. Smith*, it held that:

> the general practice of all nations in punishing all persons, whether natives or foreigners, who have committed this offense against any persons whatsoever, with whom they are in amity, is a conclusive proof that the offense is supposed to depend, not upon the particular provisions of any municipal code, but upon the law of nations, both for its definition and punishment. 5 Wheat 153, 162 (1820).

Although piracy invited the most frequent application of the doctrine of *hostes humani generis*, its breadth is explained by the pre-eminent Swiss diplomat and jurist Emmerich de Vattel, whose work, the *Law of Nations*, had particular influence on the framers of the Constitution and is viewed by the Supreme Court as an authoritative source of the founding fathers' understanding of the law of nations.[15] *United States Steel Corp. v. Multistate Tax Commission*, 434 U.S. 452, 99 S. Ct. 799, 807 (1978).

Vattel's writings show that pirates were simply one class of *hostes humani generis*, and that piracy was included not because it usually occurred on the high seas, but because of its internationally recognized nature as a heinous threat to the common safety. Noting the traditional rule that a criminal seeking refuge in a foreign country normally would not be punished for prior acts abroad, Vattel explained that the exception for international outlaws encompasses professional poisoners, assassins and incendiaries:

---

[15] The *Law of Nations*, originally published in 1758, and frequently reprinted over the next century, was the standard work on the subject an is known to have greatly influenced the founding fathers. William Seagle's *The History of Law* calls Vattel "the living embodiment of the new age" and states that "his celebrated *Droit des Gens . . .* was to be a handbook in all the cabinets of Europe for more than a century." (P. 358 (New York, 1946).) His "treatise was especially influential in the United States because his principles of liberty and equality coincided with the ideals expressed in the Declaration of Independence." The New Encyclopedia Britannica, 15th Edition, 1974. The Supreme Court recently noted that: "[i]n 1775 Benjamin Franklin acknowledged receipt of three copies of a new edition, in French, of Vattel's *Law of Nations* and remarked that the book 'has been continually in the hands of the members of our Congress now sitting . . . .' 2F. Wharton, United States Revolutionary Diplomatic Correspondence 64 (1889)." *United States Steel Corp. v. Multistate Tax Commission*, 434 U.S. 452, 98 S. Ct. 799, 807 (1978).

[A]lthough the justice of each nation ought in general to be confined to the punishment of crimes committed in its own territories, we ought to except from this rule those villains, who, by the nature and habitual frequency of their crimes, violate all public security, and declare themselves the *enemies of the human race. Poisoners, assassins, and incendiaries by profession,* may be exterminated wherever they are seized; for *they attack and injure all nations, by trampling under foot the foundation of their common safety. Thus, pirates are sent to the gibbet by the first into whose hands they fall. The Law of Nations,* §§232, 233 (1849 ed.) (which is substantially identical to earlier editions) (emphasis added).

The Supreme Court has also had occasion to affirm the applicability of the doctrine to acts not occurring on the high seas. In finding U.S. jurisdiction over a seizure which occurred on a ship anchored within the territorial waters of a foreign nation, the Court dispensed with the boundary question, holding:

Nor can it be objected that it was within the jurisdictional limits of a foreign state; for, those limits, though neutral to war, are not neutral to crimes. *Supra,* at 200, 201. *Pirates,* 5 Wheat 184 (1820).

Likewise, § 1350 was held to remove all doubt about federal jurisdiction over a seizure which took place on land of goods previously captured at sea:

I was at first doubtful whether this court had jurisdiction, Darrel's seizure, under the mortgage, having been made on land. But as the original cause arose at sea, everything dependent on it is triable in the admiralty . . . Besides, as the 9th section of the judiciary act of Congress [Act Sept. 24, 1789, 1 Stat. 77] gives this court concurrent jurisdiction with the state courts and circuit court of the United States where an alien sues for violation of the law of nations or a treaty of the United States, I dismiss all doubt upon this point. *Bolchos v. Darrel,* 3 Fed. Cas. 810 (D.S.C. 1795).

The Supreme Court has also affirmed that the doctrine of *hostes humani generis* applied not only to purely private conduct but also to that carried out under permission or pretense of law. Pirates frequently acted under color of national authority, being in some instances captains who became renegades after receiving a lawful commission. Thus, in 1790, Congress included as pirates persons acting "under color of any commission from any foreign prince, or state, or on pretense of authority from any person. . . ." 18 U.S.C. § 1652. In *United States v. Klintock,* Chief Justice

Marshall noted that a pretense of a lawful commission "can be no justification of the fact stated in the case," 5 Wheat 144, 149 (1820), and that "a belligerent character may be put off, and a piratical one assumed, even under the most unquestionable commission." *United States v. Pirates,* 5 Wheat 184, 202.

Given the early importance of the piracy problem in the eighteenth and nineteenth centuries, it is not surprising that the first two reported § 1350 cases involved claims for restitution of property allegedly seized in violation of the law of nations. *Bolchos v. Darrel, supra; Moxon v. The Fanny,* 17 Fed. Cas. 942 (D. Pa. 1793). In both cases, the courts recognized their duty to enforce that part of the law of nations giving all individuals rights against acts committed by *hostes humani generis.*

Thus, it is clear that when the framers of the Constitution, many of whom were also drafters of the First Judiciary Act, used the phrase "law of nations," they understood it to encompass universally condemned individual conduct. Dickinson emphasizes that

> it was axiomatic among them that the Law of Nations, *applicable to individuals and to states,* was an integral part of the law which they a ministered and practiced. Dickinson, *supra* at 35 (and 48). (emphasis supplied).

The long-recognized interface between state-to-state relations and internationally condemned individual conduct is discussed in Hyde's treatise on International Law, cited at length in *Abdul Rehman Omar Adra v. Clift,* 195 F. Supp. 857, 864 (D. Md., 1961):

> The commission of particular acts, regardless of the character of the actors, may be so detrimental to the welfare of the international society that its international law may either clothe a State with the privilege of punishing the offender, or impose upon it the obligation to endeavor to do so. The offender may be a private individual; and when he is subjected to the imposition of a penalty, he comes into close contact with the law of nations. *Whenever he commits acts on account of which a country not his own may not unlawfully proceed to punish him even though they are consummated beyond the limits of its territory and have no connection therewith, or whenever he commits acts which the territorial sovereign of the place where they are committed is under an obligation to endeavor to prevent or penalize, he feels the direct consequence of what the law permits an offended sovereign to do, or enjoins a law-respecting sovereign to do.* In both situations, it is not unscientific to declare that he is guilty of conduct which the law of

nations itself brands as internationally illegal. For it is by virtue of that law that such sovereign acquires the right to punish and is also burdened with the duty to prevent or prosecute. (emphasis added)

Significantly, Hyde goes on to identify § 1350 as specifically intended to provide civil redress for individual conduct, carried out here or abroad, which is proscribed by international law:

> The injunctions of international law that may be applicable to the private individual do not necessarily disappear when he enters the territory of his own or of any other State. He learns that there are acts of which that law there itself forbids the commission by any one whomsoever. Evidence of this has long been reflected in the statutory law of the United States . . . which confers upon the United States District Courts original jurisdiction of "all suits brought by any alien for a tort only, in violation of the law of nations or of a treaty of the United States." Hyde, *International Law*, Vol. 1, §11A, pp. 33-34 (2nd rev. ed., 1945).

2. *Current International Law Obliges the Court to Accept Jurisdiction in this Case.*

Appellants do not contend that the technical doctrine of *hostes humani generis*, though an evolving one,[16] is applied in its entirety, with respect to torturers. The doctrine of *hostes humani generis* has a substantive aspect and a procedural one. Substantively, it includes wrongful acts which are universally condemned; procedurally, it authorizes and, indeed, requires nations to prosecute the wrongdoer criminally. While torture is substantively an offense to all humanity, criminal prosecution is not yet required, and, without either a treaty or an act of Congress, Pena could not be pros-

---

[16] Fortunately, the slave trade, protected in *Bolchos*, later came within the doctrine as internationally held standards of justice developed. (JA 68). The International Law Association's *Report of the Fifty-Seventh Conference* held in Madrid in 1976, reflects the opinions of international jurists that terrorists and hijackers should be treated as *hostes humani generis* and subject to universal criminal sanctions. See, for example, Prof. Petko M. Radoynov of Bulgaria: "Terrorism, which razes to the ground international society and human rights, places its perpetrators outside the laws (legal and moral) of all humanity. International terrorists are, therefore, enemies of mankind (*hostes generic humani*)." *Report*, p. 122 (Great Britain, 1978), and Prof. Opperman of West Germany: "The modern terrorist has to be outlawed as 'hostes humani generis,' as was the pirate of the middle ages." *Id.* at 128. Another participant recalled the words U Thant: "Hijackers should be prosecuted in the name of the peoples of the world, for the benefit of all travelers and all pilots, irrespective of their nationality or their political system." *Id.* at 135.

[17] It should be noted, however, that Article 7 of the UN Gen. Assem. Declaration on the Protection of All Persons from Being Subjected to Torture provides that "Each state shall ensure that all acts of torture as defined in Article I are offenses under its criminal law." (Add. III.)

ecuted here.[17] The exercise of civil jurisdiction is, however, authorized by § 1350 and is an entirely different matter from the sovereign power to prosecute criminally. As discussed in Point I, the courts of the United States already have the power to provide redress under the private international law principle of transitory tort. Federal jurisdiction under § 1350 requires only that the tort involved be a wrong under international law, which torture unquestionably is. Beyond that, international legal pronouncements supported by the U.S. exhort this nation to recognize torture in every forum as a violation of the law of nations and to utilize existing and develop new mechanisms to provide redress to its victims.

Article 2 of the UN General Assembly Declaration on the Protection of All Persons From Being Subjected to Torture enjoins all nations that:

> any act of torture . . . shall be condemned as a violation of the purposes of the Charter of the United Nations and as a violation of human rights and fundamental freedoms proclaimed in the Universal Declaration of Human Rights.[18]

The International Covenant on Civil and Political Rights, which the United States has signed, condemns torture (Article 7) and obligates each state, through its legislative and judicial bodies, to "ensure that any person whose rights or freedoms as herein recognized are violated shall have an effective remedy."[19] Section 1350, inherited from the founding of this nation pro-

---

[18] Article 3 enjoins that "No state may permit or tolerate torture" and the following Articles detail the measures which states are required to take to eradicate torture. While the focus of these sections is on steps which nations must take to punish and redress torture by their own officials, universal criminal sanction (Article 5) and civil redress (Article II) is also authorized.

[19] Article 2 provides in full:

1. Each State Party to the present Covenant undertakes to respect and to ensure to all individuals within its territory and subject to its jurisdiction the rights recognized in the present Covenant, without distinction of any kind, such as race, colour, sex, language, religion, political or other opinion, national or social origin, property, birth or other status.

2. Where not already provided for by existing legislative or other measures, each State Party to the present Covenant undertakes to take the necessary steps, in accordance with its constitutional processes and with the provisions of the present Covenant, to adopt such legislative or other measures as may be necessary to give effect to the rights recognized in the present Covenant.

3. Each State Party to the present Covenant undertakes:

(a) To ensure that any person whose rights or freedoms as herein recognized are violated shall have an effective remedy, notwithstanding that the violation has been committed by persons acting in an official capacity;

vides one of the essential remedies envisaged by modern international law.

In substance then, the torturer is today the most heinous international outlaw. Defendant Pena, a professional torturer and a member of the dreaded "investigaciones" or death squad of the Paraguayan police, falls squarely into this definition of extraordinary villain. The brutal torture murder of an innocent youth clearly constitutes in Vattel's words "trampling under foot the foundation of [our] common safety." The fact that defendant Pena has relied upon corruption in Paraguay to evade action by the local courts is an additional reason why he should be brought to trial here.[20] To close the doors of the federal court to his victims would provide him refuge against any sanction and would undermine our commitment under international law to take concrete measures to condemn and eradicate torture wherever it occurs.

Thus, the principle of redress against international outlaws which was understood to be among the purposes of § 1350, together with the universal proscription of torture in current international law, form a perfect chain leading to mandatory assumption of jurisdiction by a federal court in this matter, if the court is to give effect to the law of nations as it is constitutionally required to do.

C. *Modern International Law Recognizes Individual Rights Which Are Universal in Character and Which States Are Obliged to Promote.*

In relying on the "relationship with states" language of *Vencap* and *Dreyfus*, the court below has, perhaps unwittingly, joined the ranks of the countless partisans of the great, but largely sterile, debate over whether

---

(b) To ensure that any person claiming such a remedy shall have his right thereto determined by competent judicial, administrative or legislative authorities, or by any other competent authority provided for by the legal system of the State, and to develop the possibilities of judicial remedy;

(c) To ensure that the competent authorities shall enforce such remedies when granted.

[20] Like pirates, torturers are extremely successful at evading judicial sanction. They either receive sanctuary in their own country as exemplified here (or in Chile's refusal to extradite to the U.S. the two Chileans who assassinated Orlando Letelier and Ronni Moffitt) or they are protected by foreign regimes sympathetic to their misdeeds, as for example Paraguay's shielding of the notorious Nazi Mengele. But, it should be noted that the doctrine of *hostes humani generis* depended on the nature of the acts and not on their location nor on the outlaw's resistance to capture.

[21] Some commentators, like Anzilotti, have argued that, since international law is concerned exclusively with relations between states, individuals cannot be either its subjects or objects. Others, like Scelle, contend "that states are merely convenient

individuals are objects or subjects of international law (or both, or neither, or a little of each).[21]

For most of the nineteenth century, international law theory was dominated by the positivist view that states were the subjects and the individuals were only the objects of international law. The former were the actors, the latter merely acted upon. This was a natural consequence or concomitant of the theory of the supremacy of the state, a basically undemocratic world view which saw citizens as serving their respective states, rather than the other way around.

But by the third decade of this century, a strong counter trend was making itself felt. One of its manifestations was the Advisory Opinion of the Permanent Court of International Justice concerning the Jurisdiction of the Courts of Danzig, P.C.I.J., Adv. Op. No. 15, Series B, No. 15. This held for the first time that an international treaty could create rights and obligations for individuals. Cf. discussion in Lauterpacht, *International Law and Human Rights*, New York, 1950, at pp. 28-29. Similar expressions were found in the literature of the time, e.g., Spiropoulos, *L'Individu et le Droit International*, 30 Recueil des Cours 197 (1929).

The ascent to power of the Nazi and fascist regimes in the thirties, with their glorification of the state "uber alles," led to a reappraisal and devaluation of the positive theory of state sovereignty.

The Nuremberg Charter, with its emphasis on the absolute personal responsibility of individuals for war crimes, crimes against the peace, and crimes against humanity, was, of course, the great leap forward toward the incorporation of individual duties in international law:[22]

It was submitted that international law is concerned with the

---

pieces of legal machinery for regulating the rights and duties of collectivities and individuals and that in reality individuals are the only subjects of international law." Waldock, *General Course on Public International Law*, 106 Recueil des Cours 5, 192 (1962). For one of many scholarly treatments of the subject, well endowed with bibliographical footnotes, see Manner, *The Object Theory of the Individual in International Law*, 46 Am. J. of Int'l Law 428 (1952).

[22] It is interesting to note that, three years before the adoption of the Charter on August 8, 1945, the United States Supreme Court, in *Ex parte Quirin*, 317 U.S. 1, 63 S. Ct. 2, 87 L. Ed. 3 (1942), upheld the trial of the seven German saboteurs, in part, under the 15th Article of War, proscribing offenses against "the law of war"—a branch of the law of nations—although Congress had "not itself undertaken to codify that branch of international law to work its precise boundaries, or to enumerate or define by statute all the acts which that law condemns." 317 U.S. 1, 27-29.

actions of sovereign States, and provides no punishment for individuals; and further, that where the act in question is an act of State, those who carry it out are not personally responsible but are protected by the doctrine of the sovereignty of the State. In the opinion of the Tribunal, both these submissions must be rejected. *That international law imposes duties and liabilities upon individuals as upon States has long been recognized. . . the very essence of the Charter is that individuals have international duties which transcend the national obligations of obedience imposed by the individual State. He who violates the laws of war cannot obtain immunity while acting in pursuance of the authority of the State, if the State in authorising action moves outside its competence under international law.* Brownlie, *Principles of Public International Law* (2nd ed.) (Oxford 1973), p. 545.

The next major step in bringing international law in closer contact with individuals was the coming into force, on October 24, 1945, of the UN Charter, Dept. of State Pub. 2638. The human rights provisions found throughout its text, and particularly in Article 55, were to become the fountainhead of the rapidly evolving human rights law of the post-war period. Cf. Commission to Study the Organization of the Peace, *The United Nations and Human Rights*, New York, 1968; Sohn and Buergenthal, *International Protection of Human Rights*, Bobbs Merrill, 1973.

These developments, among others, made it possible for Professor Jessup, later Judge of the World Court, to comment, in 1956, on the position that individuals as well as states are subjects of international law:

Having argued in 1948 that this was a desirable position (A Modern Law of Nations, New York Macmillan, 1948, ch. 2), I am prepared to say it is now established. Jessup, *Transnational Law*, Yale University Press, 1956.

The literature of the last several decades abounds with analytical as well as descriptive statements to the same effect. The following passages are offered merely by way of example:

The new law buried the old dogma that the individual is not a "subject" of international politics and law and that a government's behavior toward its own nationals is a matter of domestic, not international concern. It penetrated national frontiers and the veil of sovereignty. Henkin, *The Rights of Man Today*, Westview Press, 1978, p. 94.

[T]he quality of individuals as subjects of International Law is apparent from the fact that, in various spheres, they are, as such, bound by duties which International Law imposes directly upon them. The various developments since the two World Wars no longer countenance the view that, as a matter of positive law, States are the only subjects of International Law. In proportion as the realization of that fact gains ground, there must be an increasing disposition to treat individuals, within a limited sphere, as subjects of International Law. Lauterpacht's 1955 revision of Oppenheim's *International Law,* as quoted at p. 6, Sohn & Buergenthal, *International Protection of Human Right,* Bobbs-Merrill, 1973.

At present the individual has outgrown the modest classification of "subject" of international law. The individual is now the "focus" of international law. G. Syril, in International Law Association, *Report of the Fifty-Seven Conference,* 496, Great Britain, 1978.

And see *International Human Rights Law and Practice,* a Professional Education Publication prepared in cooperation with the Section of International Law, American Bar Association, 1978, passim.

Thus, the language of *Vencap* and *Dreyfus* seeming to limit international law to interstate relations, aside from being dicta, is a classic statement of the nineteenth and early twentieth century view that the individual is not a subject of international law. If narrowly construed, it is out of tune with the prevailing contemporary view that international law encompasses individual rights and duties.

Likewise, the statement in *Dreyfus* that "violations of international law do not occur when the aggrieved parties are nationals of the acting state" not only takes the holding in *Sabbatino* and *Salimoff* out of context,[23] but also ignores the unequivocal reach of modern international law. Once the position of the individual as a subject of international law is accepted, there is no exception for illegitimate acts by states against their own citizens, or, for that matter, by citizens of one state against their fellow citizens. Were there such a rule, it would be contrary to the Nuremburg Charter, which, in Article 6(c), defines as "crimes against humanity" certain acts committed against "any civilian population" not merely the population of an occupied foreign country. Such a rule would also make a sham of efforts to deal, through international law, with piracy, slavery, terrorism, aerial hijacking and, last but not least, torture. Enemies of all mankind do not escape that categorization by choosing compatriots as victims or acting on behalf of or under color of state law.

---

[23] See fn. p. 25 *supra.*

In short, the *Vencap/Dreyfus* definition of international law, if strictly interpreted, would work a gross injustice in this case. It would, in the respectful opinion of plaintiffs, place the doctrine of this Court squarely at odds with the prevailing view on the subject/object controversy in international law and with the human rights policy of this country and its international legal obligation to implement that policy. As Mr. Justice Cardozo wrote:

> Law and obedience to law are facts confirmed every day to us all in our experience of life. If the result of a definition is to make them seem to be illusions, so much the worse for the definition; we must enlarge it till it is broad enough to answer to realities. Cardozo, *The Nature of the Judicial Process,* New Haven, Yale University Press, 1921, p. 127.

Although plaintiffs suggest that the preferable course is to supplement the definition to conform it to both historical and modern precedent, the next section makes clear that the phrase "affecting the relationship between states . . . and used by them for their common safety and/or dealings *inter se*" encompasses the international condemnation of torture and the commitment of nations to protect the individual from and eradicate this heinous abuse wherever and by whomever it may be practiced.

D. *The Condemnation of Torture By The International Community Is A Rule "Affecting The Relationship Between States . . . And Used By Them For Their Common Good And/Or In Dealings Inter Se"*

The definition of the Law of Nations need not, as the District Court feared, be construed so narrowly as to exclude from § 1350 jurisdiction tort actions based on internationally condemned conduct. Rather the test must be understood to embrace the instant case if it is to comport with the intent of the drafters and the organic growth of international law. The international condemnation of torture is both in theory and in fact among the

> standards rules or customs (a) affecting the relationship between states or between an individual and a foreign state, and (b) used by those states for their common good and/or in dealings inter se. *IIT v. Vencap, supra* at 1015.

This section will demonstrate first that the universal condemnation of torture is designed to assure the common safety. Today as in 1789, flagrant disregard of fundamental norms, by individuals or by states, is an affront and a danger to all nations.

Universal condemnation implies, and modern international law enjoins upon each nation, duties with respect to the eradication of torture within their territory and abroad. The recognition and implementation of these duties by the Executive and Legislative branches of our government concretely demonstrate the inextricable impact of this modern norm on state-to-state relations, including U.S. relations with Paraguay itself.

First, the treaties, conventions and resolutions condemning torture explicitly recognize the relationship between the practice or toleration of torture and international instability. Article 55 of the UN Charter prefaces the UN obligation to promote human rights by underscoring their necessity to international harmony:

> With a view to the creation of conditions of stability and well-being which are necessary for peaceful and friendly relations among nations based on respect for the principle of equal rights and self-determination of peoples.

The Universal Declaration of Human Rights interprets Article 55 and explicates this connection further in its Preamble:

> Whereas recognition of the inherent dignity and of the equal and inalienable rights of all members of the human family is the foundation of freedom, justice and peace in the world,

> Whereas it is essential, if man is not to be compelled to have recourse, as a last resort, to rebellion against tyranny and oppression, that human rights should be protected by the rules of law,

> Whereas it is essential to promote the development of friendly relations between nations.

It is clear from these international pronouncements that that the practice of torture is viewed by the world community as a direct threat to international stability and peace, and its prohibition is "used by them for their common good." Indeed the connection between individual ethics and the common good is the mainstay of utilitarianism which so greatly inspired the framers of the Constitution.

As we have seen, international declarations to which the United States adheres, exhort and oblige every country to work towards the eradication of gross human rights violations everywhere. (Point II, C,2, *supra*).

As a result, violations by foreign officials in foreign lands, even against their own nationals, of the prohibition on torture has become a standard or rule affecting the relations between nations

Human rights which had long played an important role in U.S. foreign policy, were elevated to a preeminent role in President Carter's inaugural address. Within this last decade, the treatment of foreign nationals by their own governments has emerged as a central factor in U.S. foreign policy formulation and practice, second only to overriding consideration of national security. See *Human Rights and U.S. Policy Issues*, No. IB77056, Foreign Affairs and National Defense Division, Congressional Research Service, Library of Congress, May 6, 1977, updated April 19, 1979. (hereinafter "Human Rights and U.S. Policy Issues").

In his March 17, 1977 speech to the United Nations, President Carter stated the position of the U.S. Government on international human rights in terms pointedly applicable to this case:

All signatories of the UN Charter have pledged themselves to observe and respect basic human rights. Thus no member of the United Nations can claim that mistreatment of its citizens is solely its own business. *Equally, no member can avoid its responsibilities to service any to speak when torture or unwarranted deprivation of freedom occurs in any part of the world.* (Emphasis Supplied).[24]

In testimony before Congress in October 1977, the Deputy Assistant Secretary of Human Rights reiterated this commitment:

We have based our actions on our obligations under the United Nations Charter and other international commitments, on our responsibilities under domestic law, and on our belief that the people of this country want a foreign policy that is in accord with our values. We believe that a foreign policy that fails to reflect those values will not receive, nor deserve, the support of the American people. To those who argue that our concern for the human rights of people in other lands constitutes intervention, we say look to the Charter of the United Nations, to the Universal Declaration of Human Rights, to the Helsinki Final Act, to the Declaration Against Torture adopted by the United Nations in 1975, and to similar regional instruments and resolutions. No nation in the world today can hide torture, apartheid, arbitrary imprisonment, censorship, or other such violations of human rights behind asser-

---

[24] Human Rights and U.S. Policy Issues.

tions of sovereignty. The denial of internationally recognized human rights and fundamental freedoms is a matter of international concern. *Human Rights and U.S. Foreign Policy: A Review of the Administration Record,* Hearings before the Subcommittee on International Organizations, 95th Congress, 1st Session, October 25, 1977.

As President Carter's speech indicates, in the catalogue of human rights violations torture is at the top of the list as well as among the few violations universally condemned.

Congress has also made gross human rights violations, particularly torture, a central concern of U.S. foreign policy. Since 1976, almost every major piece of legislation relating to foreign aid has incorporated provisions that limit military and economic assistance to countries which violate internationally recognized human rights standards. See Human Rights and U.S. Policy Issues, pp. 13-21, attached hereto as Addendum I. See also Weissbrodt, Human Rights Legislation and U.S. Foreign Policy, 7 Geo. J. Int. & Compo L. 231-287 (1977). In these acts Congress incorporates explicitly or by reference the language of the UN enactments.[25] Thus norms developed in international law have become the criteria for withdrawal of aid. In some cases, torture is explicitly the first mentioned.[26]

These statutes also require the Secretary of State to report to Congress on the human rights practices of countries being considered for various forms of economic and military aid. Congress has held hearings on the human rights situation in a number of countries including Paraguay. (Addendum I).

Congressional insistence on structural changes within the State Department also underscores the importance of human rights in U.S. foreign policy.

---

[25] International Security Assistance and Arms Export Control Act, P.L. 94-329 (1976); International Development and Food Assistance Act of 1978, P.L. 95-424; Foreign Relations Authorization Act, Fiscal Year 1979, P.C. 95-426 (1978); International Monetary Fund Supplementary Financing Facility, P.L. 95-435, (Oct. 10, 1978); Appropriation for Foreign Assistance and Related Programs, P.L. 95-481, (1979); Export-Import Bank Amendments, P.L. 95-630, Nov. 10, 1978.

[26] For example Section 310 of the International Development and Food Assistance Act of 1975 (P.L. 94-161) states the criteria: "Consistent pattern of gross violations of internationally recognized human rights, including torture or cruel, inhuman, or degrading treatment or punishment, prolonged detention without charges, or other flagrant denial of the right to life, liberty, and the security of person." See also, Inter-American Development Act and African Development Fund, P.L. 34-302 (1976); Foreign Assistance Act of 1974, P.L. 94-559.

In 1976 Congress established a coordinator for Human Rights appointed by the President with the advice and consent of the Senate. International Security Assistance and Arms Export Control Act, P.L. 94-329 (June 30, 1976); in 1977, the Coordinator was elevated to the status of Assistant Secretary and was required to report on ways to strengthen the human rights component of U.S. foreign policy. Foreign Relations Authorization Act of 1978, P.L. 95-105 (August 17, 1977).

Not surprisingly, relations between the United States and numerous other nations have been directly affected by the incorporation of international standards of human rights in our foreign and military aid policy. With regard to Chile all military assistance has been prohibited since 1974 and economic assistance substantially reduced. See Addendum I pp. CRS 14-15. Military assistance to Uruguay has been eliminated since 1976. *Ibid.* In 1977, in addition to socialist countries, Congress prohibited military assistance of any kind to Ethiopia, foreign military credit sales to Argentina, Brazil, El Salvador and Guatemala, and limited appropriations, for The Philippines (*Id.* at CRS 15-18).

As a result, the diplomatic relations of this country have been affected. For example, in February of 1977, Secretary of State Vance announced that the Carter Administration had decided to reduce the 1978 Security Assistance Program budget for Argentina from $32 million recommended by the Ford Administration to $15.7 million, explicitly linking the decision to violations of human rights by the Argentina regime. The military junta responded by announcing that it considered this action an interference in Argentina's internal affairs, and rejected the $15 million left in the Security Assistance Program for FY 1978.[27] The junta's renunciation of U.S. aid was joined in by El Salvador, Brazil, Guatemala and Uruguay when shortly thereafter, the State Department transmitted its report to Congress on the Human Rights status of 82 countries. *Id.* at CRS 1.

Finally, the practice of torture by the police in Paraguay has itself directly affected the relations between this country and Paraguay. In 1978, the Senate version of the International Security Assistance Act of 1978 prohibited use of FY 1979 military education and training funds for Nicaragua and Paraguay. The Conference Committee eliminated the identities of the two countries but also eliminated $300,000, which was the amount destined to Nicaragua and Paraguay. *Id.* CRS 18-19.

---

[27] *Human Rights Conditions for Selected Countries and the U.S. Responses*, prepared for the Subcommittee on International Organizations of the Committee on International Relations, U.S. House of Representatives, by the Foreign Affairs and National Defense Division, Congressional Research Service, Library of Congress, 95th Congress, 2d Session, July 25, 1978.

More recently, in connection with the International Development Assistance Act of 1979, the Senate Committee on Foreign Relations recommended the elimination of $1.584 million in program funding for human needs for Paraguay because "human rights records and/or internal conditions . . . adversely affect the ability of the United States to implement development assistance program consistent with the 'New Direction' mandate." Paraguay was one among only 9 countries for which such bilateral aid was struck, placing it on the Senate Foreign Relations Committees' list of the worst human rights violators in the world. *Report of the Senate Foreign Relations Committee on The International Development Assistance Act of 1979*, Rep. No. 96-137 (May 11, 1979). (Addendum II).

If there is any question about the significance of the effect of human rights violations such as torture on U.S. foreign policy, generally and with respect to Paraguay in particular, appellants should be entitled to have that question fully explored in appropriate evidentiary proceedings before the District Court. At that time plaintiffs would also demonstrate, that the torture-murder of Joelito Filartiga has contributed to adverse relations between this country and Paraguay and that responsible authorities view the redress sought here as fully consistent with and supportive of U.S. efforts to eliminate torture.

III. THE FRAMERS' WISDOM IN PROVIDING CONCURRENT FEDERAL JURISDICTION UNDER § 1350 IS BORNE OUT BY THE INTERNATIONAL IMPLICATIONS OF CASES SUCH AS THIS ONE

As we have seen, § 1350 implemented the fundamental precept of our federal system that matters of national and international concern are better resolved by national rather than state institutions. (I, B, *supra*). Chief Justice Marshall issued a classic statement of the underlying principle in *Gibbons v. Ogden*, 22 U.S. (9 Wheat.) 1 (1824), when he wrote:

> The genius and character of the whole government seems to be, that its action is to be applied to all the external concerns which affect the states generally; but not to those which are completely within a particular state, which do not affect other states, and with which it is not necessary to interfere, for the purpose of executing some of the general powers of government. *Id.*

There can be no doubt that how the American courts handle tort claims by aliens involving, as here, violation of fundamental norms of international law is a matter of national and international concern and is fraught with intrinsic foreign policy implications.

The decision before this Court to entertain jurisdiction will have a bearing on the ability of this nation to carry out its international commitment to condemn torture and provide effective remedies for its victims. (II, C, 2, *supra*). The decision will affect the international perception of the seriousness with which the United States views its commitment to protect human rights. Moreover, in this case, the decision will either open Pena's conduct to real judicial inquiry and sanction, or abet his escape from justice.

Beyond that, the question before this Court is *to decide who decides*—the state courts or the federal courts—a number of issues which are pervaded with international implications and likely to arise in tort claims based on gross human rights violations. The framers' "concern for uniformity in this country's dealings with foreign nations and . . . desire to give matters of international significance to the jurisdiction of federal institutions," *Banco Nacional de Cuba*, 376 U.S. at 427, n. 25, necessitates jurisdiction because of the multiplicity of "issues of international import." *Valanga v. Metropolitan Life Insurance Co., supra* at 328.

It is clear that once jurisdiction is assumed, questions will arise about the definition of the substantive violation involved and the impact of different international agreements and doctrines. These are questions best left to determination in the first instance by the federal courts.

It is also likely that in deciding whether and how to exercise jurisdiction, a number of federal common law questions may arise. This Circuit has recognized in another context the importance of broadly construing federal jurisdiction where "even though a claim is created by state law . . . the dispositive issues stated in the complaint require application of federal common law." *Ivy Broadcasting Co. v. American Tel. and Tel. Co.*, 391 F. 2d 486, 492 (1968). Here, as the Court emphasized in *Adra*, "the importance of foreign relations to our country cautions the federal courts . . . not to decline jurisdiction . . . ." *Abdul Rahman Adra v. Clift, supra* at 865 (D. Md. 1961).

These cases will frequently involve actions where the defendant is or was a foreign government official or claims his acts to be clothed with official sanction. In some cases, traditionally federal separation of powers issues may be at issue.

---

[28] The Act of State doctrine is not at issue here because the clear official authority required by *Alfred Dunhill of London v. Cuba*, 425 U.S. 682, 694-695, 96 S. Ct. 1854, 1861 (1976) is absent. Paraguay is on record as denying that Joelito died by torture inflicted by Pena (JA 10, 44, 51). OAS, ICHR, "Report on the Situation of Human Rights in Paraguay," *supra*, p. 26.

Thus, although the Act of State doctrine is not at issue in the present case,[28] other cases involving violations of international law by foreign government officials may have to consider this doctrine. The Supreme Court has stressed that the Act of State doctrine is a topic of peculiarly federal expertise and concern. Speaking through Mr. Justice Harlan in *Banco Nacional de Cuba v. Sabbatino*, the Court declared:

> Whatever considerations are thought to predominate, it is plain that the problems involved are uniquely federal in nature. If federal authority, in this instance this Court, orders the field of judicial competence in this area for the federal courts, and the state courts are left free to formulate their own rules, the purposes behind the doctrine could be as effectively undermined as if there had been no federal pronouncement on this subject. 376 U.S. at 424.

Even though the Act of State claim should be unequivocally rejected in a case involving torture,[29] the federal courts will be better equipped to do so. On the other hand, cases may arise where Act of State should be recognized. The sensitivity and experience of the federal courts are more likely to yield proper application of the doctrine and avoid international embarrassments or entanglements over error in this respect.

Another question in this context, which was actually raised by Pena below, is the defense of *forum non conveniens*. In cases of this kind, two questions will be paramount: whether there is an alternative neutral and accessible forum, and whether the public interest requires retention of jurisdiction. See *Gulf Oil Co. v. Gilbert, supra; Schertenlieb v. Traum, supra; Mobil Tankers v. Mene Grande Oil Co., supra; Phoenix Canada Oil Co., Ltd. v. Texaco, Inc., supra.*

The public interest issue constitutes a determination of the importance of our moral and legal obligations under international law. And beyond that, the *forum non conveniens* issue will frequently require a judgment on the independence of the foreign judiciary. Indeed, to recognize an independent and competent judiciary in this case[30] would sorely undermine the credibility of this country's commitment to human rights.

Thus this case, and cases like it, involve a judgment very much like

---

[29] It can hardly be imagined that a state would have the audacity overtly to authorize torture. If it did, the unexceptional prohibition on torture in international law which renders torture always and absolutely illegitimate prevents it—consistent with our international commitments—from being cognizable as an act of state.

[30] See Statement of the Case, *supra*, pp. 1-8. Additional material and testimony supporting this conclusion would be presented on remand.

that in *Phoenix Canada Oil Co. Ltd. v. Texaco, supra*, where the federal district court rejected the suggestion that an alternative forum existed in Ecuador since procedural protections were not comparable to the United States and since

> Plaintiff has represented by affidavit that Ecuador is presently controlled by a military government which has 'assumed the power of the executive and legislative branches and rules by fiat,' 'has specifically retained the right to veto or intervene in any judicial matter which the Military Government deems to involve matters of national concern,' and 'has absolute power over all branches of government.' *supra* at 455.

Obviously, it is preferable that this decision be made by a federal court.

In addition, these cases involving gross human rights violations will also present choice of law questions. There the issue will be to what extent should the forum state recognize the foreign law when it is inconsistent, in theory or in practice, with fundamental norms of fairness recognized here and internationally. As the Court said in *Sabbatino*, paraphrasing the great professor and international jurist Philip C. Jessup, who cautioned against extending *Erie v. Tompkins* to legal problems affecting international relations "rules of international law should not be left to divergent and perhaps parochial state interpretations." *Banco Nacional de Cuba v. Sabbatino*, 376 U.S. at 425.

For all these reasons, cases involving violations of international law's proscription of torture and other undisputed human rights violations are so intimately bound up with considerations of foreign policy that the desirability of their being heard before national, as opposed to state tribunals cannot be seriously questioned. The violations complained of themselves affect American foreign policy and the courts' responses to such violations will have implications for United States participation in the world community. And it is no less apparent that disposition of such cases will require interpretation of treaties and doctrines which are uniquely federal in nature. In sum, the framers' original preference for federal fora is no less compelling today.

CONCLUSION

A finding of subject matter jurisdiction in this case is consistent with the original intent of Congress in adopting § 1350, that federal courts should have concurrent jurisdiction with the states in cases of this magnitude; it would place the judiciary in harmony with the legislative and executive branches of this nation in regard to its human rights policy; and by giving effect to the clear mandates of international law, it would evince a decent respect for the opinions of humankind.

WHEREFORE, the judgment of the District Court should be reversed.

Respectfully submitted,*

PETER WEISS
RHONDA COPELON
JOHN W. CORWIN
JOSE ANTONIO LUGO
c/o Center for Constitutional Rights
853 Broadway
New York, New York 10003

MICHAEL MAGGIO
GOREN AND MAGGIO
1801 Columbia Road,
N.W. Washington, D.C. 20009

Attorneys for Plaintiffs

Dated: New York, New York
        July 23, 1979

---

* Counsel wish to gratefully acknowledge the tremendous contributions of law students Jeff Blum, Eduardo Padro and Janet Price in the preparation of this brief.

JULY 23, 1979: UNITED STATES

Brief of Amici Curiae (International Human Rights Law Group, Council on Hemispheric Affairs, and Washington Office on Latin America) on Behalf of Appellants

UNITED STATES COURT OF APPEALS
IN THE SECOND CIRCUIT

No. 79-6090

DOLLY M.E. FILARTIGA and
DR. JOEL FILARTIGA,

Plaintiffs-Appellants,

– against –

AMERICO NORBERTO PENA-IRALA

Defendant-Appellee.

On Appeal From Judgment From New York District Court
Eastern District of New York

BRIEF OF
THE INTERNATIONAL HUMAN RIGHTS LAW GROUP,
THE COUNCIL ON HEMISPHERIC AFFAIRS, &
THE WASHINGTON OFFICE ON LATIN AMERICA
AS *AMICI CURIAE*
URGING REVERSAL.

> ALLAN ABBOT TUTTLE, ESQ.
> STEVEN M. SCHNEEBAUM, ESQ.
> 2550 M Street, N.W.
> Washington, D.C. 20037
>
> Attorneys for *Amici Curiae*
>
> July 23, 1979

TABLE OF CONTENTS

I.   STATEMENT OF THE CASE

II. THE DISTRICT COURT HAS JURISDICTION OVER THIS MATTER PURSUANT TO 28 U.S.C. § 1350

    A. This is a Suit Brought by Aliens for a Tort Only

    B. Torture Is a Violation of the Law of Nations and of Treaties of the United States

        1. Torture is a violation of the law of nations
        2. Torture is a violation of treaties to which the United States is a party
        3. Violations of the law of nations may be committed by individuals

    C. Judicial Decisions Interpreting 28 U.S.C. § 1350 Are Fully Consistent with Its Application to the Instant Case.

        1. U.S. courts recognize the changing and developing nature of international law
        2. Earlier cases applying 28 U.S.C. § 1350 have not had cause to consider contemporary norms of international law
        3. The events allegedly giving rise to this action affect the foreign relations of the United States
        4. Insofar as U.S. courts have barred the use of 28 U.S.C. § 1350 where Plaintiff and Defendant are of the same nationality, those dicta should be overruled

III. DEFENDANT IS PROTECTED FROM SUIT NEITHER BY THE ACT OF STATE DOCTRINE NOR BY SOVEREIGN IMMUNITY

    A. The Act of State Doctrine Cannot Shield Defendant's Alleged Acts from Judicial Scrutiny

    B. The Government of Paraguay Does Not Invoke Sovereign Immunity from Suit

IV. THE JURISDICTION OF THE DISTRICT COURT DOES NOT OFFEND ANY RECOGNIZABLE RIGHT OF DEFENDANT

    A. The District Court Properly Had Jurisdiction over Defendant

    B. Defendant Has Waived the Defense of Lack of Personal Jurisdiction

    C. No Constitutional Right of Defendant Would Be Infringed by the

Court's Jurisdiction

I. STATEMENT OF THE CASE

This is an action in tort for the wrongful death in Asuncion, Paraguay, on March 29, 1976, of Joelito Filartiga (hereinafter "Joelito"). The Complaint alleges that Joelito died as a direct result of willful and tortious acts of Defendant Americo N. Pena-Irala.

Plaintiffs are Dr. Joel Filartiga and Ms. Dolly Filartiga (hereinafter "the

Filartigas"), the deceased's father and sister, respectively. Dr. Filartiga sues in his individual capacity as well as in the capacity of his son's legal representative; Dolly Filartiga alleges that she too was a victim of the tortious acts that led to her brother's death.

Plaintiffs contend that Joelito died while being subjected to systematic torture by Defendant, acting under color of his apparent authority as Inspector General of the Police in Asuncion. It is alleged that Joelito was singled out for such treatment because of the dissident political activities of his father. The Complaint further alleges that Dolly Filartiga was forced by Defendant or agents acting on his behalf to view the mutilated body of her brother, and was threatened and intimidated. The Filartigas both suffered enormous emotional pain as a result of Defendant's alleged tortious conduct.

The theory of Plaintiffs' case is that insofar as torture is a tort committed in violation of international law, the district court has jurisdiction over this action pursuant to 28 U.S.C. § 1350. On May 15, 1979, the United States District Court for the Eastern District of New York dismissed the suit for lack of jurisdiction over its subject matter. Although acknowledging the "strength" of Plaintiffs' legal arguments (Opinion, p. 4), Judge Nickerson concluded that he was constrained by what he felt to be the import of precedents within this Circuit. A notice of appeal was filed on May 15, 1979.

Amici support Plaintiffs' submission that the dismissal in district court was erroneous as a matter of law. The only questions for adjudication in this Honorable Court are whether the district court properly had jurisdiction over the instant action pursuant to 28 U.S.C. § 1350, and if so, whether jurisdiction might appropriately have been declined. *Amici* respectfully submit that the lower court had and has subject matter jurisdiction, and that the dismissal should be reversed and the case remanded to the district court for trial.

Since the matter came before the district court on Defendant's motion to dismiss pursuant to Rule 12 (b)(1), Federal Rules of Civil Procedure, all factual allegations must, for the purposes of ruling on the motion and on this appeal based thereon, be taken as true. *Newport News Shipbuilding Dry Dock Co. v. Schauffer*, 303 U.S. 54 (1938); *A.F. Brod v. Perlow*, 375 F.2d 393, 395 (2d Cir. 1967); *Klanberg v. Roth*, 425 F. Supp. 440 (S.D.N.Y. 1976); *U.S. v. Bimba*, 233 F. Supp. 966, 968 (E.D.N.Y. 1964).

II. THE DISTRICT COURT HAS JURISDICTION OVER THIS MATTER

PURSUANT TO 28 U.S.C. § 1350.

Title 28, U.S. Code, section 1350 reads as follows:

The district courts shall have original jurisdiction of any civil action by an alien for a tort only, committed in violation of the law of nations or a treaty of the United States.

Amici respectfully contend that the jurisdictional prerequisites of this statute are met in the instant case.

A. *This Is a Suit Brought by Aliens for a Tort Only.*

In interpreting and applying 28 U.S.C. § 1350, the courts have consistently required that, to be subject to this section, a civil action legitimately be one in tort. Thus in *Moxon v. The Fanny*, 17 Fed. Cas. No. 9,895 (D. Fa. 1793), a suit in admiralty for recovery of a vessel seized as prize was held not properly brought under the progenitor of this statute. The court ruled that "it cannot be called a suit for a tort only, when the property, as well as damages for the supposed trespass, are sought for."

Likewise, in *Valanga v. Metropolitan Life Insurance Co.*, 259 F. Supp. 324, 327 (E.D. Fa. 1966), jurisdiction under 28 U.S.C. § 1350 was denied with respect to an action to recover funds allegedly due under an insurance policy. The court noted that "[w]hile 'tort' law embodies a broad spectrum of legal remedies, it is a word of legal art and it would be placing a severe strain on the framers' meaning" to include such an action therein.

The District Court for the District of Columbia in *Pauling v. McElrox*, 164 F. Supp. 390 (D.D.C. 1958) noted that Plaintiffs expressly declined to redraft their complaint to sound in tort, and therefore denied jurisdiction under 28 U.S.C. § 1350. In *Canadian Transport Co. v. U.S.*, 430 F. Supp. 1168, 1171 (D.D.C. 1977), the same court considered (but did not find) § 1350 jurisdiction only on the express assumption that the cause of action was in tort.

The instant allegations present a classic instance of an intentional tort. Defendant is asserted to have beaten and slashed Joelito, and to have administered electric shocks to his body. The record below contains a statement by Harold R. Berk, Esq., a member of Amnesty International (USA) Legal Committee, made to the Inter-American Commission on Human Rights, describing the nature of the injuries sustained by Joelito that led to his death.

Ordinarily for an act or omission to give rise to liability as tortious it must be actionable when and where it occurred. *See*, for example, *Black Diamond S.S. Co. v. Stewart & Sons*, 336 U.S. 386, 396 (1949); *Cuba Railroad Co. v. Crosby*, 222 U.S. 473 (1912). The conduct of Defendant Pena would, if proved, certainly constitute a tort (*delito*) under the laws of Paraguay. Indeed, Defendant admits this to be the case in his Motion to Dismiss, stating, at p. 4, that "the decedent's father has the right to file a civil suit in a Paraguayan Court under Paraguayan law for the recovery of civil damages for the wrongful death of his son."

It follows that, under the rule that the substantive law applied in an action in tort is the law of the *situs*, this cause of action qualifies as "an action in tort only." Needless to say, were the view of a minority of American courts to be adopted and recourse had to the law of the forum, the allegations of the Complaint would be found to state a cause of action "in tort only" under the laws of the State of New York.

There is no dispute that the Filartigas are aliens within the meaning of that term in 28 U.S.C. § 1350. The case is therefore "a civil action brought by an alien for a tort only," as required by the statute.

B. *Torture Is A Violation of the Law of Nations and of Treaties of the United States.*

1. *Torture is a violation of the law of nations.*

On December 9, 1975, the General Assembly of the United Nations issued a Declaration on the Protection of All Persons from Being Subjected to Torture and Other Cruel, Inhuman or Degrading Treatment or Punishment. G.A. Res. 3452 (XXX), U.N. Doc. A/1034 (1975). This Declaration, adopted by consensus of all States Members, provides that an

> act of torture . . . is an offense to human dignity and shall be condemned as a denial of the purposes of the Charter of the United Nations and as a violation of human rights and fundamental freedoms. . . .

Article 2. It goes on to forbid any State to "permit or tolerate" torture, even in cases of such "exceptional circumstances" as "a state of war or a threat of war, internal political instability, or, any other public emergency." Article 3.

Resolutions of the General Assembly are not international legislation: they do not *create* legal obligations. When, however, such resolutions "are concerned with general norms of international law, then acceptance by a majority vote constitutes *evidence* of the opinions of governments in the widest forum for the expression of such opinions." I. Brownlie, *Principles of Public International Law* (2d ed., 1973) 14, emphasis in original.

The General Assembly, then, does not *make* law, it *states* what the law *is*. In Resolution 3452 (XXX), the community of nations stated in the strongest possible terms that torture is not only a wrong but an international wrong. Nor is this the only example of emphatic and univocal denunciation of torture.

Torture was condemned in the Universal Declaration of Human Rights, G.A. Res 217A (III), U.N. Doc. A/811 (1948), Article 5, by a vote of 48-0; and in the International Covenant on Civil and Political Rights, G.A. Res. 2200 (XXI), U.N. Doc. A/6316 (1966), Article 7, which was initially signed by 45 States, and, as of January 1, 1979, had been ratified by 55. The Organization of American States outlawed torture in the 1948 American Declaration of the Rights and Duties of Man (Res *XXX*, 9th International Conference of American States), Article 26; and in the American Convention on Human Rights (O.A.S. T.S. No. 36, at 1; OEA/Ser. L/V/II.23, doc. 21, rev. 2), Article 5.

There can be no question, then, that the community of nations has condemned torture as an offense against the world's legal order. That is to say, a state that employs, permits, or tolerates torture is in violation of its solemn *international* undertakings, and this irrespective of the nationality of its victims.

The legal norm that has emerged is no doubt a relatively recent addition to the international *corpus juris*. That there is an international obligation of states not to torture their citizens is, however, less startling when one recalls the traditional prohibition against mistreating foreigners. Both stem from the recognition, set forth in the Preamble to the Universal Declaration of Human Rights (*supra*), that "recognition of the inherent dignity and of the equal and inalienable rights of all members of the human family is the foundation of freedom, justice, and peace in the world."

So well entrenched today is the notion that a State's observance of human rights is a matter of international concern that at least two regional arrangements allow access by individuals to international judicial proceedings against their own governments. Although both the European Convention on Human Rights and the American Convention on Human Rights require that individual claims be "filtered" through an international agency (the Commissions) before they are presented to the respective Courts, it is nonetheless true that both reflect the sense of the world community that States' obligations to their citizens are of international concern.

The European Court of Human Rights has held that, in carrying out its functions, it may "take cognisance of all questions of fact and law which may arise in the course of the consideration of the case." *De Wilde, et al. v. Belgium*, judgment of June 18, 1971, E.C.H.R. Publs., Series A, De Wilde Case 12. Its jurisdiction is thus as wide-ranging as that of a municipal court in matters properly brought before it.

There is no anomaly, therefore, in contending that it is a wrong with international consequences for agents of the Government of Paraguay to torture Paraguayans. Article 2(7) of the U.N. Charter, which declares the principle of non-intervention of the Organization in matters "which are essentially "within the domestic jurisdiction of any State," does not apply to human rights violations which have been repeatedly declared by the General Assembly not to be matters of exclusively domestic concern.

Nor is torture the only act forbidden to States by contemporary international law. Other systematic violations of fundamental human dignities are likewise outlawed. *See,* for example, the International Covenant on Civil and Political Rights, G.A. Res. 2200 (*XXI*), U.N. Doc. A/6316 (1966); and the Convention on the Prevention and Punishment of the Crime of Genocide, G.A. Res. 174 (*III*), U.N. Doc. A/180 (1948).

Plaintiffs are not, for the purposes of laying jurisdiction in the district court pursuant to 28 U.S.C. § 1350, constrained to argue more, however, than this simple proposition: with the development of the law of human rights, both inside and outside the United Nations, by treaties, custom, and the opinion of jurists, torture is a violation of the law of nations. This claim is amply borne out. The jurisdictional prerequisites of 28 U.S.C. § 1350 are met.

2. *Torture is a violation of treaties to which the United States is a party.*

The Charter of the United Nations is a treaty of the United States, part of the "supreme Law of the Land" under Article VI § 3 of the Constitution. Article 56 of the Charter sets out the "pledge" of all States Members "to take joint and separate action in cooperation with the Organization for the achievement" of human rights objectives.

"Joint action" was taken by the Members in espousing the principles of the Universal Declaration (*supra*). While the Declaration is not legally binding in all of its terms in the sense in which a treaty embodies obligations, it is "an authoritative guide, produced by the General Assembly, to the interpretation of the provisions in the Charter." I. Brownlie, *op. cit.*, 554.

Many publicists have contended that obligations undertaken in the Declaration contain all of the legal force of the Charter it sought to interpret. Thus, in the words of Philip C. Jessup (*A Modern Law of Nations—An Introduction* (1948) 91), "[t]he duty [of respect for fundamental human rights] is imposed by the Charter, a treaty" to which the Members are parties. Prof. Egon Schwelb compiled a list of scholars who concur with the Jessup view, in 66 Amer. Journal of Intl. Law 337 (1972): Quincy Wright, Georges Scelle, F. Blaine Sloane, Heinz Guradze, and Jacob Robinson.

Not only, however, have writers on international legal subjects concluded that the Declaration enunciates binding obligations of States, but the International Court of Justice also has embraced this view. In its *Advisory Opinion on the Legal Consequences for States of the Continued Presence of South Africa in Namibia*, (1971) I.C.J. Rep. 58, the Court found that the apartheid policies of South Africa in the former Mandatory of South-West Africa "constitute a denial of fundamental rights [that] is a flagrant violation of the purposes and principles of the Charter." At ¶ 131. The Security Council "agreed with" the Court's opinion in Resolution 301 (1971), and the General Assembly "welcomed" it in Resolution 2871 (*XXVI*).

The positing of fundamental human rights as underlying the Charter itself harks back to the dissenting opinion of Judge Tanaka, in the *Southwest Africa Cases* (Ethiopia v. South Africa; Liberia v. South Africa) (2d phase), [1966] I.C.J. Rep. 5, 293: "the Universal Declaration of Human Rights, although not binding in itself, constitutes evidence of the interpretation and application of the relevant Charter provisions."

According to Sir Hersch Lauterpacht, it is the legal duty of United Nations Members "to respect and observe fundamental human rights and freedoms." *International Law and Human Rights* (1950) 147. The key to all of these pronouncements is that respect for human rights is seen as a legal obligation coterminous with the obligations accepted with the Charter itself. And what is true of the U.N. Charter is true, *mutatis mutandis*, of the Charter of the Organization of American States, as interpreted by the American Declaration of the Rights and Duties of Man.

It will be noted that Plaintiffs need *not* contend that the Charter is self-executing. Abundant precedent in American jurisprudence has held that Article 56 does not "purport to impose legal obligations on the individual member nations or to create rights in private persons." *Sei Fujii v. State*, 38 Cal. 2d 718, 722; 242 P.2d 617, 620-21 (1952). *Accord, Pauling v. McElroy, supra*; *Hitai v. I.N.S.*, 343 F.2d 466 (2d Cir. 1965) (no provision of the Charter invalidates "*ex proprio vigore . . .* any laws of member states."); *Vlissidis v. Anadell*, 262 F.2d 398 (7th Cir. 1959) (no section of the Charter "purports to regulate the immigration policies of member nations."); *Camacho v. Rogers*, 199 F. Supp. 155 (S.D.N.Y. 1961).

This is not an action to enjoin the operation of an American statute on the basis of a perceived conflict with the Charter. Rather, *amici* respectfully direct the Court's attention to the Charter for quite another purpose. This is an action in *tort*, arising out of conduct that, as inconsistent with the Charter, was a violation of international law. It is not a suit *for* an alleged violation of the Charter; it cites a claimed violation as part of the jurisdictional prerequisites for consideration of a common law tort.

Moreover, the celebrated cases cited above may, in light of developments in international law, be of diminishing authority as precedents. It may be that after several years of robust activity in the human rights law area, American courts called upon to interpret Article 56 may find "the human rights practice of the U.N. [to] have a much more compelling domestic law relevance than would be the case with regard to other Charter provisions." L.B. Sohn and T. Buergenthal (eds.), *International Protection of Human Rights* (1973) 947.

For Defendant's alleged acts to constitute violations of treaties his country has undertaken with the United States (and of course Paraguay is a party to both the U.N. and the O.A.S. Charters), it is not necessary that any treaty independently confer on any individual a right of action in U.S. courts. *That* function—the conferring of subject-matter jurisdiction—is performed by 28 U.S.C. § 1350. Recourse is had to treaty obligations only in ascertaining the meaning of that statute.

For the reasons set out above, it is respectfully submitted that torture is a violation of treaties to which the United States is a party (whether or not any instance of torture would be separately actionable *per se* under American law). The instant action is therefore characterizable as a suit "by an alien for a tort only, committed in violation" of *both* "the law of nations" *and* "a treaty of the United States." The district court had jurisdiction over this action under the statute, and the dismissal below should be reversed.

3. *Violations of the law of nations may be committed by individuals.*

That an individual may be held responsible for violation of international legal norms is no new development. This conclusion follows even without consideration of the vexed question whether individuals are "subjects" of international law.

The pirate is but one example of individuals whose acts entail international liability. In the United States, Congress, pursuant to its Constitutional authority "to define and punish Offences against the Law of Nations" (Article I, § 8, cl. 10), has provided additional instances.

In *U.S. v. Arjona*, 120 U.S. 479 (1887), the Supreme Court upheld an indictment under a statute banning the counterfeiting of foreign banknotes by individuals. Interferences with the activities of foreign missions have been held to be "offenses against the law of nations" within the power of Congress to proscribe. *Frend v. U.S.*, 100 F.2d 691 (D.C. Cir. 1938), *cert. den.*, 306 U.S. 640 (1939); *Jewish Defense League v. Washington*, 347 F. Supp. 1300 (D.D.C. 1972).

Moreover, it has long been the case that acts committed by individuals in violation of the law of war may be punished. *Application of Yamashita*, 327 U.S. 1, 14 (1945) (the massacre of the civilian population of the Philippines is a violation entailing the individual liability of the military commander). In *Ex parte Quirin*, 317 U.S. 1 (1942), the Supreme Court held that it has always "recognized and applied the law of war as including that part of the law of nations which prescribes, for the conduct of war, the status, rights and *duties* of enemy nations, *as well as of enemy individuals*." At 27-28, emphasis added, citations omitted.

Plainly, then, within the contemplation of American courts, breaches of international obligations may be committed by individuals. Stated another way, individual human beings have rights and duties under international law as well as under the domestic legal systems with jurisdiction over them.

With the proliferation of international legal norms concerning individual rights, potential violations of international obligations too have multiplied. Thus in the Genocide Convention (*supra*), the nations of the world "confirm" (Article 1) that genocide "is a crime under international law." Jurisdiction over persons accused of this crime is vested in "a competent tribunal of the State in the territory of which the act was committed," or in an international forum. Some writers suggest that this grant of jurisdiction is not exclusive, and that the person accused of genocide may, like the pirate, be tried by the court of any state that can find him. D.P. O'Connell, for example, notes that "international law [is] flexible in the matter of permitting criminal jurisdiction over aliens for acts abroad when those acts could be related to the prosecuting state's own interest." He suggests that in the case of a crime under international law, "that interest is certainly engaged." *Op. cit.*, p. 959.

Likewise, breaches of the Geneva Conventions of 1949, relative to the Treatment of Prisoners of War and the Protection of Civilian Persons in

Time of War, 75 U.N.T.S. 287 (1950) are matters of individual responsibility. *See,* for example, Articles 129 and 130 of the former treaty.

The concept of "crimes against humanity" was developed into a body of law and legal practice after World War II. Article 6 of the Charter of the International Military Tribunal (at Nuremburg), signed on August 8, 1945, defined that term to include certain brutal and heinous acts "whether or not in violation of the domestic law of the country where perpetrated." The Tribunal was later to hold that "the very essence of the Charter is that individuals have international obligations which transcend the national obligations of obedience imposed by the individual State." These principles of international law were affirmed by the first General Assembly on December 11, 1946. G. A. Res. 95 (I).

Criminal prosecution by a domestic court of an act outside its jurisdiction may be exercised "when the act of the individual is one which the law of nations itself renders internationally illegal or regards as one which any member of the international society is free to oppose and thwart." Hyde, 1 *International Law* (2d ed., 1947) 804. Thus it is that the District Court of Jerusalem found jurisdiction over Adolf Eichmann pursuant to the Nazi Collaborators (Punishment) Law, on an indictment, *inter alia* for "crimes against humanity," as well as war crimes. *Attorney-General of Israel v. Eichmann,* Crim. No. 40/61, December 11, 1961 (excerpted in 56 Amer. Journal of Intl. Law 805 (1962)).

If criminal responsibility can, as has been shown, undoubtedly be imputed to individuals under international law, then it follows *a fortiori* that the acts of individuals may be described as violations of the law of nations for the purposes of asserting *civil* jurisdiction. It will be recalled once again that the instant case is not an action "for" a violation of international law, but rather for a *tort* only, which, if the facts alleged in the Complaint are taken as true, was committed "in violation of the law of nations and a treaty of the United States." 28 U.S.C. § 1350.

For these reasons, the dismissal of the action by the court below was incorrect as a matter of law, and should be reversed.

C. *Judicial Decisions Interpreting 28 U.S.C. § 1350 Are Fully Consistent with Its Application to the Instant Case.*

Judge Nickerson's decision turns upon what he felt to be the force of precedent in interpreting 28 U.S.C. § 1350. *Amici* respectfully submit that this view of the earlier cases is erroneous.

1. *U.S. courts recognize the changing and developing nature of international law.*

In *The Paquete Habana*, 175 U.S. 677 (1900), the Supreme Court held that customary international law, and therefore U.S. law, forbade the retention as prize of a noncommercial fishing vessel. The holding was said to be based in "an ancient usage among civilized nations, beginning centuries ago, and gradually ripening into a rule of international law." At 686. "International law," Mr. Justice Gray wrote for the Court, "is part of our law, and must be ascertained and administered by the courts of justice of appropriate jurisdiction as often as questions of right depending upon it are duly presented for their determination." At 700. The works of scholars and commentators are a source of international law "not for the speculations of their authors concerning what the law ought to be, but for trustworthy evidence of what the law really is." *Id*, citing *Hilton v. Guyot*, 159 U.S. 113 (1895).

Customary international law, which by its nature is an evolving, developing *corpus*, is part of the law of the United States. So self-evident is this principle, that it was held not unconstitutionally vague for a statute to outlaw what it describes only as "the crime of piracy, as defined by the law of nations." 18 U.S.C. § 1651; U.S. v. Smith, 5 Wheat. (5 U.S.) 153 (1820). *See, Ex parte Quirin, supra*, at 30.

References to international law in U.S. statutes include the entire body of such law of whatever provenance, save only that the law be recognized as such by the community of nations. Thus the Supreme Court is given original and exclusive jurisdiction of actions against ambassadors "not inconsistent with the law of nations." 28 U.S.C. § 1251 (a)(2). International law is defined to be part of the substantive law applied in assessment of claims against foreign nations by the Foreign Claims Settlement Commission. 22 U.S.C. § 1644b. And Congress has directed the courts to determine, for the purpose of evaluating the juridical effects of foreign expropriations, whether a violation "of the principles of international law" has occurred. 22 U.S.C. § 2370 (e)(2).

"The courts apply international custom because it is international law insofar as they have been able to ascertain." L. Erades and W.L. Gould, *The Relation Between International Law and Municipal Law in the Netherlands and in the U.S.* (1961) 292. Indeed, developments in international custom have been held to modify existing statutes. *State of the Netherlands v. Federal Reserve Bank*, 201 F.2d 455 (2d Cir. 1953). This comports with the theory of the manifold sources of international law enunciated by Article 38(1) of the Statute of the International Court of Justice.

As long ago as 1784, the Supreme Court of Pennsylvania found an assault upon a foreign consul to be "an infraction of the law of nations. This law, in its full extent, is part of the law of this State . . . [The Defendant] is guilty of a crime against the whole world." *Respublica v. De Longchamps*, 1 Dall. 111 (Sup. Ct. Pa. 1784).

It was therefore open to the district court below to consider the developing norms of customary international law in determining whether the Complaint properly alleged a violation within the meaning of 28 U.S.C. § 1350.

2. Earlier cases applying 28 U.S.C. § 1350 have not had cause to consider contemporary norms of international law.

Although the statute that is now codified as 28 U.S.C. § 1350 has been the law of the land since 1789 (Judiciary Act § 9, 1 Stat. 77), cases interpreting it are scarce. Certainly there is no reported instance of an application of the statute to facts similar to those presented in the instant action.

The only modern example of jurisdiction under 28 U.S.C. § 1350 is *Abdul-Rahman Omar Adra v. Clift*, 195 F. Supp. 857 (D. Md. 1961). There, the tort alleged was abduction by Defendant of a child properly in Plaintiff's custody. The complaint went on to accuse Defendant, in carrying out the tort, of committing the separate and additional wrong of concealing the child's nationality and having her admitted to the United States under a passport to which she had no right.

Although the court finally decided in its discretion to deny the relief sought, it did find that it had jurisdiction over the subject matter pursuant to 28 U.S.C. § 1350. It is important, in the submission of *amici*, to note that in *Clift*, the tort and the international violation were not the same act: the international wrong was part of the *modus operandi*, as it were, of the tort.

In *Nguyen Da Yen v. Kissinger*, 528 F.2d 1194 (9th Cir. 1975), the Court of Appeals held that the seizure of children in Viet Nam and their transportation to the United States "would appear to be a tort . . . and it may well be a tort in violation of the 'law of nations.'" At 1201 n. 13. The Court declined, however, to consider the issue further in the absence of adequate briefing and of a possibly indispensable party.

Plaintiff in *Lopes v. Reederei Richard Schroeder*, 225 F. Supp. 292 (E.D. Pa. 1963) was an alien seaman alleging a breach of the obligation of seaworthiness by the shipowner who employed him. Finding seaworthiness of vessels not to be mandated by international law, the court dismissed the action for lack of jurisdiction. *Accord, Benjamins v. British European Airways*, 572 F.2d 913 (2d Cir. 1978) (the Warsaw Convention does not seek to outlaw airline accidents).

The instant case differs from *Lopes* and *Benjamins* in that the tortious act alleged to have occurred *was* a violation of international legal obligations. For the same reason, it is distinguishable from the cases in which parties have sought to invoke 28 U.S.C. § 1350 in labor disputes: *Damaskinos v. Societa Navigacion Interamericana S.A. Panama*, 255 F. Supp. 919 (S.D.N.Y. 1966); *Khedivial Line v. Seafarers Intl. Union*, 278 F.2d 49 (2d Cir. 1960); *Upper Lakes Shipping v. Intl. Longshoreman's Assn.*, 33 F.R.D. 348 (S.D.N.Y. 1963); *Canadian Transport Co. v. U.S., supra.*

IIT v. Vencap, Ltd., 519 F.2d 1001 (2d Cir. 1975), presented a case of a simple fraud over which jurisdiction was alleged on the basis of 28 U.S.C. § 1350. This Honorable Court declined to find "that the Eighth Commandment 'Thou shalt not steal' is part of the law of nations." At 1015. *IIT* is wholly consistent with the exercise of jurisdiction here, where international law *does* forbid the very conduct alleged.

The same is true of *Dreyfus v. von Finck*, 534 F.2d 24 (2d Cir. 1976). Plaintiff there purely and simply failed to make out a case that certain treaty provisions forbade the expropriation of his property in Nazi Germany. Nor was there—or is there now—a general norm of international law that governs such expropriations. Since the conduct complained of was in violation of *neither* the law of nations *nor* any treaty obligation of the United States, 28 U.S.C. § 1350 jurisdiction did not lie.

Finally, the Court of Appeals for the Sixth Circuit recently had cause to consider the Statute in *Huynh Thi Anh v. Levi*, 586 F.2d 625 (6th Cir. 1978). The court held that when the effect of the law of nations is to refer back to the law of an individual state, which will provide the ultimate standard for decision making, the assertion of jurisdiction under 28 U.S.C. § 1350 was inappropriate. This problem is not present in the instant facts, however, since the substantive law by which the merits of the case will eventually be decided is not in doubt. Moreover, unlike the earlier "Vietnamese babylift" case (*Nguyen Da Yen, supra*), *Huynh Thi Anh* is arguably not a case in tort at all.

It therefore appears that in no reported precedent does a court consider the assertion of jurisdiction based on 28 U.S.C. § 1350 stemming from contemporary norms of customary international law. Such an assertion is, *Amici* respectfully submit, fully consistent with the *holdings* of the cases discussed above. Where it would be inconsistent with *dicta* in those decisions, those *dicta* should not be followed (see II.C.4 *infra*).

3. *The events giving rise to this action affect the foreign relations of the United States.*

According to the U.S. District Court for the Eastern District of Pennsylvania, in *Lopes, supra*, a "violation of the law of nations" consists of

> at least a violation by one or more individuals of those standards, rules or customs (a) affecting the relationship between states or between an individual and a foreign state, and (b) used by those states for their common good and or dealings *inter se.*

At 297; cited with approval in *IIT, supra*, at 1015, and in *Abiodun v. Martin Oil Service, Inc.*, 475 F.2d 142, 145 (7th Cir. 1973). Judge Nickerson refers to this holding in his decision, p. 4.

Amici submit that the *Lopes* standards are met by the instant case.

Human rights concerns infuse American foreign policy. Thus by law, agricultural commodity agreements may not be concluded with countries which engage "in a consistent pattern of gross violations of internationally recognized human rights, including torture . . . ." 7 U.S.C. § 1712(a). The President is required to report on the status of human rights in beneficiary nations. 7 U.S.C. § 1712(d).

United States development goals are stated by statute to include "the encouragement of development processes in which individual civil and economic rights are respected and enhanced." 22 U.S.C. § 2151(a)(3). "[A] principal goal of the foreign policy of the United States shall be to promote the increased observance of internationally recognized human rights by all countries." 22 U.S.C. § 2304(a)(1).

Congress has therefore denied security assistance to any nation "the government of which engages in a consistent pattern of gross violations of internationally recognized human rights." 22 U.S.C. § 2304 (d)(1). There are elaborate procedures for reporting by the executive branch on compliance with these principles, and for oversight by Congressional Committees. 22 U.S.C. § 2304(b), (c).

Thus the acts of which Defendant Pena stands accused are acts which, if proved, could affect the relations between the united violations of human rights norms entail a termination of (security and agricultural) *aid* programs, but they can lead to a denial of export licenses for certain articles pursuant to the Arms Export Control Act, 22 U.S.C. § 2778. 22 U.S.C. § 2304(d)(2)(c).

In this sense, the violation of the law of nations alleged by Plaintiffs *is* a matter "affecting the relationship between states" within the first *Lopes* requirement. That it is also a violation of "those standards . . . used by those states for their common good" is amply shown by the frequency with which human rights norms and declarations against such acts as torture have been espoused by the community of nations.

Torture is of international concern. American policy in this regard has often been repeated. "It rests . . . on international law and on such documents as the Universal Declaration of Human Rights, and in this hemisphere, the American Declaration of the Rights and Duties of Man." Patricia Derian, Assistant Secretary of State for Human Rights and Humanitarian Affairs, in "Current Policy" No. 68, U.S. State Department, June, 1979.

4. Insofar as U.S. courts have purportedly barred the use of 28 U.S.C. § 1350 where Plaintiff and Defendant are of the same nationality, those dicta should be overruled.

In *Dreyfus v. von Finck, supra*, this Honorable Court stated as follows: "violations of international law do not occur when the aggrieved parties are nationals of the acting state." At 31. *Amici* respectfully submit that as a general statement of the law, this statement is incorrect.

The Court relied upon the dissenting opinion of Mr. Justice White in *Banco Nacional de Cuba v. Sabbatino*, 376 U.S. 398, 44142 (1964). *Sabbatino* cannot, however, be taken to stand for anything so strident as the claim that, for an international wrong to have occurred, actor and victim must be of different nationalities. And even if that had been the holding, subsequent developments in international law (discussed in II.B *supra*) would have overtaken it.

Sabbatino and the many cases applying it hold only that a state will not be held liable in American courts for expropriations of its own nationals' property within its territory. *See*, for example, *Palicio v. Brush and Bloch*, 256 F. Supp. 481 (S.D.N.Y. 1966), *aff'd*, 375 F.2d 1011 (2d Cir. 1967), *cert. den.*, 389 U.S. 830 (1968). It is not clear from the decided cases whether this result follows because such expropriations are *not* violations of international law, or because, regardless of their legal status, they have immunity from review as acts of state.

Amici contend that there is no consensus in the international community condemning or regulating expropriations. Indeed, the General Assembly's Declaration on Permanent Sovereignty over Natural Resources, G.A. Res. 1803 (*XVII*), December 14, 1962, suggests at § 4 that expropriation is permissible if there is "appropriate" compensation. As has been illustrated above, the condemnation of torture is a legal norm *de lege lata*. The *Sabbatino* line of cases is simply inapposite.

Nor, as we have seen, was the dictum of this Court in *Dreyfus* required for the decision of the case. *Amici* therefore respectfully submit that this Court should not be bound by the erroneous proposition stated therein. For all of the foregoing reasons, the district court has jurisdiction over this matter pursuant to 28 U.S.C. § 1350, and its dismissal of the action should be reversed.

III. DEFENDANT IS PROTECTED FROM SUIT NEITHER BY THE ACT OF STATE DOCTRINE NOR BY SOVEREIGN IMMUNITY.

A. *The Act of State Doctrine Cannot Shield Defendant's Alleged Acts from Judicial Scrutiny.*

Torture is a violation of international legal norms, while simple assault is not. The former entails international responsibility precisely because of some measure of State involvement. That the facts in issue were in some sense "official"—in that they were carried out, encouraged or tolerated by or on behalf of the Government of Paraguay—is constitutive of the international offense of torture.

Thus to allow a tortfeasor to invoke the act of state defense would vitiate the very existence of the tort. Far from being a defense, his invocation of the act of state doctrine would inculpate him.

State responsibility for an act of torture would in any case not oust individual responsibility. Where *mens rea* is required for a violation of an international obligation, or where an award of damages is appropriate, justice requires that the individual answer for his acts.

Thus Lauterpacht writes, "Crimes against humanity are crimes regardless of whether they were committed in accordance with and in obedience to the national law of the accused." *Op. cit.*, at 36. The Nuremberg Charter (*supra*) took notice of this truth in Article 8: "The fact that the Defendant acted pursuant to order of his Government or of a superior shall not free him from responsibility, but may be considered in mitigation of punishment . . . ."

The act of state defense is not mandated by international law, nor does failure to apply it constitute a breach of international obligations. *Sabbatino, supra*, at 421-22. While the courts of the United States will not review the public acts of another sovereign nation that illustrate a "legitimate diversity of values on the part of two national societies," there can be no "legitimate diversity" when "an abuse of universal human rights" is entailed. Then, "domestic courts fulfill their role by refusing to further the policy of the foreign legal system." R. Falk, *The Role of Domestic Courts in the International Legal Order* (1967) 72.

No state can be heard to say that an act of torture is a publicly sanctioned act. No member of the international community can be heard to plead its own depravity as a defense to the exercise of jurisdiction over its national by an American court. To do so would be to commit a direct contravention of the judgment of the Nuremberg Tribunal: "He who violates the laws of war cannot obtain immunity while acting in pursuance of the authority of the State, if the State in authorizing action moves outside its competence under international law." Cited in Brownlie, *op. cit.*, at 545.

There is no reported case in which the act of state defense is considered in the context of 28 U.S.C. § 1350.

Neither the Government of Paraguay nor any recognized spokesman for it has been heard to suggest that the alleged acts of Defendant Pena were acts of state. Were such a plea to be entered, *Amici* would submit to the Court the foregoing reasoning.

B. *The Government of Paraguay Does Not Invoke Sovereign Immunity from Suit.*

As a rule, foreign sovereigns are immune from the exercise of jurisdiction by American courts. *See*, generally, *Alfred Dunhill of London, Inc. v. Cuba*, 425 U.S. 682 (1976). Their immunity derives from the theory that no sovereign may be required to appear before the judiciary of another.

Before 1976, United States courts often found that acts, though performed by entities that were technically agencies of foreign states, were carried out in the guise of commercial traders (*jure gestionis*) and not in that of public bodies (*jure imperii*). Thus courts began to deny defendants immunity from suit. *See*, for example, *Victory Transport, Inc. v. Comisaria General*, 336 F.2d 354 (2d Cir. 1964), *cert. den.*, 381 U.S. 934 (1965).

This distinction was codified in the Foreign Sovereign Immunities Act of 1976, Pub. L. 94-583. That statute establishes that, subject to existing international agreements, "a foreign state shall be immune from the jurisdiction of the courts of the United States . . . except as provided" by the Act. 28 U.S.C. § 1604. Exceptions cover express waivers of immunity, commercial activities, and certain matters concerning admiralty and real property.

Sovereign immunity goes to the question of a court's personal jurisdiction over the defendant. In the instant case, there is no defendant who can claim immunity.

Defendant has led no evidence to suggest that he had "been invested with sovereign authority" to act as the Complaint alleges. Absent such authority, he is not entitled to immunity from the court's jurisdiction. *See Alfred Dunhill of London, Inc., supra,* 425 U.S. at 692-94; *The Gul Djemal,* 264 U.S. 90 (1924). Nor has the Government of Paraguay come forward to wrap the mantle of immunity around Defendant. Since to do so would be to admit the Government's own violation of solemn international undertakings, it is most unlikely that such a representation will be made.

Amici do not contend that the defenses of act of state or sovereign immunity will *never* be of avail to defendants in actions under 28 U.S.C. § 1350. Act of state is no defense on *these* facts because of the nature of the international wrong alleged. State involvement or complicity is constitutive of the act that is a violation of the law of nations. This would not be the case in an action concerning, for example, a trans-border nuisance. In such a case, the act of state doctrine might preclude the adjudication of the dispute by a domestic tribunal; though it would not, of course, diminish the right of the offended state to pursue its remedy before an international forum.

Similarly, the defense of sovereign immunity could operate to oust jurisdiction under 28 U.S.C. § 1350, but only in cases where it is pleaded by a sovereign, or by a person or an entity acting in its behalf. That is not the situation here.

IV. THE JURISDICTION OF THE DISTRICT COURT DOES NOT OFFEND ANY RECOGNIZABLE RIGHT OF DEFENDANT.

A. *The District Court Properly Had Personal Jurisdiction over Defendant.*

Defendant was personally served with process at the Brooklyn Navy Yard detention facility in April, 1979. At the time he was served, he had been residing illegally in New York State for some time. He was physically present in New York, and all indications are that he exhibited the requisite *animus rimanendi* to make him a domiciliary, or at least a resident, of the State. It is not necessary that Defendant have had the intention *never* to leave the jurisdiction. *Ramey v. Rockefeller,* 348 F. Supp. 780 (E.D.N.Y. 1972).

That Defendant's presence in New York was illegal does not imply that he was not a resident. Nor does it matter that, on the day he was served, he was in detention. *Stifel v. Hopkins,* 477 F.2d 1116 (6th Cir. 1973).

In personam jurisdiction over an individual defendant is ordinarily obtained through valid service of process. *Arro Manufacturing Co. v. Automobile Body Research Corp.*, 352 F.2d 400, 402 (1st Cir. 1965); *Wagman v. Astle*, 380 F. Supp. 497 (S.D.N.Y. 1974). Service upon Defendant was valid under Rule 5(b), Federal Rules of Civil Procedure. Such service gave the district court jurisdiction over him. *See, Kulko v. California Superior Court*, 436 U.S. 84, 91 (1978).

B. *Defendant Has Waived the Defense of Lack of Personal Jurisdiction.*

Defendant's Motion to Dismiss the instant action was based on a perceived lack of subject matter jurisdiction, pursuant to Rule 12 (b) (1), Federal Rules of Civil Procedure. It therefore follows that, even if the district court for some reason lacked personal jurisdiction, Defendant has waived that defense.

According to Rule 12(h) (1) of the Federal Rules of Civil Procedure:

A defense of lack of jurisdiction over the person . . . is waived (a) if omitted from a motion . . . or (b) if it is neither made under this rule nor included in a responsive pleading or an amendment thereof. . . .

The advisory Committee Notes to Rule 12 (h) explicitly state "that certain defenses which were available to a party when he made a preanswer motion, but which he omitted from the motion, are waived. . . A party who by motion invites the court to pass upon a threshold defense should bring forward all the specified defenses he then has and thus allow the court to do a reasonably complete job. The waiver reinforces the policy of subdivision (g) forbidding successive motions."

Numerous judicial decisions support this basic rule of procedure. *Varone v. Varone*, 392 F.2d 855 (7th Cir. 1968); *Blacko v. Local 281 United Brotherhood of Carpenters & Joiners of America*, 438 F.2d 176 (2d Cir. 1970) *cert. den.*, 404 U.S. 858; *U.S. v. Gayewski*, 419 F.2d 1088 (8th Cir. 1969), *cert. den.*, 397 U.S. 1040.

Thus, it is clear that if the defense of lack of personal jurisdiction is available but omitted from the initial motion it is permanently lost. "Not only is defendant prevented from making it the subject of a second preliminary motion but he may not even assert the defense in his answer." 5 Wright & Miller, *Federal Practice and Procedure*, § 1391, pp. 852-53. Therefore, assuming *arguendo* that the district court could not have asserted personal jurisdiction over Defendant, his failure to plead this defense constitutes a waiver and permits litigation on the merits of the case.

C. *No Constitutional Right of Defendant Would Be Infringed By the Court's Jurisdiction.*

"A state may not acquire personal jurisdiction over a party without that party having certain 'minimum contacts' with the forum state. Such minimum contacts are constitutionally required." *Aanestad v. Beech Aircraft Corp.*, 521 F.2d 1298, 1300 (10th Cir. 1974), *cert. den.*, 419 U.S. 998; *Hanson v. Denckla*, 357 U.S. 233 (1958).

Where Defendant is an individual, however, "minimum contacts" may be established by physical presence. Here, Defendant was physically present in the State of New York and, until his apprehension by the Immigration and Naturalization Service, was a resident—albeit an illegal one—of the State.

Defendant's arguments, therefore, as set out in his Motion to Dismiss, to the effect that his constitutional rights are in peril, is entirely devoid of merit. If, on the other hand, Defendant's contention is that 28 U.S.C. § 1350 is unconstitutional insofar as it confers *subject-matter* jurisdiction, *Amici* respectfully direct the Court's attention to the goal of the Framers that the cases arising under the law of nations and treaties be "subjects within the purview of the Constitution." *Martin v. Hunter's Lessee*, 1 Wheat. 304, 347 (1816). *See*, generally, E. Dickinson, "The Law of Nations As Part of the National Law of the United States," (pts. 1, 2) 101 U. Pa. L. Rev. 26, 792 (1952).

V. PLAINTIFFS HAVE STANDING TO BRING THIS ACTION.

A. *Dr. Joel Filartiga Has Standing to Sue as Personal Representative of Joelito Filartiqa.*

Under the Civil Code of Paraguay, an action for the wrongful death of a child may be brought by his father. Thus in Paraguay, Joel Filartiga would have standing to bring this action. The law of New York State is that "[a] foreign legal representative may sue in New York in a wrongful death action without ancillary letters." *Wiener v. Specific Pharmaceuticals, Inc.*, 298 N.Y. 346, 83 N.E. 2d 673 (1949); *Nielson v. Avco Corp.*, 54 F.R.D. 76, 81 (S.D.N.Y. 1971).

That a non-resident of a state may bring an action for wrongful death has long been recognized. *See*, generally, Anno., 138 A.L.R. 684 (1942). Thus Dr. Joel Filartiga has standing to bring this action for the wrongful death of his son.

B. *Joel and Dolly Filartiga Have Standing to Sue in Their Own Right.*

In addition to an action brought by the representative of Joelito, however, both Filartigas have causes of action against Defendant in their own right. Both were, according to the Complaint, caused significant mental pain and suffering by the alleged acts of Defendant. Dolly Filartiga alleges that not only was she forced by Defendant to view her brother's mutilated body, but she was threatened, intimidated, and temporarily imprisoned. Joel Filartiga's injuries stem from the fact that it was he, and not his 17-year-old son, who was the target and intended victim of Defendant's alleged torts. In a very real sense, Joel and Dolly Filartiga too were tortured.

Torture was defined in General Assembly Resolution 3452 (*XXX*) (*supra*) as an "aggravated and deliberate form of cruel, inhuman or degrading treatment or punishment." Certainly the murder of one's son or brother by the methods alleged in Complaint would, if proved, qualify under this definition. It *does* instance the "particular intensity and cruelty implied by the word torture." *Ireland v. United Kingdom*, Application No. 5310/71 (Eur. Ct. of Human Rights 1978), ¶ 167. Modern, sophisticated torture techniques may abjure causing physical pain, instead seeking to provoke "the disintegration of the human personality, the destruction of man's mental and physical equilibrium and the annihilation of his will" *Id.*, separate opinion of Judge Evrigenis, 118.

In common law terms as well, the Filartigas can be said to be victims of Defendant's alleged tort. Thus one who "by intentional or wanton conduct, causes severe emotional distress to another by conduct directed at a third person is liable to the other for such distress." 38 Am. Jur. 2d 49, *sub voc.* Fright, Shock, Etc. § 38. This principle follows from a standard analysis of tort liability: Plaintiffs were foreseeably going to be injured by Defendant's alleged conduct, and they were so injured. Defendant is alleged to have acted willfully not only with respect to Joelito but with respect to Plaintiffs. He is therefore liable in tort not only to him, but to them.

VI. DEFENDANT'S OBJECTION THAT A JUDICIAL DETERMINATION OF THE MERITS OF THE CASE WOULD BE A POLITICAL SHOW TRIAL IS WITHOUT VALIDITY.

A. *28 U.S.C. § 1350 Provides No Opportunity for the District Court to Decline Jurisdiction on Political Grounds.*

The "Alien Tort Claims Act," 28 U.S.C. § 1350, lays jurisdiction in federal courts over certain tort actions. In the instant case, Defendant is an individual, who is alleged to have brought about the wrongful death of Joelito Filartiga, to the injury of his father and sister.

The Government of Paraguay is not the defendant. This action is a lawsuit alleging that Defendant killed a person brutally and maliciously. It does happen that at the time of the alleged tort, Defendant occupied an official position in Paraguay. But it cannot be inferred from this that any trial of the merits of the case would be so permeated by political concerns as to be unmanageable.

Jurisdiction may be declined by federal courts for a limited number of reasons. The inclusion in 28 U.S.C. § 1350 of reference to "the law of nations" does not create a bar to jurisdiction merely because Defendant held a public position, or because the policies of another Government may be discussed at trial.

B. *Plaintiffs Pose No Political Question of a Sort Not Usually Held Justiciable.*

"[I]t is error to suppose that every case or controversy which touches foreign relations lies beyond judicial cognizance." *Baker v. Carr*, 369 U.S. 186, 211 (1962). No issue, in the submission of *Amici*, is presented by this case that is not routinely justiciable. This is not to say that trial of an action that arose in a foreign jurisdiction will present no technical problems. But what problems there are do not affect the question of justiciability.

This is not a case in which the power of the executive branch of Government to conduct foreign affairs is in any way threatened. It is not a case in which, for example, standing to challenge official action must be shown, or where American observance of a treaty is in issue. *See*, for example, *Diggs v. Richardson*, 555 F.2d 848 (D.C. Cir. 1976). Rather, it is a simple lawsuit concerning a transitory tort, brought in the state and city where Defendant was physically located, and arising before the federal district court because of the jurisdictional provisions of 28 U.S.C. § 1350.

C. *The Court Should Not Decline to Exercise Jurisdiction on the Grounds of Forum Non Conveniens.*

"[A] court possessed of jurisdiction generally must exercise it." *Ohio v. Wyandotte Chemicals Corp.*, 401 U.S. 493, 497 (1971). *Amici* respectfully submit that this case should not be dismissed on the grounds of *forum non conveniens*.

The application of that doctrine requires that the court make an initial finding that it has jurisdiction. It lies within the discretion of the court, and its purpose is the discouraging of vexatious litigation. *Gulf Oil Corp. v. Gilbert*, 330 U.S. 501 (1947).

Plaintiffs plainly are not here "resort[ing] to a strategy of forcing the trial at a most inconvenient place for an adversary" (*Gulf, supra* at 907) in order to gain an advantage. They filed this action immediately after they became aware of Defendant's whereabouts, and they filed it in the judicial district where Defendant was found.

More importantly, however, *forum non conveniens* should never be invoked when there is no other forum in which the action could be brought. It is part of Plaintiffs' allegations that the courts of Paraguay have by various means attempted to prevent an adjudication of the facts of Joelito's death. Though an action has been instituted by Dr. Filartiga in Paraguay, no progress seems to have taken place. There is a real issue as to whether the judiciary of Paraguay possesses the independence or the will to proceed.

Furthermore, it appears that Defendant has fled Paraguay and is now living in Brazil. Conceivably, this development could cause a Paraguayan court to dismiss the case for failure of Defendant to appear.

In *Del Rio v. Ballenger Corp.*, 391 F. Supp. 1002 (D.S.C. 1975), a district court declined to entertain the case, deferring to the courts of Panama. Any resistance to the jurisdiction of that forum, however, was held sufficient to "cause this court immediately to abandon the doctrine [of *forum non conveniens*] and proceed under the jurisdiction which this court unquestionably has." At 1006.

On the instant facts, *Amici* respectfully submit that there has already been such resistance, and that jurisdiction should therefore not be declined.

D. *The Assertion of Jurisdiction Would Contain No Threat of Frivolous Litigation.*

1. *Generally, in personam jurisdiction will be lacking, and service of process will not be feasible.*

It is not true that, if the district court takes jurisdiction in the instant case, American courts will be opened to "every Kurdish rebel and every West Bank Palestinian." Motion to Dismiss, p. 2.

The facts presented by the instant case are distinguishable from the whimsical suggestions of Defendant's counsel. In this case:

  a) Defendant was personally served with process within the jurisdiction;
  b) Defendant is alleged to be the actual, individual tortfeasor; and

      c)   Plaintiffs are the victims of Defendant's alleged tort, and/or have the statutory right to represent the victim.

It is unlikely that similar facts will arise in very many cases. When they do appear, however, an action in tort may be maintainable in state court in any event, without reliance on 28 U.S.C. § 1350. That few such actions appear to have been brought speaks to the difficulty in obtaining personal service on foreign tortfeasors, a problem that is absent here.

2. *If developments in international law have enlarged the scope of 28 U.S.C. § 1350, only Congress and not the judiciary has the power to limit it.*

The expanding *corpus* of international law has increased the number of its possible violations. In 1789, torts "committed in violation of the law of nations" were fewer, comprising such offenses as abductions of ambassadors. It is clear, however, that Congress in 1789 *did* contemplate that such violations would be *individual* offenses, and *did* know that international law is an evolving body, not a static one.

If it were the case that the development of international law has made its incorporation by reference into a U.S. statute unwieldy, then Congress should amend the statute book to eliminate the anomaly. But Congress has tended in recent years to *increase*, not to diminish, statutory references to international law. *Amici* respectfully contend that this Honorable Court should construe "statutes relating to international matters . . . in accordance with international usage," and find the reference to "the law of nations" in 28 U.S.C. § 1350 to mean that law as it is today. *Empresa Hondurena de Vapores v. McLeod*, 300 F.2d 222, 231 (2d Cir. 1962).

VII. CONCLUSION

International law condemns torture. The torturer has committed a crime against humanity, and his crime is of international concern. It is not the exclusive province of his national state. As Lauterpacht noted, if the Nuremberg Charter was not "an *ad hoc* piece of vindictive legislation enacted by the victor against the vanquished," it acknowledged the existence of human rights grounded in a law superior to that of states. *Op. cit.*, at 36. The development of human rights norms since Nuremberg has been based firmly on that conception. *Amici* urge this Honorable Court to take a significant step in assuring the leadership of the United States in respect for those rights.

No court of the United States has previously been asked to hold torture to be a violation of the law of nations. That the case is one of first impression heightens its importance, and underscores its difficulty. But important, difficult cases constitute the landmarks of American jurisprudence.

In 1789, when the first Congress debated the Judiciary Act of which 28 U.S.C. § 1350 was a part, Representative John Vining of Delaware said this in support of the proposed legislation:

> He wished to see justice so equally distributed, as that every citizen of the United States should be fairly dealt by, and so impartially administered, that every subject or citizen of the world, whether foreigner or alien, friend or foe should be alike satisfied; by this means, the doors of justice would be thrown open, immigration would be encouraged from all countries into your own, and in short, the United States of America would be made not only an asylum of liberty, but a sanctuary of justice. The faith of treaties would be preserved inviolate; our extensive funded system would have its intended operation; our navigation, import and revenue laws would be executed so as to insure their many advantages, whilst the combined effect would be to establish the public and private credit of the Union.

I The Annals of Congress: 1st Congress, 1789-91, at 821.

In furtherance of these hallowed goals, and for all of the reasons set out above, *Amici* respectfully pray that this Honorable Court vacate the dismissal of the action by the district court below, and to remand the case for trial on the merits.

Respectfully submitted,

_____

Allan Abbot Tuttle

_____

Steven M. Schneebaum

Attorneys for:

THE INTERNATIONAL HUMAN RIGHTS LAW GROUP, THE COUNCIL ON HEMISPHERIC AFFAIRS, AND THE WASHINGTON OFFICE ON LATIN AMERICA

2550 M Street, N.W.
Washington, D.C. 20037

Dated: July 23, 1979

AUGUST 7, 1979: UNITED STATES

Correspondence from U.S. Attorney to Second Circuit Court of Appeals

United States Department of Justice

UNITED STATES ATTORNEY

Eastern District of New York
Federal Building
Brooklyn, N.Y. 11201

August 7, 1979

Hon. Daniel Fusaro
Clerk of the Court
United States Court of Appeals for the Second Circuit
United States Courthouse
Foley Square
New York, New York 10007

Re.   Dolly M.E. Filartiga, et al v. Americo N. Pena-Irala, et al.,
        Docket No. 79-6090

Dear Mr. Fusaro:

I am writing at the suggestion of Ms. Brullo of your staff to notify you that the federal defendants in the District Court in the above action are not parties to this appeal. In the District Court, plaintiffs-appellants sought to enjoin the federal defendants, certain Immigration officials, from proceeding with the deportation of defendant Pena-Irala pending the outcome of this action. Judge Nickerson subsequently dismissed the plaintiffs' complaint against defendant Pena-Irala on jurisdictional grounds and vacated a temporary restraining order that had been entered against the federal defendants. After unsuccessful efforts by plaintiffs to obtain a stay of defendant Pena-Irala's deportation in this Court and the United States Supreme Court, Mr. Pena-Irala was deported to Paraguay.

Plaintiffs now appeal from the judgment below insofar as it dismissed their complaint against Mr. Pena-Irala on jurisdictional grounds. Their sole claim below against the federal defendants, seeking to prevent Mr. Pena-Irala's deportation *pendente lite*, is moot and plaintiffs' counsel, Ms. Rhonda

Copelon, advised us several weeks ago that plaintiffs did not, in fact, seek any further relief on this appeal against the federal defendants.

However, since we continue to receive notices and scheduling orders from your office concerning this appeal, we wish to notify you formally that this appeal no longer involves the federal defendants and that we shall not appear or file any brief with this Court on their behalf unless otherwise advised by the Court. Thank you for your consideration in this matter.

Very truly yours,

EDWARD R. KORMAN
United States Attorney

By: _____
J. CHRISTOPHER JENSEN
Chief, Civil Division

cc: Rhonda Copelon, Esq.
Center for Constitutional Rights
853 Broadway, 14th floor
New York, New York 10003

Murry Brochin, Esq.
Lowenstein, Sandler, Brochin, Kohl, Fisher and Boyland
744 Broad Street
Newark, New Jersey 07102

AUGUST 9, 1979: UNITED STATES

Correspondence from Deputy Legal Adviser, U.S. Department of State to Department of Justice

DEPARTMENT OF STATE

Washington, D.C. 20520

August 9, 1979

Mr. John Huerta
Deputy Assistant Attorney General
Civil Rights Division
Department of Justice
Washington, D.C. 20530

Dear Mr. Huerta:

We wish to draw to your attention the concern of the Department of State regarding the case of *Filartiga v. Pena-Irala,* now on appeal from a judgment of the United States District Court for the Eastern District of New York to the United States Court of Appeals for the Second Circuit.

The District Court's judgment rejects the legal conclusion that acts of torture are in violation of international law or a treaty of the United States, relying on prior judgments of the Second Circuit Court in support of its conclusion. Its position appears to be premised on a doctrine that international law is concerned solely with the rights and duties of States in their mutual relations and their relations with aliens, and is not concerned with the rights of individual persons as subjects of international law, regardless of their nationality. This now obsolete doctrine fails to take account of 20th century (and earlier) developments of international law which firmly establish that all natural persons are entitled to fundamental human rights. The United States, and at least all other States Members of the United Nations, have participated in the establishment of such individual rights in international law, particularly as parties to the Charter of the United Nations.

The position of the Department of State on the question of international law immediately relevant to the District Court judgment in *Filartiga* is that acts of torture violate an individual's rights under international law not to be tortured. That an individual has this right is a conclusion founded on provisions of the United Nations Charter and authoritative interpretations of those provisions, on other treaties, on international custom and practice and on the general principles of law—all as recognized by the United States and other nations. It derives also from international and national judicial decisions.

In order that the Second Circuit of Appeals may have before it the reasoned legal views of the United States Government, we request that the Department of Justice seek to file a brief *amicus curiae* setting forth the position of the United States on these important questions of international law. The Department of State would welcome the opportunity to assist the Department of Justice in the preparation of such a brief.

Yours sincerely,

Stephen M. Schwebel
Deputy Legal Adviser

AUGUST 27, 1979: UNITED STATES

Correspondence from Deputy Legal Adviser, U.S. Department of State to Department of Justice

DEPARTMENT OF STATE

Washington, D.C. 20520

August 27, 1979
John Huerta, Esquire
Deputy Assistant Attorney General
Civil Rights Division
Department of Justice
Washington, D.C. 20530

Dear Mr. Huerta:

Thank you for sending to us the draft brief *amicus curiae* prepared by your office regarding the case of *Filartiga v. Pena-Irala*, now on appeal from a judgment of the United States District Court for the Eastern District of New York to the United States Court of Appeals for the Second Circuit.

The Department of State greatly appreciates preparation of the draft brief in response to our request of August 9. We believe that the draft provides a most able statement and analysis of the legal issues involved, and fully concur in its submission. We would suggest several revisions which are indicated on the attached draft brief, which we hope that your office can accept. If you should have any questions regarding these revisions, please contact Ms. Linda Baumann at 632-1217.

The Department of State wishes to confirm its view that a brief *amicus curiae* should be filed. As we have indicated previously, *Filartiga v. Pena-Irala* involves several important issues of international law. Previous judicial opinions, including the opinion in this case in the District Court, have not adequately treated these issues. Therefore, we believe it would be extremely useful for the Second Circuit Court of Appeals to have before it the reasoned legal views of the United States Government.

Yours sincerely,

Stephen M. Schwebel
Deputy Legal Adviser

Attachment:
As stated.

AUGUST 29, 1979: UNITED STATES

Memorandum from Justice Department, Civil Rights Division, to the Solicitor General

MEMORANDUM FOR THE SOLICITOR GENERAL

RE: Amicus Participation in *Filartiga v. Pena-Irala*,
        No. 79-6090 (Second Circuit)

August, 29 1979

I recommend that the United States seek leave to file an amicus brief along the lines of the attached draft brief. The Deputy Legal Adviser for the Department of State advised us on August 27, 1979 that the Department of State generally concurs in the position we have taken in the draft brief (see attached letter of August 27).

STATUS

Appellants' brief was filed on July 23, 1979. On August 9, 1979, the Deputy Legal Adviser for the Department of State requested that we prepare an amicus brief (see attached letter of August 9). Appellees' brief is due to be filed on September 18, 1979. Oral argument has not yet been scheduled. In order to give appellee an opportunity to respond, we should file our brief as expeditiously as possible. Since we are late, we will need to move for leave to file.

INTEREST OF THE UNITED STATES

The interest of the United States is set out in the draft brief (2-5).

FACTS AND PROCEDURAL HISTORY

Because the attached brief relies on appellants' statement, we briefly set forth the facts here. This civil action was brought pursuant to 28 U.S.C. 1350 for "a tort . . . committed in violation of the law of nations." The complaint, filed on April 6, 1979, alleges that the defendant Pena-Irala, an official of Paraguay, tortured and murdered Joelito Filartiga in Paraguay in retaliation for his father's out-spoken criticism of General Stroessner, the dictator-President of Paraguay (J.A. 6). Plaintiffs are Dr. Joel Filartiga, the decedent's father, and Dolly Filartiga, the decedent's sister (J.A. 5).

At the time the complaint was filed, the defendant was being held in the custody of the Immigration and Naturalization Service, and was subject to an order of deportation entered on April 5, 1979 (*ibid.*). Plaintiffs joined two INS officials as defendants in order to obtain a stay of deportation (J.A. 5, 9).

The district court dismissed the complaint for lack of jurisdiction under section 1350, on May 15, 1979 (J.A. 105-108). The court accepted defendant's argument that the torture of one foreign national by another does not violate the law of nations (J.A. 107-108). Plaintiffs filed a notice of appeal the same day and sought a stay of deportation and an order allowing them to take defendant's deposition. This motion was denied by the Second Circuit on May 22, 1979 and by the Supreme Court on May 24, 1979. On May 25, the defendant was deported.

Since the federal defendants were joined only for purposes of obtaining a temporary stay of deportation, they are not appellees. Although they have consistently argued that the pendency of a civil suit is not an adequate basis for staying deportation, the federal defendants have not taken a position on the merits of the jurisdictional question.

DISCUSSION

The attached brief fully sets forth our view that the district court's interpretation of section 1350 is unduly restrictive. Briefly, the court's holding that the law of nations can never touch the relations between a nation and its citizens fails to take into account the growth in international law since World War II, and particularly since the signing of the United Nations Charter (5-9). Section 1350, which must be given a dynamic interpretation, incorporates this development (9-12). The Second Circuit decisions relied upon the district court, did not arise in a human rights context, and did not thoroughly analyze the proper reach of Section 1350 (12–16). Application of proper legal standards leads us to conclude that official torture is prohibited by the law of nations (16-23). Finally, defendant's argument that such interpretation of section 1350 would render it unconstitutional is without merit (23-29).

CONCLUSION

For the reasons discussed in our draft brief, we recommend that the United States participate as amicus curiae.

Drew S. Days, III
Assistant Attorney General
Civil Rights Division

Cc: John Harmon   .
          Assistant Attorney General
          Office of Legal Counsel

          Stuart Schiffer
          Acting Assistant Attorney General
          Civil Division

No. 79-6090

IN THE UNITED STATES COURT OF APPEALS
FOR THE SECOND CIRCUIT

DOLLY M.E. FILARTIGA AND DR. JOEL FILARTIGA,

Plaintiffs-Appellants

v.

AMERICO NORBERTO PENA-IRALA,

Defendant-Appellee

APPEAL FROM THE UNITED STATES DISTRICT COURT
FOR THE EASTERN DISTRICT OF NEW YORK

BRIEF FOR THE UNITED STATES AS AMICUS CURIAE

EDWARD R. KORMAN
    United States Attorney

DREW S. DAYS, III
    Assistant Attorney General

JOHN E. HUERTA
    Deputy Assistant Attorney General

BRIAN K. LANDSBERG
IRVING GORNSTEIN
JOAN F. HARTMAN
    Attorneys
    Department of Justice
    Washington, D.C. 20530

IN THE UNITED STATES COURT OF APPEALS
FOR THE SECOND CIRCUIT

No. 79-6090

DOLLY M.E. FILARTIGA AND DR. JOEL FILARTIGA,

Plaintiffs-Appellants

v.

AMERICO NORBERTO PENA-IRALA,

Defendant-Appellee

APPEAL FROM THE UNITED STATES DISTRICT COURT
FOR THE EASTERN DISTRICT OF NEW YORK

BRIEF FOR THE UNITED STATES AS AMICUS CURIAE

ISSUE PRESENTED

Whether the district court erred in dismissing the complaint on the ground that jurisdiction under 28 U.S.C. 1350 was lacking because torture is not a violation of the law of nations or treaties of the United States.

STATEMENT

The United States relies upon the statement of the case in the brief for plaintiffs-appellants (Br. 1-8). Two officials[1] of the United States Immigration and Naturalization Service were joined as defendants for the purpose of obtaining a stay of deportation of Pena-Irala (J.A. 5,9), but because Pena-Irala has now been deported[2] they have not been made appellees (Br. 4). The United States files this brief in the capacity of amicus curiae.

---

[1] These officials were Leonel Castillo and George Vician (J.A. 5).

[2] Stays were denied by this Court on May 22, 1979, and by the Supreme Court on May 24, 1979.

INTEREST OF THE UNITED STATES

This case involves the interpretation and constitutionality of an Act of Congress and matters concerning international law and relations, subjects of particular interest to the United States.[3] Defendant-appellee Pena-Irala below challenged the constitutionality of 28 U.S.C. 1350 as applied to a tort committed by an alien against an alien in violation of the human rights proscriptions of the law of nations. Although this issue was not reached by the district court, it may be raised in this Court and considered if the ground for the district court's judgment of dismissal is reversed. The Attorney General has an interest in defending the constitutionality of federal statutes, as indicated by his right of intervention under 28 U.S.C. 2403 in suits drawing into question the constitutionality of an Act of Congress.

The ground for the dismissal of the complaint, that the law of nations pertains only to the relationship between states or between an individual and a foreign state, impinges on the interests of the United States. The decision applies an obsolete view of the law of nations that does not take into account United States participation in the development of international agreements and customary law concerning human rights in the period following World War II. At least since United States ratification of the United Nations Charter in 1945[4] and the proclamation of the Universal Declaration of Human Rights,[5] the federal government has recognized that international law may concern the fundamental rights of an individual vis a vis his state.

The narrow and outmoded view of the court below contradicts the numerous international treaties on human rights that have achieved wide acceptance in recent decades in the international community.[6] In addition

---

[3] The Supreme Court has recognized that the United States has a special interest in private suits involving questions of international law that have a potential impact on foreign policy and relations with other nations. The United States was requested by the Court to participate as amicus curiae in *Banco Nacional de Cuba v. Sabbatino*, 376 U.S. 398 (1964), and *Alfred Dunhill of London, Inc. v. Republic of Cuba*, 425 U.S. 682 (1976), cases involving the application of the act of state doctrine to expropriations of private property.

[4] Dept. of State Pub. 2638; 59 Stat. 1031, T.S. 993. See Brownlie, *Basic Documents in International Law* (1967) at 2 (hereafter "*Basic Documents*").

[5] UN G.A. Res. 217 (III), UN Doc. A/810 (1948); *Basic Documents, supra*, at 133.

[6] President Carter in 1978 signed and transmitted to the Senate four human rights treaties: the International Convention on the Elimination of All Forms of Racial Discrimination; the International Covenant on Civil and Political Rights; the International Covenant on Economic, Social and Cultural Rights; and the American Convention on Human Rights. S. Exec. C, D, E, F, 95th Cong., 2d Sess. (1978). The Convention on Genocide is also pending ratification in the Senate.

it could impinge upon United States participation in the development of customary human rights law through non-treaty documents such as the United Nations Declaration on the Protection of All Persons from Being Subjected to Torture and Other Cruel, Inhuman or Degrading Treatment or Punishment.[7]

The contemporary foreign policy of the United States, in which concern for human rights plays a substantial role,[8] is not in accord with the district court's limited view of international law and relations. The decision below is difficult to reconcile with the operation of foreign aid statutes that cut off or restrict funding to governments that engage in a pattern of gross violations of internationally recognized human rights.[9] The customary international law of human rights supplies the legal standard for the application of such statutes.

The United States additionally has an interest in insuring that suits brought under 28 U.S.C. 1350 not interfere with the orderly conduct of the nation's foreign affairs. This case presents an opportunity to develop standards for construing the "law of nations" in a human rights context to permit the exercise of jurisdiction over meritorious suits without an undue extension of the reach of section 1350.

SUMMARY OF ARGUMENT

This case depends upon a proper interpretation of 28 U.S.C. 1350 which gives district courts jurisdiction of cases brought by an alien for "a tort only, committed in violation of the law of nations." The district court held that "the law of nations" within the meaning of section 1350 pertains only to the relationship between states or between an individual and a foreign state.

---

[7] G.A. Res. 3452 (XXX), 30 UN GAOR Supp. (No.34) 91, UN Doc. A/1034 (1975).

[8] In a speech commemorating the 30th Anniversary of the Universal Declaration of Human Rights President Carter identified human rights as "the soul of our foreign policy." 14 Weekly Comp. of Pres. Doc. 2164 (December 11, 1978).

[9] See, *e.g.*, International Development and Food Assistance Act of 1978, Pub.L. 95-424, 92 Stat. 937 (1978), 92 Stat. 730 (1978), amending 22 U.S.C. 2151n; International Security Assistance Act of 1978, Pub.L. 95-384, 92 Stat. 730 (1978) amending 22 U.S.C. 2304. Paraguay has been subjected to aid reductions under this standard and has been the subject of congressional investigations of human rights abuses. *Human Rights in Uruguay and Paraguay: Hearings before the Subcommittee on International Organizations of the House Committee on International Relations*, 94th Cong., 2d Sess. (1976). See also, International Development and Food Assistance Act of 1977, 7 U.S.C. 1712(a); International Bank for Reconstruction and Development, 22 U.S.C. 262d, 262d-l.

1. The lower court's holding fails to take into account the growth in international law since World War II. In particular, the United Nations Charter imposes treaty obligations upon its members to promote universal respect for and observance of fundamental human rights. A growing number of specific documents and multilateral agreements evidence the international community's recognition that the manner in which a nation treats its own citizens is a proper subject of international law. Section 1350, which must be given a dynamic interpretation, incorporates these developments.

2. The district court's reliance on previous decisions of this Court is misplaced. The standard applied by the district court is derived from a 1963 district court decision, *Lopes v. Reederei Richard Schroder*, 225 F. Supp. 292 (E.D. Pa. 1963), which limited its application to the issue before it. This Court's subsequent decisions in *IIT v. Vencap, Ltd.*, 519 F.2d 1001 (2d Cir. 1975), and *Dreyfus v. Von Finck*, 534 F.2d 24 (2d Cir.), cert. denied, 429 U.S. 835 (1976), did not arise in a human rights context and did not thoroughly analyze the proper reach of section 1350.

3. The proper approach to a case such as this is no different than the approach followed in more traditional international law cases. A court must look to international instruments, federal statutes, the writings of leading commentators and the actual practice of nations to determine whether particular conduct violates a norm of international law. *The Paquete Habana*, 175 U.S. 677, 700 (1900). The relevant sources in this case uniformly point to the conclusion that torture is prohibited by international law.

4. Defendant argued below that applying section 1350 to cases of this kind would violate Article III. We perceive no constitutional difficulty. Section 1350 is not only jurisdictional but also substantive. It authorizes federal courts to fashion federal common law to resolve international law disputes. In light of the need for uniformity, Congress plainly desired federal law rather than state law to apply in such suits. Cases brought pursuant to section 1350 therefore arise under the laws of the United States within the meaning of Article III.

Finally, although Congress has no express power to provide a civil remedy for international law violations, its implied power over foreign affairs furnishes an adequate basis for such legislation. Defendant's effort to characterize this case as a local dispute overlooks the international character of the tort he has allegedly committed.

ARGUMENT

I.

THE DISTRICT COURT ERRED IN HOLDING THAT THE LAW
OF NATIONS COULD NEVER CONCERN THE RELATIONSHIP
BETWEEN A NATION AND ITS OWN CITIZENS

The resolution of this appeal turns on a proper interpretation of 28
U.S.C. 1350 which gives the district court jurisdiction in all cases where an
alien sues for "a tort only, committed in violation of the law of nations or a
treaty of the United States." The district court held that the "law of nations"
within the meaning of section 1350 includes only "those standards, rules or
customs affecting the relationship between states and between an individual and a foreign state, and used by those states for their common good
and/or dealings *inter se.*" (J.A. 108). The court then applied this formula,
derived from a 1963 district court decision and from dicta in *IIT v. Vencap,
Ltd.*, 519 F. 2d 1001, 1015 (2d Cir. 1975), and *Dreyfus v. Von Finck*, 534 F.2d
24 (2d Cir.), cert. denied, 429 U.S. 835 (1976), to the conduct alleged in
the complaint and concluded that it lacked jurisdiction under section 1350
(J.A. 108). While the court believed that plaintiffs had persuasively argued
that "the proscription of torture in numerous international instruments
accepted by nearly all the states in the international community reflects the
emergence of a norm of customary international law condemning torture,"
it felt constrained by *Vencap* and *Dreyfus* to exclude customary human rights
violations from the ambit of section 1350 (*ibid.*).

The district court's decision is premised on the obsolete doctrine that
international law never touches a nation's treatment of its own citizens.
This view of international law has been thoroughly eroded by the substantial development of a customary international law of human rights in which
the United States has participated, and section 1350 should be interpreted
to incorporate this development.

A. *International law embraces a nation's treatment of its own citizens*

The concept that a state's treatment of its own citizens is an inappropriate subject for the rule of international law was once widely held and
reflected in the writings of such influential commentators as Oppenheim.[10]
The international community began to abandon this view during the twentieth century, as evidenced by the treaties guaranteeing the religious, cultural and political rights of national minorities entered into after World

---

[10] International Law: A Treatise, Vol. I: Peace, 362-369 (1912).

War I.[11] After World War II this process accelerated, in part because the Nazi persecution of the Jews convinced many that a nation's abuse of the human rights of its citizens may have severe adverse consequences on international relations and even on the maintenance of international peace and security. Articles 55 and 56 of the United Nations Charter embody these concerns and impose treaty obligations on United Nations members to promote the observance of fundamental human rights. Articles 55 and 56 provide, in relevant part (*Basic Documents, supra,* at 17):

Article 55

With a view to the creation of conditions of stability and well-being which are necessary for peaceful and friendly relations among nations based on respect for the principle of equal/rights and self-determination of peoples, the United Nations shall promote:

***

c. universal respect for, and observance of, human rights and fundamental freedoms for all without distinction as to race, sex, language, or religion.

Article 56

All Members pledge themselves to take joint and separate action in cooperation with the Organization for the achievement of the purposes set forth in Article 55.

The United Nations Charter therefore evidences a complete break with the traditional view that a nation's treatment of its citizens is outside the pale of international law.

The Universal Declaration of Human Rights, adopted unanimously by the General Assembly in 1948, helps to define these fundamental rights.[12] Although the Universal Declaration is not a treaty and does not serve as a binding interpretation of the obligations created by the United Nations Charter, it does mark a trend toward the development of a customary inter-

---

[11] See, *e.g.,* the Treaty between the Principal Allied and Associated Powers and Poland signed at Versailles, June 28, 1919. S. Doc. No. 82, 66th Cong., 1st Sess. (1919). In addition, the general treaties of peace concluding the war included provisions aimed at guaranteeing minority rights. See, *e.g.,* Treaty of Peace With Austria, signed at *Saint Germain-en-Laye,* September 10, 1919. S. Doc. No. 348, 67th Cong., 4th Sess. (1923).

[12] Article 5 of the Universal Declaration proscribes the use of torture. *Basic Documents, supra,* at 134.

national law of human rights. This trend has been punctuated by a growing number of specific documents such as the Declaration on the Protection of All Persons from Being Subjected to Torture and Other Cruel, Inhuman or Degrading Treatment or Punishment.[13] Several multilateral agreements dealing with the protection of human rights have also entered into force in recent years.[14] These instruments not only create binding obligations among the States-Parties but contribute toward the identification of particular rights that may enter into the customary law of nations. In view of these developments the district court's formulation of the content of international law cannot be deemed to be a complete or accurate statement of international law as it is currently understood and applied.

B. *Section 1350 includes violations of the law of nations as that phrase is currently understood*

Section 1350 originated in the Judiciary Act of 1789. 1 Stat. 73, § 9 (1789). It is one of several provisions in that Act "reflecting a concern for uniformity in this country's dealings with foreign nations and indicating a desire to give matters of international significance to the jurisdiction of federal institutions." *Banco Nacional de Cuba v. Sabbatino*, 376 U.S. 398, 427 n. 25 (1964). Except for some minor differences, the language in section 1350 is essentially the same as that in the 1789 Act.

This Court may assume for the purposes of this case that in 1789 the law of nations did not govern a nation's treatment of its own citizens, however reprehensible it may have been.[15] At that time, the law of nations was primarily concerned with such matters as piracy, the treatment of ambassadors and maritime captures, as well as fundamentals such as territory and jurisdiction.

---

[13] The United Nations Human Rights Commission is currently working on a draft convention on torture that would codify the international customary law and establish procedures for securing greater compliance with that law.

[14] These include the International Covenant on Civil and Political Rights, the American Convention on Human Rights (S. Exec. Doc. No. E, F, *supra*) and the European Convention for the Protection of Human Rights and Fundamental Freedoms (*Basic Documents, supra*, at 914). The United States has not yet become a party to these major multilateral human rights treaties, though it is a party to some minor human rights treaties.

[15] While there may have been no human rights component to international law in 1789, the sense that there were fundamental human rights based upon natural law concepts was quite strong in the late 18th Century, as evidenced by the Declaration of Independence and its appeal to the "opinions of mankind." Some early international law commentators, including the seminal scholar Grotius in 1625, also recognized the concept of "humanitarian intervention," which permitted a nation to use military force to protect the oppressed citizens of another nation from the tyranny of an unjust and cruel ruler. Sohn and Buergenthal, *International Protection of Human Rights*, 138-139 (1973).

See generally, Dickenson, "The Law of Nations as Part of the National Law of the United States," 101 U. Pa. L. Rev. 26 (1952). Since the law of nations had been developed in large measure by reference to custom, however, the framers of the 1789 Act surely anticipated that the principles of international law would not remain static. And there is no evidence that the framers of the 1789 Act intended to limit the application of section 1350 to those relatively few subjects already encompassed by the law of nations in 1789, leaving the state courts free to administer those rules of international law that would develop in the future. Such a narrow interpretation of the 1789 Act would frustrate that statute's central concern for uniformity in this country's dealings with foreign nations.

Accordingly, as one lower court has stated, the phrase "law of nations" in section 1350 must be understood "as part of an 'organic growth.'" *Lopes v. Reederei Richard Schroder*, 225 F. Supp. 292, 295-296 (E.D. Pa. 1963). So viewed, the question is not whether the conduct alleged in the complaint would have been treated as a violation of the law of nations in 1789, but whether it is "customarily treated as a violation of the law of nations [today]." *Id.* at 297.

This Court's decisions do not adopt a static view of section 1350. Thus, although dicta in *Vencap, supra,* and *Dreyfus, supra,* may be read to imply that section 1350 may not reach a claim based on a nation's treatment of its own citizens, there is no indication that this conclusion is premised on a view that section 1350 is limited to violations of international law as of 1789. Similarly, in *Khedivial Line, S.A.E. v. Seafarers' International Union*, 278 F.2d 49 (2d Cir. 1960), this Court did not approach the question of a ship's right of access as one governed by the law of nations as it stood in 1789. Instead, it freely cited developments that had taken place in the twentieth century as bearing on a proper resolution of this question. *Id.* at 52 n. 1.

In sum, the fact that the law of nations may not in 1789 have touched a nation's treatment of its own citizens is of no current significance. The proper approach to a case such as this is to determine whether the conduct alleged violates the law of nations as it is currently understood.

C. *This Court's decisions should not be read to compel the result reached by the district court*

The statement that international law includes only those "rules . . . affecting the relationship between states and between an individual and a foreign state" (J.A. 108) has a curious history. It first appeared in a district court decision, *Lopes v. Reederei Richard Schroder, supra.* The issue in that case was whether negligence resulting in personal injury aboard a ship violated the law of nations. The district court held that plaintiffs had failed to show that such negligence is "customarily treated as a violation of the law of nations." 225 F. Supp. at 297. The court then expressed the view that "the phrase 'in violation of the law of nations,' for the purpose of deciding this issue, means, *inter alia*, at least a violation . . . of those standards . . . (a) affecting the relationship between states or between an individual and a foreign state, and (b) used by those states for their common good and/or in dealings *inter se*." *Ibid.*

The court appears to have derived this definition solely from early treatises on international law. 225 F. Supp. at 296-297. Moreover, the definition did not purport to be all inclusive. The court carefully stated that it was appropriate "for the purpose of deciding *this issue*, i.e., whether negligence resulting in personal injury violated the law of nations." *Id.* at 297 (emphasis added). Certainly, there is no indication that it was intended to exclude human rights violations that are customarily treated as violations of international law from the scope of section 1350.

The phrase next appears in this Court's decision in *Vencap, supra.* There plaintiffs contended that securities fraud violated the law of nations, apparently on the theory that because theft violates the domestic law of every nation, it also violates the law of nations. 519 F.2d at 1015. This Court properly rejected this erroneous argument. A violation of international law must transcend the violation of local norms and raise issues of international concern. See *Valanga v. Metropolitan Life Insurance Co.*, 259 F. Supp. 324, 328 (E.D. Pa. 1966); *Abdul-Rahman Omar Adra v. Clift*, 195 F. Supp. 857, 863-865 (D. Md. 1961). Rather than disposing of the case on this ground alone, however, the Court then quoted the Lopes formulation as support for its conclusion without any discussion of its origin or meaning. 519 F.2d at 1015.

If this Court intended in *Vencap* to adopt the *Lopes* formulation as an authoritative interpretation of section 1350, it abandoned it in *Dreyfus*, decided only one year later. *Dreyfus* involved the wrongful seizure of property. The Court began its discussion in *Dreyfus* by stating that there is no "universally accepted definition of ["the law of nations"]." 534 F.2d at 30. It further expressed the view that the law of nations "deals *primarily* with the relationship among nations . . . ." *Id.* at 30-31 (emphasis added). Although the Court discussed most of the decisions under section 1350, it did not refer to either *Vencap* or the *Lopes* formulation.

The Court in *Dreyfus* did state that "violations of international law do not occur when the aggrieved parties are nationals of the acting state." *Id.* at 31. If this statement was intended as an expression of the law governing expropriations, it is unobjectionable.[16] Due to basic differences in social and property systems there is no firmly established customary rule of international law governing a nation's confiscation of the property of its own citizens. The cases relied upon in *Dreyfus* fully support that holding. See *Sabbatino, supra*; *Salimoff & Co. v. Standard Oil Co.*, 262 N.Y. 220, 186 N.E. 679 (1933).

However, the district court apparently read *Dreyfus* as a straightforward application of the *Lopes* formulation (J.A. 108). This reading is inconsistent with this Court's deliberate avoidance of any "universal definition" of the law of nations as well as with its failure to even mention *Vencap* or the *Lopes* formulation.

This Court has never considered the reach of section 1350 in a context such as this. It is not bound by vague dicta from a district court decision that limited its application to the issue before it. In light of the manner in which it was cited in *Vencap*, its apparent abandonment in *Dreyfus* and the fact that it is fundamentally inconsistent with the development of international law, the *Lopes* formulation should now be disapproved. This Court has recognized that apparently settled interpretations of international law may sometimes have to be discarded if they were adopted without thorough analysis and have been shown to be contrary to the general practice of nations. In *Benjamins v. British European Airways*, 572 F.2d 913 (1978), cert. denied, 46 U.S.L.W. 2491 (August 22, 1978), this Court overruled a twenty-year line of decisions interpreting the Warsaw Convention for such reasons. This case as well calls for careful treatment of the question whether torture is a violation of the customary law of nations, not the application of a stale verbal formula.

II.

RESORT TO TRADITIONAL SOURCES OF INTERNATIONAL LAW LEADS TO THE CONCLUSION THAT THERE IS A CUSTOMARY NORM OF INTERNATIONAL LAW PROHIBITING TORTURE

The inclusion of the "law of nations" along with treaties in section 1350 indicates that the federal courts are expected to determine the content of customary international law in deciding tort suits brought under this statute. The same methodology may be used in a human rights case as in a more traditional case involving the law of nations. The sources to which a

---

[16] Indeed, the tort alleged in *Dreyfus* took place before the signing of the United Nations Charter and other developments made clear that a nation's treatment of its own citizens could be a proper subject of international law.

court should look are international agreements, international custom as evidence of a general practice accepted as law, the principles of law recognized by civilized nations, international judicial decisions and the teachings of learned commentators.[17]

The federal courts have long since developed techniques for defining and applying the law of nations. The leading formulation of this process was pronounced by the Supreme Court in *The Paquete Habana*, 175 U.S. 677, 700 (1900):

> International law is part of our law, and must be ascertained and administered by the courts of justice of appropriate jurisdiction, as often as questions of right depending upon it are duly presented for their determination. For this purpose, where there is no treaty, and no controlling executive or legislative act or judicial decision, resort must be had to the customs and usages of civilized nations; and, as evidence of these, to the works of jurists and commentators, who by years of labor, research and experience, have made themselves peculiarly well acquainted with the subjects of which they treat. Such works are resorted to by judicial tribunals, not for the speculations of their authors concerning what the law ought to be, but for trustworthy evidence of what the law really is.

In *United States v. Smith*, 18 U.S. (5 Wheat.) 153, 157 (1820), the Supreme Court held that a federal statute[18] making "piracy, as defined by the law of nations" a criminal offense was not unconstitutionally vague (*Id.* at 160-161):

> What the law of nations on this subject is, may be ascertained by consulting the works of jurists, writing professedly on public law; or by the general usage and practice of nations; or by judicial decisions recognizing and enforcing that law.

Since the learned writings and actual practice of nations evidenced a settled agreement on the definition of piracy, the conviction in *Smith* was upheld.

In a human rights context specific guidance may be sought from instruments such as the American Convention on Human Rights, the European Convention for the Protection of Human Rights and Fundamental Freedoms, and the International Covenant on Civil and Political Rights. These agree-

---

[17] I.C.J. Stat. art. 38; 59 Stat. 1055; T.S. 993.

[18] Act of March 3, 1819, c. 77, s.5; now codified at 18 U.S.C. 1651. Art. 5(2) of the American Convention; art. 3 of the European *Convention*; art. 7 of the International Covenant on Civil and Political Rights.

ments all provide that "no one shall be subjected to torture . . . ." Particularly since these treaties have entered into force, and despite the fact that the United States is not a party, these documents may provide an authoritative source for the definition of fundamental human rights.

However, not every provision of these treaties, which tend to be wide-ranging, can be considered to have entered into the law of nations so as to obligate observance even by nonsignatories. Where principled reservations have been attached by a significant number of signatories to specific provisions,[19] or where principled disagreement with such provisions is cited as the ground for other nations' refusal to become parties, the near-unanimity required for the adoption of a rule into the customary law of nations must be found lacking.

In this regard a federal court must be careful to distinguish between principles that are widely considered desirable but incapable of universal realization and thus not a binding rule of the law of nations, and those core rights that are regarded as truly fundamental. The former category might include the rights to rest and leisure and an adequate standard of living contained in articles 24 and 25 of the Universal Declaration of Human Rights.[20] Basic rights, such as protection against genocide and torture, would be considered core rights from the universal acknowledgement of their binding character[21] and because of their incompatibility with any rational concept of human rights and fundamental freedoms.

---

[19] For instance, article 20 of the International Covenant on Civil and Political Rights prohibits "any advocacy of national, racial or religious hatred that constitutes incitement to discrimination, hostility or violence . . . ." S. Exec. Doc. No. C, D, E, F, *supra*, at 29. This provision has been viewed as inconsistent with principles of free speech that are central to the political values of many democracies. A number of nations, including the United Kingdom, Sweden, Denmark, Norway and Finland, expressed reservations to article 20 upon ratifying the Covenant. Multilateral Treaties in Respect of Which the Secretary General Performs Depositary Functions, UN Doc. ST/LEG/SER. D/12 (1978).

[20] *Basic Documents, supra*, at 136. These rights are also protected in article 7 of the International Covenant on Economic, Social and Cultural Rights but article 2 of that Covenant specifies that these rights are to be achieved progressively (and therefore need not be fully in effect at the time a State ratifies this Covenant). Also see article 26 of the American Convention on Human Rights. S. Exec. Doc. C, D, E, F, *supra* at 14, 15, 49.

[21] Moreover, another indication of the fundamental nature of the right to protection against torture is the fact that it is one of the few rights from which derogation is never justified (See, *e.g.*, article 4(2) of the International Covenant on Civil and Political Rights; Article 3 of the Declaration on the Protection of All Persons From Being Subjected to Torture and other Cruel, Inhuman or Degrading Treatment or Punishment; and article 27(2) of the American Convention on Human Rights).

A second, and especially significant, source is the actual practice of nations. *Sabbatino, supra,* 396 U.S. at 421-422. An apparently fundamental right is not excluded from the law of nations simply because it is violated by a small number of nations.[22] Rather, the touchstone is whether the violators admit their practices and attempt to justify their transgressions on some principled ground. Where a significant number of nations by their acknowledged practices indicate that a certain right claimed to be fundamental is not considered binding, then a federal court should in all probability conclude that the asserted right is not protected by the law of nations. Here the plaintiffs argue that nations accused of torture unanimously deny the accusation and make no attempt to justify its use. The awareness of universal condemnation implicit in this conduct is highly relevant to the disposition of the issue presented by this case.

A third source is general principles of law recognized by civilized nations. Evidence of these principles may be found in non-treaty documents that have received unanimous approbation in the world community, such as the United Nations Declaration on Torture and the Universal Declaration of Human Rights.[23] The weight given these instruments must be tempered by awareness that they do not create binding treaty obligations, but they can be particularly useful in supplying a precise definition of a human rights tort. The Declaration on Torture, in article I, defines torture as:

> any act by which severe pain or suffering, whether physical or mental, is intentionally inflicted by or at the instigation of a public official on a person for such purposes as obtaining from him or a third person information or confession, punishing him for an act he has committed or is suspected of having committed, or intimidating him or other persons. It does not include pain or suffering arising only from, inherent in or incidental to lawful sanctions to

---

[22] A leading commentator, H. Lauterpacht, in describing the creation of customary international law, notes, "'Common consent' can therefore only mean the express or tacit consent of such an overwhelming majority of the members that those who dissent are of no importance as compared with the community viewed as an entity . . . . It is therefore not necessary to prove for every single rule of International Law that every single member of the international community has consented to it. . . . The body of the rules of this law can be altered by common consent only, not by a unilateral declaration on the part of one State." *International Law: A Treatise* 17-18 (1955).

[23] Article 5 of the Universal Declaration is primary evidence that the prohibition against torture is widely recognized by civilized nations. Basic Documents, *supra,* at 134. Eighteen nations have incorporated by reference the Universal Declaration into their constitutions. Torture is specifically forbidden in the constitutions of over 40 nations and is implicitly prohibited by the constitutions of over 50 nations.

the extent consistent with the Standard Minimum Rules for the Treatment of Prisoners.

The specificity of this description provides useful guidance to a federal court in a tort suit premised on a claim of torture and helps to narrow the potential range of such suits, as for instance by excluding non-official torture and much corporal punishment.

A fourth source for the identification of the law of nations is the learned commentary of international law experts. This has long been deemed a primary fountainhead of the law of nations, in such cases as *The Paquete Habana, supra,* and *United States v. Smith, supra.* Both the written works of these jurists as well as their expert testimony may appropriately be consulted. The affidavits submitted by plaintiffs of professors Falk (J.A. 61), Franck (J.A. 63), Lillich (J.A. 65) and McDougal (J.A. 71) constitute relevant evidence on the disputed question whether torture is a violation of the law of nations.

International law proscriptions against torture have also been incorporated into the statutory law of the United States. Congress has declared in 22 U.S.C. 2304(a)(1) that it is the policy of the United States, "in accordance with its international obligations as set forth in the Charter of the United Nations . . . to promote and encourage increased respect for human rights," to bar assistance (with certain exceptions) "to any country the government of which engages in a consistent pattern of gross violations of internationally recognized human rights," 22 U.S.C. 2304(a)(2), specifically including torture. 22 U.S.C. 2304(d).[24] These statutes not only evidence the existence of international law norms condemning torture and the potential effect of human rights abuses on foreign relations but indicate that these norms are certain enough to be cognizable by the federal courts.

In a section 1350 case premised on a claim of official torture, a federal court is asked to redress a violation that, if committed domestically under color of law, would be a criminal offense under 18 U.S.C. 242 and civilly actionable under 42 U.S.C. 1983 or under the Constitution. See *Bivens v. Six Unknown Fed. Narcotics Agents,* 403 U.S. 388 (1971). This Court is thus not asked to apply unfamiliar principles of law in this case or to recognize a cause of action that is entirely alien to the American legal system.

---

[24] See also, 22 U.S.C. 2151n: "No assistance may be provided . . . to the government of any country which engages in a consistent pattern of gross violations of internationally recognized human rights, including torture . . . ."

The law of nations outlawing torture is fully compatible with constitutional standards and its application under section 1350 would not in any way be repugnant to a federal court's obligation to enforce the Constitution. Section 1350, like any federal statute, is subject to the Constitution. No tort would be actionable under section 1350 if the enforcement of such a claim would run afoul of constitutional limitations.[25]

The plaintiffs below submitted undisputed expert testimony that the type of torture allegedly inflicted by defendant Pena Irala on Joelito Filartiga is a violation of the contemporary law of nations. The conclusion that torture is proscribed by customary international is also supported by the provisions of multilateral human rights treaties, such as the American Convention on Human Rights, the European Convention for the Protection of Human Rights and Fundamental Freedoms, and the International Covenant on Civil and Political Rights; by instruments evidencing the understanding of civilized nations, such as the United Nations Declaration on Torture and the Universal Declaration of Human Rights; the actual practice of nations; the statements of learned commentators; and the provisions of federal statutes. This Court should reverse the judgment of dismissal and hold that as a matter of law the "law of nations" within the meaning of section 1350 includes a prohibition against torture administered by a police official acting under color of law.[26]

III.

SECTION 1350 IS CONSTITUTIONAL AS APPLIED TO SUITS OF THIS KIND

Defendant argued below in his Memorandum of Law in Support of Motion to Dismiss Complaint and Vacate Stay (Mem.) that if section 1350 is interpreted to apply to an action by one foreigner against another for acts committed abroad it would violate Article III (Mem. 7-10). Because we believe that section 1350 should be interpreted to apply to such a suit, in appropriate cases, we address the constitutional question.

---

[25] For instance, the advocacy of racial hatred, outlawed under some human rights treaties, would not be actionable under section 1350 even if it had become proscribed by the law of nations if it were determined to be inconsistent with the First Amendment. Cf. *Reid v. Covert*, 354 U.S. 1, 16 (1957).

[26] Perhaps relying on the dicta in *Vencap* and *Dreyfus*, defendant introduced no evidence below contradicting plaintiffs' experts' affidavits. This Court might choose alternatively to vacate the judgment and remand for consideration by the district court of the existence of customary international law proscribing torture.

Defendant argued below (Mem. 9) that there are only three potential sources of Article III jurisdiction in suits brought under section 1350 for violations of the law of nations: (1) "Cases affecting Ambassadors, other public Ministers and Consuls;" (2) "Cases of admiralty and maritime Jurisdiction;" and (3) "Controversies . . . between a State or the Citizens thereof and foreign states, Citizens or Subjects." Since none of these grants of judicial power are applicable here, defendant argued, section 1350 cannot be interpreted to reach this case (*ibid.*).

Although we agree that jurisdictional grants cannot go outside Article III limits,[27] we do not believe there is any constitutional difficulty here. Article III, Section 2, extends the judicial power to cases "arising under . . . the Laws of the United States." Cases brought pursuant to section 1350 fall within the purview of this clause of Article III.

Section 1350 is not only a jurisdictional statute. It also authorizes federal courts to fashion a body of federal common law derived from the sources described in *The Paquete Habana, supra*, and discussed in Argument II, *supra*.

In this respect, it is similar to section 301 of the Taft-Hartley Act (29 U.S.C. 185), which provides that "[s]uits for violation of contracts between an employer and a labor organization . . . may be brought in any district court of the United States having jurisdiction of the parties . . . ." In *Textile Workers Union v. Lincoln Mills*, 353 U.S. 448 (1957), the Supreme Court interpreted this provision not only as a jurisdictional statute but also as a source of substantive law which federal courts "must fashion from the policy of our national labor laws." *Id.* at 456. The Court noted that it "is not uncommon for federal courts to fashion federal law" where federal interests are involved. *Id.* at 457.

In *Banco Nacional de Cuba v. Sabbatino*, supra, 376 U.S. at 425, the Supreme Court recognized that in light of the need for uniformity, questions of international law should be resolved in accordance with federal standards. The specific issue in *Sabbatino* was whether the act of state doctrine should be dealt with as a matter of state law or federal law. The Court concluded that the issue "must be treated exclusively as an aspect of federal law." *Ibid.* In reaching this result, the Court relied heavily on Professor Jessup's previous conclusion[28] that the rationale of *Erie Railroad Co. v.*

---

[27] This Court has previously indicated that section 1350 must be kept within the confines of Article III. *IIT v. Vencap, supra*, 519 F.2d at 1015. Although Justice Jackson argued in *National Ins. Co. v. Tidewater Co.*, 337 U.S. 582 (1949), that jurisdictional grants can go outside Article III limits, a majority of the Supreme Court rejected this view.

[28] "The Doctrine of *Erie R.R. v. Tompkins* Applied to International Law," 33 Am. J. Int'l. L. 740 (1939).

Tompkins 304 U.S. 64 (1938), should not be extended to questions of international law since "rules of international law should not be left to divergent and perhaps parochial state interpretations." *Sabbatino, supra,* 376 U.S. at 425. In light of this explicit statement in *Sabbatino,* disputes under section 1350 are appropriately resolved as a matter of federal common law.[29]

Such disputes may be viewed as arising either under section 1350, which is both jurisdictional and substantive, or under the federal common law which that statute authorizes federal courts to fashion. In either event, suits brought pursuant to section 1350 arise under the laws of the United States. Compare *Textile Workers Union v. Lincoln Mills, supra,* 353 U.S. at 457 (contract disputes between labor and management brought pursuant to section 301 of the Taft-Hartley Act arise under section 301 and therefore arise under the laws of the United States) with *Illinois v. City of Milwaukee,* 406 U.S. 91, 99-100 (1972) (claims arising under federal common law arise under the laws of the United States). Defendant's Article III argument is therefore wholly without merit.

Moreover, it is doubtful that defendant's argument can properly be viewed as one premised on Article III at all. The constitutional rule that Article III defines the bounds of valid jurisdictional legislation is based on fundamental principles of federalism. It reflects the framers' understanding that judicial power not specifically granted to the national judiciary by Article III is reserved to the states. See *National Ins. Co. v. Tidewater Co., supra,* 337 U.S. at 631 (Vinson, J., dissenting). Accordingly, a claim that a jurisdictional grant violates Article III is at bottom a claim that disputes arising under that jurisdictional grant should be determined in state court. See *National Ins. Co. v. Tidewater Co., supra; Textile Workers v. Lincoln Mills, supra.*

Defendant's argument does not fit this mold. Thus, defendant did not argue below that this suit belongs in state court rather than federal court.

---

[29] The Court's statement in *Sabbatino* that questions of international law should be determined under uniform federal standards is consistent with a long line of decisions recognizing that international law must be treated as an aspect of the "laws of the United States." *The Paquete Habana,* supra, at 175 U.S. at 700; *Hilton v. Guyot,* 159 U.S. 113, 163 (1895); *United States v. Arjona,* 120 U.S. 479 (1887). An early statement of this principle appears in Chief Justice Jay's charge to the jury in *Henfield's Case,* 11 Fed. Cas. 1099 (1793). In it he stated (*id.* at 1100-1101):

> [T]he laws of the United States admit of being classed under three heads of descriptions. 1st. All treaties made under the authority of the United States. 2d. The laws of nations. 3dly. The constitution, and statutes of the United States.

There is also a considerable body of evidence indicating framers of the Constitution intended the phrase "laws of the United States" in Article III to comprehend the "law of nations." For a thorough discussion of this evidence, see Note, *Federal Common Law and Article III: A Jurisdictional Approach to Erie,* 74 Yale L. J. 325, 334-337 (1964).

Instead, as we understand it, he argued that this case belongs in Paraguay rather than in the United States. This claim does not implicate Article III, since Article III is concerned solely with the distribution of judicial power between state and federal courts.

Properly viewed, defendant's claim raises the question whether Congress has constitutional power under Article I or otherwise to provide a civil remedy in cases of this kind. Thus, in his memorandum submitted below, the defendant argued as follows (Mem. 9):

> Congress has no delegated authority to make even the wrongful killing of one New Yorker by another a tort or a crime (except within the narrow range of circumstances dealt with by the Thirteenth and Fourteenth Amendments or some other specific constitutional provision). Certainly, therefore, the Constitution does not authorize Congress to empower the federal district courts to try civil damage cases by one foreigner against another for acts committed abroad!

Although no specific constitutional provision in Article I, Section 8, authorizes Congress to provide a civil remedy for violations of international law,[30] its power to do so is clear. Defendant conceded below (Mem. 9) that Congress has implied power to deal with matters of international concern. This concession was appropriate. The Supreme Court has repeatedly recognized that Congress has broad power over foreign affairs, even in the absence of an explicit grant of power in Article I. *Perez v. Brownell*, 356 U.S. 44, 57 (1958); *United States v. Curtiss-Wright Export Corp.*, 299 U.S. 304, 318 (1936); *Mackenzie v. Hare*, 239 U.S. 299, 311-312 (1915). Providing a civil remedy for violations of international law plainly falls within this residual national power.

Defendant errs in characterizing this case as a local dispute between two foreign nationals in which the United States has no interest. The complaint alleges that the defendant, an official of Paraguay, tortured and killed Joelito Filartiga in violation of an established norm of international law. At least since the signing of the United Nations Charter, nations have been obligated to promote universal respect for and observance of human rights and fundamental freedoms.

The United States has a specific obligation under the Charter to promote respect for fundamental human rights throughout the world. Pursuant

---

[30] Article I, Section 8, Clause 10, explicitly authorizes Congress to "define and punish Piracies and Felonies committed on the high Seas, and Offences against the Law of Nations."

to this obligation, the United States has passed a number of statutes barring assistance to countries engaged in a pattern of gross human rights violations. Providing a civil remedy under section 1350 for violations by State officials of the most basic human rights of that State's nationals, where the perpetrators of such violations are found in the United States is perfectly consistent with the international obligations of the United States.

CONCLUSION

For the foregoing reasons, this Court should reverse the judgment below and remand this case for further proceedings.

Respectfully submitted,

EDWARD R. KORMAN
    United States Attorney

DREW S. DAYS, III
Assistant Attorney General

JOHN E. HUERTA
Deputy Assistant Attorney General

BRIAN K. LANDSBERG
IRVING GORNSTEIN
JOAN F. HARTMAN
Attorneys
Department of Justice
Washington, D. C. 20530

SEPTEMBER 14, 1979: UNITED STATES

Correspondence from Deputy Legal Adviser, U.S. Department of State to Department of Justice

DEPARTMENT OF STATE

Washington, D.C. 20520

September 14, 1979

John Huerta, Esq.
Deputy Assistant Attorney General
Civil Rights Division
Department of Justice
Washington, D.C. 20350

Dear Mr. Huerta:

I much appreciated your telephone call the other day.

Please find enclosed a letter which we have today addressed to the Solicitor General's Office, which recommends that the United States file an amicus brief in the case of *Filartiga v. Pena-Irala*, which, however, would be of a substance which differs in important measure from that which we have both supported. I shall telephone you in that regard today.

Yours sincerely,

Stephen M. Schwebel
Deputy Legal Adviser

Enclosure: as stated.

/mers

SEPTEMBER 14, 1979: UNITED STATES

Correspondence from Deputy Legal Adviser, U.S. Department of State to U.S. Solicitor General

DEPARTMENT OF STATE

Washington, D.C. 20520

September 14, 1979

Richard Allen, Esq.
Office of the Solicitor General
Department of Justice
Room 5619
Washington, D. C. 20350

Dear Mr. Allen:

The case of *Filartiga v. Pena-Irala*, the possibility of the United States filing an amicus brief in its appeal, and your stimulating memorandum opposing such a filing, have been the subject of intensive consideration by the Legal Adviser, the Deputy Legal Advisers and a number of attorneys of the State Department's Office of the Legal Adviser.

The Office has reached the conclusion that it is important that an amicus brief be filed which embodies the points made in the enclosed note. As you will see, these points take very considerable account of the approach of the Solicitor General's Office to this case.

We hope that the Solicitor General will be prepared to authorize submission of an amicus brief of this substance. If that is not his disposition, then we would propose a meeting at an appropriately senior level between officials of the Justice and State Departments to resolve the difference between us.

Yours sincerely,

Stephen M. Schwebel
Deputy Legal Adviser

Enclosure: as stated.

/mers

In the case of *Filartiga v. Pena-Irala,* **the District Court held:**

"Jurisdiction of the court is invoked under 28 U.S.C. § 1350 which reads 'the district courts shall have original jurisdiction of any civil action by an alien for a tort only, committed in violation of the Law of Nations or a treaty of the United States.'

"Plaintiffs contend that the court has jurisdiction because the torture and murder of the decedent was 'in violation of the Law of Nations'. Plaintiffs do not contend Pena-Irala committed a tort in violation of a treaty of the United States.

"This court is bound by the decision in *ITT v. Vencap, Ltd.,* 519 F.2d 1001 (2d Cir. 1957) and *Dreyfus v. von Finck,* 534 F.2d 24 (2d Cir. 1976). Those decisions held that conduct, though tortious, is not in violation of 'the Law of Nations', as those words are used in 28 U.S.C. § 1350, unless the conduct is in violation of those standards, rules or customs affecting the relationship between states and between an individual and a foreign state, and used by those states for their common good and/or in dealings *inter se. ITT v. Vencap, Ltd., supra,* 519 F.2d at 1015.

"Plaintiffs argue cogently that 28 U.S.C. § 1350 should not be so narrowly read and that the proscription of torture in numerous international instruments accepted by nearly all the states in the international community reflects the emergence of a norm of customary international law condemning torture.

"Despite the strength of these arguments this court feels bound by the Second Circuit decisions cited above. Accordingly the complaint will be dismissed."

The position of the Department of State on the issues raised by the foregoing is as follows:

1. Contemporary international law is not limited to the relationships between States and between States and aliens. On the contrary, it does embrace relations between a State and its own nationals insofar as those relations comprehend universal respect for and observance of fundamental human rights and freedoms.

2. Torture of an individual by an agent of a State or a person acting under the color of the authority of a State is a violation of one of the most fundamental human rights and freedoms—that of being free of the physical and emotional trauma of torture. Such torture accordingly is a violation of international law.

3. The reference in 28 U.S.C. § 1350 to "the Law of Nations" should be read as referring to international law as it evolves (and not as it existed in the Eighteenth Century), and therefore must encompass certain relations of a State to its nationals. The rationale of the District Court therefore contains a serious error, and one that may prejudice the United States' efforts to promote and develop the international law of human rights. However, the reference in § 1350 not only embraces the substantive but the procedural rules and practices of international law.

4. Under customary international law, States do not ordinarily enjoy and observe universal jurisdiction in respect of violations of international law; on the contrary, they and their courts will normally exercise jurisdiction only where, in the least, their interests or those of their nationals are directly affected by the acts complained of. One exception to this rule is universal jurisdiction over the crime of piracy. States have not customarily exercised jurisdiction over criminal or civil actions flowing from allegations of acts of torture carried out beyond their territorial jurisdiction and not involving their officials or citizens.

5. While torture is proscribed expressly by some international treaties in force (notably, the International Covenant on Civil and Political Rights and the Geneva Conventions for the Protection of War Victims) and, by reasonable construction by other treaties (notably, the Charter of the United Nations), among treaties currently in force only the Geneva Conventions entrust the remedy for violations of this proscription to national courts. The United Nations Charter is not self-executing; and the International Covenant on Civil and Political Rights has created a Human Rights Committee which is charged with pursuing remedies which conduce to observance of the Covenant's provisions. Enforcement of that Covenant's provisions by national courts is not provided for (though it is not excluded).

6. There is currently under negotiation in the Commission on Human Rights of the United Nations a draft Convention on the Protection of All Persons from Being Subjected to Torture and Other Cruel, Inhuman or Degrading Treatment or Punishment. That Convention, should it be concluded and brought into force, seems likely to establish the obligation of States Parties to provide for their national courts exercising jurisdiction over acts in violation of its prescriptions wherever and by whomever committed, where there is *in personam* jurisdiction over the defendant.

7. Pending the conclusion of such a convention and ratification of it by the United States, or the evolution of customary international law as evidenced by a widespread practice of States conferring on their own courts

jurisdiction over aliens' tort claims for alleged acts of torture abroad, 28 U.S.C. § 1350 should be construed as not according federal courts the jurisdiction to entertain suits by an alien in tort for acts of torture allegedly committed by another alien abroad. This conclusion, it should be emphasized, does not derogate from the conclusion stated above that international law embraces the treatment by a State of its nationals in some respects and that one such critical respect is the torture by a State agent of an individual.

In view of the large issues of international law and public policy to which the terms of the District Court's judgment give rise, the Department of State strongly recommends that the United States file a brief *amicus curiae* which incorporates the foregoing points.

SEPTEMBER 18, 1979: UNITED STATES

Appellee's Brief

UNITED STATES COURT OF APPEALS
IN THE SECOND CIRCUIT

No. 79-6090

DOLLY M.E. FILARTIGA and
DR. JOEL FILARTIGA,

Plaintiffs-Appellants,

– against –

AMERICO NORBERTO PENA-IRALA,

Defendant-Appellee.

On Appeal From Judgment From New York District Court
Eastern District of New York

Defendant-Appellee's Brief
In Support of Judgment of Dismissal

MURRY D. BROCHIN, ESQ.
LOWENSTEIN, SANDLER, BROCHIN,
KOHL, FISHER & BOYLAN
A Professional Corporation
744 Broad Street
Newark, New Jersey 07102
(201) 624-4600
Attorneys for Defendant-Appellee

TABLE OF CONTENTS

C. Considerations of separation of powers precludes the Court from adopting plaintiffs' interpretation of 28 U.S.C. §1350

POINT III

THE JUDGMENT BELOW SHOULD BE AFFIRMED BECAUSE PLAINTIFFS' CLAIM IS BARRED BY THE ACT OF STATE DOCTRINE

CONCLUSION

STATEMENT OF THE CASE

This memorandum of law is submitted on behalf of defendant-appellee Americo N. Pena-Irala (hereinafter "defendant") and in support of the judgment of the United States District Court for the Eastern District of New York (Hon. Eugene Nickerson, U.S.D.J.), dismissing the complaint of plaintiffs appellants Joel and Dolly Filartiga (hereinafter "plaintiff") for want of federal jurisdiction.

A. *Procedural History*

Plaintiffs commenced this action by personal service of the complaint upon defendant on April 6, 1979. At the time of service, defendant was confined to the U.S. Immigration and Naturalization Service Detention Center at the Brooklyn Navy Yard pending execution of an order of deportation. (JA 18-19)

In order to pursue their claim against defendant, plaintiffs sought and obtained a stay of the order of deportation. As a result, not only defendant but also his companion and their child were detained against their will in federal custody.

On May 7, 1979, defendant moved before the District Court for an order vacating the stay of the order of deportation and dismissing plaintiffs' suit for want of federal jurisdiction or, alternatively, on the ground of *forum non conveniens.* (JA 47) The District Court heard arguments on the motion on May 14, 1979.

In its decision, filed May 16, 1979, the District Court ordered the dismissal of plaintiffs' action for want of federal jurisdiction, but continued the stay of deportation for 48 hours to permit plaintiffs time to appeal. (JA 105-108)

Plaintiffs filed their notice of appeal on May 16, 1979 (JA 109), and applied to this Court for an immediate stay. This Court rejected plaintiffs' application on of deportation May 22, 1979. (JA 1) Plaintiffs then applied to Justice Marshall in his capacity as a Circuit Justice. Justice Marshall referred the application to the full Supreme Court which, on May 24, 1979, rejected plaintiffs' arguments. On or about May 25, 1979, defendant, his companion and their child left for Paraguay.

B. *Statement of Facts*

On or about March 29, 1976, a Paraguayan youth, Joelito Filartiga, son of plaintiff Joel Filartiga and brother of plaintiff Dolly Filartiga, died in

Asuncion, Paraguay. Plaintiffs allege that the death was the result of torture inflicted upon young Filartiga by defendant in retaliation for his father's political activities. (JA 6)

The alleged killing is currently the subject of a criminal prosecution in Paraguay against defendant and another man, Hugo Duarte. Duarte has made a written statement admitting that he alone was responsible for the death of Joelito Filartiga, although he contends that the homicide was justifiable. (JA 50-51) Paraguayan law and procedure permit the decedent's father to join with the Government in the prosecution of the criminal case against both defendant and Duarte. Plaintiff Joel Filartiga has exercised this right to join in the prosecution. (JA 50)

Paraguayan law also accords the decedent's father a civil cause of action for his son's wrongful death. (JA 48, 51-52) Plaintiff Joel Filartiga, however, has not filed such a civil suit, but the period in which he may file it has not yet expired. (JA 52) Under Paraguayan law, any such civil proceeding in Paraguay would be held in abeyance pending the resolution of the criminal case. (*Id.*) Paraguayan law provides further that the criminal court must find that the act complained of, whether or not sufficient to sustain criminal liability, was in fact committed by defendant before civil liability may be imposed. (*Id.*)

ARGUMENT

POINT I.

THE JUDGMENT OF DISMISSAL SHOULD BE AFFIRMED BECAUSE THE CONSTITUTION WHOLLY PRECLUDES THE EXPANSIVE READING OF 28 U.S.C. §1350 URGED BY PLAINTIFFS TO JUSTIFY FEDERAL JURISDICTION.

A.   *Congress may not grant jurisdiction to the District Courts which is not authorized by the Constitution.*

Plaintiffs' argument, reduced to its essentials, is that, by virtue of 28 U.S.C. §1350, the District Courts of the United States have jurisdiction over any case of "torture," wherever and by whomever it may have been committed, at least when it was politically motivated. Defendant respectfully submits that the Constitution does not permit such an expansive reading of the jurisdictional grant contained in 28 U.S.C. §1350 and the language of the statute does not require it.[1]

---

[1] This section provides: "The District Court shall have original jurisdiction of any civil action by an alien for a tort only, committed in violation of the law of nations or a treaty of the United States."

The court below is, of course, a court of limited jurisdiction, constrained in the exercise of its powers by Congressional enabling legislation which may not exceed the confines of Article III. *See, e.g., Dreyfus v. Von Finck*, 534 F. 2d 24, 29 (2d Cir), *cert. denied*, 429 U.S. 835 (1976); *Lincoln Associates v. Great American Mortgage Investors*, 415 F. Supp. 351, 353 (N.D. Tex. 1976) ("It is a fundamental principle that federal courts are courts of limited jurisdiction and are empowered to hear only those cases specifically authorized to be heard by a jurisdictional grant from Congress pursuant to Article III of the Constitution"); *State of Iowa v. Union Asphalt & Roadoils, Inc.*, 291 F. Supp. 391, 395 (S.D. Iowa 1968), *aff'd*, 408 F.2d 1171 (8th Cir. 1969).

The language of §1350, therefore, must be construed in a manner consistent with Section 2 of Article III of the United States Constitution:

> Section 2. The judicial power of the United States shall extend to all Cases in Law and Equity, arising under this Constitution, the Laws of the United States, and Treaties made, or which shall be made, under their Authority; to all Cases affecting Ambassadors, other public Ministers and Consuls; to all Cases of Admiralty and maritime Jurisdiction; to Controversies in which the United States shall be a Party; to Controversies between two or more States; between a State and Citizens of another State; between Citizens of different States; between Citizens of the same State claiming Lands under Grants of different States; and between a State, or the Citizens thereof, and foreign States, Citizens or Subjects.

B. *None of the jurisdictional clauses of Article III authorizes the maintenance of this suit in the court below.*

If 28 U.S.C. §1350 were construed to extend jurisdiction to the instant case, by what clause of Article III would such a grant of jurisdiction be authorized? This suit does not "affect" any ambassador, public minister or consul. The United States is not a party to this action; nor is the suit one between citizens of different states or between a state (or its citizens) and a foreign state (or its citizens or subjects). Just as clearly, plaintiffs' claim does not implicate admiralty or maritime jurisdiction. Plaintiffs themselves have admitted, as they must, that jurisdiction in this case cannot be sustained on the basis of the citizenship of the parties, for the United States Supreme Court has held repeatedly that the Constitution precludes jurisdiction founded solely upon alienage. *See, e.g., Hodgson v. Bowerbank*, 5 Cranch (9 U.S.) 303 (1809) (where one party is an alien and the other is not shown to be a citizen of any state, jurisdiction will not lie. In the language of Chief Justice Marshall, "Turn to the article of the constitution of the United States, for the statute [the Judiciary Act of 1789] cannot extend the jurisdiction beyond the limits of the constitution"). *See also, Jackson v. Twentyman*, 2 Pet. (27 U.S.) 136 (1829); *Montlet v. Murray*, 4 Cranch (8 U.S.) 46 (1807); *Mossman v. Higginson*, 4 Dall. (4 U.S.) 12 (1800).

There remains, then, only the more general language of Article III, extending jurisdiction to "all Cases in Law and Equity, arising under this Constitution, the Laws of the United States, and Treaties . . . ." Plaintiffs do not assert that they have a claim arising under the Constitution. There would be no justification for such an assertion. The Constitution neither confers upon aliens an absolute right to sue in American courts, nor extends its guarantees to aliens outside the United States. *Johnson v. Eisentrager*, 339 U.S. 763 (1950); *Cermeno-Cerna v. Farrell*, 291 F. Supp. 521 (C.D. Cal. 1968). The Constitution does *not* govern the independent conduct of foreign officials in their own lands, *United States v. Toscanino*, 500 F.2d 267 (2d Cir.), *reh. denied*, 504 F.2d 1380 (2d Cir. 1974), nor does it provide for enforcement of rights aliens may have in their own countries. *United States v. Lira*, 515 F.2d 68 (2d Cir.), *cert. denied*, 423 U.S. 847 (1975).

Furthermore, plaintiffs' claim cannot be said to "arise under" any statute of the United States. A case does not "arise under" a jurisdictional statute—such as 28 U.S.C. §1350 or 28 U.S.C. §1331—which implements part of the constitutional grant of federal question jurisdiction by authorizing District Courts to entertain suits "arising under . . . the laws of the United States." A case "arises under" a statute only when the substantive claim depends upon the specific statute. *Gully v. First Natl. Bank of Meridian*, 299 U.S. 109, 112 (1936). Of course, no statute of the United States makes it a crime or a civil wrong for one Paraguayan to injure another Paraguayan in Paraguay and plaintiffs' substantive claim is not based on any such statute.

Similarly, in constitutional terms, a case "arises under" a treaty of the United States only when the treaty itself provides for an individual cause of action or when Congress creates such a cause of action by implementing legislation. *See, Dreyfus v. Von Finck, supra*, 534 F.2d at 30; *Foster v. Neilson*, 2 Pet. (27 U.S.) 253, 314 (1829):

> Our Constitution declares a treaty to be the law of the land. It is, consequently, to be regarded in courts of justice as equivalent to an Act of the Legislature whenever it operates by itself without the aid of any Legislative provision. But when the terms of the stipulation import a contract—when either of the parties engages to perform a particular act—the treaty addresses itself to the political, not the judicial department; and the Legislature must execute the contract before it can become a rule for the court.

As noted by this Court in *Dreyfus v. Von Finck, supra,* 534 F.2d at 28-29: "Rarely is the relationship between a private claim and a general treaty sufficiently direct so that it may be said to 'arise under' the treaty as required by Article III, §2, Cl. 1 of the Constitution." In this case, analyzing the authorities cited by plaintiffs, it is clear that none of the various "treaties" upon which plaintiffs rely provides such a direct relationship, and none has been augmented by Congressional implementing legislation.

The United Nations Charter has repeatedly been held not to grant any individual cause of action. *People of Saipan v. U.S. Interior Department,* 502 F.2d 90, 100 (9th Cir. 1974) (Trask, J., concurring) ("[T]he Charter of the United Nations is not self-executing and does not in and of itself create rights which are justiciable between individual litigants"); *Hitai v. Immigration and Naturalization Service,* 343 F.2d 466, 468 (2d Cir. 1965) ("This [Article 55, the human rights section] provision of the Charter is not self-executing . . . ."); *Camacho v. Rogers,* 199 F. Supp. 155, 158 (S.D.N.Y. 1961) ("treaties are part of the supreme law of the land . . . only if the provisions of the treaty are self-executing;" *held,* Article 55 is not self executing); *Sei Fujii v. State,* 38 Cal.2d 718, 242 P.2d 617 (Sup. Ct. 1951), *en banc* ("[N]one of the other provisions relied upon by plaintiffs [including Article 55] is self-executing").

The Universal Declaration on Human Rights, G.A. Res.217A, 3 U.N. Doc. A/810 (1948), is simply not a treaty in the constitutional sense. When it was adopted, Mrs. Franklin D. Roosevelt, then chairman of the Commission on Human Rights, declared: "It is not a treaty; it is not an international agreement. It is not and does not purport to be a statement of law or of legal obligation." 5 Whiteman, *Digest of International Law* 243 (1965). Legal scholars agree with Mrs. Roosevelt: "At the time of its approval by the United Nations, the Universal Declaration of Human Rights was not binding on the member states in the sense of an obligatory legal instrument creating enforceable rights and duties." Klayman, *The Definition of Torture in International Law,* 51 Temple L. Q. 449, 452 (1978). The delegates in accepting the language as to the condemnation of torture expressly limited it to enforcement *within national boundaries. Id.* at 477-79.

Similarly, the Declaration on the Protection of All Persons from Being Subjected to Torture and Other Cruel, Inhuman or Degrading Treatment or Punishment, G.A. Res. 3452, U.N. Doc. A/10034 (1976) is not a treaty. By its own terms, it is a declaration that every nation adhering to it will adopt measures to prevent torture "within its jurisdiction" (Article IV), and to provide redress "in accordance with national law." (Article XI). Its sponsor, Splekenbunk of The Netherlands, stated:

It should be regarded as a political document which expressed the common intent of many countries whose legal, social and economic structures were widely diverse. Without purporting to impose a legal obligation, the declaration imposed a moral obligation on states to ensure that their national legislation conformed.

30 U.N. GAOR C.3 (2160th meeting) 14, U.N. Doc. A/C.3/SR.2160 (1975).

The remaining three agreements—the American Convention on Human Rights, the International Convention on Civil and Political Rights, and the International Convention on Economic, Social and Cultural Rights—were submitted by President Carter to the Senate of the United States together with a letter of transmittal on February 23, 1978. *Senate Executive Documents C, D, E and F*, 95th Congress, 2d Session (February 23, 1978). In each case, the President recommended that the treaties (submitted together with the International Convention on the Elimination of All Forms of Racial Discrimination) be expressly held by the Senate to be non-self-executing.

As to the American Convention on Human Rights, the State Department recommendation, accepted by the President, noted: "[I]n order to avoid all possible discrepancies in the wording and to leave the implementation of all substantive provisions to the domestic legislative and judicial process, the following declaration is recommended: 'The United States declares that the provisions of Articles 1 through 32 of this Convention are not self-executing.'" *Id.*, at xviii.

The recommendation was the same as to the International Convention on Civil and Political Rights, *id*, at xv, and the International Convention on Economic, Cultural and Social Rights. *Id.*, at xi.

Thus, it is clear that, even if the latter three documents are ratified by the Senate and thereby become part of United States law, no legal rights enforceable by individuals will be created thereunder. Plaintiffs' claim does not "arise under" a treaty of the United States.

C. *The decided cases have construed 28 U.S.C. §1350 narrowly to save its constitutionality and this Court should do the same in this case.*

It is fundamental, of course, that if at all possible, a statute should be construed in a manner which will sustain its constitutionality. Hence federal courts which have interpreted the statutory phrase, "law of nations," have uniformly held it to encompass only those few cases directly implicating relations between states. Thus, in *IIT v. Vencap, Ltd.*, 519 F.2d 1001 (2d Cir. 1975), this Court held that:

[A] violation of the law of nations arises only when there has been "a violation by one or more individuals of those standards, rules or customs (a) affecting the relationship between states or between an individual and a foreign state, and (b) used by those states for their common good and/or in dealings *inter se.*"

519 F.2d at 1015, quoting from *Lopes v. Reederei Richard Schroder,* 225 F. Supp. 292, 296-97 (E.D. Pac 1963).

A similar definition was accepted in *Valanga v. Metropolitan Life Ins. Co.,* 259 F. Supp. 324, 328 (E.D. Pa. 1966): "A violation of the law of nations means a violation of those standards by which nations regulate their dealings with one another *inter se.*" In *Damaskinos v. Societa Navigacion Interamericana, S.A., Panama,* 255 F. Supp. 919 (S.D.N.Y. 1966), the court rejected a personal injury action on the grounds that the wrong complained of did not violate the standards used by nations in regulating their actions towards one another.

In *Abiodun v. Martin Oil Service, Inc.,* 475 F.2d 142 (7th Cir. 1973), plaintiffs, four Nigerian nationals, claimed they had been the victims of international fraud, and argued—as plaintiffs herein do—that the action complained of was universally condemned by all nations. The Seventh Circuit, citing the *Lopes* definition of the law of nations, rejected the claim.

Only last year, the Second Circuit was called upon again to pass on the meaning of "law of nations." Once more, the Court defined it as "a violation by one or more individuals of those standards, rules or customs (a) affecting the relation ship between states or between an individual and a foreign state, and (b) used by those states for their common good and/or in dealings *inter se.*" *Benjamin v. British European Airways,* 572 F.2d 913,916 (2d Cir. 1978). *See, also, Kalmich v. Bruno,* 450 F. Supp. 227, 229 (N.D. Ill. 1978) ("[I]nternational law, although affecting individuals, 'deals primarily with the relationship among nations rather than among individuals.'"); *Aboitiz Co. v. Price,* 99 F. Supp. 602, 609 (D. Utah 1951) ("[I]t is correct to say that international law governs only the relations between States, and that it has nothing to do directly with disputes among private individuals. . . .").

Only two reported decisions in the entire history of the federal judiciary have attempted to sustain jurisdiction under 28 U.S.C. §1350 or its predecessors, and both demonstrate that the claim must have a far more direct nexus with an interest of the United States than the tenuous link asserted here. In *Bolchos v. Darrell,* 3 Fed. Cas. 810 (No. 1607) (D.S.C. 1795), the court initially premised its jurisdiction over the action to determine title to slaves seized aboard an enemy ship upon its characterization of the action as a claim in admiralty. It noted, as an afterthought, that jurisdiction might lie under the alien's action for tort provision, since plaintiff sued in reliance upon a specific provision in a treaty which expressly provided for the disposition of neutral property found and seized aboard an enemy ship.

The only modern case in which §1350 jurisdiction was found was *Abdul-Rahman-Omar Adra v. Clift*, 195 F. Supp. 857 (D. Md. 1961), a decision which may be questionable under the more recent opinion in *Huynh Thi Anh v. Levi*, 586 F.2d 625 (6th Cir. 1978). In *Clift*, a Lebanese national sued an Iraqi national to recover custody of his teenaged daughter. Defendant had secreted the child into the United States by using a falsified passport. The court expressly premised jurisdiction on the defendant's acts of passport fraud, noting that passports are addressed by one foreign sovereign to another and serve to regulate the intercourse between them. By contrast, plaintiffs here can point to no comparable direct implication upon foreign relations.[2] (It may be significant that the *Clift* court adopted plaintiff's position on jurisdiction, but defendant's on the underlying issue of custody.)

This Court's decision in *Dreyfus v. Von Finck, supra*, construed 28 U.S.C. §1350 in a way which excludes jurisdiction in the instant suit. In that case, the tort complained of was the acquisition by an "Aryan" German of the property of a German Jew for less than its value in a coerced sale. On the issue of the availability of federal jurisdiction under the "law of nations" provision of 28 U.S.C. §1350, the Court said:

> More importantly for purposes of this lawsuit, *violations of international law do not occur when the aggrieved parties are nationals of the acting state.* . . . In the instant case, plaintiff was a citizen and resident of Germany at the time of defendants' alleged wrongdoing. Moreover his complaint did not allege that defendants played any role in the policy making decision of the German government. Defendants conduct, tortious though it may have been, was not a violation of the law of nations, which governs civilized states in their dealings with one another.

---

[2] Plaintiffs attempt, at pp. 18-19 of their brief, to argue a similarity to *Clift* in that defendant came to the United States on a visitor's visa and overstayed his welcome, thus subjecting himself to deportation. In *Clift*, the defendant's passport fraud provided the vehicle for the alleged tort. But for the passport fraud, there would have been no violation of the law of nations. Here, by contrast, unlike the protracted, multinational odyssey detailed in *Clift*, all the operative facts occurred in Paraguay. Defendant's subsequent actions neither enhance nor diminish the character of the tort allegedly committed in Paraguay. The fact that defendant at some later time arrived in the United States and overstayed his visa is irrelevant, except to emphasize how much this entire action turns on the accident of personal jurisdiction.

534 F.2d at 31, *emphasis added.* See, also, *F. Palicio y Companio, S.A v. Brush,* 256 F. Supp. 481 (S.D.N.Y.), aff'd, 375 F.2d 1011 (2d Cir.), *cert. denied,* 389 U.S. 830 (1966).

Plaintiffs appear to confuse the whole of international law, which may very well concern itself with private claims, with the law of nations, which governs "questions of right between nations." *Hilton v. Guyot,* 159 U.S. 113, 163 (1894). In clear and obvious terms, §1350 grants federal jurisdiction only over torts committed "in violation of the law of nations." It does not purport, either expressly or otherwise, to bestow jurisdiction over claims based on private international law. Insofar as plaintiffs' claim sounds in the latter, it cannot be heard in a federal forum. Such a result comports fully with the limited jurisdictional mandate set forth in Article III. In purporting to act pursuant to international law, federal courts may not exceed their constitutional and statutory limitations. When international law conflicts or is inconsistent with these limitations, it must yield to the superior domestic authority. *Tag v. Rogers,* 267 F. 2d 664 (D. C. Cir.), *cert. denied,* 362 U.S. 904, *reh. denied,* 362 U.S. 957 (1959). As §1350 limits jurisdiction to cases involving the "law of nations," and does not extend to private international law, the superior domestic authority prevails.

The controlling decisions of this Court and of other federal courts, which have construed 28 U.S.C. §1350 in accordance with the pertinent principles of constitutional law, require the same ruling here—the affirmance of Judge Nickerson's decision in the District Court which correctly held that the court was without jurisdiction to hear the case which plaintiffs have alleged.

POINT II

IF PLAINTIFFS' INTERPRETATION OF 28 U.S.C. §1350 WERE CONSTITUTIONALLY PERMISSIBLE, SUCH A CONSTRUCTION WOULD HAVE TO BE REJECTED NONETHELESS BECAUSE IT WOULD BE CONTRARY TO THE INTENT OF CONGRESS AND TO THE PUBLIC POLICY OF THE UNITED STATES

A. *Plaintiffs' interpretation of 28 U.S.C. §1350 ascribes to Congress a legislative purpose which it could not possibly have entertained in view of the international circumstances of the United States in 1789.*

The Alien Tort Statute, which is now 28 U.S.C. §1350, was first enacted as part of the Judiciary Act of 1789 by the First Congress of the United States, shortly after the ratification of the Constitution. It is a commonplace of American history that the new nation was weak, undeveloped and desirous of remaining neutral from European conflicts. George Washington's famous farewell address of September 17, 1796, summed up his doctrine of isolation as follows:

> Europe has a set of primary interests, which to us have none, or a very remote relation. Hence she must be engaged in frequent controversies, the causes of which are essentially foreign to our concerns. Hence, therefore, it must be unwise in us to implicate ourselves, by artificial ties in the ordinary vicissitudes of her politics, or the ordinary combinations and collisions of her friendships, or enmities. Our detached and distant situation invites us to pursue a different course. . . Why, by interweaving our destiny with that of any part of Europe, entangle our peace and prosperity in the toils of European ambition, rivalship, interest, humor or caprice? 'Tis our true policy to steer clear of permanent alliances, with any portion of the foreign world . . . . Taking care always to keep ourselves, by suitable establishments, on a respectable defensive posture, we may safely trust to temporary alliances for extraordinary emergencies.

* * *

> In relation to the still subsisting war in Europe, my proclamation of the 22d of April, 1793 is the index of my plan. Sanctioned by your approving voice and by that of your Representatives in both Houses of Congress, the spirit of that measure has continually governed me uninfluenced by any attempts to deter or divert me from it.

* * *

> The duty of holding a neutral conduct may be inferred. . . . The inducements of interest for observing that conduct will best be referred to your own reflections and experiences. With me, a predominant motive has been to endeavour to gain time to our country to settle and mature its recent institutions, and to progress without interruption to that degree of strength and consistency, which is necessary to give it, humanly speaking, command of its fortunes. (*American Historical Documents*, Harvard Classics 245-248 (1938 ed.).)

Thus, a primary objective of American foreign policy was to avoid giving offense to or provoking the hostility of powers stronger than itself. Indeed, a major motivation for the enactment of the Constitution in place of the Articles of Confederation was to create a national government which would have the power to restrain the states from conduct which might embroil the entire union in foreign war.

Many statements might be quoted to illustrate that the precariousness of the country's position in 1789 was clearly recognized. For example, Mr. Madison, in discussing the so called Patterson Plan for the federal government, addressed the Federal Constitutional Convention as follows:

> Will [the Patterson plan] prevent those violations of the law of nations and of treaties which if not prevented must involve us in the calamities of foreign wars? The tendency of the states to these violations has been manifested in sundry instances. The files of Congress contain complaints already, from almost every nation with which treaties have been formed. Hitherto indulgence has been shewn to us. This cannot be the permanent disposition of foreign nations. A rupture with other powers is among the greatest of national calamities. It ought therefore to be effectually provided that no part of a nation shall have it in its power to bring them on the whole. The existing confederacy does not sufficiently provide against this evil. The proposed amendment to it does not supply the omission. It leaves the will of the states as uncontrolled as ever. (I Farrand's *The Records of the Federal Convention of 1787* 316 (Yale University Press 1966)).

In the Federalist Papers, the most authoritative commentary on the Constitution and the conditions which led to its establishment, John Jay wrote:

> the safety of the people of America against dangers from foreign force depends not only on their forebearing to give just causes of war to other nations, but also on their placing and continuing themselves in such a situation as not to invite hostility or insult; for it need not be observed that there are pretended as well as just causes of war. . . (Jay, "The Federalist No. 4," *The Federalist* 18 (Cooke ed., Wesleyan University Press 1961).

The student of American history will recall that even after the formation of our national government, the United States suffered the continued English occupation of military forces on territory which was to have been ceded to the United States by the peace treaty, that American sailors were impressed for involuntary service in the British fleet, and that the Government paid ransom to protect our shipping from attacks of the Barbary Pirates. All of these grievances were suffered for years until the growing strength of the United States permitted their redress.

In this historical context, how absurd it is to suggest that the members of the First Congress determined to enact, as one of their first orders of business, a statute which would, if interpreted according to plaintiffs' urgings, authorize federal courts to provoke the antagonism and hostility of foreign powers by providing a forum in which those powers or their nationals might be tried for conduct allegedly committed in their home countries against their own countrymen!

Certainly this Court will not ascribe such an intent to the First Congress.

What problem *was* Congress seeking to deal with when it vested the District Courts with jurisdiction of suits "by an alien for a tort only, committed in violation of the law of nations or a treaty of the United States?" An answer is suggested by the following excerpt from John P. Frank, *Historical Bases of the Federal Judiciary System*, 13 Law and Contemporary Problems 3, 13 (1948):

> The Confederation had found itself powerless to conduct the international affairs of the states. It could make agreements but it could not enforce them. It could not even extend to foreign nations an assurance of protection of their representatives in America. The treaty with Great Britain, particularly in respect of debts payable to British merchants or creditors, was being ignored, and the case of *de Longchamps* had great potential of national embarrassment.

> The Chevalier de Longchamps had a standing grudge against Francis Barbe Marbois, French Consul General at Philadelphia. Epithets at the consulate were followed by blows on the streets and though the French official had the best of the battle, further punishment of de Longchamps was in order. He was prosecuted in Pennsylvania courts and heavily, almost preposterously heavily, sentenced, doubtless more as a menace to relations with France than as a threat to peace. [See *Respublica v. DeLongchamps*, 1 Dall. 111 (U.S. 1784).]

> Nonetheless, suppose Pennsylvania had not prosecuted. The foreign relations of every state were at the mercy of the one state in which the injury occurred. The Confederation was convinced that if foreign officials were either to seek justice at law or be subjected to its penalties, it should be at the hand of the national government. The Supreme Court proceeded immediately to enforce the British treaty, and the lower courts heard numerous cases like that of de Longchamps.

At the time of adoption of the Alien Tort Statute, the safeguards and jurisdictional immunities of diplomatic personnel and of their domestic servants were considered part of the law of nations. Dickinson, *The Law of Nations as Part of the National Law of the United States*, 101 Univ. of Penn. L. Rev. 26, 32 (1952) and authorities there cited. The statute thus grants the federal courts the jurisdiction to deal with the two problems of unenforced treaties and uncompensated torts against foreign ministers and consuls which had beset the Confederation.

If the statute is interpreted as intended to deal with those pressing problems of the relations of the United States with other powers, its constitutional underpinnings are clear. It is founded upon the clauses of Article III which grant jurisdiction over cases affecting ministers and consuls, alienage jurisdiction and federal question jurisdiction for treaties. Significantly, except for an 1801 statute which was repealed in 1802, no general grant of federal question jurisdiction was enacted until 1875. *See* 13 Wright-Miller-Cooper, *Federal Practice and Procedure §3561.* And, although the Judiciary Act of 1789 established alienage jurisdiction, there was a requirement of a minimum jurisdictional amount. The Alien Tort Statute filled those gaps in an area which was given particular significance by the immediately prior experience under the Articles of Confederation. *See Lynch v. Household Finance Corp.*, 405 U.S. 538, 549 n. 17 (1972) (The Alien Tort Statute is "one of a group of statutes [that] grant jurisdiction without regard to the amount in controversy in virtually all areas that would otherwise fall under the general federal question statute"). *See, also,* American Law Institute, *Study of the Division of Jurisdiction between State and Federal Courts* (1969), which recommends repeal of §1350 and its replacement by a new statute granting general federal question jurisdiction without any requirement of a minimum amount in controversy.

Considerable historical authority supports the proposition that the statutory use of the phrase "Law of Nations" to refer to "that code of public instruction which defines the rights and prescribes the duties of nations in their intercourse with each other." (I Kent, *Commentaries* 1 (1st ed. 1826)) was typical of the usage of the period. Thus, Wilson, a delegate to the Constitutional Convention and a signer of the Declaration of Independence, defined the law of nations as those "relations existing between different states and the citizens of different states and the rights and duties arising from those relations . . . ." I Wilson, *Works* 374 (Bird Wilson ed. 1804). *See, generally,* Story, III *Commentaries on the Constitution of the United States* and *Commentaries on the Conflict of Laws.* In discussing Congressional power to define "offenses. against the law of nations," James Brierly, a member of the North Carolina Ratifying Convention and Associate Justice of the United States between 1790 and 1799, noted:

"These are offenses immediately affecting the security, the honor or the interest of the United States at large." Brierly, "Observations on George Mason's Objections to the Federal Constitution, 1788," collected in Ford, *Pamphlets on the Constitution of the United States Published During Its Discussion by the People, 1787-1789 307-08* (1888). John Jay, co-author of *The Federalist* and Chief Justice of the United States Supreme Court, noted that the "law of nations" "consist[s] of those rules for regulating the conduct of nations towards each other which, resulting from right reason, receive their obligations from that principle and from general assent and practice." Jay, "Charge to Grand Juries on the Eastern Circuit, April-May 1790," III *The Correspondence and Public Papers of John Jay* 393-94 (Johnstone ed. 1891-93). Again, in his charge to the Grand Jury in Richmond, Virginia, on May 22, 1793, Jay said "those [laws] which regulate our conduct relative to foreign nations . . . comprise [] the law of nations . . . ." *Id.*, at 480.

Thus, considerations of legislative intent, to be inferred from the historical context of the adoption of the antecedent of 28 U.S.C. §1350 in the Judiciary Act of 1789 and from the meaning of the language used, strongly support the conclusion that the statute should not be interpreted in a fashion broad enough to accommodate this case, even if such a construction were constitutionally permissible.

B. *The legislative history of the phrase "law of nations" in the Constitution shows that its contemporaneous use in the statutory antecedent to 28 U.S.C. §1350 was not intended to adopt the law of nations, wholesale, as United States law.*

The phrase "law of nations" appears in Article I, section 8, clause 10 of the Constitution, which empowers Congress" to define and punish piracies[3] and felonies committed on the high seas and *offenses against the law of nations.*" (Emphasis added.) As the substance of that clause was reported to the Convention by the Committee on Style, the clause empowered the Congress:

---

[3] From the perspective of both constitutional and international law, plaintiff's reliance on the law of piracy and the so-called doctrine of *hostes humani generis* to support universal jurisdiction in the case is misplaced. Congress has express constitutional authority to declare acts of piracy criminal and prescribe appropriate sanctions. Congress has done so through the penal code, which federal courts are bound to enforce—and have the jurisdiction to enforce—as the "law of Nations." By contrast, federal courts have no constitutional or statutory jurisdiction over wrongful death claims such as that presented herein. (Congress *does* have authority to define and punish "offenses against the law of Nations." That it has not done so for cases like the present one is most significant. Indeed, under international law principles of jurisdiction, Congress is without authority to prescribe or punish such an offense. *See, Restatement (Second) of Foreign Relations Law of the United States* § 17-18 (1965).

(f) to provide for the punishment of counterfeiting securities and current coin of the United States.

(k) to define and punish piracies and felonies committed on the high seas and punish offenses against the law of nations. I *Farrand's Records of the Federal Convention of 1787, supra* at 595.

During the subsequent debate on the floor of the Convention, Mr. Gouvernor Morris moved to amend the clause to delete "punish" before the words "offenses against the law of nations." His reason was "so as to let these be definable as well as punishable, by virtue of the preceding member of the sentence." To that motion, another delegate responded that he "hoped that alteration would by no means be made [because] to pretend to define the law of nations which depended on the authority of all the civilized nations of the world would have a look of arrogance that would make us ridiculous." *Id.*, Vol. II at 614. Mr. Morris replied, "The word define is proper when applied to offenses in this case: the law of nations being often too vague and deficient to be a rule." *Id.* at 615. Mr. Morris' motion was passed and the clause assumed its present form.

Very likely, the view of the majority of delegates that the "law of nations" was too "vague and deficient to be a rule" was also the reason the phrase was consciously omitted from the definition of cases to which Article III extended the jurisdiction of the federal courts. In at least two draft proposals submitted to the Convention's Committee of Detail, the "law of nations" was expressly referred to as a category of cases to which the jurisdiction of the federal courts would extend. *Id.*, at 136, 157. Although those proposals have at least some similarity to Article III as adopted, Article III, of course, does not refer to "law of nations." The reason for the omission, undoubtedly, is the same vagueness of the phrase which prompted Governor Morris' amendment to Article I to make the "law of nations" definable by Congress.

The majority of the Congress which adopted the Judiciary Act of 1789, including the Alien Tort Statute, had been delegates to the Constitutional Convention. Warren, *New Light on the History of the Federal Judiciary Act of 1789*, 37 Harv. L. Rev. 49 (1923). Since they had considered the "law of

---

Under international law, as plaintiffs concede, universal jurisdiction is sanctioned *only* in the case of piracy, and not for any other crimes. *Restatement of Foreign Relations, supra*, § 34, Reporter Note 2. In any case, universal jurisdiction applies only to *criminal* offenses. Plaintiffs herein merely seek compensatory damages in a private law civil suit. The compelling reasons for exercise of universal jurisdiction in piracy—removing the pirate from international circulation and thereby ensuring the free flow of commerce and intercourse between nations—are absent and inapplicable here.

nations" too "vague and deficient" to provide a rule or decision unless it was defined by Congress, why did they use that phrase in the Judiciary Act which was to be a cornerstone of the judicial system? The logical explanation is that the section of the Judiciary Act in which the phrase appears is a jurisdictional statute; jurisdictional provisions of Article III (except those conferring jurisdiction on the Supreme Court) are not self-executing; in adopting the antecedent of 28 U.S.C. §1350, Congress was merely providing that the federal courts, despite the absence of a statute conferring general federal question jurisdiction, would be able to exercise jurisdiction to enforce any statute thereafter enacted by Congress pursuant to its express power "to define and punish . . . offenses against the law of nations." Of course, at least insofar as is relevant to this case, Congress has not enacted a statute defining any part of the law of nations.

The implication of this history is clear. Without having defined any relevant part of the "law of nations," Congress did not intend the Judiciary Act of 1789 to effect the wholesale incorporation of the "law of nations" as law of the United States.

C. *Considerations of separation of powers precludes the Court from adopting plaintiffs' interpretation of 28 U.S.C. §1350.*

The record below demonstrates plaintiffs' purpose in seeking to litigate this case in the Federal District Court. The bulky appendices and addenda which plaintiffs and *amici* have filed in the District Court and in this Court are directed primarily at castigating the allegedly authoritarian and repressive government and policies of Paraguay. Prior to the dismissal of the suit, plaintiffs served a notice of depositions upon the Secretary of State of the United States. (JA 77-78) That notice demanded production of all cable traffic and communications from the United States Embassy in Paraguay relating to visas granted, not only to defendant, but also to all "Paraguayan police officers or other agents of the Paraguayan government." Obviously, plaintiffs have sought to invoke the jurisdiction of the District Court in order to stage a show trial for propaganda purposes. Presumably that is the reason that they still persist in their suit even though the defendant has now left this jurisdiction and there is no showing that he has any assets here.

The effort of plaintiffs and *amici* to litigate this case in the Court below in the manner foreshadowed by the papers which they have filed is thus an effort to place the judiciary, and themselves as private litigants, in the position of determining the foreign policy of the United States. What an impact there would be upon the conduct of American foreign policy if every foreigner who has taken refuge in this country could sue any of his compatriots in a United States District Court for violations which he alleges they have committed in their homeland against the civil, political or religious rights of their own nationals! Perhaps we can best visualize the impact of such a practice if we imagine what a stir would be caused if a Moscow court tried a Brooklyn police chief for racial brutality against a black American!

Such intrusion upon the making of American foreign policy would be contrary to the fundamental constitutional principle of separation of powers. From the inception of the American Republic, each of the branches of government has been precluded from interference in the spheres set out by the Constitution for the other branches. Time after time, in case after case, federal courts have refused to involve themselves in decisions that might implicate the foreign relations of the United States because of the separation of powers doctrine. As explained by the Court in *Luther v. Borden*, 7 How. (48 U.S.) 1, 46-47 (1849), the separation of powers must be carefully observed:

> The high power has been conferred on this court of passing judgment upon the acts of the State sovereignties, and of the legislative and executive branches of the federal government, and of determining whether they are beyond the limits of power marked out for them respectively by the Constitution of the United States. This tribunal therefore, should be the last to overstep the boundaries which limit its own jurisdiction. And while it should always be ready to meet any question confided to it by the Constitution, it is equally its duty not to pass beyond its appropriate sphere of action, and take care not to involve itself in discussions which properly belong to other forums.

In *Oetjen v. Central Leather Co.*, 246 U.S. 297, 302 (1918), the Court noted: "The conduct of foreign relations of our government is committed by the Constitution to the executive and legislative—'the political'—departments of the government, and the propriety of what may be done in the exercise of this political power is not subject to judicial inquiry or decision."

In *Chicago and Southern Air Lines v. Wasserman S.S. Corp.*, 333 U.S. 103, III (1948), the Court expanded on its earlier comments on foreign relations:

> [T]he very nature of executive decisions as to foreign policy is political, not judicial. Such decisions are wholly confided by our Constitution to the political departments of the government, Executive and Legislative. They are delicate, complex, and involve large elements of prophecy. They are and should be undertaken only by those directly responsible to the people whose welfare they

advance or imperil. They are decisions of a kind for which the Judiciary has neither aptitude, facilities nor responsibility and which has long been held to belong in the domain of political power not subject to judicial intrusion or inquiry.

Accord, Harisiades v. Shaughnessy, 342 U.S. 580, 589 (1952) ("[P]olicies in regard to the conduct of foreign relations are so exclusively entrusted to the political branches of government as to be largely immune from judicial inquiry or interference."); *Farmer v. Rountree*, 252 F.2d 490, 491 (6th Cir.), *cert. denied*, 357 U.S. 906, *reh. denied*, 358 U.S. 858 (1958).

One of the primary reasons for such uniform judicial restraint in this delicate field was set forth by the Court in *Mathews v. Diaz*, 426 U.S. 67, 81 (1976): "Any rule of constitutional law that would inhibit the flexibility of the political branches of government to respond to changing world conditions should be adopted only with the greatest caution."

Should this Court decide to permit the district court to hear this case and others like it, clearly the "flexibility of the political branches of government to respond to changing world conditions" would be severely inhibited. The executive and legislative branches might one day find themselves desperately needing the assistance and cooperation of a government, only to find themselves embarrassed by a fortuitous accident of personal jurisdiction which embroiled one of that government's citizens or officials in just the kind of lawsuit here at issue.

Both the executive and legislative branches of government have adopted means by which to deal with nations whose human rights records are unsatisfactory by American standards. As noted by plaintiffs and *amici*, Congress has adopted foreign aid appropriations legislation which effectively conditions United States foreign aid on implementation of civil rights policies acceptable to the United States government. These very statutes are an expression by the political arms of the government that the promotion of individual rights in the world is the responsibility of the President and Congress, not of the courts and private litigants. In addition, the language of the various treaties and declarations on human rights to which plaintiff and the *amici* refer, and of the reservations which accompany them, demonstrate that Congress and the President have determined that advancement of those rights in other countries is not the business of courts or civil litigants.

Plaintiffs' assertion that such documents bolster their claim of federal jurisdiction is patently absurd. Nothing in the general language of any foreign aid bill, treaty, covenant or declaration suggests that they confer private rights of action in American courts upon citizens of the foreign nations involved. To the contrary, the documents cited by plaintiffs serve to emphasize that foreign relations policy decisions must be made on the political and diplomatic levels by the executive and legislative branches. Private enforcement in the federal courts would be entirely inconsistent with the structure and purpose of these enactments, which do not implicate the judicial power at all. Indeed, the absence from international treaties, covenants and declarations of any provision granting supranational jurisdiction to national courts over human rights violations is proof that most or all members of the "world community" itself would disapprove the course of action which plaintiffs are seeking to promote!

The United States long ago abjured any role as the world's policeman. Plaintiffs would now have the federal courts serve as the world's judge. That prospect is truly "fraught with intrinsic foreign policy considerations" (plaintiffs' brief at p.54) which, under the doctrine of separation of powers, should not be determined by the courts. The Alien Tort Statute should not be construed to extend jurisdiction to this case and the judgment below should be affirmed.

CONCLUSION

For the foregoing reasons, the Order of the United States District Court for the Eastern District of New York (Hon. Eugene Nickerson, U.S.D.J.) dismissing plaintiffs' complaint for want of federal jurisdiction should be affirmed.

Respectfully submitted,

LOWENSTEIN, SANDLER, BROCHIN,
KOHL, FISHER & BOYLAN
A Professional Corporation

Attorneys for Defendant-Appellee
Americo N. Pena-Irala

By. _____

Dated: September 18, 1979

SEPTEMBER 28, 1979: UNITED STATES

Correspondence from Members of Congress to the U.S. Solicitor General

Congress of the United States
House of Representatives
Washington, D.C. 20515

September 28, 1979

The Honorable Wade H. McCree
Solicitor General of the United States
Department of Justice
Washington, D.C. 20530

Dear Solicitor General McCree:

We are writing to urge you to consider filing an *amicus curiae* brief supporting the position of the plaintiffs in *Filartiga v. Pena*, a landmark case involving federal jurisdiction to redress violations of fundamental human rights. The case is presently pending before the U.S. Court of Appeals for the Second Circuit.

Filartiga v. Pena is a civil action for wrongful death, filed by Dr. Filartiga and his daughter. Dr. Filartiga is a leading opponent of the Stroessner regime in Paraguay; his 17-year old son was tortured to death by the defendant, Pena, in a futile effort to wrest from him a "confession" that would implicate his father. At the time of the torture-murder, Pena was a high-ranking official in the political police unit of the Stroessner regime known as the Investigaciones.

The lawsuit was filed in federal court in the Eastern District of New York under 28 U.S.C. Section 1350, the Alien Tort Claims Act. Section 1350 provides that an alien may sue for a tort only in violation of the treaties of the United States or the law of nations. The plaintiffs claim that torture is a violation of customary international law. The District Court agreed, but dismissed the case because of dicta in prior Second Circuit decisions under Section 1350 that appeared to adopt a pre-Nuremberg/U.N. Charter view of international law—limiting it to rules affecting the relationship between states.

We believe that the Department of Justice should urge the Court to rule for the plaintiffs-appellants because:

-to recognize jurisdiction is the only course consistent with the developments of modern international law and with the U.S.' leadership role in the area of human rights;

-civil redress in cases of gross human rights violations is explicitly authorized by private international law and Anglo-American jurisprudence as torts are generally deemed to follow the tortfeasor;

-jurisdiction should be recognized, as John Vining urged in 1789, to make clear that this country does not provide, as do so many dictatorial regimes, a sanctuary against justice for gross human rights violators;

-in the past decade, Congress and the Executive Branch have sought to make human rights more than a pious phrase by applying various sanctions to human rights violators such as the withholding of aid. It would be unfortunate if the Judicial Branch, out of hesitation to involve itself in foreign policy matters, were by its silence to place itself in conflict with such a fundamental component of U.S. foreign policy.

We greatly appreciate your attention to this request, and look forward to receiving your answer as soon as possible.

Sincerely,

Tom Moffett	Tom Harkin
Ted Weiss	James Scheur
Robert Drinan	Don Edwards
George Miller	Thomas J. Downey

OCTOBER 3, 1979: UNITED STATES

Correspondence from U.S. Solicitor General to Members of Congress

Office of the Solicitor General
Washington, D.C. 20530

October 3, 1979

Hon. Toby Moffett
Hon. Ted Weiss
Hon. Robert F. Drinan
Hon. George Miller
Hon. Tom Harkin
Hon. James Scheuer
Hon. Don Edwards
Hon. Thomas J. Downey
House of Representatives
Washington, D.C. 20515

Re: *Filartiga v. Pena-Irala*

My dear Congressmen:

Your letter of September 28, 1979, concerning the above case reached me on the afternoon of October 2, 1979.

While this Office does not itself file *amicus curiae* briefs in the courts of appeals, it is my responsibility under Departmental regulations to decide whether such a filing by one of the litigating Divisions of the Department of Justice should be authorized. In the *Filartiga* case, I am informed that both the appellants (whom you urge us to support) and the appellees have already filed their briefs, that the appellants have requested an extension to October 10, 1979, for filing a reply brief, and that the court of appeals has set the case for oral argument on October 16, 1979. An *amicus curiae* brief in support of the appellants would have been due for filing on July 23, 1979, the date the appellants filed their brief. In light of the unfairness that it would cause to the parties, only the most compelling considerations would make it appropriate for the government to seek leave to file amicus brief in such circumstances.

As it happens, this case first came to the attention of my staff on August 29, 1979. Ensuing written and oral discussions between lawyers in this

Office, in the Civil Rights Division, and on the staff of the Legal Adviser to the Department of State have revealed serious difficulties in formulating a satisfactory legal position, in light of the implication a filing by the United States on this subject would have for the treatment of our own nationals in foreign courts. At the present time, the Legal Adviser's staff is giving further consideration to this subject, in light of the questions and suggestions that have resulted from these discussions.

Further information on this subject, if desired, can be provided by Deputy Solicitor General Lawrence G. Wallace, whose telephone number is 633-2211.

Our office is pleased to be of service in this matter.

Sincerely,

Wade H. McCree, Jr.
Solicitor General

OCTOBER 9, 1979: UNITED STATES

Appellants' Reply Brief

UNITED STATES COURT OF APPEALS
FOR THE SECOND CIRCUIT

DOLLY M.E. FILARTIGA and
DR. JOEL FILARTIGA,

      Plaintiffs-Appellants,

    – against –

AMERICO N. PENA-IRALA,

    Defendants-Appellee.

APPELLANTS' REPLY BRIEF

Docket No. 79-6090

    Peter Weiss
    Rhonda Copelon
    John Corwin
    Jose Antonio Lugo
    CENTER FOR CONSTITUTIONAL
    RIGHTS
    853 Broadway
    New York, New York 10003
    (212) 674-3303

    Michael Maggio
    GOREN & MAGGIO
    1801 Columbia Road, N.W.
    Washington, D.C. 20009
    (202) 483-8055

    Attorneys for Appellants

TABLE OF CONTENTS

COMMENT ON APPELLEE'S STATEMENT OF FACT

Appellee's Statement of Facts is devoted exclusively to the recourse allegedly available to appellants under Paraguayan law, presumably to persuade this Court to deny appellants' claim of federal jurisdiction on the basis of *forum non conveniens*. But this issue is not before the Court at this time. On remand, appellants will have no difficulty demonstrating that the so-called criminal prosecution pending in Paraguay is a sham and that this is the only forum available to them.

ARGUMENT

POINT I. *Issues Not In Contest*

A. *Appellee explicitly concedes, for the purposes of this appeal, that the torture alleged violates contemporary international law.*

Appellee's motion opposing the filing of the brief amici curiae contained the following concession:

> For the purposes of defendant's motion pursuant to F.R.C.P. 12(b) to dismiss for lack of federal jurisdiction, plaintiffs' allegations that contemporary international law condemns torture, are, and remain, uncontradicted. . . . Since the testimony in support of that allegation of fact was not clearly insubstantial, the character of the norms of contemporary international law... must be taken as alleged by plaintiffs. *Movants' Memorandum Of Law In Opposition To Motion Of Amnesty International—USA, et al., For Leave To File Brief As Amici Curiae* pp. 4–5.

In his brief (pp. 14-16) appellee attempts to renege on this concession by characterizing plaintiffs' claim as based on private international law or involving simply private conduct. Private international law is relevant because, as a *procedural* matter, it confers universal civil jurisdiction—irrespective of the nationality of the parties or the place of wrongdoing—to entertain transitory actions, which include the wrongful death at issue here (Appellants' Brief pp. 11-14). The tort here is cognizable under §1350, however, because it *also* violates public international law.

It is also clear that the politically motivated act of torture alleged here, is not purely private conduct and, therefore, qualifies as a violation of the law of nations. *Dreyfus v. von Finck*, 534 F.2d 24 (2d Cir. 1976), relied on so heavily by appellee, is distinguishable not only because a state's confiscation of the property of its nationals failed to qualify as a violation of the law of nations, *Dreyfus, supra* at 31 n.10, but also because the complaint failed to allege that *von Finck* "played any role in the policy making decision of the German government." *Id.* at 31. Acquisition of property under duress by a purely private individual is no more a violation of the law of nations than is the theft at issue in *IIT v. Vencap, Ltd.*, 519 F.2d 1001 (2d Cir. 1975), or than is wife-beating under the international norm of torture. This court's *dictum*[1] in *Dreyfus*, that "violations of international law do not occur when the aggrieved parties are nationals of the acting state" must not be taken out or context and transmuted into a sweeping principle. If it were, it would make a mockery of the international law of human rights, which from the Nuremberg Judgment to this day, has added so much to the substantive law of nations.

Thus the only question is whether appellee's effort to restrict the "law of nations" exclusively to "cases directly implicating relations between states" (Appellee's Brief p.11) or "questions of rights between nations" (*id.* at 15) is constitutionally required or legally intended.

B. *Appellee implicitly concedes that even under the restrictive definition in Dreyfus, the prohibition against torture is a rule of international law affecting relations between states.*

On page 31 he acknowledges, as he must, that the practice of torture in Paraguay and elsewhere has triggered U.S. sanctions.

C. *Appellee implicitly concedes the jurisdiction of the state courts to entertain this action regardless of whether the conduct at issue violates the law of nations.*

Appellee's Brief pp. 15-16. His argument against federal jurisdiction here is thus an argument for leaving this case and others like it to the vagaries of state court determinations in accordance with state and not federal common law. (See Point II, A).

POINT II. *Article III, Section 2, Clause 1 of The Constitution Authorizes Federal Jurisdiction Under §1350 To Redress Violation Of The Law Of Nations In This Case*

Defendant's argument that recognition of 1350 jurisdiction in this case would transcend the jurisdiction conferred by Article III of the Constitution is built upon a series of distortions of law, fact and history. He truncates federal question jurisdiction under Article III, section 2 to try to

---

[1] While appellee purports simply to invoke the dictum of the earlier decisions of this Circuit, we remind the Court that appellee actually seeks to narrow that dictum. (Appellants Brief).

eliminate cases arising under the law of nations. He seeks to bolster this approach by a patently spurious reading of the legislative history of both the Constitution and the First Judiciary Act, and concludes that 1350 covers only unenforced treaties, and those torts which Congress legislates pursuant to its Article I, section 8, clause 10 powers to "define and punish . . . offenses against the law of nations."

The argument, however imaginative, is wrong. It ignores that the law of nations was incorporated into the constitution as part and parcel of the common law of the United States. It ignores the character and purposes of the constitutional grant of power to Congress under Article I, treating it as limiting judicial power rather than as clarifying and potentially expanding it. It ignores the careful mosaic of the Judiciary Act of 1789 which provided separately for cases involving foreign ministers and consuls as well as for Article I, section 8 clause 10 matters. His argument fails even to justify jurisdiction under the test previously articulated by this Circuit and renders reference in §1350 to the "law of nations" either redundant or nugatory. In this section, appellants will show that §1350 jurisdiction in this case rests on the "arising under" clause of Article III because (1) the law of nations is part of the "laws" of the United States; and (2) Section 1350 is not simply a jurisdictional statute but an exercise of power under Article I, clause 8 to "define and punish . . . offenses against the law of nations." Finally, we will demonstrate the absurdity of appellee's attempt to impress his contorted version of the law of nations on the jurisdiction conferred by § 1350.

A. *Section 1350 Implements The Constitutional Grant of Jurisdiction For Cases "Arising Under . . . the Law of the United States" Because The Law Of Nations Has And Is Part Of The Federal Common Law.*

On page 7 of his brief, appellee transforms Article III, section 2, clause 1, from a grant of jurisdiction for all cases "arising under . . . the Laws of the United States" to one which limits it to violations of statutes only. There is no question, however, that Article III, clause 1, of the Constitution authorizes federal question jurisdiction over suits which arise under federal common law as well as federal statutory law. *Illinois v. City of Milwaukee*, 406 U.S. 91, 92 S. Ct. 1385, 1390 (1972);[2] *Ivy Broadcasting Co. v. American Tel. and Tel. Co.*, 391 F. 2d 486, 492; and *Dreyfus v. Von Finck, supra* at 28.

---

[2] *City of Milwaukee* was construing 28 U.S.C. §1331(a), which implements Article III's federal question jurisdiction and which may be underinclusive but cannot exceed the authority granted by Article III, clause 2. See *Romero v. International Terminal Operating Co.*, 358 U.S. 379, 97 S. Ct. 468, 484 and cases cited, n. 51 (1959). The Convention intended Article III to embrace federal common law. Drafts of Article III had provided that the judicial power should extend to "cases arising under laws *passed by the legislature* of the United States." See authorities cited in *Romero v. International Terminal Operating Co., supra*, 79 S. Ct. at 491, n. 5.

This case arises under federal common law because from the time of
the framing of the Constitution and the drafting of the 1789 Act to the present, the law of nations has been part of the federal common law of the
land. As the eminent authority on this subject, Edwin Dickinson explains,
to the late eighteenth century leaders in law, who dominated the
Constitutional Convention, "[i]t was axiomatic that the Law of Nations,
applicable to individuals and to state[3] was an integral part of the law which
they administered or practiced." Edwin D. Dickinson, "The Law of Nations
as Part of the National Law of the United States," 101 Pa. L. Rev. 26, 35
(1952). (hereinafter, Dickinson"). Drawing upon the scholarship of legal
historians and lawmakers, he completely refutes appellee's theory of piecemeal incorporation or the law or nations into the Constitution and law of
the United States. He makes clear that in fashioning Article III, the
Convention unanimously agreed that matters of international concern
should be within the province of the federal judiciary,[4] and that therein lay
the security of the nation. See Dickinson, generally.

Moreover, Dickinson demonstrates that the framers viewed the law of
nations, even as to crimes, as automatically part of the common law of the
land, and not dependent upon Congress exercise of its Article I powers.[5]

---

[3] Dickinson explains that in the 18th century, the line between public and private
right or duty had not yet been drawn. The law of nations embraced three branches: the
law maritime, the law of merchants, and what he calls the law of states. The first two were
primarily concerned with individual commercial relations; the third was of more immediate concern to states *inter se*, but was also applicable to both individuals *inter se* and in
relation to states. On the criminal side it made piracy and attacks on ambassadors an
offense. On the civil side, it dealt with custom or agreements with regard to captures,
diplomatic privilege and treaties. Dickinson at 26-29. Plaintiffs emphasized piracy to illustrate that piracy was of the most "respectable antiquity" in the law of states. Id. at 29.
Thus the law of piracy precludes attributing to the framers and drafters a restrictive view
of the law of nations which would exclude individual conduct violative of customary
international norms from the scope of jurisdiction intended under § 1350.

[4] The itemization of the Law of Nations in the early proposals for the national judicial power are according to Dickinson illustrative of the unanimous intention to confer
the whole subject on the national judiciary and not, as appellee's spuriously contend,
(Brief, pp. 26-27) suggestive of a narrowing in the final draft of Article III. *Dickinson,
supra* at 36-38.

[5] Appellee's argument (pp. 25-28), that Article I, Section 8, Clause 10, conferring
on Congress the power to "define and punish . . . offenses against the Law of Nations"
operates as a limitation on federal jurisdiction under Section 1350 is absurd. It is clear,
before and after the framing of the Constitution that municipal courts exercised common law jurisdiction over international crimes and applied the law of nations directly. It
is also clear that the Congressional power conferred by Article I was designed to advance
uniformity and national supremacy to codify punishments where the offenses were clear
and to clarify offenses in the area of felonies where the Law of Nations was itself too
vague to enforce. The exercise of Article I powers was thus intended to assist and

On the civil side, Chief Justice Marshall made clear that in absence of an Act of Congress "the Court is bound by the law of nations which is part of the law of the land." *The Nereide*, 9 Cr. 388 (U.S. 1815). The principle of incorporation has been consistently recognized in judicial decisions[6] and is every bit as vital today.[7]

Thus, as a constitutional matter, federal question jurisdiction cannot be limited to those aspects of the Law of Nations which are either explicitly enumerated in Article III or as to which Congress exercises its Article I powers. The fallacy in appellee's argument is further underscored by the fact that absent an Act of Congress, it would preclude 1350 jurisdiction over torts which violated non-treaty-based customary international norms directly governing state-to-state relations. Thus, though appellee's argument seeks to provide a constitutional foundation for a strict reading of the *Lopes* or *IIT* test, it sweeps so broadly as to eliminate subjects which the Circuit has recognized as cognizable under Article III.

In sum, Article III, Clause 2 was intended to embrace as federal common law or the land the entire and evolving body of the law of nations, and thus, the exercise of 1350 jurisdiction in this case, where the tort alleged clearly violates international law, is constitutionally proper.[8]

---

broaden, but not to precondition or limit enforcement of the law of nations. See Dickinson, supra at 46-47, 792-795; G. Hunt and J.B. Brown (ed), *The Debates in the Federal Convention of 1787 Which Framed the Constitution of the United States of America*, (N.Y. Oxford, 1920), pp. 415-417. This is the meaning of the debates cited by appellee at p. 26. See also *United States v. Smith*, 18 U.S. (5 Wheat) 153, 159 (1820), where Justice Story wrote that legislative definition is required only where the offense "cannot be completely ascertained and defined in any public code recognized by the common consent of nations." Here the torture alleged clearly falls within the central core of the offense as defined and condemned by international law. See Applt's Br., Addendum III, Report of the European Commission of Human Rights, Applic. No. 5310/71, *Ireland v. United Kingdom*, 363 (1976); B. Klayman, "The Definition of Torture in International Law," 51 Tem. L.Q. 449 (1978).

[6] See e.g., *Respublica v. DeLongchamps*, 1 Dall. 111 (Pa. 1784); Jay, "Charge to Grand Juries, Apr-May 1790" III *Correspondence and Papers of John Jay*, 390, 393 (Johnstone ed. 1891-93); *Glass v. The Sloop Betsy*, 3 Dall (U.S. 5) 449 (1794); *Schooner Exchange v. M'Faddon*, 7 Cranch (U.S. 11) 116 (1812); *The Paquete Habana*, 175 U.S. 677 (1900); and Dickinson, generally.

[7] The Restatement 2d of Foreign Relations Law §3 states that "[i]nternational law is applied by courts in the United States without the necessity . . . of showing an affirmative acceptance by legislative or other national authority of the rule of international law applied." See also address of Leonard C. Meeker, Assistant Legal Adviser Department of State "The Law of Nations in The National Government," (April 20, 1956) in Whiteman, Digest of International Law § 11 (1963) pp. 106-108.

[8] Moreover, "where there is an overriding federal interest in the need for a uniform

B. *Section 1350 Is Not Merely A Jurisdictional Statute But Is Also A Substantive "Law" Enacted By Congress In Discharge Of Its Article I Power To "Define And Punish . . . Offenses Against The Law Of Nations."*

Congress' Article I. Section 8, Clause 10 powers to "define and punish . . . offenses against the law of nations" provide an additional fount of constitutional authority for section 1350. This is so because section 1350 is not a bare jurisdictional statute, but is also intended to create and define substantive federal rights as to which the courts are to develop federal common law. *Textile Workers of America v. Lincoln Mills*, 77 S.Ct. *supra* at 914-917.[9]

History demonstrates and appellee appears to concede (Brief pp. 7, 24-27) that Article I, section 8, clause 10 authorizes Congress to enact civil remedies to redress and punish violations of the law of nations. Section 4 of the Act of March 3, 1819 provided for condemnation of a piratical vessel when it is captured and brought into a U.S. port, a remedy which though punitive in character[10] is civil in nature.[11] Likewise, though primarily compensatory in character, tort law awards punitive or "exemplary"

---

rule of decision or where the controversy touches basic interests of federalism . . . [the federal courts] have fashioned federal common law." *Illinois v. City of Milwaukee*, 92 S.Ct. *supra* at 1394 n.6; *Banco Nacional de Cuba v. Sabbatino*, 376 U.S. 398, 84 S.Ct. 923, 938-940 (1964); *Textile Workers v. Lincoln Mills*, 353 U.S. 448, 77 S.Ct. 912 (1957). The evolving law maritime and law of states has been consistently observed either to provide a rule of decision or as a source of authority for construction of domestic laws or international agreements. See generally, Dickinson, *supra* at 796-832. Here the international condemnation of torture clearly requires the fashioning of a federal common law of tort. In so doing, federal interpretation of international norms as the law of the land, and federal disposition of choice of law, act of state and *forum non conveniens* questions will govern although state law may be resorted to and absorbed as federal law where it will best effectuate federal policy. *Textile Workers v. Lincoln Mills*, 77 S.Ct. *supra* at 918; *City of Milwaukee*, 92 S.Ct. *supra* at 1392 n.5. See, for example, *Huynh Thi Anh v. Levi*, 586 F.2d 625 (6th Cir. 1978).

9 Section 301(a) of the Labor Management Relations Act was viewed as substantive because it provided district court jurisdiction over a class of suits requiring decision according to federal common law. Compare 301(a)'s "suit for violation of contracts . . . between an employer and a labor organization . . . or between any such labor organization," with 1350's "tort[s] . . . in violation of the law of nations." By contrast 301(b) which simply gives labor organizations the right to sue in federal court was viewed as strictly jurisdictional, just as would a statute which simply gave an alien a right to sue another alien in federal court. *Lincoln Mills supra* at 914-915.

10 See e.g. *The Marianna Flora*, 24 U.S. (11 Wheat) 1, 40-57 (1826); *United States v. Brig Malek Adhel*, 43 U.S. (2 How.) 210, 233-236 (1844).

11 Thus, for example, Attorney General Bates ruled that "the condemnation of a vessel and cargo in a prize court is not a criminal sentence, and the President cannot remit the forfeiture and restore the property or its proceeds, to the claimant." 10 Opinion of Attorney General 452 (1863) cited in Moore's Digest of International Law § 1241 p. 635.

damages when defendant's misconduct has been intentional and deliberate, and is outrageous in the sense frequently associated with crime. Prosser, *Handbook on the Law of Torts*, §2 at 9-11 (4 ed. 1971); Morris, "Punitive Damages In Personal Injury Cases," 21 Ohio St. L.J. 216 (1960). There is certainly no case where punitive damages would be more appropriate than on as here, which involves the grossest human rights violation.

Thus, Section 1350 represents a proper substantive exercise of Congress' Article I, section 8, clause 10 powers and therefore qualifies as a statutory "law" under Article III, clause 2.[12] A more specific statute is not required since the offense of torture here involved can be completely ascertained and defined in "[the] . . . public code recognized by the common consent of nations." *United States v. Smith* at 59.[13]

C. *Nothing In The Legislative History of The Judiciary Act of 1789 Justifies A Narrower Definition of The Law of Nations Than That Authorized By Article III.*

Appellee's piecemeal approach to legal history reaches the height of absurdity when he argues that Congress did not mean what it said when it used the terms "law of nations."

While there is no doubt that the American nation wanted to avoid provoking hostilities with foreign nations (Appellee's Brief pp. 17-20), the creation of federal jurisdiction was responsive to this concern. The framers knew that any exercise of judicial power touching on the law of nations is fraught with implications for foreign relations. They also understood that failure to exercise judicial power could be equally inimical to the safety, peace and honor of the nation. Fidelity to international principles was and is the soundest protection of honor and against incident. See *Dickinson, supra;* C. Warren, *The Supreme Court in United States History* (1932), 106-123. To the framers and drafters the assurance lay in permitting these matters to be taken out of the hands of the states. Since all the tort claims embraced by § 1350 were otherwise cognizable in state courts, appellee's contention that this court should imply a limitation on the kinds of law of nations claims which could be brought to the federal courts makes no sense.

---

[12] Where Congress enacts criminal laws to protect a class, civil remedies can also be implied. *Reitmeister v. Reitmeister*, 162 F.2d 691, 694 (2d Cir. 1947).

[13] For example, punishing piracy or rewarding privateers might place our courts at odds with another nation. But to fail to provide redress or reward might be seen as condoning an international violation or shielding another nation's act, which are precisely the risks here.

Next, appellee speculates that the drafters intended the law of nations in section 1350 to embrace implicitly only offenses to foreign ministers and consuls (Appellee's Brief pp. 20-22).[14]

As a threshold matter, since consuls, as opposed to ambassadors and foreign ministers were not protected by the law of nations in the eighteenth century, torts involving them would not have been cognizable under § 1350. See 5 Moore, *Digest of International Law* § 702, pp. 32-35;[15] *Davis v. Packard*, 31 U.S. (6 Pet.) 276, 284 (1833). Moreover, the same section 9 of the 1789 Act today 28 U.S.C. § 1351, gave the district courts exclusive jurisdiction of suits against consuls and Section 13 of the Act provided original Supreme Court jurisdiction for all suits in which a consul or vice-consul is a party.

Section 1350 was available but certainly of minimal importance to foreign ministers in the scheme of the 1789 Judiciary Act. Section 13 gave the Supreme Court exclusive original jurisdiction over suits against them and original non-exclusive jurisdiction or proceedings they initiated.

In short, appellee's manufactured limit on the "law of nations" as used in Section 1350 renders it either nugatory or redundant. Moreover, had Congress intended to limit the scope of torts cognizable as violations of the law of nations, it would have done so explicitly. To imply a limitation on the phrase "law of nations" in Section 1350 thus ignores the fundamental assumption applicable to construction of the First Judiciary Act that "in dealing with a subject as technical as the jurisdiction of the courts, the Framers, predominately lawyers, used precise differentiating and not redundant language." *Romero v. International Terminal Operating Co.*, 358 U.S. 354, 79 S.Ct. 468, 476.

For all these reasons there is no basis for implying a limitation on the scope of §1350 jurisdiction over violations of the "law of nation," either as a constitutional or legislative matter. Consistent with the intent of the Framers and Drafters, it must be seen as a repository of evolving authority.

---

[14] Appellee would include also offenses defined by Congress under Article I, section 8, clause 10. (Appellee's Brief pp. 24-28). Clause 1 of section 9 of the 1789 Act which gave the district courts exclusive jurisdiction over all crimes and offenses that shall be cognizable under the authority of the United States, also appears to cover torts provided under Congress' Article 1, section 8, clause 10 power.

[15] See particularly the letter of Thomas Jefferson as Secretary of Foreign Affairs to Mr. Newton, September 8, 1791, 4 MS Am. Let. 283, cited in Moore, *supra* at pp. 34-35: "The law of nations does not of itself extend to consuls at all. They are not of the diplomatic class of characters to which alone that law extends of right . . . independently of [a special] law, consuls are . . . subject to the laws of the land indeed precisely as other foreigners are."

POINT III. *This Suit Arises Under Treaties Entered Into By The United States And Paraguay.*

Appellants do not question here the authorities which hold that the UN Charter is not *per se* self-executing. (Appellee's Brief pp. 8-9). Rather, our contention is (1) that §1350 implements the right to be free from torture embodied in the Charter and developed in subsequent international agreements and (2) that these developments have made, not the entire Charter, but the prohibition on torture self-executing.

First, as Appellee points out at p.7 of his brief, a case arises under a treaty "when Congress creates [an individual] cause of action by implementing legislation." This is precisely what Congress did by enacting §1350. Section 1350 is no vague, catch-all provision translating all treaty violations into private causes of actions by foreigners. The operative words are "for a tort only," reducing the class of cases to which the section is applicable to those which constitute a tort under the municipal law of the United States and in addition, violate a treaty. The Attorney General recognized the implementing character of §1350 in an Opinion which held that §1350 provided a right of action to Mexican citizens injured by a U.S. irrigation company's diversion of the Rio Grande where the Commission set up to resolve disputes under the treaty had no power to adjudicate private rights and liabilities. 26 Op. Atty Gen. 250 (1903). No court has had occasion to rule on this question.

The treaty rights involved here have their source in the UN Charter which appellee concedes is a treaty. The Universal Declaration is relied on as "an authoritative guide . . . to the interpretation of the provisions in the Charter"[16] and is today widely viewed as legally binding.[17] The United States view was recently articulated by Secretary of State Vance who characterized the Universal Declaration as "embod[ying] the fundamental tenet that international law creates obligations which all governments owe to their citizens and help[ing] to define universally recognized principles of human rights," and by President Carter who said "The Universal Declaration means that no nation can draw the cloak of sovereignty over torture." *The White House Commemoration of the 30th Anniversary of the Universal Declaration*

---

[16] I. Brownlie, *Principles of Public International Law,* (2d ed. 1973), 554; S. Schweld, *Human Rights And The International Community* (1964), 673-5; Sir Humphrey Waldock 106 *Hague Recueil* (1962, II) 199.

[17] B. Klayman, "The Definition of Torture in International Law," 51 Temple C.Q. 449, 452, n.14, 487. Indeed these references demonstrate that appellee's citation to Klayman and to Mrs. Roosevelt's disclaimers of the binding nature of the Universal Declaration at the time of its adoption is far from candid as to its status today.

of Rights, December 6, 1978 at 51. Thus, flying in the face of all accepted doctrine, appellee maintains that an international instrument which was not legally binding *ab inito* remains so for all time to come.

Second, a treaty may import a wide variety of obligations, some of which grant rights to individuals while others do not. As recognized by the Ninth Circuit:

> The extent to which an international agreement establishes affirmative and judicially enforceable obligations without implementing legislation must be determined in each case by reference to many contextual factors, the purposes of the treaty and its objectives of its creators, the extent of domestic procedural and institutions appropriate for direct implementation, the availability and feasibility of alternative enforcement methods, and the immediate and long-ranged social consequences of self-or-not-self execution. *People of Saipan v. U.S. Dept. of the Interior*, 502 F.2d 90, 97 (9th Cir. 1974).

In this case, plaintiffs submit that with respect to torture, Article 55 of the UN Charter, as interpreted in the Universal Declaration and further delineated in the "Declaration on the Protection of all Persons From Being Subjected To Torture . . . ." G.A. Res 3452, UN Doc. A/1034 (1975) (Appellants Brief, Add. III) should be viewed as self executing under *Saipan* criteria.

The prohibition against torture as interpreted has come to be recognized as flowing from obligations set out in the UN Charter. Such a prohibition meets the logical and legal requirement for the generation of rights in individuals. It states simply that individuals have the right not to be subjected to torture, and that violation of that right is an international offense.

The undertaking with regard to torture is not "an engagement to perform a particular act" on the part of states, which would require additional implementation, *Foster v. Neilson*, 2 Pet. (27 U.S.) 253 (1829) but an absolute prohibition against a particular type of conduct. The right created should be vindicated in the courts of the United States without the need for implementing legislation just as was the right at issue in *United States v. Toscanino*, 500 F.2d 278 (2d Cir. 1974).

The enforceable nature of the right not to be tortured flowing from the Charter is further demonstrated by the fact that Universal Declaration and the General Assembly Declaration are not simply a source from which to infer customary international law. These international condemnations of torture codify a norm not "simply emerging" but emerged and even entrenched—in international law.[18] *The Paquete Habana*, 175 U.S. 677 (1900) teaches that such a universal norm is part of the law of the United States, certain tortious violations of which are cognizable in the federal courts under §1350. Thus whether the international condemnation of torture is viewed as part of the law of nations or the treaties of the United States, §1350 provides civil redress for aliens against wrongdoers found on our shores.

POINT IV. *Nothing In The Doctrines of Separation of Powers Or Act of State Precludes Federal Jurisdiction Over This Suit.*

Appellee's argument that for the judiciary to entertain this lawsuit would be an "intrusion upon the making or American foreign policy . . . contrary to the fundamental principle of separation or powers" is groundless hyperbole (p.29). The cases cited (pp. 29-31) concerning challenges to political decisions of executive officials are inapposite. And Mr. Justice Harlan gave short shrift to the broad *dictum* appellee relies on from *Oetjen v. Central Leather Co.*, 246 U.S. 297, 302 (1918) when he stated that "it cannot be thought that 'every case or controversy which touches on foreign relations lies beyond judicial competence.'" *Banco Nacional de Cuba v. Sabbatino*, 376 U.S. *supra* at 423.

Under the theory espoused by appellee, a separation of powers spawned doctrine of judicial abstention would apply to every case involving an alien; every case involving a determination that the courts of another country lack judicial independence; every case involving construction of treaties; and every case involving representatives of foreign sovereigns or commerce involving foreign sovereigns or foreign laws, since all are likely to "touch[ ] on foreign relations." Indeed, appellee's theory leads one to ask why the framers did not eliminate all judicial power, rather than establish federal jurisdiction over matters affecting foreign relations.

The concerns underlying separation of powers where the conduct of a foreign official is at issue are mediated through the doctrine of Act of State. The doctrine is a flexible one and this case falls well outside its parameters as explained by Justice Harlan in *Sabbatino.*

---

[18] Appellee cites the very words of Mr. Speekenbrink of the Netherlands to illustrate that the General Assembly "is not a treaty." (Brief pp. 9-10). But he makes out plaintiffs' case, demonstrating that delegates to the Third Committee saw the Declaration as enunciating norms commonly accepted by and binding on states. See Klayman, op.cit. 487-488.

First, "the greater the degree of codification or consensus concerning a particular area of international law, the more appropriate it is for the judiciary to render decisions regarding it." *Sabbatino*, 84 S.Ct., *supra* at 940. This case involves violation of a norm which is universally accepted and to which Paraguay itself has pledged obedience.

Second, Act of State is not appropriate where the focus of judicial inquiry is on "the application of an agreed upon principle to circumstances of fact rather than on the sensitive task of establishing a principle not inconsistent with the national interest or with international justice." *Ibid.* It is thus particularly significant that international law recognizes no circumstances under which torture is legitimate (Applts' Brief, Add.III) and, therefore, precludes any defense of legality.

Third, judicial abstention is wholly inappropriate here because "the less important the implications of an issue for our foreign relations, the weaker the justification for exclusivity in the political branches." *Ibid.* Here the negative side effects of adjudication are minimal in sharp contrast to the consequences of declining jurisdiction. The fact that Congress and the Executive directly sanction foreign governments engaging in gross human rights violations decreases rather than increases the sensitivity of judicial action. Conversely, to decline jurisdiction would gravely derogate from the moral stance—not to mention the foreign policy objectives—of the United States. Our country would appear to the world as a hypocritical preacher of abstract principles, all the while providing sanctuary within our gates to the worst human rights violators. Thus there is no other conclusion possible than that "both the national interest and the progress toward the rule of law among nations," *Sabbatino, supra* at 945, are best served by recognizing rather than declining jurisdiction.

There is, indeed, no place even for consideration of judicial abstention here. It is axiomatic that Act of State operates only where an act is within the scope and authority of one's office. See A. S. Goldbert & G. Bradford, "The Act of State Doctrine: *Dunhill* and Other *Sabbatino* Progeny," 9 S.W. L. Rev. 1, n.3 (1977). In light of the unequivocal world condemnation of torture, and Paraguay's obligation to obey it, the brutal torture murder alleged in the Complaint cannot be said to be within the legitimate authority of either the defendant Pena or the dictator-president General Stroessner himself. To shield defendant's conduct from scrutiny would surely undo the fundamental principle of the Nuremberg Judgment.

Beyond that, the Court has made clear that even an act within the scope of official authority will not bar review unless the evidence demonstrates that the "conduct in question was the public act of those with authority to exercise sovereign powers and was entitled to respect in our courts." *Alfred Dunhill of London v. Republic of Cuba*, 425 U.S. 682, 96 S.Ct. 1854, 1861 (1976). In *Dunhill* as here, the only evidence was that an agent of the government did the act complained of. The Court held this insufficient and required that a "statute, decree, order or resolution of the . . . Government itself [be] offered in evidence." *Ibid*. Without that, it is inappropriate even to consider shielding this horrifying torture-murder as an Act of State.[19]

Lacking any legal basis for judicial abstention, appellee trots out that old rhetorical warhorse, the floodgate (p. 29). The court is asked to contemplate the dire consequences of "every foreigner" who has taken refuge in this country suing "any of his compatriots" for human rights violations committed in their homeland. There are three answers to this:

1. Such suits, as demonstrated in Point I,A of our Brief, can be brought in the far less appropriate forum of the state courts;
2. The extraordinary combination of circumstances leading to this case—the perpetrator of a particularly heinous crime, *clearly* in violation of international law, being found in this country at the same time as an immediate survivor of his victim, with no chance for justice in the courts of their home state—is hardly likely to be duplicated with such frequency as to materially affect the caseload of the district courts; and
3. If American courts are open to damage suits by the victims of foreign torturers or their survivors, the torturers will presumably seek refuge elsewhere.[20] By the same token, a negative attitude toward such suits on the part of our courts would be a signal to foreign torturers to seek safe haven here, which is itself a matter fraught with negative foreign policy consequences.

Similar considerations apply to the specter of the Brooklyn police chief sued in Moscow for brutality by a Black American.[21]

---

[19] Appellee cites the very words of Mr. Speekenbrink of the Netherlands to illustrate that the General Assembly "is not a treaty." (Brief pp. 9-l0). But he make out plaintiffs' case, demonstrating that delegates to the Third Committee saw the Declaration as enunciating norms commonly accepted by and binding on states. See Klayman, op.cit. 487-488.

[20] Thus, General Somoza thought it prudent to retire to Paraguay after the recent change of regime in Nicaragua, despite his well-known preference for the U.S., Paraguay apparently being the only country that would guarantee not to extradite him to Nicaragua.

[21] Even assuming the alleged conduct to violate the law of nations, it is hard to imagine both victim and attacker in Moscow at the same time, and even harder to imagine that courts which do not entertain human rights suits by their own citizens would be open to such suits by foreigners.

The ultimate answer to this far-fetched hypothetical is that the most fundamental human rights are not to be sacrificed to political convenience. Recently, the Justice Department did not shrink from seeking the extradition of a Chilean general and two of his aides for the 1976 murder of Orlando Letelier and Ronnie Moffit in Washington, *United States v. Guillermo Novo Sampol et al.*, Crim. No. 78-367 (D.D.C.), even though the revelations by the Senate Select (Church) Committee on Intelligence of past assassination plots by the CIA might lead foreign countries—including Chile—to ask for the extradition of certain Americans.

The recognition of jurisdiction here is not, like extradition, a political act directly implicating our relations with a foreign sovereign. It is a judicial one which would serve not only the international cause of justice, but also this nation's fundamental, longstanding interest in uniform and sensitive adjudication of foreign tort claims by aliens when the tort alleged violates international law.

CONCLUSION

For all the foregoing reasons, the judgment of the district court should be reversed and the case remanded for further proceedings.

Respectfully submitted,

Peter Weiss
Rhonda Copelon
John Corwin
Jose Antonio Lugo
c/o CENTER FOR CONSTITUTIONAL RIGHTS
853 Broadway
New York, New York 10003
(212) 674-3303

Michael Maggio
GOREN & MAGGIO
1801 Columbia Road, N.W.
Washington, D.C. 20009
(202) 483-8055

Attorneys for Appellants**

Dated: New York, New York
       October 9, 1979

**The attorneys gratefully acknowledge the assistance of law students Jeff Blum, Johnny Colon and Rebecca Morgan in the preparation of this Reply.

OCTOBER 29, 1979: UNITED STATES

Correspondence from the Clerk of the Second Circuit Court of Appeals to Office of the Legal Advisor, U.S. Department of State

UNITED STATES COURT OF APPEALS
SECOND CIRCUIT
UNITED STATES COURTHOUSE
FOLEY SQUARE
NEW YORK 10007

DANIEL FUSARO
CLERK   October 29, 1979

Roberts B. Owen, Esq.
Legal Advisor
Department of State
Washington, D.C. 20520

      Re: Filartiga v. Pena-Irala, Docket No. 79-6090

Dear Mr. Owen:

    The above captioned case is *sub judice* before this court. As the enclosed briefs disclose, the case involves questions of foreign policy. Accordingly, the Court has asked me to request that the Department of State submit a memorandum setting forth its position concerning the proper interpretation of 28 U.S.C. §1350 in light of the facts of this case.

                                Very truly yours,

                                Daniel Fusaro,
                                Clerk

Enclosures
cc: All Counsel
bc: IRK JJS WF

NOVEMBER 23, 1979: PARAGUAY

Telegram from American Embassy, Asunción to U.S. Department of State

Subject: Foreign Minister Nogues on Filártiga Case

UNCLASSIFIED

(REDACTED)

PAGE 01   ASUNCI   05242   252004Z
ACTION ARA-15

INFO   OCT-01   ADS-00   OC-06   CCO-00   H-01   L-03   SS-15
      NCS-05   CIAE-00   INR-10   NSAE-00   SP-02   HA-05   VO-05
      CA-01   PA-01   /   070 W

--004349 252215Z /15

R 231945Z NOV 79
FM AMEMBASSY ASUNCION
TO SECSTATE WASHDC 7601

(REDACTED) ASUNCION 5242

E.O. 12065 GDS 11/23/85 (WHITE, ROBERT E.) OR-M
TAGE: PFOR, CONS
SUBJECT: FOREIGN MINISTER NOGUES ON FILARTIGA CASE

1. C- ENTIRE TEXT.

2. FOREIGN MINISTER NOGUES ASKED ME TO MEET WITH HIM
THE AFTERNOON OF NOVEMBER 22 TO DISCUSS THE FILARTIGA
CASE. HE SAID HIS GOVERNMENT HAD RECEIVED REPORTS THAT
THE UNITED STATES EMBASSY WAS COLLABORATING WITH FILAR-
TIGA IN HIS BATTLE AGAINST THE GOVERNMENT OF PARAGUAY
TO THE EXTENT THAT IT PROVIDES HIM WITH A VEHICLE AND
IMPORTS MEDICINES FOR HIM VIA THE POUCH. NOGUES SAID
THAT FILARTIGA WOULD VISIT THE UNITED STATES THIS MONTH
AND WOULD SEEK INTERVIEWS WITH SENATOR KENNEDY AND
OTHER INFLUENTIAL AMERICANS IN AND OUT OF THE GOVERN-
MENT. HE ASKED THAT I ENSURE THAT SENATOR KENNEDY AND
OTHER OFFICIALS WHOM FILARTIGA MIGHT MEET UNDERSTAND

THAT WHAT WAS AT ISSUE WAS NOT A POLITICAL CRIME BUT "A CRIME OF PASSION."

3. I REPLIED THAT THE UNITED STATES EMBASSY HAD NOT PROVIDED A JEEP TO DR. FILARTIGA NOR HAD WE IMPORTED MEDICINES FOR HIM. I SAID IT WAS HIGHLY PROBABLE THAT VARIOUS PRIVATE GROUPS IN THE U.S. ARE SENDING MEDICINES DIRECTLY TO DR. FILARTIGA FOR HIS CHARITABLE WORK.

4. REGARDING THE MINISTER'S REQUEST I SAID THAT I COULD NOT IN CONSCIENCE REPRESENT THE FILARTIGA CASE AS HAVING NO POLITICAL SIGNIFICANCE. I POINTED OUT THAT HIS GOVERNMENT HAD DISBARRED THE LAWYER WHO FIRST ACTED ON BEHALF OF THE FILARTIGA FAMILY (A MOST UNUSUAL ACT); THAT THE GOVERNMENT HAD RELEASED THE ONLY EYE WITNESS WHO HAD THEN DISAPPEARED; THAT THE GOVERNMENT REFUSED TO ISSUE A PASSPORT TO DR. FILARTIGA AND MEMBERS OF HIS FAMILY; AND THAT THE GOVERNMENT HAD ALLOWED THIS CASE TO DRAG ON FOR YEARS WITHOUT RESOLUTION. I POINTED OUT THAT IF THE GOVERNMENT WANTED TO CONVINCE OTHERS OF ITS BONA FIDES IN THE FILARTIGA CASE IT WOULD BE A GOOD IDEA TO BEGIN BY BRINGING IT TO A SPEEDY AND JUST CONCLUSION.

5. THE FOREIGN MINISTER THEN EXPRESSED CURIOSITY OVER FILARTIGA'S ABILITY TO TRAVEL TO THE UNITED STATES AS HE HAS NO PASSPORT. I ANSWERED THAT IF THE GOVERNMENT WONDERED WHY FILARTIGA WAS SO EFFECTIVE IN BUILDING SYMPATHY IN THE UNITED STATES IT MIGHT BEGIN BY LOOKING AT ITS POLICY OF DENYING PASSPORTS TO FILARTIGA AND OTHER PEOPLE WHO HAVE DIFFERENCES WITH THE GOVERNMENT. THE MINISTER SAID WHILE HE SYMPATHIZED WITH FILARTIGA'S PERSONAL TRAGEDY, IT WAS HIS OPINION THAT HE WAS SOMEWHAT DERANGED. I RESPONDED BY SAYING THAT DR. FILARTIGA IS A FINE ARTIST AND AN EXCELLENT MEDICAL DOCTOR WHO SPENDS A GREAT DEAL OF HIS TIME HELPING THE POOR. AS FAR AS I COULD TELL, HE IS NOT ACTIVE POLITICALLY BUT I ADDED THAT DR. FILARTIGA HAS A FLARE FOR PUBLIC RELATIONS AND UNDERSTANDS THE VALUE OF POINTING OUT TO ALL HIS AUDIENCES THAT THE GOVERNMENT OF PARAGUAY IS DENYING HIM HIS CONSTITUTIONAL RIGHT TO A PASSPORT. I THEN EXPLAINED OUR POLICY OF GRANTING VISAS TO PEOPLE WHO ARE ARBITRARILY DENIED PASSPORTS IF WE CONSIDER THEM TO HAVE LEGITIMATE BUSINESS IN THE UNITED STATES.

6. THE DISCUSSION OF IRAN WILL BE TREATED IN A SEPARATE MESSAGE.

WHITE

(REDACTED)

MAY 29, 1980: UNITED STATES

Memorandum for United States as Amicus Curiae

IN THE UNITED STATES COURT OF APPEALS
FOR THE SECOND CIRCUIT

No. 79-6090

DOLLY M.E. FILARTIGA AND DR. JOEL FILARTIGA,

Plaintiffs-Appellants,

v.

AMERICO NORBERTO PENA-IRALA,

Defendant-Appellee.

APPEAL FROM THE UNITED STATES DISTRICT COURT
FOR THE EASTERN DISTRICT OF NEW YORK

MEMORANDUM FOR THE UNITED STATES
AS AMICUS CURIAE

ROBERTS B. OWEN
Legal Advisor

WILLIAM T. LAKE
Deputy Legal Advisor
General

STEFAN A. RIESENFELD
CHARLES RUNYON
LINDA A. BAUMANN
Attorneys
Department of State
Washington, D.C. 20520

DREW S. DAYS, III
Assistant Attorney General

JOHN E. HUERTA
Deputy Assistant Attorney

BRIAN K. LANDSBERG
IRVING GORNSTEIN
Attorneys
Department of Justice
Washington, D.C. 20530

TABLE OF CONTENTS

INTRODUCTION

The United States files this memorandum in response to the Court's request that "the Department of State submit a memorandum setting forth its position concerning the proper interpretation of 28 U.S.C. § 1350 in light of the facts of this case."[1] The memorandum addresses the following questions:

1. Whether the torture of a foreign citizen by an official of the same country is a violation of the law of nations within the meaning of 28 U.S.C. 1350?

2. If so, whether such a violation gives rise to a judicially enforceable remedy and is therefore a tort within the meaning of that provision?

---

[1] Letter from Daniel Fusaro, Clerk, to Roberts B. Owen, October 29, 1979. Under 28 U.S.C. 516, the conduct of litigation in which the United States or an agency is interested is reserved to the Department of Justice. For that reason, the Department of Justice is filing this memorandum, developed jointly by the Department of Justice and the Department of State.

STATEMENT

This appeal involves the interpretation of 28 U.S.C. 1350, which gives the district courts jurisdiction in all cases where an alien sues for "a tort only, committed in violation of the law of nations or a treaty of the United States." The complaint alleges that defendant, acting under color of his authority as a Paraguayan official, tortured and killed Joel Filartiga, a Paraguayan national, and that this conduct was a tort in violation of the law of nations. The district court nonetheless held that it lacked jurisdiction. The court acknowledged the strength of plaintiffs' argument that torture violates international law, but concluded that dismissal was compelled by two prior decisions of this Court, *IIT v. Vencap, Ltd.*, 534 F.2d 1001 (1975), and *Dreyfus v. Von Finck*, 534 F.2d 24 (1976), cert. denied, 429 U.S. 835, which it read to establish that (A. 107-108)[2]

> conduct, though tortious, is not in violation of 'the Law of Nations', as those words are used in 28 U.S.C. §1350, unless the conduct is in violation of those standards, rules or customs affecting the relationship between states and between an individual and a foreign state, and used by those states for their common good and/or in dealings *inter se.*

Because the court dismissed the complaint for lack of jurisdiction, it did not reach defendant's alternative argument for dismissal based on *forum non conveniens.* Plaintiffs appealed to this Court.

ARGUMENT

I
OFFICIAL TORTURE VIOLATES THE LAW OF NATIONS

The district court dismissed the complaint because it believed that the torture of a foreign citizen by an official of the same country does not violate the law of nations as that term is used in 28 U.S.C. 1350. If Section 1350 reached only those practices that historically have been viewed as violations of international law, the court's decision would very likely be correct. Before the turn of the century and even after, it was generally thought that a nation's treatment of its own citizens was beyond the purview of international law. But as we demonstrate below, Section 1350 encompasses international law as it has evolved over time. And whatever may have been true before the turn of the century, today a nation has an obligation under international law to respect the right of its citizens to be free of official torture.

---

[2] "A." references are to the joint appendix.

A. *Section 1350 encompasses the law of nations as that body of law may evolve*

Section 1350 originated as Section 9 of the Judiciary Act of 1789 (1 Stat. 76 (1789)) and has not changed significantly since that time. It provides that:

> The district courts shall have original jurisdiction of any civil action by an alien for a tort only, committed in violation of the law of nations or a treaty of the United States.

This is one of several provisions in the Judiciary Act "reflecting a concern for uniformity in this country's dealings with foreign nations and indicating a desire to give matters of international significance to the jurisdiction of federal institutions." *Banco Nacional de Cuba v. Sabbatino,* 376 U.S. 398, 427 n. 25 (1964).

The law of nations in Section 1350 refers to the law of nations as that body of law may evolve. There is no reason to believe that Congress intended to freeze the meaning of the law of nations in this statute as of 1789, any more than it intended the simultaneous grant of jurisdiction over maritime actions to be limited to maritime law as it then existed.[3] Since the law of nations had developed in large measure by reference to evolving customary practice, the framers of the first Judiciary Act surely anticipated that international law would not be static after 1789.

The *Paquete Habana,* 175 U.S. 677 (1900), illustrates this evolutionary process. There, the question was whether international law protected fishing ships from capture during times of war. Although a 1798 British case had held that the protection of such ships was a rule of comity only, the Court held that (*id.* at 694)

> the period of a hundred years which has since elapsed is amply sufficient to have enabled what originally may have rested in custom or comity, courtesy or concession, to grow, by the general assent of civilized nations, into a settled rule of international law.

If the application of Section 1350 were limited to the subjects encompassed by the law of nations in 1789, leaving only the state courts competent to administer any rules of international law that might subsequently develop, the result would be to frustrate the statute's central concern for

---

[3] Maritime law has evolved significantly since 1789. See *Moragne v. State Marine Lines,* 398 U.S. 375 (1970) (overruling an 1886 decision and holding that maritime law affords a remedy for wrongful death on navigable waters).

uniformity in this country's dealings with foreign nations. Accordingly, the district court's jurisdiction in this case turns not on whether the conduct alleged in the complaint would have been a violation of the law of nations in 1789, but on whether it is customarily treated as a violation of the law of nations today.

B. *International law now embraces the obligation of a state to respect the fundamental human rights of its citizens*

The view that a state's treatment of its own citizens is beyond the purview of international law was once widely held and is reflected in traditional works on the subject.[4] However, as we have stated, customary international law evolves with the changing customs and standards of behavior in the international community. Early in this century, as a consequence of those changing customs, an international law of human rights began to develop. This evolutionary process has produced wide recognition that certain fundamental human rights are now guaranteed to individuals as a matter of customary international law.

As we demonstrate in Part II, *infra*, this does not mean that all such rights may be judicially enforced. Indeed, it is likely that only a few rights have the degree of specificity and universality to permit private enforcement and that the protection of other asserted rights must be left to the political branches of government. But this distinction between judicially enforceable rights and rights enforceable only by the political branches should not obscure the central point we make here. The district court's assumption that a nation has no obligation under international law to respect the human rights of its citizens is fundamentally incorrect. The sources of international law are international agreements, international custom, general principles of law recognized by civilized nations, and judicial decisions and the teachings of learned commentators.[5] Developments in each of these areas have had a role in establishing the twentieth century international law of human rights.

The first significant treaty development was the Covenant of the League of Nations in 1919, which declared that the members of the League would attempt to secure and maintain fair and humane conditions of labor, and secure just treatment for the inhabitants of territory under their control.[6]

---

[4] *E.g.*, L. Oppenheim, *International Law: A Treatise*, Vol. 1, 362-369 (2d Ed. 1912).

[5] Statute of the International Court of Justice, Article 38, June 26, 1945, 59 Stat. 1055, 1060 (effective October 24, 1945). See also, *The Paquete Habana, supra*, 175 U.S. at 700.

[6] The Covenant of the League of Nations, Articles 22, 23, June 28, 1919, reprinted

Other early developments were the treaties entered into after World War I guaranteeing the religious, cultural, and political rights of national minorities.[7]

Treaty activity accelerated after World War II. In 1945, the United Nations Charter imposed on U.N. members a general obligation to promote "universal respect for, and observance of, human rights and fundamental freedoms for all without distinction as to race, sex, language, or religion."[8] The U.N. Charter represents a clear break with the traditional view that a nation's treatment of its citizens is beyond the concern of international law—a break also evidenced by recognition in the Charter of the Organization of American States of "the fundamental rights of the individual without distinction as to race, nationality, creed, or sex."[9]

More recently, the obligation of states to respect fundamental human rights has been reiterated in a growing number of more specific multilateral treaties. These include The International Covenant on Civil and Political Rights,[10] The American Convention on Human Rights[11] and The European Convention for the Protection of Human Rights and Fundamental Freedoms.[12]

---

in *Treaties and Other International Agreements of the United States of America 1776-1949*, 2 Bevans, 55-57(1969).

[7] See, *e.g.*, Treaty Between the Principal Allied and Associated Powers and Poland, signed at Versailles, June 28, 1919, reprinted in *Treaties, Conventions, International Acts, Protocol and Agreements Between the United States of America and Other Powers 1910-1923*, 3 Malloy-Redmond 3714 (1923). In addition, the general treaties of peace concluding the war included provisions aimed at guaranteeing minority rights. See, *e.g.*, Treaty of Peace with Austria, Part 3, Sec. 5, signed at St. Germaine-en-Laye, September 10, 1919, reprinted in 3 Malloy-Redmond 3149.

[8] United Nations Charter, June 26, 1945, Arts. 55, 56, 59 Stat. 1031, 1045-1046, 3 Bevans 1153, 1166-1167 (1969).

[9] Charter of the Organization of American States, Articles 3(j), 16, 43(a) (entered into force December 13, 1951), as amended by the Protocol of Buenos Aires of 1967 (entered into force February 27, 1970), OAS Treaty Series No. 1-C, OAS, OR, OEA/Ser.A/2 (English), Rev. (1970), 21 U.S.T. 607, T.I.A.S. 6847. See also American Declaration of the Rights and Duties of Man, ch. 1 (1948), OAS, OR, OEA/Ser. L/V/E.23, Doc. 21, Rev. 2.

[10] General Assembly Resolution 2200 (XXI)A (December 16, 1966), entered into force March 23, 1976: *Four Treaties Pertaining to Human Rights*, Message from the President of the United States, S. Doc. No. Exec. C, D, E, and F, 95th Cong., 2d Sess. (1978).

[11] Signed at San Jose, Costa Rica, November 22, 1969, entered into force July 18, 1978, OAS Treaty Series No. 36, OAS, OR, OEA/Ser.A/16 (English).

[12] Signed November 4, 1950, entered into force September 3, 1953, Council of Europe, European Treaty Series No. 5 (1968), 213 U.N.T.S. 221.

International custom also indicates that nations have accepted as law an obligation to observe fundamental human rights. In 1948, The United Nations General Assembly unanimously adopted the Universal Declaration of Human Rights,[13] which goes beyond the UN Charter in specifying and defining the fundamental rights to which all individuals are entitled. The Universal Declaration has been followed by a growing number of U.N. resolutions clarifying and elaborating on these rights[14] or invoking them in specific cases.[15] In a parallel development, the International Conference on Security and Cooperation in Europe, which met in Helsinki and Geneva between 1973 and 1975, adopted a Final Act declaring that the participating nations would respect the human rights of their nationals.[16] The Final Act, like the UN resolutions, does not have the legal effect of a treaty but provides evidence of customary international law.[17]

General principles of law recognized by civilized nations also establish that there are certain fundamental human rights to which all individuals are entitled, regardless of nationality. Although specific practices differ widely among nations, all nations with organized legal systems recognize constraints on the power of the state to invade their citizens' human rights. In the period 1948-1973, the constitutions or other important laws of over 75 states either expressly referred to or clearly borrowed from the Universal Declaration of Human Rights.[18] In the same period, the Declaration was referred to in at least 16 cases in domestic courts of various nations.[19]

---

[13] General Assembly Resolution 217 (III)A (December 10, 1948).

[14] See Addendum.

[15] See *United Nations Action in the Field of Human Rights* (1974), ST/HR/2 (Pub. Sales No. E.74.XIV.2), at 14-15.

[16] *Conference on Security and Cooperation in Europe: Final Act* (Helsinki, 1975), 73 Dep't State Bull. 323, 325 (1975).

[17] As further evidence, see Declaration on Principles of International Law concerning Friendly Relations and Cooperation among States in accordance with the Charter of the United Nations, General Assembly Resolution 2625(XXV) (October 24, 1970). The Declaration proclaims that:

> Every State has the duty to promote through joint and separate action universal respect for and observance of human rights and fundamental freedoms in accordance with the Charter.

It further states:

> The principles of the Charter which are embodied in this Declaration constitute basic principles of international law . . . .

[18] *United Nations Action in the Field of Human Rights, supra,* at 17-18.

[19] *United Nations Action in the Field of Human Rights, supra,* at 19.

The decisions of the International Court of Justice also reflect and confirm the existence of a customary international law of human rights.[20] And the affidavits of four American experts in international law, filed by plaintiffs below, document the broad recognition among legal scholars that human rights obligations are now part of customary international law.[21]

In sum, as the Department of State said in a recent report to Congress on human rights practices:

> There now exists an international consensus that recognizes basic human rights and obligations owed by all governments to their citizens . . . . There is no doubt that these rights are often violated; but virtually all governments acknowledge their validity.[22]

We recognize that a panel of this Court has said that "violations of international law do not occur when the aggrieved parties are nationals of the acting state." *Dreyfus, supra*, 534 F.2d at 31. As we have shown, however, this statement is incorrect and should not be followed.[23]

---

[20] *Nuclear Tests (Australia v. France)*, Judgment of December 20, 1974, [1974] J I.C.J. 253, 303 (Opinion of Judge Petren); Advisory Opinion on *Legal Consequences for States of the Continued Presence of South Africa in Namibia (South West Africa) Notwithstanding Security Council Resolution 276 (1970)*, [1971] I.C.J. 16.

[21] See Affidavit of Richard B. Lillich (A. 65-70); Affidavit of Thomas M. Franck (A. 63-64); Affidavit of Myres S. MacDougal (A. 71); Affidavit of Richard Anderson Falk (A. 61-62).

[22] Department of State, *Country Reports on Human Rights Practices for 1979*, published as Joint Committee Print, House Comm. on Foreign Affairs & Senate Comm. on Foreign Relations, 96th Cong., 2d Sess. (February 4, 1980) Introduction at 1.

[23] *Dreyfus* mistakenly relied on Mr. Justice White's dissent in *Sabbatino* for its conclusion. At one point in his opinion Mr. Justice White does distinguish several cases decided long before the turn of the century as cases where violations of international law were not present because the parties were nationals of the acting state. 376 U.S. at 442, n. 2. However, Mr. Justice White makes clear elsewhere in his opinion that this is not the law today. In discussing a case in which an individual brought suit to recover property expropriated by the Nazis, Mr. Justice White specifically explained that "racial and religious expropriations, while involving nationals of the foreign state and therefore customarily not cognizable under international law, had been condemned in multinational agreements and declarations as crimes against humanity." *Id.* at 457 n. 18. Accordingly, Mr. Justice White concluded, "the acts could . . . be measured in local courts against widely held principle rather than judged by the parochial views of the forum." *Ibid.* Mr. Justice White's opinion thus reinforces our view that international law prohibits a nation from violating the fundamental human rights of its citizens.

C. *Freedom from torture is among the fundamental human rights protected by international law*

Every multilateral treaty dealing generally with civil and political human rights proscribes torture. These include The American Convention on Human Rights,[24] The International Covenant on Civil and Political Rights[25] and The European Convention for the Protection of Human Rights and Fundamental Freedoms.[26] In addition, the Geneva Conventions of 1949 forbid torture in international or domestic conflicts and declare it to be a "grave breach" of the conventions.[27] This uniform treaty condemnation of torture provides a strong indication that the proscription of torture has entered into customary international law.[28]

We do not suggest that every provision of these treaties states a binding rule of customary international law. Where reservations have been attached by a significant number of nations to specific provisions or where disagreement with provisions is cited as the ground for a nation's refusal to become a party, the near-unanimity required for the adoption of a rule into customary international law may be lacking.[29] No such disagreement has been expressed about the provisions forbidding torture.

---

[24] Article 5 provides in relevant part, that "No one shall be subjected to torture or to cruel, inhuman, or degrading punishment or treatment." OAS Treaty Series No. 36, *supra*, at 2.

[25] Article 7: "No one shall be subjected to torture or to cruel, inhuman or degrading treatment or punishment." General Assembly Resolution 2200 (XXI)A, *supra*.

[26] Article 3: "No one shall be subjected to torture or to inhuman or degrading treatment or punishment." Council of Europe, European Treaty Series No. 5 (1968), 213 U.N.T.S. 221.

[27] Geneva Convention Relative to the Treatment of Prisoners of War of August 12, 1949, 6 U.S.T. 3316, T.I.A.S. No. 3364, Articles 3, 13, 129, 130.

[28] These treaty provisions, in conjunction with other evidence, are persuasive of the existence of an international norm that is binding as a matter of customary law on all nations, not merely those that are parties to the treaties. A, D'Amato, *The Concept of Custom in International Law* 103, 124-128 (1971).

The United States has signed both the American Convention on Human Rights and the International Covenant on Civil and Political Rights, and those instruments await the advice and consent of the Senate. See *Four Treaties Pertaining to Human Rights, supra*. Only European countries are entitled to be parties to the third treaty.

[29] For instance, Article 20 of the International Covenant on Civil and Political Rights prohibits "advocacy of national, racial, or religious hatred that constitutes incitement to discrimination, hostility or violence . . . ." *Four Treaties Pertaining to Human Rights, supra*, at 29. This provision conflicts with principles of free speech that are central to the political values of many democracies. A number of nations, including the United Kingdom,

A court also must distinguish between provisions that reflect principles that are considered desirable but incapable of immediate realization and those provisions that codify fundamental human rights. Illustrative of the former category are the declarations in the International Covenant on Economic, Social and Cultural Rights that individuals are entitled to favorable working conditions and to social security.[30] In proposing that the Senate ratify that treaty, the President observed:

> Some of the standards established under these articles may not readily be translated into legally enforceable rights, while others are in accord with United States policy, but have not yet been fully achieved. It is accordingly important to make clear that these provisions are understood to be goals whose realization will be sought rather than obligations requiring immediate implementation.[31]

The President further recommended that the Senate express its understanding that these and like provisions "described goals to be achieved progressively rather than through immediate implementation."[32] The Covenant itself casts these principles in this light.[33] In contrast, because torture is universally condemned and incompatible with accepted concepts of human behavior, the protection against torture must be considered a fundamental human right.

International custom also evidences a universal condemnation of torture. While some nations still practice torture, it appears that no state asserts a right to torture its nationals. Rather, nations accused of torture unanimously deny the accusation and make no attempt to justify its use.[34]

Sweden, Denmark, Norway, and Finland, expressed reservations to Article 20 upon ratifying the Covenant. *Multilateral Treaties in Respect of Which the Secretary General Performs Depository Functions*, UN Doc. ST/LEG/Ser. D/12 108, 112, 114 (1978). President Carter has proposed a similar reservation in connection with United States ratification. *Four Treaties Pertaining to Human Rights, supra*, at XI-XII.

[30] International Covenant on Economic, Social, and Cultural Rights, Articles 7, 9. *Four Treaties Pertaining to Human Rights, supra*, at 15-16.

[31] *Four Treaties Pertaining to Human Rights, supra*, at X.

[32] *Id.* at IX.

[33] International Covenant on Economic, Social, and Cultural Rights, Article 2(1), *Four Treaties Pertaining to Human Rights, supra*, at 14.

[34] See, *e.g.*, Affidavit of Richard Anderson Falk (A. 62); Affidavit of Thomas M. Franck, (A. 64). In exchanges between United States embassies and all foreign states with which the United States maintains relations, it has been the Department of State's general experience that no government has asserted a right to torture its own nationals. Where reports of such torture elicit some credence, a state usually responds by denial

That conduct evidences an awareness that torture is universally condemned. This universal condemnation is made explicit in The Universal Declaration of Human Rights, which declares that "No one shall be subjected to torture . . . ."[35] That principle has been reiterated in a number of unanimous UN resolutions, including the 1975 Declaration on the Protection of All Persons from Being Subjected to Torture and Other Cruel, Inhuman or Degrading Treatment or Punishment ("UN Declaration on Torture").[36]

The UN Declaration on Torture not only confirms that international custom outlaws torture, but also supplies a precise definition of the conduct proscribed. The UN Declaration on Torture defines torture as

> any act by which severe pain or suffering, whether physical or mental, is intentionally inflicted by or at the instigation of a public official on a person for such purposes as obtaining from him or a third person information or a confession, punishing him for an act he has committed or is suspected of having committed, or intimidating him or other persons. It does not include pain or suffering arising only from, inherent in or incidental to, lawful sanctions to the extent consistent with the Standard Minimum Rules for the Treatment of Prisoners.[37]

---

or, less frequently, by asserting that the conduct was unauthorized or constituted rough treatment short of torture. The Department's *Country Reports on Human Rights, supra*, reports no assertion by any nation that torture is justified.

[35] General Assembly Resolution 217(III)A (December 10, 1948), Art. 5.

[36] General Assembly Resolution 3452(XXX) (December 9, 1975). Article 2 of the Declaration provides:

> Any act of torture or other cruel, inhuman or degrading treatment or punishment is an offence to human dignity and shall be condemned as a denial of the purposes of the Charter of the United Nations and as a violation of the human rights and fundamental freedoms proclaimed in the Universal Declaration of Human Rights.

Article 3 provides:

> No State may permit or tolerate torture or other cruel, inhuman or degrading treatment or punishment. Exceptional circumstances such as a state of war or a threat of war, internal political instability or any other public emergency may not be invoked as a justification of torture or other cruel, inhuman or degrading treatment or punishment.

[37] General Assembly Resolution 3452 (XXX) (December 9, 1975), Annex, Art. 1 (1). The United Nations Human Rights Commission is now drafting a Convention Against Torture and Other Cruel, Inhuman or Degrading Treatment or Punishment. That draft Convention would require each party to make torture criminally punishable within its jurisdiction. It contains a very similar definition of torture (E/CN.4/1367, Annex at 1):

This definition provides guidance to any court that may be required to determine whether particular conduct violates the proscription of torture in customary international law.

Analysis of general principles of law also discloses consistent condemnation of torture in national constitutions and legislation. Torture is specifically forbidden in the constitutions of over 40 nations.[38] The constitutions of over 15 additional nations contain implicit prohibitions against torture.[39] Eighteen states have incorporated the Universal Declaration of Human Rights in their constitutions and therefore have accepted the prohibition against torture contained in Article 5 of the Declaration.[40]

Condemnation of torture is reflected in both constitutional and statutory law in the United States. Conduct falling within the definition of torture in the UN Declaration on Torture would be a criminal offense under 18 U.S.C. 242 and civilly actionable under 42 U.S.C. 1983 or under the United States Constitution. Moreover, with certain exceptions, federal statutes bar assistance "to any country the government of which engages in a consistent pattern of gross violations of internationally recognized human rights", specifically including "torture."[41] These statutes evidence the United States' acceptance of the international norm condemning torture and reflect the fact that the norm is certain enough to be cognizable by federal courts.

Finally, judicial decisions and the commentary of experts confirm that official torture violates international law. As shown in Part I-B, these authorities recognize the modern emergence of human rights norms in customary international law. Plaintiffs have submitted the affidavits of four American scholars confirming that the proscription of torture is such a

---

For the purpose of this Convention, torture means any act by which severe pain or suffering, whether physical or mental, is intentionally inflicted on a person for such purposes as obtaining from him or a third person information or a confession, punishing him for an act he or a third person has committed or is suspected of having committed, or intimidating or coercing him or a third person, or for any reason based on discrimination of any kind, when such pain or suffering is inflicted by or at the instigation of or with the consent or acquiescence of a public official or other person acting in an official capacity. It does not include pain or suffering arising only from, inherent in or incidental to lawful sanctions.

[38] 48 Revue Internationale de Droit Penal Nos. 3 and 4, at 208 (1977). Paraguay is one such nation.

[39] *Id.* at 208-209.

[40] *Id.* at 211.

[41] 22 U.S.C. 2304(a)(2), (d); 22 U.S.C. 2151.

norm.[42] And published commentary is to the same effect.[43] In these circumstances, the conclusion that international law prohibits torture is inescapable.

II
OFFICIAL TORTURE IS A TORT AND
GIVES RISE TO A JUDICIALLY ENFORCEABLE REMEDY

Not every violation of international law is a tort within the meaning of Section 1350. However, some such violations are judicially cognizable as torts. A corollary to the traditional view that the law of nations dealt primarily with the relationship among nations rather than individuals was the doctrine that generally only states, not individuals, could seek to enforce rules of international law. *Sabbatino, supra,* 376 U.S. at 422-423. Just as the traditional view no longer reflects the state of customary international law, neither does the latter doctrine.

Indeed, it has long been established that in certain situations, individuals may sue to enforce their rights under international law. For example, when a ship is seized on the high seas in violation of international law, the owner of the ship may sue to recover the ship as well as seek damages. *The Paquete Habana, supra.* Similarly, when there has been an assault on a foreign ambassador in violation of international law, domestic courts may properly furnish a remedy. Cf. *Respublica v. De Longchamps,* 1 U.S. (1 Dall.) 111 (1784).

The more recently evolved international law of human rights similarly endows individuals with the right to invoke international law in a competent forum and under appropriate circumstances. The highly respected Constitutional Court of Germany has recognized this right of individuals. The court declared that, although "contemporary generally recognized principles of international law include only a few legal rules, that directly create rights and duties of private individuals by virtue of the international law itself," an area in which they do create such rights and duties is "the sphere of the minimum standard for the protection of human rights."[44]

---

[42] Affidavit of Richard Anderson Falk (A. 61-62); Affidavit of Thomas M. Franck (A. 63-64); Affidavit of Richard B. Lillich (A. 65-70); Affidavit of Myres S. MacDougal (A. 71).

[43] O'Boyle, *Torture and Emergency Powers Under the European Convention on Human Rights: Ireland v. The United Kingdom,* 71 Am. J. Int'l L. 674, 687-688 (1977).

[44] *In Matter of the Republic of the Philippines,* 46 BVerfGE 342, 362 (2 BvM 1/76, December 13, 1977) (translated from the German by Stefan A. Riesenfeld); see also *Borovsky v. Commissioner of Immigration,* Judgment of September 28, 1951 (S.Ct. Philippines), summarized in [1951] United Nations Yearbook on Human Rights 287-

As a result, in nations such as the United States where international law is part of the law of the land, an individual's fundamental human rights are in certain situations directly enforceable in domestic courts. As the Supreme Court said in *The Paquete Habana, supra,* 175 U.S. at 700:

> International law is part of our law, and must be ascertained and administered by the courts of justice of appropriate jurisdiction, as often as questions of right depending upon it are duly presented for their determination.

Because foreign officials are among the prospective defendants in suits alleging violations of fundamental human rights, such suits unquestionably implicate foreign policy considerations. But not every case or controversy which touches foreign relations lies beyond judicial cognizance. *Baker v. Carr,* 369 U.S. 186, 211 (1962). Like many other areas affecting international relations, the protection of fundamental human rights is not committed exclusively to the political branches of government. See *Sabbatino, supra,* 376 U.S. at 423, 430 n. 34.

This does not mean that Section 1350 appoints the United States courts as Commissions to evaluate the human rights performance of foreign nations. Cf. *Sabbatino, supra,* 376 U.S. at 423. The courts are properly confined to determining whether an individual has suffered a denial of rights guaranteed him as an individual by customary international law. Accordingly, before entertaining a suit alleging a violation of human rights, a court must first conclude that there is a consensus in the international community that the right is protected and that there is a widely shared understanding of the scope of this protection. *Sabbatino, supra,* 376 U.S. at 428, 430 n. 34. When these conditions have been satisfied, there is little danger that judicial enforcement will impair our foreign policy efforts. To the contrary, a refusal to recognize a private cause of action in these circumstances might seriously damage the credibility of our nation's commitment to the protection of human rights. As we have shown in Part I-C, official torture is both clearly defined and universally condemned. Therefore, private enforcement is entirely appropriate.[45]

288; *Chirskoff v. Commissioner of Immigration,* Judgment of October 26, 1951 (S.Ct. Philippines), summarized in *id.* at 288-289; *Judgment of Court of First Instance of Courtrai* (Belgium) of June 10, 1954, summarized in [1954] United Nations Yearbook on Human Rights 21 (courts relied on Universal Declaration of Human Rights in ordering release from detention).

[45] There are few decisions which base judgments against torturers directly on customary international law. But this attests to the longstanding condemnation of torture under municipal law and the more recent evolution of international human rights law. Courts have, nonetheless, invoked customary international law along with municipal and

From what we have said, it should be clear that a court is not at liberty to enforce its own views of policy under the guise of interpreting the requirements of international law. On the other hand, as the Supreme Court stated in *Sabbatino, supra*, 376 U.S. at 428:

> It should be apparent that the greater the degree of codification or consensus concerning a particular area of international law, the more appropriate it is for the judiciary to render decisions regarding it, since the courts can then focus on the application of an agreed principle to circumstances of fact rather than on the sensitive task of establishing a principle not inconsistent with the national interest or with international justice.

In this case, not only is there a consensus in the international community that official torture is unlawful, but Paraguay's Constitution expressly prohibits official torture[46] and Paraguayan law recognizes a tort action as an appropriate remedy.[47] The compatibility of international law and Paraguayan law significantly reduces the likelihood that court enforcement would cause undesirable international consequences and is therefore an additional reason to permit private enforcement.

Because international law and Paraguayan law both prohibit torture, this Court need not decide whether considerations of comity or a proper construction of section 1350 might require a different result if, despite the nearly universal condemnation implicit in the existence of a rule of customary international law, the jurisdiction with the most immediate interest in the controversy did not prohibit torture. Similarly, this case does not present any questions concerning whether international law, Paraguayan law or federal common law will govern other aspects of this lawsuit. The only question presented is whether official torture is a "tort . . . committed in violation of the law of nations . . . ."[48] Because the district court erred in

---

treaty law in cases involving torture. *Ireland v. United Kingdom,* Judgment of January 18, 1978 (European Ct. of Human Rights) summarized in [1978] Y.B. Eur. Conv. on Human Rights 602 (Council of Europe) (UN Declaration of Torture relied on in interpreting the European Convention of Human Rights); *Auditeur Militaire v. Krumkamp,* Pasicrisie Belge, 1950.3.37 (February 8, 1950) (Belgian Counseil de guerre de Brabant), summarized in 46 Am. J. Int'l L. 162-163 (1952) (Article 5 of Universal Declaration of Human Rights, which prohibits torture and cruel treatment, cited as authority that under customary international law the defendant accused of war crimes was not free to use torture).

[46] Article 45 of the Paraguayan Constitution.

[47] A. 51-53, 80.

[48] Because the lower court dismissed for lack of jurisdiction, it did not decide whether the case should be dismissed on the ground of *forum non conveniens.* Although

concluding that it is not, its judgment should be reversed and the case remanded for further proceedings.[49]

CONCLUSION

The judgment of the district court should be reversed and the case remanded for further proceedings.

Respectfully submitted,

ROBERTS B. OWEN	DREW S. DAYS, III
Legal Advisor	Assistant Attorney General
WILLIAM T. LAKE	JOHN E. HUERTA
Deputy Legal Advisor	Deputy Assistant Attorney General
STEFAN A. RIESENFELD	BRIAN K. LANDSBERG
CHARLES RUNYON	IRVING GORNSTEIN
LINDA A. BAUMANN	Attorneys
Attorneys	Department of Justice
Department of State	Washington, D.C. 20530
Washington, D.C. 20520	

---

we agree with plaintiffs that this question should be addressed by the district court first, we note that when the parties and the conduct alleged in the complaint have as little contact with the United States as they have here, abstention is generally appropriate. *Romero v. International Terminal Operating Co.*, 358 U.S. 354 (1959); *Lauritzen v. Larsen*, 345 U.S. 571 (1953). Plaintiffs assert that abstention is inappropriate because a tort suit in Paraguay would be a sham. For reasons of comity among nations, however, such an assertion should not be accepted absent a very clear and persuasive showing. In determining whether abstention is appropriate, the court should also consider the fact that the defendant has been deported. Compare *United States v. Castillo*, 615 F.2d 878, 882 (9th Cir. 1980).

[49] Defendant erroneously suggests (Br. 4-16) that Section 1350 is unconstitutional in conferring jurisdiction on federal courts to entertain tort actions under the law of nations. Customary international law is federal law, to be enunciated authoritatively by the federal courts. *Sabbatino, supra*, 376 U.S. at 425; see *The Paquete Habana, supra*, 175 U.S. at 700. An action for tort under international law is therefore a case "arising under . . . the laws of the United States" within Article III of the Constitution. See Note, *Federal Common Law and Article III: A Jurisdictional Approach to Erie*, 74 Yale L.J. 325, 331-336 (1964).

ADDENDUM

1. Standard Minimum Rules for the Treatment of Prisoners, adopted by the First United Nations Congress on the Prevention of Crime and Treatment of Offenders, held at Geneva in 1955, and approved by the Economic and Social Council by its resolutions 663 (XXIV) C (July 31, 1957) and 2076 (LXII) (May 13, 1977).

2. Declaration of the Rights of the Child, General Assembly Resolution 1386 (XIV) (November 20, 1959).

3. Declaration on the Granting of Independence to Colonial Countries and Peoples, General Assembly Resolution 1514 (XV) (December 14, 1960).

4. United Nations Declaration on the Elimination of All Forms of Racial Discrimination, General Assembly Resolution 1904 (XVIII) (November 20, 1963).

5. Declaration on the Elimination of Discrimination Against Women, General Assembly Resolution 2263 (XXII) (November 7, 1967).

6. Declaration on Territorial Asylum, General Assembly Resolution 2312 (XXII) (December 14, 1967).

7. The Proclamation of Tehran, unanimously proclaimed by the International Conference on Human Rights at Tehran, May 13, 1968, (convened pursuant to General Assembly Resolutions 2081 (XX) (December 20, 1965), 2217 (XXI) C (December 19, 1966) and 2339 (XXII) (December 18, 1967), Final Act of the International Conference on Human Rights, Tehran, Iran, May 13, 1968, *Human Rights: A Compilation of International Instruments of the United Nations* (1973) ST/HR/1 (Pub. Sales No. E.73.XIV.2).

8. Principles of International Cooperation in the Detection, Arrest, Extradition and Punishment of Persons Guilty of War Crimes and Crimes against Humanity, General Assembly Resolution 3074 (XXVIII) (December 3, 1973).

9. Declaration on the Protection of Women and Children in Emergency and Armed Conflict, General Assembly Resolution 3318 (XXIX) (December 14, 1974).

10. Declaration on the Protection of All Persons from Being Subjected to Torture and Other Cruel, Inhuman or Degrading Treatment or Punishment, General Assembly Resolution 3452 (XXX) (December 9, 1975).

JUNE 30, 1980: UNITED STATES

Second Circuit Court of Appeals: Decision

United States Court of Appeals
Second Circuit

Dolly M. E. FILARTIGA and Joel Filartiga,
Plaintiffs-Appellants,
v.

Americo Norberto PENA-IRALA,
Defendant-Appellee.

No. 191, Docket 79-6090.

Argued Oct. 16, 1979.
Decided June 30, 1980.

Peter Weiss, New York City (Rhonda Copelon, John Corwin and Jose Antonio Lugo, Center for Constitutional Rights, New York City, and Michael Maggio, Goren & Maggio, Washington, D.C., of counsel), for plaintiffs-appellants.

Murry D. Brochin, Newark, N. J. (Lowenstein, Sandler, Brochin, Kohl, Fisher & Boylan, P. C., Newark, N. J., of counsel), for defendant-appellee.

Irving Gornstein, Atty., Dept. of Justice, Washington, D. C. (Drew S. Days, III, Asst. Atty. Gen., John E. Huerta, Deputy Asst. Atty. Gen., Roberts B. Owen, Legal Advisor, William T. Lake, Deputy Legal Advisor, Stefan A. Riesenfeld, Charles Runyon and Linda A. Baumann, Attys., Dept. of State, Washington, D. C.), for the U.S. as amicus curiae.

Donald L. Doernberg, New York City, and David S. Weissbrodt, Minneapolis, Minn., for Amnesty International-U.S.A., Intern. League for Human Rights, and the Lawyers' Committee for Intern. Human Rights as amici curiae.

Allan Abbot Tuttle, and Steven M. Schneebaum, Washington, D. C., for The Intern. Human Rights Law Group, The Council on Hemispheric Affairs and the Washington Office on Latin America as amici curiae.

Before FEINBERG, Chief Judge, KAUFMAN and KEARSE, Circuit Judges.*

---

* The late Judge Smith was a member of the original panel in this case. After his unfortunate death, Judge Kearse was designated to fill his place pursuant to Local Rule § 0.14(b).

IRVING R. KAUFMAN, Circuit Judge:

Upon ratification of the Constitution, the thirteen former colonies were fused into a single nation, one which, in its relations with foreign states, is bound both to observe and construe the accepted norms of international law, formerly known as the law of nations. Under the Articles of Confederation, the several states had interpreted and applied this body of doctrine as a part of their common law, but with the founding of the "more perfect Union" of 1789, the law of nations became preeminently a federal concern.

Implementing the constitutional mandate for national control over foreign relations, the First Congress established original district court jurisdiction over "all causes where an alien sues for a tort only (committed) in violation of the law of nations." Judiciary Act of 1789, ch. 20, § 9(b), 1 Stat. 73, 77 (1789), *codified at* 28 U.S.C. § 1350. Construing this rarely-invoked provision, we hold that deliberate torture perpetrated under color of official authority violates universally accepted norms of the international law of human rights, regardless of the nationality of the parties. Thus, whenever an alleged torturer is found and served with process by an alien within our borders, § 1350 provides federal jurisdiction. Accordingly, we reverse the judgment of the district court dismissing the complaint for want of federal jurisdiction.

I

The appellants, plaintiffs below, are citizens of the Republic of Paraguay. Dr. Joel Filartiga, a physician, describes himself as a longstanding opponent of the government of President Alfredo Stroessner, which has held power in Paraguay since 1954. His daughter, Dolly Filartiga, arrived in the United States in 1978 under a visitor's visa, and has since applied for permanent political asylum. The Filartigas brought this action in the Eastern District of New York against Americo Norberto Pena-Irala (Pena), also a citizen of Paraguay, for wrongfully causing the death of Dr. Filartiga's seventeen-year old son, Joelito. Because the district court dismissed the action for want of subject matter jurisdiction, we must accept as true the allegations contained in the Filartigas' complaint and affidavits for purposes of this appeal.

The appellants contend that on March 29, 1976, Joelito Filartiga was kidnapped and tortured to death by Pena, who was then Inspector General of Police in Asuncion, Paraguay. Later that day, the police brought Dolly Filartiga to Pena's home where she was confronted with the body of her brother, which evidenced marks of severe torture. As she fled, horrified, from the house, Pena followed after her shouting, "Here you have what you have been looking for for so long and what you deserve. Now shut up." The Filartigas claim that Joelito was tortured and killed in retaliation for his father's political activities and beliefs.

Shortly thereafter, Dr. Filartiga commenced a criminal action in the Paraguayan courts against Pena and the police for the murder of his son. As a result, Dr. Filartiga's attorney was arrested and brought to police headquarters where, shackled to a wall, Pena threatened him with death. This attorney, it is alleged, has since been disbarred without just cause.

During the course of the Paraguayan criminal proceeding, which is apparently still pending after four years, another man, Hugo Duarte, confessed to the murder. Duarte, who was a member of the Pena household,[1] claimed that he had discovered his wife and Joelito *in flagrante delicto*, and that the crime was one of passion. The Filartigas have submitted a photograph of Joelito's corpse showing injuries they believe refute this claim. Dolly Filartiga, moreover, has stated that she will offer evidence of three independent autopsies demonstrating that her brother's death "was the result of professional methods of torture." Despite his confession, Duarte, we are told, has never been convicted or sentenced in connection with the crime.

In July of 1978, Pena sold his house in Paraguay and entered the United States under a visitor's visa. He was accompanied by Juana Bautista Fernandez Villalba, who had lived with him in Paraguay. The couple remained in the United States beyond the term of their visas, and were living in Brooklyn, New York, when Dolly Filartiga, who was then living in Washington, D. C., learned of their presence. Acting on information provided by Dolly the Immigration and Naturalization Service arrested Pena and his companion, both of whom were subsequently ordered deported on April 5, 1979 following a hearing. They had then resided in the United States for more than nine months.

Almost immediately, Dolly caused Pena to be served with a summons and civil complaint at the Brooklyn Navy Yard, where he was being held pending deportation. The complaint alleged that Pena had wrongfully caused Joelito's death by torture and sought compensatory and punitive damages of $10,000,000. The Filartigas also sought to enjoin Pena's deportation to ensure his availability for testimony at trial.[2] The cause of action

---

[1] Duarte is the son of Pena's companion, Juana Bautista Fernandez Villalba, who later accompanied Pena to the United States.

[2] Several officials of the Immigration and Naturalization Service were named as

is stated as arising under "wrongful death statutes; the U.N. Charter; the Universal Declaration on Human Rights; the U.N. Declaration Against Torture; the American Declaration of the Rights and Duties of Man; and other pertinent declarations, documents and practices constituting the customary international law of human rights and the law of nations," as well as 28 U.S.C. § 1350, Article II, sec. 2 and the Supremacy Clause of the U. S. Constitution. Jurisdiction is claimed under the general federal question provision, 28 U.S.C. § 1331 and, principally on this appeal, under the Alien Tort Statute, 28 U.S.C. § 1350.[3]

Judge Nickerson stayed the order of deportation, and Pena immediately moved to dismiss the complaint on the grounds that subject matter jurisdiction was absent and for *forum non conveniens*. On the jurisdictional issue, there has been no suggestion that Pena claims diplomatic immunity from suit. The Filartigas submitted the affidavits of a number of distinguished international legal scholars, who stated unanimously that the law of nations prohibits absolutely the use of torture as alleged in the complaint.[4] Pena, in support of his motion to dismiss on the ground of *forum non conveniens*, submitted the affidavit of his Paraguayan counsel, Jose Emilio Gorostiaga, who averred that Paraguayan law provides a full and adequate civil remedy for the wrong alleged.[5] Dr. Filartiga has not com-

---

defendants in connection with this portion of the action. Because Pena has now been deported, the federal defendants are no longer parties to this suit, and the claims against them are not before us on this appeal.

[3] Jurisdiction was also invoked pursuant to 28 U.S.C. §§ 1651, 2201 & 2202, presumably in connection with appellants' attempt to delay Pena's return to Paraguay.

[4] Richard Falk, the Albert G. Milbank Professor of International Law and Practice at Princeton University, and a former Vice President of the American Society of International Law, avers that, in his judgment, "it is now beyond reasonable doubt that torture of a person held in detention that results in severe harm or death is a violation of the law of nations." Thomas Franck, professor of international law at New York University and Director of the New York University Center for International Studies offers his opinion that torture has now been rejected by virtually all nations, although it was once commonly used to extract confessions. Richard Lillich, the Howard W. Smith Professor of Law at the University of Virginia School of Law, concludes, after a lengthy review of the authorities, that officially perpetrated torture is "a violation of international law (formerly called the law of nations)." Finally, Myres MacDougal, a former Sterling Professor of Law at the Yale Law School, and a past President of the American Society of International Law, states that torture is an offense against the law of nations, and that "it has long been recognized that such offenses vitally affect relations between states."

[5] The Gorostiaga affidavit states that

a father whose son has been wrongfully killed may in addition to commencing a criminal proceeding bring a civil action for damages against the person responsible. Accordingly, Mr. Filartiga has the right to commence a civil action against Mr. Duarte and Mr. Pena-Irala since he accuses them both of responsibility for his son's death.

menced such an action, however, believing that further resort to the courts of his own country would be futile.

Judge Nickerson heard argument on the motion to dismiss on May 14, 1979, and on May 15 dismissed the complaint on jurisdictional grounds.[6] The district judge recognized the strength of appellants' argument that official torture violates an emerging norm of customary international law. Nonetheless, he felt constrained by dicta contained in two recent opinions of this Court, *Dreyfus v. von Finck*, 534 F.2d 24 (2d Cir.), *cert. denied*, 429 U.S. 835, 97 S.Ct. 102, 50 L.Ed.2d 101 (1976); *IIT v. Vencap*, Ltd., 519 F.2d 1001 (2d Cir. 1975), to construe narrowly "the law of nations," as employed in § 1350, as excluding that law which governs a state's treatment of its own citizens.

The district court continued the stay of deportation for forty-eight hours while appellants applied for further stays. These applications were denied by a panel of this Court on May 22, 1979, and by the Supreme Court two days later. Shortly thereafter, Pena and his companion returned to Paraguay.

II

Appellants rest their principal argument in support of federal jurisdiction upon the Alien Tort Statute, 28 U.S.C. § 1350, which provides: "The district courts shall have original jurisdiction of any civil action by an alien for a tort only, committed in violation of the law of nations or a treaty of the United States." Since appellants do not contend that their action arises directly under a treaty of the United States,[7] a threshold question on the jurisdictional issue is whether the conduct alleged violates the law of

---

He may commence such a civil action either simultaneously with the commencement of the criminal proceeding, during the time that the criminal proceeding lasts, or within a year after the criminal proceeding has terminated. In either event, however, the civil action may not proceed to judgment until the criminal proceeding has been disposed of. If the defendant is found not guilty because he was not the author of the case under investigation in the criminal proceeding, no civil action for indemnity for damages based upon the same deed investigated in the criminal proceeding, can prosper or succeed.

[6] The court below accordingly did not consider the motion to dismiss on *forum non conveniens* grounds, which is not before us on this appeal.

[7] Appellants "associate themselves with" the argument of some of the amici curiae that their claim arises directly under a treaty of the United States, Brief for Appellants at 23, but nonetheless primarily rely upon treaties and other international instruments as evidence of an emerging norm of customary international law, rather then independent sources of law.

nations. In light of the universal condemnation of torture in numerous international agreements, and the renunciation of torture as an instrument of official policy by virtually all of the nations of the world (in principle if not in practice), we find that an act of torture committed by a state official against one held in detention violates established norms of the international law of human rights, and hence the law of nations.

The Supreme Court has enumerated the appropriate sources of international law. The law of nations "may be ascertained by consulting the works of jurists, writing professedly on public law; or by the general usage and practice of nations; or by judicial decisions recognizing and enforcing that law." *United States v. Smith*, 18 U.S. (5 Wheat.) 153, 160-61, 5 L.Ed. 57 (1820); *Lopes v. Reederei Richard Schroder*, 225 F.Supp. 292, 295 (E.D. Pa. 1963). In *Smith*, a statute proscribing "the crime of piracy (on the high seas) as defined by the law of nations," 3 Stat. 510(a) (1819), was held sufficiently determinate in meaning to afford the basis for a death sentence. The Smith Court discovered among the works of Lord Bacon, Grotius, Bochard and other commentators a genuine consensus that rendered the crime "sufficiently and constitutionally defined." *Smith, supra*, 18 U.S. (5 Wheat.) at 162, 5 L.Ed. 57.

The Paquete Habana, 175 U.S. 677, 20 S.Ct. 290, 44 L.Ed. 320 (1900), reaffirmed that

> where there is no treaty, and no controlling executive or legislative act or judicial decision, resort must be had to the customs and usages of civilized nations; and, as evidence of these, to the works of jurists and commentators, who by years of labor, research and experience, have made themselves peculiarly well acquainted with the subjects of which they treat. Such works are resorted to by judicial tribunals, not for the speculations of their authors concerning what the law ought to be, but for trustworthy evidence of what the law really is.

Id. at 700, 20 S.Ct. at 299. Modern international sources confirm the propriety of this approach.[8]

---

[8] The Statute of the International Court of Justice, Arts. 38 & 59, June 26, 1945, 59 Stat. 1055, 1060 (1945) provides:

Art. 38

1. The Court, whose function is to decide in accordance with international law such disputes as are submitted to it, shall apply:

> (a) international conventions, whether general or particular, establishing rules expressly recognized by the contesting states;

Habana is particularly instructive for present purposes, for it held that the traditional prohibition against seizure of an enemy's coastal fishing vessels during wartime, a standard that began as one of comity only, had ripened over the preceding century into "a settled rule of international law" by "the general assent of civilized nations." *Id.* at 694, 20 S.Ct. at 297; *accord, id.* at 686, 20 S.Ct. at 297. Thus it is clear that courts must interpret international law not as it was in 1789, but as it has evolved and exists among the nations of the world today. *See Ware v. Hylton*, 3 U.S. (3 Dall.) 198, 1 L.Ed. 568 (1796) (distinguishing between "ancient" and "modern" law of nations).

The requirement that a rule command the "general assent of civilized nations" to become binding upon them all is a stringent one. Were this not so, the courts of one nation might feel free to impose idiosyncratic legal rules upon others, in the name of applying international law. Thus, in *Banco Nacional de Cuba v. Sabbatino*, 376 U.S. 398, 84 S.Ct. 923, 11 L.Ed.2d 804 (1964), the Court declined to pass on the validity of the Cuban government's expropriation of a foreign-owned corporation's assets, noting the sharply conflicting views on the issue propounded by the capital-exporting, capital-importing, socialist and capitalist nations. *Id.* at 428-30, 84 S.Ct. at 940-41.

The case at bar presents us with a situation diametrically opposed to the conflicted state of law that confronted the *Sabbatino* Court. Indeed, to paraphrase that Court's statement, *id.* at 428, 84 S.Ct. at 940, there are few, if any, issues in international law today on which opinion seems to be so united as the limitations on a state's power to torture persons held in its custody.

The United Nations Charter (a treaty of the United States, see 59 Stat. 1033 (1945)) makes it clear that in this modern age a state's treatment of its own citizens is a matter of international concern. It provides:

(b) international custom, as evidence of a general practice accepted as law;

(c) the general principles of law recognized by civilized nations;

(d) subject to the provisions of Article 59, judicial decisions and the teachings of the most highly qualified publicists of the various nations, as subsidiary means for the determination of the rules of law.

2. This provision shall not prejudice the power of the Court to decide a case *ex aequo et bono*, if the parties agree thereto.

Art. 59

The decision of the Court has no binding force except between the parties and in respect of that particular case.

With a view to the creation of conditions of stability and well-being which are necessary for peaceful and friendly relations among nations . . . the United Nations shall promote . . . universal respect for, and observance of, human rights and fundamental freedoms for all without distinctions as to race, sex, language or religion.

Id. Art. 55. And further:

All members pledge themselves to take joint and separate action in cooperation with the Organization for the achievement of the purposes set forth in Article 55.

Id. Art. 56.

While this broad mandate has been held not to be wholly self-executing, *Hitai v. Immigration and Naturalization Service*, 343 F.2d 466, 468 (2d Cir. 1965), this observation alone does not end our inquiry.[9] For although there is no universal agreement as to the precise extent of the "human rights and fundamental freedoms" guaranteed to all by the Charter, there is at present no dissent from the view that the guaranties include, at a bare minimum, the right to be free from torture. This prohibition has become part of customary international law, as evidenced and defined by the Universal Declaration of Human Rights, General Assembly Resolution 217 (III)(A) (Dec. 10, 1948) which states, in the plainest of terms, "no one shall be subjected to torture."[10] The General Assembly has declared that the Charter

---

[9] We observe that this Court has previously utilized the U.N. Charter and the Charter of the Organization of American States, another non-self-executing agreement, as evidence of binding principles of international law. *United States v. Toscanino*, 500 F.2d 267 (2d Cir. 1974). In that case, our government's duty under international law to refrain from kidnapping a criminal defendant from within the borders of another nation, where formal extradition procedures existed, infringed the personal rights of the defendant, whose international law claims were thereupon remanded for a hearing in the district court.

[10] Eighteen nations have incorporated the Universal Declaration into their own constitutions. 48 *Revue Internationale de Droit Penal Nos.* 3 & 4, at 211 (1977).

[11] Article 1

1. For the purpose of this Declaration, torture means any act by which severe pain or suffering, whether physical or mental, is intentionally inflicted by or at the instigation of a public official on a person for such purposes as obtaining from him or a third person information or confession, punishing him for an act he has committed or is suspected of having committed, or intimidating him or other persons. It does not include pain or suffering arising only from, inherent or incidental to lawful sanctions to the extent consistent with the Standard Minimum Rules for the Treatment of Prisoners.

precepts embodied in this Universal Declaration "constitute basic princi-ples of international law." G.A.Res. 2625 (XXV) (Oct. 24, 1970).

Particularly relevant is the Declaration on the Protection of All Persons from Being Subjected to Torture, General Assembly Resolution 3452, 30 U.N. GAOR Supp. (No. 34) 91, U.N.Doc. A/1034 (1975), which is set out

---

2. Torture constitutes an aggravated and deliberate form of cruel, inhuman or degrading treatment or punishment.

Article 2

Any act of torture or other cruel, inhuman or degrading treatment or punishment is an offense to human dignity and shall be condemned as a denial of the purposes of the Charter of the United Nations and as a violation of human rights and funda-mental freedoms proclaimed in the Universal Declaration of Human Rights.

Article 3

No state may permit or tolerate torture or other cruel, inhuman or degrading treatment or punishment. Exceptional circumstances such as a state of war or a threat of war, internal political instability or any other public emergency may not be invoked as a justification of torture or other cruel, inhuman or degrading treat-ment or punishment.

Article 4

Each state shall, in accordance with the provisions of this Declaration, take effective measures to prevent torture and other cruel, inhuman or degrading treatment or punishment from being practiced within its jurisdiction.

Article 5

The training of law enforcement personnel and of other public officials who may be responsible for persons deprived of their liberty shall ensure that full account is taken of the prohibition against torture and other cruel, inhuman or degrading treatment or punishment. This prohibition shall also, where appropriate, be included in such general rules or instructions as are issued in regard to the duties and functions of any-one who may be involved in the custody or treatment of such persons.

Article 6

Each state shall keep under systematic review interrogation methods and practices as well as arrangements for the custody and treatment of persons deprived of their liberty in its territory, with a view to preventing any cases of torture or other cruel, inhuman or degrading treatment or punishment.

Article 7

Each state shall ensure that all acts of torture as defined in Article I are offenses under its criminal law. The same shall apply in regard to acts which constitute par-ticipation in, complicity in, incitement to or an attempt to commit torture.

Article 8

Any person who alleges he has been subjected to torture or other cruel, inhuman or degrading treatment or punishment by or at the instigation of a public official

in full in the margin.[11] The Declaration expressly prohibits any state from permitting the dastardly and totally inhuman act of torture. Torture, in turn, is defined as "any act by which severe pain and suffering, whether physical or mental, is intentionally inflicted by or at the instigation of a public official on a person for such purposes as . . . intimidating him or other persons." The Declaration goes on to provide that "(w)here it is proved that an act of torture or other cruel, inhuman or degrading treatment or punishment has been committed by or at the instigation of a public official, the victim shall be afforded redress and compensation, in accordance with national law." This Declaration, like the Declaration of Human Rights before it, was adopted without dissent by the General Assembly. Nayar, "Human Rights: The United Nations and United States Foreign Policy," 19 *Harv. Int'l L.J.* 813, 816 n.18 (1978).

These U.N. declarations are significant because they specify with great precision the obligations of member nations under the Charter. Since their adoption, "(m)embers can no longer contend that they do not know what human rights they promised in the Charter to promote." Sohn, "A Short History of United Nations Documents on Human Rights," in *The United Nations and Human Rights, 18th Report of the Commission* (Commission to

---

shall have the right to complain to, and to have his case impartially examined by, the competent authorities of the state concerned.

Article 9

Wherever there is reasonable ground to believe that an act of torture as defined in Article 1 has been committed, the competent authorities of the state concerned shall promptly proceed to an impartial investigation even if there has been no formal complaint.

Article 10

If an investigation under Article 8 or Article 9 establishes that an act of torture as defined in Article 1 appears to have been committed, criminal proceedings shall be instituted against the alleged offender or offenders in accordance with national law. If an allegation of other forms of cruel, inhuman or degrading treatment or punishment is considered to be well founded, the alleged offender or offenders shall be subject to criminal, disciplinary or other appropriate proceedings.

Article 11

Where it is proved that an act of torture or other cruel, inhuman or degrading treatment or punishment has been committed by or at the instigation of a public official, the victim shall be afforded redress and compensation, in accordance with national law.

Article 12

Any statement which is established to have been made as a result of torture or other cruel, inhuman or degrading treatment or punishment may not be invoked as evidence against the person concerned or against any other person in any proceeding.

Study the Organization of Peace ed. 1968). Moreover, a U.N. Declaration is, according to one authoritative definition, "a formal and solemn instrument, suitable for rare occasions when principles of great and lasting importance are being enunciated." 34 U.N. ESCOR, Supp. (No. 8) 15, U.N. Doc. E/CN.4/1/610 (1962) (memorandum of Office of Legal Affairs, U.N. Secretariat). Accordingly, it has been observed that the Universal Declaration of Human Rights "no longer fits into the dichotomy of 'binding treaty' against 'non-binding pronouncement,' but is rather an authoritative statement of the international community." *E. Schwelb, Human Rights and the International Community* 70 (1964). Thus, a Declaration creates an expectation of adherence, and "insofar as the expectation is gradually justified by State practice, a declaration may by custom become recognized as laying down rules binding upon the States." 34 U.N. ESCOR, *supra*. Indeed, several commentators have concluded that the Universal Declaration has become, *in toto*, a part of binding, customary international law. Nayar, *supra*, at 816-17; Waldlock, "Human Rights in Contemporary International Law and the Significance of the European Convention," *Int'l & Comp. L.Q.*, Supp. Publ. No. 11 at 15 (1965).

Turning to the act of torture, we have little difficulty discerning its universal renunciation in the modern usage and practice of nations. *Smith, supra*, 18 U.S. (5 Wheat.) at 160-61, 5 L.Ed. 57. The international consensus surrounding torture has found expression in numerous international treaties and accords. *E.g., American Convention on Human Rights*, Art. 5, OAS Treaty Series No. 36 at 1, OAS Off. Rec. OEA/Ser 4 v/II 23, doc. 21, rev. 2 (English ed., 1975) ("No one shall be subjected to torture or to cruel, inhuman or degrading punishment or treatment"); International Covenant on Civil and Political Rights, U.N. General Assembly Res. 2200 (XXI)A, U.N. Doc. A/6316 (Dec. 16, 1966) (identical language); European Convention for the Protection of Human Rights and Fundamental Freedoms, Art. 3, Council of Europe, European Treaty Series No. 5 (1968), 213 U.N.T.S. 211 (*semble*). The substance of these international agreements is reflected in modern municipal i.e. national law as well. Although torture was once a routine concomitant of criminal interrogations in many nations, during the modern and hopefully more enlightened era it has been universally renounced. According to one survey, torture is prohibited, expressly or implicitly, by the constitutions of over fifty-five nations,[12] including both the United States[13] and Paraguay.[14] Our State Department reports a general recognition of this principle:

---

[12] 48 *Revue Internationale de Droit Penal Nos.* 3 & 4 at 208 (1977).

[13] U.S. Const., Amend. VIII ("cruel and unusual punishments" prohibited); *id.* Amend. XIV.

[14] Constitution of Paraguay, Art. 45 (prohibiting torture and other cruel treatment).

There now exists an international consensus that recognizes basic human rights and obligations owed by all governments to their citizens . . . . There is no doubt that these rights are often violated; but virtually all governments acknowledge their validity.

Department of State, *Country Reports on Human Rights for 1979*, published as Joint Comm. Print, House Comm. on Foreign Affairs, and Senate Comm. on Foreign Relations, 96th Cong. 2d Sess. (Feb. 4, 1980), Introduction at 1. We have been directed to no assertion by any contemporary state of a right to torture its own or another nation's citizens. Indeed, United States diplomatic contacts confirm the universal abhorrence with which torture is viewed:

In exchanges between United States embassies and all foreign states with which the United States maintains relations, it has been the Department of State's general experience that no government has asserted a right to torture its own nationals. Where reports of torture elicit some credence, a state usually responds by denial or, less frequently, by asserting that the conduct was unauthorized or constituted rough treatment short of torture.[15]

Memorandum of the United States as *Amicus Curiae* at 16 n.34.

Having examined the sources from which customary international law is derived—the usage of nations, judicial opinions and the works of jurists[16]—we conclude that official torture is now prohibited by the law of nations. The prohibition is clear and unambiguous, and admits of no distinction between treatment of aliens and citizens. Accordingly, we must conclude that the dictum in *Dreyfus v. von Finck, supra*, 534 F.2d at 31, to the effect that "violations of international law do not occur when the aggrieved parties are nationals of the acting state," is clearly out of tune with the cur-

---

[15] The fact that the prohibition of torture is often honored in the breach does not diminish its binding effect as a norm of international law. As one commentator has put it, "The best evidence for the existence of international law is that every actual State recognizes that it does exist and that it is itself under an obligation to observe it. States often violate international law, just as individuals often violate municipal law; but no more than individuals do States defend their violations by claiming that they are above the law." J. Brierly, *The Outlook for International Law* 4-5 (Oxford 1944).

[16] *See* note 4, *supra; see also Ireland v. United Kingdom*, Judgment of Jan. 18, 1978 (European Court of Human Rights), *summarized in* (1978) Yearbook, European Convention on Human Rights 602 (Council of Europe) (holding that Britain's subjection of prisoners to sleep deprivation, hooding, exposure to hissing noise, reduced diet and standing against a wall for hours was "inhuman and degrading," but not "torture" within meaning of European Convention on Human Rights).

rent usage and practice of international law. The treaties and accords cited above, as well as the express foreign policy of our own government,[17] all make it clear that international law confers fundamental rights upon all people vis-a-vis their own governments. While the ultimate scope of those rights will be a subject for continuing refinement and elaboration, we hold that the right to be free from torture is now among them. We therefore turn to the question whether the other requirements for jurisdiction are met.

III

Appellee submits that even if the tort alleged is a violation of modern international law, federal jurisdiction may not be exercised consistent with the dictates of Article III of the Constitution. The claim is without merit. Common law courts of general jurisdiction regularly adjudicate transitory tort claims between individuals over whom they exercise personal jurisdiction, wherever the tort occurred. Moreover, as part of an articulated scheme of federal control over external affairs, Congress provided, in the first Judiciary Act, § 9(b), 1 Stat. 73, 77 (1789), for federal jurisdiction over suits by aliens where principles of international law are in issue. The constitutional basis for the Alien Tort Statute is the law of nations, which has always been part of the federal common law.

It is not extraordinary for a court to adjudicate a tort claim arising outside of its territorial jurisdiction. A state or nation has a legitimate interest in the orderly resolution of disputes among those within its borders, and where the *lex loci delicti commissi* is applied, it is an expression of comity to give effect to the laws of the state where the wrong occurred. Thus, Lord Mansfield in *Mostyn v. Fabrigas*, 1 Cowp. 161 (1774), *quoted in McKenna v. Fisk*, 42 U.S. (1 How.) 241, 248, 11 L.Ed. 117 (1843) said:

> [I]f A becomes indebted to B, or commits a tort upon his person or upon his personal property in Paris, an action in either case may be maintained against A in England, if he is there found . . . . As to transitory actions, there is not a colour of doubt but that any action which is transitory may be laid in any county in England, though the matter arises beyond the seas.

---

[17] *E. g.*, 22 U.S.C. § 2304(a)(2) ("Except under circumstances specified in this section, no security assistance may be provided to any country the government of which engages in a consistent pattern of gross violations of internationally recognized human rights."); 22 U.S.C. § 2151(a) ("The Congress finds that fundamental political, economic, and technological changes have resulted in the interdependence of nations. The Congress declares that the individual liberties, economic prosperity, and security of the people of the United States are best sustained and enhanced in a community of nations which respect individual civil and economic rights and freedoms.").

Mostyn came into our law as the original basis for state court jurisdiction over out-of-state torts, *McKenna v. Fisk, supra,* 42 U.S. (1 How.) 241, 11 L.Ed. 117 (personal injury suits held transitory); *Dennick v. Railroad Co.,* 103 U.S. 11, 26 L.Ed. 439 (1880) (wrongful death action held transitory), and it has not lost its force in suits to recover for a wrongful death occurring upon foreign soil, *Slater v. Mexican National Railroad Co.,* 194 U.S. 120, 24 S.Ct. 581, 48 L.Ed. 900 (1904), as long as the conduct complained of was unlawful where performed. *Restatement (Second) of Foreign Relations Law of the United States* § 19 (1965). Here, where in personam jurisdiction has been obtained over the defendant, the parties agree that the acts alleged would violate Paraguayan law, and the policies of the forum are consistent with the foreign law,[18] state court jurisdiction would be proper. Indeed, appellees conceded as much at oral argument.

Recalling that *Mostyn* was freshly decided at the time the Constitution was ratified, we proceed to consider whether the First Congress acted constitutionally in vesting jurisdiction over "foreign suits," *Slater, supra,* 194 U.S. at 124, 24 S.Ct. at 582, alleging torts committed in violation of the law of nations. A case properly "aris(es) under the . . . laws of the United States" for Article III purposes if grounded upon statutes enacted by Congress or upon the common law of the United States. *See Illinois v. City of Milwaukee,* 406 U.S. 91, 99-100, 92 S.Ct. 1385, 1390-91, 31 L.Ed.2d 712 (1972); *Ivy Broadcasting Co., Inc. v. American Tel. & Tel. Co.,* 391 F.2d 486, 492 (2d Cir. 1968). The law of nations forms an integral part of the common law, and a review of the history surrounding the adoption of the Constitution demonstrates that it became a part of the common law of the *United States* upon the adoption of the Constitution. Therefore, the enactment of the Alien Tort Statute was authorized by Article III.

During the eighteenth century, it was taken for granted on both sides of the Atlantic that the law of nations forms a part of the common law. 1 Blackstone, Commentaries 263-64 (1st Ed. 1765-69); 4 *id.* at 67.[19] Under the Articles of Confederation, the Pennsylvania Court of Oyer and Terminer at Philadelphia, *per* McKean, Chief Justice, applied the law of nations to the

---

[18] Conduct of the type alleged here would be actionable under 42 U.S.C. § 1983 or, undoubtedly, the Constitution, if performed by a government official.

[19] As Lord Stowell said in *The Maria,* 165 Eng. Rep. 955, 958 (Adm. 1807): "In the first place it is to be recollected, that this is a Court of the Law of Nations, though sitting here under the authority of the King of Great Britain. It belongs to other nations as well as to our own; and what foreigners have a right to demand from it, is the administration of the law of nations, simply, and exclusively of the introduction of principles borrowed from our own municipal jurisprudence, to which it is well known, they have at all times expressed no inconsiderable repugnance."

criminal prosecution of the Chevalier de Longchamps for his assault upon the person of the French Consul-General to the United States, noting that "(t)his law, in its full extent, is a part of the law of this state . . . ." *Republica v. DeLongchamps*, 1 U.S. (1 Dall.) 113, 119, 1 L.Ed. 59 (1784). Thus, a leading commentator has written:

> It is an ancient and a salutary feature of the Anglo-American legal tradition that the Law of Nations is a part of the law of the land to be ascertained and administered, like any other, in the appropriate case. This doctrine was originally conceived and formulated in England in response to the demands of an expanding commerce and under the influence of theories widely accepted in the late sixteenth, the seventeenth and the eighteenth centuries. It was brought to America in the colonial years as part of the legal heritage from England. It was well understood by men of legal learning in America in the eighteenth century when the United Colonies broke away from England to unite effectively, a little later, in the United States of America.

Dickenson, "The Law of Nations as Part of the National Law of the United States," 101 *U. Pa. L. Rev.* 26, 27 (1952).

Indeed, Dickenson goes on to demonstrate, *id.* at 34-41, that one of the principal defects of the Confederation that our Constitution was intended to remedy was the central government's inability to "cause infractions of treaties or of the law of nations, to be punished." 1 Farrand, Records of the Federal Convention 19 (Rev. ed. 1937) (Notes of James Madison). And, in Jefferson's words, the very purpose of the proposed Union was "(t)o make us one nation as to foreign concerns, and keep us distinct in domestic ones." Dickenson, *supra*, at 36 n. 28.

As ratified, the judiciary article contained no express reference to cases arising under the law of nations. Indeed, the only express reference to that body of law is contained in Article I, sec. 8, cl. 10, which grants to the Congress the power to "define and punish . . . offenses against the law of nations." Appellees seize upon this circumstance and advance the proposition that the law of nations forms a part of the laws of the United States only to the extent that Congress has acted to define it. This extravagant claim is amply refuted by the numerous decisions applying rules of international law uncodified in any act of Congress. *E.g., Ware v. Hylton*, 3 U.S. (3 Dall.) 198, 1 L.Ed. 568 (1796); *The Paquete Habana, supra*, 175 U.S. 677, 20 S.Ct. 290, 44 L.Ed. 320; *Sabbatino, supra*, 376 U.S. 398, 84 S.Ct. 923, 11 L.Ed.2d 804 (1964). A similar argument was offered to and rejected by the Supreme Court in *United States v. Smith, supra*, 18 U.S. (5 Wheat.) 153, 158-

60, 5 L.Ed. 57 and we reject it today. As John Jay wrote in *The Federalist* No. 3, at 22 (1 Bourne ed. 1901), "Under the national government, treaties and articles of treaties, as well as the laws of nations, will always be expounded in one sense and executed in the same manner, whereas adjudications on the same points and questions in the thirteen states will not always accord or be consistent." Federal jurisdiction over cases involving international law is clear.

Thus, it was hardly a radical initiative for Chief Justice Marshall to state in *The Nereide*, 13 U.S. (9 Cranch) 388, 422, 3 L.Ed. 769 (1815), that in the absence of a congressional enactment,[20] United States courts are "bound by the law of nations, which is a part of the law of the land." These words were echoed in *The Paquete Habana, supra,* 175 U.S. at 700, 20 S.Ct. at 299: "[i]nternational law is part of our law, and must be ascertained and administered by the courts of justice of appropriate jurisdiction, as often as questions of right depending upon it are duly presented for their determination."

The Filartigas urge that 28 U.S.C. § 1350 be treated as an exercise of Congress's power to define offenses against the law of nations. While such a reading is possible, *see Lincoln Mills v. Textile Workers*, 353 U.S. 488, 77 S.Ct. 912, 1 L.Ed.2d 972 (1957) (jurisdictional statute authorizes judicial explication of federal common law), we believe it is sufficient here to construe the Alien Tort Statute, not as granting new rights to aliens, but simply as opening the federal courts for adjudication of the rights already recognized by international law. The statute nonetheless does inform our analysis of Article III, for we recognize that questions of jurisdiction "must be considered part of an organic growth part of an evolutionary process," and that the history of the judiciary article gives meaning to its pithy phrases. *Romero v. International Terminal Operating Co.*, 358 U.S. 354, 360, 79 S.Ct. 468, 473, 3 L.Ed.2d 368 (1959). The Framers' overarching concern that control over international affairs be vested in the new national government to safeguard the standing of the United States among the nations of the world therefore reinforces the result we reach today.

Although the Alien Tort Statute has rarely been the basis for jurisdiction during its long history,[21] in light of the foregoing discussion, there can

---

[20] The plainest evidence that international law has an existence in the federal courts independent of acts of Congress is the long-standing rule of construction first enunciated by Chief Justice Marshall: "an act of congress ought never to be construed to violate the law of nations, if any other possible construction remains . . . ." *The Charming Betsy,* 6 U.S. (2 Cranch), 34, 67, 2 L.Ed. 208 (1804), *quoted in Lauritzen v. Larsen,* 345 U.S. 571, 578, 73 S.Ct. 921, 926, 97 L.Ed. 1254 (1953).

[21] Section 1350 afforded the basis for jurisdiction over a child custody suit between aliens in *Adra v. Clift,* 195 F. Supp. 857 (D.Md. 1961), with a falsified passport supplying

be little doubt that this action is properly brought in federal court.[22] This is undeniably an action by an alien, for a tort only, committed in violation of the law of nations. The paucity of suits successfully maintained under the section is readily attributable to the statute's requirement of alleging a "*violation* of the law of nations" (emphasis supplied) at the jurisdictional threshold. Courts have, accordingly, engaged in a more searching preliminary review of the merits than is required, for example, under the more flexible "arising under" formulation. *Compare O'Reilly de Camara v. Brooke*, 209 U.S. 45, 52, 28 S.Ct. 439, 441, 52 L.Ed. 676 (1907) (question of Alien Tort Statute jurisdiction disposed of "on the merits") (Holmes, J.), *with Bell v. Hood*, 327 U.S. 678, 66 S.Ct. 773, 90 L.Ed. 939 (1946) (general federal question jurisdiction not defeated by the possibility that the averments in the complaint may fail to state a cause of action). Thus, the narrowing construction that the Alien Tort Statute has previously received reflects the fact that earlier cases did not involve such well-established, universally recognized norms of international law that are here at issue.

For example, the statute does not confer jurisdiction over an action by a Luxembourgeois international investment trust's suit for fraud, conversion and corporate waste. *IIT v. Vencap*, 519 F.2d 1001, 1015 (1975). In *IIT*, Judge Friendly astutely noted that the mere fact that every nation's municipal law may prohibit theft does not incorporate "the Eighth Commandment, 'Thou Shalt not steal' . . . (into) the law of nations." It is only where the nations of the world have demonstrated that the wrong is of mutual, and not merely several, concern, by means of express international accords, that a wrong generally recognized becomes an international law violation within the meaning of the statute. Other recent § 1350 cases are similarly distinguishable.[23]

---

the requisite international law violation. In *Bolchos v. Darrell*, 3 Fed.Cas. 810 (D.S.C.1795), the Alien Tort Statute provided an alternative basis of jurisdiction over a suit to determine title to slaves on board an enemy vessel taken on the high seas.

[22] We recognize that our reasoning might also sustain jurisdiction under the general federal question provision, 28 U.S.C. § 1331. We prefer, however, to rest our decision upon the Alien Tort Statute, in light of that provision's close coincidence with the jurisdictional facts presented in this case. *See Romero v. International Terminal Operating Co.*, 358 U.S. 354, 79 S.Ct. 468, 3 L.Ed.2d 368 (1959).

[23] *Dreyfus v. von Finck*, 534 F.2d 24 (2d Cir.), cert. denied, 429 U.S. 835, 97 S.Ct. 102, 50 L.Ed.2d 101 (1976), concerned a forced sale of property, and thus sought to invoke international law in an area in which no consensus view existed. *See Sabbatino, supra*, 376 U.S. at 428, 84 S.Ct. at 940. Similarly, *Benjamins v. British European Airways*, 572 F.2d 913 (2d Cir. 1978), *cert. denied*, 439 U.S. 1114, 99 S.Ct. 1016, 59 L.Ed.2d 72 (1979), held only that an air disaster, even if caused by "willful" negligence, does not constitute a law of nations violation. *Id.* at 916. In *Khedivial Line, S.A.E. v. Seafarers' International Union*, 278 F.2d 49 (2d Cir. 1960), we found that the "right" to free access to the ports of a foreign nation was at best a rule of comity, and not a binding rule of international law.

IIT adopted a dictum from *Lopes v. Reederei Richard Schroder*, 225 F.Supp. 292 (E.D. Pa. 1963) to the effect that "a violation of the law of nations arises only when there has been 'a violation by one or more individuals of those standards, rules or customs (a) affecting the relationship between states or between an individual and a foreign state and (b) used by those states for their common good and/or in dealings *inter se*.'" *IIT, supra*, 519 F.2d at 1015, *quoting Lopes, supra*, 225 F.Supp. at 297. We have no quarrel with this formulation so long as it be understood that the courts are not to prejudge the scope of the issues that the nations of the world may deem important to their interrelationships, and thus to their common good. As one commentator has noted:

> the sphere of domestic jurisdiction is not an irreducible sphere of rights which are somehow inherent, natural, or fundamental. It does not create an impenetrable barrier to the development of international law. Matters of domestic jurisdiction are not those which are unregulated by international law, but those which are left by international law for regulation by States. There are, therefore, no matters which are domestic by their 'nature.' All are susceptible of international legal regulation and may become the subjects of new rules of customary law of treaty obligations.

Preuss, "Article 2, Paragraph 7 of the Charter of the United Nations and Matters of Domestic Jurisdiction," Hague *Receuil* (Extract, 149) at 8, *reprinted in* H. Briggs, The Law of Nations 24 (1952). Here, the nations have made it their business, both through international accords and unilateral action,[24] to be concerned with domestic human rights violations of this magnitude. The case before us therefore falls within the *Lopes/IIT* rule.

Since federal jurisdiction may properly be exercised over the Filartigas' claim, the action must be remanded for further proceedings. Appellee Pena, however, advances several additional points that lie beyond the scope of our holding on jurisdiction. Both to emphasize the boundaries of our

---

The cases from other circuits are distinguishable in like manner. The court in *Huynh Thi Anh v. Levi*, 586 F.2d 625 (6th Cir. 1978), was unable to discern from the traditional sources of the law of nations "a universal or generally accepted substantive rule or principle" governing child custody, *id.* at 629, and therefore held jurisdiction to be lacking. *Cf. Nguyen Da Yen v. Kissinger*, 528 F.2d 1194, 1201 n.13 (9th Cir. 1975) ("the illegal seizure, removal and detention of an alien against his will in a foreign country would appear to be a tort . . . and it may well be a tort in violation of the 'law of nations'") (§ 1350 question not reached due to inadequate briefing). Finally, the district court in *Lopes v. Reederei Richard Schroder*, 225 F.Supp. 292 (E.D.Pa. 1963) simply found that the doctrine of seaworthiness, upon which the plaintiff relied, was a uniquely American concept, and therefore not a part of the law of nations.

holding, and to clarify some of the issues reserved for the district court on remand, we will address these contentions briefly.

IV

Pena argues that the customary law of nations, as reflected in treaties and declarations that are not self-executing, should not be applied as rules of decision in this case. In doing so, he confuses the question of federal jurisdiction under the Alien Tort Statute, which requires consideration of the law of nations, with the issue of the choice of law to be applied, which will be addressed at a later stage in the proceedings. The two issues are distinct. Our holding on subject matter jurisdiction decides only whether Congress intended to confer judicial power, and whether it is authorized to do so by Article III. The choice of law inquiry is a much broader one, primarily concerned with fairness, *see Home Insurance Co. v. Dick*, 281 U.S. 397, 50 S.Ct. 338, 74 L.Ed. 926 (1930); consequently, it looks to wholly different considerations. *See Lauritzen v. Larsen*, 345 U.S. 571, 73 S.Ct. 921, 97 L.Ed. 1254 (1954). Should the district court decide that the *Lauritzen* analysis requires it to apply Paraguayan law, our courts will not have occasion to consider what law would govern a suit under the Alien Tort Statute where the challenged conduct is actionable under the law of the forum and the law of nations, but not the law of the jurisdiction in which the tort occurred.[25]

---

[24] As President Carter stated in his address to the United Nations on March 17, 1977:

All the signatories of the United Nations Charter have pledged themselves to observe and to respect basic human rights. Thus, no member of the United Nations can claim that mistreatment of the citizens is solely its own business. Equally, no member can avoid its responsibilities to review and to speak when torture or unwarranted deprivation occurs in any part of the world.

Reprinted in 78 *Department of State Bull.* 322 (1977); see note 17, *supra.*

[25] In taking that broad range of factors into account, the district court may well decide that fairness requires it to apply Paraguayan law to the instant case. *See Slater v. Mexican National Railway Co.*, 194 U.S. 120, 24 S.Ct. 581, 48 L.Ed. 900 (1904). Such a decision would not retroactively oust the federal court of subject matter jurisdiction, even though plaintiff's cause of action would no longer properly be "created" by a law of the United States. *See American Well Works Co. v. Layne & Bowler Co.*, 241 U.S. 257, 260, 36 S.Ct. 585, 586, 60 L.Ed. 987 (1916) (Holmes, J.). Once federal jurisdiction is established by a colorable claim under federal law at a preliminary stage of the proceeding, subsequent dismissal of that claim (here, the claim under the general international proscription of torture) does not deprive the court of jurisdiction previously established. *See Hagans v. Lavine*, 415 U.S. 528, 94 S.Ct. 1372, 39 L.Ed.2d 577 (1974); *Romero v. International Terminal Operating Co.*, 358 U.S. 354, 79 S.Ct. 468, 3 L.Ed.2d 368 (1959); *Bell v. Hood*, 327 U.S. 678, 66 S.Ct. 773, 90 L.Ed. 939 (1946). *Cf. Huynh Thi Ahn, supra*, 586 F.2d at 633 (choice of municipal law ousts § 1350 jurisdiction when no international norms exist).

Pena also argues that "[i]f the conduct complained of is alleged to be the act of the Paraguayan government, the suit is barred by the Act of State doctrine." This argument was not advanced below, and is therefore not before us on this appeal. We note in passing, however, that we doubt whether action by a state official in violation of the Constitution and laws of the Republic of Paraguay, and wholly unratified by that nation's government, could properly be characterized as an act of state. *See Banco Nacional de Cuba v. Sabbatino, supra,* 376 U.S. 398, 84 S.Ct. 923, 11 L.Ed.2d 804; *Underhill v. Hernandez,* 168 U.S. 250, 18 S.Ct. 83, 42 L.Ed. 456 (1897). Paraguay's renunciation of torture as a legitimate instrument of state policy, however, does not strip the tort of its character as an international law violation, if it in fact occurred under color of government authority. *See* Declaration on the Protection of All Persons from Being Subjected to Torture, *supra* note 11; *cf. Ex parte Young,* 209 U.S. 123, 28 S.Ct. 441, 52 L.Ed. 714 (1908) (state official subject to suit for constitutional violations despite immunity of state).

Finally, we have already stated that we do not reach the critical question of *forum non conveniens,* since it was not considered below. In closing, however, we note that the foreign relations implications of this and other issues the district court will be required to adjudicate on remand underscores the wisdom of the First Congress in vesting jurisdiction over such claims in the federal district courts through the Alien Tort Statute. Questions of this nature are fraught with implications for the nation as a whole, and therefore should not be left to the potentially varying adjudications of the courts of the fifty states.

In the twentieth century the international community has come to recognize the common danger posed by the flagrant disregard of basic human rights and particularly the right to be free of torture. Spurred first by the Great War, and then the Second, civilized nations have banded together to prescribe acceptable norms of international behavior. From the ashes of the Second World War arose the United Nations Organization, amid hopes that an era of peace and cooperation had at last begun. Though many of these aspirations have remained elusive goals, that circumstance cannot diminish the true progress that has been made. In the modern age, humanitarian and practical considerations have combined to lead the nations of the world to recognize that respect for fundamental human rights is in their individual and collective interest. Among the rights universally proclaimed by all nations, as we have noted, is the right to be free of physical torture. Indeed, for purposes of civil liability, the torturer has become—like the pirate and slave trader before him—*hostis humani generis,* an enemy of all mankind. Our holding today, giving effect to a jurisdictional provision enacted by our First Congress, is a small but important step in the fulfillment of the ageless dream to free all people from brutal violence.

SEPTEMBER 3, 1980: UNITED STATES

Correspondence from Defense Counsel Murry Brochin to U.S. District Court Judge Nickerson

LOWENSTEIN, SANDLER, BROCHIN, KOHL, FISHER & BOYLAN
A PROFESSIONAL CORPORATION

September 3, 1980

PLEASE REPLY TO ROSELAND
REFER TO FILE NO. P 4136

Honorable Eugene H. Nickerson
United States District Court
Eastern District of New York
United States Court House
225 Cadman Plaza East
Brooklyn, New York

Re: 79 C 917
Filartiga v.Pena-Irala, et als

My dear Judge Nickerson:

I enclose a copy of a Notice of Motion returnable before your Honor on October 3, 1980 for leave to withdraw as attorneys for defendants in the above-entitled matter. I have filed the original with the clerk of the court.

I respectfully request that your Honor accept the enclosed affidavit in lieu of a brief. My grounds for leave to withdraw are as appears from the affidavit, that we have not been paid the balance of an agreed fee for services heretofore rendered and we have been advised that we would not be paid for any further services. In addition, it appears that it would be difficult or impossible to communicate readily with Mr. Pena Irala.

This motion is being submitted to your Honor on the enclosed papers. I do not believe that oral argument will be necessary although, of course, I am ready to appear in person before your Honor at your direction.

Respectfully yours,

Murry D. Brochin

MDB : abc
Encl.

cc: All Counsel, w/encl.
Norberto Pena-Irala, w/encl.

SEPTEMBER 3, 1980: UNITED STATES

Affidavit of Murry D. Brochin in Support of Motion to Withdraw as Attorney

UNITED STATES DISTRICT COURT
EASTERN DISTRICT OF NEW YORK

DOLLY M.E. FILARTIGA and DR. JOEL FILARTIGA,	**AFFIDAVIT OF MURRY D. BROCHIN IN SUPPORT OF MOTION TO WITHDRAW AS ATTORNEY**
Plaintiffs,	**79 Civ. 917**
— against –	
AMERICO NORBERTO PENA-IRALA, LEONEL CASTILLO, et als.	
Defendants.	

MURRY D. BROCHIN, of full age, being duly sworn according to law upon his oath deposes and says that:

1. I am an attorney at law of the State of New Jersey and a member of the firm of Lowenstein, Sandler, Brochin, Kohl, Fisher & Boylan, A Professional Corporation, with our offices at 65 Livingston Avenue, Roseland, New Jersey, 07068. I am not a member of the bar of the United States District Court for the Eastern District of New York, but I was admitted *pro hoc vice* for purposes of the above-entitled case.

2. Our firm was first contacted about representing the individual defendants in this matter shortly before May 1, 1979. We were introduced to the case by Robert G. Rebollo, Esq., of the firm of Fragano, Rebollo & Barone, 4044 Hylan Boulevard, Staten Island, New York 10308. Mr. Robollo's representation of defendants began on or about April 9, 1979. The firm of Fragano, Rebollo & Barone, Esq., was retained on behalf of the individual defendants by Dr. Jose Emilio Gorostiaga, a Paraguayan attorney whose offices are located at 14 de Mayo Street, Asuncion, Paraguay

3. Prior to our firm's entry into the case, Mr. Rebollo conferred at length with Dr. Gorostiaga and others and made various applications to the Court

in connection with the individual defendants' detention, the stay of their deportation and this Court's Order to Show Cause dated April 9, 1979. Mr. Rebollo recommended the retention of our firm as co-counsel in the matter and, with the authorization of Dr. Jose Emilio Gorostiaga on behalf of the individual defendants, contacted us to discuss the nature of the case and to request us to join with him in representing the individual defendants. Our assistance was requested because of the difficulties presented by the fact that the individual defendants were being held in detention, the short return date of the Order to Show Cause and the novel, complicated and somewhat esoteric issues raised by the case.

4. Neither I nor any representative of our law firm, nor, I am advised Mr. Rebollo or anyone from his law firm has ever communicated directly with Mr. Norberto Pena-Irala or any of the other individual defendants. All of our communications have been with Dr. Jose Emilio Gorostiaga, Mr. Pena-Irala's Paraguayan attorney. The only time that I have ever seen Mr. Pena-Irala was in court on the return date of the Order to Show Cause. I do not speak Spanish and, insofar as I am aware, Mr. Pena-Irala does not speak English. During the period when I was present in the courtroom while Mr. Pena-Irala was there, Dr. Gorostiaga had not yet arrived and so there was no one available through whom I could speak to Mr. Pena-Irala. I am advised that Mr. Rebollo has met Mr. Pena-Irala only once or twice in the courtroom or in the corridors of the courthouse. Accordingly, the arrangements for our fees were made with Dr. Gorostiaga and he has transmitted whatever payments we have received.

5. The financial arrangements which Mr. Rebollo and I on behalf of our respective firms made with the individual defendants through Dr. Gorostiaga were that in return for an agreed fee, we would undertake to represent the individual defendants to obtain the court's determination of our motions to dismiss the suit for lack of jurisdiction and to vacate the stay of the deportation order on various procedural and substantive grounds. In fact, for that agreed fee, we not only represented the individual defendants through the decision by the United States District Court for the Eastern District of New York, but we also defended actively against the plaintiffs' application for a stay to the United States Court of Appeals for the Second Circuit, submitting a letter memorandum and presenting oral argument in opposition to the motion, and we also filed papers on behalf of the individual defendants in opposition to plaintiffs' application for a stay to the United States Supreme Court. At the standard rates customarily charged by Mr. Rebollo's firm and mine, our fees for the time expended on behalf of the individual defendants through the denial of plaintiffs' application for a stay to the United States Supreme Court substantially exceeded the amount of our agreed fee.

6. When the United States Supreme Court denied plaintiffs' application for a further stay of the deportation of the individual defendants, they immediately left the country. Thereafter, a Notice of Appeal was filed on behalf of defendants and I wrote a letter to Dr. Gorostiaga advising him of the appeal and informing him what our further fees would be for representing Mr. Norberto Pena-Irala in connection with the Appeal. In due course, we were advised by Dr. Jose Emilio Gorostiaga that our requested fees were acceptable to Mr. Pena-Irala and we received a partial payment on account. After receipt of that initial payment, we continued with preparation of our papers for the Court of Appeals and did, in fact, file a brief and present oral argument on behalf of defendant Pena-Irala. However, no part of the agreed fee for our services in connection with the defense of the appeal to the Court of Appeals for the Second Circuit was paid except for the initial payment on account. The greater part of the agreed fee for those services still remains unpaid.

7. Following receipt of the Opinion of the United States Court of Appeals for the Second Circuit which reversed the judgment below, I immediately communicated with Dr. Gorostiaga, sending him a copy of the Opinion, advising him of the legal implications of the decision and of the time limits for further action, and requesting his instructions.

8. On July 28, 1980, I received a written reply from Dr. Gorostiaga. He informed me that Mr. Pena-Irala was unable to pay the balance due for our legal services thus far rendered or to pay any further fees to represent him, either to file a petition for certiorari or to defend the suit in the United States District Court. Dr. Gorostiaga's letter recognized that under those circumstances we would probably seek leave to withdraw as attorneys.

9. Obviously the further defense of this suit will be extremely time consuming and expensive. The difficulties and expenses are increased because of the fact that Mr. Pena-Irala is, as far as I am aware, in Paraguay. Under the circumstances, we respectfully request permission of the Court to withdraw as attorneys for the individual defendants.

———————————————

Murry D. Brochin

Dated: Sept. 3, 1980

APRIL 8, 1981: UNITED STATES

Revised Notice of Plaintiffs' Application for Default Judgment

UNITED STATES DISTRICT COURT
EASTERN DISTRICT OF NEW YORK

DOLLY M.E. FILARTIGA and DR. JOEL FILARTIGA,	**REVISED NOTICE OF PLAINTIFFS' APPLICATION FOR DEFAULT PURSUANT TO FEDERAL RULES OF CIVIL**
Plaintiffs,	**PROCEDURE 55(b)(2)**
– against –	
AMERICO NORBERTO PENA-IRALA, et al.,	
Defendants.	

TO: Jose Emilio Gorostiaga
     14 de Mayo No. 158 Of. 315
     Asuncion, Paraguay

PLEASE TAKE NOTICE that the undersigned will make application pursuant to Federal Rules of Civil Procedure 55(b)(2) to this Court in Room 11, United States Courthouse, 225 Cadman Plaza East, Brooklyn, New York 11201, on the 15th day of May, 1981 at 9:30 o'clock in the forenoon of that day for entry of a default judgment of liability for the kidnapping, torture and murder, of plaintiffs' decedent Joelito Filartiga and for the intentional infliction of emotional suffering upon plaintiff Dolly Filartiga, in favor of plaintiffs and against the defendant Pena Irala in a sum not to exceed $10,000,000 plus costs and fees.

> PETER WEISS
> RHONDA COPELON
> JOSE ANTONIO LUGO
> c/o Center for Constitutional Rights
> 853 Broadway
> New York, New York 10003
> (212) 674-3303
>
> MICHAEL MAGGIO
> Goren & Maggio
> 1801 Columbia Rd. N.W.
> Washington, D.C. 20009

Dated: April 8, 1981

UNITED STATES DISTRICT COURT
FOR THE EASTERN DISTRICT OF NEW YORK

DOLLY M.E. FILARTIGA and
JOEL FILARTIGA,

Plaintiffs,

v.

AMERICO NORBERTO PEÑA-
IRALA,

Defendant.

**AFFIRMATION IN SUPPORT
OF MOTION FOR JUDGMENT
BY DEFAULT PURSUANT
F.R. CIV. P. 55(b)(2)**

79 CIV 917

RHONDA COPELON hereby affirms under penalties of perjury that:

1. I am one of counsel for plaintiffs and make this affirmation in support of plaintiffs' motion for default judgment against defendant America Norberto Pena-Irala (hereinafter Pena).

2. As set forth below, a default judgment on the question of liability should be entered by the Court pursuant to F.R.Civ.P. 55(b)(2) because the defendant had failed to answer the Complaint in timely fashion as prescribed by F.R.Civ.P. 12(a)(1).

3. In accordance with the Circuit Court's procedures, one of the clerks, Ms. Chin, advised Audrey Seniors a legal worker under my direction, that a copy of the decision and order of the court was duly sent to all counsel of record which included at that time the law firm of Lowenstein, Sandler, Brochin, Kohl, Fisher and Boylan of Newark, New Jersey and Fragano, Rebollo & Barone of Staten Island, New York. Mr. Murry D. Brochin has acknowledged receipt of the opinion. (Affidavit of Murry D. Brochin In Support of Motion to Withdraw As Attorney, dated September 3, 1980 ¶ 7 p.4).

4. In addition, Mr. Brochin avers that he thereafter "immediately communicated with Dr. Gorostiaga (the defendant's Paraguayan attorney), sending him a copy of the decision and of the time limits for further action . . . ." Ibid. In response Dr. Gorostiga advised that the defendant could not pay for further services and anticipated the motion of the attorneys to withdraw (*id.* at p.4 ¶ 4) which was granted by this Court on November 7, 1980. (Endorsement on Notice of Motion For Leave to Withdraw).

5. It is thus clear from the affidavit of Mr. Brochin that the defendant, by and through his attorneys, has been properly served with the Opinion of the Circuit Court, and has had over seven months to answer the complaint. The failure to answer is, therefore, far in excess of the 13 days following service of the Court's action, as allowed by Rule 12 (a)(1). See 2A Moore's Federal Practice §12.06 [1-3].

6. This case is accordingly ripe for entry of a default judgment pursuant to F.R.Civ.P. 55(b)(2). While the rules allow 3 day notice of a hearing on an application for a default judgment, plaintiffs have scheduled the hearing date for 30 days from the filing of this motion given that this Notice must be sent to the defendant via his attorney Dr. Gorostiaga in Paraguay.

7. At that time, plaintiffs will ask the Court for a judgment by default pursuant to F.R.Civ.P. 55 (b)(2) holding defendant liable for kidnapping and torture resulting in the death of Joelito Filartiga and the intentional infliction of emotional suffering upon plaintiffs as alleged in the Complaint.

8. Thereafter, at a time to be set by the Court, plaintiffs will present evidence necessary to determining the amount of damages to which plaintiffs are entitled.

RHONDA COPELON

Dated: New York, New York
        April 3, 1981

U.S. District Court for the Eastern District of New York: Order Entering Default Judgment

UNITED STATES DISTRICT COURT
EASTERN DISTRICT OF NEW YORK

DOLLY M.E. FILARTIGA and **ORDER**
DR. JOEL FILARTIGA,
79 Civ 917
      Plaintiffs,

  – against –

AMERICO NORBERTO PENA-
IRALA, ET AL.,
      Defendants.

NICKERSON, District Judge

This is a motion by plaintiffs for the entry of a judgment of default against defendant Pena-Irala pursuant to Federal Rule of Civil Procedure 55(b)(2).

Plaintiffs brought this action "for damages for violation of human rights for the wrongful torture and murder of the decedent Joel Filartiga" against the former Inspector General of Police of Asuncion, Paraguay, who was then being held in custody by the Immigration and Naturalization Service as an illegal alien. Defendant Pena-Irala made a timely motion to dismiss the complaint for lack of subject matter jurisdiction. Defendant was represented by two firms of American attorneys and by Paraguayan counsel, Dr. Jose Emilio Gorostiaga. By a Memorandum and Order of this court filed on May 16, 1979, the motion to dismiss was granted and the stay of defendant's deportation was continued for 48 hours to enable plaintiffs to apply to the Court of Appeals for the Second Circuit for a further stay.

On May 22, 1979 the Court of Appeals denied plaintiff's motion for a further stay and defendant shortly thereafter returned to Paraguay. He has apparently not returned to this jurisdiction since that time.

On June 30, 1980, the Court of Appeals reversed this court's grant of defendant's motion to dismiss and remanded the action for further proceedings. Since that decision was rendered, defendant has failed to answer or otherwise take part in this action. Defendant's American attorneys thereafter moved for leave to withdraw from this action, stating, in an affidavit of Murry D. Brochin, Esq., that they had sent a copy of the Opinion of the Court of Appeals to defendant through his Paraguayan counsel, and that they had been informed by Dr. Gorostiaga that defendant was unable to pay for further services. On November 7, 1980, the motion to withdraw was granted.

Federal Rule of Civil Procedure 12(a)(1) provides that a responsive pleading shall be filed within 10 days of notice of the denial of a motion made pursuant to Rule 12. As is established in the affidavit of Mr. Brochin, defendant Pena-Irala received notice of the decision of the Court of Appeals denying his motion to dismiss shortly after it was rendered, through his American and Paraguayan attorneys. By affidavit of Rhonda Copelon, Esq., plaintiff states that notice of the instant motion was sent to defendant Pena-Irala through his Paraguayan attorney thirty days prior to its presentation to the court.

The motion for entry of a default judgment is granted. The issue of the amount of damages due plaintiffs is respectfully referred to Magistrate John Caden for determination. So ordered.

_____

Eugene H. Nickerson, U.S.D.J.

Dated: Brooklyn, New York
June 23, 1981

The Clerk shall make copies of this Memorandum and Order and serve it upon the parties and Magistrate John Caden.

FEBRUARY 12, 1982: UNITED STATES

Transcript of Hearing on Damages Before the U.S. District Court for the Eastern District of New York

**UNITED STATES DISTRICT COURT
EASTERN DISTRICT OF NEW YORK**

DOLLY M.E. FILARTIGA and DR. JOEL FILARTIGA,	**HEARING ON DAMAGES**
	79 Civ 917
Plaintiffs, – against –	
AMERICO NORBERTO PENA- IRALA, et al,	
Defendants.	

United States Courthouse
Brooklyn, New York

February 12, 1982
9:00 A.M. o'clock

Before:

     HONORABLE JOHN L. CADEN, U.S. MAGISTRATE

Appearances:

     RHONDA COPELON, ESQ.,
     BETTY LAWRENCE BAILEY, ESQ.,
     PETER WEISS, ESQ.,
     Center for Constitutional Rights
     853 Broadway
     New York, New York 10003

     MICHAEL MAGGIO, ESQ.,
     1800 Belmont Road, N.W.
     Washington, D.C. 20009

MS. COPELON: We were going to begin this morning with Miss Bailey who is going to make a brief opening, just to set the stage for what we are considering here today.

THE COURT: All right. Miss Bailey, are you ready?

MS. BAILEY: Yes, sir. We just want to point out the importance of this case, that today for the first time in history, a United States Court will sit to vindicate the international guarantee of the human right to be free from torture. These unprecedented proceedings arise out of the landmark decision in the U.S. Court of Appeals for the Second Circuit, in June of 1980.

This decision recognized the right of aliens under the Alien Tort Claims Act to sue in federal court to redress violations of the International Law of Human Rights; in cases where the defendant can be found and sued in this country. We are not here to determine whether the defendant is liable. The issue of liability is settled. This Court has ordered that a default judgment be entered because of defendant's failure to answer plaintiff's complaint.

A default judgment on the issue of liability means that all of the allegations in plaintiffs' complaint are to be taken as true. Accordingly, the following allegations are considered true.

On March 29, 1976, 17 year old Joelito Filartiga was kidnapped and tortured to death by the defendant Pena. His sister, plaintiff Dolly Filartiga was subjected to intentional infliction of emotional pain and suffering when she was summoned a few hours after his death to the defendant's house and led to the mutilated body of her brother, and threatened with a similar fate. Joelito was murdered and tortured by the defendant in retaliation for the political activities and opinions of his father. Further, Dolly Filartiga and her mother were arrested and kept in jail without cause right after the murder.

This hearing will examine the extent of suffering of the plaintiffs. We will present four witnesses; Joelito's father, Mr. Filartiga, and his sister, Dolly, will describe the terrible and lasting impact of the torture and murder upon them. Robert White, the former U.S. Ambassador to Paraguay and later El Salvador will describe the role and impact of torture in maintaining Latin America's most repressive dictator, General Stroessner. Finally, Jacobo Timmerman, the former editor of the Argentinian paper La Opinion, will discuss torture from the perspective of an observer of a society decimated by torture as well as a victim trying to understand the impact of torture on the life of a person.

We will seek damages for the following: The pain and suffering of decedent Joelito Filartiga as a result of the torture. Damages for the wrongful death of Joelito, the pain and suffering which was intentionally inflicted on the plaintiffs as a result of Joelito's torture. And punitive damages to punish the defendant for this most inhuman crime against Joelito, his family, and as Judge Kauffman stated, all humanity.

No amount of money—

THE COURT: Whose law are you applying?

MS. BAILEY: Well, that—we will present additional evidence to you in the form of affidavits and we will present memoranda of law to you addressing those issues.

No amount of money could right the wrong done to Joelito, his family and humanity. However, money damages are the only way the law provides to compensate for the injuries suffered by plaintiffs. Thus, we ask for compensatory and punitive damages in the amount of $10,000,000, not as an evaluation of Joelito. His worth as a human being is beyond monetary evaluation. Nor as an evaluation of the endless suffering of his family. That can never be fully compensated in dollars. But to respond to the wrong done in the only way possible, under our laws. This Court has the responsibility of acting on behalf of the international community, to vindicate the critical international interests of freeing society from torture.

THE COURT: Thank you. Are you ready to proceed?

MS. COPELON: Yes. The first thing I would like to do is qualify Martin Poblete as the translator.

THE COURT: All right.

MS. COPELON: Do you want the witnesses sworn?

THE COURT: Absolutely. I'll do that far as the interpreter is concerned, you can state your qualifications and that will be fine with me.

THE INTERPRETER: Martin Poblete, P-o-b-l-e-t-e. Yes. I am a former professor of European contemporary history at the University of Chile. Here I am teaching Spanish language at the St. Thomas Aquinas College, and I am teaching contemporary history at the Latin American seminar of Columbia University.

THE COURT: That's fine. You can stop right there. You may—who will be your first witness?

MS. COPELON: The first witness is Dolly Filartiga.

THE COURT: All right. Miss Filartiga, raise your right hand, please.

DOLLY FILARTIGA, called as a witness, having been first duly sworn by the Court, testified as follows:

DIRECT EXAMINATION

BY MS. COPELON:

    Q   Dolly, will you tell the Court where you reside today, where you live today?
    A   I live in United States, Manhattan.

MS. COPELON: Magistrate Caden, let me just interrupt for a minute to say that Dolly will testify in part in English and will revert to Spanish when she has troubles.

THE COURT: Fine.

    Q   Dolly, what is your occupation?

THE COURT: Why don't we do it all in Spanish? It is a lot easier, I think. In other words, every question that Miss Copelon asks, you will translate in Spanish. It will be a lot easier.

THE INTERPRETER: Yes, sir.

    A   At this moment I am unemployed.
    Q   In Paraguay, did you have an occupation?
    A   I studied when I was in Paraguay.
    Q   And what did you study in Paraguay?
    A   I finished my primary school and after finishing my high school, I was expecting to continue my studies at the School of Medicine.
    Q   And what was your ambition in studying medicine?
    A   What I was expecting to accomplish was to help people.
    Q   Did you want to become a doctor?
    A   Yes.
    Q   Dolly, are you employed today?
    A   No.
    Q   And are you one of the plaintiffs in this action?

A   Yes.

Q   What is your relationship to this case?

A   I am Joelito Filartiga's sister.

Q   Where do you come from originally?

A   I am from Paraguay.

Q   When did you come to this country?

A   I arrived in the United States three months ago.

Q   How did you come here?

A   I came through Amnesty International and with a waiver visa.

Q   Why did you need a waiver visa?

A   Because I did not have a passport.

Q   What is your legal status here today?

A   I have my application for political asylum pending.

Q   Dolly, could you explain to the Court why you didn't have a passport?

A   Because my passport was taken by the authorities while I was in prison.

Q   Dolly, can you identify this document, which is marked Plaintiff's Exhibit 1-A and 1-B?

A   Yes. This is my application for political asylum.

Q   When did you make that application?

A   I presented this application three months after my arrival in the United States.

MS. COPELON: Magistrate Caden, we'd like to move that as an exhibit, Plaintiff's Exhibits 1-A and 1-B.

THE COURT: Both 1-A and 1-B will be received. (So marked.)

Q   Dolly, what happened precisely that caused you to come when you did to the United States?

A   The tremendous pressure I was receiving in my country by the police, the lack of security I was experiencing. Another reason was that I wanted to have some form of justice.

Q   What happened to make you think that that might—that you should come to this country? What was your purpose in coming here?

A   The purpose of my trip was to search for Pena, whom I knew was living in the United States.

Q   How do you know that?

A   I knew it by a wrong—a mistake. I received a letter he had sent to his family.

Q   What did you learn from the letter?

A   I knew his address.

Q   I want you to turn your attention, Dolly, to the period of time before your brother Joelito was killed.

A   Okay.

Q   How old were you then?

A   I was 20 years old.

Q   How old was he?

A   He was just 17 years old.

Q   Were there other brothers or sisters in your family?

A   Yes, there were some younger brothers.

Q   Who was that?

A   Fourteen year old and eleven year old.

Q   They were your sisters or brothers?

A   They were my sisters.

Q   And where were you living at the time?

A   We had to leave, or our status in Asuncion.

Q   Were your parents living with you at the time?

A   No, they didn't.

Q   Where were they?

A   They lived in Ybycui.

Q   Why were they living in Ybycui?

A   Because they worked there.

Q   How often did you see them?

A   I used to see them for the weekends.

Q   And so who took care of the family during the week when your parents were in Ybycui?

A   My father asked a sailor to take care of us.

Q   Did you also take care of the family?

A   Yes. I was the head of household.

Q   And can you explain what you were doing? Is this the period when you were a student, studying medicine?

A   Yes.

Q   And can you tell us a little about what your life was like in that time?

A   It was as the normal, regular life of any normal family, with the exception that we were the Filartiga family and we were against the Government of Stroessner.

Q   What was your social life like during that time? Did you have friends? Did you go out? What did you do?

A   Yes, we had friends. We used to go out with my brother.

Q   Did you spend a lot of time with your brother?

A   Yes, because we were more or less the same age.

Q   Dolly, I know this is hard, but would you try to tell the Court what your relationship was like with your brother?

A   We were great friends, great companions because our parents were far from us, far away, so we tried to get together as best as we can.

Q   Did you go out together a lot?

A   Yes.

Q   Did you share friends together?

A   Yes.

Q   Did you confide in each other about your lives?

A   Yes, we trusted each other very much.

Q   Dolly, I'm going to show you Plaintiff's Exhibit 2-A and 2-B and ask you to identify them.

A   Yes. This is Joelito when he was five years old. This is Joelito shortly before his death with my sister.

THE COURT: 2-A and 2-B will be received. (So marked.)

Q   What was the date, Dolly, that your brother was killed?

A   He had just arrived from school. We spent a few hours together. Then we went to sleep. About—it was more or less 4:00 o'clock in the morning, we heard a person strong knocking on the door, somebody was strongly knocking on the door. We were awakened by Galeano, the Chief of Police, of the precinct in the neighborhood where we lived.

Because I wanted to know what was going on, I asked him what happened. He answered me that there was small problem with my brother at Pena's house.

Q   Where was Pena's house, Dolly, in relationship to your own house?

A   Both houses were in a row of houses and ours was separated by one house from the house of Pena.

Q   And then what happened? When Galeano came?

A   We walked together to the house of Pena and as soon as we got there, I saw a platoon of policemen in the street and also in the house and I asked where was my brother. I was told that he was at the room, at the back of the house. Knowing the house, I walked to that room.

A   Dolly, when you got to the door of that room, what did you see?

Q   I saw police there, who was making a sign, sort of showing something, and telling me where my brother was. When I turned and I saw the horrible scene. I just couldn't believe it. I ran to where my brother was and tried to awake him, but he didn't answer. One time after another time. I wanted to cry but they didn't let me. I wanted to ask for help but they didn't let me do that. They told me to be as quiet as possible because it was dawn. They also asked me to take away the body of my brother as soon as possible and bury it. To which I answered them that they should let me think, that I didn't know what to do. In my desperation, I ran to the street and I met Pena in the hall of the house.

Q   Did you say anything to Pena and did he say anything to you?

A   I asked him, sir, what have you done to my brother. He answered me, shut up. Here you have what you have been looking for and deserved.

Q   Dolly, are you certain those were his words?

A   I cannot forget.

Q   Dolly, I'm going to show you Plaintiff's Exhibit 3 and ask you if that's the way you found your brother in that room.

A   Yes.

Q   Would you tell the Court when those photographs were taken?

A   They were taken at my house, he was on the same mattress.

THE COURT: Exhibit 3-A will be received. (So marked.)

MS. COPELON: It's 3.

THE COURT: 3 will be received. (So marked 3 in evidence.)

Q   After the confrontation with Pena, what did you do?

A   I kept running to the street but there the Chief Galeano stopped me and told me, where are you going. I answered him, I was going home. You have to take away the body of your brother from there. I told him I don't know what to do. I cannot touch the body. Then he said, all has been done. He introduced me to the coroner and other person whose identity I don't remember. I told him to excuse me, but I was going home. In my desperation, I started to walk in circles at home. I didn't know what to do. I didn't know how to call my father, what to do.

Q   Was anyone else at home at this time?

A   My sister.

Q   What did you do when you saw your sister?

A   We hold each other.

Q   Did you try to get, to reach your father?

A   First I tried to reach my grandmother. Because she was my closest relative living in Asuncion.

Q   Then—did she come over to the house?

A   Yes. She came home.

Q   Did you have any trouble reaching your father and your mother in Ybycui?

A   Yes.

Q   What happened?

A   We tried unsuccessfully for six hours to reach my father and my mother.

Q   Have you ever had so much trouble reaching them before?

A   Yes, the night before.

Q   What happened at that time, your brother was still at Pena's? What happened? Did they continue to ask you to bring him over?

A   Yes.

Q   What did you do?

A Yes, time and time, over and over again, they insisted. Until the moment they threatened me with throwing the body to the street.

Q What did you do, Dolly?

A With the help of the sailor who was living with us at home, and a policeman, I took the body of my brother.

Q You helped carry the mattress that your brother's body was on?

A Yes.

Q About how many hours was it until your parents got home?

A I think almost seven or seven and a half hours.

Q What happened when they came home?

A I am not sure. There were so many people at home. All I can remember is that there was crying.

Q Do you remember seeing your mother when home?

A Yes, I do.

Q And what happened when she came home, when you saw her?

A My mother got mad.

Q What do you mean "mad?"

A She got mad. She didn't want to believe.

Q What did your father do?

A He went to the room where my brother was, trying to understand what was going on. He took charge of the situation. He took pictures. He began a new diagnosis of the death.

Q Do you remember what happened around the funeral of your brother?

A Yes. More or less, I remember.

Q Can you describe that for the Court?

A Yes. We had his body at home for two days, undressing it and showing it, the tortured body, to all those who came home.

Q Was it—then there was a funeral?

A Yes.

Q Did a lot of people come during this time?

A Yes, many people attended. We think that probably 2,000 people.

Q What did you do during this period?

A So many things happened after the death of my brother that we didn't know. We received threats that probably we might be killed.

Q Did you—did you see police?

A All night. All day, in groups, on trucks, 20, 50 policemen.

Q Were the policemen there all the time that the people kept coming to the house?

A Yes, yes, they were in front of my house.

Q Was your brother known to a lot of people in the community?

A Yes, he was well known.

Q What did people say to you about your brother?

A   They loved him very much. He was full of life.

Q   After the funeral, Dolly, do you remember what your feelings were about what had happened?

A   I didn't believe what was going on.

Q   Were you afraid during that period?

A   Yes.

Q   Did you try to imagine what they had done to Joelito?

A   Yes, of course. Because I have seen before my father suffering the same.

Q   What happened to your life after your brother's death, in the first six months? What was your life like then?

A   We received many threats and persecution.

Q   Describe those a little bit.

A   On the phone, in the court, when we had to appear.

Q   What do you mean in the court? How did you happen to come to court?

A   When we had to go to court in the morning, the yard, the court was always filled with policemen. We were shadowed. They followed us in cars.

Q   Dolly, why did you go to court? What was the case?

A   Because we were trying to present the case of my brother before the court.

Q   Was that—how did you feel about trying to do that?

A   I had deep—I was very angered because I knew that there was no justice.

Q   Did you feel when you got home from court, did you feel safe at home?

A   No.

Q   Tell the Court what it felt like to be living in your house during that period.

A   We had to sleep behind the bed. We had to watch through the night because we heard the noise of weapons being prepared.

Q   Where were these weapons?

A   Weapons were in the street. And the house was surrounded.

Q   Who was carrying the weapons, Dolly?

A   The policemen.

Q   What do you mean you heard the noise of weapons?

A   I think it was a form to make us feel the fear of—to scare us.

Q   What else happened during this period? Did you get any other threats during this period?

A   Yes. My father—my parents received threats that myself and my younger sister would be kidnapped if we didn't withdraw the case before the court.

Q   What did you feel when the telephone rang in your house?

A   So difficult to explain. Fear, anger, powerlessness, and the knowledge that one is struggling against something which is very strong.

Q   Did you sleep very much during this period?

A   No.

Q   About how much did you sleep?

A   There were people who came to accompany me for the night. Sometimes I couldn't sleep one hour.

Q   Did there come a time during this period when you were yourself summoned to court and charged with criminal charges?

A   Yes, my mother and myself.

Q   When did that happen? How much after the death of Joelito?

A   Twenty-five days after the death of Joelito.

Q   What happened? What were the charges?

A   We were accused of breaking into a house.

Q   Into whose house?

A   Pena's house.

Q   Was there any other charge against you?

A   Yes. That we had scratched one of the son-in-law of Pena.

Q   What happened with these charges? Did you go to court? Did you have a trial? What—describe what happened.

A   We were summoned before the court. The Judge read us the charges and we were sent to jail.

Q   Were the charges true?

A   No. They couldn't be true because the house of Pena was under the control of the police. And we were so afraid.

Q   Did you have any chance to present any evidence or to say anything in this trial?

A   No. We—but we were helped by public opinion.

Q   Were you sentenced as a result of these charges?

A   Yes, we were sentenced.

Q   Did you go to jail?

A   Yes.

Q   When you went to jail, did you know how long you might stay in jail?

A   No.

Q   The Judge didn't say how long you were to be in jail?

A   No, he didn't.

Q   What did you feel?

A   I was afraid for what would happen to the family.

Q   How long did you finally spend in jail, Dolly?

A   One day.

Q   Is it unusual that you spend one day?

A   Yes, it is unusual.

Q   Why do you think you only spent a day in jail?

A   Because we had the help of public opinion.

Q   How did that happen?

A   My father published an advertisement in the newspaper, asking for security for our lives.

Q   There was—that is what you mean by public opinion?

A   Yes.

Q   During this period in these first six months when you were going to court, when you were in jail, when you came out of jail, can you tell the Court what you felt emotionally, how you dealt with this emotionally?

A   It was terrible because I couldn't speak. We couldn't emotionally help each other in the family because we were all going through the same.

Q   You—go ahead.

A   I tried to work, to fill the time. But I couldn't.

Q   You said earlier that you couldn't believe that Joelito was dead. In this period of time, did you believe that he was dead?

A   No.

Q   What happened in that regard?

A   I kept listening to voices in the house. I kept waiting for my brother during one year.

MS. COPELON: Could we take a little break?

THE COURT: Why don't we take another witness all right?

MS. COPELON: I think if we took a little break.

THE COURT: We can. But I'd like to take another witness. Why don't you take a break, okay? It's been very difficult. I think you can step outside of the courtroom and maybe one of the—somebody can go with you. But I'd like to take another witness. So can we take Mr. Filartiga, please? My office is located in room 621. My secretary will be more than happy to help Dolly Filartiga. Just take a break and relax, please.

MR. MAGGIO: Thank you, Magistrate Caden.

THE COURT: Surely. Would you take Mr. Filartiga?

MR. MAGGIO: Yes, your Honor.

THE COURT: Good morning, Mr. Filartiga. Would you raise your right hand, please?

JOEL FILARTIGA called as a witness, having been first duly sworn by the Court, through an interpreter, testified as follows:

DIRECT EXAMINATION

BY MR. MAGGIO:

Q   Would you state your name, address and occupation for the Court?

A   My name is Joel Filartiga. I'm a medical doctor, drawer and poet. I am a permanent opponent to the dictatorial regime.

Q   Where do you reside, Dr. Filartiga?

A   I live in Paraguay, in a small town in the countryside, where I have a small clinic to provide free attention for poor people. I live there during the week and in the weekend I go to Asuncion with my family.

Q   How do you support yourself if the medical services you deliver are without cost for your patients?

A   I give free medical care to poor people and to those who have some resources I do charge. I present my drawings at exhibitions. I have been eight times in the United States before, presenting my exhibitions, lecturing on my work on rural medicine.

Q   Could you please tell us a bit about your family, Dr. Filartiga?

A   We are a family normally studied, my wife and four sons, Dolly, Joel, Analida and Catya. Joel on March 30, 1976 was killed under brutal torture.

MR. MAGGIO: Could I have Exhibit 2-B, please?

Q   Why was Joel murdered?

A   Joel was killed as a retaliation for my opposition.

Q   I would like to show you a copy of Plaintiff's Exhibit 2-B. Is this an accurate picture of Joel shortly before his death?

A   Yes. It is a picture taken seven months before his death on the occasion of the birthday of his sister Analida.

Q   Could you tell the Court about your relationship with Joel, what his goals were in life, his activities.

A   We were close friends. We talked about justice in our country and in the world. We had long dialogues. We even talked about the danger on our lives, of a situation of opposition to the regime, that in danger of our lives, of the possibility of being tortured and I had been four times in prison and three times tortured. I talked to him about my experience and how to behave before the torturer.

Q   How was Joel's health? Was there anything unusual about your son's health?

A   He was a very strong kid, very healthy. He's what in medicine we would call—

THE INTERPRETER: That's a very specialized—

THE COURT: I got the idea.

THE INTERPRETER: Thank you.

    A   (Continuing) Temperamental. It is the type of a kid for whom is very dangerous to have some—to have some sudden fear because they may have a heart stroke. It is the problem of health that can be overcome once adolescence is over.
    Q   This problem would not interfere with his life expectancy?
    A   Absolutely not. I suffer the same symptoms when I was a kid and I was operated from the—from the adenoids.
    Q   What did Joel want to do with his life?
    A   He had two projects for his life in the future. In regard to profession. He was a good drawer. And he wanted to be an architect. But once he started helping me in my medical work, he said that he thought he could be more helpful to people by being a medical doctor. Lately that was his—that was his decision, to become a medical doctor.
    Q   Did Dolly also help you in your clinic?
    A   Yes, she helped me very much in the clinic. Dolly also helped me as a nurse.
    Q   What kind of help specifically would Dolly and Joel give you in your clinic?
    A   If Dolly had continued there, she would be at this time a student of medicine and probably she would be helping me with surgical operations. And Joel would have also been studying medicine.
    Q   Dr. Filartiga, you said that you had been arrested and tortured yourself in Paraguay. Could you tell us about your detention and torture in Paraguay?
    A   I was arrested four times and tortured three times. In 1958, there was a movement of workers and students against the dictatorial regime of Stroessner in which I was the coordinator of student front with the workers. I was taken prisoner and tortured during 11 days continuously, without food and under forced labor. Almost to the limit of death. Afterwards, in 1963, I was tortured in more classical forms.
    Q   Could you tell us about the forms of torture that were used against you?
    A   The telephone, which is a—with both hands, violently, they put both hands and violently strike on the ears simultaneously both. They also kept me standing, in a standing position for more than 76 hours without sleep. I was also beaten in my lungs, in my kidneys. I was urinating blood for six days as a result of being beaten in the kidneys. And then I was subjected to what they called the submarine. I was submersed in water almost

to the point of exhaustion under the supervision of medical doctors to avoid being killed. Then they also put salt in the water to stimulate the capacity of the water to communicate electricity, conduct electricity and I was subjected to electric shocks which resulted in lack of control of the sphincters and so that one has to deficate and urinate in the water and one is kept permanently submersed in that water approximately for three hours each session, lasts three hours. This is very painful but more painful is to be a spectator for two or three hours and I had to be—I had to be a spectator of the torture of a veteran of the war of Chaco, a man of 67 years of age, who was taken almost to the point of death.

Q   Did the victims cry out, that you saw tortured?

A   Yes, they did scream, brutally. There was also some stereo equipment being played loudly so that they could—that sound could cover the screams.

Q   Were electrical shocks also placed directly on your body in these torture sessions?

A   No. They did it by means of water, to avoid leaving marks.

Q   Dr. Filartiga, what thoughts linger about your experiences under torture?

A   It is a sensation of being tremendously isolated. A sensation of sudden fear, of feeling prisoner. And thinking that almost all the people do not know what's going on in that place because one knows that people just walk in front of the building of the police and in that backyard I could count 70 or 80 of us and that night ten were tortured and they would do the same next night, another ten. And the people weren't conscious of the criminality of that regime.

Q   How many people did you see being tortured, just this one man from the Chaco War or were there others?

A   No. I have seen 300 persons tortured. I have seen people dead by torture. I have seen people who were left in poor health as a result of torture. A man by the name of Inchausti, I-n-c-h-a-u-s-t-i, they beat him in the eyes and the eyes was blown out of the orbit. His head was a mass without form as a result of being beaten. I visited his brother and learned that he died in Brazil one year after, after being—as a result of having been tortured.

Q   Dr. Filartiga, did you see this man in prison or did you treat this man as a doctor?

A   I saw him in prison. But I have also provided medical care for many people who have been tortured, about 500 persons who have been tortured.

Q   Have you treated—

A   I know the immediate effect of torture.

Q   Have you treated persons who have had electric shocks put to their body as part of their torture?

A   Yes. Yes, I have seen the—that—the electric shock and I have also seen the marks left by the use of the Picana, p-i-c-a-n-a, which is a prod, a rod, something.

Q   So that we are clear on this fact, Doctor, you have both seen persons had electric shocks applied to their bodies while in prison and you have also treated individuals who have come to you with injuries as a result of being tortured with electricity in Paraguay; is that accurate, Doctor?

A   Yes, it is correct.

Q   You said that you discussed torture with your son Joel. What were these discussions like?

A   I told him—I told him that I was living under a state of permanent depression and of permanent fear for myself and for my family. I think that's the way 80 percent of the population of Paraguay lives permanently. One of the instruments for the stability of, the Government of Stroessner is fear.

Q   Doctor, calling your attention to late March, 1976, in this constant state of political oppression, was there anything unusual or particularly frightening at this time in Paraguay?

A   Yes. I was in January in 1976 in Los Angeles, California, lecturing on the situation of health in Paraguay. I was interviewed by both the ABC and NBC TV networks, where I spoke about the regrettable situation of Paraguayan peasants. Then I was in Buenos Aires and I was interviewed at Channel 9 and the program was interrupted and I was almost kidnapped. That left me terribly scared, that something might happen to me in Paraguay. Previously in November and December, 1975, many people were taken prisoner in Paraguay. We had information that at least four or five of those were killed and brutally tortured. I spoke about all this with my son and I told him to take care, that we were in danger.

Q   Doctor—

A   That if you are taken by the police, don't say anything because you don't know anything, but don't lie because a lie brings another and they will not know. It is better to say that you don't know anything.

Q   In addition to explaining to your son Joel that he should be careful, were there any other precautions that you took for the safety of your family at this time?

A   Yes.

Q   Would you please—

A   One of them was that sometimes I made a visit in the middle of the week. My wife has a cousin who is a high navy official in Paraguay and thanks to him, we obtained a sailor to guard our house. It was a way to obtain some guarantees.

Q   Doctor, at this time, late March, 1976, you were living in Ybycui; is that right, and the children were in Asuncion?

A   Yes, correct.

Q   Where was this sailor at that time?

A   The sailor was at my house in Asuncion. In the day he went to the Navy base, which was close to my house and at 4:00 o'clock he was back home. He slept in the room next door to a room of Joelito.

Q   How long had you known this sailor?

A   I had treated him medically since he was four years old. He is from Ybycui, from the countryside near Ybycui. In such a way that I helped him to enter the Navy for his military service.

Q   What was the environment in Ybycui in late March, 1976?

A   There was a lot of repression and there was also great fear. Eight days after the death of Joel, at a population near Ybycui called Cimbron, C-i-m-b-r-o-n, one thousand peasants were arrested and all of them were tortured and kept on a concentration camp which was very well known by its name of Emboscada, E-m-b-o-s-c-a-d-a.

Q   Dr. Filartiga, calling your attention to March 30, 1976, did anything unusual happen that day?

A   At the beginning it was just as another day. I awoke at 7:00 o'clock. I had some Paraguayan tea. We made a list of the patients we were waiting to be given care. We had 21. We gave them their numbers and began to work. We thought it was a day as any other, but at 10:05 in the morning, while I was taking care of the 10th patient, a messenger from the telephone office in town arrived to tell me that my son Joelito had suffered a tragedy and he gave no further explanations.

Q   How did you feel at that time and what did you do in response to this message?

A   I was very scared. I felt like a robot. I took my wife and within three minutes we were on the road. I told my patients that I couldn't continue giving them attention. They insisted, they tried to come in but I violently locked the door and told my wife, let's hurry up. We have to go to Asuncion. I had a secretary there, his name is Leandro, L-e-a-n-d-r-o, and we made the 80 miles separating Ybycui from Asuncion in one hour, a distance that usually takes two hours to cover.

Q   What did you find when you arrived at your neighborhood in Asuncion?

A   I want to explain something which I omitted before. One of the strange things before the death of my son Joel is that I noticed that in the road to Ybycui there was a police control, which was really very surprising to me. I asked them once, why do you do this, and I was told that there were many Paraguayan gorilla fighters being persecuted in Argentina and trying to reenter Paraguay so they wanted to arrest them. I noticed that on that day, there was no control at all. The day before, in the afternoon, I asked a colleague who was visiting if there was a control and he said yes. And I called attention of my wife to the fact that the control was no longer there. As we arrived to our neighborhood where we lived, it was known as Sajonia, S-a-j-o-n-i-a, there was an unusual number of police patrols, a hundred soldiers, the police, and in front of my house there were many of them, two patrol cars filled with—filled with armed policemen and many policemen armed keeping watch on my house. They were blocking the way so they opened the door of the garage for me to enter the house. As I entered the house, I greeted my mother and brother. My brother told me that they killed your son, and in a moment my wife went crazy. I took her to a nearby room and asked her to go to bed and two friends tried to stay with her. Then I returned to the room where the body of my son was being washed.

    Q Dr. Filartiga, I'd like to show you Plaintiff's Exhibits 5-A and 5-B and I'd like you to identify them, please.

    A Yes. They are pictures taken from the body of my son.

    Q Dr. Filartiga, could you please describe the injuries?

    A Yes. He has marks from being beaten with—

THE INTERPRETER: I had doubts of the word, your Honor.

THE COURT: Then we will just go on.

THE INTERPRETER: I want to be accurate.

THE COURT: Yes. I appreciate your effort.

    A (Continuing) Cables, high tension electricity cables, one and a half inch and rods covered with wet cotton. Besides, I notice burns, burns, cuts in the skin as a result of electrical because the electric Picana is an instrument of high voltage, but can be controlled and when it is applied at high voltage it can burn. Another thing that is also important in this picture is that a—is that a wire, an aluminum wire was removed from the penis of my son. I was surprised to see his penis erect as a ruler. In that picture you can see that we took off that wire.

    Q How long would it take to inflict this kind of damage in your experience of torture and as a medical doctor who has treated victims of torture?

    A According to my experience of tortures, a group of torturers is—is composed of six members and a medical doctor who supervises, and I think that my son might have been tortured for three quarters of an hour, 45 minutes. And he died as a result of cardiac stroke. The wounds were probably inflicted after his death, to hide the torture and I think—I think that this is the reality because in the previous pictures we had seen, the blood is—the blood is falling downwards but when we have a body alive, the work of the heart makes blood to spill so blood would have been spilled in several directions.

Q   Doctor, what kind of wounds were inflicted after he had died, in your opinion?

A   Yes. I think that the wounds after his death were knife wounds, with intention of hiding the reality of torture. Because torturers are criminals and they try to hide their crime.

Q   Dr. Filartiga, is that how you found your son's body when you arrived at your home in Asuncion?

A   Yes, that is the state in which the body was. And I understand perfectly all that had happened, including the intention of those who had done it and they knew that I knew. And when they noticed that I was trying to have all the necessary documentation to make a case, to present, they—we were afraid and that was the beginning of tremendous pressure of threats.

Q   Dr. Filartiga, did you have these pictures taken?

A   Yes. The first thing I thought was I know what happened, but how could I make the world to know what happened.

Q   How did you feel right then when you saw your son's body?

A   I told myself everything has happened, but this martyrdom is—it's document for the future. And it is good if it's good that as a result of it it will not happen to others what is happening to me now.

Q   Did you at all think of your own experiences in prison under torture, seeing victims of torture when you first saw your son there?

A   Yes, I thought in my own experience and I also though in other victims. And it was hard to believe. Three days after the death, a massive wave of arrests took place in Asuncion. Many of them were killed in their houses. Two thousand persons were in prisons. Paraguay as a country and Asuncion the city was under military occupation. Without living in that country is really hard to believe how that is. Truckloads of armed soldiers with machine guns, houses broken.

Q   Dr. Filartiga, when you arrived at your home and found your son's body, was the sailor that you were paying to guard your family, was he around?

A   The person indeed was looked for, the sailor, but he had disappeared to today. Nobody knows where he is. His relatives don't know. He never appeared again.

Q   Dr. Filartiga, could you tell the Court about the funeral arrangements that you made for your son?

A   I thought that the most important thing was to document facts. As part of the documentation, I took pictures. I drafted a—with other three doctors, a letter and the crime was the greatest scandal in the city. Many people came to the house. I undressed and dressed again the body of my son for 15 times. I took him in my arms for two consecutive days. There was permanently many people there, at dawn, in the afternoon, at night.

Q   Was this at some risk to you that you laid the tortured body out, dangerous?

A   Yes, it was dangerous. That same day marks the beginning of the telephone threats. I remember that the first threat I was told ironically "Doctor, you are being wrinkled. Be careful, we're going to iron you."

Q   Dr. Filartiga, could you please tell the Court of the other efforts that you undertook to both—to both inform people as to what happened to your son and to obtain justice in the courts in Paraguay?

A   I had friends in the United States. I wrote to them. Historian Richard White, from UCLA. I sent two letters, one by the mail, which he didn't receive, and another by the diplomatic pouch of the Ambassador of Peru, requesting his help and asking him to communicate with Amnesty International. Surprisingly, four days later, I received a call from him and he told me that he was with me and one month after, he arrived in Paraguay to stay with us for four months. He was also threatened with death. And one night we had to leave the house because we had a situation of alarm. Our daughters stayed under the bed and we escaped.

Q   Dr. Filartiga, did you institute any legal proceedings in Paraguay, to try and obtain justice for the death of your son?

A   The death of my son with suffering, but the recovery of trying to obtain justice in Paraguay is another suffering. It would be something like reading the Process by Franz Kafka. That's Paraguayan justice. It is something without end. It is a machine that deteriorates people psychologically.

Q   What were the experiences you had and your lawyers had with the Paraguayan system in your efforts to obtain justice for the murder of your son?

A   We had all the evidence to prove the truth, which we could have proved. It was just a question of small doses of equity from them. When we asked for that key police officers be summoned, my lawyer was arrested, threatened and put into an iron cage at one of the prisons of the Paraguayan police. They deprived him of his authorization to work professionally as a lawyer. To today. Two other lawyers I had, they left the case. They were afraid. For eight months I had no lawyer to defend me. That was the moment in which the scandal of Pena erupted in the United States. Then the Paraguayan police themselves sends me a lawyer of the police and I took it. Because it's better to have that lawyer than to have none. But once the case of Pena begun to be treated in the United States, then I was left without lawyer at all and I ended all the cases in Paraguay without lawyer. Nobody wanted to take the case.

Q   Dr. Filartiga, you said that you had proof, did that include any other evaluation of the cause of Joelito's death other than your own?

A   Yes, we did have other proofs. We had information given us by members of the police who told us about all the details, how it happened and where it happened. Not only that, but when Pena was here arrested, I was threatened and almost killed by accident. It was a fabricated accident in the road. At the same time, I received an envoy from the Government who told me that I should withdraw the case here and that they would take care of doing justice there. That I should keep myself quiet, to withdraw the case here in the United States and that they would take me the bodies of those who killed my son. I told him, I don't want more people killed. It's enough. Besides, the case of my son is now out of my hands. I am no longer in control of it.

Q   Dr. Filartiga, did any other doctor than yourself examine your son's body?

A   The first doctor, the coroner, he gave a completely false diagnosis.

Q   What was his diagnosis?

A   The diagnosis said penetrating wound between the fifth—between the fifth and fourth ribs, and death. That wound does not exist. Besides, he ignored all the other wounds. So we prepared with three other doctors a detailed diagnosis of all the wounds. One of these doctors was an army coroner, the other was the Director of Health for Indigenous, an official position. The other was a doctor of a hospital in one of the neighborhoods of Asuncion. None of them stated a term such as the burns, so I had to call another coroner. We exhumed the body three days after and that doctor is Dr. Hernan, H-e-r-n-a-n G-o-d-o-y, and he stated that those were burns. Surprisingly for us, the Judge wrote, put that word "burns" in parenthesis and with a question mark, and he said, what's this. Now, the same thing as the lawyers couldn't take my case, we also had six different judges. It was a case who was burning both, lawyers and judges.

Q   Dr. Filartiga, what was the official Paraguayan Government explanation for the death of your son?

A   The Government never gave any explanation. The president is a personal friend of my mother and my mother went to see him. He told her, this is a great tragedy. We will try to investigate this mystery. My mother was never again received after that and—on the ground of dignity, she never tried to be received again. Justice was evidently not done.

Q   Did the Paraguayan police have an explanation as to why and how your son died?

A   Yes, there is official police statement which tried to present the case in a very devious way, tried to present it as a passionate crime. There is a very machisto law in Paraguay which says that the husband can kill any person whom he thinks is cheating and the try—they tried to explain this crime as a passionate crime.

Q   Does that happen often in Paraguay, where there are deaths explained as crimes of passion or is this unusual?

A   No. It is very—it is usual to have people killed as tortured as it was the case of my son.

Q   Doctor, you said they alleged it was a crime of passion, so where is the woman that the police allege your husband—your son was having an affair with?

A   She was the wife of the step-son of Policeman Pena.

Q   Where is she?

A   She has disappeared. Coincidentally, all the key witnesses that might explain the case have disappeared.

Q   Where did she disappear? Where was the last time she was seen?

A   She was in prison at the women's jail, the same prison where my wife and my daughter were. When she was called to appear before the Court, the Judge released her immediately. And a woman of the Paraguayan police went with her to Buenos Aires on a chartered flight. And we knew that she was being kept under tight police control of the Paraguayan police in Buenos Aires. One of my cousins tried to see her and he found her. And this cousin of mine was kidnapped January 3, 1978 in Buenos Aires, and until today he remains disappeared. His name, J-u-a-n, Alberta, Filartiga.

Q   Dr. Filartiga, could you tell the Court, the impact that your son's death has had on your family and your relationship with your wife and other children?

A   Life has changed completely for me. I lost my capacity to work 50%. My sight has also been impaired. 15 days after, I had to wear glasses and two months later I had to change the glasses, and six months later I had to change them again, because evidently I was losing sight. My hair grayed in less than six months. I had terrible guilt feelings whether I had some guilt of the death of my son as a result of my militancy in defending those Paraguayan peasants. But if it was just the willingness of the regime to make me feel guilty, when those who were really guilty were them. This is the problem on my personal level and also in my relationship with my family. My wife many times has repeatedly become very hostile to me, seeing me as perhaps a monster who is perhaps guilty for the death of my son. She has even written so also to my daughters, telling them that I will go to the U.S. and leave your father.

There were also psychological changes in all my daughters. The youngest one who was 11 years old at the time is just now beginning to recover her psychological equilibrium, which Dolly lost completely. In one opportunity she became very aggressive, physically. Unconsciously I think they saw me as guilty for the death of my son and all this in addition, in addition to all this, we had the Paraguayan justice march to destroy consciousness. My—my near death, because of accidents on the road, then the U.S. Ambassador Landau called the Minister of Interior to request guarantees for me. The Minister of Interior was Montanero. And for six months I just couldn't work. Afterwards I tried to rebuild my life. But evidently that life was abruptly changed, and now here I am in this room trying to continue this struggle. There is no way to add up the feelings, but of course there is mounting feelings.

Q   Dr. Filartiga, how often do you think of your son Joel, and what are your thoughts when you do think of him?

A   I am always thinking of him. Practically Joel has become the owner of me. I can't say that I am not a friend, but I can say I am less a friend than before, and consciously I felt sometimes a little suicidal. I had never used weapons before the death of my son, but after, I took weapons, and regardless of my being a medical doctor I felt that there was within me a desire to kill. I had to fight with myself for two years to recover myself from this situation; to understand that the right way wasn't that way.

Q   Dr. Filartiga, you testified earlier that you support yourself through the sale of your drawings as well as to your medical practice. Could you identify this drawing and briefly describe what it shows?

A   Below, you can see peasants, but if united they might be able to rise up, and that's part of my experience with peasants. I give them free health care. In my whole life there I never had to buy anything to eat, and the clinic under my direction was built by peasants with their work. As I said before that's Joelito, and in the back my wife suffering. Joelito is crying for the future generations of kids, and it is a flag that should be lifted up by all of us.

Q   Dr. Filartiga, this drawing is dated 1979. Would you describe it for us, please?

A   That's the documentation of what a peasant told me, a peasant by the name Barbosa told me. You may not understand, Doctor, what is happening to you, but because you are too close to it, but we do understand. Your son was killed not because he was the son of Filartiga, but because he was the son of serving us, poor people. The punishment is not just for you, but it is also for us, the poor.

Q   Who is this, Joelito?

A   Those are electric picanas, an electric rod, and that arm, with the machete, that symbolizes the spirit of the peasants, which is still there regardless of the persecutions. It is the resistance of the peasants to persecution and death.

Q   This is dated 1981. What does this picture represent?

A   You can see three tunnels. One tunnel represents a hand within a prison, and the fingers praying and a hand which gives freedom and below, the body of myself as a document to the future to be exchanged for the Paraguayan freedom. So people say that the one who dies lives, but I think that the one who dies remains, and people who learn how to die are people who deserve to be free.

Q   In this drawing of yours, Dr. Filartiga?

A   A poor peasant's girl, Paraguayan, the map of Paraguay made of wood, Christ, as one of the vehicles for the liberation of our people. The scream of Joelito tortured and the bars of the prison broken.

Q   And lastly, Dr. Filartiga, this picture here, dated 1976.

A   That's the much pain and consolation within the spirit of suffering together with compassion.

Q   And here, Doctor?

A   A mother carrying a jug or jar and a poor child on her arm, and the sun rising.

Q   You have a man and a woman here crying with their hearts with screws in them. Who are they?

A   They represent my wife and myself, giving us much consolation, fighting the pain with our isolation, with our powerlessness.

MR. MAGGIO: Thank you very much for your testimony, Dr. Filartiga.

THE COURT: Any other witnesses?

MR. COPELON: I would like to call, recall Dolly.

THE COURT: Is Mr. Timmerman here?

MR. COPELON: Yes.

THE COURT: Would you come up, please. All right, all of the exhibits have been received into evidence.

JACOB TIMMERMAN, a witness called herein, having been first duly sworn by the Clerk, took the stand and testified as follows:

EXAMINATION BY MR. COPELON:

Q   Would you tell the Court where you live and what your present occupation is?

A   I live in Tel Aviv, Israel. I am a journalist.

Q   And where are you presently living?

A   I am spending a semester at the Institute for Advanced Study at Princeton. I was invited to work on a book about the way the time I spent under torture, destroyed my relationship with normal intellectual life.

Q   Have you written one book?

A   I have written one book which is my testimony about my being in prison. The name is, "Prisoner Without the Name, Cell Without a Number." It was published in 13 languages, all over the world.

Q   Could you tell the Court a little about your work and experience in Argentina, the country from which you come?

A   Well, I arrived there, I was born in the Soviet Union from where my family went out, running away from the Communist life. I arrived in Argentina when I was five years old. I spent all my life there. I went through college and the university, and I was a journalist all my life; professional journalist. That was my only profession. I started from the beginning as a street reporter. I went up to be an editor. I created three weekly magazines, a book publishing house and a daily newspaper. I had my own program of the T.V.; something like "Meet the Press." The name was "Pressroom," translated into English. And I had my radio program. I was always a journalist.

Q   And was there a particular character to your role as a journalist in Argentina?

A   Well, I was always very independent, to describe it more precisely. I would say that during the eight years that I was editor and publisher of my newspaper there in Argentina, six presidents and the six at some point closed my newspaper and punished my business. There were six different presidents from the left to the right to the center, military dictatorships as well as elected presidents. I was always, as the New York Times said in an editorial, a troublemaker. Very independent. And I didn't belong to any political party.

Q   Mr. Timmerman, we have asked you to testify here today to inform the Court about torture as it is experienced in a country which has similarity to Paraguay, and I would like to ask you to preface your testimony by explaining the ways that you have come into touch with an understanding of and experience of torture.

A   You want me to describe the way I was tortured, or the reflections and the problems of torture?

Q   Why don't we start with your experience—

THE COURT: I think we can only have so much of that one day. I prefer not to have the witness tell us about his personal experiences.

Q   Would you like to tell us your reflections?

A   My personal experiences was not different than everybody's experience in the way of pain and in the way of despair and horror. So there is nothing new I could say to you, your Honor.

Reflections is quite different. You know, that this is the first time, that a Judge is going to judge torture. That is quite different from condemning torture. Torture was condemned as a crime. It was never judged as a problem of our civilization, and this is quite different. I am working on that, because there is not one judgment about torture in the way that justice showed different guidelines to the people who have been tortured, to the people who were never connected with torture and to the torturers. What is the meaning of torture in our civilization and in our society, and this is absolutely new. And believe me, I am working on that, and I have been reading a lot, and this is the first time in which there is nobody to be accused except for torture itself. And this is something absolutely unusual, and I really hope that from here, as so many other times in the history from the U.S., will come a guideline about what is the relation of our civilization with torture.

Very recently in the Indiana University Press has published a book by a writer, James Amery, who had been tortured by the Gestapo when he was a Belgium fighter, underground fighter, and that was in 1943. He committed suicide in 1978, and all those times, all those years he was living with the problem of torture, and he wrote about that; and that was published in this book. He said that once you have been tortured, torture is with you forever and there is nothing you can do about it.

I am trying to describe what it means, and it is quite difficult, because it is like another kind of civilization, not another kind of society. The history of mankind we have seen every kind of society, middle ages, the mother revolution, the communists; everything. But we had always one civilization.

Torture is something quite different. It is pain and humiliation, but more than that, the moment you are tortured, and the days after torture, and the years after torture, they have changed your human condition. It is a biological change. Your feelings have difference, your feelings are different. Your relations with the rest of the people is different. You are like, they transform you from a human being to another planet. This is very different. And something should be said about that.

Usually in a criminal court the most horrible of the crimes is to kill somebody, death, and this is the biggest crime that anybody can commit. Not under torture, because I have heard dozens of people when they were tortured asking, kill me. So you see, death was not the biggest crime, they wanted to be killed. And this is what changed everything when we talk about torture.

I have my reflections and my problems, and this is the second time that I have to live with the problem, and I am very grateful to you that you didn't want to hear more about the details because the last time I was in a problem about explaining, and I collapsed because it is very difficult; not only to remind, to remember, but to try to transmit to you, to transfer to you the feelings you have. The biggest humiliation, the moment they are changing your world of ideas and your world of values and your biological structure. And now, I still, after two years and having written a book and having the support of my family and my sons, friends, human rights institutions, and many people all over the world, I still cannot accept that it happened. I have to find a way in which acceptance doesn't mean approval, in which acceptance doesn't mean that I accept as a realization that torture can be a part of our civilization. This is why I couldn't accept torture.

I couldn't go back to the man I used to be. This is something that I couldn't deal with. I don't remember who I was. And I am trying very hard and still I don't remember; because to remember who I was, I have to go back through torture, to the time before that, and this is very difficult to do. I was a businessman and a journalist and a professional, and I, my work now is very painfully writing. I couldn't be an editor. I haven't the strength to be an editor. I have fear for the rest of the people. There is, I hope the word is correct that I am using in English, there is a kind of syndrome.

You see I am invited to a party. So the day before, I begin to work psychologically, what is going to happen in the party and it can be hours and hours; who is going to be there, what are they going to ask me. So suddenly, I realize that I am rebuilding in me the hours before interrogation, like going again into being interrogated. This is something I couldn't overcome. I am living under permanent interrogation. If I go to take a train at Princeton Station, I begin to ask myself do I have the money and if they will sell me the tickets, if I am going to say the normal words; and it is again like being under interrogation. I am permanently under interrogation. Imagine the life in the Institute of Advanced Study in Princeton, 180 of the most important scientists and professors all over the world to write or think or do whatever they want. It is a very unique institution all over the world. And there is, of course, relations between everybody; discussions and conversations. Everybody has a house. And I spend all the time, all the time, practically in my house; three or four or five days without going out.

Suddenly I discovered I was repeating the life of a prisoner. I couldn't overcome that. Because I am afraid, the moment I leave and go outside, interrogation and torture comes back. This is quite different from any prisoner. And I have seen prisoners, they are very happy to leave the prison, and they very quickly adjust to a free life. People who have been—I have met people who haven't been tortured and were in prison for 10 and 15 years. I was only three years. They adjust very quickly to life. But the people who have been tortured, they couldn't adjust to life because they don't know how to deal with the big destruction of their life that has been made under this moment in which several people are over you and there is only pain, your Honor, pain and pain and pain and pain, and there is nothing you can do about it. Absolutely nothing. This is the horrible thing.

And this is the judgment that I mean, I was in many human rights conventions, especially dedicated to journalism. In Argentina 100 journalists are missing. This is a genocide, genocide of journalists. It is enormous. I received the golden pen of freedom from the International Federation of Publishers. And I was in Congresses of many institutions all over the world and always trying to explain to them that we need some kind of judgment about torture. We need some kind of guidelines about torture. It is not only to condemn torture as a horrible scene. There is also something to say what we feel about it, what we think about that. This kind of condemnation. And everything has been destroyed, the relation with my sons, with my wife; there is something, always something between us. The time we suffered, the way they suffered, the way I suffered, looking at them, looking at my wife when she came to my prison and asked me if I was tortured again. All those feelings are inside us and it is not easy to destroy them and overcome them.

There is always in the lives of my sons a moment in which they could not depend on their father, and there is always in me a feeling that I have punished them in a terrible way when there were nights, after night, thinking, where was his father and if he has or is being tortured. This is another aspect of the punishment that the torturers are giving us.

Q   Mr. Timmerman, working from your experience, what can you say about the impact of torture on the people, society on a whole?

A   I had this discussion in a place in which there is no torture practically and people live always in danger, like the State of Israel. We have to live with a terrorism of the Arabs. Once I had the discussion, because the police in Israel discovered a terrorist the moment he was placing a bomb in a bus station. They disarmed the bomb but they realized he has placed two other bombs in two public places. They tortured him to discover where the bombs were placed and they find it out and the bombs were dismantled. I protested and the answer was that if those two bombs would have been exploded, they would kill probably 30 people, and I tried to explain as a journalist, in my writings, and the statements I made about this subject to columnists of the New York Times who was in Jerusalem at that time, Anthony Lewis, I was trying to explain to him that the police who succeeded and discovered two bombs through torture will think now forever that torture is a very positive and important instrument to solve the problems of our everyday life, and from that moment on torture is incorporated to our society, and who is going to decide who to torture. How many innocent people are going to be tortured now.

So the incorporation of torture to a society or civilization means that there is somebody, many people who believe that they have in their hands an instrument to discover everything they want, to obtain anything they want to obtain. They act like God because they have the power not only to kill you, that it is nothing, because to kill is a power that is in the hands of every human being. They have a bigger power to torture and to discover, find out and change everything they want to do. And this is the danger.

Torture is the moment it is incorporated to a society as routine, a permanent feature of life, an instrument permanent, normally as the American philosopher H. Arendt said about Eichmann, the banality of everything; the moment you accept that, you haven't changed society, you have changed our civilization. This is going on in countries like Paraguay, Argentina, Chile, in which torture is an inevitable instrument of the way this society, this country has been built up.

Q   Can you describe the effects of some people in Argentina that you have observed while you were there?

A   It is very curious that how difficult it is to understand torture. I was an editor and journalist in a country where people have been tortured and I was informed of that, and I published many articles and stories, many articles, editorials protesting torture; but still after the moment I was tortured and I saw other people tortured, I couldn't understand exactly what it means. After that, well, the reactions are so different, and it depends on so many psychological things. I wouldn't dare to give a general theory. My second man in my newspaper was kidnapped two weeks before me, like the assistant editor, he was kidnapped two weeks before me, and he was kidnapped one day after Miss Patricia Darien, Undersecretary of Human Rights came to Argentina. I was the only editor to invite her to my newspaper. All the other newspapers, editors and publishers rejected the idea. She asked for discussions for visits and everybody rejected and didn't want to have her. I was the only one. It was March 31st, the 31st of '77 and April 1st, my second man was kidnapped. He disappeared forever, a man of 40 years; and two weeks later I was kidnapped. The wife of this man, whose name is—Sajon, from 1977 up to now, his wife is every night cooking a dinner and waiting for her husband, with four children.

There are different kinds of reactions. A lot of people who have been tortured couldn't live together any more after that, with the families. Divorce, suicide in adaptation to life, impossibility to adjust to life. Many have overcome in a way at least openly, but you never know what is happening inside them during the nights when they couldn't sleep. The nightmares. It is a unique experience, your Honor, a unique experience. After my release from prison I spent 10 days resting as a guest of the writer Elie Weisel, who wrote many books about the holocaust, and he is a survivor or Auschwitz, and he has been appointed by the Government of the U.S. President of the Commission of Holocaust of the U.S., that is a presidential commission. In talking about our experiences, he in Auschwitz and I in the prisons of Argentina, he said to me, that, my experience was much more painful than his, because he was with thousands and thousands of people together. That is quite different; of being lonely, tortured, without any hope of nothing. There is more hope in a concentration camp, and Elie Weisel saw his father going to the gas chambers, but there is more hope in that collective experience than in the loneliness of the tortured man in which there is nothing, nothing left to you; not your body, not your mind, not your imagination, not your dreams, absolutely nothing.

MR. COPELON: I have no further questions, Mr. Timmerman.

THE COURT: All right. We will take a recess and we will come back at about 12 o'clock.

MS. COPELON: If you would like, your Honor, we can begin with the former Ambassador to Paraguay, then—

THE COURT: May I have your name, please?

THE WITNESS: Robert White.

THE COURT: Mr. White, would you raise your right hand, please?

ROBERT WHITE called as a witness, having been first duly sworn by the Court, testified as follows:

DIRECT EXAMINATION

BY MS. COPELON:

Q   Could you state your current residence and occupation?

A   Yes. My name is Robert White. I live at 500 Jefferson Court, Alexandria, Virginia. I'm a senior associate with the Carnegie Endowment for International Peace.

Q   Could you outline very briefly your experience in the foreign service?

A   I spent almost 20 years in Latin America, in various capacities, with the United States Government, as a career diplomat. I served as Ambassador to Paraguay and Ambassador to El Salvador.

Q   During what years were you Ambassador to Paraguay?

A   1977 to 1979.

Q   Could you, Mr. White, give sort of a brief description of Paraguay under General Stroessner?

A   Well, Paraguay—with the exception of Cuba, Paraguay is the closest thing to a totalitarian state that we have in the Western Hemisphere, in the sense of total arbitrariness. There, in effect, is no law. The only law is the law that the president decides on.

Q   And is—is it fair to describe Paraguay as under martial law? Is that—

A   It's not only fair. It's accurate. Because by the—the Government every three month declares that—a state of siege exists. They do that because—this government is very legalistic, likes to follow legal norms. So they keep the state of siege in being, even though there is no justification for it, in order to be able to take any measure which, you know, under an emergency rule.

Q   Could you describe the situation in terms of the existence of political opposition in Paraguay?

A   Well, the political—political opposition exists but it is a very dangerous profession. And if you intend on being effective in a political opposition, your chances of being arrested, tortured, kept, detained for a long time or exiled are very great.

Q   Is there anything that one could describe as an independent judiciary system in Paraguay?

A   No. The total power belongs to the president and the president gives the order whether to free or sentence. Now, I don't want to overstate it, in the sense there are numerous cases, civil cases, where nothing is really at stake, except, you know, a suite of one person against another. This will indeed function in a normal and proper way.

But if we are talking about an issue in which the government is interested, then the law is what the president says it is.

Q   Could you describe briefly the economic conditions in Paraguay?

A   Paraguay—what comes to mind when you say "economic conditions" to me is corruption, and corruption is endemic in Paraguay. One of the reasons for torture, one of the reasons for arbitrary behavior is so they could maintain themselves in power and continue the immense profits. For example, Paraguay is the largest importer of cigarettes in the world, this very small country. That's because they bring them in on the Air Force planes and then scatter them out all over the Western Hemisphere. They contraband them in. So these give huge profits to the military.

Q   Now, have you studied the three reports of the International League for Human Rights and do you know their work and do you consider that they are an accurate portrayal of the situation in Paraguay? We have the three reports here.

A   Yes, I am familiar with all three reports. I have studied them. I know the authors very well. They're all three of them highly professional works.

MS. COPELON: These are marked as Exhibits 10-A, 10-B and 10-C, for the record.

Q   Could you discuss particularly, Mr. White, the role of torture in maintaining the regime in Paraguay?

A   I think torture is basic to the repression. It's at the heart of the system that enables the Stroessner dictatorship to maintain itself in power.

Q   And against whom is torture used?

A   Anyone who has the capacity to play a leadership role, or anyone who challenges the system in any way.

Q   Do you have a view regarding to what extent torture is calculated to keep people in line and to what extent it is an expression of sheer viciousness?

A   Well, there is certainly certain people in power in Paraguay who are vicious. But I think that really it's something—it's routine. I mean, perfectly normal people who appear normal get up and go to work and their work is torture, and then they come home after work and do whatever normal people do. It is institutionalized in Paraguay.

Q   Have you had occasion to observe the impact of torture on torture victims?

A   Oh, yes. I can give you two examples that come to mind.

A very intelligent young doctor named Bogado Gondra, came to see me to thank me for my help in getting him out of prison, and he described for me the torture and—which consisted of being put into a pool of dirty water, excrement, and being in effect caused to drown repeatedly, and he told me that by the time he was through with this torture, his only desire was to find out what they wanted him to confess to. He didn't care whether it was true or false, he just wanted to find out what they wanted. And that way—and he would sign it. And he—so they left him alone in a room and they fabricated the type of story that the torturers wanted to hear.

The other example is a man came up to me when I was at a—just leaving a building and asked, and thanked me for my help. I had no idea who the man was. So I asked him to come to see me at the Embassy. He came in and told me how he had helped the high school friend, the high school friend, because he was jobless. The high school friend was then arrested and under torture, they asked—he told them that he was staying at the house of this man. So they then arrested him, tortured him, kept him in prison for five years and he had no idea why. He was released and they wouldn't—they refused to give him an identity card and without an identity card you can't work in Paraguay. So he was literally without work, without means to feed his family and no way could he function as a human being. So I—he went to work for us in the Embassy as a gardener. But it's a—this type of thing has terrible psychological impact. For example, Bogado Gondra left the country and said no longer can I live in this place.

Q   What is the effect of torture beyond the direct victims?

A   Well, there is no—almost no one in Paraguay who hasn't been touched by torture, in the sense that either they or someone in their family or—has been tortured. This is true—this is true in the upper class as well as—if it's true there, where people have connections and so forth, you can imagine what it's like in the countryside, where the people are poor and illiterate.

Q   Is anyone immune? Does class position immunize one from torture?

A   The only people who would be immune would be the people who are part of the apparatus.

Q   So how does it come that anyone is able to retain any independence in Paraguay?

A   Well, you retain your independence, what little independence you can retain, either because you are attached to an institution, even though the church in Paraguay, the Catholic Church in Paraguay, has described itself at one point as a persecuted church, it is still true that being part of the church, priest, nun, gives you some assistance in—in an institutional framework, which will try to help you should you fall into—into the hands of the authorities. Secondly, certain international groups take an interest in Paraguay, Amnesty, International League of Human Rights, the Embassy of the United States and other western embassies. But, you know, what happens in most cases is that people just operate out of any kind of activity that could possibly get them into trouble.

Q And yet, that hasn't reduced the amount of torture or repression?

A It may. It may reduce it. In other words, I don't think these people torture just for the fun of it. I think they only—mostly torture when it is necessary, and if you torture for a certain period, you cow the people. Then you no longer—it's because the—I wouldn't want to be thought that the torture is at a sort of constantly ascending level. That's not true. It goes in waves, depending upon the pressures on the government.

Q Do you have an opinion, Mr. White, whether General Stroessner's regime could survive or not if it did not employ torture?

A I think—torture, which is at the heart of it—overall repression, no. That's what keeps the government in place.

Q From your experience in Paraguay, El Salvador, but Paraguay in particular, do you have a view about how the use of torture can be stopped?

A Well, the only thing that Paraguay responds to are international pressures. Traditionally Paraguay—the Stroessner regime has survived pressures by keeping—by not responding to them, by postponing action, by waiting things out. There was—I think that the Carter administration with emphasis on human rights had a great effect in Paraguay and—but now that—in the—that there has been a change in the priorities of the administration, it probably has less effect. But international pressures are the only way.

Q What role do you think the existence of civil remedies for the victims of torture as we are here in this court for might play in the overall effort to stop torture?

A Well, let me give you—I think one example might illustrate this. After the case was decided in favor of Dr. Filartiga, a Paraguay official, one of the people closest to General Stroessner, told me that I just had to do everything possible to get this decision reversed. They don't really understand independence of the court system here. And he stressed to me that no Paraguayan government figure would feel free to travel to the United States if this judgment was upheld because, you know, they would feel that they would be liable to arrest for just even being in any state in the United States.

Q Were you aware that the Filartigas filed a lawsuit in Paraguay?

A Oh, yes.

Q Were you involved in that in any respect?

A No. You can't say—as an Embassy—as the Ambassador or any embassy officer, it is very difficult for us to involve ourselves in the—what are really, strictly speaking, internal affairs of another country. We can do a lot, but not that much.

Q   I guess I might better rephrase my question. Did you become engaged—did you know Dr. Filartiga while you were in Paraguay and did you ever become involved in providing him the sort of protection, the assistance that the Embassy could give?

A   I knew Dr. Filartiga from perhaps the first month that I was in Paraguay. Knew his family. We became very interested in the Filartiga case, not only because it was our mandate under the Carter administration to be vigilant about human rights and to report on them and to do whatever we could to protect them, but also because we were deluged with letters from the United States after every trip that, Dr. Filartiga made here and we would get letters from university professors, human rights organizations and just ordinary citizens, Senators, Congressmen, etc., in effect saying, please do everything you can to protect Dr. Filartiga.

Q   Do you think that that international opinion provided him some protection in Paraguay?

A   Yes, I do. I think that—I think that one of the purposes that I had in my—in putting forward the human rights policies was to try to spread an umbrella of protection not only over Dr. Filartiga, but people who were conducting themselves according to the norms of the Constitution of Paraguay and sort of generally accepted civilized norms, and so that the government could not without expecting a reaction from the United States, kidnap, torture, kill, whatever.

Q   Going back to their lawsuit, are you aware of the result in their lawsuit?

A   Yes.

Q   What was that?

A   That Dr. Filartiga, the Judge awarded the decision to—in favor of the Filartigas against—

Q   Here, no. The lawsuit in Paraguay.

A   Oh. As far as I know, it's still pending. There is no there is no determination of the case at all, as far as I know.

Q   Based upon your knowledge of the system in Paraguay, do you have an opinion whether or not the Filartigas could get justice in Paraguay?

A   No, it's impossible.

MS. COPELON: I have no further questions.

THE COURT: Thank you, Mr. White. Any other witnesses?

MS. COPELON: Just the completion of Dolly Filartiga's testimony.

THE COURT: All right.

DOLLY FILARTGA, having been previously sworn by the Clerk of the Court, through an interpreter, resumed the witness stand and testified further as follows:

EXAMINATION

BY MS. COPELON: (Continues through an interpreter.)

Q   Dolly, I want to turn your attention back to the period after your brother was killed. I want you to tell the Court about the dreams that you began having during that period.
A   There are moments in which those dreams come to me continuously. And other times it's from time to time.
Q   Do you want to describe the dream?

THE COURT: Why don't we go on to something else?

Q   Dolly, I want to ask you about coming to the United States. What were your feelings about coming to this country.
A   First of all, I want justice, and secondly, to escape from the pressure I was living under in Paraguay.
Q   If Joelito had not been killed, do you think you would have come to this country?
A   Yes, I may have came, but in a different way.
Q   What do you mean?
A   As a tourist. Or maybe to study.
Q   What caused you to file your application for political asylum?
A   The regime of Stroessner.
Q   Did your filing of the—when you came to this country, did you in fact locate the defendant Pena?
A   I knew where he lived. I wasn't familiar with the country yet. But I had some Paraguayan friends living here and they helped me.
Q   And together, did you report to the Immigration and Naturalization Service the whereabouts of the defendant Pena?
A   Yes. First we had the help of an American friend and with his help, we were able to locate him.
Q   When you undertook to report his whereabouts and have him arrested, what implication did that have for you about returning to Paraguay?
A   The implication for me and my family was that we all might get killed, but with the regime of Stroessner, you never know what's going to happen.
Q   Did it have an implication for you regarding whether or not you could return to Paraguay?

A   I was once in prison in Paraguay and I was released on bail. That means that if am back, I might be in prison again at any moment.

Q   Could you tell the Court what it has felt like to try to adjust to life in the United States?

A   First we have to think about things such as culture, language.

Q   Did you know English before you came here?

A   I had studied, but it's not the same.

Q   How does it feel—have you been able to recommence your studies here?

A   My papers in Paraguay were destroyed. I have my application for political asylum pending. I had no money when I came, so I had to defend myself as I could. And up to now what I have been able to do is strictly to survive.

Q   At the beginning of your testimony you said that you were studying medicine and you had wanted to be a doctor. Do you still want to be a doctor?

A   No. My life has changed a lot. Seeing my father and the work he does, I think I may not be prepared to handle more pain.

Q   Do you want to tell the Court the other ways in which your brother's death has affected your life, physically, emotionally?

A   I have moments in which all I want is to be alone. I don't know if this action of masturbation of the mind is something like being mad or it is something too strong and I cannot forget it.

Q   Have you had therapy since you've been in this country?

A   Yes, I had.

Q   Do you feel like you will have to continue that in the future?

A   Yes, I think so.

Q   How do you feel in social situations, with other people?

A   I feel different to others.

Q   How do you feel about engaging in normal activities like reading? Can you read? Can you do things like that?

A   I cannot concentrate myself. Regardless of the problem of what happened with my brother, I also have the problem of my family who still lives there and I know what they are going through.

Q   Dolly, how often do you think of your brother?

A   Always.

Q   Do you feel you'll ever be free of that?

A   I think that only if I could be brainwashed.

MS. COPELON: I don't have any further questions.

Q   Is there anything else you want to say to the Court?

A   Everything is fine.

MS. COPELON: Magistrate Caden, I did not go through two parts of Dolly's testimony that have to do with the aftermath of the period and asking her to relive what in fact was the most painful, devastating period. I think that you have observed her and since you have indicated in the past that we could submit additional material on affidavits, I think it would be—

THE COURT: It is agreeable with me. If you like, you can submit an affidavit or submit it in the form a letter. However you choose to do it. Do you have any other witnesses?

MS. COPELON: No. That completes the testimony for today. And we believe that that completes the oral component of this submission. If it is acceptable to you, we can project with the difficulties of getting additional material from Paraguay and the things ahead of us, that we would like to submit the additional evidence and the legal memoranda regarding the underlying law of damages here within a month.

THE COURT: Let's agree on one thing. As far as the submission is concerned, as I indicated before, we need a transcript—

MS. COPELON: Right.

THE COURT: —of what occurred here today. We need an exhibit list. We need—if the exhibits as they were being marked today have not already been received into evidence, all of those that have been marked and identified will be received in evidence. That includes, I guess, to the extent that a book was used, I think we should at least keep the book as an exhibit even though only portion of the book were referred to.

MS. COPELON: We have that marked here.

THE COURT: Then to the extent that this Court indicates that there are a number of affidavits that have been filed in the Court, to the extent you want this Court to consider any specific, for example, I note that there were a number of affidavits that were offered, if you like just indicate on the exhibit list, at least to incorporate by reference the prior exhibits that have been filed that you wish this Court specifically to consider when it files its memorandum and order. And, as I indicated to you previously, if you wish to submit anything else, as long as we agree on some outside date that you think you can comply, you tell me what time you need and we will agree to it.

MS. COPELON: Can we learn from the court reporter how long it will take to get a transcript?

THE COURT: Let's assume that—whatever period of time that is, it will be whatever period of time, a couple of weeks. My only question is, when everything comes to me, I'd like it to come in one. I don't think it is going to be helpful to me or any of the people that—it's not going to be helpful unless I have it all together. After I receive anything, if I have any further questions or I think we should meet again, I'll advise you in writing of that. If there is anything, especially with regard to the applicable law, because it seems to me in this particular case one of the more difficult problems that this case poses is not so much the testimony of the witnesses and what occurred, but assuming for a moment the law that applies in this case is the law of Paraguay. That seems to me to pose some interesting legal problems.

MS. COPELON: We'll have an affidavit from an expert in Paraguayan law to give you a background of that. On the other hand, it is not because there is any deficiency in the law of Paraguay but rather because we think that what is presented here, since it is an issue of remedy under international law, that it may not be that the traditional rules, for example, cited by Judge Kaufman, that apply to admiralty law, necessarily apply to determining what the law should be in this case. That's what we will address in our memorandum.

THE COURT: That's the $64 question.

MS. COPELON: That's right.

THE COURT: In any event, what we will do is we will at this point let a month go by and see where we stand at that time. On the assumption that everything will come to me together. Then after I receive that, I'll be in correspondence with you, either by order or by letter, indicating whether or not we need to do anything further or whether I just at that point have to take it on my own. Okay. This hearing is closed.

MS. COPELON: Thank you very much.

MR. MAGGIO: Thank you, your Honor.

THE COURT: I am going to ask you, if you would, to please take all of these exhibits back. I will leave everything with you.

MR. MAGGIO: Yes.

THE COURT: Double check it. I have my own file here.

(Whereupon this matter was concluded for this date.)

FEBRUARY 25, 1982: PARAGUAY

Telegram from American Embassy, Asunción to U.S. Department of State

Subject: The Filartiga Case in the News

UNCLASSIFIED

UNCLASSIFIED

PAGE 01   ASUNCI   00799   251547Z
ACTION ARA-16

INFO   OCT-00   ADS-00   INR-10   CIAE-00   NSAE-00   HA-06   L-03
        PA-02   ICAE-00   JUSE-00   SPRS-02   /039 W.
        ------------------------------------376361   251839Z   /45

R 251504Z FEB 82
FM AMEMBASSY ASUNCION
TO SECSTATE WASHDC 3165

UNCLAS ASUNCION 0799

E.O. 12065: N/A
TAGS: SHUM, PA
SUBJECT: THE FILARTIGA CASE IN THE NEWS

1. BASED ON WIRE SERVICE REPORTS CONCERNING DR. JOEL FILARTIGA'S CONTINUING CASE IN U.S. FEDERAL COURTS WHICH NOW SEEKS INDEMNIFICATION FROM THE GOVERNMENT OF PARAGUAY FOR THE MARCH 29, 1976 MURDER OF HIS SON, JOELITO, IN ASUNCION, PARAGUAY, THE LOCAL PRESS HAS CARRIED SEVERAL STORIES ON RECENT DEVELOPMENTS. THE LEADING DAILY, "ABC COLOR", ON FEBRUARY 14 REPORTED THE TESTIMONY GIVEN BY THE FORMER U.S. AMBASSADOR TO PARAGUAY ROBERT WHITE AND JACOBO TIMMERMAN CONCERNING HUMAN RIGHTS IN LATIN AMERICA AND PARAGUAY. AMBASSADOR WHITE IS QUOTED AS SAYING THAT DURING HIS TIME IN PARAGUAY IT WAS A SOCIETY SEIZED BY FEAR WHERE TORTURE IS A BASIC MEANS OF REPRESSION AND HAS BEEN INSTITUTIONALIZED. THE ASSOCIATED PRESS STORY WHICH QUOTED AMBASSADOR WHITE PROVOKED A LENGTHY EDITORIAL FROM "PATRIA", THE PAPER OF THE RULING COLORADO PARTY, WHICH WITHOUT MENTIONING THE FILARTIGA CASE BY NAME, CALLED AMBASSADOR WHITE "THE MAN OF INTRIGUES AND FRICTIONS, BOTH

HERE AND IN CENTRAL AMERICA" AND THEN RECOUNTED THE HISTORY OF DEMOCRACY AND JUSTICE IN PARAGUAY.

2. ON FEBRUARY 19 ANOTHER ASUNCION DAILY, "HOY", STATED THAT PARAGUAYAN COURTS ARE REVIEWING THE RECORDS IN THE CASE OF HUGO DERLIS DUARTE ARREDONDO, THE CONFESSED MURDERER OF JOELITO FILARTIGA, AS THE RESULT OF AN APPEAL AGAINST THE SEPTEMBER 1981 DECISION WHICH ABSOLVED DUARTE ARREDONDO OF GUILT AND PUNISHMENT AND FREED HIM AFTER ALMOST FIVE-AND-A-HALF YEARS IN JAIL. THE "HOY" ARTICLE STRESSES THAT DR. FILARTIGA DOES NOT BELIEVE THE VERSION OF THE CASE WHICH CLAIMS THAT DUARTE ARREDONDO KILLED YOUNG FILARTIGA IN A FIT OF PASSION WHEN HE FOUND HIS WIFE IN BED WITH JOELITO.

LANE

UNCLASSIFIED

MARCH 10, 1982: PARAGUAY

Telegram from American Embassy, Asunción to U.S. Department of State

Subject: The Filartiga Case

DECONTROLLED/UNCLASSIFIED
[Excised]
n/a

[Excised]

PAGE 01   ASUNCI   01024   111243Z
ACTION ARA-16

INFO   OCT-00   ADS-00   INR-10   CIAE-00   NSAE-00   HA-06   L-03
       PA-01   ICAE-00   JUSE-00   SPRS-02   /038 W
       ---------------------------------- 137560   111320Z   /41

R 101900Z MAR 82
FM AMEMBASSY ASUNCION
TO SECSTATE WASHDC 3278

[Excised]   ASUNCION 1024

E.O. 12065: N/A
TAGS: SHUM, PA
SUBJECT: THE FILARTIGA CASE

REF: ASUNCION 0799

1. THE COVERAGE IN THE ASUNCION PRESS OF DR. FILARTIGA'S REQUEST FOR DAMAGES IN THE CASE OF THE DEATH OF HIS SON (REFTEL) HAS IMPLIED THAT HE IS SEEKING DAMAGES FROM THE GOVERNMENT OF PARAGUAY. THE LEADING DAILY, ABC COLOR, ON FEBRUARY 13 RAN THE HEADLINE "FILARTIGA ENTERS AN ACTION AGAINST PARAGUAY." HOWEVER, WE HAVE SEEN A COPY OF A MID-FEBRUARY ASSOCIATED PRESS STORY ON THE FILARTIGA CASE WHICH, WHILE QUOTING DR. FILARTIGA AS SAYING "TORTURE IS ON TRIAL AND TORTURE IN PARAGUAY IS ON TRIAL", LEAVES UNANSWERED THE QUESTION OF WHETHER DR. FILARTIGA IS SEEKING DAMAGES FROM AMERICO PENA OR FROM THE GOP.

2. EMBASSY WOULD APPRECIATE REPORT ON CURRENT STATUS OF U.S. DISTRICT COURT ACTION ON FILARTIGA'S DAMAGE SUIT AND

CLARIFICATION OF WHO OR WHAT ENTITY IS LIABLE FOR DAMAGES, IF ANY. GOP OFFICIALS ALSO LACK SPECIFIC INFORMATION ON THIS SUBJECT AND HAVE INDICATED THEY WOULD BE CONCERNED IF THE CASE IN U.S. COURTS COULD CONCEIVABLY LEAD TO SOME DEMAND AGAINST GOP ASSETS IN THE U.S.

LANE

DECEMBER 10, 1982: UNITED STATES

Plaintiffs' Post-Trial Memorandum of Facts and Law; Affidavits of Dolly Filartiga, Joel Filartiga, and Dr. Glenn Randall and Dr. Jose Quiroga

UNITED STATES DISTRICT COURT
EASTERN DISTRICT OF NEW YORK

DR. JOEL FILARTIGA and   **PLAINTIFFS' POST-TRIAL**
DOLLY M.E. FILARTIGA,   **MEMORANDUM OF FACTS**
     AND LAW

        Plaintiffs,

     79 Civ. 917

   – against –

AMERICO NORBERTO PENA-
IRALA, et al.,
     Defendants.

> Rhonda Copelon
> Betty Lawrence Bailey
> Peter Weiss
> c/o CENTER FOR CONSTITUTIONAL RIGHTS
> 853 Broadway
> New York, New York 10003
> (212) 674-3303
>
> Michael Maggio
> 1800 Belmont Road, N.W.
> Washington, D.C. 20009
> (202) 483-0052
>
> Attorneys for Plaintiffs

TABLE OF CONTENTS

A. Funeral and Memorial Expenses

B. Legal Cost

C. Medical Expenses

D. Dolly Filartiga's Medical Expenses

E. Dr. Filartiga Lost Income

Point IV

PLAINTIFFS ARE ENTITLED TO RECOVER FOR THEIR NON-PECUNIARY LOSSES AS A MATTER OF COMPENSATION FOR "MORAL DAMAGE" AND AS A MATTER OF PUNITIVE OR EXEMPLARY DAMAGES UNDER INTERNATIONAL LAW

A. Compensation For Moral Damage Is Required Under Paraguayan And International Law And Must Take Into Account The Heinousness Of Torture And Its Impact On The Suffering Of The Plaintiffs

1. Paraguayan Law

2. Compensation Under International Law

B. The Precedents And Evolving Principles of International Law Warrant This Court's Recognition of Punitive Damages In The Circumstances of This Case

CONCLUSION

I. PROCEDURAL HISTORY

This case arose out of a complaint seeking damages for the wrongful torture and murder of the decedent, Joel (Joelito) Filartiga, in violation of the law of nations and the laws of the United States and Paraguay.

This Court attained personal jurisdiction when the defendant, Norberto Pena-Irala, (Pena), who, having illegally entered this country was found and served with process. The district court dismissed the complaint for want of jurisdiction (Opinion dated May 15, 1979) and an appeal was taken.

On June 30, 1980, the United States Court of Appeals for the Second Circuit, in an unprecedented opinion, held that

deliberate torture perpetrated under color of official authority violated universally accepted norms or the international law of
human rights, regardless of the nationality of the parties. Thus,
whenever an alleged torturer is found and served with process by
an alien within our borders, §1350 provides federal jurisdiction.

Filartiga v. Pena, 630 F.2d 876, 878 (2nd Cir. 1980). Subsequent to this decision, defendant Pena failed to answer the complaint, and after proper
notice a default judgment was entered by the district court (Opinion dated
June 26, 1981) thereby eliminating the issue of liability.

The only issue before this Court is the valuation of damages. On
February 12, 1982, a hearing was held before this Court.[1] At the hearing,
Dr. Filartiga, Joelito's father, and Dolly Filartiga, his sister, testified about
the impact of the torture and the murder of Joelito on them as a family.
Robert White, the former U.S. Ambassador to Paraguay and later El
Salvador described the role and impact of torture in maintaining Latin
America's most repressive dictator, General Stroessner. Jacobo Timerman,
the former editor of the Argentinian paper, "La Opinion" and author of
Prisoner Without A Name, Cell Without A Number discussed torture from the
perspective of an observer of a society decimated by torture as well as a vic-
tim trying to understand the impact of torture on the life of a person.

Additional affidavits and evidence are now being submitted to supplement the oral testimony and the exhibits introduced at the hearing. This
memorandum will summarize the facts relevant to the valuation of damages and in light of the international ramifications of this case, propose a
theory for the application of choice of law, principles to this case.

II. STATEMENT OF FACTS

A. *The Death of Joelito Filartiga*

On March 29, 1976, in the middle of the night, seventeen year old
Joelito Filartiga was kidnapped from his bed while his three sisters and a
sailor lay sleeping in the house (Pictures of Joelito Filartiga at age 5 and
shortly before his death were submitted to this court as Exhibit 2A and 2B).
He was taken two doors down to the house of Americo Norberto Pena-Irala
(Pena), then Inspector General of Police of Asuncion, Paraguay and the
defendant herein. Complaint ¶7. He was whipped, beaten, slashed across
his body and appeared to have been subjected to extremely high levels of
electric shock. An aluminum wire was placed in his penis for the purpose

---

[1] TR. cites refer to the transcript of these proceedings.

of applying electric shock. He was tortured in this manner for approximately forty-five minutes[2] until his young body reached its endurance limit and he died. (Complaint ¶11) The torture of Joelito was in retaliation for the political activities and opinions of his father. (Complaint ¶¶14-15).

At approximately 4:00 a.m. in the morning, Dolly Filartiga, the sister of Joelito and one of the plaintiffs herein was awakened by a loud knock on the front door. The person knocking was Galeano, the Chief of Police for the precinct in that area. He informed her that "there was a small problem with [her] brother at Pena's house." TR. 14. She followed Galeano to Pena's house which was surrounded by land filled with policemen. She asked for her brother and was told he was in the back room. TR. 15.

Knowing the house, she walked to that room and there she was confronted with the brutally tortured body of her beloved brother. The body lay on a mattress in a pool of blood. Complaint ¶12. (A picture of the body, as it was found, was submitted to this Court as Exhibit 3).

In disbelief, she ran to her brother and tried to awaken him. She wanted to cry, but they did not let her. She wanted to ask for help, but she was stopped. She was told to take her brother's body and bury it quickly. (TR. 15). But she could not think of what to do. In desperation, she ran to the street.

On her way out, Dolly Filartiga met defendant Pena in the hall of the house. She asked him what he had done to her brother and he replied with a confession and a threat: "here you have what you have been looking for for so long and what you deserved. Now shut up." (Complaint, ¶ 13, TR 16). He further threatened Dolly with a similar fate. With this, Dolly ran into the streets in circles, finally finding her way home where she and a younger sister consoled each other and attempted to call relatives. Still Pena insisted that Dolly remove the body of her brother, or it would be thrown into the streets. (TR. 18). With the help of the sailor and a policeman, Dolly took Joelito's body home on the bloody mattress on which she found it.

---

[2] Dr. Filartiga testified that, based on his experience as an observer of the torture of over 300 victims, as well as his experience in treating over 500 victims of torture in his medical practice, that it would take approximately 45 minutes to inflict the degree of torture inflicted on Joelito. TR. 33. This estimate was supported by Dr. Glenn Randall and Dr. Jose Quiroga in their affidavits.

Dr. Filartiga testified that he believed his son had endured at least 45 minutes of extreme torture and his son died of cardiac arrest (TR. 40). Drs. Randall and Quiroga note this as one possibility indicating that shock, hemorrhage and an intracerebral bleed as a result of the injuries he suffered could also explain his death. (Affd. of Randall and Quiroga, ¶8, p.6).

At the time Joelito was killed, Dolly's parents were in rural Ybycui where they ran a medical clinic for the poor. Dolly had tried unsuccessfully to reach them since the night before and she tried in vain for six hours to summon them after she discovered Joelito. (TR. 18). Over seven hours after Dolly had been led to Joelito, her parents arrived, having been informed by a messenger that "Joelito has suffered a tragedy." (TR. 37).

Both parents were totally devastated by the sight of their son's tortured body. Dr. Filartiga, having seen over 300 victims tortured during his four imprisonments, having treated over 500 victims of torture in his medical practice and having been a torture victim himself on three occasions, knew exactly what had happened to his son. (TR. 39-42). He also knew immediately that his son was killed to punish him. (TR. 28).

His immediate thought, in the midst of all of his grief, was to document what had happened to his son, in order to prevent it from happening to others. (TR. 41-43). Thus immediately upon his arrival home, he took pictures of Joelito's tortured body. (Four of the pictures were submitted to this Court as Exhibits 5A and 5B). In addition, he summoned three doctors, who along with himself performed an autopsy on Joelito to supplement the false official autopsy. (The text of these reports is contained in Exhibit 11A). Joelito's naked body lay in state at the Filartiga home so that the entire community could pay their respects and be made aware of the brutality that was done to Joelito. Subsequent to his burial and fourteen days after his death, his body was exhumed and a third autopsy was performed on him. (Exhibit 11B). The last autopsy established that there had been burn marks on Joelito's body. (Exhibit 11B). See affidavit of Joel Filartiga ¶4).

The evidence demonstrates that Joelito suffered the most brutal forms of physical torture.

> The torture to which Joelito was subjected probably consisted of the elements suggested in the autopsy report. That is, beating with a fist and other devices, including a looped cord, kicking, removing the nails from their proper places, (although the nails on the photograph provided seem to be intact on the left hand, and the report therefore may suggest loosening as a postmortem change) burning with electricity (or with chemical or other thermal agent) and penetration with sharp objects. These resulted in wounds and ecchymoses of the head and face, lips, malar region, periorbital, temporal aspect of the skull (fracture of the right temporal bone, parietal, and nasal), right shoulder, right and left arms, hands, tho-

rax, abdominal flanks, back, hips, thighs, legs, and feet. These have been described in the autopsy report. There were also penetrating wounds of the thorax and right leg. There were three reportedly burned areas measuring 2 cm. in diameter, 3 x 4 cm., and 5 x 2 cm. respectively. The genitalia were reportedly mutilated and a wire was removed from Joelito's penis by Dr. Filartiga. The photograph of the body of Joelito Filartiga shows direct evidence of torture in the form of whipping and beating. The patterned marks over the right side of the body are classical for whip marks by a looped flexible cord. The injuries of Joelito were deliberately forceful, multiple and inflicted over a period of time. For example, the mark on the right thigh appears to be older than others. The other marks on the skin were certainly inflicted during life and were intended to produce severe pain. The cause of death probably was not a single stab wound but rather the result of shock and hemorrhage due to multiple traumatic injuries. If the burns were caused by electricity, the amount of current used may have caused his death by cardiac arrest. An intracerebral bleed may have also been responsible. This possibility must be raised because of the fracture of the temporal bone of the skull. To my knowledge no examination of the internal organs or the brain was made. While the pain associated with the beating and stabbing can be imagine to some degree by anyone, the amount of pain from the considerable number of wounds inflicted upon Joelito must be outside the experience of any of us. Joelito's torture and pain may have been more severe than any of the victims we have examined in the United States. We say this because it was severe enough to cause his death. In our research experience 100% of the victims were beaten. The electric shock torture is customarily administered, either by conduction through an electrolyte solution or wet rags, thus, leaving no physical trace. Or through more direct means, by direct application of the electrodes to the skin. This is an extremely painful torture. In the usual apparatus the amount of electricity applied to the electrode can be varied and the electrode can be moved from place to place. The genitalia are often shocked in this way and the urethal wire removed by Dr. Filartiga was probably used for electric torture. 75% of the victims that we have examined were subjected to electric shock torture. After inflicting an unbearable amount of pain, the electric torture commonly causes the loss of consciousness. Only the most severe cases have more than minor evidence of burns, either immediately after torture or years later. Thus, the burns on Joelito, if caused by electricity, represent an agonizing amount of electrical torture.

(Affidavit of Dr. Glenn Randall and Dr. Jose Quiroga ¶¶ 8, 9). See also TR 32 (J. Filartiga). It can be assumed that Joelito was also subjected to psychological torture in the form of taunting and humiliation including "threats against the family, threats of death and other vague threats." Affidavit of Drs. Randall and Quiroga ¶9. Jacobo Timerman describes the humiliation of torture as worse than death. (TR. 60).

The harassment of the Filartiga family by agents of the government did not end with Joelito's death. Immediately thereafter, armed guards surrounded the family home twenty-four hours per day. The clicking of guns could be heard throughout the night. Dr. and Mrs. Filartiga and their three children lived in constant fear that they would be harmed by these guards. (TR. 22). The family was so fearful for the safety of one another that they took turns watching the guards during the night. (TR. 22). They slept under the bed for protection. Threats were made by telephone. Every time the telephone rang they answered it apprehensively. The entire family was threatened with a similar fate as Joelito. See also sealed Affidavit. ¶16, (TR. 20, 23).

Twenty-five days after Joelito's death, Dolly and Mrs. Filartiga were arrested and without being allowed to present any evidence in their own behalf, thrown in jail. They were falsely accused of breaking into defendant Pena's house and scratching one of his sons-in-law. Complaint ¶16. They were released from jail only after Dr. Filartiga published an advertisement in the newspaper asking for security for their lives. (TR. 25).

Nor was it possible for the family to achieve justice. All the key witnesses that might explain the case have disappeared. (TR. 49). Dr. Filartiga brought a lawsuit in Paraguay in which he was represented by Horacio Galeano Perrone, a Paraguayan lawyer. He did not get a hearing on his claim, instead, his lawyer was thrown in jail and disbarred. (TR. 45). See also affidavit of Dr. William L. Wipler ¶12. Other lawyers left his case because they were afraid. (TR. 45).

We were not allowed to submit evidence or obtain discovery in the proceeding in Paraguay. The court was just sitting on the case until we brought this suit in the United States.

Affidavit ¶8 J. Filartiga.

As former Ambassador White testified:

Q: Based upon your knowledge of the system in Paraguay, do you have an opinion whether or not the Filartigas could get justice in Paraguay?

A. No it's impossible. (TR. 80)

Moreover, as the family persisted in their quest for justice and as they tried to survive the death of their beloved brother and son, agents of the government would appear in the house undercover pretending to be suitors of the Filartiga daughters. The harassment was constant and never ending.[3] Pena had fled to the United States. When Pena was arrested here Dr. Filartiga was threatened and almost killed in a fabricated traffic accident. (TR. 45-46).

Still being strong individuals, the family was determined to endure the continued harassment. However, they could not escape the traumatic effect that Joelito's death had on each family member and the family as a whole. Although Joelito's death had a devastating impact on all the family members, the effect with which we are concerned here is as to the plaintiffs: Dolly, his best friend and the one who was first confronted with his brutally tortured body; and Dr. Filartiga, his father, his friend and the person at whom this terrible brutality was directed, and who blamed himself for the suffering and death of his son and that of the entire family.

B. *The Impact of Joelito's Death on Dr. Filartiga*

Dr. Filartiga's suffering was threefold. He suffered because he lost his only son. He suffered because Joelito was tortured in retaliation for Dr. Filartiga's political beliefs. Finally, he suffered because his entire family was suffering and he blamed himself for their suffering. His suffering was both emotional and physical.[4]

First, Dr. Filartiga suffers because he lost a companion, comforter, helper, and friend and the person he thought would carry on his work. Joelito and Dr. Filartiga enjoyed each other's company. They went fishing together. They took walks. They talked about their respective views of life with each other. Joelito shared his father's concern for the Paraguayan poor, and would show this by frequently assisting his father in the clinic in Ybycui. His father's work became so important to him that Joelito decided to devote his life to helping heal people. Like his father, he was going to become a doctor. Further, Joelito enjoyed art as a form of expression, as did his father. He wanted to also become an architect. (TR. 30). He strongly

---

[3] At one point the youngest of the Filartiga daughters was kidnapped by a police officer, kept away from the family for eighteen hours and was found only after the family went to the American Embassy to protest. (Sealed affidavit p. 5).

[4] Reference is made to the Transcript of the Filartigas testimony and to the sealed affidavit and those of Dr. Filartiga, Dolly Filartiga, Dr. Frederico Allodi, Drs. Randall and Quiroga, Michele Anna Burgess.

identified with his father in many ways. Dr. Filartiga expressed this sentiment in a poem:

TO ANOTHER JOEL
by Joel Filartiga
On a sinister and pitch-black night
on a Monday, 29th of March
another way of being Joel
departed.
A painful journey without end.
Youth cut off
cruelly chopped off
by the bearers of death and nothingness.
Others will be what you couldn't become:
soldier of a new dawn.
Joel, your father, another Joel but Joel just
the same.

Translated by Robert Cohen.

(Exhibit 8).

Second, Dr. Filartiga suffers severe mental anguish and grief not just because he lost his son, but because of the manner in which he lost him. He understood and suffered vicariously the intensity of Joelito's pain because he had been a victim as well as observer of torture while in prison.

As a lifetime opponent of the Stroessner regime, Dr. Filartiga has been imprisoned four times and was tortured three of those times. In 1958, while coordinator of students and workers against the Stroessner dictatorial regime, he was arrested and tortured continuously for eleven days without food and under force labor. (TR. 31). He was also tortured in 1963 and on another occasion. Several forms of torture were used against Dr. Filartiga. A torture method called "telephone" was used which involved striking his ears with both hands. He was kept standing for 76 hours without sleep. His lungs and kidneys were battered, causing him to urinate blood for six days. He was "submarined," which involved submersing him in water almost to the point of exhaustion. This was done under the supervision of a doctor to avoid killing him. (TR. 31). Dr. Filartiga testified that

> they put salt in the water to stimulate the capacity of the water to communicate electricity, conduct electricity and I was subjected to electric shocks which resulted in lack of control of the sphincters and so that one has to defecate and urinate in the water and one is kept permanently submerged in that water approximately 3 hours each session. (TR. 31-32).

He was further tortured psychologically being forced to watch the torture of others. Most notably, he watched a sixty-seven year old man tortured almost to the point of death. As painful as it was to be a victim of torture, Dr. Filartiga found that being a spectator to torture was more painful—it was psychological torture. Having seen 300 persons tortured, Dr. Filartiga has been psychologically tortured 300 times. To Dr. Filartiga, Joelito's death was the ultimate torture and it has left him in permanent pain. When he saw Joelito's body, he remembered all of the torture he experienced and witnessed and he knew exactly how his son felt when he was brutalized. (TR. 42). Joelito's death has affected every aspect of Dr. Filartiga's life.

He blamed himself for Joelito's death, he felt the accusations of his family and he wished it had been him instead. (See, sealed affidavit ¶10, affidavit of Drs. Randall and Quiroga ¶12,14, TR 50, 51). He felt anger and despair because of his son's death which he expressed in his drawings. (Examples of Dr. Filartiga's drawings after Joelito's death are submitted as Exhibits 6A, 6E, 6C and 7.) Additionally, he lived in great fear almost to the point of paranoia. Sealed affidavit, ¶18. He constantly worried that what happened to Joelito would happen to other family members. Soon his emotional response to Joelito's death triggered a physical response.

Dr. Filartiga lost 50% of his capacity to work. (TR. 50). His eyesight weakened. His hair grayed. He experienced circulatory problems. He developed an ulcer and he developed a borderline case of diabetes—which is a known result of extreme stress. Finally, he watched his family suffer and blamed himself for their suffering. Affidavit of Dr. Filartiga, Dr. Allodi, Dr. Randall and Quiroga.

His wife lived in a state of constant fear for the entire family. She feared when any family members left the house and protested whenever Dr. Filartiga left home. She was angry and hostile towards him on the one hand, since she verbally blamed him for Joelito's death, while she was over-protective on the other. (Sealed affidavit). He watched Joelito's death impact on all of his daughters, most notably his oldest daughter, Dolly. When Dolly was forced to seek asylum in the United States, Dr. Filartiga and the family lost not only a son, but for all practical purposes, the companionship, comfort and substantial assistance at home and in the clinic of their oldest daughter, Dolly.

C. *The Impact of Joelito's Death on Dolly Filartiga.*

Dolly had a very close relationship with her brother. As she described it, they "were great friends, great companions . . . ." (TR. 13). They had mutual friends. They went out together and spent a great deal of time with each other. They trusted and confided in each other. As the oldest Filartiga children, they also shared the responsibility of taking care of the house and their younger sisters during the week when their parents were working in the clinic in Ybycui. They also shared the dream of becoming doctors. Both assisted their parents in the clinic whenever it was possible. Both were working towards the eventual goal of attending medical school. Although the family felt the repression of the regime, their lives were relatively normal—they went to school, worked, took care of the household, went out socially and always had a houseful of people, until Joelito was brutally tortured to death. His death had a devastating impact on Dolly's life. Her life, since that time, has been a nightmare. TR. 21-26. Affidavit of Dolly Filartiga, ¶¶2, 3, 4, 6, 9, 10, 13.

For the first year following her brother's death, Dolly refused to believe that he was dead. She often thought that she heard the sound of his footsteps or his voice, only to be filled with terrible fear and despair when he did not appear.

Dolly had constant nightmares. In these nightmares, she would see Joelito "raising from the blood-soaked mattress upon which [she] found him with all his wounds and that he [would tell her] that nothing happened." Through the dreams, she constantly relived her forced confrontation in defendant Pena's house, with the brutally tortured body of her beloved friend and brother. Each time, she would wake up screaming, covering her mouth with a pillow to drown the sound.

During this period, Dolly could not sleep. On average, she slept for one hour per day. She could not concentrate, she could not hold a job. She wandered at times, not knowing where she was going. She lost her identity. She felt helpless and insecure. All of her difficulties were apparent in her family interactions which were marked by anger and isolation. Affidavits of Dolly Filartiga ¶8, Drs. Randall and Quiroga ¶12.

Dolly became a compulsive cleaner. She basically cleaned "the same thing over and over . . . [she could not] stand anything messy" as she had found her brother. Affidavit of Dolly Filartiga ¶3. She was a picky eater. Her family frequently had to beg her to eat her food. Michele Burgess' affidavit ¶8.

Even so Dolly did not acknowledge Joelito's death until one year after it had occurred. During the middle of a mass, exactly one year after Joelito's death, Dolly realized that he was never corning back. Several days later, she tried to kill herself and was taken to the hospital where her stomach was pumped. Subsequently, severe depression set in. She began to spend a substantial period of time in the house, where she usually remained in bed. She could not communicate with any one. Dolly stated, "I thought I should have died so my brother could live - I wished it had been me. I wanted to die; I felt that he was my only hope, and I could never possibly feel normal again." Affidavits of Dolly Filartiga ¶6, Drs Randall and Quiroga ¶12,13, Deutsch ¶7,10 Dr. Allodi ¶7. Dolly withdrew from both family life and life in her community—she had no friends. She lost her capacity to enjoy life.

These symptoms' exhibited by Dolly closely fit the pattern of post-traumatic stress disorder. (A discussion of this disorder is in the appendix of the affidavit of Dr. Glenn Randall and Dr. Jose Quiroga.) See also, affidavit of Ana Deutsch and Exhibit 21.[5]

---

[5] The-American Psychiatric Association, states that "Post-traumatic Stress Disorder" can be produced by "deliberate man-made disasters (bombing, torture, camps)." DMS III American Psychiatric Association Diagnostic and Statistical Manual. 1980.

The traumatic event can be reexperienced in a variety of ways. Commonly the individual has a recurrent painful, intrusive recollections of the event or recurrent dreams or nightmares during which the event is reexperienced. In rare instances there are dissociative like states, lasting from a few minutes to several hours or even days, during which components of the events are relived and the individual behaves as though experiencing the event at that moment. Such states have been reported in combat veterans. Diminished responsiveness to the external world, referred to as "psychic numbing" or "emotional anesthesia," usually begins soon after the traumatic event. A person may complain of feeling detached or estranged from other people, that he or she has lost the ability to become interested in previously enjoyed significant activities, or that the ability to feel emotions of any type, especially those associated with intimacy, tenderness, and sexuality, is markedly decreased.

After experiencing the stressor, many develop symptoms of excessive autonomic arousal, such as hyper-alertness, exaggerated startle response, and difficulty falling asleep. Recurrent nightmares during which the traumatic event is relived and which are sometimes accompanied by middle or terminal sleep disturbance may be present. Some complain of impaired memory or difficulty in concentrating or completing tasks. In the case of a life-threatening trauma shared with others, survivors often describe painful guilt feelings about surviving when many did not, or about the things they had to do in order to survive. Activities or situations that may arouse recollections of the traumatic events are often avoided. Symptoms characteristic of Post-traumatic Stress Disorder are often intensified when the individual is exposed to situations or activities that resemble or symbolize the original trauma (e.g., cold snowy weather or uniformed guards for death-camp survivors, hot humid weather for veterans of the South Pacific).

In her affidavit Ana Deutch found that Dolly exhibited the following symptoms of the above disorder:

(a) sleep disturbance (nightmares, insomnia); (b) incapacity to concentrate; (c) incapacity to work; (d) identity confusion ("When people . . . asked me my name, I drew a blank"); (e) helplessness, insecurity ("I felt that I would never

Joelito's death also affected the way Dolly perceived her country and her family:

> She could not see anything positive about her own country; she only saw that they let the brutal torture and death occur. Dolly blamed not only the government but also her family, specifically her father, for the death of her brother and for the pain she experienced as a result of her loss. Her hostility was tremendous. Reason or logic left her. She was alone. (Sealed affidavit ¶21, p.6).

Subsequent to her suicide attempt and as a result of the symptoms discussed herein, Dolly went into psychoanalysis for one year. However, the pain would not cease. Finally, as the pain over Joelito's death increased, and as the harassment of her family continued, Dolly left home. She came to the United States not only to find defendant Pena, but because life in Paraguay had become unbearable. (Sealed Affidavit ¶22, 23). Her problems did not end.

In the United States, Dolly was estranged from her family, and in unfamiliar surroundings. She had to learn a new language and go through a process of assimilation while still struggling to deal with her loss. Now she had lost not only her best friend and brother, but also the comfort and assistance of her entire family. Further, by pursuing Pena in this country, and by bringing the lawsuit in federal court, she had lost all hope of ever returning to the country of her birth—a country which she loved and hated at the same time. She abandoned as well her ambition to become a doctor—because she was not "prepared to handle more pain." TR. 83 Affidavit of Dolly Filartiga ¶13.

Six years after Joelito's death, Dolly still cannot read or concentrate, is afraid of social situations, feels estranged from normal life and despairs of ever feeling normal again. All of this pain, dislocation, and suffering should not have occurred but for the brutal slaying of her brother by defendant Pena and others. Six years after her brother's death Dolly is still tormented and there seems to be no end in sight. Even with extensive ther-

---

possibly feel normal again"); (f) self-pity, worthlessness ("I wanted to die, I felt that was the only hope"); (g) withdrawals ("I had no friends"); (h) incapacity to enjoy life ("I had no life in Paraguay"); (i) anxiety (Implied into the context of her description and "I could not study, I could not live, I could not work, I had no friends, and I felt constantly persecuted"); (j) survivor guilt (her tendency to clean compulsively is a reactive formation against guilt feelings; "I tried to kill myself," or it could be an attempt to defend herself against guilty feelings); and (k) difficulties in establishing interpersonal relationship ("I am fearful of social situations and strangers").

apy, it is unlikely she will ever feel normal again. (See affidavits of Dolly Filartiga ¶6, Drs. Randall and Quiroga ¶¶12,13, Deutch ¶7,10 and Dr. Allodi ¶7.) Dolly summarizes the way she feels today:

> I don't think there is a moment in my life when I feel free of the torture of my brother's torture and death. I have always the memory of his tortured body and his death; always the weight of this experience, of my identity; always the great hole in my life left by his death. I used to want to be a doctor and I functioned like a nurse in my father's clinic. Today, I do not think I could bear the pain, just as I still cannot bear to read; or use my intellect; I am fearful of social situations and strangers. I always feel different, and like I will never know what it is like to live a relatively normal life. Affidavit, p.5, ¶13.

D. *The Role of Torture in Paraguay*

This terrible brutality and its intended consequences for the family members, was no isolated incident in Paraguay but part of a system of lawlessness and cruelty which destroys humanity and sustains Latin America's most brutal dictatorship.

As former Ambassador Robert White testified, "Torture is basic to the repression [in Paraguay]. It's at the heart of the system that enables the Stroessner dictatorship to maintain itself in power." (TR. 72). Anyone who has the capacity to play a leadership role, or anyone who challenges the system in any way, can be subjected to torture. "[P]eople who appear normal get up and go to work and their work is torture, and then they come home after work and do whatever normal people do. [Torture] is institutionalized in Paraguay." (TR. 73). An understanding of the Paraguayan legal system is necessary to put the role of torture in context.

In Paraguay there exists a dual system of authoritative norms, which perpetuates violations of human rights including the use of torture. The first of these laws

> consists of the Constitution, Code, laws and administrative rules and regulations which make up the country's official legal system. The second is an unwritten code of norms assigning rank and influence within a hierarchy of power. The second bears the name in Guarani of *mbarete*, which in English means "superior power over others." In Paraguay when the code of *mbarete* clashes with the legal system, it is the latter which must and does give way. *Mbarete* is the higher law, superior to any and all norms postulated by the legal system.

Affidavit of Dr. William L. Wipfler, p.2, and Exhibits 10A,B,C. *Mbarete* exists throughout the authoritative system. It allows the will of President Stroessner to be pre-eminent. It allows police, prosecutors and judges to feel a sense of immunity no matter the extent of their lawlessness. "No police official fears retribution for murder, torture or the violation of other basic human rights, nor do prosecutors or judges feel the slightest sense of insecurity about subverting the law." Its corrupting effects are pervasive and deep-seated. (Wipfler affidavit, p.3).

However, the servants of the *mbarete* system, only occasionally exercise it openly and nakedly.

> The government shows a marked preference for legal formality, even when *mbarete* is at the heart of a decision. Thus state of siege decrees are issued every three months, police reports are filed, prosecutors prepare and present briefs and judges take statements, hear testimony and render opinions and sentences. The police never admit to torture or the murder of prisoners, nor do judges refer to the intervention of illegal pressures in the cases they decide. An effort is made to maintain at least some formal compliance with norms of the legal system.

Wipfler affidavit p.4. Thus, the torture-murder of Joelito, and the clumsy attempt to cover it up as a crime of passion and exonerate Pena fits squarely into the manner in which *mbarete* operates.

Under the *mbarete* system "political dissent is repressed through the use of torture, imprisonment and other means. Torture is a perfectly acceptable and almost commonplace instrument of interrogation and repression." (Wipfler affidavit, p.4).

To understand how torture could become so commonplace, one must understand the theory behind the use of torture. According to Jean-Paul Sartre:

> The purpose of torture is not only to make a person talk, but to make him betray others. The victim must turn himself by his screams and by his submission into a lower animal, in the eyes of all and in his own eyes. His betrayal must destroy him and take away his human dignity. He who gives way under questioning is not only constrained from talking again, but is given a new status, that of a sub-man.

Quoted in M. Ruthven *Torture The Grand Conspiracy*. (1978), p.284. The *Amnesty International Report on Torture* 34-35 (Farras, Straus and Giroux) (1975) (Exhibit 15) explains:

Torture implies a systematic activity with a rational purpose. The unwitting, and thus accidental, infliction of pain, is not torture. Torture is the deliberate infliction of pain, and it cannot occur without the specific intent of the torturer. Inherent in this element of purpose are the goals or motives for employing torture, and while torture can be used for a variety of purposes, it is most generally used to obtain confessions or information, for punishment, and for the intimidation of the victim and third persons. The first two motives relate directly to the victim, while the purpose of intimidation, in wide use today as a political weapon, is intended to be a deterrent to others as well as the victim.

The motives for torture in Paraguay are equally consistent with the above:

In Paraguay, motives for torture are varied since charges of communism are often used as an excuse for arrest and maltreatment in order to dispose of rivals. The most extreme opponents of the regime are summarily disposed of, so that those who are tortured do not usually represent violent opposition, but may simply be the relatives of suspects or persons whom the government deems it desirable to intimidate.

Amnesty International Report on Torture, p.215. Thus, in this case, when Dr. Filartiga's opposition was not stopped by his own torture, the Stroessner regime turned to a more cruel form of repression, the torture and death of his son. Joelito and his father were not the only ones subjected to political repression during the period in which Joelito was brutally killed. The entire political climate was especially repressive at that time. The sealed affidavit describes the situation:

Just before Joelito was murder, Paraguayan police killed several alleged "guerrillas" shortly after they had crossed the Argentine border and entered Paraguay. The next week several other members of a new formed "guerilla" group, OPM, the political military organization were killed in an alleged shootout in Asuncion. A few days later the police raided the Catholic Jesuit school Cristo Rey which they claimed was the center of "guerilla" operation. The government offered no proof of their charges and found no evidence that support their action. Later that month, they raided the agricultural school of Santa Maria in Coronel Oviedo not far from where I lived, saying that it had been a center for communist cell groups operations and that they had found a tremendous amount of subversive literature on the property. Three years later I learned that this material was planted by the police to support their accusations that it was a center for cell groups operations. Just shortly after Joelito's death, over two thousand of our peasant leaders were jailed without being brought before the court and held on the mere accusations that they all had connections or relationships with subversive groups, or with the communist party. It is worth noting that holding citizens without presenting charges against them is in itself a violation of the Paraguayan Constitution. P.2 ¶13.

No doubt many of those arrested were tortured. So long as *mbarete* exists, torture as a form of repression will exist, since "it is . . . the suspension of the rule of law, often accompanied by putting a specific group of individuals beyond the limits of a society, which seems to create the matrix for the growth of torture." (*Amnesty International Report on Torture*, p.242).

The inhumanity of torture is beyond demonstration, and beyond the imagination of those who have never been subjected to it. We can only stretch our imagination through hearing the experiences of victims of torture to glimpse the enormity of this crime and understand why the community of nations has joined to condemn its use without qualification and work towards redress of its victims and its ultimate elimination.

To Jacobo Timerman and indeed to Dr. Filartiga, torture is worse than death. It is "the biggest humiliation, the moment they are changing your world of ideas and your world of values and your biological structure." (TR 60). Torture is something one never forgets—it can never be overcome. Further, it is something that international law condemns and society should never accept for any reason; torture cannot be rationalized under any set of circumstances. (TR. 61, 65). Mr. Timerman explained that the torturer

> act[s] like God because they have the power not only to kill you—that it is nothing—because to kill is a power that is in the hands of every human being.

> They have a bigger power to torture and to discover, find out and change everything they want to do. And this is the danger.

> The moment [torture] is incorporated to a society as routine, a permanent feature of life, as American philosopher H. Arendt said about Eichmann, the banality of everything; the moment you accept that, you haven't changed society, you have changed our civilization.

> This is going on in countries like Paraguay, Argentina, Chile, in which torture is an inevitable instrument of the way this society, this country has been built up.

(TR. 66). In the words of Mr. Timerman, torture destroys life not only through death, as in the case of Joelito Filartiga, but it destroys the essence of life by permanently becoming a part of the lives of its victims.[6] (TR. 59). Torture is a permanent part of the life of Mr. Timerman and his family, as well as of the Filartiga family. Indeed in Paraguay, it is a part of the lives of almost everyone since, as former Ambassador Robert White testified, "there is . . . almost no one in Paraguay who hasn't been touched by torture, in the sense that either they or someone in their family . . . has been tortured." (TR. 75).

In addition, the problem of torture is international[7] and torture is internationally condemned. As stated in the opinion in this case: "[f]or purposes of civil liability, the torturer has become—like the pirate and slave trader before him—hostis humani generis," an enemy of all mankind." *Filartiga v. Pena-Irala*, 630 F.2d at 890. Thus, present in this case is the compelling interest of the community of nations as well as this nation in the condemnation of torture. It is not a simple crime, but a crime which transcends the bounds of civilization itself. As Jacobo Timerman stated:

> Torture was condemned as a crime. It was never judged as a problem of our civilization, and this is quite different. . . . And this (the Filartiga case) is something absolutely unusual, and I really hope that from here, as so many other times in the history from the U.S. will come a guideline about what is the relation of our civilization with torture. (TR. 58).

Robert White's testimony illustrates the deterrent effect a judgment against torture would have in Paraguay:

> The only thing that Paraguay responds to are international pressures. Traditionally Paraguay—the Stroessner regime has survived pressures of keeping—by not responding to them, by postponing action, by waiting things out.

> There was—I think, that the Carter administration with emphasis on human rights had a great effect in Paraguay and—but now that—in the—that there has been a change in the priorities of the

---

[6] A compelling illustration of this point was made by Mr. Timerman, when he told the story of author James Amery, who was tortured by the Gestapo when he was a Belgium fighter in 1943. "He committed suicide in 1978, and all those times, all those years he was living with the problem of torture." TR. 59.

[7] See e.g., plaintiffs' exhibit 10a-c, 13-19 and affidavit of international legal experts on torture: Arens, Falk, Franck, Lillich and MacDougal (plaintiffs' exhibit 20A-E).

administration, it probably has less effect. But international pressures are the only way.

[I] think one example might illustrate this. After the case was decided in favor of Dr. Filartiga, a Paraguayan official, one of the people closest to General Stroessner, told me that I just had to do everything possible to get this decision reversed. They don't really understand independence of the court system here. And he stressed to me that no Paraguayan government figure would feel free to travel to the United States after every trip that Dr. Filartiga made here and we would get letters from university professors, human rights organizations and just ordinary citizens, Senators, Congressmen, etc., in effect saying, please do everything you can to protect Dr. Filartiga. (TR. 78-79).

Former Ambassador White feels that taking action in this case will spread,

[a]n umbrella of protection not only over Dr. Filartiga, but people who were conducting themselves according to the norms of the Constitution of Paraguay and sort of generally accepted civilized norms and so that the government could not without expecting a reaction from the United States, kidnap, torture, kill, whatever. (TR. 79).

Dr. William L. Wipfler in his affidavit concluded that:

Given the immunity that *mbarete* provides to violators of the international human rights norms in Paraguay, this case is crucially important, both practically and symbolically. It challenges the system of *mbarete* and puts its participants on notice that the freedom they have assumed to travel to this country and potentially others around the world is constrained. Moreover, the damage award—whether ultimately enforceable or not—will stand as a symbol of the value the international community places on the protection against torture and the heinousness with which such deeds are viewed.

CONCLUSION

No judgment that this Court can render can possibly compensate or full reflect the condemnation of torture or the ineffable life-long suffering it has inflicted on these plaintiffs and all other victims of the system that makes it possible. This Court has the power only to award damages. Money can never repair, can never compensate and cannot adequately punish. It can never bring Joelito back to life or even change his death from the vehicle for the torture and punishment of the family into a normal accidental or natural death of a loved one.

The damage award from this Court must compensate for the identifiable pecuniary losses which are explained in the attached chart. But it has a higher function. In considering the pain and suffering of the plaintiffs and the heinousness of the defendants' crime, this Court must vindicate the right to be free from torture and express the condemnation of the entire international community of this intolerable offense. The award will not be for the personal benefit of the plaintiffs, but will be put in a Foundation "La Esperanza Fund" (The Hope Fund) "devoted to protecting and advancing the health and welfare of the poor people of Paraguay and a symbol that Joelito lives and is helping them." Affidavit of Dr. Filartiga ¶16.

ARGUMENT

Introduction

Plaintiffs submit that damages in this case must be assessed in light of the dual character of the torture-murder at issue. On the one hand, all the acts committed against plaintiffs and their decedent, Joelito Filartiga, are torts under the relevant municipal law which prescribes the scope of damages recoverable. On the other, the torture-murder of Joelito also violates the customary international law. The assessment of damages is, therefore, not confined to what municipal law provides, but must account as well for the international character of the tort and the interest of the international community in just satisfaction. (Point I).

If this case involved a purely domestic offense then choice of law principles would point to the law of Paraguay. (Point II-A). Given the international condemnation of torture, however, choice of law doctrine demands primary consideration of whether the domestic remedy provides just and full satisfaction as that is understood in international law. (Point II-B). Alternatively, insofar as this case involves the customary international law which is incorporated into the federal common law, this court should apply international principles directly. (Point II-C). In either case, the measure of damage must be sufficient to vindicate the interest of the community of nations in full reparation of the damage and vindication of the world's condemnation of torture.

Plaintiffs have documented $439,734 in pecuniary losses flowing from the torture-murder of Joelito and the consequences they entailed. (Point III). The major aspect of damage in this case does not involve pecuniary losses, however, but rather non-pecuniary ones.[8] This involves what is referred to in Paraguayan, and at times in international law, as "moral" damage, e.g. for mental suffering, loss of companionship and security, injury to feelings, the suffering of illness and physical deterioration, the disruption of relations and way of life and the like; and it includes "punitive" or "exemplary" damages designed to express outrage and deter future offenses.

As we shall show, both Paraguayan and international law require this court to take punitive aspects such as malice, the heinousness of the crime and the severity of the consequences, into account in assessing "compensatory" damages. (Point IV-A). But in addition the precedents and the principles reflected in the evolving customary international norms with respect to damages[9] justify an award of explicitly punitive damages in view of the international condemnation and demand that torture be punished. This is particularly so in light of the fact that the defendant has escaped all sanction in Paraguay, being immunized by the system of *mbarete* from criminal as well as civil liability. (Point IV-B).

POINT I.   DAMAGES FOR TORTURE WHICH IS BOTH A MUNICIPAL AND INTERNATIONAL WRONG MUST BE ASSESSED IN LIGHT OF BOTH MUNICIPAL AND INTERNATIONAL PRINCIPLES.

The decision of the Second Circuit in this case makes clear the dual nature of the wrong at issue. It is at once, a tort subject to the principle that

> [C]ommon law courts of general jurisdiction regularly adjudicate transitory tort claims between individuals over whom they exercise personal jurisdiction, wherever the tort occurred. Moreover, as part of an articulated scheme of federal control over external affairs, Congress provided . . . for federal jurisdiction over suits by aliens where principles of international law are in issue."

630 F.2d 876, 885 (2d Cir. 1980).

In this respect, the torture and the related wrongs enumerated in the complaint are violations of domestic law which are actionable here because of the principle that torts are transitory and follow the wrongdoer. The concurrent federal jurisdiction affords a national rather than a state forum for

---

[8]   See also: *Letelier v. Republic of Chile*, 503 F.Supp 259, 266-267 (D.D.C. 1980).

[9]   International law has never addressed the question of individual recovery against individual wrongdoers directly. The principles referred to are drawn primarily from the international approach to questions of state responsibility. See Point III-B, *infra*.

redress of claims involving international law because of the significance of the federal concern with the international relations and obligations.

But the torture for which the defendant Pena is liable here, is not simply a constitutionally condemned domestic crime, giving rise to civil remedy, under the laws of Paraguay. It is also, as the Circuit held, 630 F.2d at 884, a violation of the customary international law. Because Article III jurisdiction rests on the fact that the "law of nations forms an integral part of the common law of the United States," 630 F.2d at 886, torture is also subject to redress in accordance with international law principles and this court is empowered to enforce those principles. The Circuit made clear that the federal court's authority to discern and apply the principles of international law does not depend upon whether Congress has acted to define it, pursuant to its Article I sec. 8 cl. 10 powers. The Circuit held:

> Thus, it was hardly a radical initiative for Chief Justice Marshall to state in *The Nereide*, 13 U.S. (9 Cranch) 388, 422, 3 L.Ed. 769 (1815), that in the absence of a Congressional enactment, United States courts are "bound by the law of nations, which is a part of the law of the land." These words were echoed in *The Paquete Habana*, supra, 175 U.S. at 700, 20 S.Ct. at 299. "International law is part of our law, and must be ascertained and administered by the courts of justice of appropriate jurisdiction, as often as questions of right depending upon it are duly presented for their determination."

630 F.2d at 887. Also cited as evidencing this principle are, e.g. *Ware v. Hylton*, 3 U.S. (3 Dall.) 1 L.Ed. 568 (1796); *Banco Nacional de Cuba v. Sabbatino*, 376 U.S. 398 (1964); *United States v. Smith*, 18 U.S. (5 Wheat.) 153, 158-60 (1820); Dickinson, "The Law of Nations as Part of the National Law of the United States," 101 U.Pa.L.Rev. 26, 27 (1952) 630 F.2d at 886-87.[10]

In sum, because of the dual nature of the tort, this Court must fashion a rule of damages that takes into account remedies available to the plaintiffs under the appropriate law and the international interest in vindicating the right to be free from torture.

---

[10] Moreover, while the Circuit found it unnecessary to treat §1350 as an exercise of Congress' Article I power to "define and punish . . . offenses against the law of nations" because the automatic absorption of international law provided sufficient justification for the jurisdictional grant under Article III, it is nonetheless clear that the federal court's duty to apply the principles of international law is further justified by the principle established by *Lincoln Mills v. Textile Works*, 353 U.S. 488 (1957) that a jurisdictional statute authorizes judicial explication of the federal common law. See 630 F.2d at 877.

In its decision, the Circuit made passing reference in *dicta* to the question of what law provides the rules for decision in this case. Given that torture is actionable in Paraguay, the Circuit suggested that Paraguayan law would probably govern. 630 F.2d at 889. It made clear that, should this be the case, federal jurisdiction established by the international nature of the wrong would not be ousted. *Id.* at 889 n.25.

The Circuit's reference to Paraguayan law was clearly not intended to settle the question whether Paraguayan law should govern even at the expense of proper vindication of the international interests at stake. Rather in suggesting the applicability of Paraguayan law, the Circuit explicitly left open the possibility that some other rule of decision would be required when the "challenged conduct is actionable under the law of the forum and the law of nations, but not the law of the jurisdiction in which the tort occurred." *id.* Here we have a situation where the tort is actionable under Paraguayan law, but where the recovery allowed under Paraguayan does not satisfy the unusually strong interest of the international community in explicitly penalizing the torturer given his status as *hostes humani generis.* 630 F.2d at 890. It is, therefore, appropriate for this Court to look to international principles to assure that full satisfaction is made. It derives the authority and, indeed, the duty to do this because these international principles and the commitment of each nation to them is the primary consideration under general choice of law principles (II-B, *infra*), and because the international principles are a part of the federal common law which this court is bound to apply. (Point II-C, *infra*).

POINT II.   CHOICE OF LAW PRINCIPLES APPLIED BY FEDERAL COURTS IN CASES INVOLVING A PARAMOUNT INTERNATIONAL INTEREST REQUIRE FORMULATION OF THE DAMAGE REMEDY IN ACCORDANCE WITH INTERNATIONAL LAW

A. *If Torture Were A Purely Domestic Wrong, Choice Of Law Principles Would Direct Application Of The Law Of Paraguay.*

To the extent this case is viewed as a municipal tort, stripped of its international aspect, the Circuit's suggestion that Paraguayan law as opposed to New York law, should govern is consonant with choice of law principles applicable to torts. See 630 F.2d at 889.

Section 145 (1) of the Restatement (Second) of Conflict of Laws 2d states that the court should apply the "law of the state which, with respect to that issue (as to the tort) has the most significant relationship to the occurrence and the parties under the principles stated in §6." Section 145(2) outlines the relevant contacts:

"(a) the place where the injury occurred, (b) the place where the conduct causing the injury occurred, (c) the domicile, residence, nationality, place of incorporation and place of business of the parties, and (d) the place where the relationship, if any, between the parties is centered."

New York is not without significant relationship to this matter. One of the plaintiffs, Dolly Filartiga, is domiciled here and has been granted political asylum as a consequence of the wrongs in question. Pena was found and served in this jurisdiction as a consequence of his effort to escape trial and notoriety in Paraguay. *Compare Home Insurance Co. v. Dick.*, 281 U.S. 391 (1930). Nonetheless, we agree that the most significant relationship exists to the state of Paraguay primarily because it is the place where the injury and the conduct causing injury occurred, and where the decedent and his family lived, but also because it is where Dr. Filartiga still lives, and where the defendant lived and continues to lives.[11] Moreover the appropriateness of looking first to Paraguayan law because it has the most significant relationship with the offense and parties is consistent with the approach of international law itself, discussed in section B, *infra.*[12]

B.   *Choice Of Law Principles Treat The International Character Of The Tort As Primary And Require Recovery In Accordance with International Law.*

Section 6 of the Restatement (Second) of Conflict of Law sets out the general principles governing all choice of law questions governed by §145 and §146:

1. A court, subject to constitutional restrictions, will follow a statutory directive of its own state on choice of law.
2. When there is no such directive, the factors relevant to the choice of the applicable rule of law includes:
(a) the needs of the interstate and international system,
(b) the relevant policies of the forum,

---

[11] See also: Section 146, which sets out the choice of law for personal injuries directs application of the law of the situs except where "with respect to the particular issue, some other state has a more significant relationship under the principles stated in ¶6 to the occurrence and the parties, in which event the local law of the other state will apply."

[12] It should be noted that were it not for the propriety of applying international law here, a strong argument could be made that United States law rather than international law should apply or at least override or supplement any aspect of the situs laws which are inconsistent with United States public policy. But since this country's commitment to condemn torture and provide effective redress is adequately and more properly effectuated through international principles, plaintiffs do not address this question.

    (c) the relevant policies of other interested states and the relative interest of those states in the determination of the particular issue,

    (d) the protection of justified expectations,

    (e) the basic policies underlying the particular field of law,

    (f) certainty, predictability and uniformity of result, and

    (g) ease in the determination and application of the law to be applied.

At the outset it should be noted that the drafters of the Restatement (Second) clearly intended that it govern international as well as interstate conflicts of law. Restatement (Second) of Conflicts of Law, §10. In fact, international considerations, head the list of relevant factors precisely because they are considered paramount.

Comment (d) to §6 states: "Probably the most important function of choice—of law rules is to make the interstate and international systems work well." Moreover, examination of all the factors listed in section 6(2) in light of the international character of the wrong inflicted upon plaintiffs and their decedent, overwhelmingly direct application of international standards as the choice of law in cases involving human rights violations.

(a) *The Needs of the Interstate and International System.*

The existence of this case in the federal court today is a function of the fact that the nations of this earth have combined to condemn torture and guarantee to every individual the right to be free from torture. As the Circuit concluded in this case:

> In the twentieth century the international community has come to recognize the common danger posed by the flagrant disregard of basic human rights and particularly the right to be free of torture. Spurred by the Great War, and then the Second, civilized nations have banded together to prescribe acceptable norms of international behavior. From the ashes of the Second World War arose the United Nation Organization, amid hopes that an era of peace and cooperation had at last begun. . . . In the modern age, humanitarian and practical considerations have combined to lead the nations of the world to recognize that respect for fundamental human rights is in their individual and collective interest.

630 F.2d at 890. See also: 630 F.2d at 888-889. Thus only a remedy tailored to effectuate the purposes of the international guarantees of human rights is consistent with the concurrence of the nations that torture is absolutely forbidden and that its practice violates international law. In such a setting, it is clear that the needs of the international community can be met not by

mere application of the law of one or another nation-state having an interest in the matter, but by application of the law directed by international principles and practice itself.

(b) *The relevant policies of the forum.*

As the circuit explained, the enactment of §1350 reflects in significant part the concern of the founders of this nation that disputes of an international character be settled in a manner consistent with international law. See 630 F.2d at 886-887. More recently, this nation has made explicit, its commitment to further respect for human rights guaranteed by the customary international law. See Amicus Brief of the United States; U.S. 630 F.2d at 884. This commitment is embodied as well in congressional statutes denying aid to governments which engage in "gross violations of human rights" including torture. See e.g. 22 U.S.C. 2151 n (a) and 22 U.S.C. §2304 (Foreign Assistance Act of 1961; as amended); 7 U.S.C. §1712 (Agricultural Trade Development and Assistance Act as amended); 22 U.S.C.A. §262c note and §262d note (International Financial Institutions Act of 1977).

The interest of the United States, here, is not in the application of its own laws, but in the fulfillment of its duty to see that international wrongs are properly redressed in its courts. The fact that the federal courts are "bound by the law of nations" makes clear the duty of this court to provide a remedy which is consistent with international law. *The Nereide*, 13 U.S. (9 Cranch.) at 422. See also: *The Paquete Habana*, 175 U.S. at 700.[13]

(c) *The Relevant Policies of Other Interested States . . .*

As the Circuit noted, the human rights proscriptions on torture are perhaps the most universally subscribed to of all international norms. 630 F.2d at 884. There is no area of law in which an international remedy is more appropriate, and no area wherein an international remedy would more reflect the common policies of nation-states.

---

[13] To the same effect is the Commentary on Article 19 of the Draft Articles on state responsibility, relying on *Barcelona, Light and Power Company, Ltd.*, judgment, I.C.J. Reports (1970), for the proposition that every state has an interest in redressing breach of certain international obligations "in whose fulfillment all states have a legal interest." The Commentary states: "in the event of a breach of these obligations every state must be considered justified in invoking—probably through judicial channels—the responsibility of the state committing the internationally wrongful act." Yearbook of the International Law Commission, Vol. II, Part 2, 99 (1976).

(d) *The Protection of Justified Expectations*

It might be argued that this factor dictates the application of Paraguayan law since the parties are Paraguayan and the torture-death occurred in Paraguay. Such a conclusion is inappropriate, however, since Paraguay, as a signatory of the American Convention on Human Rights has ascribed to the prohibition on torture. Thus neither the state nor its officials have any legitimate expectations of avoiding redress consonant with minimum international standards. Indeed, the Convention obliges the state to adopt measures necessary to give effect to this right. Articles 1, 2 and 5, reprinted in Brownlie, *Basic Documents on Human Rights*, 392-93 (2d ed. 1981).

(e) *The Basic Policies Underlying the Particular Field of Law.*

This factor hardly needs explication. The policies of discouraging torture worldwide and attempting to alleviate the humiliation, fear and oppression that torture causes, demand the creation of an international minimum remedy that reflects these human rights goals.

(f) *Certainty, Predictability and Uniformity of Result.*

A remedy fashioned by this Court that reflects the human rights concerns of the international community rather than one that reflects only the situs of the torture will promote the certainty of an effective remedy and enhance the predictability and uniformity of the outcome. Absolute uniformity—i.e. as would be accomplished by an exclusive international standard is not required. Rather, it is important that international law guarantee a minimum recovery consonant to the offense; if the state of wrongdoing provides more, that will undermine neither international nor national goals.

(g) *Ease in the Determination and Application of the Law to be Applied.*

It could be argued that, since international law has only recently begun to develop standards for the redress of individual human rights, the safer course is reliance on traditional domestic law. But this ignores recognition by the international community of the necessity, as well as the progress it has made heretofore, in fashioning international principles for the redress of human rights.

Thus the principles of §6 of the Restatement (Second) all point to international law as the source of rules for assessing damages for a violation of international human rights. Indeed, not to do so could well be viewed as a defalcation of the responsibility of this nation. If this Court were to allow national rules to frustrate vindication of a matter of fundamental international concern, our standing in the world of nations could well be compromised.

The question then is what does international law direct on this question. Interestingly, the international approach is a hybrid. It commands the states to develop and provide remedies, civil and criminal, for violations of the prohibition against torture. See "Declaration on the Protection of All Persons from Being Subjected to Torture," General Assembly Resolution 3452, 30 U.S. GAOR Supp. (No. 34) 91, U.N. Doc. A/1034 (1975), Articles 4-11, set forth in 630 F.2d at 882. But it does not rest on this alone. For example, European Court on Human Rights, which hears state and individual applications against states only, must assure that the domestic remedy available is an adequate one and if not supplement it in accordance with international standards. This progressive principle is found in Article 50 of the European Convention on Human Rights which provides:

> If the court finds that a decision or measure taken by a legal authority of a High Contracting Party is completely and partially in conflict with the obligations arising from the present Convention, and if the internal law of said Party allows only partial reparation to be made for the consequences of this decision or measure, the decision of the court shall, if necessary, afford just satisfaction to the injured party.

Brownlie, *Basic Documents* at 242. Article 63 of the American Convention sets forth the power of the Inter-American Court on Human Rights to provide a remedy. It is less detailed than Article 50, but likewise calls for a remedy fashioned by international law standards. It provides that upon finding a violation

> The court shall rule that the injured party be ensured the enjoyment of his right or freedom that was violated. It shall also rule, if appropriate, that the consequences of the measure or situation that constituted the breach of such right or freedom be remedied and that fair compensation be paid to the injured part.

Brownlie, *Basic Documents*, at 411.

Plaintiffs, therefore suggest that the appropriate course for this Court is to look to the practice under international law. This means that the ultimate remedy must satisfy international standards, but that domestic remedies should be taken into account and ignored or supplemented when they frustrate rather than fulfill the goals of the international community.[14]

---

[14] Since this Court sits as an enforcer of the law of nations as part of the federal common law, the rules applied by the federal courts in deciding whether to incorporate state

C. *Principle Derived From The Customary International Law Should Govern The Remedy In This Case.*

From the principle that our federal common law incorporates the law of nations and obliges our courts to apply it flows the startlingly simple and logical principle that they are bound to apply the rules of international decision. See *supra*, Point I. In this light, the choice of law inquiry, suggested by the Circuit, as between the forum, the state of the wrong and the law of nations becomes unnecessary. The choice of law applicable is determined by international principles and practice, and the federal court acts, as it should, as the machinery of the international community. The result under this approach is the same as under the choice of law analysis undertaken in the preceding section. The route, however, appears more consonant with the principle that international law is incorporated into United States law.

Whichever approach this Court chooses, it should be underscored that both safeguard the primary interest of the international community in providing appropriate redress; and both avoid the ridiculous spectacle of allowing matters of such fundamental international dimension to be defeated by parochial or self-serving state interests. While the difference here between the Paraguayan and international law of remedies is not so great, see Point IV *infra*, the principle that local law must not be permitted to defeat international law where gross violations of human rights are involved is essential.

---

law or fashion a wholly independent federal common law also guide this court to apply international principles here.

In *Banco Nacional de Cuba v. Sabbatino*, 376 U.S. 398, 426 27 (1964), the importance to the Union of uniformity and consistency in matters affecting international relations required exclusive application of federal law. See also *Texas Industries Inc. v. Readcliff Materials, Inc.*, __U.S.__, 101 S.Ct. 2061, 2067 (1981). In addition, where tort remedies are concerned, the Court has frequently held that federal law governs or supplants contrary state law. *See* e.g. *United States v. Standard Oil of California*, 332 U.S. 301 (1947); *Massachusetts Bonding & Insurance Co. v. United States*, 352 U.S. 120 (1956). These holdings emphasize, by analogy, the importance of looking to international standards rather than to the vagaries of the laws of the many nations. They also provide an analogy for the international approach of "borrowing" or incorporating national law where it is consistent with the overriding international police. *United States v. Little Lake Misere Land Co. Inc*, 412 U.S. 580, 605 (1973). *See also: Massachusetts Bonding & Insur. Co. v. United States*, 352 U.S. 120 (1957); *DeSylva v. Ballentine*, 351 U.S. 570, 581 (1946); *United States v. Standard Oil Co.*, 332 U.S. 301, 309-10 (1942); *RFC v. Beaver County*, 328 U.S. 204, 210 (1946); *Royal Indemnity Co. v. United States*, 313 U.S. 289 (1941); *Board of Commissioners v. United States*, 308 U.S. 343 (1940).

POINT III.   PLAINTIFFS ARE ENTITLED TO COMPENSATION FOR
THE PECUNIARY LOSSES CLAIMED.

Plaintiffs claim a total of $439,734.00 in pecuniary losses as a result of
Joelito's torture and death. These are not, as explained in the affidavit of
Dr. Filartiga, in any sense a complete statement of past and future losses.[15]

The affidavit of Alexandro Miguel Garro, an expert in Latin American
and Paraguayan law is submitted herewith to explain to the Court the bases
in Paraguayan law for recovery of the itemized losses. Since Paraguayan law
provides compensation for these matters, it is unnecessary to turn in detail
to an examination of international law, which also recognizes recovery for
the losses claimed.[16]

A. *Funeral and Memorial Expenses.*

These expenses totaled $27,670 and are itemized and explained in Dr.
Filartiga's affidavit, ¶7. As Mr. Garro explains Articles 1118 and 1119 of the
Civil Code of Paraguay explicitly provide for the right of the statutory heirs,
here Dr. Filartiga, to recover funeral expenses. Garro Affidavit ¶11, 15(b).
Court decisions have construed this to include the erection of monuments
such as the pantheon for Joelito's grave, *id.*, which was modest and appropriate to the family's circumstances. Dr. Filartiga's Affidavit ¶7(e).

In addition, the Filartigas seek recovery ($8,770) for the cost of peri-
odic memorial services for Joelito. Affidavit of Dr. Filartiga, ¶7(h). Mr.
Garro explains, that while these services would not technically be recoverable under Article 1118, they are recoverable under Articles 939, 940 and
1113 of the Civil Code of Paraguay as incidental consequences of an international wrongful act. Garro Affidavit, ¶15(c), 20.

---

[15] As Dr. Filartiga explains:

To talk about this terrible suffering in terms of money is very difficult and very
inadequate, but I realize I must to do to help the Court in its job of trying to set
a dollar amount on our damages. The costs outlined below are only the most
obvious expenses; there are many I have not tried to remember or itemize. In
addition, for the most part, I have no records of these expenses and payments.
We do not keep financial records of file financial returns as you do in this country. Therefore I have only certified expenses that I can clearly reconstruct in my
memory." ¶6.

[16] See generally Whiteman, Damages Under International Law (1943). With respect to
legal expenses, the practice of the European Court on Human Rights is to include them in
an award of just compensation. *See, e.g., The Nenmeister Case,* Judgment, 7 May, 1974.

B. *Legal Costs.*

The Filartigas' futile efforts to bring the defendant to justice in Paraguay have been very costly, as has the suit here.[17] The total cost is $101,364. Affidavit of Dr. Filartiga, ¶8-10. The expense continues as Dr. Filartiga has been, without any notice of a proceeding against him, assessed a fine of $12,000 at the request of Hugo Duarte who was inserted into this case to confess to the murder of Joelito but plead excuse based on the hidebound notion that a husband has the right to kill his wife's lover, thereby protecting both Pena and himself from criminal liability. This fine, which has been secured by an attachment against his clinic in Asuncion requires continued legal expense. Affidavit of Dr. Filartiga, ¶8(f).

Mr. Garro tells us that the legal expenses, court costs, travel and living expenses connected with litigation, as well as the fine and its attendant costs, are recoverable under Paraguayan law. ¶17-21. The expenses of suit in Paraguay are recoverable under two theories. Had the Filartiga's criminal suit prevailed in Paraguay, he would have been entitled to his fees. Furthermore, the unsuccessful lawsuit is a "mediate" consequence of the torture murder of Joelito according to Article 935. ¶19-21. Even if this suit, which represented an act of extraordinary courage given the conditions in Paraguay, was not have been foreseeable to the defendant, the expenses associated with it are recoverable as incidental consequences of an intentional wrong under Articles 939 of the Civil Code. Garro Affidavit, ¶21-22. Under the same principle, the expenses of suing here, which could be said to be even less foreseeable, are also recoverable as incidental expenses. *id* at ¶21. So also is the fine assessed against Dr. Filartiga as a consequence of the suit against Duarte and the legal expenses associated with fighting that fee and the attachment of his clinic in Paraguay. *id.*

C. *Medical expenses incurred by Dr Filartiga for himself and his family as a consequence of Joelito's torture-murder.*

The torture-murder of Joelito has had devastating effects on the physical and mental health of the plaintiffs and their family. Here Dr. Filartiga claims compensation for the medical costs associated with the health problems of himself and his wife as a consequence of the extreme emotional trauma and stress they have undergone. Although they were not the direct victims of the torture in a technical legal sense, they were its intended victims and have suffered psychological and somatic disturbances which are

---

[17] The Center for Constitutional Rights provides services without fee. If the possibility of recovering the damages materializes, the Center will request the Court to order attorneys fees.

characteristic of torture victims and their families. See Affidavits of Randall and Quiroga, ¶18, Allodi, ¶7, TR. 50. The total cost of out-of-pocket medical expenses (i.e., not including the values of Dr. Filartiga's own medical services) is $50,740.

The Paraguayan Civil Code explicitly provides for compensation for these expenses. Article 1113 of the Paraguayan Code obliges the torfeasor to repair the damage suffered "by any person who has suffered therefrom even in an indirect manner." Garro Affidavit, ¶13. Article 1112 provides for the recovery of moral damages where the wrong, as here *id.* at ¶31, constitutes an offense under the criminal law. Moral damage arises from suffering as a result of the offense caused by "molesting him in his personal security, or in his enjoyment of his property, or wounding his legitimate affections." *id* at ¶9.

In addition, Mr. Garro advises that Paraguayan law accepts that physical disablements can flow from psychological stress: "Should Dr. Filartiga prove that his health problems appeared for the first time or were seriously exacerbated after Joelito's death, it is reasonable to assume that a Paraguayan court could find that those health injuries are more probably than not related to the wrongful act imputed to the defendant." *id* at ¶29. This same principle applies as well to the medical problems of Mrs. Filartiga, for which Dr. Filartiga bears the expense. Since Dr. Filartiga functions as his own doctor and the physician for his family and since there are no medical people in this country who know their medical history, Dr. Filartiga's affidavit is the only direct evidence of the sudden and increasing physical deterioration. Affidavit of Dr. Filartiga ¶12-14, TR. 50.

He describes the rapid deterioration of his eyesight, circulatory problems, an ulcer and, since the attachment of the Asuncion clinic, the development of borderline diabetes, ¶13(a-d), and avers that prior to Joelito's death his health at the age of 43 was normal. *id.* at ¶13(e).

He also describes his wife Nydia as having been 36 years old and in good health when Joelito was killed. She also experienced a rapid loss of eyesight which required several vitamin treatments. She suffers from the recurrence of kidney stones, which are clearly stress-produced, as she had previously suffered this problem only when Dr. Filartiga was jailed and tortured and had been free of it for four years before Joelito's death. Now this problem, exacerbated by great weight loss continues to plague her with pain and requires treatment. ¶14(b)b. In addition, she has suffered severe memory loss since Joelito's death for which she requires expensive vitamin treatments. ¶14 (c).

Dr. Filartiga's information is corroborated by the sealed affidavit which describes the pain and rapid aging of Dr. and Mrs. Filartiga following Joelito's torture and death. ¶28. In addition, the expert doctors who examine torture victims and examined the affidavits and testimony in this case corroborate the onset or aggravation of stress-related somatic disorders as a consequence of torture. Allodi affidavit, ¶7; Randall and Quiroga, ¶18.

D. *Dolly Filartiga's medical expenses.*

Dolly Filartiga suffered from severe suicidal depression, in Paraguay and required hospitalization and therapy the expense of which plaintiffs have not yet been able to reconstruct. The expense sought here is for therapy, past and projected in this country totaling $29,120.

Dolly describes her trauma in her affidavit. Ana Deutsch, a clinical psychologist who has been involved with Amnesty International's investigation on the Medical and Psychological Sequelae of Torture, (affd. ¶1-3), examined the documents describing Dolly's reaction to her brother's torture and acts directed against her. Ms. Deutsch projects that Dolly will need at least 4 years, amounting to 337 sessions, of decreasingly intensive therapy to work on the effects of this trauma. ¶12-14. At an average United States rate (affidavit of Michael Schneider) this will cost $26,960. In addition, Dolly claims $2,160 for earlier treatment here. This is demonstrated by Exhibit 12. The psychiatric problems that plague her are typical of the consequences of torture-induced stress. Affidavits of Ana Deutsch, ¶7-8; Dr. Allodi, ¶7; Drs. Randall and Quiroga, ¶12.

Mr. Garro's affidavit explains that although Dolly is not considered a direct heir under the laws of Paraguay and, therefore, not entitled to recover under Articles 1118 and 1119, she is entitled to recover for her pecuniary and non-pecuniary losses under Article 1113 and related provisions of the Code. Garro Affidavit ¶24-25.

E. *Dr. Filartiga's lost income.*

Dr. Filartiga estimates having lost $71,300 in the last 6 years since Joelito's death and projects the loss of $162,500 over the next ten years. His losses are explained as a consequence of Joelito's death and his efforts to have Pena prosecuted and convicted in Paraguay, as well as his reduced capacity to work as a product of the physical and mental disorders produced by the torture-murder. Affidavit of Dr. Filartiga, ¶15.

Mr. Garro's affidavit makes clear that Dr. Filartiga is entitled to recover his lost income as a result of his son's death under Articles 1102 and 1103, which defines the scope of pecuniary losses, and under Article 1113, which recognizes damage suffered by a person other than the direct victim. *id.* at ¶¶9, 13 and 27.

POINT IV.   PLAINTIFFS ARE ENTITLED TO RECOVER FOR THEIR NON-PECUNIARY LOSSES AS A MATTER OF COMPEN-SATION FOR "MORAL DAMAGE" AND AS A MATTER OF PUNITIVE OR EXEMPLARY DAMAGE UNDER INTERNATIONAL LAW

The heinousness of the crime of torture, the virtually unparalleled brutality of the torture inflicted upon Joelito, the intentional and enduring psychological torture and resulting physical suffering of Dr. Filartiga, Dolly, and their family, the systemic encouragement of torture and immunization of its perpetrators from both criminal and civil sanction in Paraguay—all these call for the harshest sanction of which this Court is capable.

The pecuniary losses discussed in Point III reflect but the tip of the iceberg of plaintiffs' true and irreparable losses as a result of Joelito's torture and death. In this point, we discuss the non-material aspects of their suffering which have endured for over 6 years and will affect them, physically and emotionally, on a daily basis for the rest of their lives.

As a legal matter, the plaintiffs pain and suffering flowing from the physical, psychological, political and legal consequences of the torture and murder of Joelito is recoverable under alternative theories of compensatory and punitive damages. In subsection A, we discuss the principles of awarding damages under compensation for "moral damage" or non-pecuniary losses recognized under both Paraguayan and international law. Though described as "compensation," it is important to note that under the principles of both legal systems, factors which are considered punitive under United States law must be taken into account in the assessment of adequate compensation. Subsection B discusses the evidence that punitive damages would be awarded in the extraordinary circumstances of this case in accordance with the norms of the customary international law and the explicit interest of the international community in seeing the torturer—"the modern day *hostes humani generic*"—punished.

A.   *Compensation For Moral Damage Is Required Under Paraguayan And International Law And Must Take Into Account The Heinousness Of Torture And Its Impact On The Suffering Of The Plaintiffs*

1. *Paraguayan Law*

The affidavit of Mr. Garro sets forth the entitlement of plaintiffs under the Civil Code of Paraguay to recover for "moral injury" (*agravio moral*) which the offense may have caused the person to suffer either "by molesting him in his personal security, or in the enjoyment of his property, or wounding his legitimate affections," because the wrong inflicted is a crime under the laws of Paraguay. Article 1112. ¶¶9, 22. He indicates further that "moral damage" is recoverable both by Dr. Filartiga as Joelito's "necessary heir," and Dolly as her brother's death entails a wound to her "legitimate affections." *Id.*, ¶¶12 and 25.

Because the Paraguayan system so effectively immunizes the common practice of torture, there is no case which comes close to this one to cite as a direct precedent of the approval of the Paraguayan courts of punitive damage. Nor is there a case which involves international crimes notwithstanding that they are clearly committed in Paraguay. Thus the ascertainment of Paraguayan law provided here by Mr. Garro must, of necessity, be based entirely on the precedents and theories applicable to common place wrongs and crimes of and purely domestic character. Garro affidavit ¶31.

In the normal case, Paraguayan law would not recognize punitive damages as a separate and explicit category of damages. Mr. Garro states:

> ¶32. In the civil law tradition, the line between civil and criminal law is more sharply drawn than in common law jurisdictions. Thus, the ideal of punitive damages, as known in this country, designed to express society's outrage at the offense, to punish the defendant, and to deter future violations is foreign to the civil law, at least since the recognition of the state's monopoly over criminal sanctions. The punishment of morally reprehensible (i.e., malicious or grossly negligent) actions are generally matters for the criminal court rather than for the civil law. Thus in the prevailing view reflected in court decisions and the opinions of most legal commentators, recovery for non-pecuniary losses (*agravio moral*) under article 1112 of the Civil Code is not aimed at punishing the defendant but at compensating the victim.

This does not mean, however, that punitive considerations play no role in the assessment of moral damages for pain and suffering caused the direct and indirect victims of an intentional tort which violates the criminal law. Rather the Paraguayan courts can and do take into account factors that United States law commonly characterizes as "punitive;" but they term them "compensatory." As Mr. Garro explains the law:

> ¶33. Civil liability is concerned with reparation: a just and adequate compensation to the injured person for the losses arising from the wrongful act. It must be acknowledged, however, that the

nature of compensation for non-pecuniary harm is hardly free of punitive connotations. In spite of the compensatory nature of the award of damages for moral injuries, there is an unavoidable connection between the gravity or seriousness of defendant's fault and the harm inflicted to the victim. This close relationship existing between fault and damage, as pointed out by Givord, shows that blurred line between punishment and compensation in the award for moral damage. F. Givord, La reparation du prejudice moral 123 (1938). The Court of Appeals of Asuncion has held:

> "The award of damages to compensate moral injuries must be left to the prudence and discretion of the judges. It is obvious that no mathematical rule can be fixed in order to measure the award. All sorts of considerations must be taken into account: *the seriousness of the harm*, the age, sex, and social position of the victim, the mediate and immediate consequences resulting from the injuries, etc."

Fernandez v. Melgarejo, Court of Appeals of Asuncion, June 20, 1977 reported in 1 La Ley 36 (1977) (emphasis supplied). In fact, some court decisions in Argentina have explicitly based recovery for moral injuries (*agravio moral*) on a punitive rather than compensatory theory, holding, for example, that the loss of child is non-compensable. E.g., 93 L.L. 504.

¶34. Thus, in awarding moral damages to compensate for pain and suffering, a Paraguayan court would have discretion to consider factors which in this country are treated as punitive damages. It is likely that a Paraguayan court would view the pain and suffering produced by the death of a son by means of torture as of a different intensity and duration than the suffering produced by the death of a son in an automobile accident. Thus, the more heinous the tort, the greater is the pain to the survivors and, consequently, the larger the award which must be given in order to "compensate" them for moral damage. The increase of the award is not justified by the desire to punish the defendant, however, but by the purpose of compensating the greater pain suffered by the plaintiff.

The Paraguayan authorization of moral damages for pain and suffering as a result of offenses which are classed as criminal corresponds, therefore, in some part, to what we describe as punitive damages:

Where the defendant's wrongdoing has been intentional and deliberate, and has the character of outrage frequently associated with crime, all but a few (U.S. State) courts have permitted the jury to award in the tort action "punitive" or "exemplary" damages . . . . Such damages are given to the plaintiff over and above the full compensation for his injuries, for the purpose of punishing the defendant, of teaching him not to do it again, and of deterring others from following his example. Occasional decisions have mentioned the additional purpose of reimbursing the plaintiff for elements of damage which are not legally compensable, such as his wounded feelings or the expenses of suit. Something more than the mere commission of a tort is always required for punitive damages. There must be circumstances of aggravation or outrage, such as spite or "malice," or a fraudulent or evil motive on the part of the defendant.

Prosser, *Law of Torts* ¶2 4th ed. (1974).

Thus if this Court were applying solely Paraguayan law, it would be permissible and appropriate for it to enhance the award of moral damages for the pain and suffering entrained by this act to Dr. Filartiga and Dolly, because their suffering is inseparable from the heinous and malicious nature of the act. And, while Paraguayan law does not compensate the pain and suffering of the decedent, Garro affidavit ¶¶12-14, the pain and suffering caused to Joelito should be accounted for in the award to the plaintiffs since their daily suffering is certainly a consequence of the indelible vision of his battered body with which they live and Dr. Filartiga's ability from his own experience of torture, to imagine all too clearly the enormity of the abuse his son endured. Mr. Garro states: "Insofar as those indirectly harmed suffer moral injury on account of pre-death suffering of the deceased, they would be entitled to recover for the pain it caused them." *id* ¶14.

Finally, Paraguay's refusal to recognize distinct category of punitive damages is rooted in the view that the criminal justice machinery is the proper mechanism for imposing punishment. ¶32, quoted *supra*. Here, the defendant has evaded criminal sanction as a function of fleeing to this country and of the extra-legal immunity which the Paraguayan system gives him. If the system were not corrupt, we can only speculate whether the enormity of his crime and his avoidance of criminal sanction would move a Paraguayan court to assess punitive damages contrary to the normal rule. It is clear, however, that as with Joelito's suffering under torture, the defendant's immunity from criminal sanction and the protection he has enjoyed have substantially aggravated the Filartiga's terrible anguish and should be accounted for in the award of moral damages. Garro affidavit ¶14.

2. *"Compensation Under International Law"*

As in Paraguayan law, international law has consistently recognized that the traditional conception of responsibility already contained not only the idea of reparation in the strict sense of the word but also the idea of punishment [and] . . . that in practice some of the forms of reparation had a distinctly punitive purpose Garcia-Amador, "Draft Article on the Responsibility of the State for Injuries Caused in its Territory To The Person or Property of Aliens," in Garcia-Amador, Sohn & Baxter, *Recent Codifications of the Law of State Responsibility for Injuries to Aliens,* 10 (1974).[18] The famous discussion by Umpire Parker of damages in the *Lusitania* Cases recognizes that elements which are embodied in the concept of punitive damages in this country have been traditionally treated as part of compensation in international cases:

> That one injured is, under the rules of international law, entitled to be compensated for an injury inflicted resulting in mental suffering, injury to his feelings, humiliation, shame, degradation, loss of social position or injury to his credit or to his reputation, there can be no doubt, and such compensation should be commensurate to the injury. Such damages are very real, and the mere fact that they are difficult to measure or estimate by money standards make them none the less real and affords no reason why the injured person should not be compensated therefor as compensatory damages, but not as a penalty. The tendency of the decisions and statutes of the several American States seems to be to broaden the scope of the elements to be considered in assessing actual and compensatory damages, with the corresponding result of narrowing the application of the exemplary damages rule.

cited in: I. Whiteman, Damages In International Law, 718-19 (1943) (hereinafter "Whiteman"). One of the most recent discussions of the problem of distinguishing punitive and compensatory remedies underscores their inextricable interrelationship. In the "Second Report on the Content, Forms and Degree of State Responsibility (Part Two of the Draft Articles) by Mr. Riphagen, The Special Rapporteur for the International Law Commission, group on State Responsibility, U.N. Doct. A/CN. 4/344 (May 1, 1981), it is stated:

> ¶74 . . . [I]t should be noted that the term "reparation" is often used in a sense covering [*inter alia*] . . . "punitive damages" and other forms of "Penalty," *id* at 16.

---

[18] Hereinafter *Recent Codifications.*

. . .

¶82 . . . [T] he "quantitative" factors of the "attitude" of the author State in respect of the breach, and the "seriousness" of the result of the breach from the point of view of the injured State, cannot but influence the opinion of the international judicial body dealing with the case.

. . .

¶84 . . . [I]t is understandable that controversy exists between learned writers, e.g., as to whether pecuniary compensation for moral damage has or has not a "punitive character." Actually in all cases where, somehow or other, a pecuniary compensation is awarded as a counterpart of an irreparable loss, the, obvious incomparability between the receipt of a sum of money and the loss suffered invites analogy with a "penalty." Nevertheless in many national legal systems such pecuniary compensation is awarded under the title of damages rather than under any other title.

id at 16-19. Thus, the traditional reluctance of international law to recognize an explicit and separate category of punitive damages is, in significant part, semantical.

B. *The Precedents And Evolving Principles of International Law Warrant This Court's Recognition of Punitive Damages In the Circumstances of This Case.*

Given that torture is an international crime, the job of this Court, as enforcer of the federal common law of nations, is to vindicate the interest of the world of nations in accomplishing the elimination of torture through assuring appropriate sanctions, and to express the moral outrage which the status of torture as a violation of the customary international law demands. While there are no established conventions or codifications in international law concerning the occasions for imposition of punitive damages, there is both precedent and authoritative evidence of evolving doctrine that justify application of punitive damages in this case.

Since the traditional international law of damages has developed primarily through resolution of claims made by one state against the other on behalf of its injured nationals, it is rare to see awards of punitive damages. Whiteman explains this as follows:

Punitive, vindictive, or exemplary damages are generally based in local law upon the presence of gross fraud, malice, willful negligence, or oppression, etc. The refusal of international tribunals to assess punitive, vindictive, or exemplary damages, as such, against respondent governments may be explained in part by the absence of malice, or *mala mens,* on the part of government of the respondent state. This is especially true in cases where the wrong against the alien was committed in the first instance by someone other than an official within the jurisdiction of the respondent.

In other cases where the original wrong is committed by an officer of the respondent government, those charged with the settling of the claim may feel that the people of the state as a whole should not be charged with additional damages for a wrong on the part of one or more officers, of which they had neither knowledge nor wrongful intent. Apart from this, it is plain that international tribunals have hesitated, *eo nomine,* to pass judgment upon the actions of states in the form of punishment. . . . Where a state is held responsible in damages by an international tribunal or through diplomatic channels, the wrong is not denominated a crime, but merely an international delinquency which gives rise to the payment of compensatory damages.

Whiteman, 716-17 (1943). (footnotes omitted).

There are exceptions even to this general rule, which involves considerations of the appropriateness of directly punishing a state that are not present in this case where the defendant is an individual. Whiteman cites in a footnote the case of the *I'm Alone* (*Canada v. United States*) where the American and Canadian claims Commissioners recommended, in addition to compensatory damages, the payment of $25,000 for the "wrong" done to Canada by the *Responsibility for Injuries to Aliens,* 9-11 (1974). While the International Law Commission's work on state responsibility has taken on different focus not limited to injuries to aliens, it has continued to examine the question of distinction between international wrongs that are criminal and those that are simply delicts.[19] This distinction is embodied in Part I of the Draft Articles on State Responsibility. Yearbook of the International Law Commission, Vol. II, Part 2, pp. 69-122 (1976). In particular Article XIX of Part I distinguishes international delicts and international crimes defined in subsection (2) as

---

[19] Codification is not essential in international law for evolving principles to be evidence of the customary international law and carry legal authority as such. This is particularly true of the reports and draft articles approved by the International Law Commission. See, Jennings, Recent Developments in the International Law Commission: Its Relation to the Sources of International Law, 13 Int'l & Comp. L.Q., 385-93 (1964) cited in Henkin, Pugh, Schachter & Smit, *International Law,* Cases and Materials, 95 & 98 (1980). See also: Henkin at 91 *et seq.*

An internationally wrongful act which results from the breach by a state of an international obligation so essential for the protection of fundamental interests of the international community that its breach is recognized as a crime by that community as a whole, constitutes an international crime.

The purpose of this distinction, as explained by the commentary is "not purely descriptive or didactic, but 'normative'":

[I]t should be known that the establishment of a distinction between internationally wrongful acts, based on the differences in importance—for the international community as a whole—of the subject matter of the obligations breached, and at the same time of the extent of the breaches, will necessarily be reflected in the legal consequences attached to the internationally wrongful acts falling into one or the other of the two categories, and on the determination of the subject or subjects of international law authorized to implement . . . those consequences.

id. at 97. The provisional adoption by ILC part I of these draft articles is persuasive authority for the acceptance of a distinction between punitive and reparative consequences, particularly since it involves the ultimate question of state responsibility and punitive sanction against the state. *Supra* at 18.

Moreover, the work on Part II of the draft articles which is intended to deal with remedies continues to explore the role and function of establishing explicit punitive sanctions in addition to their inclusion in concepts of reparation, as previously discussed, *supra* at *Riphagen Report*, at 15-41. It states: "if a breach 'is recognized as a crime' by the international community as a whole, it may be assumed that such "recognition" particularly relates to what this international community and its members consider to be an adequate response on their part to such a breach." *id* at 24.

It should be again noted that this discussion of penalties relates to the far stickier questions of imposing penalties directly on states and the need for some international organization to do so, unlike this case where the question is only what should be exacted from the individual wrongdoer.

There is also precedent for awarding punitive damages here in the rules and practice of the Nuremberg and other war crimes tribunals, as well as Denazification proceedings in Germany following World War II.

The International Military Tribunal, Nuremberg sentenced Alfred Krupp to forfeit all real and personal property, United Nations War Crimes

Commission, X Law Reports of Trials of War Criminals, 158 (1949);[20] and the penalty of forfeiture was imposed by other war crimes tribunals. *See*, e.g., Trial of Ganleiter Arthur Greiser before the Supreme National Tribunal. United Nations War Crimes Commission, XIII Law Reports of Trials of War Criminals, 104 (1949). Moreover in the Denazification proceedings crimes of lesser dimension than war crimes were also punished by forfeiture. To fulfill the mandate to denazify, these proceedings, established by agreement of the occupying forces, were designed to eliminate nazis from positions of any importance and mete out appropriate punishment. They regularly imposed severe fines and forfeitures on individuals for varying degrees of participation in Nazi activities. These financial sanctions were intended as punitive and not to compensate the victims. *See:* Dept. of State, *Germany, 1947-49: The Story in Documents*, 107-111 (1950); Friedman, *The Allied Military Government of Germany*, 110-25 (1947).

Perhaps the closest analogy for this case derives from the original class of "enemies of all mankind," the pirate. The international law has always recognized punitive damages in instances that are analogous to intentional torts at common law: in war prize claims, where a hostile relationship exists between the states that are party to the litigation. *The Paquete Habana*, 175 U.S. 677, 20 S.Ct. 290, 44 L.Ed. 320 (1900), though reversing the award of a Cuban fishing vessel as war prizes, reflects the standard rules that ships of an enemy state, combatant or non-combatant, are subject to seizure as war prizes when captured under both customary international law and such codification as the Hague Convention Relative to Certain Restrictions with Regard to the Exercise of the Right to Capture in Naval Warfare, of 1907.

Now that individuals are able to sue under international law, it is important to note that in the only area of traditional international law where the legal claim was based on a hostility between the parties, punitive damages in the form of condemnation of capture property was awarded. As this court now has before it two private parties with a claim based on intentional commission of a universally condemned practice, it should conclude that, just as traditional international law awarded punitive damages in such cases should this court, in this case.

There is thus substantial support in past practice and in the progressive developments of international law through the work of the International Law Commission for the proposition that vindication of the international guarantee against torture warrants an award of punitive dam-

---

[20] Counsel has been advised by one of the former U.S. prosecutors at Nuremberg that the forfeiture was commutated thereafter. As no evidence has been found of this in the Nuremberg records, she believes the commutation was given by German authorities.

ages against the defendant, rather than incorporating the punitive elements into a compensatory award for moral damage and irreparable loss.

The Circuit has recognized the criminal nature of the torturer as *hostes humani generis*. 630 F.2d at 890. The criminal character of torture under international law is evidenced by the fact that it is universally condemned by the nations. 630 F.2d at 884.[21] Finally, the view of the international community that torture should be criminally punished is explicit in the Declaration on the Protection of All Persons From Being Subjected to Torture, General Assembly 3452, 30 U.N. GAOR Supp. (No. 34) 91, U.N. Doc. A/l034 (1975) which requires that states shall (1) "ensure that all acts of torture . . . are offenses under its criminal law," (Article 7); (2) impartially investigate, *sua sponte*, a reasonable belief that torture occurred (Article 9); (3) institute criminal proceedings against the alleged offender or offenders in accordance with national law. (Article 10); as well as (4) afford redress and compensation to the victims in accord with natural law. 630 F.2d at 883-84 n.11.

Thus need for redress of a punitive nature is not only made express by this Declaration. It is made essential by the fact that Paraguay has immunized this defendant from appropriate criminal sanction. Had sanctions been imposed in Paraguay, it might be argued that punishment had been exacted and is unnecessary here. But this is not the case. If this Court's award fails to take into account the international demand for punishment, then the defendant escapes all sanction both real and symbolic. Since this Court has a responsibility under the customary international law to respect and enforce its norms and to express the condemnation of the community of nations, it is crucial that the remedy of money damages,—which is inherently inadequate to compensate an irreparable loss and irreversible consequences of this dimension, but which is the only remedy available to this Court,—be used to the fullest.

---

[21] See Article 38 (1)(c) of. the Statute of the International Court of Justice, T.S. 99313 Bevans 1179. It should be noted that while Article XIX of Part I discussed in the 1976 Report of the International Law Commission does not explicitly mention torture. Article XIX (3) describes as an international crime *inter alia:* "(c) a serious breach on a widespread scale of an international obligation of essential importance for safeguarding the human being, such as those prohibiting slavery, genocide and *apartheid.*" The guarantee of freedom from torture has become in recent years a peremptory norm in the eyes of the international community of states as a whole. See authorities cited, *Filartiga v. Pena*, 630 F.2d at 881-884, and therefore qualifies under Article XIX (2) and (3) (c), which is explicitly not an inclusive list. In all cases the gravity of the act is taken into account as well as whether it is as, in Paraguay, part of a systematic or persistent pattern of violations of the obligations set forth in the Universal Declaration of Human Rights. 1976 Yearbook, Vol. II, part 2 at 110.

In connection with this Court's computation of an award for both compensatory and punitive damages, whether on the theory that they are separate or that the one incorporates the other, there follows a necessarily incomplete and inadequate list of the physical and emotional pain and suffering inflicted upon plaintiffs:

For Dolly Filartiga:
Apprehension at being awakened and called to Pena's house Confrontation with her brother's tortured, blood-soaked body
Being harassed and forced to carry his body home
Having to tell her younger sisters
Being threatened by Pena and told to shut up, or it would happen again and that they got what they were looking for
Having to endure the sight of her brother's body in their home during the wake
Recurrent nightmares reenacting the discovery of her brother's body and expressing the wish that he were still alive
Arrest and false imprisonment, without knowing for 6 hours whether she and her mother would ever be released
Constant surveillance and threatening actions around her home by the police
One year of frequent episodes of believing that her brother would reappear; and then no one came
Loss of his friendship, society and her closest confidant
Isolation within her family
Anger and withdrawal
Guilt that she blames her father; anger at her father
Realization, one year later, that her brother would never return
Severe depression, loss of appetite, ability to read, concentrate, study, mostly confined to bed
Inability to sleep, and fear of attack during the night
Contemplation of and attempt to commit suicide
Loss of companionship of friends; people being afraid to associate with the Filartigas due to fear of reprisals
Difficulty establishing personal relationships, apprehension at social occasions
Constant feeling of being different
Constant consciousness of the torture-murder and loss of her brother
Inability to continue school in Paraguay
Inability to maintain a job, to find work
Worry about other family members, the kidnapping of her sister, whether she'd be found
Personal harassment, rumors and slander; police agents pretending to be suitors, impugn her reputation

Inability to obtain justice in Paraguay
Apprehension at leaving Paraguay
Separation from home, family and her country
Inability to go home; to leave the United States
Traumas of adjustment to a strange culture, new language, no job
Apprehension at the filing of the lawsuit in this country; knowing she could never go back; fearing for her family
Homelessness; waiting in limbo for three years for processing of political asylum
Having to be strong

For Dr. Filartiga
Apprehension on hearing in Ybycui that something was wrong at home; reckless drive back to Asuncion
Apprehension entering his home
Confrontation with his son's tortured body
Watching his wife's inconsolable hysteria; his children's suffering
Experiencing his son's pain; reliving his own torture and the others he witnessed being tortured over and over
Mourning at the wake; watching his family, anger
Finding photographers, doctors to conduct second autopsy
Exhuming his son's body for a third autopsy
Blaming himself; feeling blamed by his family, feeling fury
Wishing it had been himself who had been tortured and died
Constant police harassment; fear for himself and his family; paranoia
Recklessness and anger; desire to destroy himself
Missing his son, his companionship
Anger and grief over his death; late nights all alone drawing, writing poems, imagining the instruments of torture, the screams, the taunts
Loss of potential colleague, Joelito, who loved the rural people and would have carried on his work
Preparing and trying to prosecute a lawsuit; constant surveillance; constant roadblocks; constant threats; losing lawyers; lawyer arrested
Fearing Dolly and his wife would not be released from prison; fearing his youngest daughter would not be returned by her kidnappers
Watching his wife's suffering—her loss of eyesight, memory, weight; her terrible pain with kidney stones; feeling responsible
Experiencing the loss in her two miscarriages; her sadness
Feeling numbness, pain and cramps in his limbs from circulatory problems
Severe pains from ulcer; losing eyesight; borderline diabetes
Inability to work; loss of half his capacity to work and anguish at being the only source of health care for the people of Ybycui

Inability to obtain justice; persistence
Isolation and aloneness
Separation from Dolly; loss of her care of the younger children, her work in the clinic
Feeling responsible for the upset of his younger daughters
Separation from his family on trips to the United States
Apprehension for his family's safety; threats against him on his return to Paraguay
Facing death and torture
Anger and responsibility
Going on.

CONCLUSION

It is obvious in this case that so long as Paraguay continues to immunize the defendant, it is unlikely that he will ever pay just redress or compensation or be subject to sanction. It is not in expectation of money that plaintiffs pursue this suit, but out of the conviction that this Court can, in a symbolic way, vindicate the enduring personal anguish of the victims of torture and take another "small but important step in the fulfillment of the ageless dream to free all people from brutal violence." 630 F.2d at 890.

Respectfully submitted,

Rhonda Copelon
Peter Weiss
Betty Lawrence Bailey
c/o Center for Constitutional Rights
853 Broadway
New York, New York 10003
(212) 674-3303

Michael Maggio
1800 Belmont Road, N.W.
Washington, D.C. 20009
(202) 483-0052

Attorneys for Plaintiffs

Dated: New York, New York
        December 10, 1982

APPENDIX

TABLE I

TABLE OF PAST PECUNIARY LOSSES AS A
CONSEQUENCE OF JOELITO'S TORTURE AND DEATH

	TYPE OF EXPENSES	AMOUNT	SOURCE*
1.	Funeral Expenses	$18,900	Dr. Filartiga's Affidavit, ¶7
2.	Memorial Services	5,810	Dr. Filartiga's Affidavit, ¶9
3.	Legal Costs (Paraguayan suit)	71,000	Dr. Filartiga's Affidavit, ¶10
4.	Costs connected to U.S. lawsuit	10,364	Dr. Filartiga's Affidavit, ¶10
5.	Medical Expenses (Dr. Filartiga)	4,100	Dr. Filartiga's Affidavit, ¶13
6.	Medical Expenses (Mrs. Filartiga)	19,340	Dr. Filartiga's Affidavit, ¶14
7.	Medical Expenses (Dolly Filartiga's past psychiatric care)	2,160	
8.	Lost Earnings	71,300	Dr. Filartiga's Affidavit, ¶15

	TOTAL	$202,974

---

* See the designated affidavit or document for itemized account.

TABLE II

TABLE OF FUTURE PECUNIARY LOSSES AS A
CONSEQUENCE OF JOELITO'S TORTURE AND DEATH

	TYPE OF EXPENSES	AMOUNT	SOURCE*
1.	Medical Expenses (Dr. Filartiga)	$10,600	Dr. Filartiga's Affidavit ¶13
2.	Medical Expenses (Mrs. Filartiga)	16,700	Dr. Filartiga's Affidavit ¶14
3.	Medical Expenses (Dolly Filartiga's psychiatric care)	26,960	Affidavit of Ana Deutsch ¶14 & Michael Schneider ¶3.**
4.	Future Lost Earnings (Dr. Filartiga)	162,500	Dr. Filartiga's Affidavit ¶15
5.	Future Legal Expenses	20,000	Dr. Filartiga's Affidavit ¶9 (f) and (g)
	TOTAL	236,760	

---

* See the designated affidavit or document for itemized account.

**This figure was computed by assuming the cost per session to be an average of the going rates as set forth in the affidavit of Michael Schneider and, on the basis of Ana Deutsch's estimate of Dolly's need for 337 sessions spanning 4 years.

UNITED STATES DISTRICT COURT
FOR THE EASTERN DISTRICT OF NEW YORK

DOLLY M.E. FILARTIGA and JOEL FILARTIGA,	**AFFIDAVIT OF DR. JOEL FILARTIGA**
	79 Civ. 917
Plaintiffs,	
v.	
AMERICO NORBERTO PEÑA-IRALA,	
Defendant.	

Dr. Joel Filartiga, being duly sworn deposes and says:

1. I am one of plaintiffs in this case and I make this affidavit to explain certain exhibits relevant to this case and some of the expenses I incurred as a result of the torture-death of my son.

The Autopsies

1. In this part of the affidavit I want to explain the three autopsies attached to this affidavit.

2. Exhibit 11A, between the "x's" is a complete copy of the medical information contained in the first autopsy. It was performed by Dr. Arnulfo Malinas, who was the medical coroner. As I testified, this autopsy was completely false.

3. Exhibit 11B, contains the second autopsy performed by three doctors whom I solicited to examine the body of my son. They are: Sinforiano Rodriguez Doldan, Indigenous Association of Paraguay; Isidor Caceres Marin, doctor at the state hospital at Kaaguazu; and David Cicioli, medical army colonel.

The doctors' autopsies are only descriptive. They did not include their opinions or interpretations in regards to the cause of the wounds they discovered. This information was not necessary for the first part of the autopsy and when it was asked for, the judge did not allow it, although we asked twice.

4. Exhibit 11C is a copy of the third autopsy performed by Dr. Hernon Godoy, coroner of the court of Paraguay. His autopsy was performed after my son's body was exhumed on the 13 of April 1976, thirteen days after his death. On line 25 of the autopsy, you will note the word "quemadura" (burn) between parentheses. The parentheses and the exclamation point were added by the judge after the autopsies were submitted to the court as part of the legal proceedings in Paraguay. It is unusual for a judge to add his own notations on the submitted evidence.

5. I have not been able to obtain the original documents in order to submit them here for the following reasons:

(1) The copies which were in my possession were stolen by the police when they broke into my house four months after the death of Joelito.

(2) It is difficult to obtain a certified copy from the archives of the court in Paraguay. It is different from the United States. In Paraguay, one has to retain an attorney and the process takes a few days before the judge's approval is obtained. As the court knows, it has been more than difficult for me to obtain legal representation in Paraguay. I presently have an attorney. I have asked him to obtain the documents from the archives of the court several times, but he has not responded. For these reasons, the attached copies are the best I can submit at this time and I can certify that they are accurate copies of the original documents.

6. The remainder of this affidavit outlines some of the expenses I have incurred or expect to incur as a result of Joelito's torture and death. On this I would like to say several things: To talk about this terrible suffering in terms of money is very difficult and very inadequate, but I realize I must do so to help the court in its job of trying to set a dollar amount on our damages. The costs outlined below are only the most obvious expenses; there are many I have not tried to remember or itemize. In addition, for the most part, I have no records of these expenses and payments. We do not keep financial records or file financial returns as you do in this country. Therefore, I have only certified expenses that I can clearly reconstruct in my memory.

Funeral and Memorial Expenses.

7. The following is a list of funeral and memorial expenses. Each item is explained in the appropriate lettered paragraph that follows:

(a) Burial and Funeral	3,500
(b) Legal Certificate and Burial Cost	1,500
(c) Food and Drink for Funeral	500
(d) Black Clothes for the Family	1,500
(e) Pantheon for Grave of Joelito	10,000
(f) Burial site rental	1,700
(g) Transfer of Body (1981)	200
(h) Memorial Services	8,770

Total $27,670

(a) Paid for funeral cost to Crichigno funeral home. This represents a middle-level cost for a funeral in Paraguay, appropriate to the family's station and the circumstances. We had additional costs because of the large number of people—2500-3000—who came to the funeral.

(b) Legal certification and burial were paid in a lump sum to a person who took care of all the requirements and details necessary to allow Joelito to be buried. These are typical expenses in addition to the funeral expenses.

(c) It is traditional to feed people when they come to the home and we did so during the two days that Joelito's body lay in our home. Thereafter, the house was full of people who came to pray the rosary for 9 days following Joelito's death. On the ninth day, it is traditional to give food to the poor and the children.

(d) The entire family had to dress in black for a year following Joelito's death.

(e) The Pantheon is the burial place for the family and is the traditional Catholic way of marking a grave in Paraguay. This represents a low-average cost in Paraguay.

(f) Burial site rental. There is a yearly cost for rental of the plot of $100. We have paid this already for six years. In addition, because Joelito was killed so young, I have estimated this cost for an additional eleven years as a flat rate, with no inflation. Our family would not be likely to have this cost until I, as the oldest member, would die. Since the life-expectancy of a man of my class in Paraguay is 60 years, and I am presently 49, I have estimated this additional cost for 11 years.

(g) Transfer of body. We were not able, until last year, to purchase the Pantheon and prepare the final resting place of Joelito. We had had him temporarily buried and had to have his body moved.

(h) Memorial services. Following the funeral, we had services every day for the first three months, then every three months to the end of the first year after death. After that memorial services are held every 6 months. The costs associated with this are $25.00 for each church service and $15.00 for each newspaper notice. The breakdown is as follows:

First 9 days:	
– newspaper notice	135.00
– Services in Asunción and Ybycui daily	450.00
Following 12 weeks:	
– weekly newspaper notice	180.00
– daily service in Asunción and Ybycui	4200.00
Until end of first year:	
– notice and service in 2 churches every 3 months	195.00
Annual to present:	
– notice and service in 2 churches every 6 months	650.00
Future memorial service cost	
– notice and one church service every 6 months for 37 years (to Joelito's life expectancy of 60).	2960.00
Total	$8,770.00

Legal Costs

8. In this part I will list and explain the expenses I incurred in connection with the lawsuit our family brought against Pena and Duarte, the latter as an accomplice for having tried to cover up the crime by saying he killed Joelito in a "crime of passion." I explained in my testimony that we were not allowed to submit evidence or obtain discovery in the proceeding in Paraguay. The court was just sitting on the case until we brought this suit in the U.S. Thereafter, when the court in Paraguay declared Duarte responsible, but freed him based on an old, forgotten, sexist law which allows a man to kill another if he is found in bed with his wife. Duarte received his absolution in September 1981. This occurred during a time that I had no legal representation. My attorneys had been disbarred and threatened.

9. The total legal costs in connection with our lawsuit in Paraguay were:

(a) Autopsy (second)	400.00
(b) Exhumation for autopsy (third)	1000.00
(c) Notarization of Photographs	600.00
(d) Newspaper notice	
—To prevent killing of Duarte in prison	500.00
—To seek release of my wife and Dolly from prison	500.00

(e) Legal fees and costs	66,000.00
(f) Damages claimed by Duarte	12,000.00
(g) Legal fees defending damage claim	10,000.00
Total	$91,000.00

These expenses are lettered and explained in corresponding lettered paragraph below:

(a) The second autopsy was performed at my request to counter the spurious official autopsy and to show there were burn marks.

(b) The third autopsy required exhumation of the body and was performed to explain the cause of wounds.

(c) Notarization can be a very expensive thing in Paraguay and, given the danger that accompanied notarization of the photographs of Joelito's body, I was charged a lot. In addition, I had 150 copies of the photographs made and notarized to prevent this important proof from being stolen and seized by the police.

(d) These were large notices in the newspaper. I put in one to save Duarte's life as he had had his life threatened in prison. He was in danger of being killed by the police because he had denied being the murderer and the coverup would have been more successful if he had been dead. I had the second notice published when Dolly and my wife were arrested and put in jail. I felt that the only chance of getting them freed was to advise the public of this injustice.

(e) In pursuit of our lawsuit in Paraguay I spent the following in legal fees:

1976	12,000
1977	12,000
1978	12,000
1979	12,000
1980	12,000
1981	6,000
Total	66,000

(f) On October 28, 1981, I received notice from the Marshall of the court in Paraguay. The notice of attachment against my clinic in Asunción was for 1.5 million guaranies, the equivalent of $12,000 United States dollars in damages for having brought the case against Duarte. Before this notice, I had no knowledge of their pending suit.

(g) I have spent so far $2,000 for an attorney to defend against the attachment. I have estimated an additional $8,000. On February 23, 1982, my wife informed me that Pena was also suing for damages, but I don't know for how much. I have retained an attorney to defend me in these suits by Pena and Duarte. The 12,000 and the continuous demands of Pena, who has not responded to the charges in the U.S. are completely unjustified and are a way of punishing my efforts to obtain justice in the torture and death of my son.

10. In connection with the lawsuit here, we have been represented without fee. I have, however, incurred the following expenses in connection with pursuit of the suit here:

(1) October 1978—airfare	
Dr. Filartiga-New York-Paraguay	1,140.00
Dolly Filartiga—to New York	
for purposes of locating Pena.	680.00
(2) April 1979—airfare Dr. and Mrs. Filartiga:	
New York-Paraguay for purposes of filing lawsuit	2,280.00
(3) February-April 7, 1982 Dr. Filartiga for and as	
a result of hearing on damages.	
Airfare—Paraguay-New York	1,474.00
Living expenses: rent (1/2 share)	400.00
Other living expenses	990.00
Telephone to Paraguay	3400.00
Total	$10,364.00

11. I was advised to remain longer in the United States this winter than I had intended because, as a result of the publicity generated by the hearing on damages, my family and friends received threats from people in positions in the Stroessner regime that I should not return to Paraguay. I was advised not to return for several months to allow the situation to cool down. While many people urged me not to return at all, I believe that the health care I provide to peasants in Paraguay is so important and that I must return. I also do not want other people to be intimidated about filing human rights suit in this country believing that, if they should do so, they would have to go into permanent exile.

Medical Expenses Of Family As a Result of Joelito's Torture and Murder

12. Dolly, my wife and I have all suffered serious medical problems as a result of our grief and anguish at Joelito's death and the stress it has created for our everyday life. Our emotional pain is almost beyond descrip-

tion, but, because of its severity, we have all suffered serious concrete physical problems. In this section of the affidavit, I will outline the expenses of
myself and my wife, that I paid for. The expenses I paid for in regard to
Dolly will be explained in Dolly's affidavit

Dr. Filartiga:

13. My out-of-pocket expenses, explained in corresponding lettered
paragraphs below are as follows:

(a) deterioration of eyesight	500.00
(b) circulation problems (medicine) expended already	1440.00
– for life expectancy	2640.00
(c) ulcer medication since Joelito's death	2160.00
– for life expectancy	3960.00
(d) projected diabetes medication	4000.00
Total	$14,700.00

(a) My eyesight, which was normal before Joelito's death, deteriorated
rapidly thereafter so that now I have the sight of a 60 year old person. In
the first 3 years after Joelito's death, I changed my prescription substantially
three times. My eyesight is 3 D positive. The cost of examinations and prescriptions has been $500.00. Such deterioration is a known consequence of
extreme stress.

(b) Following Joelito's death, I also began to experience for the first
time circulatory problems which are also known to be a product of extreme
tension. The result is numbness and cold in my hands and feet, painful
cramps and muscle tension in my arms, legs and feet. As I treat myself, the
cost associated with this problem is medicine which has cost $20.00 per
month since Joelito's death and which, in my medical judgment, I will have
to take for the rest of my life. (Estimated on basis of 60 years average life
expectancy).

(c) Following Joelito's death, I also developed, for the first time, an
ulcer. Prior to that I had had some discomfort from gastritis, but the severe
tension and constant threats following his death produced the ulcer. It
gives me severe pain and, in the past five months, given the attachment of
my clinic in Asunción Paraguay which resulted in my staff of 6 doctors quit-
ting, and the tension about returning, I have experienced 6 severe crises.
For this condition I take the drug cimetidin ("tagamet") every other month
at a cost of $60 per month. I also expect to have to continue this for the
rest of my life.

(d) I have also recently discovered, as a result of the terrible strain I have experienced recently with the attachment of the Asunción clinic, loss of the staff and concern about being here and returning, a grave concern about the financial situation my wife faces in Paraguay in my absence, along with her illness during my absence as a result of her concern over me, I have developed a borderline case of diabetes, and this too is a disease, the emergence of which is often associated with extreme stress which causes blood sugar levels to rise. Presently I am treating this condition by diet, but I expect to have medication expenses in the future.

(e) When Joelito was killed I was 43 years old and in a normal condition of health for a person my age. My physical health has deteriorated very severely as a result of the trauma and continuing tension I have experienced.

Mrs. Filartiga

14. I have paid for the following expenses amounted with my wife Nydia suffering as a consequence of Joelito's death:

(a) treatment of loss of eyesight	1000.00
– future medication (estimated 5 years)	12200.00
(b) treatment of kidney dysfunction medication	14640.00
– doctors services (1982)	1000.00
(c) treatment for loss of memory since Joelito's death	2700.00
– future treatments (10 years)	4500.00
Total	$36,040.00

My wife was 36 years old and in good health when Joelito was killed. Since that time she has suffered a number of stress-related problems. In addition, she tried to have another child and suffered two miscarriages, one at 6 months and one at 3 months gestation. In my medical opinion, these were a product of the trauma and stress from Joelito's death and threats that continue to this day as a result. Watching her suffer has caused and continues to cause me unspeakable anguish.

(a) Nydia's eyesight also seriously deteriorated as a product of the trauma of Joelito's torture and death. Before his death her eyes were fine. They deteriorated so quickly that we tried to save her sight with vitamin treatment as well as providing corrective glasses. The cost of treatment was approximately $1000.00.

(b) Over four years before Joelito's death, Nydia had suffered from kidney stones but was cured. Her problem first emerged when I was put in jail for 6 months and she was under extraordinary stress. She had no kidney problem for four years prior to Joelito's death. After he died, however, she lost 40 pounds, her weight dropping from 132 to 92 pounds. She is about 5'3" tall. The weight loss caused her kidneys to drop and she suffered great pain from stones, which sometimes caused her to have to stay in bed for 3-4 days at a time. The pain is so great that I have had to administer a spinal anesthetic approximately five times per year. The anesthetic is very expensive to obtain and costs $200 or $1000 per year. In addition, she takes antibiotics with cost $120 per month. This has been going on for six years already. The trauma of Joelito's death is so deep and so permanent that it is impossible to say whether she will be able to be cured again. I have estimated that she will at least require another 5 years of anesthetic and antibiotic treatment at a cost of $2440.00 per year.

(c) Also a common response to an extreme trauma, my wife has suffered serious memory loss. We have been treating this with a regime of vitamin imported from Germany which costs $75 for 6 months of treatment annually, or a total of $450 annually. It is likely she will continue these treatments for another 10 years.

Dr. Filartiga's Lost Income

15. As a result of Joelito's torture and death I estimate the following income losses since 1976 and project the following for the future:

(a)	1976	9,000
(b)	1977-79	19,000
(c)	1980-81	23,000
(d)	1982 (4 months)	7,650
(e)	1982 (8 months)	7,650
(f)	1983-87	57,500
(g)	1988-93	105,000
	Total	227,800

(a) In 1976 I did not work at all following Joelito's death. I had been earning 12,000 a year in fees and 12,000 a year in kind exchange from the peasants for medical services. While I continued to receive in kind assistance from the people, I lost 9,000 in fees that year.

(b) In 1977 and 1978 I worked at half my capacity, losing $6,000 annually in fees. In 1979, with the filing of the lawsuit I worked more sporadically, forfeiting $7,000 in income.

(c) In 1980 and 1981 my income more than doubled despite the fact that there was a devaluation of Paraguayan guarani compared to the dollar in 1980 as well. I opened a clinic in Asunción with 6 other doctors as well as continuing my clinic in Yucca. As I testified however, I had lost 50% of my working capacity and, therefore, considered that my fees in those years, $11,500 annually, represent only one-half my earning capacity.

(d) Since I have been forced to be in the United States for the last 4 months, I have forfeited my entire earning capacity for this period. I have figured this loss as one-third of my previous $23,000 full earning capacity.

(e) For the remaining 8 months of 1982 my estimated earning loss will be $1/2$ of the salary I would have normally earned.

(f) I estimate that I have five years remaining during which I can work at the level at which I am now capable. On the basis of my prior salary, this means a earning loss of $11,500 per year.

(g) Had Joelito not been killed, I would have expected to work to full capacity until I am 60 years old. I have suffered greatly, however, and I expect I will have to cut back my work even more severely in 5 years. After that point I have estimated that I will be able to work only one-quarter of normal capacity, and have calculated a 3/4 lost earning capacity based on the $25,000 annual base.

16. My lost working capacity is worth far more than the income it fails to produce for my family. I cannot take care of as many poor people either and this loss, in terms of their health, is inestimable. I hope the court can give consideration to this very concrete loss to the community as a consequence of the debilitation of my health and the time I have had to spend away from medical practice.

17. All funds that I would receive in damages will be put in a foundation *La Esperanza Fund* devoted to protecting and advancing the health and welfare of the poor people of Paraguay and a symbol that Joelito lives and is helping them. I seek no personal gain from this award and ask the court to consider, not only the continuing suffering and debilitation—a form of torture itself—that we have suffered as a family, but also the loss this has caused to the people I am devoted to serve.

18. The contents of this affidavit have been read to me in Spanish and I affirm that everything is accurate and true to the best of my knowledge.

DR. JOEL FILARTIGA

April 7, 1982

UNITED STATES DISTRICT COURT
FOR THE EASTERN DISTRICT OF NEW YORK

DOLLY M.E. FILARTIGA and JOEL FILARTIGA,	**AFFIDAVIT OF DOLLY FILARTIGA**

Plaintiffs,

v.

AMERICO NORBERTO PEÑA-IRALA,

Defendant.

Dolly Filartiga being duly sworn, deposes, and says:

1. I am one of the plaintiffs herein and make this affidavit to complete the testimony I was unable to finish in the court hearing.

2. For a full year following my brother's death, I could not believe he was dead. I kept thinking he would come back and that I heard the sound of his footsteps or of his voice. This happened often and each time I would rush to see if he was there; each time he did not appear filled me with terrible fear and despair.

3. I also constantly had the same dream—almost every night and I still have this dream from time to time. I dream that Joelito is rising from the blood-soaked mattress upon which I found him with all his wounds and that he is telling me that nothing happened. It is like I am continually confronted with the vision of my brother as he was when I was led to him. I wake up screaming. When I was home I would put pillows in my mouth so my mother wouldn't hear my screams and turn on the water faucets in the bathroom so that she couldn't hear me sobbing. During that first year I could hardly sleep. I guess I slept actually about one hour a day. When I couldn't sleep I would start cleaning in a frenzy. Cleaning the house, sweeping the pavement in front of the house. I would clean the same thing over and over and I still am a compulsive cleaner. I cannot stand anything messy.

4. After Joelito died I had to learn everything again. I tried to go back to school but my papers had mysteriously disappeared from the Ministry of Education. I used to read a lot and after Joelito's death I couldn't stand to read; I could not concentrate. I tried to work and had a job for about six months but I couldn't continue. It became harder and harder for me to

concentrate. I began to wander, not knowing where I was. I would take the wrong bus, one after another. I did not know what was happening. The only thing I could do was clean.

5. In Paraguay, it is customary to commemorate a person's death on a periodic basis with masses. In the beginning we had mass every day for the first three months, then we had mass once every three months for a year after Joelito's death. We would put notices in the paper of each mass and many people came. Sometimes several hundred people came because Joelito was very beloved and had also become a symbol of resistance. The mass was, in a sense, the safest way for people to express this.

6. On year from the day my brother died, we had a large mass. Suddenly, in the middle of this ceremony, it hit me that Joelito was never going to come back—that he was dead. Several days later, I tried to kill myself by taking a lot of pills; I was taken to the hospital where they pumped my stomach. After that I became so depressed. I hardly ever went out of the house or even out of my room, or my bed. I couldn't remember who I was. When people asked me a question, I would have to repeat it to myself to try to understand. If they asked me my name, I drew a blank. I felt I was losing my mind and my memory completely. I thought I should have died so my brother could live—I wished it had been me. I wanted to die; I felt that was the only hope, and that I could never possibly feel normal again.

7. I remained in this state for about six months. I would try very hard to go out or just to go on the street. I felt I had to try to do it for my sisters, but I felt I was always noticed, that people would single me out. I still feel that when I meet people, people single me out as Joelito's sister—I always wonder if people know who I am, wish I could be someone else.

8. I guess I fought to get out of this constant depression. I was in psychiatric therapy in Paraguay for about one year. I had to speak to someone about my pain, but it was never enough. I couldn't talk about it at home or with people I knew. When the family was together, I felt completely alone. It was very hard to be alone together. We couldn't look at each other and we couldn't talk. Although I knew it was wrong, I couldn't help but blame my father for my brother's death, my father who would not accede to the Stroessner system like other Paraguayans. I knew how tormented he was but I was so angry, I made his pain worse. I loved him and I hated him for this. It was only during his recent visit here that we began to feel like friends again.

9. After about six months I also tried to go back to work but that was too difficult. Sometimes I felt strong and it was o.k. But we kept having crises at home because of harassment by the police. For example, my little sister, Katia was kidnapped, strangers would come to the house, we would

get threatening phone calls. Under these conditions it was hard to work. I was often very tired or simply unable to go.

10. Before Joelito was killed we had many friends in common. The doors of our house were always open and there were always people there. I went out with my brother and our friends and had a relatively normal social life. Afterwards, I had no friends. People said they were afraid to come to the house and hardly ever called. Instead of friends, police agents would come pretending to be suitors. One of the tactics the regime uses in Paraguay is to try to paint someone as immoral. So, if you are seen with different companions you can get a bad reputation. Or, for example, after this suit was filed and reported in Paraguay, some of the stories designed to impugn the suit, said falsely I was having an affair with one of my attorneys Michael Maggio.

11. When the letter from Pena was delivered to our house, I decided that the only thing I could do was to come to the United States to find him. I had no life in Paraguay. I could not study, I could not live, I could not work, I had no friends, and I felt constantly persecuted. I knew if I came here I might never be able to go back, but I had no choice.

12. When I finally found Pena and, with the help of friends, identified him to the Immigration and Naturalization Service, I knew I could never return to Paraguay. My life was very hard then. I knew very little English and was suffering terrible culture shock. Everything was different and I felt completely alone. But I had to report Pena and have him arrested because I had to try to have him brought to justice, even though I knew I would have to file for political asylum here. I did not know I would be in limbo for years waiting for processing. I still have not found a life here—either work or a society of friends. I had six months of therapy to try to help me adjust but I feel like I need years more of very hard in depth help. Years ago I would have wanted to come to this country on a vacation; now because I am not free either to leave or go back home, I feel sometimes like I am in a big jail.

13. I don't think there is a moment in my life when I feel free of the torture of my brother's torture and death. I have always the memory of his tortured body and his death; always the weight of this experience, of my identity; always the great hole in my life left by his death. I used to want to be a doctor and I functioned like a nurse in my father's clinic. Today, I do not think I could bear the pain, just as I still cannot bear to read; or use my intellect; I am fearful of social situations and strangers. I always feel different, and like I will never know what it is like to live a relatively normal life.

DOLLY FILARTIGA

May 17, 1982

UNITED STATES DISTRICT COURT
FOR THE EASTERN DISTRICT OF NEW YORK

DOLLY M.E. FILARTIGA and JOEL FILARTIGA, Plaintiffs, v. AMERICO NORBERTO PEÑA-IRALA, Defendant.	**AFFIDAVITS OF DR. GLENN RANDALL AND DR. JOSE QUIROGA**

Dr. Glenn Randall and Dr. Jose Quiroga being duly sworn, deposes and says:

1. I, Dr. Glenn Randall am an internist, Board certified by the American Board of Internal Medicine. I am a graduate of the Medical School at Rush Medical College in Chicago, Illinois. I am chairman of the San Francisco Medical Group of Amnesty International, U.S.A. I, Dr. Jose Quiroga am a cardiologist now working as an Adjunct Assistant Professor of Medicine and Public Health at the University of California in Los Angeles. I received my medical training at the University of Chile. I am chairman of the Los Angeles Medical Group of Amnesty International, U.S.A.

2. We make this affidavit to help explain the physical and psychological suffering of Joelito Filartiga and the psychological suffering of the Filartiga family. We make this affidavit jointly because much of our research was done jointly.

3. In our capacities as chairmen of two branches of Amnesty International we have spent over two and one half years doing a research study of victims of torture and its medical and psychological consequences. Among us we have examined a total of over 55 victims of torture. These victims were from various countries including Chile, Uruguay, Colombia, Argentina, and Honduras. We have not examined any victims from Paraguay. However, the physical and psychological methods of torture used in the above countries are similar. The methods of torture used in Paraguay, as have been described in the autopsy reports, testimony and affidavits and judging by the sequelae described, are similar in Paraguay as well.

4. Our expertise in the matter of examination, care, and treatment of torture victims—approximately 55 cases is not staggering; however, in the

United States, to our knowledge there are no other physicians with this amount of experience. In addition to our experience we have access to the data from a five city multi-center study investigating the physical and psychological sequelae of torture and as such we have the records of an additional twenty victims.

5. The victims that we have examined are those that now reside in the United States. In addition, during the course of our examination and treatment of the victims we have come to know some of the families, both in therapeutic settings and in social ones, thus allowing us to know the impact of torture on these families in the United States.

6. There are several differences between the Filartiga case and many of the cases we have studied. First, the victim is deceased and we do not have access to him except as in the autopsy records and by descriptions of him in testimonies and affidavits. The materials we have, while not complete, is sufficient for analysis. The family in this case is represented by the affidavit of Dolly Filartiga, the affidavit of Dr. Joel Filartiga, the testimony of Dolly Filartiga and the testimony of Dr. Joel Filartiga. From these documents we are most familiar with Dolly Filartiga, Dr. Joel Filartiga, Joelito Filartiga and somewhat less familiar with his wife. We have much less information on his two youngest daughters, Analida and Katia.

7. The suffering of this family has been immense and to a large degree typical of the suffering of torture victims we have examined. Each suffers from a variety of psychological and physical complaints with the onset occurring after the death of Joelito. The family structure has been altered, with Analida, Katia and the mother living in Paraguay. Dolly is living in the United States and the father has had to travel extensively and was able to work less than usual. Each family members' life has been dramatically changed by the death of Joelito, the fact that it was accomplished by torture, and their efforts to achieve justice. These efforts have further strained the family. As a family their working capacity is decreased. Their ability to work and concentrate is decreased. They have been isolated and they have difficulty establishing new relationships. All of these changes contribute to the suffering of this family. After six years we know that Dr. Filartiga, his wife, Nydia, and Dolly have not been able to return to a normal life.

Joelito Filartiga

8. The torture to which Joelito was subjected probably consisted of the elements suggested in the autopsy report. That is, beating with a fist and other devices, including a looped cord, kicking, removing the nails from their proper places, (although the nails on the photograph provided seem

to be intact on the left hand, and the report therefore may suggest loosening as a postmortem change), burning with electricity (or with chemical or other thermal agent) and penetration with sharp objects. These resulted in wounds and ecchymoses of the head and face, lips, malar region, periorbital, temporal aspect of the skull (fracture of the right temporal bone, parietal, and nasal), right shoulder, right and left arms, hands, thorax, abdominal flanks, back, hips, thighs, legs, and feet. These have been described in the autopsy report. There were also penetrating wounds of the thorax and right leg. There were three reportedly burned areas measuring 2 cm. in diameter, 3 x 4 cm, and 5 x 2 cm. respectively. The genitalia were reportedly mutilated and a wire was removed from Joelito's penis by Dr. Filartiga. The photograph of the body of Joelito Filartiga shows direct evidence of torture in the form of whipping and beating. The patterned marks over the right side of the body are classical for whip marks by a looped flexible cord. The injuries to Joelito were deliberately forceful, multiple and inflicted over a period of time. For example, the mark on the right thigh appears to be older than others. The other marks on the skin were certainly inflicted during life and were intended to produce severe pain. The cause of death probably was not a single stab wound but rather the result of shock and hemorrhage due to multiple traumatic injuries. If the burns were caused by electricity, the amount of current used may have caused his death by cardiac arrest. An intracerebral bleed may have also been responsible. This possibility must be raised because of the fracture of the temporal bone of the skull. To my knowledge no examination of the internal organs or the brain was made. While the pain associated with the beating and stabbing can be imagined to some degree by anyone, the amount of pain from the considerable number of wounds inflicted upon Joelito must be outside the experience of any of us.

9. Joelito's torture and pain may have been more severe than any of the victims we have examined in the United States. We say this because it was severe enough to cause his death. In our research experience 100% of the victims were beaten. The electric shock torture is customarily administered, either by conduction through an electrolyte solution or wet rags, thus, leaving no physical trace. Or through more direct means, by direct application of the electrodes to the skin. This *is* an extremely painful torture. In the usual apparatus the amount of electricity applied to the electrode can be varied and the electrode cane moved from place to place. The genitalia are often shocked in this way and the urethral wire removed by Dr. Filartiga was probably used for electric torture. 75% of the victims that we have examined were subjected to electric shock torture. After inflicting an unbearable amount of pain, the electric torture commonly causes the loss of consciousness. Only the most severe cases have more than minor evidence of burns, either immediately after torture or years later. Thus, the burns on

Joelito, if caused by electricity, represent an agonizing amount of electrical torture.

10. Torture is not limited to physical methods, although this is all that can be documented from the autopsy results. A great part of the torture and often the most devastating aspect consist of psychological torture. All of the victims we examined experienced threats against the family, threats of death, verbal abuse and other vague threats.

11. As have been presented in direct testimony and affidavits, it is evident that members of the Filartiga family are also victims of Joelito's torture and have suffered heavily. As victims they suffer in ways similar to the victim, but not as a result of physical torture. Their suffering is psychological. In our study the long term psychological difficulties have often been more devastating than the physical problems. This is because the physical problems often heal, while the psychological ones are more difficult to treat and less evident initially. Another reason the psychological torture predominates in our studies, is that the victims of severe torture die.

Dolly Filartiga

12. Dolly's experiences as a result of her brother's death are characteristic of post-traumatic stress disorder. (A discussion of the disorder is in the appendix.) Her difficulties and losses were easier to ascertain because we have more information about her than her younger sisters. However, by any means of measurement, her anguish is severe in degree. At the time of Joelito's death she was 20 years old and had an extremely close relationship with her brother. She has been sequentially traumatized from the time of her brother's death; she was the first family member to see him dead, was subjected to the continual harassment in Paraguay, and, finally, by virtue of her relocation to the United States was forced to adjust to a new culture, was isolated from her family and needed to learn a new language. She was deprived of the significant relationship with her brother. The relationship with her entire family was instantly changed. She blamed Joelito's death on her father. Her mother was unable to cope with this situation. She was immediately intimidated by Pena at the site of her brother's body when he said, 'here you have what you have been looking for and deserved.' While in Paraguay she was threatened with death, kidnapping, legal accusations by Pena (spending one night in jail), harassed with constant surveillance of her home by police who were constantly preparing their weapons, and disappearance of her papers from the Ministry of Education. For over a year in Paraguay she had difficulty with sleep, recurrent nightmares, decrease in memory and concentration, feelings of persecution and of being singled out. She used denial when she thought that her brother

would come back to life. She felt alone even when in the company of her family. Her friends deserted her because people were afraid to come to the house. She was unable to study, she was unable to work and had a constant feeling of pessimism. After approximately one year she attempted suicide and was again depressed for months. She had psychotherapy for one year in Paraguay. After she came to the United States in search of Pena 'to bring him to justice,' she applied for political asylum and still years later has not been able to lead a normal life. She has had to adjust to a new culture, a new language, and is unable to return to Paraguay. After an additional 6 months of psychotherapy in the United States she reported in May 1982 that she was not free of the thought of her brother's torture and death, she was unable to read or think as well as she could previously, she remained fearful of social situations and strangers and she doubted that she will ever be able to lead a normal life.

13. She is still very much a victim of the circumstances into which she was placed by the death of her brother. Certainly, her thoughts about herself and relationships with others are abnormal. She still has recurrent nightmares, is isolated socially and isolated from her family emotionally and geographically, and cannot function in a normal manner cognitively. It is likely that since these symptoms have continued for 6 years that they will continue for years more, even if she has the proper psychiatric treatment.

Dr. Joel Filartiga

14. Dr. Filartiga's present condition and suffering are more complicated to evaluate because of his prior experience in detention (4 times) and torture (3 times). When asked about lingering thoughts surrounding his prior experience he mentions feelings of isolation, fear, and that people did not know that torture occurred in the buildings which they passed. In 1958 he was subjected to tortures that are still widely used. Deprivation of food and sleep, forced labor, telephone, submarino, electric shock, and watching others being tortured. He seems to have been able to recover from these episodes of torture with opposition to the Stroessner regime and through his work benefiting the peasants in Ybycui. Evidence of Dr. Filartiga's immense emotional strength is shown when he has the presence of mind to photograph Joelito's body just after death and to arrange for the autopsies, which were performed. These two acts would be extremely difficult for any father. His art work has also probably had a therapeutic, in addition to an educational and artistic function. Dr. Filartiga's paintings, done after Joelito's death showed the day without any sun, a garden without flowers, and a river without water suggesting anguish, despair and rage. His emotionally bland testimony suggests that he continues to repress very powerful feelings and materials. Dr. Filartiga suffers from

thoughts of his son's experience under torture, of guilt feelings because his family views him as being partially responsible for Joelito's death, and with a variety of physical problems which he ascribes to his emotional pain and severe distress.

15. His wife has also suffered from this experience by the loss of her son, constant harassment in Paraguay, alteration in the family structure and frequent medical problems which are outlined in Dr. Filartiga's testimony and affidavit. Her suffering and that of her children have added to Dr. Filartiga's pain

16. The burden placed on Dr. Filartiga was made more intense by the suffering of his younger daughters. Anilida and Catia were cared for by their brother, Joelito, and their sister, Dolly. The parents worked in Ybycui and usually were present only on weekends. After Joelito's death, Joelito was obviously no longer a caretaker. Their mother and Dolly were unable to function at a high level because of their grief, legal battles, and fear from constant threats. After a number of years Dolly came to the United States seeking Pena and this further changed Analida's and Catia's environment. Dr. Filartiga has not been able to spend as much time in Paraguay with his family because of travel to the United States, and, at times, because of the fear of returning to Paraguay. Moreover, he is unable to support his family as easily because of decreased work capacity. He was also not as effective in family interactions because of his guilt about Joelito's death and the blame from other family members he received regarding the death.

17. In an article by Dr. F. Allodi, a Canadian psychiatrist, entitled, 'The Psychiatric Effects in Children and Families of Victims of Political Persecution and Torture,' he reports on three studies concerning this subject, as published in the Danish Medical Bulletin, Vol.27 No. 5/November 1980; pages 229-232. We have reproduced part of this article in the appendix. While these studies are not identical to the situation of the Filartiga family, they describe many of the stresses to which the Filartiga family and, in particular, the younger children, were subjected. As in these articles, the family had been subjected to violence, social ostracism and stigma, economic injury (Dr. Filartiga was unable to work as much as before), and emotional pain. The experience of the Filartiga family may be further compared to families in which one member of the family mourns and continues their life. Because there has been no finality the family has had a constant reminder of Joelito's death and this process has been prolonged and delayed. These reminders include disruption of family life with Dolly Filartiga in the United States, Dr. Filartiga in the United States periodically, a decrease in Dr. Filartiga's earning power, and continued legal involvement.

18. In summary, the whole family has suffered since 1976 following Joelito's death. From what we know, the suffering is characterized by recollection of traumatic events, disintegration of family ties, both geographically and emotionally, feelings of guilt, multipicsomatic complaints, reduced involvement with the external world, feelings of estrangement with other people, loss of interest in previously enjoyed social activities, sleep disorders and nightmares. These symptoms present in multiple members of the Filartiga family constitute the psychiatric diagnosis of Post-traumatic Stress Disorder. This diagnostic category is from the Diagnostic and Statistical Manual III. This manual is the official diagnostic and classification manual for psychiatric disease in the United States. We reproduced a portion if the DMS III dealing with the Post-traumatic Stress Disorder. (That portion is attached to this affidavit). The suffering of this family has been immense and has been of a greater degree than any of the other families that I have examined. This may be because the whole family has been involved continuously from the time of Joelito's death. By reading their testimony and affidavits, it is only possible to glimpse the suffering this family endures. They experience it and think of it constantly as they have done for the past 6 years.

_____

DR. GLENN R. RANDALL
    August 20, 1982

_____

DR. JOSE QUIROGA
    August 25, 1982

DECEMBER 15, 1982: PARAGUAY

Paraguayan Investigation File

CAPITAL POLICE*
DEPARTMENT OF INVESTIGATIONS
DIRECTOR OF POLITICS

Asuncion, 15 December 1982

D.P.A. No. 1519
Purpose: Update report

To: Senior Chief of the Department of Investigations
      Mr. Pastor M. Coronel
      E.S.D.

I have the honor of writing you in order to provide the following information:

I received a visit from Mr. HUGO DERLIS DUARTE ARREDONDO, who lives on Alas Paraguayas No. 850, Mariscal Estigarribia Barrio, and who provided the following information: after leaving the National Penitentiary, where he was imprisoned for the death of Joel Filartiga, he had his second marriage to Elena Vysokolan, daughter of General Estephan Vysokolan. His current brother-in-law, Oleg Vysokolan, is a lawyer and sociologist, and works with the Committee of Churches. On more than one occasion, Vysokolan told Duarte that the death of Joel Filartiga was a political crime and that they considered Duarte a professional assassin at the service of the government and that all of the case history was perfectly documented by the Committee of Churches. This caused on Sunday the 15th, in the afternoon hours an incident between the two, causing Duarte wounds that were looked at by a competent medical professional.

I also report that during his stay in prison he was visited by the lawyer HORACIO GALEANO PERRONE, who asked Duarte that he retract his confession of the murder of Joel Filartiga, a fact that would then be utilized by the press to attack the government. He, Duarte, declared that he rejected the proposal and asked that the lawyer leave and that he not visit anymore.

Alberto Cantero
Director of Politics

Asuncion,
15 December 1982

---

* Document located in the *Centro de Documentacion y Archivo*, Asunción, Paraguay. Translated into Spanish by author.

MAY 13, 1983: UNITED STATES

U.S. District Court for the Eastern District of New York: Magistrate's Report and Recommendation

UNITED STATES DISTRICT COURT
FOR THE EASTERN DISTRICT OF NEW YORK

DOLLY M.E. FILARTIGA and JOEL FILARTIGA,	**MAGISTRATE REPORT AND RECOMMENDATION**
Plaintiffs,	**79 Civ. 917**
v.	
AMERICO NORBERTO PEÑA-IRALA,	
Defendant.	

By an Order dated June 23, 1981, Your Honor granted plaintiffs' motion for entry of a default judgment against the defendant, Americo Norberto Pena-Irala. The order referred to the undersigned the issue of the damages to be awarded to plaintiffs. An evidentiary hearing concerning damages was held on February 12, 1982.

PRIOR PROCEEDINGS

Plaintiffs brought this action "for damages for the violation of human rights for the wrongful torture and murder of the decedent, Joel Filartiga" by the defendant, Americo Norberto Pena-Irala ("Pena"), and for related wrongs, all of which events were alleged to have occurred in Paraguay. Plaintiffs are Dr. Joel Filartiga, the decedent's father, a resident, of Paraguay, and Dolly Filartiga, the decedent's sister, who now resides in New York, having arrived on a visitor's visa and applied for political asylum in the United States. Defendant is the former Inspector General of Police of Asuncion, Paraguay. Defendant was served with process in this action while in Brooklyn, in the custody of the Immigration and Naturalization Service as an illegal alien. Defendant has since returned to Paraguay.

Jurisdiction was invoked under the Alien Tort Statute, 28 U.S.C. § 1350, which provides that "[t]he district courts shall have original jurisdiction of any civil action by an alien for a tort only, committed in violation of the law of nations or a treaty of the United States."

By a Memorandum and Order dated May 16, 1978, Your Honor granted defendant's motion to dismiss the complaint for lack of subject matter jurisdiction.

On June 30, 1980, the Court of Appeals, in what has been recognized as a landmark decision,[1] reversed and remanded the case for further proceedings. *Filartiga v. Pena-Irala*, 630 F.2d 876 (2d Cir. 1980).

The Court of Appeals held that the Congressional grant of jurisdiction in §1350 was authorized by Article III of the Constitution. The court reasoned:

> [A] case properly arise(s) under the . . . laws of the United States for Article III purposes if grounded upon the common law of the United States. . . . The law of nations forms an integral part of the common law, and a review of the history surrounding the adoption of the Constitution demonstrates that it became a part of the common law *of the United States* upon the adoption of the Constitution. Therefore, the enactment of the Alien Tort Statute was authorized by Article III.

Filartiga, supra at 886 (citations omitted) (emphasis in original)

In finding the allegations of the complaint sufficient to invoke §1350 jurisdiction, the court held that:

> [D]eliberate torture perpetrated under color of official authority violates universally accepted norms of the international law of human rights, regardless of the nationality of the parties. Thus, whenever an alleged torturer is found and served within our borders, § 1350 provides federal jurisdiction.

Filartiga, supra at 878.

The court held that §1350 jurisdiction did not depend upon the existence of a private remedy under international law; rather, plaintiffs' remedy was to be determined by the district court, guided by the choice of law considerations set forth by the Supreme Court in *Lauritzen v. Larsen*, 345 U.S. 571, 73 S.Ct. 921, 97 L.Ed 1254 (1954). The Court of Appeals recognized that "fairness" might require application of Paraguayan law and

---

[1] E.g., Blum & Steinhardt, *Federal Jurisdiction Over International Human Rights Claims: The Alien Tort Claims Act After Filartiga v. Pena-Irala*, 22 Harv. Int'l. L. J. 53 (1981); Case Comment, *Torture as a Tort in Violation of International Law; Filartiga v. Pena-Irala*, 33 Stan. L. Rev. 353 (1981); Note, *Terrorism as a Tort in Violation of The Law of Nations*, 6 Fordham L. Rev. 236, 247-264 (1982).

noted that, in such case, federal subject matter jurisdiction would not be ousted, even though plaintiff's claim under the general international proscription of torture would be dismissed. *Filartiga, supra* at 889 and n.25.

DAMAGES CLAIMS

Familiarity with the facts of the case as set forth in the opinion of the Court of Appeals and Your Honor's previous memorandum and order dismissing the action is assumed. Those facts were confirmed by the evidence adduced at the damages hearing before the undersigned.

Plaintiffs seek a total of $10,000,000.00 in compensatory and punitive damages, as follows:

(1) Dr. Filartiga, in his capacity under Paraguayan law as the personal representative of the decedent, claims an unspecified amount of damages for the bodily injuries, pain and suffering of the decedent caused by defendant's acts of torture;

(2) Dr. Filartiga and Dolly Filartiga each claim specific damages for his/her pecuniary losses and unspecified damages for emotional pain and suffering caused by decedent's wrongful death as a result of defendants acts of torture;

(3) Dolly Filartiga claims an unspecified amount of damages for her emotional pain and suffering caused by being led to the mutilated and lifeless body of her brother, the decedent;

(4) Dolly Filartiga claims an unspecified amount of damages for being wrongfully charged in Paraguay with harassment of Pena's house and battery on his stepson and for being sentenced to jail without trial, and for being incarcerated for six hours;

(5) Dr. Filartiga seeks to recover court costs, attorneys fees and other specified expenses incurred by him in prosecuting a criminal action against the defendant in Paraguay, based upon the same acts of torture and murder as are alleged here, which prosecution was subverted by defendant's abuse of process, and false imprisonment of, and physical threats to, Dr. Filartiga's Paraguayan attorney;

(6) Dr. Filartiga seeks to recover attorneys fees incurred and anticipated by him in defending a civil action brought against him by the defendant herein and Jose Duarte in Paraguay, as well as the amount of the damages claimed against him in that action; and

(7) Plaintiffs seek to recover court costs, attorneys fees and other specified expenses incurred by them in pursuing the instant litigation.

The undersigned observes initially that Dr. Filartiga's claim ((6) above) for his expenses in the civil action brought against him in Paraguay is not mentioned in the complaint. Defendant, therefore, had no notice of such claim and it cannot properly be the subject of a default judgment.

Furthermore, there is no independent basis of federal jurisdiction for that claim, or for Dr. Filartiga's claim ((5) above) for his expenses in the Paraguayan criminal prosecution of defendant, or for Dolly Filartiga's claims ((3) and (4) above) for intentional infliction of emotional distress, abuse of process and false imprisonment in Paraguay.

The complaint, without reference to any particular claim made therein, asserts that the doctrine of pendent Jurisdiction is applicable here. However, the undersigned concludes that the court has power to hear only Dolly Filartiga's claim ((3) above) for intentional infliction of emotional distress.

> Pendent jurisdiction, in the sense of judicial *power*, exists whenever there is a claim "arising under [the] Constitution, the Laws of the United States, and Treaties made, or which shall be made, under their Authority. . . ." U.S. Const., Art. III, §2 and the relationship between that claim and the state claim permits the conclusion that the entire action before the court comprises but one constitutional "case." The federal claim must have substance sufficient to confer subject matter jurisdiction on the court. *Levering & Garrigues Co. v. Morrin*, 289 U.S. 103, 53 S.Ct. 549, 77 L.Ed. 1062. The state and federal claims must derive from a common nucleus of operative fact. But if, considered without regard to their federal or state character, a plaintiff's claims are such that he would ordinarily be expected to try them all in one judicial proceeding, then, assuming substantiality of the federal issues, there is power in federal courts to hear the whole.

United Mine Workers v. Gibbs, 383 U.S. 715, 725, 86 S.Ct. 1130, 1138, 16 L.Ed.2d 218 (1966) (emphasis in original). The requirements of a common nucleus of operative fact and that the claims be such that they ordinarily would be expected to be tried in a single proceeding are cumulative. *Almenares v. Wyman*, 453 F.2d 1075, 1083 (2d Cir. 1971); *cert. denied*, 405 U.S. 944, 92 S.Ct. 962, 30 L.Ed.2d 815 (1972); 13 Wright, Miller & Cooper, *Federal Practice and Procedure*, § 3567 at 445 and n.2. (1975).

Dolly Filartiga's claim for intentional infliction of emotional distress is the only one of the local claims that "derives from a common nucleus of operative fact" with plaintiffs' federal claim based upon defendant's torture and murder of the decedent in violation of international law. Also, it is such a claim as would ordinarily be expected to be tried together with the federal claim. Because of the factual connection with the federal claim, considerations of judicial economy, convenience and fairness to the litigants argue persuasively for exercise of pendent jurisdiction in the case of this particular local claim. *E.g., Claridge House One, Inc. v. Borough of Verona,* 490 F. Supp. 706, 710 (D.N.J. 1980). The other local claims (4), (5) and (6) above should be dismissed without prejudice.[2]

The cognizable damages claims remaining in the case are numbers (1), (2) and (3) above. However, Dr. Filartiga's claim ((2) above) for damages for the wrongful death of the decedent includes a claim for the medical expenses of Mrs. Filartiga, who allegedly suffered emotional and psychosomatic harm as a result of the decedent's death. Affidavit of Dr. Joel Filartiga (hereinafter "Dr. Filartiga Aff."), ¶4. Mrs. Filartiga is not a plaintiff in this action; hence, no damages award can be made for her injuries.

APPLICABLE LAW

The relevant choice of law considerations set forth in the *Lauritzen* decision include: (1) the place of the injury; (2) the place of the conduct causing the injury; (3) the nationality and domicile of the respective parties; (4) the place where the relationship between the parties is centered; (5) the relevant policies of the forum, including respect for international law; and (6) the possibility of prejudice to the plaintiff in having the forum court apply a foreign nation's law.

In the instant case, Paraguay was the place of the tort and the injury caused by it. Both the plaintiffs and the defendant were Paraguayans. The only connection of the case to the United States is that defendant was served with process here. "Thus, the Filartigas' cause of action should be brought under Paraguayan Tort law." Case Comment, *Torture as a Tort in Violation of International Law: Filartiga v. Pena-Irala,* 33, Stan. L.Rev 353, 362 (1981); *Slater v. Mexican National Railway,* 194 U.S. 120, 24 S.Ct. 581, 48 L.Ed. 900 (1904); Restatement (Second) of Conflicts of Laws, §145.

Moreover, plaintiffs concede that the laws of Paraguay afford them adequate remedies consonant with the international proscription of torture.

---

[2] It is unclear whether the order granting plaintiffs' motion for entry of a default judgment may put the case beyond discussions of pendent jurisdiction, *see Mayor of Philadelphia v. Educational Equity League,* 415 U.S. 605, 627, 94 S.Ct. 1323, 1336, 39 L.Ed.2d 630 (1974).

Tr. 88;[3] Plaintiffs' Post-Trial Memorandum of Facts and Law, 45-48. A review of the relevant Paraguayan laws indicates that they conform to and compliment Articles 3-11 of the Declaration on the Protection of All Persons from Being Subjected to Torture, General Assembly Resolution 3452, 30 U.N. GAOR Supp. (No. 34) 91, U.N.Doc. A/1034 (1975). That document was relied upon by the Court of Appeals in discerning the international norm, *Filartiga, supra* at 882-889 and n.11. Articles 3-11 provide, essentially, that each nation shall make torture a crime and that victims of torture by public officials shall be afforded redress and compensation "in accordance with national law." Furthermore, our own domestic policies favor upholding human rights conventions, *Filartiga, supra* at 884-85 and n.17, 889 and n.24, and would, therefore, be advanced by application of Paraguayan laws providing redress to those injured as a result of acts of torture perpetrated under color of official authority, 33 Stan. L. Rev., *supra* at 362-63. Finally, plaintiffs do not contend that they would be in any way prejudiced by this court's application of Paraguayan law in computing damages.

Thus, considering the choice of law factors outlined in the *Lauritzen* decision and the circumstances of this case, the undersigned concludes that the laws of Paraguay should be applied in determining the plaintiffs' damages.

The Paraguayan Constitution prohibits torture. *Filartiga, supra* at 884 and n.14; Affidavit of Alexandro Miguel Garro, December 9, 1982 (hereinafter "Garro Aff."), 16.[4] Also, Article 337 of the Paraguayan Penal Code prohibits torture; and, homicide by torture is an offense punishable by a prison term of 15-20 years. Garro Aff., 16.

In the case of an intentional homicide, such as is alleged here, the Paraguayan Civil Code ("C.C.") provides for a wrongful death action in favor of the decedent's father (C.C. art. 1118, 1119). Garro Aff., 5-7; Affidavit of Ramiro Rodriguez, May 2, 1979, in Support of Defendant's Motion to Dismiss the Complaint, 2; Affidavit of Emilio Gorostiaga, May 3, 1979, in Support of Defendant's Motion to Dismiss the Complaint (hereinafter "Gorostiaga Aff."), ¶ ¶ 8, 10.[5] The Paraguayan Civil Code also provides for a right of action in favor of anyone who has "indirectly" suffered

---

[3] "Tr." denotes a reference to the transcript of the damages hearing.

[4] By his credentials set forth in the affidavit, Mr. Garro qualifies as an expert on the laws of Latin American countries, including Paraguay. Garro Aff., 1. "[T]he testimony of an expert as to the accepted or proper construction of [the statutes of a foreign nation] is admissible upon any matter open to reasonable doubt." *Slater v. Mexican National Railway Co.*, 194 U.S. at 130.

[5] Messrs. Rodriguez and Gorostiaga both qualify as experts on the laws of Paraguay.

a compensable injury as a result of the decedent's death (C.C. art. 1113). Garro Aff. 5-7, 11-13. In the former action, the plaintiff can recover for both his out-of-pocket pecuniary losses and his expected share of the decedent's future earnings (C.C. art. 1102-1103); Garro Aff., 4-13; Gorostiga Aff., ¶10.[6] In the latter action, the plaintiff can recover for his/her pecuniary losses causally related to the decedent's death and also for his/her non-pecuniary "moral injuries" (agravio moral) (C.C. art. 1112, 1113). Garro Aff., 5-6, 13-15. Punitive damages are not recoverable; rather, under Paraguayan law, the punishment of the tortfeasor is a function of the criminal law.[7] Garro Aff., 16-18; Gorostiaga Aff., ¶10.

Under the Paraguayan Civil Code, compensable pecuniary injuries may include (1) customary funeral, burial and memorial service expenses; (2) the plaintiff's expected share of the future income; and (3) plaintiff's own lost income and medical expenses resulting from emotional or psychoso-

---

[6] As noted by the Court of Appeals, *Filartiga*, 630 F.2d at 879 n.5, the Gorostiaga affidavit asserts that under Paraguayan law a civil action for wrongful death "may not proceed to judgment until the criminal action has been disposed of" and, "[i]f the defendant is found not guilty because he was not the author of the case under investigation in the criminal proceeding, no civil action for indemnity for damages based upon the same deed investigated in the criminal proceeding can succeed or prosper." Gorostiaga Aff., ¶8. Assuming this is the law in Paraguay, the other submissions before the court, including the evidence adduced at the evidentiary hearing, do not clearly show that the criminal prosecution instituted against Pena by Dr. Filartiga in Paraguay has reached a conclusion or that Pena has been found not guilty of the torture and murder of the decedent. Defendant's exoneration in the Paraguayan criminal proceeding was not asserted by him in defense of this action, prior to his default. The mere possibility that Pena may have a meritorious defense to this action does not bar entry of a default judgment against him. *Cf. Meehan v. Snow*, 652 F.2d 1274, 277 (2d Cir. 1981) (Under R.Civ.P. 55(c), principal factors bearing an appropriateness of relieving a party of a default include, *inter alia*, whether a meritorious defense is presented); *Moldwood v. Stutts*, 410 F. 2d 351, 352 (5th Cir. 1969). (Under F.R.Civ.P. 55(c), party seeking relief from default must show "by definite recitation of fact," *inter alia*, "that there was a valid defense to it"). Moreover, while Paraguayan law applies here as the substantive rule of decision, the Federal Rules govern the procedural aspects of the case, including the appropriateness of entering a default judgment. *See Erie Railroad Co. v. Tompkins*, 304 U.S. 64, 58 S.Ct. 817, 82 L.Ed. 1188 (1938). Were defendant to seek relief from the default judgment to be entered in this case, plaintiffs' allegations regarding the corruption of the Paraguayan judicial system by the principle of "mbarete," Plaintiffs' Post-Trial Memorandum of Facts and Law, 20-24, which, if true, would put Paraguayan law in conflict with United States policy, might be considered by the court in determining the meritorious nature of the defense of exoneration in the Paraguayan criminal prosecution. However, that issue need not be resolved at this time.

[7] Nor are punitive damages normally awarded by courts of international jurisdiction, as plaintiffs admit. Plaintiffs' Post-Trial Memorandum of Facts and Law, 61-70. Furthermore, it is not at all clear, as plaintiffs suggest, that the defendant has been immunized from criminal sanctions in Paraguay. *See* note 6, *supra.*

matic impairments caused or exacerbated by the decedent's death. Garro Aff., 7-10; Gorostiaga Aff., ¶10. Compensable moral injuries may include (1) emotional pain and suffering; (2) loss of companionship; and (3) disruption of family life. Garro Aff., 14. The plaintiff will additionally be entitled to recover court costs and attorneys fees. Garro Aff., 10-12; Gorostiaga Aff., ¶10.

The plaintiff in a Paraguayan wrongful death action under C.C. art. 1118 and 1119, or in an action for indirect injuries under C.C. art. 1113 has no right of recovery for the decedent's own pain and suffering. Garro Aff., 4-5, 7; Gorostiaga Aff., ¶10. Furthermore, such claim cannot pass to the decedent's estate unless the decedent had instituted it prior to death. Garro Aff., 14.

The Paraguayan Civil Code recognizes a cause of action for pecuniary and non-pecuniary damages for the intentional infliction of emotional distress (See, C. C. art. 1102, 1103). Garro Aff., 4, 14.

RECOMMENDED DAMAGES AWARD

Dr. Filartiga and Dolly Filartiga each claim that he/she has experienced emotional pain and suffering, loss of companionship and disruption of family life as a result of the decedent's death. Dolly Filartiga claims additionally that she has experienced emotional pain and suffering as a result of being led to the body of her brother. These claims are well supported by the testimony at the hearing, as well as by affidavits in evidence from psychiatrists and psychologists and from visitors to the Filartiga home in Paraguay. These injuries are compensable under Paraguayan law as outlined above. Based upon the evidence adduced, the undersigned recommends that the plaintiffs be awarded the sum of $150,000.00 each as compensation for his/her emotional pain and suffering, loss of companionship and disruption of family life resulting from the above described events.

Dolly Filartiga also claims pecuniary losses in the form of past and future medical expenses for treatment of a psychiatric impairment resulting from the decedent's wrongful death and her encounter with the decedent's tortured body. Such loss is compensable under Paraguayan law. The existence of the alleged psychiatric impairment is well supported by the testimony and affidavits in evidence. Likewise, there is evidence that treatment should continue for approximately three years at a cost of between $60 and $100 per session. Affidavit of Ana Deutsch, August, 1982; Affidavit of Michael Schneider, August 5, 1982. Based upon this evidence, the undersigned recommends an award to Dolly Filartiga of $25,000.00 as compensation for her future medical expenses for treatment of her psychiatric impairment resulting from the above described events. There is no evidence of the cost of Dolly Filartiga's past psychiatric treatment, and the undersigned will not speculate as to such cost; therefore, it is recommended that no award be made for these expenses.

Dr. Filartiga also claims pecuniary losses resulting from the wrongful death of the decedent. These losses allegedly include the costs of a funeral, burial and memorial services for the decedent, Dr. Filartiga's own past and future medical expenses for treatment of psychosomatic impairments resulting from his emotional distress caused by decedent's death by torture, and Dr. Filartiga's lost income from 1976 (following the decedent's death) to 1993 (Dr. Filartiga's remaining life expectancy) due to a diminution of his work capacity resulting from said emotional distress. Dr. Filartiga alleges that these various losses total upwards of $200,000.00. Dr. Filartiga Aff., ¶ ¶ 7; 13, 15. These pecuniary losses are not documented by financial records or invoices. His projected future losses are speculative only. Furthermore, there is scant medical evidence confirming the physical aspects of Dr. Filartiga's alleged impairments. Based upon all the evidence, the undersigned recommends that Dr. Filartiga be awarded the sum of $50,000.00 as compensatory damages for past funeral-related and medical expenses and for his lost income, resulting from the decedent's death by torture.

As stated above, punitive damages are not recoverable in a civil action under Paraguayan law. Therefore, the undersigned recommends that no award of punitive damages be made to plaintiffs.

Plaintiffs also claim attorneys fees in this action. Such fees are recoverable under Paraguayan law, as discussed. However, Dr. Filartiga has admitted that neither he nor Dolly Filartiga has incurred any attorneys fees in connection with this lawsuit. Dr. Filartiga Aff. ¶10. Therefore, the undersigned recommends that no award of attorneys fees be made to plaintiffs.

Dr. Filartiga also seeks to recover certain other expenses incurred by him in this action, including airfare between Paraguay and New York for himself, Dolly Filartiga and Mrs. Filartiga, housing rental and other living expenses in the United States at times during the pendency of this action, and the costs of telephone calls between the United States and Paraguay. These expenses allegedly total $10,364.00; however, Dr. Filartiga has submitted no documentation. Dr. Filartiga asserts that said expenses are recoverable on the theory that defendant's relocation to the United States was an act bearing such relationship to the wrongful conduct as to render the costs of pursuing him here compensable "mediate consequences" of the wrongful acts, under articles 935, 938 and 1102 of the Paraguayan Civil Code. Garro Aff., 10-13. Considering the statutory scheme relied upon, as quoted in Mr. Garro's affidavit at pages 4 and 11, and the facts in this case, the undersigned finds no merit whatsoever in this claim. Furthermore, such an award would be contrary to our own policy against encouraging forum shopping. Therefore, it is recommended that no award be granted for these expenses.

CONCLUSION

Based upon the foregoing discussion, the undersigned recommends that the court enter judgment in favor of the plaintiffs for $375,000.00 in compensatory damages as follows:

(1) For Dr. Joel Filartiga $200,000.00

(2) For Dolly Filartiga $175,000.00

Any objections to the recommendation of this report must be filed with the Honorable Eugene H. Nickerson within 30 days of your receipt of this report.

Respectfully submitted,

JOHN L. CADEN. United States Magistrate
Eastern District of New York

Dated: Brooklyn, New York
          May 13, 1983

MAY 20, 1983: UNITED STATES

U.S. District Court for the Eastern District of New York: Addendum to Magistrate's Report and Recommendation

UNITED STATES DISTRICT COURT
FOR THE EASTERN DISTRICT OF NEW YORK

DOLLY M.E. FILARTIGA and JOEL FILARTIGA,	**ADDENDUM TO REPORT AND RECOMMENDATION**
Plaintiffs,	**79 Civ. 917**
v.	
AMERICO NORBERTO PEÑA-IRALA,	
Defendant.	

The report issued by the undersigned on May 13, 1983 in the above-captioned case is hereby amended to include the following two recommendations, which were inadvertently omitted:

(1) (Add to penultimate paragraph, page 9)

Plaintiffs' claim under the general international proscription of torture should, therefore, be dismissed. *See Filartiga, supra* at 889 n. 25;

(2) (Add as final paragraph, page 13)

Similarly, under Paraguayan law, the decedent's potential claim for his bodily injuries, pain and suffering caused by defendant's acts cannot be asserted by his estate, as it was not instituted by the decedent, prior to his death. Therefore, the undersigned recommends that no damages be awarded on the claim for those injuries asserted by Dr. Filartiga in his capacity as the decedent's personal representative.

In addition, the first sentence of the second paragraph at page 7 of the report, listing the cognizable damages claims in the case, must be amended to conform it to the remainder of the report and thereby avoid unnecessary confusion. Therefore, that sentence is hereby amended to read as follows:

The cognizable damages claims remaining in the case are numbers (1), (2), (3) and (7) above.

Respectfully submitted,

John L. Caden
United States Magistrate
Eastern District of New York

Dated: Brooklyn, New York
        May 20, 1983

JULY 12, 1983: UNITED STATES

Plaintiffs' Objections to Magistrate's Report

UNITED STATES DISTRICT COURT
FOR THE EASTERN DISTRICT OF NEW YORK

DOLLY M.E. FILARTIGA and JOEL FILARTIGA,	**PLAINTIFFS' OBJECTIONS TO MAGISTRATE'S REPORT**
Plaintiffs,	
v.	
AMERICO NORBERTO PEÑA-IRALA,	
Defendant.	

After conducting an evidentiary hearing on February 12, 1983 and considering Plaintiff's Post-Trial Memorandum of Facts and Law and attached affidavits and exhibits (hereinafter "PTM"), Magistrate John L. Caden, on May 13, 1983, filed with this court his Report and Recommendation (hereinafter "Report") on the issue of damages to be awarded to plaintiffs. On May 20, 1983, Magistrate Caden filed an Addendum to his Report (hereinafter "Addendum"). Plaintiffs herewith submit certain objections to the Report and Addendum, which they respectfully ask the court to consider before acting on the Magistrate's Report.

APPLICABLE LAW

Plaintiffs have no quarrel with the Magistrate's recommendation that, under the doctrine of *Lauritzen v. Larsen*, 345 U.S. 571 (1954), the court should look to the law of Paraguay as the appropriate municipal law in initially determining their damages. Report, 9. They do, however, take exception to his view that it follows from this that "Plaintiff's claim under the general international proscription of torture should. . . be dismissed." Addendum, 1.

A holding that the act of torture underlying this suit violates Paraguayan law in no way mandates a corollary holding that it does not simultaneously violate the law of nations. Indeed, the whole doctrine of pendent jurisdiction teaches that, when a suit is brought in federal court, alleging, on the basis of the same facts, violation of federal as well as state law, one of four results may follow. The court may find that

1) neither federal nor state law was violated;
2) both federal and state law were violated;
3) only federal law was violated;
4) only state law was violated.

Here, federal law, which incorporates the international law of human rights, was violated, as the Circuit Court decision makes abundantly clear. Paraguayan law, which corresponds to state law in the analogy with pendent Jurisdiction, was also violated, but this does not mean that the federal law/international law claim should be dismissed, any more than a holding of, say, violation of state unfair competition law, in a suit alleging such violation as well as infringement of a federally registered trademark, would justify dismissal of the federal claim. *National Fruit Product Co. v. Dwinnell-Wright Co.*, 47 F. Supp. 499, 501 (D. Mass. 1942)

The Magistrate's theory of mutual exclusivity of the applicable law seems to be based on a misreading of the Circuit Court's holding that

> "Should the district court decide that the *Lauritzen* analysis requires it to apply Paraguayan law, our courts will not have occasion to consider what law would govern a suit under the Alien Tort Statute where the challenged conduct is actionable under the law of the forum and the law of nations *but not the law of the jurisdiction in which the tort occurred.*" (emphasis supplied), 630 F.2d 876, 889.

As the emphasized portion of the above passage indicates, the Circuit was commenting on a situation in which the alleged tort violates the law of the forum and the law of nations, but not the law of the jurisdiction in which the tort occurred. Here, there was a twofold violation: of the law of nations *and* of the law of Paraguay; hence both claims are valid and neither should be dismissed.

Plaintiffs are exceedingly puzzled by the Magistrate's finding that they "concede that the laws of Paraguay afford them adequate remedies consonant with the international proscription of torture," Report, 8, and that they "do not contend that they would in any way be prejudiced by this court's application of Paraguayan law in computing damages." Report, 9. On the contrary, plaintiffs began their post-trial argument by stating

> "The assessment of damages is, therefore, not confined to what municipal law provides, but must account as well for the interna-

tional character of the tort and the interest of the international community in just satisfaction." PTM, 29

and devoted the next sixteen pages of their post-trial memorandum, to which they respectfully call the court's attention, to elaborating on this point.

An international tort requires an international remedy. This basic proposition underlies Article 50 of the European Convention for the Protection of Human Rights and Fundamental Freedoms, which, in laying down guidelines for the remedial functions at the European Court of Human Rights, provides as follows:

"If the Court finds that a decision or a measure taken by a legal authority or any other authority of a High Contracting Party is completely or partially in conflict with the obligations arising from the present Convention, and if the internal law of the said Party allows only partial reparation to be made for the consequences of this decision or measure, the decision of the Court shall, if necessary, afford just satisfaction to the injured party."

Sohn and Buergenthal, Basic Documents in International Protection of Human Rights, p. 137.[1]

COSTS OF THE ACTION

The Magistrate's holding that an award to Dr. Filartiga of the costs incurred by law in bringing this action would encourage forum shopping, Report, 14, is contrary to the spirit of the Circuit Court decision and to the facts of the case. Dolly Filartiga came to the United States to escape harassment and possible imprisonment and torture in Paraguay, not to file a lawsuit. The defendant certainly did not come here in order to be sued. If Paraguay had an independent judiciary, Dr. Filartiga would by now have obtained redress from the courts of his own country. The policy of this country is to maximize the international enforcement of human rights, not to relegate plaintiffs to fora in which the only consequence of an attempt to vindicate human rights is a further deprivation of such rights.

THE QUESTION OF PUNITIVE DAMAGES

It may be that, if Paraguayan law provided for punitive damages, the issue of exclusivity of the applicable law would be academic. But it is pre-

---

[1] See *The Sunday Times v. United Kingdom*, 3 EHRR 317 (1980), in which the European Court of Human Rights awarded the plaintiff its expenses for attendance

cisely because punitive damages are not available under Paraguayan law—
although there is a certain overlap between the "moral damages" provided
for in Paraguayan law and the punitive damages familiar to United States
lawyers and judges[2]—that the matter of dual applicability is of cardinal
importance.

"It is a generally accepted rule that where two theories of damages
lie, claimant is entitled to the greater of the two." *McLean v. Alexander*, 449
F.Supp. 1251, 1260 (Del 1978), reversed on other grounds 599 F.2d 1190
(3rd Cir. 1979).[3] Plaintiffs have shown in their Post-Trial Memorandum
that, under international law, they are entitled to punitive damages. PTM,
59-73. Hence, dismissal of their international law claim, for reasons other
than lack of merit, deprives them of their entitlement to punitive damages, which, in the circumstances, could well be a multiple of their actual
damages.[4]

CONCLUSION

The Circuit Court, in what the Magistrate correctly called a landmark
decision, Report, 2, said that it considered that decision "a small but important step in the fulfillment of the ageless dream to free all people from brutal violence." 630 F.2d 876, 890. It would be ironic if the final result of this
case were an overly strict application of choice of law principles, resulting
in an award totally incommensurate with the heinousness of the tort. "The
general problem," as Professor Cavers argued in his classic article "The
Choice of Law Problem," 47 Harvard Law Review, 173, 179 (1933), is not
to apply mechanistic rules to conflict situations, but to satisfy "the demands
of justice."

Plaintiffs therefore request the court not to dismiss their claim under
international law and to increase the damages recommended by the

---

before the European Commission on Human Rights, although no such award would
have been made under British law.

[2] For a discussion of this point, see PTM, 55-58.

[3] Cf. *Friend v. H.A. Friend & Col*, 416 F.2d 526, 534 (8th Cir. 1969), cert. den. 397
U.S. 914 (1970), upholding an award of attorneys' fees under a pendent state claim
although no such award would have been available under the federal claim.

[4] For a European Court of Human Rights case awarding punitive damages under
international law, see *Ringeisen v. Austria (No. 2)*, 1 EHRR 504 (1972).

Magistrate to an amount commensurate with the gravity of defendant's acts and with the interest and obligation of the United States to make torture an unacceptable form of human conduct.

Respectfully submitted,

Peter Weiss
Rhonda Copelon
Betty Lawrence Bailey
c/o Center for Constitutional Rights
853 Broadway
New York, New York 10003

Michael Maggio
1800 Belmont Road, N.W.
Washington, D.C. 20009

Attorneys for Plaintiffs

Dated: New York, New York
July 12, 1983

JANUARY 10, 1984: UNITED STATES

U.S. District Court for the Eastern District of New York: Memorandum and Order

UNITED STATES DISTRICT COURT
FOR THE EASTERN DISTRICT OF NEW YORK

DOLLY M.E. FILARTIGA and
JOEL FILARTIGA,

Plaintiffs,

v.

AMERICO NORBERTO PEÑA-
IRALA,

Defendant.

MEMORANDUM AND ORDER

79 Civ. 917

NICKERSON, District Judge

Plaintiffs, Dolly M.E. and Dr. Joel Filartiga, citizens of Paraguay, brought this action against defendant Pena, also a Paraguayan citizen, and the former Inspector General of Police of Asuncion. They alleged that Pena tortured and murdered Joelito Filartiga, the seventeen year old brother and son, respectively, of plaintiffs, in retaliation for Dr. Filartiga's opposition to President Alfredo Stroessner's government. Plaintiffs invoked jurisdiction under, among other provisions, 28 U.S.C. §1350, giving the district, court "original jurisdiction of any civil action by an alien for a tort only, committed in violation of the law of nations or a treaty of the United States."

This court followed what it deemed the binding precedents of *IIT v. Vencap, Ltd.*, 519 F.2d 1001 (2d Cir. 1975) and *Dreyfus v. von Finck*, 534 F.2d 24 (2d Cir.), *cert. denied*, 429 U.S. 835 (1976), and dismissed for lack of jurisdiction on the ground that violations of the law of nations "do not occur when the aggrieved parties are nationals of the acting state," *id.* at 31.

The Court of Appeals reversed and remanded, concluding that the above quoted language from the Dreyfus opinion was "clearly out of tune with the current usage and practice of international law." *Filartiga v. Pena-Irala*, 630 F.2d 876, 884 (2d Cir. 1980). The Court of Appeals held that "deliberate torture perpetrated under color of official authority violates universally accepted norms of the international law of human rights, regardless of the nationality of the parties," and that 28 U.S.C. §1350 gave jurisdiction over an action asserting such a tort committed in violation of the law of nations. *Id.* at 878.

Following remand Pena took no further part in the action. This court granted a default and referred the question of damages to Magistrate John L. Caden for a report. The Magistrate, after a hearing, recommended damages of 200,000 for Dr. Joel Filartiga and $175,000 for Dolly Filartiga. Plaintiffs filed objections to the report, and the matter is now here for determination.

I

Before addressing damages the court considers two matters urged before but not decided by the Court of Appeals. Both go to whether the court should decline to exercise jurisdiction.

The first is whether the court should abstain in deference to the so-called act of state doctrine. See *Banco Nacional de Cuba v. Sabbatino*, 376 U.S. 398 (1964). Were the government of Paraguay concerned that a judgment by the court as to the propriety of Pena's conduct would so offend that government as to affect adversely its relations with the United States, presumably Paraguay would have had the means so to advise the court.

In any event, the Court of Appeals held that the alleged acts constitute, by the "general assent of civilized nations," a "clear and unambiguous" violation of the law of nations. 630 F.2d at 881, 884. As the Supreme Court noted in discussing the act of state doctrine in the *Sabbatino* decision, "the greater the degree of codification or consensus concerning a particular area of international law, the more appropriate it is for the judiciary to render decisions regarding it." 376 U.S. at 428. Where the principle of international law is as clear and universal as the Court of Appeals has found it to be, there is no reason to suppose that this court's assumption of jurisdiction would give justifiable offense to Paraguay.

Moreover, as the Court of Appeals noted, Paraguay has not ratified Pena's acts, 630 F.2d at 889, and this alone is sufficient to show that they were not acts of state. *See Alfred Dunhill of London, Inc. v. Republic of Cuba*, 425 U.S. 682, 684, 694 (1976).

Pena argued here on the original motion and in the Court of Appeals that this court should decline to proceed because Paraguay and not the United States is the convenient forum. Pena's default now casts doubt on the good faith of this contention. Its merits depend on whether the courts of Paraguay are not only more convenient than this court but as available and prepared to do justice. *Piper Aircraft Co. v. Reyno*, 454 U.S. 235, 254 n.22 (1981). Pena submitted nothing to cast doubt on plaintiffs' evidence showing that further resort to Paraguayan courts would be futile. This, court will therefore retain jurisdiction.

II

The Court of Appeals decided only that Section 1350 gave jurisdiction. We must now face the issue left open by the Court of Appeals, namely, the nature of the "action" over which the section affords jurisdiction. Does the "tort" to which the statute refers mean a wrong "in violation of the law of nations" or merely a wrong actionable under the law of the appropriate sovereign state? The latter construction would make the violation of international law pertinent only to afford jurisdiction. The court would then, in accordance with traditional conflict of laws principles, apply the substantive law of Paraguay. If the "tort" to which the statute refers is the violation of international law, the court must look to that body of law to determine what substantive principles to apply.

The word "tort" has historically meant simply "wrong" or "the opposite of right," so-called, according to Lord Coke, because it is "wrested" or "crooked," being contrary to that which is "right" and "straight." Sir Edward Coke on Littleton 158b; *see also* W. Prosser, Law of Torts 2 (1971). There was nothing about the contemporary usage of the word in 1789, when Section 1350 was adopted, to suggest that it should be read to encompass wrongs defined as such by a national state but not by international law. Even before the adoption of the Constitution piracy was defined as a crime by the law of nations. *United States v. Smith*, 18 U.S. (5 Wheat.) 153, 157 (1820). As late as 1819 Congress passed legislation, now 18 U.S.C. § 1651, providing for punishment of "the crime of piracy, as defined by the law of nations." 3 Stat. 510 (1819). Congress would hardly have supposed when it enacted Section 1350 that a "crime," but not the comparable "tort," was definable by the law of nations. Nor is there any legislative history of the section to suggest such a limitation.

Accordingly, there is no basis for adopting a narrow interpretation of Section 1350 inviting frustration of the purposes of international law by individual states that enact immunities for government personnel or other such exemptions or limitations. The court concludes that it should determine the substantive principles to be applied by looking to international law, which, as the Court of Appeals stated, "became a part of the common law of the United States upon the adoption of the Constitution." 630 F.2d at 886 (emphasis in original); *see also The Nereide*, 13 U.S. (9 Cranch) 388, 422 (1815) (Marshall, C.J.); *The Paquete Habana*, 175 U.S. 677, 700 (1900).

The international law described by the Court of Appeals does not ordain detailed remedies but sets forth norms. But plainly international "law" does not consist of mere benevolent yearnings never to be given effect. Indeed, the Declaration on the Protection of All Persons from Being Subjected to Torture, General Assembly Resolution 3452, 30 U.N. GAOR Supp. (No.34) 91, U.N. Doc. A/1034 (1975), adopted without dissent by the General Assembly, recites that where, an act of torture has been committed by or at the instigation of a public official, the victim shall be afforded redress and compensation "in accordance with national law," art. 11, and that "[e]ach state" shall ensure that all acts of torture are offenses under its criminal law, art. 7.

The international law prohibiting torture established the standard and referred to the national states the task of enforcing it. By enacting Section 1350 Congress entrusted that task to the federal courts and gave them power to choose and develop federal remedies to effectuate the purposes of the international law incorporated into United States common law.

In order to take the international condemnation of torture seriously this court must adopt a remedy appropriate to the ends and reflective of the nature of the condemnation. Torture is viewed with universal abhorrence; the prohibition of torture by international consensus and express international accords is clear and unambiguous; and "for purposes of civil liability, the torturer has become—like the pirate and the slave trader before him—*hostis humani generis*, an enemy of all mankind." 630 F. 2d at 884, 888, 890. We are dealing not with an ordinary case of assault and battery. If the courts of the United States are to adhere to the consensus of the community of humankind, any remedy they fashion must recognize that this case concerns an act so monstrous as to make its perpetrator an outlaw around the globe.

III

The common law of the United States includes, of course, the principles collected under the rubric of conflict of laws. For the most part in international matters those principles have been concerned with the relevant policies of the interested national states, and with "the needs" of the "international systems." Restatement (Second) of Conflict of Laws (1971) §6 (2). The chief function of international choice-of-law rules has been said to be to further harmonious relations and commercial intercourse between states. *Id.*, comment d.

However, where the nations of the world have adopted a norm in terms so formal and unambiguous as to make it international "law," the interests of the global community transcend those of anyone state. That does not mean that traditional choice-of-law principles are irrelevant. Clearly the court should consider the interests of Paraguay to the extent they do not inhibit the appropriate enforcement of the applicable international law or conflict with the public policy of the United States.

In this case the torture and death of Joelito occurred in Paraguay. The plaintiffs and Pena are Paraguayan and lived in Paraguay when the torture took place, although Dolly Filartiga has applied for permanent asylum in the United States. It was in Paraguay that plaintiffs suffered the claimed injuries, with the exception of the emotional trauma which followed Dolly Filartiga to this country. The parties' relationships with each other and with Joelito were centered in Paraguay.

Moreover, the written Paraguayan law prohibits torture. The Constitution of Paraguay, art. 50. The Paraguayan Penal Code, art. 337, provides that homicide by torture is punishable by imprisonment for 15 to 20 years. Affidavit of Alejandro Miguel Garro, December 9, 1982 (Garro Aff.), ¶ 31. Paraguay is a signatory to the American Convention on Human Rights, which proscribes the use of torture. Paraguayan law purports to allow recovery for wrongful death, including specific pecuniary damages, "moral damage," and court costs and attorney's fees. Thus, the pertinent formal Paraguayan law is ascertainable.

All these factors make it appropriate to look first to Paraguayan law in determining the remedy for the violation of international law. *See Lauritzen v. Larson*, 345 U.S. 571 (1953); Restatement (Second) of Conflict of Laws (1971) § 145(2). It might be objected that, despite Paraguay's official ban on torture, the "law" of that country is what it does in fact, Holmes, *The Path of the Law*, 10 Harv. L. Rev. 457, 461 (1897), and torture persists throughout the country. Amnesty International Report on Torture (1975) 214-16; D. Helfield and W. Wipfler, Mbarete: The Higher Law of Paraguay (The International League for Human Rights, 1980).

Where a nation's pronouncements form part of the consensus establishing an international law, however, it does not lie in the mouth of a citizen of that nation, though it professes one thing and does another, to claim that his country did not mean what it said. In concert with the other nations of the world Paraguay prohibited torture and thereby reaped the benefits the condemnation brought with it. Paraguayan citizens may not pretend that no such condemnation exists. If there be hypocrisy, we can only say with La Rochefoucauld that "hypocrisy is the homage which vice pays to virtue." Reflections; or Sentences and Moral Maxims 218 (1678).

To the extent that Pena might have expected that Paraguay would not hold him responsible for his official acts, that was not a "justified" expectation, Restatement (Second) of Conflict of Laws (1971) §6(2)(d) and comment g, so as to make unfair the application to him of the written law of Paraguay.

IV

Plaintiffs claim punitive damages, and the Magistrate recommended they be denied on the ground that they are not recoverable under the Paraguayan Civil Code. While compensable "moral" injuries under that code include emotional pain and suffering, loss of companionship and disruption of family life, Paraguayan Civil Code, arts. 1102, 1103, 1112, plaintiffs' expert agrees that the code does not provide for what United States courts would call punitive damages. Paraguayan law, in determining the intensity and duration of the suffering and the consequent "moral" damages, takes into account the heinous nature of the tort. However, such damages are not justified by the desire to punish the defendant. They are designed to compensate for the greater pain caused by the atrocious nature of the act. Garro Aff. ¶¶ 33, 34.

Yet because, as the record establishes, Paraguay will not undertake to prosecute Pena for his acts, the objective of the international law making torture punishable as a crime can only be vindicated by imposing punitive damages. It is true, as plaintiffs concede, that damages designated punitive have rarely been awarded by international tribunals. As explained in M. Whiteman, Damages in International Law 716-17 (1937), the international law of damages has developed chiefly in the resolution of claims by one state on behalf of its nationals against the other state, and the failure to assess exemplary damages as such against a respondent government may be explained by the absence of malice or *mala mens* on the part of an impersonal government. Here Pena and not Paraguay is the defendant. There is no question of punishing a sovereign state or of attempting to hold the people of that state liable for a governmental act in which they played no part.

Moreover, there is some precedent for the award of punitive damages in tort even against a national government. In *I'm Alone* (Canada v. United States), U.N. Rep. Int. Arb. Awards, vol. 3, at 1609, the American and Canadian claims Commissioners recommended, in addition to compensatory damages, payment of $25,000 by the United States to Canada for intentionally sinking a Canadian ship. In *de Letelier v. Republic of Chile*, 502 F. Supp. 259, 266, 267 (D.D.C. 1980), the court awarded $2,000,000 in punitive damages against the Republic of Chile and various of its employees to the survivors and personal representatives of the former Chilean Ambassador to the United States and a passenger in his car, both killed by the explosion of a bomb. While the court imposed the damages under domestic laws, it mentioned that the "tortuous actions" proven were "in violation of international law." *Id.* at 266. Where the defendant is an individual, the same diplomatic considerations that prompt reluctance to impose punitive damages are not present. The Supreme Court in *dicta* has recognized that punishment is an appropriate objective under the law of nations, saying in *The Mariana Flora*, 24 U.S. (11 Wheat.) 1, 41 (1826), that "an attack from revenge and malignity, from gross abuse of power, and a settled purpose of mischief . . . may be punished by all the penalties which the law of nations can properly administer." In developing common law remedies to implement the rights secured by the Constitution, the Supreme Court has stated that courts may award punitive damages in actions based on the Constitution alone, *Carlson v. Green*, 446 U.S. 14, 21-22 (1980), and based on 42 U.S.C. § 1983, where the legislation makes no reference to the nature and extent of the damages to be awarded. *Smith v. Wade*, 103 S. Ct. 1625 (1983); *Carey v. Piphus*, 435 U.S. 247, 257 n.11 (1978).

This court concludes that it is essential and proper to grant the remedy of punitive damages in order to give effect to the manifest objectives of the international prohibition against torture.

V

In concluding that the plaintiffs were entitled only to damages recoverable under Paraguayan law, the Magistrate recommended they be awarded $150,000 each as compensation for emotional pain and suffering, loss of companionship and disruption of family life. He also suggested that Dolly Filartiga receive $25,000 for her future medical expenses for treatment of her psychiatric impairment and that Dr. Filartiga receive $50,000 for past expenses related to funeral and medical expenses and to lost income. The Magistrate recommended against an award of punitive damages and of $10,364 in expenses incurred in connection with this action. Plaintiffs object only to these last recommendations.

The court finds no reason to reject the opinion of the plaintiffs' expert that the expenses incurred by them in prosecuting this action are compensable under Paraguayan law. Garro Aff. ¶¶ 21, 22. The United States policy against forum shopping does not warrant a denial. Plaintiffs could get no redress in Paraguay and sued Pena where they found him.

In deciding to grant punitive damages the court is aware of the concern that such awards, designed to attain objectives fostered chiefly by the criminal law, are nevertheless made without at least some of the safeguards afforded by that law, such as proof beyond a reasonable doubt and the presumption of innocence. *Cf. Curtis Publishing Co. v. Butts*, 388 U.S. 130, 159 (1967); *Malandria v. Merrill Lynch, Pierce, Fenner & Smith*, 703 F.2d, 1152, 1172-73 (10th Cir. 1981). However, this concern, which may obtain increasing attention in the future, is not pertinent here. Pena has defaulted and has not sought such protections.

In determining the amount of punitive damages the court must consider a variety of factors. Pena's assets are pertinent. *Brink's Inc. v. City of New York*, 546 F. Supp. 403, 413 (S.D.N.Y. 1982), but the burden is on the defendant to show his modest means if he wishes them considered in mitigation. *Zarcone v. Perry*, 572 F.2d 52, 56 (2d Cir. 1978). The court has received no evidence on the subject.

The nature of the acts is plainly important. *Flaks v. Kuegel*, 504 F.2d 702, 707 (2d Cir. 1974); *Pomovoyage, S.A.R.L. v. Bosco*, 557 F. Supp. 1366, 1372 (S.D.N.Y. 1983). The court need not comment upon the malice that prompts one man to torture another in reprisal for the deeds of his father or to say to the dead man's sister as she left the corpse "shut up. Here you have what you have been looking for and deserved." (Transcript at 16). Nor would any purpose be served by detailing Pena's conduct. Spread upon the records of this court is the evidence of wounds and of fractures, of burning and beating and of electric shock, of stabbing and whipping and of mutilation, and finally, perhaps mercifully, of death, in short, of the ultimate in human cruelty and brutality.

Chief among the considerations the court must weigh is the fact that this case concerns not a local tort but a wrong as to which the world has seen fit to speak. Punitive damages are designed not merely to teach a defendant not to repeat his conduct but to deter others from following his example. *Zarcone v. Perry, supra*, 572 F.2d at 55. To accomplish that purpose this court must make clear the depth of the international revulsion against torture and measure the award in accordance with the enormity of the offense. Thereby the judgment may perhaps have some deterrent effect.

There are no binding precedents to guide the court in determining what amount lies within those respectable bounds that hedge the judiciary and yet may serve to come to the attention of those who think to practice torture. There have been large jury verdicts for punitive damages against the press for conduct that no one would claim is comparable to Pena's, for example, $25,000,000, reduced by the district court to $14,000,000, *Pring v. Penthouse International, Ltd.*, No. 79-351 (D. Wyo. May 23, 1979), to Miss Wyoming who claimed that Penthouse Magazine unfavorably identified her in a fictional piece; $2,500,000 against the Alton Telegraph in Illinois for reporting alleged wrongdoing of a contractor to the Justice Department; and $1,300,000 to an actress who asserted that the National Enquirer had implied she had been drunk in a restaurant. Goodale, *Getting Even with the Press*, N.Y. Law J., Aug. 11, 1982, at 1. col. 2. But often such verdicts have been overturned as inconsistent with the First Amendment, *see, e.g., Pring v. Penthouse International, Ltd.*, 695 F.2d 438 (10th Cir. 1982), and they are hardly persuasive here.

More pertinent is the punitive award of $2,000,000 by the court in *de Letelier v. Republic of Chile, supra,* for the murder by bombing of the former Chilean Ambassador and his companion. Also germane is *Malandris v. Merrill Lynch, Pierce, Fenner & Smith,* 447 F. Supp. 543 (D. Colo. 1977), where the District Court sustained a verdict of $3,000,000 in punitive damages for acts far less reprehensible than those of Pena. There the defendant deceived the plaintiff and invested her life savings of $60,000 in stock options, thereby causing a loss of $30,000 and emotional injury. The court upheld the verdict of $1,030,000 in compensatory damages and $3,000,000 in punitive damages. The Court of Appeals affirmed on condition that plaintiff accept a reduction in the punitive award to $1,000,000 and a total judgment of $2,030,000. 703 F.2d 1152 (10th Cir. 1981).

The decision in *Brink's Inc. v. City of New York, supra,* is also apposite, particularly for the reasoning distinguishing it from this case. There employees of a firm collecting parking meter coins for the City stole some of the proceeds. The jury found punitive damages of $5,000,000 because the firm's management, knowing of repeated illicit activities, recklessly failed to investigate and discharge the employees. The court granted a new trial unless the City agreed to a remittitur in punitive damages to $1,500,000. The court reasoned that the potential of injury to others was minimal because there was little likelihood of a recurrence, and the injury, even assuming repetition, was loss of money "not death or severe personal injury." 546 F. Supp. at 413-14.

The record in this case shows that torture and death are bound to recur unless deterred. This court concludes that an award of punitive damages of no less than $5,000,000 to each plaintiff is appropriate to reflect adherence to the world community's proscription of torture and to attempt to deter its practice.

VI

Judgment may be entered for plaintiff Dolly M.E. Filartiga in the amount of $5,175,000 and for plaintiff Joel Filartiga in the amount of $5,210,364, a total judgment of $10,385,364. So ordered.

Eugene H. Nickerson,
U.S.D.J.

Dated: Brooklyn, New York
      January 10, 1984.

JANUARY 31, 1984: PARAGUAY

Telegram from American Embassy, Asunción to U.S. Department of State

Subject: Human Rights—Case of Dr. Joel Filartiga

UNCLASSIFIED

[Excised]
n/a

[Excised]

PAGE 01   ASUNCI   00585   311658Z
ACTION HA-08

INFO   OCT-00   COPY-01   ADS-00   INR-10   CIAE-00   DODE-00
        ARA-00   NSAE-00   SY-06   L-03PA-01   SYE-00   USIE-00
        SP-02   PRS-01   /032 W
        --------------------------366100   311750Z   /40

P   311501Z   JAN 84
FM AMEMBASSY ASUNCION
TO SECSTATE WASHDC PRIORITY 8341

[Excised] ASUNCION 0585

E.O. 12356: DECL: OADR
TAGS: SHUM, PA
SUBJECT: (U) HUMAN RIGHTS: CASE OF DR. JOEL FILARTIGA
REF: ASUNCION 0380

1. [Excised]-ENTIRE TEXT.

2. DR. JOEL FILARTIGA CAME TO THE EMBASSY JANUARY 30 AT OUR
REQUEST TO DISCUSS LATEST DEVELOPMENTS IN HIS SITUATION.
HE CONFIRMED THAT HE HAD HEARD INFORMALLY THAT THE
SUPREME COURT HAD RULED HIM LIABLE FOR THE COURT COSTS
ARISING FROM HIS LEGAL ACTIONS AGAINST FORMER POLICE
OFFICIAL AMERICA PENA AND OTHERS IN THE DEATH OF HIS SON,
AND THAT THE SUM INVOLVED WAS APPROXIMATELY 5 MILLION
GUARANIES (REFTEL). HOWEVER, HE HAS NOT YET BEEN
INFORMED OF THIS OFFICIALLY BY THE COURT. FILARTIGA HAS
NONETHELESS ENGAGED A LAWYER TO APPEAL THIS RULING,
MAINLY, HE SAID, AS A STALLING TACTIC, SINCE HE DOES NOT

HAVE SUFFICIENT FUNDS TO PAY SUCH A JUDGMENT. HE EXPECTS THAT ULTIMATELY HIS LEGAL MANEUVERING WILL FAIL, AND THAT HE WILL HAVE TO FACE THE PROSPECT OF PAYING. HE HOPES IN THE MEANTIME TO BE ABLE TO RAISE FUNDS FROM FRIENDLY ORGANIZATIONS IN THE UNITED STATES.

3. FILARTIGA SAID THAT IN THE IMMEDIATE WAKE OF THE ARTI-CLES IN THE PRESS HERE ABOUT THIS LATEST DEVELOPMENT (REFTEL), HE HAD RECEIVED A RASH OF THREATENING AND ANONYMOUS PHONE CALLS, AND THAT HE HAD BEEN TIPPED OFF ABOUT AN ALLEGED PLOT TO ELIMINATE HIM BY FAKING AN AUTOMOBILE ACCIDENT IN WHICH HE WOULD BE KILLED. HE CONTINUED THAT IN THE LAST WEEK OR SO THE HARASSMENT OF HIM AND HIS FAMILY HAD WANED, BUT HE REMAINS CON-CERNED FOR HIS OWN AND HIS FAMILY'S SAFETY. EMBASSY OFFI-CER SAID THAT HE SHOULD FEEL FREE TO STAY IN CLOSE TOUCH WITH THE EMBASSY AND KEEP US INFORMED OF ANY FURTHER DEVELOPMENTS IN THE CASE. THE EMBASSY WILL ALSO FIND OCCASION TO TALK TO APPROPRIATE GOP OFFICIALS ABOUT FILARTIGA'S CASE, TO REMIND THEM OF OUR CONTINUED INTER-EST IN HIS WELL-BEING.

DAVIS

[Excised]

FEBRUARY 2, 1984: UNITED STATES

U.S. District Court for the Eastern District of New York: Judgment

UNITED STATES DISTRICT COURT
FOR THE EASTERN DISTRICT OF NEW YORK

DOLLY M.E. FILARTIGA and   **JUDGMENT**
JOEL FILARTIGA,
                                  79 Civ. 917
      Plaintiffs,

      v.

AMERICO NORBERTO PEÑA-
IRALA,

      Defendant.

A memorandum and order of Honorable Eugene H. Nickerson, United States District Judge, having been filed on January 12, 1984, directing that judgment be entered for plaintiff Dolly M.E. Filartiga in the amount of $5,175,000.00 and for plaintiff Joel Filartiga in the amount of $5,210,364.00, for a total judgment of $10,385,364.00, it is

ORDERED and ADJUDGED that judgment is entered for plaintiff Dolly M.E. Filartiga in the amount of $5,175,000.00 and for plaintiff Joel Filartiga in the amount of $5,210,364.00 for a total judgment of $10,385,364.00.

        Robert C. Heinemann
        Clerk of Court

Dated: Brooklyn, New York
      February 2, 1984

SEPTEMBER 20, 1984: PARAGUAY

Telegram from American Embassy, Asunción to U.S. Department of State

Subject: Paraguay Restores Human Rights Activist's Passport

                    DECONTROLLED/UNCLASSIFIED
                           [REDACTED]
                              n/a
[REDACTED]

Page 01   ASUNCI   05891   201501Z
ACTION ARA-00

INFO   OCT-00   COPY-01   ADS-00   INR-10   SS-00   CIAE-00
        NSAE-00   HA-08   PM-10   SP-02   SLPD-01   /032W

-------------------------------------- 322754   210953Z   /62

R 201350Z SEP 84
FM: AMEMBASSY ASUNCION
TO: SECSTATE WASHDC 9865

[REDACTED] ASUNCION 5891

FOR ARA/SC

E.O. 12356: N/A
TAGS: PINS, PINR, SHUM, PA, CVIS (FILARTIGA, JOEL HOLDEN)
SUBJECT: PARAGUAY RESTORES HUMAN RIGHTS ACTIVIST'S
PASSPORT

1. (U) PARAGUAY RECENTLY RESTORED A VALID PASSPORT TO
WIDELY KNOWN HUMAN RIGHTS ACTIVIST DR. JOEL H. FILARTIGA.
DR. FILARTIGA'S NEXT TRIP ABROAD WILL BE IN OCTOBER TO
ATTEND A CONFERENCE OF THE CHICAGO LAWYER'S COMMITTEE
OF AMNESTY INTERNATIONAL.

2. (U) THIS WAS THE FIRST TIME THE GOP HAD DOCUMENTED
FILARTIGA FOR INTERNATIONAL TRAVEL SINCE HE BEGAN TO
INVESTIGATE AND PUBLICIZE HIS SON'S 1976 MURDER AT THE
HANDS OF PARAGUAYAN POLICE. FILARTIGA'S PERSISTENCE ON
HIS SON'S CASE HAD LED THE PARAGUAYANS TO REFUSE TO
RENEW HIS PASSPORT SINCE 1977. THEY HOPED THIS WOULD PRE-

VENT THE DOCTOR FROM TRAVELLING ABROAD AND SMOTHER THE STORY.

3. (U) THIS HARASSMENT BACKFIRED. WE, AMONG OTHER, WAIVED THE PASSPORT REQUIREMENT FOR FILARTIGA. MOREOVER, HIS STATURE AS A HUMAN RIGHTS SPOKESMAN GREW AND AMPLIFIED HIS MESSAGE. IN AN UNPRECEDENTED SUIT IN 1979, A U.S. COURT AWARDED HIM CIVIL DAMAGES AGAINST A FORMER PARAGUAYAN POLICE OFFICIAL THEN IN NEW YORK.

4. (LOU) COMMENT: WE DO NOT KNOW FOR SURE WHY THE PARAGUAYANS CHOSE TO RESTORE FILARTIGA'S PASSPORT. THE GOP, REALIZING THAT CONTINUING TO DENY HIM DOCUMENTA-TION WOULD NOT KEEP HIM HOME, MAY HAVE WANTED TO WIPE A SMUDGE OFF ITS HUMAN RIGHTS RECORD. END COMMENT.

DAVIS

[REDACTED]

JANUARY 29, 2004: UNITED STATES

Civil Complaint Filed in U.S. District Court for the Eastern District of New York

**UNITED STATES DISTRICT COURT
FOR THE EASTERN DISTRICT OF NEW YORK**

DOLLY M. E. FILARTIGA and   **COMPLAINT**
JOEL FILARTIGA,

         Plaintiffs,

         v.

AMERICO NORBERTO PEÑA-
IRALA,

         Defendant.

Dolly M.E. Filartiga and Joel Filartiga, for their Complaint, allege as follows:

PRELIMINARY STATEMENT

1. This is an action upon a money judgment, brought pursuant to Federal Rule of Civil Procedure 69(a) and New York Civil Practice Law and Rules 5014, filed in this Court on February 3, 1984.

JURISDICTION

2. This Court has jurisdiction over this matter pursuant to 28 U.S.C. §§ 1331 and 1350.

PARTIES

3. Plaintiff Dolly M.E. Filartiga is a citizen of the United States and a resident of Brooklyn, New York.

4. Plaintiff Dr. Joel Filartiga is a citizen and resident of Paraguay.

5. Americo Norberto Peña-Irala is a citizen and resident of Paraguay.

STATEMENT OF FACTS

6. Plaintiffs commenced the action, Filartiga v. Peña-Irala, Case No. 79-CV-917 (E.D.N.Y. 1979), on April 6, 1979 for damages arising out of the violation of human rights for the wrongful torture and murder of Joel Filartiga,

under the treaties of the United States, the law of nations and the laws of the states of the United States.

7. This Court awarded plaintiff Dolly M.E. Filartiga judgment in the amount of $5,175,000 and awarded plaintiff Joel Filartiga judgment in the amount of $5,210,364, a total judgment of $10,385,364 (the "Judgment"), for plaintiffs by memorandum and order dated January 10, 1984. *Filartiga v. Peña-Irala*, 577 F. Supp. 860 (E.D.N.Y. 1984).

8. The Judgment was filed on February 3, 1984. A copy of the Judgment is attached hereto as Exhibit A.

9. No payment on the Judgment has been made.

FIRST CAUSE OF ACTION

10. Plaintiffs repeat and reallege each and every allegation contained in paragraphs 1-9 above as if fully set forth herein.

11. Plaintiffs and defendants are the original parties to the action *Filartiga v. Peña-Irala*, 79-CV-917 (E.D.N.Y. 1979).

12. More than ten years have elapsed since the Judgment was first docketed.

13. Plaintiffs have been unable to collect on the Judgment.

REQUEST FOR RELIEF

For the foregoing reasons, plaintiffs pray that this Court:

1. Enter a renewal judgment in the amount of $5,175,000 for plaintiff Dolly M.E. Filartiga and enter a renewal judgment in the amount of $5,210,364 for plaintiff Joel Filartiga for a total renewal judgment of $10,385,364 plus accrued interest, and

2. Award plaintiffs such other and further relief as this Court deems reasonable and proper.

Respectfully submitted,

_____

Jennifer M. Green, JG 3169
Center for Constitutional Rights
666 Broadway, 7th floor
New York, New York 10012
(212) 614-6431

Attorney for Plaintiffs

Dated: New York, New York
           January 29, 2004

BIBLIOGRAPHY

BOOKS AND MONOGRAPHS

ABRAMS, NORMAN, ANTI-TERRORISM AND CRIMINAL ENFORCEMENT (2003).

ADLER, DAVID G. & LARRY N. GEORGE EDS., THE CONSTITUTION AND THE CONDUCT OF AMERICAN FOREIGN POLICY (1996).

AFRICA WATCH, ETHIOPIA: RECKONING UNDER THE LAW (1994).

AMNESTY INTERNATIONAL, END IMPUNITY: JUSTICE FOR THE VICTIMS OF TORTURE (2001).

AMNESTY INTERNATIONAL, DEATHS UNDER TORTURE AND DISAPPEARANCES OF POLITICAL PRISONERS IN PARAGUAY (1977).

AMNESTY INTERNATIONAL USA, USA: A SAFE HAVEN FOR TORTURERS (2002).

ARDITTI, RITA, SEARCHING FOR LIFE: THE GRANDMOTHERS OF THE PLAZA DE MAYO AND THE DISAPPEARED CHILDREN OF ARGENTINA (1999).

ASPEN INSTITUTE ED., STATE CRIMES: PUNISHMENT OR PARDON (1989).

BARNHIZER, DAVID ED., EFFECTIVE STRATEGIES FOR PROTECTING HUMAN RIGHTS (2000).

BASS, GARY JONATHAN, STAY THE HAND OF VENGEANCE: THE POLITICS OF WAR CRIMES TRIBUNALS (2000).

BAZYLER, MICHAEL, HOLOCAUST JUSTICE: THE BATTLE FOR RESTITUTION IN AMERICA'S COURTS (2003).

BAZYLER, MICHAEL J. & ROGER ALFORD EDS., HOLOCAUST RESTITUTION: PERSPECTIVES ON THE LITIGATION AND ITS LEGACY (2006).

BIGGAR, NIGEL ED., BURYING THE PAST: MAKING PEACE AND DOING JUSTICE AFTER CIVIL CONFLICT (2001).

BLACKSTONE, WILLIAM, 4 COMMENTARIES ON THE LAWS OF ENGLAND (1769).

BLUM, DEBORAH, BAD KARMA: A TRUE STORY OF OBSESSION AND MURDER (1986).

BORAINE, ALEX ET AL. EDS., DEALING WITH THE PAST: TRUTH AND RECONCILIATION IN SOUTH AFRICA (1994).

BORK, ROBERT H., COERCING VIRTUE: THE WORLDWIDE RULE OF JUDGES (2003).

BOTTIGLIERO, ILARIA, REDRESS FOR VICTIMS OF CRIMES UNDER INTERNATIONAL LAW (2004).

BOUVARD, MARGUERITE GUZMAN, REVOLUTIONIZING MOTHERHOOD: THE MOTHERS OF THE PLAZA DE MAYO (1994).

BOUVIER, VIRGINIA M., DECLINE OF THE DICTATOR: PARAGUAY AT A CROSSROADS (1988).

BRADLEY, CURTIS A. & JACK L. GOLDSMITH, FOREIGN RELATIONS LAW (2d ed. 2006).

BRIERLY, J.L., THE OUTLOOK FOR INTERNATIONAL LAW (1944).

BRODY, REED & MICHAEL RATNER EDS., THE PINOCHET PAPERS: THE CASE OF AUGUSTO PINOCHET IN SPAIN AND BRITAIN (2000).

BROOKS, ROY L. ED., WHEN SORRY ISN'T ENOUGH: THE CONTROVERSY OVER APOLOGIES AND REPARATIONS FOR HUMAN INJUSTICE (1999).

BROOMHALL, BRUCE, INTERNATIONAL JUSTICE AND THE INTERNATIONAL CRIMINAL COURT: BETWEEN SOVEREIGNTY AND THE RULE OF LAW (2002).

BURGERS, J. HERMAN & HANS DANELIUS, THE UNITED NATIONS CONVENTION AGAINST TORTURE: A HANDBOOK ON THE CONVENTION AGAINST TORTURE AND OTHER CRUEL, INHUMAN OR DEGRADING TREATMENT OR PUNISHMENT (1988).

CARTER, BARRY ET AL., INTERNATIONAL LAW (4th ed. 2003).

CASSESE, ANTONIO ET AL. EDS., I THE ROME STATUTE OF THE INTERNATIONAL CRIMINAL COURT: A COMMENTARY (2002).

CLERMONT, KEVIN M. ED., CIVIL PROCEDURE STORIES (2004).

COMISIÓN NACIONAL SOBRE LA DESAPARICIÓN DE PERSONAS, NUNCA MAS (1986).

COUNCIL ON FOREIGN RELATIONS, TERRORIST FINANCING (2002).

CRUMP, DAVID & JEFFREY B. BERMAN, THE STORY OF A CIVIL CASE: DOMINGUEZ V. SCOTT'S FOOD STORES (3d ed. 2001).

DAMROSCH, LORI F. ET AL., INTERNATIONAL LAW: CASES AND MATERIALS (4th ed. 2001).

DANZIG, RICHARD & GEOFFREY R. WATSON, THE CAPABILITY PROBLEM IN CONTRACT LAW: FURTHER READINGS ON WELL-KNOWN CASES (2d ed. 2004).

DE NIKE, HOWARD J. ET AL. EDS., GENOCIDE IN CAMBODIA: DOCUMENTS FROM THE TRIAL OF POL POT AND IENG SARY (2000).

DE WAAL, ALEXANDER, EVIL DAYS: THIRTY YEARS OF WAR AND FAMINE IN ETHIOPIA (1991).

DOOLAN, BRIAN, LAWLESS V. IRELAND: THE FIRST CASE BEFORE THE EUROPEAN COURT OF HUMAN RIGHTS (2001).

DORF, MICHAEL ED., CONSTITUTIONAL LAW STORIES (2004).

DORFMAN, ARIEL, EXORCISING TERROR: THE INCREDIBLE UNENDING TRIAL OF AUGUSTO PINOCHET (2002).

DRAGNICH, ALEX N., SERBS & CROATS: THE STRUGGLE IN YUGOSLAVIA (1992).

EARTHRIGHTS INTERNATIONAL, IN OUR COURT: ATCA, SOSA AND THE TRIUMPH OF HUMAN RIGHTS (2004).

EIZENSTAT, STUART E., IMPERFECT JUSTICE: LOOTED ASSETS, SLAVE LABOR, AND THE UNFINISHED BUSINESS OF WORLD WAR II (2003).

ENGLADE, KEN, BEYOND REASON (1990).

FITZPATRICK, J.C. ED., 28 JOURNALS OF THE CONTINENTAL CONGRESS 1774–1789 (1933).

FRANCK, THOMAS M., POLITICAL QUESTIONS/JUDICIAL ANSWERS (1992).

GERSON, ALLAN & JERRY ADLER, THE PRICE OF TERROR: LESSONS OF LOCKER-
BIE FOR A WORLD ON THE BRINK (2001).

JOHN GIMLETTE, ALLAN, AT THE TOMB OF THE INFLATABLE PIG: TRAVELS
THROUGH PARAGUAY (2003).

GIUTTARI, THEODORE R. ED., PROCEEDINGS AND COMMITTEE REPORTS OF
THE AMERICAN BRANCH OF THE INTERNATIONAL LAW ASSOCIATION
(1982).

GOLDSTEIN, BRANDT, STORMING THE COURT: HOW A BAND OF YALE LAW STU-
DENTS SUED THE PRESIDENT—AND WON (2005).

GROSSMAN, LEWIS A. & ROBERT G. VAUGHN, A DOCUMENTARY COMPANION
TO A CIVIL ACTION (3d ed. 2006).

GUEST, IAIN, BEHIND THE DISAPPEARANCES (1990).

HEERE, WYBO P. ED., CONTEMPORARY INTERNATIONAL LAW ISSUES: NEW
FORMS, NEW APPLICATIONS (1998).

HELFELD, DAVID M. & WILLIAM L. WIPFLER, MBARETÉ: THE HIGHER LAW OF
PARAGUAY (1980).

HENKIN, LOUIS, THE AGE OF RIGHTS (1990).

HENKIN, LOUIS ET AL., HUMAN RIGHTS (1999).

HERZ, JOHN H. ED., FROM DICTATORSHIP TO DEMOCRACY: COPING WITH THE
LEGACIES OF AUTHORITARIANISM AND TOTALITARIANISM (1982).

HOLBROOK, RICHARD, TO END A WAR (1998).

HUFBAUER, GARY CLYDE & NICHOLAS K. MITROKOSTAS, AWAKENING MON-
STER: THE ALIEN TORT STATUTE OF 1789 (2003).

HUMAN RIGHTS WATCH, RELUCTANT PARTNER: THE ARGENTINE GOVERN-
MENT'S FAILURE TO BACK TRIALS OF HUMAN RIGHTS VIOLATORS (2001).

HUNTER, NAN D., THE POWER OF PROCEDURE: THE LITIGATION OF JONES V.
CLINTON (2002).

INTERNATIONAL HUMAN RIGHTS LAW GROUP & COMITE DE IGLESIAS PARA
AYUDAS DE EMERGENCIA, PARAGUAY: HUMAN RIGHTS AND THE TRANSI-
TION TOWARDS THE RULE OF LAW (1996).

INTERNATIONAL LEAGUE FOR HUMAN RIGHTS, MBARETE: TWO YEARS LATER
(1982).

JANIS, MARK W. & JOHN E. NOYES, TEACHER'S MANUAL, CASES AND COM-
MENTARY ON INTERNATIONAL LAW (3d ed. 2006).

JESSUP, PHILIP, TRANSNATIONAL LAW (1956).

JOSEPH, SARAH, CORPORATIONS AND TRANSNATIONAL HUMAN RIGHTS LITI-
GATION (2004).

KAPLAN, ROBERT, BALKAN GHOSTS: A JOURNEY THROUGH HISTORY (1993).

KECK, MARGARET & KATHRYN SIKKINK, ACTIVISTS BEYOND BORDERS: ADVO-
CACY NETWORKS IN INTERNATIONAL POLITICS (1998).

KISSINGER, HENRY, DOES AMERICA NEED A FOREIGN POLICY? TOWARD A
DIPLOMACY FOR THE 21ST CENTURY (2001).

KLEBER, ROLF J. ET AL. EDS., BEYOND TRAUMA: CULTURAL AND SOCIETAL
DYNAMICS (1995).

KLUGER, RICHARD, SIMPLE JUSTICE (1975).

KORNBLUH, PETER, THE PINOCHET FILE: A DECLASSIFIED DOSSIER ON ATROC-
ITY AND ACCOUNTABILITY (2003).

KRITZ, NEIL J. ED., II TRANSITIONAL JUSTICE: HOW EMERGING DEMOCRACIES
RECKON WITH FORMER REGIMES (1995).

LAWYERS COMMITTEE FOR HUMAN RIGHTS, PROSECUTING GENOCIDE IN
RWANDA: THE ICTR AND NATIONAL TRIALS (1997).

LEWIS, PAUL H., PARAGUAY UNDER STROESSNER (1980).

LILLICH, RICHARD B. ET AL., INTERNATIONAL HUMAN RIGHTS: PROBLEMS OF
LAW, POLICY, AND PRACTICE (4th ed. 2006).

LINZ, JUAN J. & ALFRED STEPAN, THE BREAKDOWN OF DEMOCRATIC REGIMES:
CRISIS, BREAKDOWN & REEQUILIBRIUM (1978).

MACEDO, STEPHEN ED., UNIVERSAL JURISDICTION: NATIONAL COURTS AND
THE PROSECUTION OF SERIOUS CRIMES UNDER INTERNATIONAL LAW
(2003).

MALCOLM, NOEL, BOSNIA: A SHORT HISTORY (1994).

MARCUS, MAEVA ED., ORIGINS OF THE FEDERAL JUDICIARY: ESSAYS ON THE
JUDICIARY ACT OF 1789 (1992).

MARTIN, DAVID A. & PETER H. SCHUCK EDS., IMMIGRATION STORIES (2005).

MCADAMS, A. JAMES ED., TRANSITIONAL JUSTICE AND THE RULE OF LAW IN
NEW DEMOCRACIES (1997).

MEAD, WALTER RUSSELL, SPECIAL PROVIDENCE: AMERICAN FOREIGN POLICY
AND HOW IT CHANGED THE WORLD (2001).

MENDEZ, JUAN, TRUTH AND PARTIAL JUSTICE IN ARGENTINA: AN UPDATE
(1991).

MINOW, MARTHA, BETWEEN VENGEANCE AND FORGIVENESS: FACING HISTORY
AFTER GENOCIDE AND MASS VIOLENCE (1998).

MIRANDA, ANIBAL & ANALY FILARTIGA, EL CASO FILARTIGA (1992).

MIRANDA, CARLOS R., THE STROESSNER ERA: AUTHORITARIAN RULE IN
PARAGUAY (1990).

MOORE, JOHN NORTON, CIVIL LITIGATION AGAINST TERRORISM (2004).

NASH (LEICH), MARIAN ED., I CUMULATIVE DIGEST OF UNITED STATES PRAC-
TICE IN INTERNATIONAL LAW 1981–1988 (1993).

NASH (LEICH), MARIAN ED., CUMULATIVE DIGEST OF UNITED STATES PRAC-
TICE IN INTERNATIONAL LAW 1979 (1983).

NINO, CARLOS SANTIAGO, RADICAL EVIL ON TRIAL (1996).

NORDEN, DEBORAH L., MILITARY REBELLION IN ARGENTINA (1996).

O'DONNELL, GUILLERMO & PHILIPPE C. SCHMITTER, TRANSITIONS FROM
AUTHORITARIAN RULE: TENTATIVE CONCLUSIONS ABOUT UNCERTAIN
DEMOCRACIES (1986).

O'SHAUGHNESSY, HUGH, PINOCHET: THE POLITICS OF TORTURE (2000).

O'SHEA, ANDREAS, AMNESTY FOR CRIME IN INTERNATIONAL LAW AND PRAC-
TICE (2002).

PAUST, JORDAN, INTERNATIONAL LAW AS LAW OF THE UNITED STATES (2d ed. 2003).

PAUST, JORDAN ET AL., INTERNATIONAL LAW AND LITIGATION IN THE U.S. (2d ed. 2003).

PAZ, ALFREDO BOCCIA ET AL., ES MI INFORME: LOS ARCHIVOS SECRETOS DE LA POLICIA DE STROESSNER (1994).

RABKIN, JEREMY, WHY SOVEREIGNTY MATTERS (1998).

RADOSH, RONALD & JOYCE MILTON, THE ROSENBERG FILES (2d ed. 1984).

RANDALL, KENNETH, FEDERAL COURTS AND THE INTERNATIONAL HUMAN RIGHTS PARADIGM (1990).

REDRESS TRUST, ENFORCEMENT OF AWARDS FOR VICTIMS OF TORTURE AND OTHER INTERNATIONAL CRIMES (2006).

REDRESS TRUST, IMMUNITY V. ACCOUNTABILITY: CONSIDERING THE RELATIONSHIP BETWEEN STATE IMMUNITY AND ACCOUNTABILITY FOR TORTURE AND OTHER SERIOUS INTERNATIONAL CRIMES (2005).

REDRESS TRUST, REPARATION: A SOURCEBOOK FOR VICTIMS OF TORTURE AND OTHER VIOLATIONS OF HUMAN RIGHTS AND INTERNATIONAL HUMANITARIAN LAW (2003).

REDRESS TRUST, TORTURE SURVIVORS' PERCEPTIONS OF REPARATION (2001).

RESTATEMENT (THIRD) OF THE FOREIGN RELATIONS LAW OF THE UNITED STATES (1987).

REYDAMS, LUC, UNIVERSAL JURISDICTION: INTERNATIONAL AND MUNICIPAL LEGAL PERSPECTIVES (2003).

RITZ, WILFRED J., REWRITING THE HISTORY OF THE JUDICIARY ACT OF 1789 (1990).

ROHT-ARRIAZA, NAOMI ED., IMPUNITY IN INTERNATIONAL HUMAN RIGHTS LAW AND PRACTICE (1995).

ROHT-ARRIAZA, NAOMI, THE PINOCHET EFFECT: TRANSNATIONAL JUSTICE IN THE AGE OF HUMAN RIGHTS (2005).

SADAT, LEILA NADYA, THE INTERNATIONAL CRIMINAL COURT AND THE TRANSFORMATION OF INTERNATIONAL LAW: JUSTICE FOR THE NEW MILLENNIUM (2002).

SCHAPIRO, JANE, INSIDE A CLASS ACTION: THE HOLOCAUST AND THE SWISS BANKS (2003).

SCHUMAN, DANIEL W. & ALEXANDER MCCALL SMITH, JUSTICE AND THE PROSECUTION OF OLD CRIMES: BALANCING LEGAL, PSYCHOLOGICAL, AND MORAL CONCERNS (2000).

SCOTT, CRAIG ED., TORTURE AS TORT: COMPARATIVE PERSPECTIVES ON THE DEVELOPMENT OF TRANSNATIONAL HUMAN RIGHTS LITIGATION (2001).

SHAPO, MARSHALL, COMPENSATION FOR VICTIMS OF TERRORISM (2005).

SHELTON, DINAH, REMEDIES IN INTERNATIONAL HUMAN RIGHTS LAW (2d ed. 2006).

SIMPSON, A.W. BRIAN, LEADING CASES IN THE COMMON LAW (1995).

STEINER, HENRY J. & PHILIP ALSTON, INTERNATIONAL HUMAN RIGHTS IN CONTEXT (2d ed. 2000).

STEINHARDT, RALPH G. & ANTHONY D'AMATO EDS., THE ALIEN TORT CLAIMS ACT: AN ANALYTICAL ANTHOLOGY (1999).

STEINMETZ, SARA, DEMOCRATIC TRANSITION AND HUMAN RIGHTS: PERSPECTIVES ON U.S. FOREIGN POLICY (1994).

STEPHENS, BETH & MICHAEL RATNER, INTERNATIONAL HUMAN RIGHTS LITIGATION IN U.S. COURTS (1996).

STERN, GERALD M., THE BUFFALO CREEK DISASTER (1976).

STIGLMAYER, ALEXANDRA ED., THE ENTRENCHMENT OF SYSTEMATIC ABUSE: MASS RAPE IN FORMER YUGOSLAVIA (1994).

STOVER, ERIC & ELENA O. NIGHTINGALE EDS., THE BREAKING OF BODIES AND MINDS: TORTURE, PSYCHIATRIC ABUSE, AND THE HEALTH PROFESSIONS (1985).

STOVER, ERIC & HARVEY M. WEINSTEIN EDS., MY NEIGHBOR, MY ENEMY: JUSTICE AND COMMUNITY IN THE AFTERMATH OF MASS ATROCITY (2004).

STROZIER, CHARLES B. & MICHAEL FLYNN EDS., GENOCIDE, WAR, AND HUMAN SURVIVAL (1996).

STROMSETH, JANE E. ED., ACCOUNTABILITY FOR ATROCITIES: NATIONAL AND INTERNATIONAL RESPONSES (2003).

TEITEL, RUTI, TRANSITIONAL JUSTICE (2000).

TIMERMAN, JACOBO, PRISONER WITHOUT A NAME, CELL WITHOUT A NUMBER (1981).

TRIFFTERER, OTTO ED., COMMENTARY ON THE ROME STATUTE OF THE INTERNATIONAL CRIMINAL COURT (1999).

WAGNER, RICHARD, THE AUTHENTIC LIBRETTOS OF THE WAGNER OPERAS (1938).

WEISSBRODT, DAVID ET AL., INTERNATIONAL HUMAN RIGHTS: LAW, POLICY, AND PROCESS (3d ed. 2001).

WESCHLER, LAWRENCE, A MIRACLE, A UNIVERSE: SETTLING ACCOUNTS WITH TORTURERS (1990).

WHITE, RICHARD ALAN, BREAKING SILENCE: THE CASE THAT CHANGED THE FACE OF HUMAN RIGHTS (2004).

YORE, FATIMA MYRIAM, LA DOMINACION STRONISTA: ORIGENES Y CONSOLIDACION (1992).

ZITTRAIN, JONATHAN L. & JENNIFER HARRISON, THE TORTS GAME: DEFENDING MEAN JOE GREENE (2004).

SCHOLARLY ARTICLES AND BOOK CHAPTERS

Aceves, William J., *Liberalism and International Legal Scholarship: The Pinochet Case and the Move Toward a Universal System of Transnational Law Litigation*, 41 HARV. INT'L L.J. 129 (2000).

Aceves, William J., *Prosecuting Violations of Human Rights in U.S. Courts: A Primer for the Justice Department on the Convention against Torture, in* EFFECTIVE STRATEGIES FOR PROTECTING HUMAN RIGHTS (David Barnhizer ed., 2000).

Aceves, William J., *The Legality of Transborder Abductions: A Study of United States v. Alvarez-Machain*, 3 SW. J. L. & TRADE 101 (1996).

Akhavan, Payam, *Beyond Impunity: Can International Criminal Justice Prevent Future Atrocities?*, 95 AM. J. INT'L L. 7 (2001).

Alvarez, Jose, *Rush to Closure: Lessons of the Tadic Judgment*, 96 MICH. L. REV. 2031 (1998).

Amley, Edward A., *Sue and Be Recognized: Collecting § 1350 Judgments Abroad*, 107 YALE L.J. 2177 (1998).

Arsanjani, Mahnoush H., *Developments in International Criminal Law: The Rome Statute of the International Criminal Court*, 93 AM. J. INT'L L. 22 (1999).

Barkan, Elazar, *Between Restitution and International Morality*, 25 FORDHAM INT'L L.J. 46 (2001).

Bass, Peter Evan, *Ex-Head of State Immunity: A Proposed Statutory Tool of Foreign Policy*, 97 YALE L.J. 299 (1987).

Bassiouni, M. Cherif, *Universal Jurisdiction for International Crimes: Historical Perspectives and Contemporary Practice*, 42 VA. J. INT'L L. 81 (2001).

Bazyler, Michael J., *Nuremberg in America: Litigating the Holocaust in United States Courts*, 34 U. RICH. L. REV. 1 (2000).

Bederman, David et al., *The Enforcement of Human Rights and Humanitarian Law by Civil Suits in Municipal Courts: The Civil Dimension of Universal Jurisdiction, in* CONTEMPORARY INTERNATIONAL LAW ISSUES: NEW FORMS, NEW APPLICATIONS (Wybo P. Heere ed., 1998).

Bello, Judith Hippler, *Chile: Criminal Jurisdiction: Prosecution of Official of Secret Service for Assassination of Former Ambassador to United States*, 90 AM. J. INT'L L. 290 (1996).

Belsky, Adam C. et al., *Implied Waiver Under the FSIA: A Proposed Exception to Immunity for Violations of Peremptory Norms of International Law*, 77 CAL. L. REV. 365 (1989).

Benomar, Jamal, *Justice After Transitions*, 4 J. DEMOCRACY 3 (1993).

Berkowitz, Benjamin, *Sosa v. Alvarez-Machain: United States Courts as Forums for Human Rights Cases and the New Incorporation Debate*, 40 HARV. C.R.-C.L. L. REV. 289 (2005).

Bianchi, Andrea, *Denying State Immunity to Violators of Human Rights*, 46 AUSTRIAN J. PUB. & INT'L L. 195 (1994).

Blum, Jeffrey M. & Ralph G. Steinhardt, *Federal Jurisdiction over International Human Rights Claims: The Alien Tort Claims Act After Filartiga v. Pena-Irala*, 22 HARV. INT'L L.J. 53 (1981).

Boed, Roman, *The Effect of a Domestic Amnesty on the Ability of Foreign States to Prosecute Alleged Perpetrators of Serious Human Rights Violations*, 33 CORNELL INT'L L.J. 297 (2000).

Boyd, K. Lee, *Are Human Rights Political Questions?*, 53 RUTGERS L. REV. 277 (2001).

Boyd, Kathryn Lee, *Universal Jurisdiction and Structural Reasonableness*, 40 TEX. INT'L L.J. 1 (2004).

Boyd, Kathryn Lee, *The Inconvenience of Victims: Abolishing Forum Non Conveniens in Human Rights Litigation*, 39 VA. J. INT'L L. 41 (1998).

Bradley, Curtis A., *The Alien Tort Statute and Article III*, 42 VA. J. INT'L L. 587 (2002).

Bradley, Curtis A., *The Costs of International Human Rights Litigation*, 2 CHI. J. INT'L L. 457 (2001).

Bradley, Curtis A., *Universal Jurisdiction and U.S. Law*, 2001 U. CHI. LEGAL F. 323.

Bradley, Curtis A. & Jack L. Goldsmith, *Customary International Law as Federal Common Law: A Critique of the Modern Position*, 110 HARV. L. REV. 815 (1997).

Brandt, Michele, *Doe v. Karadzic: Redressing Non-State Acts of Gender-Specific Abuse Under the Alien Tort Statute*, 79 MINN. L. REV. 1413 (1995).

Brav, Ehren J., *Opening the Courtroom Doors to Non-Citizens: Cautiously Affirming Filartiga for the Alien Tort Statute*, 46 HARV. INT'L L.J. 265 (2005).

Brilmayer, Lea, *International Law in U.S. Courts: A Modest Proposal*, 100 YALE L.J. 2277 (1991).

Brown, Bartram S., *Primacy or Complementarity: Reconciling the Jurisdiction of National Courts and International Criminal Tribunals*, 23 YALE J. INT'L L. 383 (1998).

Burgess, Michele, *Physician-Artist Is the Schweitzer of Paraguay*, MARYKNOLL 8 (Sept. 1978).

Burley, Anne-Marie, *The Alien Tort Statute and the Judiciary Act of 1789: A Badge of Honor*, 83 AM. J. INT'L L. 461 (1989).

Bush, Jonathan A., *How Did We Get Here? Foreign Abduction After Alvarez-Machain*, 45 STAN. L. REV. 939 (1993).

Cabraser, Elizabeth J., *Human Rights Violations as Mass Torts: Compensation as a Proxy for Justice in the United States Civil Litigation System*, 57 VAND. L. REV. 2211 (2004).

Calloni, Stella, *The Horror Archives of Operation Condor*, 50 COVERT ACTION 7 (Fall 1994).

Caron, Paul L., *Back to the Future*, 71 U. CIN. L. REV. 405 (2003).

Cassese, Antonio, *When May Senior State Officials Be Tried for International Crimes? Some Comments on the Congo v. Belgium Case*, 13 EUR. J. INT'L L. 853 (2002).

Casto, William, *The Federal Courts' Protective Jurisdiction over Torts Committed in Violation of the Law of Nations*, 18 CONN. L. REV. 467 (1986).

Chibundu, M.O., *Making Customary International Law Through Municipal Adjudication: A Structural Inquiry*, 39 VA. J. INT'L L. 1069 (1999).

Christenson, Gordon A., *The Uses of Human Rights Norms to Inform Constitutional Interpretation*, 4 HOUS. J. INT'L L. 39 (1981).

Claude, Richard Pierre, *The Case of Joelito Filartiga and the Clinic of Hope*, 5 HUM. RTS. Q. 275 (1983).

Clermont, Kevin M., *Teaching Civil Procedure Through its Top Ten Cases, Plus or Minus Two*, 47 ST. LOUIS L.J. 111 (2003).

Cobban, Helena, *International Courts*, FOREIGN POL'Y, Mar.–Apr. 2006, at 22.

Cole, David et al., *Interpreting the Alien Tort Statute: Amicus Curiae Memorandum of International Law Scholars and Practitioners in Trajano v. Marcos*, 12 HASTINGS INT'L & COMP. L. REV. 1 (1988).

Coliver, Sandra, *Bringing Human Rights Abusers to Justice in U.S. Courts: Carrying Forward the Legacy of the Nuremberg Trials*, 27 CARDOZO L. REV. 1689 (2006).

Coliver, Sandra et al., *Holding Human Rights Violators Accountable by Using International Law in U.S. Courts: Advocacy Efforts and Complementary Strategies*, 19 EMORY INT'L L. REV. 169 (2005).

Collingsworth, Terry, *Separating Fact from Fiction in the Debate over Application of the Alien Tort Claims Act to Violations of Fundamental Human Rights by Corporations*, 37 U.S.F. L. REV. 563 (2003).

Collingsworth, Terry, *The Key Human Rights Challenge: Developing Enforcement Mechanisms*, 15 HARV. HUM. RTS. J. 183 (2002).

Crocker, David A., *Punishment, Reconciliation, and Democratic Deliberation*, 5 BUFF. CRIM. L. REV. 509 (2002).

Crocker, David, *Reckoning with Past Wrongs: A Normative Framework*, 13 ETHICS & INT'L AFF. 43 (1999).

Crotly, Thomas P., *The Law of Nations in the District Court: Federal Jurisdiction Over Tort Claims By Aliens Under 28 U.S.C. § 1350*, 1 B.C. INT'L & COMP. L.J. 71 (1977).

Curran, William J., *Official Torture and Human Rights: The American Courts and International Law*, 304 NEW ENG. J. MED. 1342 (May 28, 1981).

D'Amato, Anthony, *The Alien Tort Statute and the Founding of the Constitution*, 82 AM. J. INT'L L. 62 (1988).

D'Amato, Anthony, *What Does Tel-Oren Tell Lawyers? Judge Bork's Concept of the Law of Nations is Seriously Mistaken*, 79 AM. J. INT'L L. 92 (1985).

D'Amore, Carolyn A., *Sosa v. Alvarez-Machain and the Alien Tort Statute: How Wide Has the Door to Human Rights Litigation Been Left Open?*, 39 AKRON L. REV. 593 (2006).

d'Argent, Pierre, *Wrongs of the Past, History of the Future?*, 17 EUR. J. INT'L L. 279 (2006).

Daneher, Michael, *Case Comment: Torture as a Tort in Violation of International Law: Filartiga v. Pena-Irala*, 33 STAN. L. REV. 353 (1981).

Danieli, Yael, *Preliminary Reflections from a Psychological Perspective, in* TRAN-
SITIONAL JUSTICE: HOW EMERGING DEMOCRACIES RECKON WITH FORMER
REGIMES (Neil J. Kritz ed., 1995).

Davis, Jeffrey, *Justice Without Borders: Human Rights Cases in U.S. Courts*, 28
LAW & POL'Y 60 (2006).

Deutsch, Ruthanne M., *Suing State Sponsors of Terrorism Under the Foreign
Sovereign Immunities Act*, 38 INT'L LAW. 891 (2004).

Dicker, Richard & Helen Duffy, *National Courts and the ICC*, 6 BROWN J.
WORLD AFF. 53 (1999).

Dickinson, Edwin D., *The Law of Nations as Part of the National Law of the
United States*, 101 U. PA. L. REV. 26 (1952).

Dodge, William S., *The Constitutionality of the Alien Tort Statute: Some Observations on Text and Context*, 42 VA. J. INT'L L. 687 (2002).

Dodge, William S., *The Historical Origins of the Alien Tort Statute: A Response
to the Originalists*, 19 HASTINGS INT'L & COMP. L. REV. 221 (1996).

Dokos, Daniel S., *Enforcement of International Human Rights in the Federal
Courts After Filartiga v. Pena-Irala*, 67 VA. L. REV. 1379 (1981).

Donovan, Donald Francis & Anthea Roberts, *The Emerging Recognition of
Universal Civil Jurisdiction*, 100 AM. J. INT'L L. 142 (2006).

Dwyer, Susan, *Reconciliation for Realists*, 13 ETHICS & INT'L AFF. 81 (1999).

D'Zurilla, William T., *International Responsibility for Torture Under International
Law*, 56 TUL. L. REV. 186 (1981).

Fitzgerald, Amber, *The Pinochet Case: Head of State Immunity Within the United
States*, 22 WHITTIER L. REV. 987 (2001).

Fitzpatrick, Joan, *The Future of the Alien Tort Claims Act of 1789: Lessons from
In Re Marcos Human Rights Litigation*, 67 ST. JOHN'S L. REV. 491 (1993).

Fletcher, Laurel F. & Harvey M. Weinstein, *Violence and Social Repair:
Rethinking the Contribution of Justice to Reconciliation*, 24 HUM. RTS. Q. 573
(2002).

Fox, Hazel, *State Immunity and the International Crime of Torture*, 2006 EUR.
HUM. RTS. L. REV. 142 (2006).

Franck, Thomas M., *The Emerging Right to Democratic Governance*, 86 AM. J.
INT'L L. 46 (1992).

Free, Brian C., *Comment: Awaiting Doe v. Exxon Mobil Corp.: Advocating the
Cautious Use of Executive Opinions in Alien Tort Claims Act Litigation*, 12
PAC. RIM L. & POL'Y J. 467 (2003).

Fuks, Igor, *Sosa v. Alvarez-Machain and the Future of ATCA Litigation*, 106
COLUM. L. REV. 112 (2006).

Garro, Alejandro M. & Henry Dahl, *Legal Accountability for Human Rights
Violations in Argentina: One Step Forward and Two Steps Backward*, 8 HUM.
RTS. L.J. 283 (1987).

Garvey, Jack I., *Judicial Foreign Policy-Making in International Civil Litigation:
Ending the Charade of Separation of Powers*, 24 LAW & POL'Y INT'L BUS. 461
(1993).

Gery, Yoav, *The Torture Victim Protection Act: Raising Issues of Legitimacy*, 26 GEO. WASH. J. INT'L L. & ECON. 597 (1993).

Glannon, Joseph W. & Jeffery Atik, *Politics and Personal Jurisdiction: Suing State Sponsors of Terrorism Under the 1996 Amendments to the Foreign Sovereign Immunities Act*, 87 GEO. L.J. 675 (1999).

Glennon, Michael J., *Foreign Affairs and the Political Question Doctrine*, 83 AM. J. INT'L L. 814 (1989).

Goldsmith, Jack L., *The New Formalism in United States Foreign Relations Law*, 70 U. COLO. L. REV. 1395 (1999).

Gomez, Virginia Monken, *The Sosa Standard: What Does it Mean for Future ATS Litigation?*, 33 PEPP. L. REV. 469 (2006).

Goodman, Ryan, *Congressional Support for Customary International Human Rights as Federal Common Law: Lessons of the Torture Victim Protection Act*, 4 ILSA J. INT'L & COMP. L. 455 (1998).

Goodman, Ryan & Derek P. Jinks, *Filartiga's Firm Footing: International Human Rights and Federal Common Law*, 66 FORDHAM L. REV. 463 (1997).

Gray, David, *An Excuse-Centered Approach to Transitional Justice*, 74 FORDHAM L. REV. 2621 (2006).

Haffke, Christopher W., *Torture Victim Protection Act: More Symbol Than Substance*, 43 EMORY L.J. 1467 (1994).

Hassan, Farooq, *A Conflict of Philosophies: The Filartiga Jurisprudence*, 32 INT'L & COMP. L.Q. 250 (1983).

Henkin, Louis, *Lexical Priority or "Political Question": A Response*, 101 HARV. L. REV. 524 (1987).

Herz, Richard L., *Doe v. Unocal and the Poverty of the Corporate Attack on the Alien Tort Statute*, 56 RUTGERS L. REV. 1005 (2004).

Herz, Richard L., *Litigating Environmental Abuses Under the Alien Tort Claims Act: A Practical Assessment*, 40 VA. J. INT'L L. 545 (2000).

Herz, Richard L. et al., *Alien Tort Claims and Business Liability*, 95 AM. SOC'Y INT'L L. PROC. 42 (2001).

Hibey, Richard A., *U.S. Courts Shouldn't Meddle in Foreign Policy*, ABA J. 35 (Feb. 1990).

Hoffman, Paul, *Symposium Panel: War Crimes and Other Human Rights Abuses in the Former Yugoslavia*, 16 WHITTIER L. REV. 433 (1995).

Holmes, John T., *Complementarity: National Courts versus the ICC*, in I THE ROME STATUTE OF THE INTERNATIONAL CRIMINAL COURT: A COMMENTARY 667 (Antonio Cassese et al. eds., 2002).

Humphrey, Jay M. Lewis, *Note: A Legal Lohengrin: Federal Jurisdiction Under the Alien Tort Claims Act of 1789*, 14 U.S.F. L. REV. 105 (1979).

Huyse, Luc, *Justice After Transition: On the Choices Successor Elites Make in Dealing with the Past*, 20 L. & SOC. INQUIRY 51 (1995).

Issacharoff, Samuel, *The Content of our Casebooks: Why Do Cases Get Litigated?*, 29 FLA. ST. U. L. REV. 1265 (2002).

Jacobius, Arleen, *Collection Next Step for Marcos Victims: Getting Money for Human Rights Abuse is Hardest Part of International Cases*, 81 ABA J. 24 (Apr. 1995).

Kaufman, Irving R., *The Anatomy of Decisionmaking*, 53 FORDHAM L. REV. 1 (1984).

Keller, Joseph, *The Flatow Amendment and State-Sponsored Terrorism*, 28 SEATTLE U. L. REV. 1029 (2005).

Kinley, David & Junko Tadaki, *From Talk to Walk: The Emergence of Human Rights Responsibilities for Corporations at International Law*, 44 VA. J. INT'L L. 931 (2004).

Koh, Harold Hongju, *Agora: The United States Constitution and International Law: International Law as Part of Our Law*, 98 AM. J. INT'L L. 43 (2004).

Koh, Harold Hongju, *Is International Law Really State Law?*, 111 HARV. L. REV. 1824 (1998).

Koh, Harold Hongju, *The 1998 Frankel Lecture: Bringing International Law Home*, 35 HOUS. L. REV. 623 (1998).

Koh, Harold Hongju, *Transnational Legal Process*, 75 NEB. L. REV. 181 (1996).

Koh, Harold Hongju, *Reflections on Refoulement and Haitian Centers Council*, 35 HARV. INT'L L.J. 1 (1994).

Koh, Harold Hongju, *Transnational Public Law Litigation*, 100 YALE L.J. 2347 (1991).

Koh, Harold Hongju, *Civil Remedies for Uncivil Wrongs: Combatting Terrorism Through Transnational Public Law Litigation*, 22 TEXAS INT'L L.J. 169 (1987).

Kohn, Elizabeth, *Rape as a Weapon of War: Women's Human Rights During the Dissolution of Yugoslavia*, 24 GOLDEN GATE U. L. REV. 199 (1994).

Kontorovich, Eugene, *Implementing Sosa v. Alvarez-Machain: What Piracy Reveals About the Limits of the Alien Tort Statute*, 80 NOTRE DAME L. REV. 111 (2004).

Kontorovich, Eugene, *The Piracy Analogy: Modern Universal Jurisdiction's Hollow Foundation*, 45 HARV. INT'L L.J. 183 (2004).

Ku, Julian G., *The Third Wave: The Alien Tort Statute and the War on Terrorism*, 19 EMORY INT'L L. REV. 105 (2005).

Ku, Julian & John Yoo, *Beyond Formalism in Foreign Affairs: A Functional Approach to the Alien Tort Statute*, 2004 SUP. CT. REV. 153.

Lavinbuk, Ariel N., *Note, Rethinking Early Judicial Involvement in Foreign Affairs: An Empirical Study of the Supreme Court's Docket*, 114 YALE L.J. 855 (2005).

Lee, Aimee, *United States v. Alvarez-Machain: The Deleterious Ramifications of Illegal Abductions*, 17 FORDHAM INT'L L.J. 126 (1993).

Lee, Thomas H., *The Safe-Conduct Theory of the Alien Tort Statute*, 106 COLUM. L. REV. 830 (2006).

Lillich, Richard B., *Damages for Gross Violations of International Human Rights Awarded by U.S. Courts*, 15 HUM. RTS. Q. 207 (1993).

Lind, E. Allan et al., *In the Eye of the Beholder: Tort Litigants' Evaluations of Their Experiences in the Civil Justice System*, 24 L. & SOC'Y REV. 953 (1990).

Lite, Allyn, *Another Attempt to Heal the Wounds of the Holocaust*, 27 HUM. RTS. 12 (Spring 2000).

Little, David, *A Different Kind of Justice: Dealing with Human Rights Violations in Transitional Societies*, 13 ETHICS & INT'L AFF. 65 (1999).

Louden, Jeffrey Hadley, *Note: The Domestic Application of International Human Rights Law*, 5 HAST. INT'L & COMP. L. REV. 161 (1981).

Lutz, Ellen, *The Marcos Human Rights Litigation: Can Justice Be Achieved in U.S. Courts for Abuses that Occurred Abroad?*, 14 B.C. THIRD WORLD L.J. 43 (1994).

Lutz, Ellen & Kathryn Sikkink, *The Justice Cascade: The Evolution and Impact of Foreign Human Rights Trials in Latin America*, 2 CHI. J. INT'L L. 1 (2001).

MacKinnon, Catherine A., *Collective Harms Under the Alien Tort Statute: A Cautionary Note on Class Actions*, 6 ILSA J. INT'L & COMP. L. 567 (2000).

Martinez, Michael L. & Stuart H. Newberger, *Combating State-Sponsored Terrorism with Civil Lawsuits*, VICTIM ADVOCATE 5 (Spring/Summer 2002).

McLachlan, Campbell, *Transnational Tort Litigation: An Overview, in* TRANS-NATIONAL TORT LITIGATION: JURISDICTIONAL PRINCIPLES 1 (Campbell McLachlan & Peter Nygh eds., 1996).

Mendez, Jose E., *In Defense of Transitional Justice, in* TRANSITIONAL JUSTICE AND THE RULE OF LAW IN NEW DEMOCRACIES (A. James McAdams ed., 1997).

Mendlovitz, Saul & John Fousek, *The Prevention and Punishment of the Crime of Genocide, in* GENOCIDE, WAR, AND HUMAN SURVIVAL (Charles B. Strozier & Michael Flynn eds., 1996).

Morgan, Amanda L., *U.S. Officials' Vulnerability to "Global Justice": Will Universal Jurisdiction over War Crimes Make Traveling for Pleasure Less Pleasurable?*, 57 HAST. L.J. 423 (2005).

Munoz, Heraldo & Ricardo Lagos, *The Pinochet Dilemma*, FOREIGN POL'Y, Spring 1999, at 26.

Murphy, John F., *Civil Liability for the Commission of International Crimes as an Alternative to Criminal Prosecution*, 12 HARV. HUM. RTS. J. 1 (1999).

Nash, Marian, *Claims for Wrongful Death*, 86 AM. J. INT'L L. 347 (1992).

Neuborne, Burt, *Preliminary Reflections on Aspects of Holocaust-era Litigation in American Courts*, 80 WASH. U. L.Q. 795 (2002).

Nickson, Andrew, *The Overthrow of the Stroessner Regime: Re-establishing the Status Quo*, 8 BULL. LATIN AM. RES. 185 (1989).

Note: An Objection to Sosa—And to the New Federal Common Law, 119 HARV. L. REV. 2077 (2006).

O'Connell, Jamie, *Gambling with the Psyche: Does Prosecuting Human Rights Violators Console Their Victims?* 46 HARV. INT'L L.J. 295 (2005).

Oliver, Covey T., *Problems of Cognition and Interpretation in Applying Norms of a Customary International Law of Human Rights in United States Courts*, 4 HOUS. J. INT'L L. 59 (1981).

Orentlicher, Diane F., *Whose Justice? Reconciling Universal Jurisdiction with Democratic Principles*, 92 GEO. L.J. 1057 (2004).

Orentlicher, Diane F., *Settling Accounts: The Duty to Prosecute Human Rights Violations of a Prior Regime*, 100 YALE L.J. 2537 (1991).

Parlett, Kate, *Immunity in Civil Proceedings for Torture: The Emerging Exception*, 2006 EUR. HUM. RTS. L. REV. 49.

Patel, Krishna R., *Recognizing the Rape of Bosnian Women as Gender-Based Persecution*, 60 BROOK. L. REV. 929 (1994).

Paust, Jordan, *The History, Nature, and Reach of the Alien Tort Claims Act*, 16 FLA. J. INT'L L. 249 (2004).

Pell, Owen, *Historical Reparation Claims: The Defense Perspective, in* HOLO-CAUST RESTITUTION: PERSPECTIVES ON THE LITIGATION AND ITS LEGACY (Michael J. Bazyler & Roger Alford eds., 2006).

Pion-Berlin, David, *To Prosecute or to Pardon? Human Rights Decisions in the Latin American Southern Cone*, 16 HUM. RTS. Q. 105 (1993).

Popkin, Margaret & Nehal Bhuta, *Latin American Amnesties in Comparative Perspective: Can the Past Be Buried?*, 13 ETHICS & INT'L AFF. 99 (1999).

Posner, Eric A. & Cass R. Sunstein, *Dollars and Death*, 72 U. CHI. L. REV. 537 (2005).

Posner, Eric A. & Adrian Vermeule, *Transitional Justice as Ordinary Justice*, 117 HARV. L. REV. 761 (2004).

Proceedings: Conference on International Human Rights Law in State and Federal Courts, 17 U.S.F. L. REV. 1 (1982).

Quigley, John, *Our Men in Guadalajara and the Abduction of Suspects Abroad: A Comment on United States v. Alvarez-Machain*, 68 NOTRE DAME L. REV. 723 (1993).

Ramasastry, Anita, *Secrets and Lies? Swiss Banks and International Human Rights*, 31 VAND. J. TRANSNAT'L L. 325 (1998).

Randall, Kenneth C., *Federal Jurisdiction over International Law Claims: Inquiries into the Alien Tort Statute*, 18 N.Y.U. J. INT'L L. & POL. 1 (1995).

Ratner, Morris A., *Factors Impacting the Selection and Positioning of Human Rights Class Actions in United States Courts: A Practical Overview*, 58 N.Y.U. ANN. SURV. AM. L. 623 (2003).

Ratner, Morris A., *The Settlement of Nazi-era Litigation Through the Executive and Judicial Branches*, 20 BERKELEY J. INT'L L. 212 (2002).

Ratner, Steven R., *Corporations and Human Rights: A Theory of Legal Responsibility*, 111 YALE L.J. 443, (2001).

Ratner, Steven R., *New Democracies, Old Atrocities: An Inquiry in International Law*, 87 GEO. L.J. 707 (1999).

Ratner, Steven R., *The Schizophrenias of International Criminal Law*, 33 TEX. INT'L L.J. 237 (1998).

Relyea-Bowman, Susan, *Second Circuit Expands Reach of Alien Tort Claims Act and Rejects Statist Definition of "Law of Nations,"* 12 INT'L PRAC. HANDBOOK 10 (Nov. 1980).

Rickard, Lisa A., *Filartiga v. Pena-Irala: A New Forum for Violations of International Human Rights*, 30 AM. U. L. REV. 807 (1981).

Rispin, Sarah C., *Implications of Democratic Republic of the Congo v. Belgium on the Pinochet Precedent: A Setback for International Human Rights Litigation?*, 3 CHI. J. INT'L L. 527 (2002).

Roht-Arriaza, Naomi, *The Pinochet Precedent and Universal Jurisdiction*, 35 NEW ENG. L. REV. 311 (2001).

Roht-Arriaza, Naomi, *Introduction, in* IMPUNITY AND HUMAN RIGHTS IN INTERNATIONAL LAW AND PRACTICE 3 (Naomi Roht-Arriaza ed., 1995).

Roht-Arriaza, Naomi & Lauren Gibson, *The Developing Jurisprudence on Amnesty*, 20 HUM. RTS. Q. 843 (1998).

Rosen, Edward J., *Decision: Filartiga v. Pena-Irala*, 75 AM. J. INT'L L. 149 (1981).

Rosenfeld, Jennifer A., *The Antiterrorism Act of 1990: Bringing International Terrorists to Justice the American Way*, 15 SUFFOLK TRANSNAT'L L. REV. 726 (1992).

Roth, Brad R., *International Decision: Sosa v. Alvarez-Machain*, 98 AM. J. INT'L L. 798 (2004).

Roth, Kenneth, *The Case for Universal Jurisdiction*, FOREIGN AFF., Sept.–Oct. 2001, at 150.

Rubin, Alfred P., *U.S. Tort Suits By Aliens Based on International Law*, THE FLETCHER FORUM 66 (Summer/Fall 1994).

Rubin, Alfred P., *What Does Tel-Oren Tell Lawyers? Professor D'Amato's Concept of American Jurisdiction is Seriously Mistaken*, 79 AM. J. INT'L L. 105 (1985).

Rubin, Alfred P., *U.S. Tort Suits By Aliens*, 21 INT'L PRAC. HANDBOOK 19 (1983).

Russo, Frank A., *Recent Development: The Alien Tort Statute of 178—International Law as the Rule of Decision*, 49 FORDHAM L. REV. 874 (1981).

Ryngaert, Cedric, *Universal Criminal Jurisdiction Over Torture*, 23 NETHERLANDS Q. HUM. RTS. 571 (2005).

Sadat, Leila Nadya, *Exile, Amnesty and International Law*, 81 NOTRE DAME L. REV. 955 (2006).

Sansani, Inbal, *The Pinochet Precedent in Africa: Prosecution of Hissene Habre*, 8 HUM. RTS. BR. 32 (2001).

Schabas, William A., *Sentencing by International Tribunals: A Human Rights Approach*, 7 DUKE J. COMP. & INT'L L. 461 (1997).

Schneebaum, Steven M., *Human Rights in the United States Courts: The Role of Lawyers*, 55 WASH. & LEE L. REV. 737 (1998).

Schneebaum, Steven M., *Freedom from Torture Is a Legal Right*, ABA J. 34 (Feb. 1990).

Schneebaum, Steven M., *International Law as a Guarantor of Judicially-Enforceable Rights: A Reply to Professor Oliver*, 4 HOUS. J. INT'L L. 65 (1981).

Schrage, Elliot, *Judging Corporate Accountability in the Global Economy*, 42 COLUM. J. TRANSNAT'L L. 153 (2003).

Schreiber, Sol & Laura D. Weissbach, *In re Estate of Ferdinand E. Marcos Human Rights Litigation: A Personal Account of the Role of the Special Master*, 31 LOY. L.A. L. REV. 475 (1998).

Schwartz, Rachel, *"And Tomorrow?" The Torture Victim Protection Act*, 11 ARIZ. J. INT'L & COMP. L. 271 (1994).

Setear, John K., *A Forest with No Trees: The Supreme Court and International Law in the 2003 Term*, 91 VA. L. REV. 579 (2005).

Sherman, Mark Andrew, *Some Thoughts on Restoration, Reintegration, and Justice in the Transnational Context*, 23 FORDHAM INT'L L.J. 1397 (2000).

Short, Aric K., *Is the Alien Tort Statute Sacrosanct? Retaining Forum Non Conveniens in Human Rights Litigation*, 33 N.Y.U. J. INT'L L. & POL. 1001 (2001).

Silove, Derrick et al., *The Psychological Effects of Torture, Mass Human Rights Violations, and Refugee Trauma: Toward an Integrated Conceptual Framework*, 187 J. NERVOUS & MENTAL DISEASES 200 (1999).

Slack, Keith M., *Operation Condor and Human Rights: A Report from Paraguay's Archive of Terror*, 18 HUM. RTS. Q. 492 (1996).

Slaughter, Anne-Marie & David Bosco, *Plaintiff's Diplomacy*, FOREIGN AFF., Sept.–Oct., 2000, at 102.

Slaughter (Burley), Anne-Marie, *Are Foreign Affairs Different?*, 106 HARV. L. REV. 1980 (1993).

Slawson, W. David, *Changing How We Teach: A Critique of the Case Method*, 74 S. CAL. L. REV. 343 (2000).

Steinhardt, Ralph G., *International Humanitarian Law in the Courts of the United States: Yamashita, Filartiga and 9–11*, 36 GEO. WASH. INT'L L. REV. 1 (2004).

Steinhardt, Ralph G., *Laying One Bankrupt Critique to Rest: Sosa v. Alvarez-Machain and the Future of International Human Rights Litigation in U.S. Courts*, 57 VAND. L. REV. 2241 (2004).

Steinhardt, Ralph G., *Fulfilling the Promise of Filartiga: Litigating Human Rights Claims Against the Estate of Ferdinand Marcos*, 20 YALE J. INT'L L. 65 (1995).

Stephens, Beth, *Sosa v. Alvarez-Machain: "The Door Is Still Ajar" For Human Rights Litigation in U.S. Courts*, 70 BROOK. L. REV. 533 (2004).

Stephens, Beth, *Upsetting Checks and Balances: The Bush Administration's Efforts to Limit Human Rights Litigation*, 17 HARV. HUM. RTS. J. 169 (2004).

Stephens, Beth, *Translating Filartiga: A Comparative and International Law Analysis of Domestic Remedies for International Human Rights Violations*, 27 YALE J. INT'L L. 1 (2002).

Strauss, Debra M., *Enlisting the U.S. Courts in a New Front: Dismantling the International Business Holdings of Terrorist Groups Through Federal Statutory and Common Law Suits*, 38 VAND. J. TRANSNAT'L L. 679 (2005).

Sveaass, Nora & Nils Johan Lavik, *Psychological Aspects of Human Rights Violations: The Importance of Justice & Reconciliation*, 69 NORDIC J. INT'L L. 35 (2000).

Sweeney, Joseph, *A Tort Only in Violation of the Law of Nations*, 18 HASTINGS INT'L & COMP. L. REV. 445 (1995).

Swift, Robert A., *Holocaust Litigation and Human Rights Jurisprudence, in* HOLOCAUST RESTITUTION: PERSPECTIVES ON THE LITIGATION AND ITS LEGACY 50 (Michael J. Bazyler & Roger Alford eds., 2006).

Symposium—Federal Jurisdiction, Human Rights, and the Law of Nations: Essays on Filartiga v. Pena-Irala, 11 GA. J. INT'L & COMP. L. 305 (1981).

Symposium, Legal Archaeology, 2000 UTAH L. REV. 183 (2000).

Symposium: Teaching Law Stories, 55 J. LEGAL EDUC. 108 (2005).

Thorp, Jodi, *Welcome Ex-Dictators, Torturers, and Tyrants: Comparative Approaches to Handling Ex-Dictators and Past Human Rights Abuses*, 37 GONZ. L. REV. 167 (2001/2002).

Teitel, Ruti, *Transitional Jurisprudence: The Role of Law in Political Transformation*, 106 YALE L.J. 2009 (1997).

Tzeutschler, Gregory G.A., *Corporate Violator: The Alien Tort Liability of Transnational Corporations for Human Rights Abuses Abroad*, 30 COLUM. HUM. RTS. L. REV. 359 (1999).

Van Dyke, Jon M., *Promoting Accountability for Human Rights Abuses*, 8 CHAP. L. REV. 153 (2005).

Van Schaack, Beth, *With All Deliberate Speed: Civil Human Rights Litigation as a Tool for Social Change*, 57 VAND. L. REV. 2305 (2004).

Van Schaack, Beth, *In Defense of Civil Redress: The Domestic Enforcement of Human Rights Norms in the Context of the Proposed Hague Judgments Convention*, 42 HARV. INT'L L.J. 141 (2001).

Weaver, Russell L., *Langdell's Legacy: Living with the Case Method*, 36 VILL. L. REV. 517 (1991).

White, Patricia D., *Afterword and Response: What Digging Does and Does Not Do*, 2000 UTAH L. REV. 301.

Wilson, Richard J., *Book Review: The Pinochet Effect*, 28 HUM. RTS. Q. 528 (2006).

Wippman, David, *Atrocities, Deterrence, and the Limits of International Justice*, 23 FORDHAM INT'L L.J. 473 (1999).

Wirth, Steffen, *Immunity for Core Crimes?*, 13 EUR. J. INT'L L. 877 (2002).

Wu, Yolanda, *Genocidal Rape in Bosnia: Redress in U.S. Courts Under the Alien Tort Claims Act*, 4 UCLA WOMEN'S L.J. 101 (1993).

Zalaquett, Jose, *Confronting Human Rights Violations Committed by Former Governments: Principles Applicable and Political Constraints, in* STATE CRIMES: PUNISHMENT OR PARDON 23 (The Aspen Inst. ed., 1989).

Zappala, Salvatore, *Do Heads of State in Office Enjoy Immunity from Jurisdiction for International Crimes? The Ghaddafi Case Before the French Cour de Cassation*, 12 EUR. J. INT'L L. 595 (2001).

Zoglin, Katie, *Paraguay's Archive of Terror: International Cooperation and Operation Condor*, 32 U. MIAMI INTER-AM. L. REV. 57 (2001).

NEWSPAPERS AND PERIODICALS

Adams, David, *27 Years Later, Chile's Caravan of Death Touches U.S.*, ST. PETERSBURG TIMES, Mar. 13, 2000, at A1.

Artner, Alan G., *All That Glitters is Golden*, CHI. TRIBUNE, June 22, 2006, at C3.

Beyette, Beverly, *A 6-Year Quest for Justice*, L.A. TIMES, Apr. 28, 1982, at F1.

Cabral, Alberto, *Political Murder in Paraguay*, AMERICA, Apr. 23, 1977, at 376.

Chambers, Marcia, *Court Says Alien Can Sue for Torture in Paraguay*, N.Y. TIMES, July 1, 1980, at B3.

Clinton in Africa: Ethiopia's Uglier Past Recalled Closer to Home, CNN MORNING NEWS, Mar. 31, 1998.

Crossette, Barbara, *$2.6 Million Awarded Families in Letelier Case*, N.Y. TIMES, Jan. 13, 1992, at A11.

Dorfman, Ariel, *Why Chile is Hopeful*, N.Y. TIMES, Sept. 11, 2004, at A15.

Duarte Arredondo habla en prision, ULTIMA HORA (Asunción), Apr. 21, 1979, at 10.

El estudiante no murio a las 2,30, HOY (Asunción), Apr. 9, 1979, at 11.

El juez Nickerson postergo la audiencia por dos semanas, ABC (Asunción), May 1, 1979.

Es un ataque a nuestra soberanía, HOY (Asunción), Apr. 19, 1979, at 11.

Foreign Torture, American Justice, N.Y. TIMES, Aug. 20, 1980, at A18.

Fried, Joseph P., *Brooklyn Court Told of Torture of Paraguayan*, N.Y. TIMES, Feb. 13, 1982, at 27.

Gertner, Reni, *Human Rights Claims Against Corporations May Go Forward*, LAW. WKLY. USA, July 19, 2004, at 1.

Girion, Lisa, *Court OKs Foreign-Abuse Suits*, L.A. TIMES, June 30, 2004, at C1.

Glaberson, William, *U.S. Courts Become Arbiters of Global Rights and Wrongs*, N.Y. TIMES, June 21, 2001, at A1.

Goldstone, Richard J., *Ethnic Reconciliation Needs the Help of a Truth Commission*, INT'L HERALD TRIB., Oct. 24, 1998, at 6.

Greenberger, Robert S. & Pui-Wing Tam, *Human Rights Suits Against U.S. Firms Curbed*, WALL ST. J., June 30, 2004, at A3.

Greenhouse, Linda, *Justices Hear Case About Foreigners' Use of Federal Courts*, N.Y. TIMES, Mar. 31, 2004, at A16.

Greenhouse, Linda, *Supreme Court Roundup*, N.Y. TIMES, June 18, 1996, at A20.

Haithman, Diane & Christopher Reynolds, *Court Awards Nazi-Looted Artworks to L.A. Woman*, L.A. TIMES, Jan. 17, 2006, at A1.

Hall, Carla, *In Paraguay, A Death in the Family; Dolly Filartiga's Crusade for Human Rights*, WASH. POST, Mar. 25, 1982, at B1.

Informaran hoy sobre el caso Pena a periodistas de EE.UU., ABC (Asunción), Apr. 18, 1979.

Johnson, Reed, *Alfredo Stoessner, 93: Ruled Paraguay for 3 Decades With Repression and Paternalism*, L.A. TIMES, Aug. 17, 2006, at B6.

Jones, Gregg, *Marcos Wealth Remains Elusive*, DALLAS MORNING NEWS, Feb. 22, 2001, at 1A.

Kaufman, Irving R., *A Legal Remedy for International Torture?*, N.Y. TIMES MAG., Nov. 9, 1980, at 44.

Koch, Janet, *Dr. Filártiga—A Picture of Hope*, NEW HAVEN JOURNAL-COURIER, Nov. 11, 1978, at 41.

Kohn, Alan, *1789 Alien Tort Act Invoked To Allow $10 Million Suit*, NEW YORK L.J., July 1, 1980, at 1.

Kostianovsky, Pepa, *La democracia es la unica vacuna contra el comunismo*, ABC REVISTA (Asunción), May 13, 1979, at 4.

Kurlantzick, Joshua, *Pirates of the Corporation: Alien Tort Statute and Slave Labor Cases*, MOTHER JONES, July 2005, at 19.

La justicia nunca tuvo trabas, HOY (Asunción), May 9, 1979, at 9.

Lane, Charles, *Court Hears Cases on Agents' Actions Abroad*, WASH. POST, Mar. 31, 2004, at A6.

Large, Jerry, *A Life of Justice*, SEATTLE TIMES, Aug. 24, 1995, at A1.

Lescaze, Lee, *Justice and State Back Right to Sue in Torture Cases*, WASH. POST, June 3, 1980, at A10.

Lescaze, Lee, *Paraguayan Police Figure is Arrested in New York*, WASH. POST, Apr. 5, 1979, at A17.

Lifsher, Marc, *Unocal Settles Human Rights Lawsuit Over Alleged Abuses at Myanmar Pipeline*, L.A. TIMES, Mar. 22, 2005, at C1.

Magnusson, Paul, *A Milestone for Human Rights*, BUSINESS WEEK, Jan. 24, 2005, at 63.

McDonnell, Patrick J., *Pinochet Loses Immunity in Abuse Case*, L.A. TIMES, Jan. 21, 2006, at A3.

McDonnell, Patrick J., *A Long Battle for Vindication Pays Off*, L.A. TIMES, Sept. 16, 1996, at A1.

Mexico Hails Man's Acquittal, DALLAS MORNING NEWS, Dec. 16, 1992, at A13.

Mine, Douglas Grant, *The Assassin Next Door, Part 2*, MIAMI NEW TIMES, Oct. 12, 2000, at 25.

Mine, Douglas Grant, *The Assassin Next Door*, MIAMI NEW TIMES, Nov. 18, 1999, at 32.

Morris, Mike, *Ethiopian to be Deported*, ATLANTA J. CONST., Aug. 2, 2005, at B5.

Muchnic, Suzanne, *LACMA to Show Klimts*, L.A. TIMES, Mar. 16, 2006, at E4.

Nadler, Eric, *Paraguay Torture in U.S. Courts*, THE NATION, May 8, 1982, at 551.

Nesmith, Jeff, *U.S. Probe of Visas Resisted*, ATLANTA CONSTITUTION, Apr. 9, 1979, at 1-A.

New Taiwanese Law May Free Journalist's Killer, S.F. CHRON., Jan. 2, 1991, at A3.

Nuestra justicia no trabo a nadie, HOY (Asunción), May 9, 1979, at 1.

O'Connor, Anne-Marie, *Attorney's Perseverance Yields a Legal Masterpiece,* L.A. TIMES, Jan. 23, 2006, at A1.

Oliver, Myrna, *G. Suarez Mason, 81; Ex-General Linked to Argentina's 'Dirty War,'* L.A. TIMES, June 22, 2005, at B10.

Peña: Rechazaron la demanda y dejarian libre al ex policía, ULTIMA HORA (Asunción), May 16, 1979, at 14.

Raab, Selwyn, *Judge Rules Pena Can Be Sued Here on Death in Paraguay,* N.Y. TIMES, Apr. 10, 1979, at B1.

Raab, Selwyn, *Paraguay Alien Tied to Murders in Native Land,* N.Y. TIMES, Apr. 5, 1979, at B1.

Rice, Andrew, *The Long Interrogation,* N.Y. TIMES MAG., June 4, 2006, at 50.

Richey, Warren, *Ruling Makes it Harder for Foreigners to Sue in U.S. Courts,* CHRISTIAN SCI. MONITOR, June 30, 2004, at 3.

Richey, Warren, *When Can Foreigners Sue in U.S. Courts?,* CHRISTIAN SCI. MONITOR, Mar. 30, 2004, at 2.

Rivkin, Jr., David B. & Lee Casey, *Crimes Outside the World's Jurisdiction,* N.Y. TIMES, July 22, 2003, at A19.

Rohde, David, *Jury in New York Orders Bosnian Serb to Pay Billions,* N.Y. TIMES, Sept. 26, 2000, at A10.

Rohter, Larry, *A Web of Investigations Increasingly Entangles Pinochet,* INT'L HERALD TRIB., Feb. 8, 2005, at 3.

Rohter, Larry, *Judge Finds Pinochet Fit for Trial,* INT'L HERALD TRIB., Dec. 5, 2004, at 7.

Rohter, Larry, *Dramatizing a Family That Took on Dictatorship,* L.A. TIMES, Apr. 18, 1991, at C15.

Scheffey, Thomas, *Bosnian Serb Leader on Trial,* LEGAL TIMES, Nov. 13, 1995, at 2.

Schemo, Diana Jean, *Gen. Alfredo Stroessner, Colorful Dictator of Paraguay for 35 Years, Dies in Exile at 93,* N.Y. TIMES, Aug. 17, 2006, at A25.

Smith, Greg B., *N.Y.C. Jury Orders Serb Leader to Pay 4B for War Crimes,* DAILY NEWS (New York), Sept. 28, 2000, at 8.

Smothers, Ronald, *Nightmare of Torture in Ethiopia is Relived in an Atlanta Court,* N.Y. TIMES, May 22, 1993, at A6.

Sonado caso Filartiga reactivan ante Corte Superior neoyorquina, ULTIMA HORA (Asunción), Aug. 6, 1979, at 26.

Specter, Arlen, *The Court of Last Resort,* N.Y. TIMES, Aug. 7, 2003, at A23.

Strickland, Eliza, *Was DiFi Batting for Big Oil?,* EAST BAY EXPRESS, Nov. 9, 2005, at 9.

Taking Tyrants to Court, AM. LAW., Oct. 1991, at 56.

Tell, Larry, *U.S. Court Hears of Torture: "A Death in Asuncion,"* NAT'L L.J., Mar. 1, 1982, at 6.

Teves, Oliver, *Filipino Victims Left Waiting for Cash*, SOUTH FLORIDA SUN-SEN-TINEL, June 29, 2006, at 14A.

Total Settles Rights Case, INT'L HERALD TRIB., Nov. 29, 2005, at 14.

Un precedente en la justicia de EE.UU., ABC (Asunción), July 4, 1980, at 9.

Villamil, Oscar Alzaga, *Es Espana un buen juez de la transicion Chilena?*, ABC (Madrid), Dec. 1, 1998.

Warder, Michael, *Let Chileans Handle Their Own Tyrant*, L.A. TIMES, Jan. 5, 1999, at B7.

Waxman, Sharon, *A Homecoming, in Los Angeles, for Looted Klimts*, N.Y. TIMES, Apr. 6, 2006, at E1.

Weinstein, Henry, *U.S. Settles Suit with Holocaust Survivors*, L.A. TIMES, Mar. 12, 2005, at A1.

CONGRESSIONAL MATERIAL

123 CONG. REC. 3048 (Feb. 1, 1977) (statement of Sen. Kennedy).

123 CONG. REC. 4014 (Feb. 9, 1977) (statement of Rep. Koch).

136 CONG. REC. S17486-01 (Oct. 27, 1990).

137 CONG. REC. S4511-04 (Apr. 16, 1991) (statement of Senator Grassley).

151 CONG. REC. S 11423 (Oct. 17, 2005) (statement of Senator Feinstein).

Anti-Terrorism Act of 1990, Hearing Before the Subcommittee on Courts and Administrative Practice of Committee on the Judiciary, United States Senate, 101st Congress, Second Session, July 25, 1990.

Anti-Terrorism and Effective Death Penalty Act, Pub. L. No. 104-132, § 221, 110 Stat. 1214, 1241 (1996).

Civil Liability for Victims of State Sponsored Terrorism, Pub. L. No. 104-208, 100 Stat. 3009-172 (Sept. 30, 1996).

Federal Efforts Related to the Exclusion, Removal and Prosecution of Aliens and Naturalized U.S. Citizens Who Have Committed War Crimes or Human Rights Abuses Outside the U.S. Testimony: Hearing Before the Committee on Appropriations, 109th Cong. (Dec. 8, 2005) (statement of Eli M. Rosenbaum, Director, Office of Special Investigations Criminal Division Department of Justice).

H.R. Rep. No. 102-367 (1991).

S. Rep. No. 102-249 (1991).

S. 1874, 109th Cong., § 2(a) (2005).

OTHER INTERNATIONAL MATERIALS

Agreement Concerning the Foundation "Remembrance, Responsibility and the Future," 39 I.L.M. 1298 (2000).

Convention against Torture and Other Cruel, Inhuman or Degrading Treatment or Punishment, Dec. 10, 1984, 1465 U.N.T.S. 85.

Convention on the Prevention and Punishment of the Crime of Genocide, Jan. 12, 1951, 78 U.N.T.S. 277.

Human Rights Committee, General Comment 20 (1992), Compilation of
  General Comments and General Recommendations Adopted by
  Human Rights Treaty Bodies, U.N. Doc. HRI/GEN/1/Rev.7 (2004).
Inter-Am. C.H.R., OEA/Ser.L/V/II.43, Report on the Situation of Human
  Rights in Paraguay, doc. 13 corr. 1 (1978).
International Covenant on Civil and Political Rights, Mar. 23, 1976, 999
  U.N.T.S. 171.
Rome Statute of the International Criminal Court, July 17, 1998, 2187
  U.N.T.S. 90.
U.N. General Assembly, Basic Principles and Guidelines on the Right to a
  Remedy and Reparation for Victims of Gross Violations of Inter-
  national Human Rights Law and Serious Violations of International
  Humanitarian Law, U.N. Doc. A/C.3/60/L.24 (2005).

MISCELLANEOUS SOURCES

Abduction and Restitution of Slaves, 1 Op. Att'y Gen. 29 (1792).
Arrest Warrant of 11 April 2000 (Dem. Rep. Congo v. Belg.) 2002 ICJ REP.
  1 (Feb. 14).
Breach of Neutrality, 1 Op. Att'y Gen. 57 (1795).
Zita Cabello-Barrett, Address at the University of Santiago, Chile (Oct. 20,
  2002).
John Huerta, General Counsel, The Smithsonian Institution and Former
  Deputy Assistant Attorney General, Department of Justice, Remarks at
  the Association of the Bar of the City of New York (Nov. 2, 2005).
Mexico Boundary—Diversion of the Rio Grande, 26 Op. Att'y Gen. 250
  (1907).
ONE MAN'S WAR (HBO Studios 1991).
Press Release, Center for Justice & Accountability, Judgment Final Against
  Generals Responsible for Torture in El Salvador (July 10, 2006).
Press Release, Council on Hemispheric Affairs, The Strange Case of
  Americo Pena (Apr. 17, 1978).
Press Release, Earthrights International, Historic Advance for Universal
  Human Rights: Unocal to Compensate Burmese Villagers (Apr. 2,
  2005).
Press Release, Human Rights First, Human Rights First Welcomes Senator's
  About Face on Bill Limiting Human Rights Accountability (Nov. 3,
  2005).
Press Release, Unocal, Settlement Reached in Yadana Pipeline Lawsuit
  (Mar. 21, 2005).
Ratner, Michael & Beth Stephens, *The Center for Constitutional Rights: Using
  Law and the Filartiga Principle in the Fight for Human Rights, in* ACLU
  INTERNATIONAL CIVIL LIBERTIES REPORT (Dec. 1993).
Statement on Signing the Torture Victim Protection Act of 1991, Mar. 12,
  1992, 28 WEEKLY COMP. PRES. DOC. 465 (Mar. 16, 1992).

Testimony of Edward B. O'Donnell, Jr., U.S. Special Envoy for Holocaust Issues, Bureau of International Information Programs, U.S. Department of State (Nov. 11, 2004).

TRIAL OF THE MAJOR WAR CRIMINALS BEFORE THE INTERNATIONAL MILITARY TRIBUNAL, NUREMBERG, 14 NOVEMBER 1945–1 OCTOBER 1946, 1 OFFICIAL DOCUMENTS 223 (1947).

U.S. Dep't of State, Country Reports on Human Rights Practices 2001: Argentina (Mar. 4, 2002).

U.S. Dep't of State, Initial Report of the United States of America to the U.N. Committee against Torture, U.N. Doc. CAT/C/28/Add.5 (2000).

U.S. Dep't of State, Second Periodic Report of the United States of America to the U.N. Committee against Torture, U.N. Doc. CAT/C/48/Add.3 (2005).

Peter Weiss, Vice-President, Center for Constitutional Rights, Remarks at the Association of the Bar of the City of New York (Nov. 2, 2005).

INTERNET RESOURCES

BBC News, *Argentina Generals Get Life* (Dec. 6, 2000), *available at* http://news.bbc.co.uk/1/hi/world/americas/1058205.stm.

BBC News, *Argentine General Jailed for Racist Remarks* (June 25, 2003), *available at* http://news.bbc.co.uk/1/hi/world/americas/3019090.stm.

Center for Constitutional Rights, *available at* www.ccr-ny.org.

Center for Justice & Accountability, *available at* www.cja.org.

International Labor Rights Fund, *available at* www.laborrights.org.

INDEX